THE GLENCOE PRESS POLICE SCIENCE SERIES

General Editor:

G. DOUGLAS GOURLEY

Inspector (Ret.), Los Angeles Police Department
Chairman, Department of Police Science and Administration
California State College at Los Angeles
Los Angeles, California

.

Foreword by Quinn Tamm

EXECUTIVE DIRECTOR, INTERNATIONAL ASSOCIATION OF CHIEFS OF POLICE

Police and Community Relations:
a sourcebook

A. F. Brandstatter

DIRECTOR, SCHOOL OF POLICE ADMINISTRATION AND PUBLIC SAFETY
MICHIGAN STATE UNIVERSITY

Louis A. Radelet

DIRECTOR, NATIONAL CENTER ON POLICE AND COMMUNITY RELATIONS
MICHIGAN STATE UNIVERSITY

The Glencoe Press

A DIVISION OF THE MACMILLAN COMPANY / BEVERLY HILLS, CALIFORNIA
COLLIER-MACMILLAN LIMITED, LONDON

HV
7936
.P8
N37

For further information write to:

The Glencoe Press
A Division of The Macmillan Company
8701 Wilshire Boulevard
Beverly Hills, California 90211

Collier-Macmillan Canada, Ltd., Toronto, Ontario
Library of Congress Catalog Card Number: 68-19968
Printed in the United States of America

Foreword

The various sociological, economic, and psychological factors that contribute to the social ferment of our times have been studied, discussed, and debated by a variety of experts, self-appointed as well as actual. Each factor has its elements of pro and con with correspondingly vociferous advocates. But one point that cannot be debated is the fact that in every case of social disturbance, the police are the ones in the middle. They are maligned by the rebellious as brutes and by the reactionaries as ineffectives. Why? Because it is the police who stand alone and distinctive with the ultimate responsibility to enforce the law and maintain order; and this does not mean some of the laws some of the time, but all of the laws all of the time.

Fulfillment of the police mission to maintain law and order requires the attainment of two objectives: first, prevention of crime, and second, detection and apprehension of lawbreakers. While leading police administrators have long known that crime prevention is a primary objective, the use of police–community relations programs as a major tool in attaining this objective has generally been nonexistent or rudimentary except in the more progressive departments. Apathy and noninvolvement on the part of the general public have contributed greatly to this situation.

The widespread social dissension that has erupted into virtual civil war in many of our cities during the past two summers makes it painfully obvious that this indifference can no longer be tolerated. Today, our citizens of every complexion are finding that it is their stores that are being looted and burned; it is they, and their sons and daughters, who suffer directly when law and order collapse and anarchy reigns.

Today the police officer who believes "social work" is beneath him, who thinks police–community relations programs are merely "publicity gimmicks," is living in a fool's paradise. More importantly, he isn't getting the job done. We of the police are inextricably involved in the complex, fast-moving social changes of the times and many of our traditional methods of operation must be modified accordingly. The unprecedented police problems of today and tomorrow will not be solved by ignoring them, nor by an unwillingness to take the initiative in securing understanding and support from all of the citizens in the community.

It has been said repeatedly that a community gets the kind of law enforcement is deserves — that respect for the law and support of law enforcement are every citizen's responsibilities. These truths are fundamental, but that doesn't absolve us from supplying the initiative and definitive action to insure that they remain true.

We must go to the people and actively enlist their support. We must continuously promote understanding and goodwill. We must earn such understanding and support by providing the finest possible protection to all of the people, all of the time, regardless of whether they are rich or poor, black or white, young or old. And, of primary importance, we must insure that they realize that this principle is being observed in spirit and in action. This must be done on a face to face, day to day basis.

Those departments which are actively adhering to this principle are, in the main, taking a two-pronged approach: first, they have established a specialized community services unit manned by highly trained, carefully chosen officers with well developed communications skills; second, they have insured that all members of the department receive training in the understanding of ethnic groups with emphasis on human and race relations, linguistics and cultural variations.

The several thousand law enforcement executives who comprise the International Association of Chiefs of Police have recognized the importance of concerted professional progress in this area. To this end we have, during the past three years, prepared and disseminated detailed studies and texts on the subject, and have held numerous conferences, seminars and workshops throughout the nation. Much of this service has been possible through the cooperation of such governmental agencies as the Office of Law Enforcement Assistance and various civic, professional and industrial organizations.

We have been fortunate to have received important guidance in this area from the pioneer work done at Michigan State University by its National Institute, and subsequently by its National Center on Police and Community Relations. Under the guidance of Professor Arthur Brandstatter, Director of the University's School of Police Administration and Public Safety, and Professor Louis Radelet, Director of its National Center on Police and Community Relations, notable progress has been made. This is particularly evidenced in the compilation of studies, speeches, lectures, and other authoritative material on the subject.

It is, therefore, most gratifying that these two leaders in this field have distilled their knowledge and that of other authorities into this Sourcebook in Police and Community Relations. It should be a most valuable guide and tool for law enforcement administrators throughout the world, and an invaluable contribution to the literary annals of the police profession.

Quinn Tamm
Executive Director
International Association of
Chiefs of Police

Preface

This work is dedicated by the coeditors to the cause of better police and community relations. Royalties accruing from it will be invested in this cause, specifically to further the research and program services of the National Center on Police and Community Relations at Michigan State University.

The authors of the essays contained in this volume join us in this investment. Their is clearly the greater contribution, for it was their handiwork which inspired the idea of this book initially, and which now constitutes its substance. To each of them, we extend hearty thanks.

We are also grateful to others who have helped considerably in producing this text, including particularly our staff associates and secretaries who worked with us on the manuscript. Appreciation is also extended to the National Conference of Christians and Jews, without whom there would not have been an annual Institute as a forum for presentation of these papers.

The reader should keep in mind the circumstances in which these papers were originally presented. Each paper was prepared as an oral presentation to a "live" audience. Some were done in manuscript form; some were transcribed from tapes, for inclusion in the Institute *Proceedings*, each year — and subsequently selected for inclusion in this book. In style and in rhetoric, therefore, the papers are rather informal, and there are instances where liberties are taken with prescribed rules for literary expression. We have endeavored to retain, insofar as possible, the individual style of the particular author; in fact, each author has had the opportunity to review his or her essay, for publication in this anthology.

One further point should be noted. These papers were also prepared and presented at a particular time. Thus, it is important that the perspective of the reader be adjusted to the time when the paper was created. In matters such as prevailing judicial decisions, for example, many changes have occurred since the earliest of the papers contained herein was presented.

Finally, we wish to acknowledge our agreement with many of the views expressed in these essays. We also wish to acknowledge our disagreement with some of the views expressed. But on one thing we agree completely: these are outstanding papers presented at the annual National Institute on Police and Community Relations since its inception at Michigan State University in 1955.

As such, they merit a larger audience.

A. F. Brandstatter
Louis A. Radelet

East Lansing, Michigan
September, 1967

Acknowledgements

Grateful acknowledgement is made to the following for their permission to include the articles listed:

The Constitution and the Citizen, by Paul C. Bartholomew, reprinted with permission from POLICE Magazine, Vol. 10, No. 4, March–April 1966, pp. 32–37. Charles C Thomas, Publisher, Springfield, Illinois.

Police and the Community: A Judicial View, by Hon. George Edwards, an adaptation of an article by Judge Edwards appearing in the MICHIGAN LAW REVIEW, Nov. 1965, Vol. 64, No. 1; Copyright 1965, Michigan Law Review Association.

Police Practices and the Citizen, by B. J. George, Jr., reprinted with permission from POLICE Magazine, Vol. 10, No. 4, March–April 1966, pp. 38–42. Charles C Thomas, Publisher, Springfield, Illinois.

New Frontiers for the Police, by A. F. Brandstatter, reprinted with permission from POLICE Magazine, Nov.–Dec. 1962. Charles C Thomas, Publisher, Springfield, Illinois.

The Police as Community Leaders, by E. Wilson Purdy, reprinted with permission from POLICE Magazine, Vol. 10, No. 5, May–June 1966, pp. 57–63. Charles C Thomas, Publisher, Springfield, Illinois.

The Police and Community Conflict, by William P. Brown, reprinted with permission from THE POLICE CHIEF Magazine, May–June 1964, pp. 51–59. International Association of Chiefs of Police, Inc., publisher, Washington, D.C.

The Police Role in Community Relations, by William H. Parker, from Wilson, O. W., (Ed.), PARKER ON POLICE, 1957. Courtesy of Charles C Thomas, Publisher, Springfield, Illinois.

Full Enforcement vs. Police Discretion Not to Invoke Criminal Process, by Herman Goldstein, reprinted with permission from PUBLIC ADMINISTRATION REVIEW, Vol. XXIII, No. 3 (Sept. 1963). American Society for Public Administration, Washington, D.C.

Police Planning and Research, as Related to Police-Community Relations, by A. C. Germann, reprinted with permission from POLICE Magazine, Vol. 6, No. 3, Jan.–Feb. 1962. Charles C Thomas, Publisher, Springfield, Illinois.

The Police and Their Problems, by Marvin E. Wolfgang, reprinted with permission from POLICE Magazine, Vol. 10, No. 4, March–April 1966, pp. 50–56. Charles C Thomas, Publisher, Springfield, Illinois.

Contents

PREFACE

FOREWORD

INTRODUCTION

section 1:   THE RULE OF LAW   1
              Editors' Commentary

      1. *The Rule of Law in the Republic*, 1
         Don Hyndman

      2. *The Constitution and the Citizen*, 7
         Paul C. Bartholomew

      3. *Equal Protection Under Law —*
         Fact or Fiction?, 16
         John A. Hannah

      4. *Police and the Community — A Judicial View*, 24
         George Edwards

      5. *Police Practices and the Citizen*, 36
         B. J. George, Jr.

section 2:   PSYCHOLOGICAL AND SOCIOLOGICAL
              ASPECTS OF POLICE-COMMUNITY RELATIONS   45
              Editors' Commentary

      1. *What Makes Us Behave as People?*, 46
         G. M. Gilbert

      2. *Police and Community —*
         As Viewed by a Psychologist, 50
         Milton Rokeach

      3. *A Look at Ourselves:*
         Elements of Misunderstanding, 53
         Mildred Peters

      4. *Personal and Social Disorganization*, 61
         John J. Kane

      5. *The Implications of Population Trends for*
         Urban Communities, 66
         Paul Mundy

      6. *Contra-Cultural Conflict in the Metropolitan*
         Community, 72
         Mel Ravitz

      7. *The Idea of Community*, 80
         Louis A. Radelet

      8. *Special Problems of Police-Community Relations*, 84
         Gordon W. Lovejoy

9. *Police and the Community:*
A Law-Medicine View, 92
Oliver Schroeder, Jr.

10. *Reflections on Police-Community Relations,* 96
H. G. Pope

11. *Group Behavior and Civil Disobedience,* 103
Nelson A. Watson

12. *Understanding the Community,* 113
James B. McKee

section 3:   THE POLICE AND MINORITY GROUPS   121
Editors' Commentary

1. *A Look at Others: Minority Groups and*
Police-Community Relations, 121
Harold A. Lett

2. *Understanding Minority Groups,* 128
John A. Buggs

3. *Two Case Studies:*
Los Angeles and Philadelphia, 137, 140
Noel A. McQuown
Edward M. Payne

4. *A Rationale For Racial Demonstrations,* 144
John A. Morsell

5. *The Constitution and the Citizen:*
The Quest For Balance, 151
George Edwards

6. *Racial Factors in Law Enforcement,* 161
Thurgood Marshall

7. *Understanding the Community:*
Community Change As It Affects
Police-Community Relations, 166
Herbert Jenkins

8. *A Sense of Responsibility,* 168
Harold A. Lett

9. *Challenges in Contemporary Law Enforcement,* 178
Thomas J. Cahill

section 4:   SOCIAL CHANGE AND LAW ENFORCEMENT   185
Editors' Commentary

1. *Defining Police-Community Relations,* 185
Manuel Lopez-Rey

2. *Changing Attitudes Toward Crime,* 190
Robert H. Scott

3. *Community Development For Better*
Police and Community Relations, 196
Nelson A. Watson

4. *New Frontiers For the Police,* 202
A. F. Brandstatter

5. *Professionalization of the Police*, 215
   Albert J. Reiss, Jr.

6. *Understanding Others: Police and the Citizen*, 230
   Bernard L. Garmire

7. *Social Change, the Law and the Common Good*, 235
   Frank J. Remington

8. *Police and the Community:*
   Probing For Mutual Understanding, 241
   Patrick V. Murphy

9. *The Police As Community Leaders*, 247
   Wayne E. Thompson

10. *Guidelines In Seeing Ourselves*, 253
    C. G. Conner

11. *Police and Community Relations As a*
    Political Issue, 259
    Dan W. Dodson

12. *Police Conduct and the Public*, 266
    Monrad G. Paulsen

13. *Police and Community Partnership in*
    Crime Prevention — As Related to Poverty and
    Unequal Justice Under the Law, 273
    William T. Downs

14. *The Police Role In A Democratic Society*, 276
    Frederick Routh

15. *The Police As Community Leaders*, 281
    E. Wilson Purdy

16. *Police and the Community —*
    Probing For Mutual Understanding, 290
    Lawrence W. Pierce

section 5: PRINCIPLES OF PROGRAMMING IN POLICE
            AND COMMUNITY RELATIONS   297
            Editors' Commentary

   1. *A Police Administrator Looks At*
      Police-Community Relations, 297
      Howard R. Leary

   2. *Professional Development of Law*
      Enforcement Personnel, 302
      Bernard C. Brannon

   3. *Why Human Relations Training For Police?*, 316
      Joseph D. Lohman

   4. *The Police and Community Conflict*, 322
      William P. Brown

   5. *The Police Role in Community Relations*, 335
      William H. Parker

   6. *Tale of Two Cities — The Crucial Role of the*
      Police in Community Change, 347, 352
      Jesse E. Curry
      Lawrence W. Fultz

7. *Police Working in the Neighborhood,* 355
   Allen B. Ballard

8. *The St. Louis Story,* 361
   James T. McCrory

9. *Preparing For Police Leadership in
   Community Relations,* 369
   Harry G. Fox

10. *Understanding the Police,* 375
    Quinn Tamm

section 6:   SPECIAL CONSIDERATIONS   381
             Editors' Commentary

1. *Full Enforcement vs. Police Discretion
   Not To Invoke Criminal Process,* 381
   Herman Goldstein

2. *Police Planning and Research, as Related To
   Police-Community Relations,* 392, 398
   A. C. Germann
   Robert R. J. Gallati

3. *Youth and Police,* 403
   James J. Brennan

4. *Administration of Criminal Justice:
   From Arrest to Sentence,* 409
   Edmond F. DeVine

5. *Administration of Criminal Justice:
   The Correctional Process,* 414
   Richard A. McGee

6. *Problems in Communication and Cooperation in the
   Administration of Criminal Justice,* 430
   Robert H. Scott

7. *Police-Press Relations,* 435
   Patrick V. Murphy

8. *Communication Within the Community,* 440
   William R. Carmack

9. *Police and Community —
   As Viewed By a Religious Leader,* 446
   Paul O. Cardwell

10. *Police-Community Relations — A Personal View,* 448
    Jackie Robinson

11. *Police-Citizen Interaction As a Problem in
    Communication,* 453
    Hideya Kumata

12. *The Police and Their Problems,* 459
    Marvin E. Wolfgang

A SELECTED BIBLIOGRAPHY ON POLICE AND
COMMUNITY RELATIONS   473
Compiled by Martin G. Miller

I. Books, 473
II. Articles, 477
III. Unpublished Materials, 480

Introduction

In 1955, the original of the nation's land-grant institutions, Michigan State University, observed its centennial. There were many special activities on the campus, designed in one way or another to celebrate the occasion. The School of Police Administration and Public Safety at Michigan State itself, that year, marked its twentieth anniversary. It was seeking appropriate ways to underscore the significance of both anniversaries.

Community service had long been a high priority for the School, in keeping with the land-grant history and philosophy of the University. Moreover, the School was committed to the idea of the police officer as a community leader, an important *part of* not *apart from* the community he serves. In subsequent years, this was to be underlined as the School became part of the College of Social Science. In 1955, as its graduate program at the master's level was initiated, the School was recognized as the nation's largest facility of its type, already beginning to retreat from an earlier orientation in the technical and "tooling" aspects of law enforcement education, moving toward a broader-based curriculum, with heavy emphasis on social and behavioral science.

The National Conference of Christians and Jews was founded in 1928, against the background of the religious bigotry which characterized the presidential election campaign of that year. It was conceived as a civic organization of religiously motivated individuals, seeking through education to promote cooperation and mutual understanding among men of goodwill of diverse religious belief, racial and ethnic origin, without compromise of any particular creed or faith. Through the years, this organization fostered multiple programs via its regional offices across the country, developing into America's largest national private intergroup relations agency. Its programs were directed toward leaders in the social institutional "trunklines" of society having great influence in the formulation of attitudes: churches and synagogues, schools and colleges, parents, youth, community organizations, the mass media of public information, labor and management groups, etc. Beginning in 1934, the National Conference sponsored the annual observance of Brotherhood Week; Religious News Service was another of its creations.

Some months prior to the epochal decision of the U.S. Supreme Court in the school desegregation cases, May, 1954, certain NCCJ officials began stressing the increasing demands upon law enforcement officers which were emerging as a result of a complex of social factors in our large cities. It was determined that steps should be taken to mount a new phase in the NCCJ program nationally, to be called *Police and Community Relations*. It was further determined that a logical first step would be some sort of national conference, a meeting to bring together interested police and other community leaders, to study problems of police–citizen interaction, police–minority group relations, the police role in social conflict, and other questions of the same nature. One purpose of such a conference would be to provide leadership and inspiration for localized problem-solving endeavors, which might be promoted by NCCJ local and regional operations. In a nutshell, the central concern was for an orderly and just society. It was recognized that the policeman, in his "peace officer" function, is a vitally important part of society's apparatus for order and justice. This, in itself, was hardly a startling discovery. What was new was the rather sudden realization that this function of the police officer had become extremely complicated, and that very little was being done to help police officers cope effectively and sensitively with "people problems," increasingly threatening domestic tranquility.

This was the background for the first National Institute on Police and Community Relations, which took place at Michigan State University May 15–20, 1955, repeated annually since that time. Thus was arranged the partnership, in planning and conducting the Institute, of the School of Police Administration and Public Safety and the National Conference of Christians and Jews.

Only fifty-eight people registered for the Institute the first year, about two-thirds of them police officers with command or supervisory responsibilities in their departments. Others attending were other types of community leaders, i.e., school officials, clergymen, youth agency and human relations professionals, corrections personnel and social workers, civic–social organization leaders, labor, management and mass media people. A primary aim was to make the Institute, as nearly as possible, a laboratory of the actual community, to encourage an interprofessional "dialogue" focusing upon community problems in which the police and other leadership forces of the community felt a common sense of social and moral "stake."

In the ensuing years, attendance at the Institute increased to more than four hundred in recent years, still maintaining roughly the same ratio of police to non-police. Represented in the Institute population in a given year have been as many as 160 communities in 30 states and several foreign countries. Its total "alumni association" today numbers approximately 2500; only eight states have never been represented. Literally hundreds of counterpart programs developed throughout the country, traceable directly or indirectly to the Institute at Michigan State. Each year, the Institute program has featured speakers of national prestige in their fields of academic scholarship, administrative or operational endeavor. Some of the more outstanding papers have been selected for inclusion in this book.

Historically, specialized police training in the subject matter of community relations goes back about twenty-five years. Its development has been a phase of the broader context of professionalization of the police during the same period. This type of training, as it developed in the police departments of twenty or twenty-five major cities during World War II, dealt almost exclusively with racial problems. The sociological factors in the background were apparent; for example, unprecedented migration of Southern Negroes (and whites) to Northern and Western big cities, in search of better economic opportunities in war production industries. The pace of the social change involved created serious problems of metropolitan adjustment for the newcomers, conditions in which the police task of maintaining civic peace became more challenging. Logically, police training programs began to reflect efforts to meet this need.

It was not, however, until the 1950's that a "police–community relations concept" was identified in the literature beginning to converge in "the sociology of the police." The purposes of Police and Community Relations programs were formulated as a result of expanding experiences, as follows:

1. To encourage police–citizen partnership in the cause of crime prevention.

2. To foster and improve communication and mutual understanding between the police and the *total* community.

3. To promote interprofessional approaches to the solution of community problems, and stress the principle that the administration of justice is a *total* community responsibility.

4. To enhance cooperation among the police, prosecution, the courts, and corrections.

5. To assist police and other community leaders to achieve an understanding of the nature and causes of complex problems in people-to-people relations, and especially to improve police–minority group relationships.

6. To strengthen implementation of equal protection under the law for all persons.

Certain basic assumptions came to be delineated in Police and Community Relations programs — these, for instance:

. . . that the law enforcement officer occupies a crucially important position in the maintenance of order in the community. Yet it is vital that the police recognize that order, in itself, is NOT the ultimate end of government in the free society.

. . . that, therefore, the principle of equal protection of the law for ALL citizens, and respect for their rights AS PERSONS, is absolutely fundamental under our system of government.

. . . that police interested in police–community relations are police committed to their own professional development and advancement. At a minimum, this means — at least — fair and impartial law enforcement, regardless of personal opinions, prejudices or other irrelevant considerations in the administration of justice.

. . . that today's community, which the police officer is endeavoring to serve, is vastly different from the community of yesteryear, in the sense of its community relations. This implies a vital need for new concepts in police education and police training, especially with regard to social and behavioral science.

. . . that Police–Community Relations programs must involve a genuine educational process, the cultivation of "dialogue" across lines of diversty, and real effort to make communication more effective and mutual understanding a practical objective.

. . . that the administration of justice is, indeed, the responsibility of the TOTAL community, and not merely that of the police — who are too often the scapegoat for all manner of social bankruptcy.

. . . that each of us has something to learn from others regarding complex community problems, in their definition, diagnosis and remedies. For the police officer, as an example, this means recognition that he may have something to learn from people who are not policemen. For others, it means the reverse.

. . . that police education in community relations does not add new burdens for law enforcement officers. The police are always in the position of dealing with the effects of social and personal disorganization. What we seek is to deal more effectively with situations involving community conflict. We see this as proper police function, not "do gooding" or "social engineering."

. . . that current problems in race relations and civil rights represent extremely important subject matter in any Police–Community Relations Institution. Yet it is also important to recognize that there are many problems affecting the police–community relationships which have little or nothing to do with race, and which beg for our attention also. As an example, what about the communication problems between the police and corrections personnel? How are things in the relationship between the police and the courts? Are police happy with their treatment by the press and mass media?

. . . that there is much more to the field of Police–Community Relations than the traditional (and important!) notion of "public relations."

. . . that the improvement of the police–community relationship is not to be seen as an end in itself. The relationship is improved as the dialogue matures, and this in the process of working together in interprofessional approaches to the solution of community problems. Thus, a good police–community relations program may very well be, chiefly, a program in crime prevention . . . or a series of discussions focusing on the attitudes of youth toward law and authority . . . or an action project in traffic safety. All the great issues in the administration of justice today are pertinent as a focus or pivot for police–community relations programs or projects.

In 1961, on a grant of funds from the Field Foundation, the School of Police Administration and Public Safety conducted a national survey of 168 law enforcement agencies. The results of this survey strongly established a case for establishment of a National Center on Police and Community Relations. This Center, with year-round services available, was launched August 1, 1965 at Michigan State, on the basis of a substantial grant from the Field Foundation. The Center's functions include:

1. Undertaking action-related research projects.

2. Preparing, publishing and circulating reports, manuals, pamphlets, booklets and other literature in the field of its interest.

3. Developing and conducting educational and training programs.

4. Providing direct consultative service to interested police and community agencies and organizations.

5. Training young professionals for work in the field of police and community relations.

The Center has been the recipient of several Federal grants, including one with which it conducted the national survey of Police and Community Relations for the President's Commission on Law Enforcement and Administration of Justice, completed in January, 1967.

The subject of Police and Community Relations, in our time, prompts a variety of meanings and definitions. To some, it means public relations, in the traditional sense, i.e., the development of a favorable public impression of a given product — what in the jargon is called "imagery." In this conception of Police and Community Relations, the police largely determine what is good for the community. Sometimes the tendency is to place more emphasis upon *looking good* than upon *being good*. Sometimes there is a tendency, in this conception of Police and Community Relations, to suggest that what is good for the police department is also good for the community, and for the common welfare. It ain't necessarily so!

To be sure, a sound *public relations* program is vitally important in a police agency. Too many such agencies neglect it, at their peril. Properly understood, it is a vital *part* of a Police and Community Relations program. But it is not synonymous, it is not identical.

To some, Police and Community Relations means racial and civil rights problems, police–minority group relationships, handling demonstrations and civil disturbances, parrying charges of "police brutality" and clamor for establishment of citizen review boards, etc. There is little doubt that the rather spectacular popularity, in recent years, of institutes and workshops and conferences on Police and Community Relations is explainable largely in the terms and ramifications of this particular conception of the subject. But again, "the police and racial tensions" is not the same thing as Police and Community Relations. As with public relations, the one is an important aspect of the other, but only an aspect. The substance of one is not wholly the substance of the other.

What, then, constitutes an adequate, comprehensive definition of community relations, for our purpose? Properly understood, Police and Community Relations in its generic sense means the variety of ways in which it may be emphasized that the police are indeed an important *part of,* not *apart from* the communities they serve. Properly understood, Police and Community Relations is a concept for total police organization, functionally speaking — a *total orientation,* not merely the preoccupation of a special unit or bureau within the department. It bears upon administrative policy, it bears upon supervision, it bears upon every aspect of personnel practices, it bears up records and communications, it bears upon complaint procedures, it bears upon all aspects of internal as well as external relations, it bears upon planning and research, and perhaps most significantly, it bears upon line service through the uniformed patrol division. In short, Police and Community Relations, ideally, is an emphasis, an attitude, a way of viewing police responsibilities that ought to permeate the entire organization. Every major issue in American law enforcement today is, in a substantial sense, a challenge and an opportunity in terms of Police and Community Relations. For it is only in an effective partnership of police and community that there is any prospect of dealing constructively with these issues.

It is absurd, therefore, to settle for a concept of Police and Community Relations that amounts to nothing more than efforts to persuade the public to *like* the police. It is absurd from several standpoints. So, too, is a concept that amounts to nothing more than efforts to secure better pay for deserving police officers. There is a kind of social myopia implied in such, rather common notions of Police and Community Relations. The fundamental Police and Community Relations question of our time pertains to what the proper role and function of the police should be, under contemporary social circumstances in the free society. It is to this basic question that much of the relevant literature in the field is currently being addressed.

Community relations is like a three-legged stool, each leg of equal importance in holding the stool upright. One leg is *public relations,* in its traditional sense. Another leg is *community service.* The third leg is *community participation,* * and this is the facet of the total community relations job that is being emphasized

---

* Murray G. Ross, COMMUNITY ORGANIZATION: THEORY AND PRINCIPLE, New York: Harper Brothers, 1955.

today in Police and Community Relations programs. In effect, it involves an inter-professional or teamwork approach to a wide number and variety of community problems in which the police and other social institutions have a common sense of stake, of consequence. In and through meaningful problem-solving endeavors, in which community leaders — including police officers — participate, the relationships among and between the diverse parties to these endeavors tend to improve. Stated another way, we learn from one another as we develop respect for those who are in some ways different from ourselves. This suggests that problem-solving can be an exciting educational experience. It suggests the idea of the police officer as a *community leader*, profoundly engaged in the *preventative* policing that is the metabolism of effective Police and Community Relations — as distinguished from *tactical* policing, concerned only with what is to be done after the fact of a riot or major social disorder. It is to portray the police officer as a "professional citizen,"† gradually to rid the police officer of what has been called the "pariah" complex.‡

We have reviewed a bit of the historical background for contemporary interest in the field of Police and Community Relations. We have "positioned" the National Institute in this background, as the annual forum at Michigan State University where the papers appearing in this book were originally presented. We have outlined the purposes and assumptions which have come to be identified with programs and projects in the field of Police and Community Relations in recent years. We have suggested a definition of the term for our purposes herein, and something of what may be called the philosophy of today's work in the field. A bit more of the latter may be useful, by way of concluding this introductory commentary by the coeditors.

We maintain that law enforcement must examine its "image" and modify it from that of a purely repressive social influence to one willing to experiment with positive programs in a sociological context. The social aspects of police work offer rich rewards, if expanded in cooperation with the community in crime prevention programs. For the police to be static, to be isolated from the citizenry, to pursue traditional practices blindly, and without regard to community relations factors, can only result in serious retardation of the professionalization process and wasted human resources. Such a posture ignores an increasingly important part of the social responsibility of the police.

The police are a social institution concerned with social problems. They are the agency around which the community often rallies in times of tension and emergency. They cannot respond by force alone. They must have other means of developing and sustaining civic peace, with greater emphasis than in the past upon *preventative* policing, i.e., programs aimed at anticipating and heading off social conflict, the causes of which are so intimately related to the causes of crime and delinquency. Crime prevention is generally recognized as an important police function. But the police can do little without community cooperation and assistance. The police must take the initiative, and show the way — in effect, to assist

---

†Michael Banton, *Social Integration and Police Authority:* THE POLICE CHIEF, April, 1963, Vol. XXX, No. 4, pp. 8 ff.

‡William A. Westley, *Violence and the Police,* THE AMERICAN JOURNAL OF SOCIOLOGY, 1953, 59(1), pp. 34–41. Also James Q. Wilson, *The Police and Their Problems: A Theory,* PUBLIC POLICY: YEARBOOK OF THE GRADUATE SCHOOL OF PUBLIC ADMINISTRATION, Harvard University, 1963, pp. 189–216.

the community to meet its responsibility, and at the same time, hopefully, to improve police–community relations. If the police fail in providing such leadership, as has been the case too often in the past, the community tends to blame the police for all manner of social bankruptcy. The police cry out defensively at such scapegoating, but they have only themselves to blame for the situation.

Recognition and status as true professionals must be earned, in any field. Professional status is not all privilege; it also involves responsibility. The community ought to be able to expect forthright and visionary police leadership, in constructive efforts to cope with problems in which the police have a profound concern. Crime prevention through police–community teamwork, and the improvement of police–community relations go together. Good work in one will be good work in the other. We reject the premise that a police department is only as good as the community wants it to be. We subscribe rather to the principle that the community will respond to public education, sparked by the police, as to how good law enforcement can be.

Something better than bumper-sticker pleas to "Support Your Local Police" is required. However well-intentioned, slogans will not get the job done. The quality of law enforcement service must be elevated in every respect, beginning with educational qualifications for entry into police service. A high school diploma is no longer adequate. Training merely in the technical aspects of police work is no longer adequate. Personnel standards which ascribe greater importance to an applicant's height than to his ability to deal sensitively with people of many backgrounds are no longer adequate. Police work performed without benefit of proper planning and research is no longer adequate.

What, then, is adequate? Our reply to this question would be: a police department is adequate when it is viewed as *our* police by all segments of the population of the community it serves. This, it seems to us, is the measure of the professional integrity of law enforcement in our time and society.

The Editors

Police and Community
Relations: a sourcebook

Section 1
The Rule of Law

It is self-evident that a society depends for its survival upon formal and informal instrumentalities of social control, by and through which the behavior of most of its population is made predictable, most of the time. Social control and social stability go together: the sum total of the processes by which groups and societies secure conformity to prevailing, generally accepted standards.

Public opinion is an important instrumentality of social control. So is propaganda. So is law, i.e., the expressed will of the state. Relatively few laws are needed in a culturally homogeneous society, in which there is little spacial and social mobility. But in a society such as ours has become, more and more social control is sought through the medium of law.

It is important, therefore, that we consider initially the place of law in the social constellation. The substance of our legal system in the United States consists chiefly of the common law, statutory law, and court decisions. Our common law had its origin in the ideals and customs which prevailed in ninth and tenth century England. The principles upon which judicial decisions have rested were not the creation of judges. Our judges do not pretend to make the law. They have attempted, rather, to expound the law, on the assumption that there are fixed principles applicable to the forms of behavior which a given society regards as inimical to its well-being.

In the United States, it is the Constitution which broadly delineates these principles. In an ostensibly democratic society, functioning as a Constitutional system, the principle of equal protection under the law for every citizen is obviously fundamental. The ultimate end of government in the free society is the preservation of the liberty of the individual person, properly understood. The phrase, *ordered liberty with justice* captures the spirit of the American creed, with its clear implication of respect for the rights of *persons as persons*. In a very basic sense, this bears upon the "product" of law enforcement in our society.

These are the ideas discussed in the essays in this section.

The Rule of Law in the Republic

DON HYNDMAN

Director, Public Relations, American Bar Association,
Chicago, Illinois

MAY 23, 1961

The rule of law covers a great deal of ground. So I'm going to confine myself to a few observations about the more obvious facets, and then consider with you one phase that seems to me particularly important just now—how the rule of law is faring as it relates to indigent defendants accused of crime.

One highly publicized aspect of the rule of law these days involves court congestion. Dockets *are* badly overcrowded in many big cities. In most of the small cities and towns, it fortunately isn't much of a problem. But any candid appraisal of how the rule of law is functioning would have to recognize that calendar backlogs add up to a serious problem. When it takes five or six years to get a lawsuit to trial, which it does in some jurisdictions, it certainly cannot be said that justice is swift and sure.

Admittedly, too, the structure of our courts is outmoded. Most court systems were devised over a century ago under the altogether different conditions then prevailing. They need modernizing as to organic arrangement, personnel and facilities. They need more full-time administrators, expediters with authority to employ business management methods and assign judges where judicial business requires. Despite a lot of effort on the part of the legal profession through the years to take the selection of judges out of politics, most of the judges in our country still are elected on party ballots. That system has produced some fine judges, but the advantages of an appointive system are pretty apparent to most people. Generally speaking, too, it can be said that traffic and juvenile courts need upgrading and modernizing to meet demands which have outstripped their manpower and facilities.

But perhaps most difficult of all are the problems involved in seeing to it that everyone—including the poor, the unpopular and the eccentric—receives fair and equal treatment in the processes of criminal justice.

That problem is especially important because it goes to the heart of the vital relationship between government and the individual citizen. It is what distinguishes our whole concept of freedom under law from the communist system and its denial of individual rights. And it is important, too, from the standpoint of the numbers of people involved.

Just how important it is from this latter standpoint is indicated by this: more than half of all the persons accused of crime in our country every year lack funds with which to employ private counsel. And many thousands of these men and women— no one knows exactly how many—are arraigned, tried and sentenced without the benefit of a lawyer to advise them of their rights or to plead their case.

From all this I hope no one concludes that I think there are more things wrong than right about our system for the administration of justice. Far from it. The basic values of our system far out weigh the weaknesses, and in the aggregate, the system works pretty well. Generally speaking, we have held firm to the basic ideals of our system—the presumption of innocence, the right to be free from arbitrary arrest, the privilege against self-incrimination, the right to bail and *habeas corpus,* the right to a prompt judicial hearing. In recent years, the trend of court decisions has been to assert these rights in louder tones than ever.

The imperfections I mentioned a moment ago are not faults inherent in our system of justice. They are correctable shortcomings arising from the fact that the great growth of the country, and the immense changes that have occurred in the pattern of American life, have put strains on the court systems which they have not been equipped to meet fully. A prime example is the revolution wrought by that relatively commonplace mechanism, the automobile. When most of our courts were created, long before the invention of the motor car, personal injury litigation made up only a small part of the courts' business. Today, it represents up to 90 per cent of the civil litigation in many jurisdictions and accounts for most of the court congestion we read about.

When we get enough judges, court personnel and facilities, the congestion can and will be relieved. And resources for the defense of indigents can and will be broadened, as they are being increased now, even though the tempo of that growth needs to be faster.

A large part of the trouble in keeping courts geared to present day requirements is traceable to a curious public indifference. The courts have been taken for granted. The average person has seemed to feel that the courts always have managed to get along and that they always would—that it wasn't his problem. In a way, I suppose that's a tribute to the courts, but it has made it difficult to arouse the public support needed for court reorganizations and increased judicial manpower.

Just out of curiosity I asked the administrative office of the United States Courts in Washington what part of the Federal budget goes for maintenance of the Federal court system. You'd never guess the answer. Last year it was ¼₄th of one per cent. One fourteenth of a penny out of each Federal tax dollar goes to support the judiciary, one of the three coequal and coordinate branches of our government. As far as I could learn there are no reliable, comparable figures as to the proportionate cost of the state courts, but I've heard educated guesses that this, too, represents only a minute fraction of the total cost of state and local governments.

There are some hopeful signs of progress, however. After seven years or more of indecisive sparring around on how many—if any—additional Federal judges were needed, the Congress has now decided we need 73 more, all at once. One of our leading TV commentators observed this was an interesting lesson in political science. Whatever it was, it will help a lot to relieve congestion in the Federal courts.

Then too, there is a trend running in the country toward court reorganization. Many nonlegal groups are beginning to join hands with the legal profession in this effort. It's slow, often discouraging work because it involves the ponderous business of amending state constitutions. For example, in my own State of Illinois, the organized bar, after strenuous effort, has twice in this generation managed to get a popular referendum on revising the judicial system created by the Constitution of 1870. The first vote in 1922 failed badly. Then, three years ago, the proposed revision of the judicial article received a solid majority, but failed by a handful of votes to get the required two-thirds majority. Again this year the never-say-die bar associations are trying to get a Constitutional amendment before Illinois voters in 1962. One of these years, they will make it.

But back to the problem of the indigent defendant. If anything about the rule of law relates closely to the objectives of this Institute, I think this does. And certainly, the quality of justice is very much a part of the democracy which we like to hold up as an example to the world. In a Law Day speech three weeks ago, U. S. Supreme Court Justice Tom Clark said something I thought was very much to the point. He said that if we hope to export more democracy around the world, we are going to have to produce more of it here at home. He said, in effect, that if we don't really practice equality of justice in America—if we deny or dilute the Constitutional rights of certain people or groups because they are poor or because they are minorities or hold unorthodox views—we can be sure the failure will not go unnoticed among the peoples of the world.

What can a penniless defendant expect when he is brought into court on a criminal charge? If this happens in one of the 95 communities in the country that have organized defender services, he can look to that source for legal advice. If the charge against him is a capital offense, the court will appoint a lawyer to represent him. All of the states provide for court assigned counsel in capital cases.

But if he is accused of any number of lesser offenses, including felonies, he may or may not be able to obtain counsel. In eight states, assigned counsel is required *only* in capital cases. And in only 18 states is court assignment of counsel mandatory in *all* felonies. In the others, it depends on whether or not the defendant requests counsel, and whether the court believes a lawyer should be appointed.

And in just 21 states—less than half—is anything paid to the lawyer who takes a case on court appointment, even though it may require days or even weeks of his time. In the states that do have statutory fees, the fees range from $5 (that's for the case as a whole) to "reasonable." Lawyers have traditionally recognized an obligation to accept court appointment to represent indigents, but only a relatively small proportion of the bar practices in criminal court. The result is that a disproportionate share of the responsibility of defending indigents falls on a few lawyers. That isn't good, either from their standpoint or the defendants'.

The American Bar Association and the National Legal Aid and Defender Association have together been trying hard to cope with this growing problem. They work with bar associations and local communities encouraging more defender services. They have established minimum standards for legal aid and defender organizations. They have helped provide and organize local community financial support. They have not taken sides in the argument that still goes on over whether defender services should be publicly or privately supported; they say only that this is for local decision, that the main thing is to get the services. They say, further, that with the vast growth and urbanization of the country, the assigned counsel system, which worked well enough in an earlier, simpler era, no longer is adequate. Like public health services, legal assistance needs have reached dimensions making them a community responsibility.

Organized legal aid is growing, but it is scarcely keeping pace with population growth and need. Here is an interesting example: In the decade of the 1950's, the number of cities of over 100,000 without organized legal aid was reduced from 27 to 6. Then along came the 1960 census, and overnight the number of cities over 100,000 that lacked legal aid offices was back up to 14. So the race is on again, to try to catch up with the census.

What I am saying touches only part of the problem. I have been talking about counsel for indigents after they are in court. There is today a growing concern about *when* the arrested person is entitled to have a lawyer. Many feel that the need is as great between the time of arrest and arraignment as at any other time. That is especially true when the defendant is a minor, or friendless, or mentally incapable of knowing his rights.

This is an area in which there is little or no uniformity of opinion among law enforcement people, state legislatures, or the courts themselves. Efforts to bring about some uniformity in arrest procedures haven't progressed very far. Back in 1942, the Interstate Commission on Crime drafted the Uniform Arrest Act which undertook to lay down some ground rules on search and seizure, and on such things as how long a suspect could be detained for questioning before arraignment (two hours, suggests the Uniform Act). In the intervening 19 years, only three states have adopted the Act—Delaware, Rhode Island and New Hampshire.

The Mallory decision of the Supreme Court in 1957 has violently agitated the issue again. That was the case, as most of you will recall, in which the high court threw out a confession of a Washington, D.C., rape suspect, on the ground too much time elapsed between his arrest at 2:30 in the afternoon and his arraignment about eight hours later, at 10:30 that evening.

As a direct result of that decision, an Advisory Committee on the Federal Rules of Criminal Procedure, composed of lawyers and judges, is now trying to draft a revised rule covering this point. The report of that committee ultimately will go to the Supreme Court for its consideration. Already, before its report has been formulated, something of a controversy has developed over how the rule should be changed. Prosecutors and some judges think the rule should give police and other law enforcement agencies more leeway than the courts have accorded them in recent decisions; some lawyers and others want the emphasis to be on greater safeguards of the rights of arrested persons.

If an acceptable formula evolves that will protect due process without hamstringing police investigations—and if the rights of police and defendants can become more clearly defined and recognized in this area—it will be an important forward step. And if the new Federal rules gain some degree of acceptance, it may serve as a spur to clarification of the widely diverse state rules.

There exists, presently, a twilight zone, where the rights of arrested persons seem to come into conflict with procedures that the state feels are necessary to protect the public. The deepest shadow surrounds the interval between the time a suspect is picked up by the police until he is brought to trial. This is the interval which concerns police officials most, because it confronts them every day.

It's a healthy sign that thoughtful leaders in law enforcement and criminal law administration are trying to bring some new enlightenment to the problem. The glory of our system is that we do seek constantly to improve it—that we regard the rule of law as more than a phrase, and *do* worry about protecting the rights of the individual, as well as the interests of the state.

It isn't an easy problem to solve, and it often has been a source of friction between police and lawyers, tending to generate an unfortunate atmosphere of conflict between them. Actually, the police and the bar are partners in the business of administering justice, even though our adversary system may put them on opposite sides in the courtroom. It's natural that police investigators want as much time as possible to interrogate suspects, and it's understandable that they might prefer that a defense lawyer not be there because he might advise the suspect to say nothing. That frequently has happened, of course, but it is well to remember that the Constitutional safeguard against self-incrimination is basic to our system. It also is well to remember that only about 5 percent of criminal convictions stem from confessions. A great many prosecutions have failed which relied too heavily on statements taken from defendants during long questioning in police stations. Recently, I read some figures that purported to show there had been no decline in the rate of criminal convictions in the District of Columbia, for example, since the Mallory decision. And since then, a number of police officials have been quoted as saying they thought the Mallory case and similar decisions of the Supreme Court had helped to encourage more thorough police investigations.

We can be sure of this: the syndicate hoodlum, the racketeer, the "con man" and the professional burglar, all know what their rights are when arrested. They know all about when they can call a lawyer, and about *habeas corpus,* and how to avoid self-incrimination. And of course other suspects who are mature in age and intellect, and who are familiar with their rights—and those of financial means—know how to get legal help when they need it. The ones who need the protections we are discussing here are the frightened, confused, the ignorant, or the friendless, who frequently fall under suspicion. Their numbers are not insignificant. If we compare the number of persons arrested with the number actually charged with a crime in any given jurisdiction, we realize a great many more are arrested than are accused. So it is not just a few obscure individuals who are involved.

It would be comforting to be able to conclude these rather rambling observations with some helpful suggestions. But there are no ready solutions, and no set of rules is going to be foolproof. New issues and questions of interpretation always will arise, because no two cases are exactly alike. That's why the courts bear such a heavy burden of responsibility, and why Justice Holmes once wrote that the life of the law is not logic, but experience.

There is one suggestion I would advance that may have some pertinence here. Would it not be mutually beneficial to the police departments, the courts, the bar and the public if the law enforcement agencies and the bar associations in any given community got together to jointly seek a closer working relationship between them in this sensitive area of balancing the public interest and individual rights? My guess is that most bar associations would, as a public service, be glad to set up a panel of leading lawyers who would meet regularly with police officers for informal guidance clinics, to consider the basic legal aspects of police work—what constitutes legal search, detention, admissible evidence, arraignment procedures, and the like. Such clinics could serve as a kind of in-service training for policemen. Questions arising in the day-to-day conduct of police investigative work might be raised, discussed informally and perhaps clarified. A better understanding of some of these difficult problems might save trouble for the police, the prosecutor, the courts, and everyone else concerned.

Great progress is being made in the scientific phases of police work. Educational qualifications and training of police personnel is being upgraded everywhere. Voluntary, cooperative instruction classes for working policemen might provide a practical supplement to the regular training programs in that they would deal with new problems, situations and relevant court decisions as they arise.

One further point in conclusion: all the problems under consideration in this Institute are related in one way or another to maintaining this delicate balance between state authority and individual rights. All of us have a direct and personal stake in helping to preserve that balance. When the Supreme Court of the United States reverses a conviction and condemns coercive methods of a few police officers, all police officers share, to a degree at least, the unfavorable public reaction. When a newspaper accuses police of extralegal methods of making an arrest or gaining a confession, the resulting public reaction often harms the whole department.

Those in the front line of law enforcement have a difficult task, perhaps the most difficult of all, in making our rule of law work. They must deal with the hard facts of a mounting crime rate, and the complex intergroup tensions in our communities. Frequently, they must exercise judicial judgment in meeting the problems these tensions generate, yet they may not usurp the judicial authority of the courts. They must face the sometimes loud and insistent clamor of the public for action—as for example the quick solution of a heinous crime—and at the same time not throw overboard the procedural safeguards, the "technicalities" as they seem at such times, that go with justice under law as we understand it.

It is indeed a difficult task, but it also is a great opportunity, to help to bring our system closer to its ideal of truly equal treatment for everyone. A wise Englishman, Lord Moulton, once said that "the measure of a civilization is the degree of its obedience to the unenforceable." We have in this country a high degree of voluntary obedience to the rule of law; we have reached the point where we can concentrate on strengthening the few weak points. In helping to make our system work even better, we are striking multiple blows for better community relations, better law enforcement, for increased public respect and, incidentally, for a legitimate self-interest—better public relations for all officers of the law.

The Constitution and the Citizen*

PAUL C. BARTHOLOMEW

Professor, Department of Government, University of Notre Dame

MAY 19, 1965

The more one explores the Constitution of the United States and tries to determine its real meaning, the more he finds that this is a document established primarily to be effective *against* government, and that its provisions for the most part do not apply to the individual citizen as such. To be sure, the provisions of our supreme law affect the individual, be he citizen or alien, and affect him very deeply, but in most instances by indirect rather than direct application of the dictates of that document, regardless of whether the effect is positive or negative. To put it another way, the individual is the *object* rather than the subject of this great law. This is a generalization, but as a general proposition, it is defensible. The Federal government and, to a lesser extent, the states are the ones to whom the Constitution attributes rights and duties, to whom are made direct authorizations and legal obligations. The Federal and state governments are thus the *subjects* of our supreme law. Individual persons, citizens and aliens, are those in respect to which rights are held and duties imposed.

This brings up another matter on which there is, at times, some misrepresentation, and that is the relative legal position of citizens and aliens under our Constitution. Almost all of our Constitutional guaranty provisions are held in respect to aliens as well as citizens. Almost without exception, where there are guarantees to restrict the operations of Federal or state government in a way that would infringe on the rights of individuals, the term "person" is used rather than "citizen," or the phraseology is in such general terms that all individuals, regardless of citizenship, are included and thus protected.

Bearing these two points in mind, we can proceed to a third point, which is that the problems in law which are so much the concern of almost all persons today, and of professional groups in particular, would in all probability not be with us if we had not had what is sometimes called the "revolution of 1868," that is, the

* Reprinted with permission from POLICE Magazine, Vol. 10, No. 4, March–April, 1966, pp. 32–37. Charles C Thomas, Publisher, Springfield, Ill.

adoption of the Fourteenth Amendment. Prior to this there were only a very few, fewer than a half dozen, provisions in the Constitution which restricted the states in their operations in matters that would affect individual persons — such things as *ex post facto* laws, bills of attainder, the obligation of contract, and mutual recognition by states of rights acquired by individuals under the laws of other states. In his last message from the Court bench, John Marshall had held that the general provisions of the Constitution, specifically the guarantees of the so-called Bill of Rights, were not applicable to the states. "The Constitution was ordained and established by the people of the United States for themselves, for their own government, and not for the government of the individual states. . . . Limitations on power, if expressed in general terms, are naturally, and, we think, necessarily applicable to the government created by the instrument."

Then came the Fourteenth Amendment, which provided that no state should deprive any citizen of the privileges or immunities he possessed as a United States citizen (one of the few instances where aliens are excluded), no state should deprive a person of life, liberty, or property without due process of law, and no state should deny a person equal protection of the laws. For a considerable length of time, the Amendment was applied almost entirely to legal persons, that is, corporations, and virtually not at all to natural persons, that is, individuals. Then in 1925, and again in 1952, came two judicial revolutions in which the entire interpretation and application of the Amendment's provisions were changed.

In 1925, in the case of *Gitlow* v. *New York* (268 U.S. 652), the Supreme Court of the United States held that the abstract term "liberty," which by the provisions of the Amendment no state could deprive a person without due process of law, was to be defined and made concrete in certain of the specifics of the first eight amendments, the Bill of Rights. In this opinion, the Court said that "for present purposes we may and do assume that freedom of speech and of the press—which are protected by the First Amendment from abridgment by Congress—are among the fundamental personal rights and 'liberties' protected by the due process clause of the Fourteenth Amendment from impairment by the states."

The process begun by the Court in this case has been continued and is still continuing in a steady but gradual absorption of more and more of these provisions into the definition of the term "liberty." What the Court did was to divide the twenty-odd provisions of the first eight amendments into two categories, formal and fundamental. In reality, there was nothing new in this particular approach, since this had been done in the *Insular Cases* near the turn of the century. Later this was "spelled out" better by the Court in *Palko* v. *Connecticut* (302 U.S. 319, 1937) when it noted that the line of division between the formal and fundamental categories "may seem to be wavering and broken if there is a hasty catalogue of the cases on one side and the other. Reflection and analysis will induce a different view. There emerges the perception of a rationalizing principle which gives to discrete instances a proper order and coherence. The right to trial by jury and the immunity from prosecution except as the result of an indictment may have value and importance. Even so, they are not of the very essence of a scheme of ordered liberty. To abolish them is not to violate a 'principle of justice so rooted in the traditions and conscience of our people as to be ranked as fundamental.' " (302 U.S. 319 at 325.)

Thus was the first of the two judicial revolutions in the interpretation of the Fourteenth Amendment brought about. The principle of the *Barron* case, that this is a *Federal* constitution and its general provisions apply only to the Federal government still held, but two things new had been added. The Fourteenth Amendment now said that no state could deprive any person of liberty without due process, and a Supreme Court interpretation of that liberty had begun to "snowball" its way to including more and more of the specifics of the Bill of Rights, that is, the first eight amendments of the Constitution. Thus the individual person was being given, in an expanding way, the protection against certain state activities directed to the individual, activities of the sort against which all persons had long been protected when these actions were Federally sponsored. Government was still the subject of the Constitution, and people the object, but more and more state governments were being forced to recognize this object of our supreme law; more and more total governmental action against individuals was being restricted.

As terms of the Court have rolled by, additions have been made to the high rank of *fundamental* liberty attributed to speech and press in the *Gitlow* decision. Religion (*Cantwell* v. *Connecticut,* 310 U.S. 296, 1940), assembly and petition (*De Jonge* v. *Oregon,* 299 U.S. 353, 1937), search and seizure (*Mapp* v. *Ohio,* 367 U.S. 643, 1961), self-incrimination (*Malloy* v. *Hogan,* 378 U.S. 1, 1964), confrontation of witnesses (*Pointer* v. *Texas,* 380 U.S. 400, 1965), counsel in all criminal cases (*Gideon* v. *Wainwright,* 372 U.S. 335, 1963), and cruel and unusual punishments (*Robinson* v. *California,* 370 U.S. 660, 1962). From time to time over the years, some of the justices of the Court have maintained that the Fourteenth Amendment should be interpreted to include all of the specific guarantees of the Bill of Rights, so-called, and not only those deemed by the Court to be "fundamental." However, a majority of the Court has never subscribed to this notion.

Two other rather basic matters need to be noted. The first is that even if a particular provision of the guarantees of the first eight amendments is not ruled as "fundamental" by the Court, it may still be applied to state actions. If under the particular circumstances of a case, the facts show that an accused person has been denied essential justice or fairness, the Court will hold that due process has been violated. The First and Fourteenth amendments combine to hold that both Federal and state activities must adhere to due process. As we said on another occasion, "The effective difference between the two tests applied by the Court is pretty obvious for all to see. Under the definition-of-liberty test, where the Court distinguishes between 'formal' and 'fundamental' rights, the inclusion of a specific guarantee means that henceforth that provision of the Constitution is to be as applicable in the areas of state operations as it is in regard to Federal matters. In the second type of test, where the Court determines that a particular procedure denies essential justice and is thus violative of due process, there is much more flexibility involved while at the same time the rights of accused persons are safeguarded. Here the particular provisions are not henceforth to be applied rigidly at all times, but only when under a given set of circumstances there will be lack of essential fairness.

"If the Court should ever arrive at the point, either directly or by indirection, of declaring that the entire Bill of Rights is to be regarded as applicable to the states through the Fourteenth Amendment, the result would be a 'can of worms' of difficulties that would almost defy adequate solution. State cases without number could be reopened. Criminal cases where the convicted person had not been brought to trial by grand jury indictment would line up alongside civil cases where a jury trial had been denied. Under the present arrangement, conduct that 'shocks the conscience' is voided, but in other matters that lack a 'fundamental' character, the states are left free.

"This freedom of the states also has the salutary effect of encouraging experimentation. Justice should not be static. Improvement and greater efficiency should always be sought if basic justice is to be preserved. Without such freedom we might never have had the process involved in the information, where the Court has held that there is certainly due process. The expanding application of the *Gitlow* doctrine may one day reach the saturation point, but in the meantime this approach offers the Court an eclectic arrangement the advantages of which seem undeniable." (*American Bar Association Journal,* February, 1964, p. 141.)

The second basic matter to be noted directly concerns both law enforcement officers and individual citizens. As has been repeatedly noted, the provisions of the Constitution, almost without exception, do not inhibit activities of individual persons. It is to the states or the Federal government that the restrictive words of the Constitution are aimed. In recent years, however, the Court has held that, while granting the truth of this, certain provisions may be applied to individual law enforcement *officers* when they are "acting under color of state law." Under the Federal Criminal Code (U.S. Code, Title 18, Sec. 242) "whoever, under color of any law, statute, ordinance, regulation, or custom, willfully subjects any inhabitant of any State, Territory, or District to the deprivation of any rights, privileges, or immunities secured or protected by the Constitution or laws of the United States, . . . shall be fined not more than $1,000 or imprisoned not more than one year, or both." A state officer who thus offends is regarded as the personification of the state and is subject to the provisions of the Constitution that stipulate that "no state" shall do certain things.

Under another provision of the Federal code, Title 18, Sec. 241, the Court has indicated (*United States* v. *Williams,* 341 U.S. 70, 1951) that Congress may legally secure against interference by *private individuals* rights that flow from the substantive powers of the Federal government, rights which arise from the relationship of the individual and the Federal government, such as the right of citizens to vote in Congressional elections. Such things are to be clearly distinguished from interests which the Constitution only guarantees from interference by states. Thus there are, on the one hand, the rights and privileges "granted or secured" to *citizens* of the United States as such, and on the other hand rights extended to all *persons* and "secured or protected" against state interference. In the case of the former, Congress may and has legislated to protect them against conspiracy by *individuals* to violate them. In the case of the latter, Congress can legislate only to apply to situations where there is *state* involvement in some way, such as action by an officer under color of state law. Incidentally, officers may be held to have acted "under color of state law," even if there is no authority for them to act under state law, state custom, or state usage, or if they may even possibly be acting in violation of state laws. (See *Monroe* v. *Pape,* 365 U.S. 167, 1961.)

By way of illustration of the relationship that exists between the Constitution, an individual person, and law enforcement officers, let us consider the matter of search and seizure, a provision that is not applicable to both Federal and state governments. (*Mapp* v. *Ohio,* 367 U.S. 643, 1961.) The Fourth Amendment forbids unreasonable searches and seizures. The qualification "unreasonable" should be given proper emphasis. Not all searches and seizures are forbidden, but only such as are *unreasonable.* Over the years, the Court in this type of case has been trying to determine in situations as they have arisen whether in the context of those circumstances and conditions, a search has been reasonable or not. The results of the Court's inquiries can be summarized, although not with complete satisfaction.

To begin with, there is no argument about a search that results from a properly issued search warrant. The real difficulties arise when there is search without a warrant. In general this can be done on two occasions: (1) in connection with a valid arrest; (2) when a crime is committed in the presence of an officer. As to the first of these, the constitutional validity of the search depends on the constitutional validity of the arrest, and this depends in turn upon whether at the moment the arrest was made, the officers had probable cause to make the arrest. The Court has said that the validity of an arrest must be determined by a court on whether "the facts available to the officers at the moment of arrest would 'warrant a man of reasonable caution in the belief' that an offense had been committed." (*Beck* v. *State of Ohio*, 379, U.S. 89, 1964.) The extent of search that may be made in connection with a valid arrest, or when a crime is committed in the presence of an officer, has varied with different decisions by the Supreme Court, ranging from the person of the individual to the room or even the apartment in which the arrest takes place—although the Court has tended to become less "liberal" on this matter in recent years. Certainly search may not validly extend to a place removed from the location of the valid arrest. (*Harris* v. *United States*, 331 U.S. 145, 1947; *United States* v. *Rabinowitz*, 339 U.S. 56, 1950; *Agnello* v. *United States*, 269 U.S. 20, 1925.)

There have been a number of recent cases before the Court involving some exploration, and presumed clarification of this problem of when is a search valid. District of Columbia police, without a warrant, knocked on the door of William Miller's apartment there. When he inquired as to who was at the door, one of the officers replied in a low voice, "Police." The officers admitted that this reply might not have been heard inside the door. Miller opened the door, and when he saw the officers, quickly tried to close it. Then the officers broke the door, entered the apartment, and arrested Miller. Evidence seized at the time was admitted at the trial, and Miller was convicted of violations of the narcotics laws. The Supreme Court held that the validity of an arrest without a warrant is to be determined by reference to local law. Under District of Columbia law, peace officers may break the door of a house to make an arrest only if denied admittance after notice of their authority and purpose. "Because the petitioner did not receive that notice before the officers broke the door to invade his home, the arrest was unlawful, and the evidence seized should have been suppressed. (*Miller* v. *United States*, 357 U.S. 301, 1958.)

In Denver an experienced Federal narcotics agent was told by a reliable informer that a man named Draper, whom the agent did not know but who was described by the informer, would return from Chicago on a certain train. The agent recognized Draper and, without a warrant, arrested him, searched him, and seized narcotics found in his possession. The Supreme Court held that the arresting officer "had probable cause and reasonable grounds to believe the petitioner was committing a violation of the laws of the United States relating to narcotic drugs at the time he was arrested. The arrest was therefore lawful, and the subsequent search and seizure, having been made incident to that lawful arrest, were likewise valid." (*Draper* v. *United States*, 358 U.S. 307, 1959.)

The problem of the search of automobiles has always posed a particularly difficult problem for police officers. Years ago in *Carroll* v. *United States* (267 U.S. 132, 1925), the Court emphasized that an automobile may be treated differently because of the mobility of the vehicle. It is simply a matter of emphasizing the pragmatic. As the Court said, "Where the securing of a warrant is reasonably practical, it must be used. . . . In cases where seizure is impossible except without a warrant, the seizing

officer acts unlawfully and at his peril unless he can show the court probable cause."
This same problem was involved in *Henry* v. *United States* (361 U.S. 98, 1959),
where Federal officers were investigating a theft from an interstate shipment of
whiskey. They observed Henry loading cartons into a car. After search and arrest,
these cartons were found to contain radios stolen from an interstate shipment. Henry
was brought to trial and convicted for the illegal possession of the radios. The
Supreme Court reversed the conviction, pointing to the lack of probable cause for
the arrest, which was without a warrant. The arrest, both prosecution and defense
agreed, took place when the Federal agents stopped the car. "Probable cause exists
if the facts and circumstances known to the officer warrant a prudent man in believing that the offense has been committed. . . . If the officer acts with probable cause,
he is protected even though it turns out that the citizen is innocent. . . . And while a
search without a warrant is, within limits, permissible if incident to a lawful arrest,
if an arrest without a warrant is to support an incidental search, it must be made with
probable cause. . . . An arrest is not justified by what the subsequent search discloses.
Under our system, suspicion is not enough for an officer to lay hands on a citizen.
It is better, so the Fourth Amendment teaches, that the guilty sometimes go free
than that citizens be subject to easy arrest."

The most important single case decided by the Court in recent years in the field
of search and seizure was *Mapp* v. *Ohio* in 1961. (367 U.S. 643) This case arose
in Cleveland, where three police officers requested entrance to a house to look for
a person they had been advised was hiding in the house, wanted for questioning in
connection with a recent bombing. They had been further advised that there was a
large amount of policy paraphernalia hidden in the house. Later, additional officers
arrived, and—without a warrant—forced their way into the house. Obscene materials
were found, for possession of which Mrs. Mapp was tried and convicted. The
Supreme Court held that this evidence was inadmissible, and reversed the conviction.
In a sense, the decision was anticlimactic, since years before in *Wolf* v. *Colorado*
(338 U.S. 25, 1949) the court had declared that the security of one's privacy against
arbitrary intrusion by the police is implicit in the concept of ordered liberty in the
Fourteenth Amendment—in other words, a "fundamental" right. However, the Court
in *Wolf* had then proceeded to note that the Fourteenth Amendment did not forbid
the admission, in a state court, of evidence obtained by an unreasonable search and
seizure. So what *Mapp* did was simply to add to the situation the sanction of exclusion of unreasonably secured evidence, the same sanction that had been used against
the use of such evidence in Federal courts for almost half a century.

An interesting and different situation was before the Court in *Lanza* v. *New York*
(370 U.S. 139, 1962). Here Lanza had visited his brother in a New York jail. Their
conversation had been electronically intercepted and recorded by state officials.
Later, during an investigation by a committee of the New York legislature of possible
corruption in the state parole system, Lanza refused to answer questions, even though
he was granted immunity under state statute. He claimed that the transcript of the
conversation with his brother furnished the basis of the committee's questions. His
argument was simply that the interception of the jail conversation was a violation of
those principles of the Fourth Amendment which have found recognition in the due
process clause of the Fourteenth. This the Court denied. "To say that a public jail
is the equivalent of a man's 'house,' or that it is a place where he can claim constitutional immunity from search or seizure of his person, his papers, or his effects, is at
best a novel argument. . . . It is obvious that a jail shares none of the attributes of
privacy of a home, an automobile, an office, or a hotel room."

As has already been noted, local law is a real factor in determining the reasonableness of a search and seizure, and that this is still very much a viable proposition was recognized in the recent case of *Ker* v. *California*. (374 U.S. 23, 1963.) Here the accused, husband and wife, had been convicted of possession of marijuana in violation of a California statute. The arresting officers had no search warrant, but the Supreme Court upheld the conviction by noting two basic points. First, there was probable cause for the arrest, since the information within the knowledge of the officers at the time they arrived at the Kers' apartment clearly furnished grounds for a reasonable belief that Ker had committed and was committing the offense of possession of marijuana. This information was the result, chiefly, of observation of his movements, his meeting with a person from whom a police sergeant had purchased marijuana, and information secured from a reliable informer.

Second, the Court noted that, even after *Mapp,* the states are not precluded from developing workable rules governing arrests and searches and seizures to meet the practical demands of effective criminal investigation and law enforcement, so long as the rules themselves are not unreasonable. Conditions and circumstances vary, just as do investigative and enforcement techniques. California's Penal Code (Section 844) permits peace officers to break into a dwelling for the purpose of arrest, after demanding admittance and explaining their purpose. Admittedly, the officers did not comply with the terms of this statute, since they entered quietly and without announcement, in order to prevent the destruction of contraband. The California District Court of Appeal held that this came within a judicial exception which had been engrafted upon the statute by a series of court decisions, and the Supreme Court of the United States agreed. "Here justification for the officers' failure to give notice is uniquely present. In addition to the officers' belief that Ker was in possession of narcotics, which could be quickly and easily destroyed, Ker's furtive conduct in eluding them shortly before the arrest was ground for the belief that he might well have been expecting the police. We therefore hold that in the particular circumstances of this case, the officers' method of entry, sanctioned by the law of California, was not unreasonable under the standards of the Fourth Amendment as applied to the States through the Fourteenth Amendment." (374 U.S. 23 at 40–41.)

It may be worthy of emphasis that even when officers are armed with a warrant, that warrant must have been issued on a finding of probable cause. Two cases illustrate the problem. In Chicago, Rugendorf had been convicted of knowingly concealing stolen fur garments. The furs were found in the basement of his home, pursuant to a search warrant which had been issued by the United States Commissioner on the strength of an affidavit which was found to be factually inaccurate in two respects, and to have been based partly on hearsay statements of confidential informants. The Court, in upholding the validity of the warrant, noted that the factual inaccuracies "were of only peripheral relevancy to the showing of probable cause. . . . We believe that there was substantial basis for the Commissioner to conclude that stolen furs were probably in the petitioner's basement. No more is required." (*Rugendorf* v. *United States,* 376 U.S. 528 at 532–533.)

A second case illustrative of the workings of the rule came out of Houston. Two police officers had applied to a local Justice of the Peace for a warrant to search for narcotics in Aguilar's home. In executing the warrant, the police officers announced at the door of Aguilar's home that they were officers, with a warrant. Upon hearing a commotion within the house, the officers forced their way into the house and seized Aguilar in the act of attempting to dispose of a packet of narcotics.

On appeal, the Supreme Court noted that "the search warrant should not have been issued because the affidavit did not provide a sufficient basis for a finding of probable cause and that the evidence obtained as a result of the search warrant was inadmissible in petitioner's trial." (*Aguilar* v. *State of Texas*, 378 U.S. 108, 1964.) The Court noted that while an affidavit may be based on hearsay information, the magistrate must be informed of some of the underlying circumstances from which the informant concluded that a crime was being committed, and some of the underlying circumstances from which the officer concluded that the informant, whose identity need not be disclosed, was "credible" or his information "reliable."

Another case in the short series that has developed explaining the application of constitutional guarantees in the matter of automobiles came out of Newport, Kentucky, a year ago. (*Preston* v. *United States*, 376 U.S. 364, 1964.) Three men who had been seated for several hours in a parked car were arrested by the police for vagrancy, searched for weapons, and taken to the police station. The car was not searched at the time of arrest, but was driven by an officer to the station, then was towed to a garage, and shortly after, was searched. Articles found in the car were turned over to Federal authorities and were later used as evidence in a trial in Federal court which resulted in conviction of conspiracy to rob a Federally-insured bank. Upon appeal, the Supreme Court noted that "Common sense dictates, of course, that questions involving searches of motor cars or other things readily moved cannot be treated as identical to questions arising out of searches of fixed structures, like houses. For this reason, what may be an unreasonable search of a house may be reasonable in the case of a motor car. . . . But even in the case of motor cars, the test still is, was the search unreasonable? . . . We think that the search was too remote in time or place to have been made as incidental to arrest and conclude, therefore, that the search of the car without a warrant failed to meet the test of reasonableness under the Fourth Amendment, rendering the evidence obtained as a result of the search inadmissible." (376 U.S. 364 at 366–368, 1964.)

Cases decided by the Court recently continue to underline the indispensable need for probable cause, either for the issuance of a warrant or for a valid arrest. For example, a United States Commissioner had issued a warrant on the basis of an affidavit by an investigator for the Internal Revenue Service. This affidavit specified a number of occasions when Federal investigators had by sight, smell, and hearing detected suspicious activities. Pursuant to the search warrant, a still was found and a conviction for possession and operation followed. Appeal was taken on the basis that there was not probable cause for the issuance of the warrant, but the Supreme Court upheld the conviction. The Court emphasized that preference is accorded police action taken under a warrant, as against searches and seizures without one. The Court went on to note that it "has long held that 'the term "probable cause" means less than evidence which would justify condemnation' . . . and that a finding of 'probable cause' may rest upon evidence which is not legally competent in a criminal trial. . . . The affidavit in this case, if read in a commonsense way rather than technically, shows ample facts to establish probable cause and allow the Commissioner to issue the search warrant." (*United States* v. *Ventresca*, 380 U.S. 102 at 107, 109, 1965.)

In another recent instance, police in Cleveland had neither a search warrant nor an arrest warrant but had received unspecified "information" and "reports" about a William Beck. They knew what he looked like and that he had a gambling record and stopped him one day in his automobile. They arrested him and searched his car but found nothing incriminating. The officers then took him to a police station where they searched his person and found some clearing house slips in his sock. Once again, there was the matter of the validity of the search depending on the validity of the arrest, and this depending on whether at the moment of arrest, there was probable cause to make it. The Court reversed the conviction and noted, "We may assume that the officers acted in good faith in arresting the petitioner. But 'good faith on the part of the arresting officers is not enough.' . . . If subjective good faith alone were the test, the protections of the Fourth Amendment would evaporate, and the people would be 'secure in their persons, houses, papers, and effects,' only in the discretion of the police." (*Beck* v. *State of Ohio,* 379 U.S. 89 at 97, 1964.)

Finally, the Court has had occasion to call attention to another specific requirement for the issuance of a warrant. The Fourth Amendment requires that a warrant may issue only on probable cause, supported by oath or affirmation, and with a particular description of the place, persons, or things to be searched or seized. In San Antonio, Texas, several officers presented themselves at John Stanford's home for the purpose of searching it, under authority of a warrant issued by a local magistrate. The object of the search was to find evidence of activity by the Communist Party, which had been outlawed by a Texas statute. The officers seized fourteen cartons of books and documents ranging from books by Hugo Black and Pope John to insurance policies, Stanford's marriage certificate, and household bills, but there were no Communist Party records or lists. Altogether there were some 2,000 items. Action was brought to annul the warrant, and to order the return of the property seized. On appeal, the Supreme Court of the United States said that "we think it is clear that this warrant was of a kind which it was the purpose of the Fourth Amendment to forbid—a general warrant." (*Stanford* v. *State of Texas,* 379 U.S. 476 at 480, 1965.) The Court then went on to note that "the constitutional requirement that warrants must particularly describe the 'things to be seized' is to be accorded the most scrupulous exactitude when the 'things' are books, and the basis for their seizure is the ideas which they contain. . . . The constitutional impossibility of leaving the protection of those freedoms to the whim of the officers charged with executing the warrant is dramatically underscored by what the officers saw fit to seize under the warrant in this case." (*Stanford* v. *State of Texas,* 379 U.S. 476 at 485, 1965.)

These are the cases, the precedents, the rules governing this matter of search and seizure at this time. We have confirmed our discussion to the more recent cases and have not even mentioned the older, classical cases such as *Rochin* v. *California* (342 U.S. 465, 1952), involving a stomach-pumping episode; *Irvine* v. *California* (347 U.S. 128, 1954), involving the placing of microphones in a home and actual trespass; and *Breithaupt* v. *Abram* (352 U.S. 432, 1957), in which there was brought into question the taking of a blood test from an unconscious man. These are older cases and of such importance that we assume knowledge of them. They are presumably still good law, even though there might be some incompatibility between *Rochin* and *Breithaupt.*

This is the relationship that exists between the Constitution and a citizen, with particular emphasis on that relationship in the narrow confines of one clause of the Constitution. This Constitution is primarily a document that applies to governmental activity, only rarely directed to citizen or individual activity. Moreover, it is a document whose applicability to government has been radically changed and expanded by the adoption of the Fourteenth Amendment and subsequent judicial interpreta-

tion of the provisions of that Amendment. Any constitution is at least two constitutions—the one establishing the organization of the government and its powers,
and the other setting down procedural and substantive restrictions on that government. In a country which spans a continent and which takes some pride in the
Federal solution to its governmental problems, we have in recent times gone far
toward a unitary scheme of things in the field of rights and liberties, again primarily
by means of the Fourteenth Amendment and subsequent interpretations. One of
these areas in which we have this "uniformity" is that of the search and seizure
guarantee, a matter with which police officers probably have more to do than with
any other single provision of the entire Constitution.

Equal Protection Under Law—Fact or Fiction

JOHN A. HANNAH

President, Michigan State University,
Chairman, U.S. Commission on Civil Rights

MAY 21, 1962

I

Michigan State University is gratified that it has been actively interested in
problems of community relations for a long, long time, and proud that its Department of Police Administration was among the pioneers in the movement to place
police and community relations on a sounder basis.

Equal protection under the law is an American ideal older than the nation itself.
It was set forth both as principle and objective in the Declaration of Independence,
reemphasized in the original Constitution, and reinforced by subsequent amendments
to that document.

Because the Constitution is essentially a legal document, we tend to overlook the
fact that it is a declaration of political and social ideals as well. Those who wrote it
were practical men, and clearly understood that their ideals would not be achieved
automatically upon ratification of the document. Hence, they wove an amazing
flexibility into it by laying down the basic ground rules, and leaving it to future generations to work out the procedures by which conditions they then considered to be
ideal would eventually be reached. For example, the original Constitution did not
provide for the direct election of senators and did not extend the franchise to
American women. This was changed by subsequent amendment, without doing
violence to the original idea of placing political power in the hands of the people.

We should not apologize for the fact that equal protection under the law remains
an ideal not yet fully realized. It probably will never be complete and absolute,
human nature being what it is. The important considerations are the size of the gap
between the ideal and today's reality, and the progress being made in narrowing
the gap.

In its 1961 Report, the U.S. Commission on Civil Rights stated that this gap
between ideal and reality was sufficiently wide as to be considered a great challenge
to all Americans. In Volume 1, it was stated:

The great American experiment in self-governing began for white people only. The inconsistency between the Nation's principles and its practices has diminished over the years. . . . The gains have been considerable . . . more people than ever before are exercising more fully their rights as citizens of the United States. The American people are increasingly aware that professions of belief in the dignity of man have meaning only if they are realized by all people in all aspects of life. The gap between the promise of liberty and its fulfillment is narrower today than it ever has been. Yet a gap remains.

The five volumes of the Commission Report set out in detail the authenticated facts of inequality in the fields of voting, education, housing, employment, and the administration of justice. All of these have significance for those interested in human relations, and the actions and attitudes of police officers have some impact for good or ill in all these areas.

There is not time to explore all five of these areas here, and because police officers are more concerned with the administration of justice, my discussion will be concentrated in that area primarily.

II

While the Constitution is not entirely clear regarding discrimination involving some private or personal prejudice, it is extremely clear that such discrimination has no place in the temples of justice. Not only is the Constitution color blind, but it requires that every judge, every jury commissioner, and every police officer be oblivious to the color of the individuals to whom the law is to be impartially applied, and to their religions and national origins as well.

Although the ideal of impartial administration of the law has by no means been fully recognized, the Commission's 1961 Justice Report makes the following statement:

It is the considered judgment of the Commission that in most respects criminal justice is administered in the United States on a non-discriminatory basis. Indeed, our progress towards the ideal of equal justice under law should be a source of pride for all Americans. The Commission is particularly impressed by the fact that most police officers never resort to brutal practices. Because of this fact, instances of brutality or discrimination in law enforcement stand out in bold relief.

That is the Commission's considered judgment. In most respects, criminal justice is administered on a non-discriminatory basis, and Americans should take pride in that fact.

But because it is the exceptions in which we are interested here, let us look at some of the instances of brutality or discrimination in the administration of justice. Here I shall draw heavily on the Justice section of the Commission's 1961 report as being the best available source of fact.

The Commission found that "police brutality by some State and local officers presents a serious and continuing problem in many parts of the United States. Both whites and Negroes are the victims, but Negroes are the victims . . . far more, proportionately, than any other group in American society."

It is not necessary to explain to most Americans that relatively few policemen are involved in brutal acts, that enlightened police leaders do everything in their power to discourage them, but that even one brutal act is too many, for it frequently suffices to convince the poor and minority group members of a community that no policeman can be trusted.

Consequently, valuable sources of information may be cut off from law enforce-ment authorities, and the entire tone of justice is coarsened and cheapened. The humane and dedicated efforts of police leaders, of judges, and other impartial offi-cials may be enervated or come to naught because of a few bad actors on the police force.

It is legitimate to argue that at least as important as the *fact* of impartial justice is the *image* of justice in a community. Do the poor and minority group members of a community *believe* that justice is administered on an impartial basis?

Police Chief E. C. Hale, of Lexington, Kentucky, summed it up when he said: "The true victims of police brutality are the police themselves, since it develops widespread hostility and disrespect for the law among members of minority groups."

As you know, brutality in administering justice frequently is not due to police action at all, but is inflicted by vigilantes or others who seek to take the law into their own hands. The Commission found that while police connivance in violence by private persons is becoming less of a problem than in the past, unfortunately such denials of equal protection still occur.

The Constitution demands that law enforcement officers show no partiality in their actions, nor use unnecessary violence. It also demands that they do not give passive or active support to the violent actions of private conspirators. Perhaps no one has ever stated this in plainer terms than the Federal judge who said almost 10 years ago: "One charged with the duty of keeping the peace cannot be an inno-cent bystander where the constitutionally protected rights of persons are being in-vaded. He must stand on the side of law and order or be counted among the mob."

A third area of discrimination and partiality dealt with by the Commission in its Justice Report was jury exclusion. This is not directly a matter of police con-cern, but it certainly is a matter of community concern, and so deserves consider-ation here.

This is what the Commission found:

> The practice of excluding Negroes from juries on account of their race still per-sists in a few States. The burden of combating such racial exclusion from juries now rests entirely on private persons—almost invariably defendants in criminal trials.

It should be added that our state-by-state study of the status of civil rights in this country turned up instances of members of other races, principally American Indians, being excluded from juries in some states where there are sizable groups of such persons. However, the problem is principally one of discrimination against Negroes.

It should seem shocking that this practice continues despite the fact that a Federal criminal statute has specifically prohibited jury exclusion since 1875—and for 80 years the Supreme Court has clearly held it to be a denial of the equal pro-tection clause of the Fourteenth Amendment. Yet, in 1959, a judge on the United States Court of Appeals for the Fifth Circuit could say: ". . . we have long known that there are counties not only in Mississippi but in the writer's own state of Alabama, in which Negroes constitute the majority of the residents but take no part in government either as voters or as jurors. Familiarity with such a condition thus prevents shock, but it all the more increases our concern over its existence."

The Supreme Court said over 80 years ago: "The very fact that colored people are singled out and expressly denied by a statute all right to participate in the administration of the law, as jurors, because of their color, though they are citizens and may be in other respects fully qualified, is practically a brand upon them, affixed by law; an assertion of their inferiority, and a stimulant to that race prejudice which is an impediment to securing to individuals of the race that equal justice which the law aims to secure to all others."

This thought applies today, not only to jury exclusion by court officials, but also to any discriminatory action by any law enforcement or court official.

There are other practices which, like jury exclusion, are not directly within the control of police officers, but which are of direct concern to them because they raise questions about the equality of justice in the United States—and distort the image of justice.

For example, there is nothing more shocking to a minority community than the news that another Negro or another Mexican has been put to death at the state prison. While one may get into many debatable issues if he enters the thorny thicket of the capital punishment question, a review of the statistics shows one clear fact: those who are executed are most often economically poor or are members of racial minorities.

A compilation by the Federal Bureau of Prisons found that 3,666 persons were executed for all offenses during the 30-year period from 1930–1959; more than half were Negroes—1,972. The statistics on executions for rape are even more disconcerting. Nine out of ten of those persons executed for rape in the United States from 1930 to 1959 were Negroes—382 out of a total of 426. All but 10 of these 426 executions took place in the Southern states. Seven of those states executed *only* Negroes for rape during this period. For example, Virginia executed 20 Negroes and no whites; Florida, 34 Negroes and no whites; Mississippi, 17 Negroes and no whites; Louisiana, 17 Negroes and no whites; and Oklahoma, 4 Negroes and no whites.

Whatever arguments may be used to justify these lopsided figures, the image of justice in the minds of many Negroes and whites stands tarnished by the shocking thought that even in matters of life and death, there may be discrimination in the administration of justice. While the police officer cannot control the imposition of the death penalty, he will be affected by its unhappy results. A community belief that sentences are being unfairly imposed makes the job of the impartial officer that much more difficult.

There is still another little known but important aspect to the matter of equal protection of the law. Many people believe that "you can't send a million dollars to jail." This widespread belief finds some support in practices that promote inequality in justice primarily because of economic rather than racial reasons—although race also may be somewhat involved. The most obvious difference in the administration of justice between the rich and the poor is found in regard to defense counsel.

Thirty years ago Mr. Justice Sutherland stated the basic proposition clearly: "Even the intelligent and educated layman . . . requires the guiding hand of counsel at every step in the proceedings against him. Without it, though he be not guilty, he faces the danger of conviction because he does not known how to establish his innocence."

So the proposition reduces itself to this: if you are poor—no matter what race or color—and you cannot afford a competent attorney, it is extremely likely that you will not get "justice" equal to that of a man who can afford a competent attorney.

This is no small problem. Indeed, one of the most extensive gaps which must be closed to get within sight of equal justice for all is that made by the problem of the indigent defendant. No one knows how many impoverished defendants are prosecuted every year, but legal aid experts place the number at hundreds of thousands of indigents prosecuted for serious offenses every year. According to Mr. Justice Douglas, "Thirty-five states provide for appointment of counsel as a matter of course on behalf of an indigent in any felony case; 15 states either make no explicit provision for appointment of counsel or make provision therefore only in capital cases or leave appointment of counsel to the discretion of the trial judge." In misdemeanor cases, there is actually no provision for the appointment of counsel to the indigent.

Even more important than legal provisions relating to the right to assigned counsel are the organized agencies that provide defender service. It has long been accepted by many lawyers and legal scholars that the traditional assigned counsel system is a failure in most American courts, and that professional organized defender systems usually provide a better standard of protection for the indigent person. As long ago as 1919, Reginald Heber Smith wrote: ". . . the truth about the assignment system in criminal cases is that as a whole, it has proved a dismal failure, and that at times it has been worse than a failure."

There were 98 defender agencies in the United States as of September 21, 1961, according to listings in the National Legal Aid and Defender Association Directory. During 1960, some 71 of these agencies reported 116,568 new cases to the National Legal Aid and Defender Association. Adding the cases probably handled by the agencies that didn't report, it is likely that no more than 130,000 cases were handled by all professional defenders during 1960. Therefore, it is probable that hundreds of thousands of indigent defendants were not represented by professional defenders —they had to rely upon court-appointed counsel or none at all. Most of those attorneys appointed by the court served either without compensation or for a totally inadequate fee. Defenders operated in 16 states and the District of Columbia. Approximately half of all defenders were concentrated in two states—California and Illinois. In 34 states, there is not single professional agency.

One of the toughest questions about the right to counsel is: when does it begin? This question concerns the ideal of equal justice and the police. The law on this point is quite unclear. While a few states make it a crime for a police officer to refuse a prisoner's request to communicate with his counsel, most states have no such provision. And the Supreme Court of the United States has never overruled a conviction solely because the police refused a man's request to see his counsel while being interrogated.

If policemen permitted every person's request to see his attorney, many officers argue, the solution of crimes would be made immensely more difficult. As Mr. Justice Jackson stated in 1949: "To bring in a lawyer means a real peril to solution of the crime, because, under our adversary system, he deems that his sole duty is to protect his client—guilty or not—and that in such a capacity he holds no duty whatever to help society solve its crime problem. Under this conception of criminal procedure, any lawyer worth his salt will tell the suspect in no uncertain terms to make no statement to police under any circumstances."

But a competent law enforcement officer realizes that evidence should come from some source other than the suspect's confession. Modern law enforcement plays down the confession and emphasizes scientific, systematic investigation— regardless of the counsel factor.

For many people, of course, there is no need of a lawyer's advice not to talk to the police. A man of some education or a professional gangster will often be fully aware of his right to keep quiet. So it is the poor, the uneducated, and the intimidated who most need lawyers during the initial stages of criminal prosecution. If the present procedure continues whereby policemen do not have to allow counsel to confer with their clients while under interrogation, it amounts to preying on the ignorance of the poor and the uneducated to solve crimes. Again, we come face to face with a situation which may result in unequal justice.*

III

What can be done to make the ideal of equal protection under law less a fiction, more a fact?

When a police officer violates the law, it is possible to bring a civil or a criminal suit against him. However, the U. S. Commission on Civil Rights found that the Federal Civil Rights Acts are not, in their present state, effective remedies. In a recent two-and-one-half-year period, 1,328 complaints of brutality against police officers were received at the United States Department of Justice. Six of these resulted in convictions. During a comparable 2-year period, 42 civil suits for money damages were filed by victims of alleged police brutality in Federal courts. None of these was successful.

To improve the effectiveness of the Federal criminal remedies for unlawful official violence, the Commission on Civil Rights recommended a more tightly drawn criminal statute and an amendment to the civil statute which would allow suits against any local government that employs officers who deprive persons of rights.

While such court actions have their place on the path of progress, the Commission on Civil Rights found that "Perhaps the single most potent weapon against unlawful police activity is a police commander who will not tolerate it. The converse is also true: where police leaders assume a permissive attitude toward violence by their men, they are often licensing brutality."

A police leader determined to have his organization fight crime within the law must have a system for handling complaints from citizens. Whether it is done within the police department, or through an independent police advisory board composed of private citizens may make no essential difference, so long as the cases are investigated impartially, and so long as punishment is imposed where punishment is deserved.

The Justice Report stated: "The ultimate factor in any study of police misconduct must be . . . the individual policeman. The manner of his selection and of his training are crucial factors. When a police department fails to screen out the strongly prejudiced, the emotionally unstable, or the unintelligent, it is inviting official misconduct."

---

* Editors' Note: Subsequent decisions of the Supreme Court, in the *Escobedo* and *Miranda* cases, have dealt with this issue.

More gratifying to me personally, as President of a University which for many years has fought for higher standards of police training of a professional kind at the college level, was this finding of the Commission:

The most effective "remedies" for illegal official violence are those that tend to prevent such misconduct, rather than those which provide sanctions after the fact. The application of professional standards to the selection and training of policemen is one such preventive measure.

There is growing acceptance among enlightened police leaders that social science has great contributions to make in the field of police science. For example, the New York City police department is now sponsoring a comprehensive research program which is aimed at developing tests to identify the proper personality types for police work, and in establishing training programs which will further the establishment of professional standards.

Training courses in scientific crime detection and in human relations and constitutional rights will also have their impact. An officer trained to fight crime with some sophistication will not resort to such crude and unsophisticated methods as brutality or coercion of confessions. And an officer trained to understand, both the nature of constitutional rights and the vital democratic reasons for their existence, may be expected to respect them, not only in theory but also in practice.

It is clear that there is greater interest than ever before among policemen of all ranks in making police work a fine profession. Nothing is more eloquent testimony of that fact than this conference. Further proof is found in the growth of interest across the land in police–community relations meetings and institutes, which have spread from the nucleus of this Institute. Every enlightened police leader realizes that we now stand on the threshold of great advances, that with a concerted effort now there will be a breakthrough in the struggle for police progress in both law enforcement and in the observance of rights.

One of the major obstacles on the path of progress is a very old one: lack of money. Students of police science know that much research is possible, but it remains only possible and not accomplished because of a lack of funds for research in this field.

There are now many college-level schools of police administration in existence, including that at Michigan State University. But there are extremely few scholarships to aid worthy students in attending them. Police leaders know that they must attract good men in order to carry on the fight against crime, and they know that they must train these men properly in methods of crime control, and how to handle mob situations, and how to observe the Constitution. Police leaders know also that the states and localities which want all of these things done by their police force are not willing to provide the necessary funds. No community that pays its policemen the salaries of day laborers should expect that they be and act like professionals.

In recognition of the great problems facing state and local police forces because of inadequate funds, the Commission on Civil Rights recommended a Federal grant-in-aid program to assist state and local governments, upon their request, to increase the professional quality of their police forces.

The Commission stated: "Such grants-in-aid might apply to the development and maintenance of (1) recruit selection tests and standards; (2) training programs in scientific crime detection; (3) training programs in constitutional rights and human relations; (4) college-level schools of police administration; and (5) scholarship programs that assist policemen to receive training in schools of police administration."

Since this Commission recommendation was made, several bills have been introduced into both houses of Congress which would establish such a grant-in-aid program. If Congress were to pass these bills, for the first time in history the Federal government would be giving direct monetary aid to help state and local police forces in the fight against crime and in the fight for constitutional rights. For a modest sum, the Federal government would be pushing our nation ever closer to the ideal of equal justice under law.*

IV

The emphasis has been on the policeman and his role in the administration of justice. It would be unfair to leave the impression that the police officer and the police leaders are free agents in this matter. We should acknowledge that those in other positions of authority and respect in the community can, through their actions and words, either stimulate race prejudice, or stimulate respect for the Constitution, for the law, and for democratic progress through the efforts and contributions of all of our citizens, regardless of skin pigmentation, religion, or national origin.

When community or government officials advocate defiance of the Constitution, or even of specific court orders, they are setting examples which others in the community may follow all too faithfully in their own way. Government officials and community leaders usually content themselves with rather sophisticated devices: the oratorical harangue, the printed word, the lawyer's brief. But others in the community may be excited by such exhortations to use less sophisticated weapons in order to defy the law: the fist, the booted foot, the torch, even the loaded pistol.

Police leaders frequently find themselves in the middle when community tensions mount. For example, they will receive demands from some citizen groups to fight a "crime wave" by any method available, such as indiscriminate arrests, searches, and seizures. Other community leaders may make it clear that they expect their police force to keep minority group members "in their places" by enforcing local segregation customs, or by allowing local vigilante groups to handle the situation in their own violent way.

On the other hand, leaders of the minority groups may be accusing police, without justification, of practicing discrimination in the enforcement of the law.

One needs to be reminded that when faced with such demands and charges, a policeman's lot is more than unhappy—it is extremely difficult.

With no intention to intrude upon another's profession, it seems appropriate to say that the conscientious police leader, when faced with a situation such as described, must strive to accomplish two difficult tasks.

First, he must honor the constitutional and legal guarantees of the rights of all citizens. It is a contradiction in terms when a law enforcement officer claims the right to violate the law in order to enforce it. It is a contradiction in terms when a law enforcement officer lets his personal opinions or community pressures affect his duty to apply the law equally to all persons, regardless of their race, economic status, or social views. Unequal justice is not justice at all. A Dallas Police Department manual states the principle succinctly: "An officer of the law . . . stands as a symbol of the impartial authority of society."

---

* Editor's Note: Subsequently accomplished via establishment of the Office of Law Enforcement Assistance, U. S. Department of Justice.

The second difficult task confronting the police leader in a situation of high tension is to convince every segment of the community that the police department as a whole is impartial, and that it will apply the law within the law. To do this requires more than demonstration by action, although this is a major part of the task; it requires constant contact with community leaders as well, and a good job of explaining, so they understand clearly why the police department must be impartial, no matter whose ox is gored.

But this chore of developing community understanding of the necessity that the police be impartial should not rest on the police leader alone. Other leaders in the community share the responsibility for convincing the citizens of the community that the police can properly take no other posture than one of impartial administration of justice.

In this presentation, we have gone at length into the responsibilities of the police leader to train his officers to perform as professionals, and to understand their roles in the community. If they do their part, the remainder of the community is under equal obligation to learn about, to understand, and to support what the police are seeking to do. The leaders of the community have the right to expect their police force to do its duty, but they have no right to make the discharge of that duty more difficult or impossible.

This is a matter of education, in the broadest sense of the word, and brings us back to where we began—the notion that education is and will be a prime factor in the solution of the kinds of problems with which this Institute concerns itself. Education, in this sense, can take forms ranging from simple over-the-fence conversations between neighbors, to the formal professional training of policemen, to community discussion groups, to national conferences such as this. We cannot hope for sudden miracles in the complex area of civil rights; the record shows that such progress as we have made has been made slowly and painfully over many years.

The important thing is to make progress all of the time in all of the communities across the land; the rate of advance may be uneven, and here and there it will be discouragingly slow. But if we continue to make some progress all of the time, the cumulative effect will be tremendous, and this decade will be remembered as the one in which the gap between American idealism and practical reality was narrowed sharply. We can even look forward to the day when it will no longer be of interest to ask whether equal protection of the law is fact or fiction, because it has become accomplished fact.

Police and the Community:
a Judicial View*

THE HONORABLE GEORGE EDWARDS

Judge, Sixth Circuit, United States Court of Appeals

MAY 15, 1966

This article expresses the views of a man well qualified to discuss the vital topic of law enforcement and its relation to minority groups. In 1961 the resi-

* An adaptation of an article by Judge Edwards appearing in the MICHIGAN REVIEW, November 1965, Vol. 64, No. 1; Copyright 1965, Michigan Law Review Association.

dents and newly-elected city administration of Detroit felt that there was a real possibility of a major riot similar to the one in 1943. Mayor Cavanagh therefore persuaded Judge Edwards to leave his position as a Justice of the Supreme Court of Michigan and assume the responsibilities of Police Commissioner of Detroit.

After we join all public authority in decrying mob violence and disrespect for law, the problems of causation and of recurrence still remain. I pretend no competence to solve these problems with specific reference to any city other than my own. However, the discussion that follows represents the result of a quarter of a century of study of the same problems in Detroit, and I have no reason to believe that the factors which produced the 1943 race riot in Detroit, or the methods by which Detroit has sought (successfully to date) to prevent recurrence in the 1960's, are of importance only in Michigan.

I. The Detroit Riot of 1943

I cannot overemphasize the fact that race hatred is not a one-way street. There are extremists with names other than Ku Klux Klan. There are extremists who have black faces as well as those who have white faces, and extremists of both varieties took over the streets of Detroit for twenty-four bloody hours in 1943. Thirty-six people died during that reign of terror. I believe that I can fully illustrate the pattern by describing the fate of two of the victims.

One of these was a Dr. de Horatius, who was of Italian origin, I believe; certainly of white skin. Dr. de Horatius had served on the east side of Detroit for many years, and among his patients he had many Negroes. At approximately ten o'clock on the morning the riot broke out, he was called to assist a patient on the east side of the city. In pursuance of his duty, he responded. He was met on the streets by a mob full of anger and race hatred. They didn't know Dr. de Horatius from a bale of hay; all they knew about him was that they, the mob, had black faces and that he had a white face. They stoned him to death with no more knowledge than that.

Later in that twenty-four-hour period, a Negro workman was going home from his job, driving alone. He was stopped by a mob with anger and race hatred in their hearts. They did not know any more about him than that the mob's faces were white and this man's face was black. They overturned his car, and when the gasoline spilled out of the tank, they lit a match and set fire to it, burning up the man inside the car.

The Honorable Edward J. Jeffries was Mayor of the City of Detroit at the time. He was a great mayor, but he had not known that this terror was imminent or that it was even possible. This attitude was shared by most of the city's residents, and to say that Detroit was not ready for this outburst of racial strife would be to put it mildly. In this respect, every mayor in America would find it useful to read a recent journalistic account of the events of that twenty-four-hour period.[1] The authors of this commentary were not very kind in their judgment of Detroit. With the benefit of twenty-two years of hindsight, it is easy to criticize the lack of preparation and the failure of performance which left thirty-six people dead on the streets of Detroit and army units in command of the city. Nevertheless, whatever may have precipitated this violence in 1943, it is clear that in 1966 no one will make excuses for any city's inability to foresee the possibility of racial trouble in any large city in this country. The warnings from the summer of 1964 and the 1965

Los Angeles riot are too recent. Therefore, the following discussion is dedicated to seeking answers—in advance of disaster.

II. The Impact of a Changing Society

The police function is in trouble in every section of our nation. This fact may be attributed to the impact of four historic trends: the increasing urbanization of our country; the increasing insistence of the United States Supreme Court on strict compliance by the police with the principles of the Bill of Rights; the vast and continuing migration of millions of Negro citizens, principally from southern rural areas to the great metropolitan centers; and the civil rights revolution of the 1960's, which is seeking to establish within this decade full freedom and equality for all Negro citizens.[2] I do not decry any of these trends, but it is quite evident that each of them imposes certain problems upon the metropolitan police function.

A. Effects of Urbanization

Social order has always been the basic function of every organized government. However, our American government, while plainly designed to preserve order, has also made the signal contribution to history of avowing as a government objective the achieving of individual liberty for its citizens. Thus, the policeman has the responsibility of reconciling these two objectives of order and freedom; in a large city, this is a complex task.

Freedom in a metropolitan area is entirely different from the freedom that was once enjoyed on the frontier. In relation to the man of the frontier, liberty could almost be defined as the right to do what one wished, without hindrance. In a big city, however, liberty might be more accurately referred to as the maximum freedom of choice consistent with the maintenance of similar freedom for the other members of society.

In the days of Daniel Boone, there would have been little point to a traffic light at a crossing of foot trails; today we accept the interference with our liberty represented by traffic signals because we know that without them, there would be hopeless confusion. Similarly, when a generation or two ago a farm boy on a spring day yelled, ran, or picked up a rock and threw it—who cared? He was a boy. However, today this same conduct in a large city—with perhaps no more basic motivation than the animal spirits which moved the boy's rural grandfather—would almost inevitably produce a police call and a police statistic. In an earlier period, few people would have been bothered by bitter and violent words uttered by a pioneer to a few companions around a campfire. However, in the hot city streets of summer, words of equal violence addressed to a Ku Klux Klan-minded crowd in St. Augustine, or to a Black Muslim-minded crowd in Philadelphia could prove to be a major public hazard.

These examples are provided only to remind us that law enforcement in a rural society and law enforcement in our modern urban society are vastly different. Today, most Americans live in metropolitan areas, where millions of people who do not know one another, nevertheless live and work in close proximity and with greatly increased chances for conflict.[3] At least partly from necessity — and frequently without recognizing what we have done—we have turned over to the police officers of our big cities many functions which used to be among the most important duties of the individual and the family. A modern policeman's tour of duty is full of radio runs which require him to correct the conduct of children, to mediate family quarrels, to determine the right of way between over-eager drivers, to care for the injured on the streets, and to protect our homes at night and our persons in the daytime. All this is expected to be done with the concern of a social worker, the wisdom of a Solomon, and the prompt courage of a combat soldier. It is interesting to note that in our day, when the parable of the Good Samaritan is re-enacted on a city street, almost invariably the modern Good Samaritan wears a blue coat.

B. Effect of Recent Supreme Court Rulings

For the moment, let us leave the frontline defender of society—the police officer—and turn abruptly to another agency of our law: the Supreme Court of the United States. Notwithstanding the foregoing complimentary remarks about our police departments, I do not intend to attack the recent Court decisions in which the rights of persons suspected of crime have been vigorously upheld. Indeed, I see nothing inconsistent about simultaneously praising both the police function and the protective policies laid down by the Supreme Court.

For over a decade, our Supreme Court has been engaged in leading this country toward making more effective the high ideals of our American Constitution. It has been setting ever higher standards of law enforcement; it has told us that equality before the law and the equal protection of the laws must be made realities of everyday life; it has told us that deprivation of human liberty is essentially a decision for the judiciary; it has told us that as far as the Constitution is concerned, absent probable cause or a judicial warrant, there is no such thing as a lawful arrest for investigation only; and it has told us that forced confessions are anathema to American law and that a citizen has a right to counsel in all felony prosecutions. Thus, it seems clear that the Constitution and the Supreme Court has ruled out of our system of law such old-fashioned police measures as dragnet arrests, detention for investigation only, and third-degree procurement of confessions.[4] However, no matter how much we approve, in general, of the objectives just outlined, it must be recognized that they demand more intensive police training and increased police manpower.

C. Effect of Mass Migration of Negroes

The third tremendous change which has taken place in this nation, and which has had a concomitant impact on law enforcement and social order, has been the redistribution of millions of Negro citizens who have departed from rural areas in the South. To some degree, this movement is still continuing. The problems which confront American cities as a result of this human migration were well summarized by one recent writer:

> [The solution] is not, as so many assume, to bring the wandering middle class back from the suburbs. The large city . . . cannot import a middle class; it must manufacture its own. . . . [B]ringing people from society's backwaters into the mainstream of American life has always been the principal business, and the principal glory, of the American city. . . .
>
> It isn't any longer; the city is in trouble today because it isn't dealing successfully with its newcomers. They are still pouring in—not from County Cork, or Bavaria, or Sicily, or Galicia, but from Jackson, Mississippi, and Memphis, Tennessee, and a host of towns and hamlets with names like Sunflower, Rolling Fork, and Dyersburg. The new immigrants are distinguished from the old residents not by religion or national origin, but by color. Between 1950 and 1960 the twelve largest cities lost over two million white residents; they gained nearly two million Negro residents.
>
> It is the explosive growth of their Negro populations, in fact, that constitutes the large cities' principal problem and concern.[5]

The writer of this commentary also observed that city slum problems are regarded by city officials as primarily the product of physical deterioration of areas inhabited by Negroes. He also noted that juvenile delinquency and mounting welfare payments are frequently associated with the problems encountered by Negroes because of their failure to adjust to city life.

My reporting of these general observations should not be taken as an indication that I am not identifying crime in big cities as a race problem. On the contrary, I think crime is a problem which is produced by human degradation. If you subject any portion of a population, regardless of its national origin or color, to conditions of poverty, lack of education, lack of culture, and lack of employment opportunities, that segment of society will, in relatively short order, begin to produce a disproportionately large number of delinquents and criminals. Although it is true that in most of our large cities a higher percentage of recorded crimes are committed by Negro citizens than by whites, it also is true that statistically a far higher percentage of Negro citizens reside in slums. They constitute a much higher percentage of employees with the lowest paid jobs, a greater percentage of the unemployed, a far higher percentage of school dropouts, and a far higher percentage of people who have known degradation, poverty, and discrimination throughout the past three hundred years.[6]

In every one of our large cities, there are two other factors which should be obvious to any who will look. First, it is clear that the portion of our society with the greatest stake in effective, vigilant, and vigorous law enforcement is the Negro community. Although more crimes are committed by Negroes than by white in the core areas of our cities, Negroes also constitute a higher percentage of the victims than do whites.[7] For example, 84 per cent of the assault victims in Washington, D.C., are Negroes. A study conducted in one of Detroit's precincts heavily populated with Negroes disclosed that although 78 per cent of the identified assault offenders were Negroes, 76 per cent of the victims were also Negroes. Similarly, a 1963 survey undertaken in Dallas revealed that 68 per cent of the persons arrested on suspicion of homicide were Negroes, and that 69 per cent of the victims were likewise of Negro extraction. Finally, in Philadelphia a five-year study of homicides indicated that all but 6.6 per cent of the crimes were committed by offenders belonging to the same race as the victim. With respect to the small number of interracial homicides, 2.7 per cent were committed by whites and 3.9 per cent by Negroes. Thus, it can be seen that, contrary to widely held beliefs about the nature of crime in the United States, Negroes are much more likely to be victims of crimes involving violence than are whites.

The second factor that deserves emphasis is that just as it is true that it is easy to police the better sections of the white-occupied portions of any city, so it is also far easier to police the better sections which are occupied by Negro residents. A good example of this exists in Detroit, where for approximately forty years a particular neighborhood has attracted Negro businessmen, lawyers, doctors, and skilled craftsmen, who have built homes and reared their children in a pleasant residential atmosphere. Indeed, this neighborhood—Conant Gardens—is known as one of the quietest areas in the entire city of Detroit. Thus, it should be evident that the notion that crime is a race problem is totally false. But wherever there has been discrimination, impoverishment, and denial of rights, automatically there will also be built-in problems in relation to social order.

D. Effect of the Civil Rights Revolution

The foregoing observations provide a background for a discussion of the fourth major influence upon the law enforcement function—the civil rights revolution of the 1960's. As a nation, we are engaged in the historic task of seeking to raise eleven per cent of our people from the effects of the slavery, segregation, and degradation in which they have lived for the past three hundred years. This is a stupendous challenge, and none of us can assume that it will be easy to accomplish in any respect. However, it is certainly obvious that the role of the police in this historic revolution is crucial.

The local police should always be the representatives of the law; it is, therefore, a tragedy to have their energies diverted to defiance of the law, the Constitution, and the courts. It requires condemnation from every law-abiding citizen in this country. Episodes like those experienced in Birmingham and Selma, Alabama, and in Oxford and Neshoba County, Mississippi, add to the police problems in every section of the country. These episodes represent the most futile exhibitions of this century. There is no real question about whether such fundamental constitutional rights as equal education and equal voting will be granted to all citizens in this country; it is only a question as to when and how this result will be achieved. Equal treatment with respect to these essential rights is required by the basic religious concepts of the American people, and is mandated by every aspect of our constitutional law. Even those persons who are engaged in leading the resistance activities must know in their hearts that they must accede to this result.[8]

It is not enough, however, merely to condemn the use of local police to defeat implementation of constitutional rights for Negro citizens. Positive measures must also be applied to dispel the deep-seated belief held by many Negro citizens that equal law enforcement does not exist anywhere in the country. For this reason, the demand for equal law enforcement is increasingly one of the fundamental objectives of the civil rights revolution. No matter how frequently this demand is stated in exaggerated terms, there remains a fundamental problem that must be recognized. Although local police forces generally regard themselves as public servants with the responsibility of maintaining law and order, they tend to minimize this attitude when they are patrolling areas that are heavily populated with Negro citizens. There they tend to view each person on the streets as a potential criminal or enemy, and all too often that attitude is reciprocated. Indeed, hostility between the Negro communities in our large cities and the police departments is the major problem in law enforcement in this decade. It has been a major cause of all recent race riots. The elimination of this hostility will require attention and reason, and great local and national effort.

III. Origin and Magnitude of the Hostilities and Suggestions for Improvement

Conflict between the police and the Negro people is deep-rooted in our history. The Negro citizen sees the police officer in blue coat, with a white face, as the representative of the white man's law, who for nearly 300 years has enforced the laws—first of slavery, and more recently of legally sanctioned segregation.[9] Similarly, the bitterness that has been demonstrated by Negro rioters may be the product of a long series of unforgettable personal experiences. For example, in the 1930's, if a teenage Negro boy met a white police officer in the late afternoon on the streets of a town in eastern Texas near where I grew up, his first contact with the law would probably be the command: "Nigger, don't let the sun set on you in this town!" Thirty years later in a large northern city, the bitterness engendered by the memory could turn a Saturday night party that has become loud enough for a police call into a dangerous melee.[10]

Feelings of hostility also exist on the other side of the conflict. Police officers have grown up in a tradition in which part of their historic function assigned by the community has been "keeping the Negro in his place." This history produces current attitudes which are illustrated by the great number of present-day police officers who invariably use the hated term "nigger" in talking about (and sometimes to) Negro citizens.

However, some police hostility is based upon personal observations made during the course of duty. A thoroughly unbiased officer making the run to the Saturday night party referred to above could not miss the hostility which greeted him—and he would neither know nor think about its source. Similarly, many white police officers work daily in core area precincts where they are constantly in contact with crimes committed by Negroes. These same officers probably live in neighborhoods occupied by white residents where there is relatively less crime and disorder; this fact alone makes them tend to identify Negroes with crime, and whites with peace and order. We have already seen that such a conclusion is an erroneous over-simplification, but it is nevertheless a part of the hostility problem with which we must deal. Indeed, it is the pressure exerted by these hostilities which makes it so very important that top policymaking be in civilian control, and that mayors and civilian police commissioners exercise, in fact, the control which the law grants to them.

This analysis of the problem leads me inevitably to two simple conclusions, each an enormously difficult goal to achieve: (1) that we should greatly strengthen law enforcement and (2) that we should move in every way possible to guarantee equal law enforcement.

While I was Police Commissioner of Detroit during 1962 and 1963, we formulated a policy for the police department which was specifically designed to achieve these two goals. It provided: (1) More law enforcement and more vigorous law enforcement. (2) Equal protection of the law for all law-abiding citizens; equal enforcement of the law against all law violators. (3) The support of law-abiding citizens for law enforcement. We posted this policy statement above the admitting desk in each of the precinct stations. I always thought that the mere statement of these very general principles was of real value, because they were read by both the men on the force and the general public. However, awareness of such a policy is only the initial phase; the real problem relates to the method of implementation. That is, how does one actually guarantee equal and effective law enforcement? The answer to this question is crucial to the task of ending the feelings of hostility, fear, and distrust which currently affect a major portion of the people in American cities. The following guidelines are offered as a means to this vital end.

A. The Fact-Finding Function

First, it is essential to find the facts and face them. Unfortunately, this has not always been the practice. "The police officer is always right" is a familiar slogan in precinct station houses, and the temptation, regardless of the facts, to defend police conduct which violates the book of procedure, and the law, is a temptation to which many police officers are, by social pressure in their own ranks, quite inclined to yield.

However, facts are frequently misstated against the police as well as in their favor. The criminal arrested on the street almost invariably wants to find something on the policeman. The fact that he would lie to achieve this should surprise nobody. Therefore, some suspicion is justified in relation to almost anything that such a person may offer in mitigation or expiation of his conduct.

Fortunately, there are certain well-defined ways of finding facts. Most things that happen on the streets of large cities are seen by a number of people. If you ask, and take down what is said by those who saw the incident, and look at what is there to be seen, the chances are good of coming out with an accurate picture of what actually occurred.

There are, of course, some questions which cannot be completely resolved. For example, it is impossible to determine exactly how hard an arresting officer should have hit a belligerent drunk who took a swing at him. There is, of necessity, a basic discretion vested in a police officer dealing with such a situation. Thus, no one can fairly determine after the fact whether the pounds of pressure exerted by the policeman's fist, or by his billy, were scientifically calculated to be the least amount of physical force necessary to subdue his antagonist. Similarly, when dealing with violent crime, the police officer who knows that his own life is in jeopardy has legal discretion to utilize any reasonable means to protect himself; in such measures, he deserves the support of the community he serves.

However, some police hostility is based upon personal observations made during the course of study. A thoroughly unbiased officer making the run to the Saturday night party referred to above could not miss the hostility which greeted him— and he would neither know nor think about its source. Similarly, many white police by "falling on the precinct steps." Nevertheless, in the early months of my administration as Police Commissioner, I reviewed reports that described this somewhat fantastic feat as having been accomplished by a shackled prisoner.

This does not mean that every error in judgment made by a police officer should result in his discharge, for policemen are required to deal with difficult and complicated problems. However, as in any other walk of life, if an officer deserves correction, he should have it. As a matter of fact, any situation where the truth is allowed to be covered up by official reports is productive of a great amount of hostility toward, and disregard for, law enforcement agencies. For this reason, the community relations or complaint bureau in every police department should be manned by permanently assigned officers who have demonstrated sufficient intelligence and courage to face hostilities, both inside and outside the department. Their reports should go directly to the civilian head of the department, who should in turn make a thorough investigation of all significant complaints, and who should exercise the final decision-making authority.

B. Communication with the Public

The second means suggested to achieve impartial and effective law enforcement involves knowing the community. The administrative branch of every police department should open and maintain lines of communication between the department and all sections of the community it serves. Particularly in this decade, meaningful communication with the Negro community and its leaders is essential. Police administrators should always be available to meet with them, to exchange information, and to try earnestly to resolve problems. Furthermore, if the administrators are conscious of a problem, they should themselves initiate the discussion, instead of waiting for someone else to call.

C. Abolition of "Alley Court"

The administration of every police department should also make it known that it will not tolerate the institution commonly referred to in police circles as "alley court." No legal concept or constitutional theory sanctions the use of such disciplinary devices. Nevertheless, a few police officers are sincerely convinced that they are unable to maintain peace and order unless they are allowed to bolster their authority in the streets by use of a fist or billy when they feel it is necessary. Our total society prohibits "alley court." Punishment is not the function of the police; their function is to detect and apprehend and bring into court for punishment.

"Alley court" is ordinarily used against minority groups. It is easy to see how such a practice can inflame the attitude of such a group—in this case, the Negro population. It produces cries of "police brutality," and it deprives the police department of its most important weapon against crime—the support of the law-abiding populace residing in the core areas of our big cities. There are relatively few police officers who believe in "alley court"; they cannot be allowed to perpetuate an utterly indefensible institution.

D. Suggestions for Additional Measures

The remaining suggestions designed to achieve impartial law enforcement do not require elaboration; I have therefore incorporated them into the following checklist:

1. Identify police troublemakers on the force and transfer them to non-critical jobs.
2. Ban "trigger words" in police station.
3. Enforce politeness in the giving of traffic tickets.
4. End investigative arrests.
5. Increase law enforcement in high-crime precincts.
6. Drive out organized crime and pay particular attention to its manifestations in the core areas.
7. Make certain that equal opportunity exists in all phases of department operation—recruitment, assignments, and promotion.
8. Ban the use of police dogs in core areas. A dog companion for a single patrolman on a lonely beat may be useful, but that same dog at a racial demonstration is a symbol of race hatred.[11]
9. Integrate police teams—particularly details employed at racial demonstrations and "ready forces" employed to respond to street conflicts.
10. Seek more police officers.
11. Seek better training for police officers.
12. Seek better pay for police officers.

I make no suggestion that any of these items is so elementary that it can be the subject of a simple order, and then forgotten. Even more important, I do not wish to suggest that any police department with which I am familiar has completely accomplished all of them. However, I do feel that if these policies are adopted as sincere objectives, and if they are tenaciously adhered to, then significant progress can be achieved. In fact, these policies have been adopted as goals by the Police Department of the City of Detroit. Although the inauguration of this program brought many predictions of dire consequences from prophets of doom both inside and outside the Police Department, the results have been quite gratifying. Since the implementation of this program, Detroit's figures have been significantly below the national trend as indicated by the FBI crime trend index.

By what I have said, it must be obvious that I believe wholeheartedly in civilian control of police forces. There are many proposals for achievement of this, including civilian review boards. The best mechanism in my view, by far, is that of a civilian police administration—dedicated to vigorous, effective, fair and equal law enforcement—which has both responsibility for law enforcement and control of police practice.

The great majority of police officers, I believe, want no part of any abusive practices. They want and will support higher standards of training, of pay, and of performance in their profession.

Federal assistance in relation to some local police needs should be sought—particularly, I believe, in relation to police training. In Washington, I recently proposed the founding of a National Police Training College, to be organized, staffed, and financed on a level which would make it comparable to a West Point or an Annapolis. Such an institution could do more to enhance the quality of local law enforcement than any other single program I can imagine.

IV. The Need for Community Support

Finally, I wish to emphasize that I would like to see more public concern about police work—not less. I would like to see citizens feel that they have a tremendous stake in how their police department operates and feel a duty to support it in the proper discharge of its duties. I would like to see them willing to "get involved."

A woman was murdered in Queens last year within sight or hearing of thirty-eight people, not one of whom called the police. They did not want to get involved. A police officer was engaged in a desperate struggle to prevent a would-be suicide from throwing himself off an expressway bridge in Detroit. When the officer asked for help in trying to lift the man to safety, one citizen gave it. Others passed by, not wanting to get involved. What commentaries these are on our civilization!

Indeed, the element of citizen support for law enforcement is basic in a democratic society. Without it, the police effort can degenerate into an occupation-army attitude.[12] With citizen support, the police are the community's right arm in fighting the evils which make city living difficult.

In the press, by television and radio, and at neighborhood meetings, we openly sought the active support of the civilian population while I was Police Commissioner of Detroit. At that time, Precinct 10 was the most difficult area to patrol in the city, and it also happened to be heavily populated by Negroes. The topic of "community relations" had been scheduled for one of the regular quarterly precinct meetings. The occasion did not turn out to be an ordinary affair. The overflowing crowd (ninety per cent were Negroes) was seated on hard folding chairs, but the people remained for three hours to talk in detail with the precinct officers about law enforcement problems in their area.

The most popular man at the meeting was the precinct inspector, who had been responsible for a vigorous program of law enforcement. During the course of this entire meeting, there was not one complaint about police discrimination or brutality. In fact, these residents were asking for stricter enforcement measures in their particular block or neighborhood, rather than wanting to have the police removed. They were telling us where stills and "blind pigs" were operating, and who was pushing people around in that area. This is the kind of information which makes the job of law enforcement a great deal easier than it might otherwise be.

During this same meeting, we also awarded ten department citations in recognition of outstanding assistance to the police. The circumstances of one of these awards are particularly interesting. Two gunmen had held up a bar; when they left with the loot, three Negro citizens followed them out the door, chased them, caught them, and held them until the police arrived. Although we did not advocate such dangerously active civilian participation, we felt compelled to acknowledge that it was an act of considerable courage. However, we did encourage people to tell us when they were aware of illegal activities, and most of the other nine citations were awarded for this type of service.

V. Conclusion

The sort of communication that was represented by that precinct meeting is the very essence of democratic participation in law enforcement. Such avenues of communication will permit us to make further progress in human relations without the eruptions of violence which plagued many of our great cities this past summer.

All good law is basically the codification of the wisdom and morality of past ages. It is never safe to deal with practical problems for long without eventually relating them to moral standards. I feel it is fitting to conclude with such a statement:

Owe no man anything, but to love one another: for he that loveth another hath fulfilled the law. . . .

Love worketh no ill to his neighbor: therefore love is the fulfilling of the law.

And that, knowing the time, that now it is high time to awake out of sleep: for now is our salvation nearer than when we believed.

The night is far spent, the day is at hand: let us therefore cast off the works of darkness, and let us put on the armor of light.[13]

References

1. Shogan & Craig, THE DETROIT RACE RIOT (1964).

2. "[T]he Negroes' impatience, bitterness, and anger . . . are likely to increase the closer they come to full equality. This is not a quirk of Negro character but a characteristic of all disadvantaged groups: the closer they are to their goals, the harder it is to understand or justify the disparities that remain." Silberman, CRISIS IN BLACK AND WHITE, 357 (1964).

3. "[T]he most important factor [affecting crime and law enforcement] is the simplest. It is the trend of concentration of our population in a few large metropolitan centers—it is people living closer together than ever before. Crime as well as other human behavior, is a function both of the number of persons involved and their proximity to each other. This is probably the most difficult single problem with which law enforcement must deal." Acheson, Remarks at the Semi-Annual Meeting, Central Eastern Area Armed Forces Disciplinary Central Board, Bolling Air Force Base, October 15, 1964.

4. To a large extent, recent Supreme Court decisions have not *changed* substantive standards as much as they have sought *compliance* with existing standards, and have not imposed "tighter

restriction" on police powers, as much as they have sought tighter *enforcement* of long standing restrictions. See generally Kamisar, *On the Tactics of Police–Prosecution Oriented Critics of the Courts,* 49 CORNELL L.Q. 436, 440–46 (1964).

5. Siberman, *The City and the Negro,* FORTUNE, March 1962, pp. 88–89.

6. "On any scale of economic adequacy or inadequacy — measured, e.g., in terms of number unemployed, number on relief, number in unskilled occupations, number in professional work, income levels—the Negro would have to be rated as from two to four times worse than the white man." Johnson, *The Negro and Crime,* ANNALS, Sept. 1941, p. 94. He concluded that "the position of the Negro in American society, with all that this means in terms of subordination, frustration, economic insecurity, and incomplete participation, enters significantly into almost every possible aspect of Negro crime causation. Indeed, it is so important as to constitute virtually a special and major set of sociological and psychological factors which can 'explain' Negro crime in so far as it needs special explanation." *idem* at 103.

7. "[T]he damming-up of resentment is one reason for the high incidence of crime among lower-class Negroes; this is further supported by the fact that the vast majority of violent acts by Negroes are directed towards other Negroes. To put it another way, one might say that for the lower-class Negro, avenues have been closed off by the social structure, so that violent crime against members of his own race is one of the channels of least resistance open to him for the expression of aggression." Solomon, Walker, O'Connor, & Fishman, *Civil Rights Activity and Reduction in Crime Among Negroes,* 12 ARCHIVES OF GENERAL PSYCHIATRY 227, 234 (1965).

8. Perhaps the same may be said for recent Supreme Court decisions dealing with the procedural rights of the accused, although a number of law enforcement spokesmen are fighting a desperate rear-guard action in the mass media. The sharp, and too often intemperate, criticism of the Supreme Court by police–prosecution spokesmen is collected and appraised in Kamisar, *supra* note 4; Kamisar, *Public Safety* v. *Individual Liberties — Some "Facts" and "Theories,"* 53 J. CRIM. L., C & P.S. 171 (1962).

9. "This sense of rejection by American society, a sense which dominates the lower-class Negro's life, tends to destroy his feeling of responsibility to law and authority; law and authority are always white and middle class and always seem designed to keep the lower-class Negro in his place." Silberman, *op. cit. supra* note 2, at 53.

10. "[T]he Southern Negro comes to Harlem not necessarily in search of freedom, but expecting to find it there and determined to enjoy it. He resents any curb on his personal activities by policemen and it seems likely to many that he takes out on Northern

policemen the angers he built up against Southern policemen but didn't dare to show. But even many Northern Negroes seem to have a latent hostility to policemen, often traceable to the times that ignorant or unthinking cops gave them the 'move on' or 'what are you doing in this neighborhood, buddy' treatment." Shapiro & Sullivan, RACE RIOTS: NEW YORK 1964, p. 40–41 (1964). See also Lomax, THE NEGRO REVOLT, p. 72 (1962): "I don't know of a single Negro who doesn't get a flutter in his stomach when approached by a white policeman. Anything can happen: sometimes it does."

11. "No one would deny that we need vigorous law enforcement. But should this entail, for example, the use of terror evoked by the threat of setting beasts against human beings? I refer, of course, to the use of police dogs in many of our cities — in the North and West, as well as in the South. Although I am not aware that police dogs have reduced the crime rate, the police assert that they are 'effective.' Assume for the moment that this is so. A full scale reign of terror might be 'effective,' too. But could we respect ourselves if we instituted one? Can we pretend that resort to such tactics will foster respect for the law and not merely respect for brute force? By measures such as these, perhaps even the most unsocialized and antisocial people can be forced into a kind of submission — and we wouldn't have to bother to look at the reasons for their plight. *But what a price!*" Bazelon, *Law, Morality, and Civil Liberties*, 12 U.C.L.A. L. Rev. 13, 25 (1964).

12. The charge has been made that in some places this has already occurred: "The officer moves through Harlem like an occupying soldier in a bitterly hostile country; which is precisely what and where he is and the reason he walks in twos and threes." Baldwin, NOBODY KNOWS MY NAME, 62 (1961).

13. Romans 13:8, 10–12 (King James).

Police Practices and the Citizen*

B. J. GEORGE, JR.

Professor of Law, University of Michigan, Ann Arbor

MAY 19, 1965

United States Supreme Court activity during the past several terms of the Court has been designed to bring about major changes in police practices. Certainly the decisions which Professor Bartholomew describes in the preceding article have been the cause of much debate among judges and lawyers. One can if he wishes utilize them either to attack the Supreme Court or come to its defense. This is, however, essentially negative action, since the decisions are still law whatever we say about them. Affirmative action remains ours to take at the community level. The community itself is not only a prime cause of crime, but also the primary source of

* Reprinted with permission from POLICE Magazine, Vol. 10, No. 4, March–April, 1966, pp. 38–42; Charles C Thomas, Publisher, Springfield, Ill.

crime control. All of us who form the community must consider the problem of crime in our midst not as casual spectators of a bout between police and criminals with judges as referees, but as active participants whose shifting roles include now support to the police, against protection of the criminal against deliberate invasions of his basic procedural rights, and then perhaps an appraisal of the judicial referee's effectiveness in balancing conflicting claims which cannot be totally reconciled. We can solve the practical problems of law enforcement in the community only by participating as citizens, not by dispassionately looking on.

The Chinese Puzzle of Judicial Decisions

It is undeniable that United States Supreme Court and state supreme court decisions in recent years have done much to promote an atmosphere protective of the rights of defendants in federal and state courts. At the same time, there have been several by-products of this judicial activity which should be a legitimate matter of concern to all of us. While I do not want to duplicate Professor Bartholomew's exposition of legal doctrine, I feel we must be aware of the impact which these recent decisions have on us as we try to work with the police to combat crime in our cities and towns. How do these decisions affect our police and us today at the state and local level?

Police Confusion Over the Rules by Which They Are to Operate

Most of us who read about Supreme Court decisions in the newspaper are interested in what individual justices have had to say about the general problem which the particular case illustrates, such as police interrogation, limitations on searches, wire tapping, and the like. We equate their essays with a solution of a great and grave social problem. The only concrete result, however, is the decision in that case. Is the conviction to be reversed because the defendant had no lawyer?[1] Is the particular evidence to be excluded because the police did not know before they entered the defendant's apartment to serve a warrant?[2] Is a confession not to be used because it was obtained through questioning at the police station while the defendant's lawyer waited outside vainly trying to get in to see his client?[3] The historian now has the case for his leisurely consideration. On other days, however, police officers must make other arrests under different conditions. They must decide whether to search cars stopped for a traffic offense now, later, or not at all. They must make split-second decisions whether to delay long enough to obtain a warrant to search pawnshops or barns or houses for stolen property, or whether to enter now to arrest before the property, if it is there, disappears. The appellate judges' beloved abstractions are of little assistance to them in making these pressure-ridden decisions. Even these judicial abstractions are not as clear as they might appear to be when you scan the evening paper. As evidence of this, appellate judges, trial judges, and lawyers are split into a score of camps as to what the recent landmark *Escobedo* case[4] on the constitutional limits on receiving confessions means. If they are in confusion, what do we expect of the men manning the patrol cars in Marquette, Michigan?

---

[1] *Gideon* v. *Wainwright,* 372 U.S. 335, 1963.

[2] *Miller* v. *United States,* 357 U.S. 301, 1958, and *cf. Ker* v. *California,* 374 U.S. 23, 1963.

[3] *Escobedo* v. *Illinois,* 378 U.S. 478, 1964.

[4] *Ibid.*

A Freezing of Legislative Experimentation at the State Level

Our traditions of constitutional government permit the United States Supreme Court to control state practices only if it feels strongly enough to invoke some applicable provision of the federal Constitution, which in the criminal law administration area usually means the due process clause of the Fourteenth Amendment. This amendment has of course been instrumental in safeguarding the "ordered liberty" in which we all have a stake. Judicial decisions on constitutional grounds, however, are to a degree self-defeating. The Court's objective is to tailor constitutional concepts to a modern society. To use constitutional terms, however, to delineate contemporary social rights is to paint one's self into a corner. If that corner happens to have in it the door opening into the hall, so that one can go elsewhere, all is well. But if it has no exit, the alternatives are less attractive. One way is to wait for the problem to disappear, for the paint to dry. The Supreme Court seems to be adept at this through the expedient of denying certiorari, and thus refusing to review cases which might force it to qualify some of its earlier sweeping pronouncements. A second is to walk to the nearest exit while pretending that the paint is not there at all. This is the process of overruling or distinguishing earlier decisions, which to the judges deciding them were clear expositions of unalterable constitutional propositions. The third is to batter another door in the wall behind, which in this instance is to amend the Constitution to extricate one's self from an intolerable conflict between the abstractions of constitutional interpretation and the inexorable pressures of a modern society. There is a difficulty in this, however. With too many new exits, the house collapses. A constitution frequently amended in small detail soon resembles nothing more than a "senior-citizen" statute.

What does this mean to the states? First, the Supreme Court, in interpreting its leading case on the applicability of the exclusionary rule of evidence to the states whenever there has been an illegal search and seizure, has said that the test of reasonableness is a federal one.[5] The federal standard, however, is not based on Congressional legislation, which can be changed by a new statute, but on a series of court cases which interpret and apply eighteenth and nineteenth century arrest law as a matter of constitutional law. This law is in many respects unsuited to modern conditions. I assume that most citizens would accept new state legislation which (a) permits police to arrest on reasonable grounds to believe that a misdemeanor has been committed, (b) permits police to stop and question a suspicious person on the street, and to detain him under certain circumstances up to two hours to check his story,[6] (c) permits an officer to frisk a suspect when the officer has reason to believe the suspect is armed,[7] or (d) permits a search or arrest warrant to dispense with requirements that the officer knock and announce himself as an officer if there is reason to believe that the officer's life will be in danger if he gives warning of his entry, or that evidence of the crime will be quickly and efficiently disposed of before the officer can succeed in entering.[8] If the test by which we judged the constitutionality of statutes like these were one of the reasonableness of the legislature's evaluation of the problem of arrest, search, and seizure under twentieth-century conditions, all this legislation and much more would be quite acceptable to most people except, perhaps, criminals. All, however, would

---

[5] See, Uniform arrest law. § 2. Comment, 65 COLUM. L. REV. 848, (1965).

[6] *Ibid.*

[7] New York Code of Criminal Procedure, Sec. 180-a.

[8] New York Code of Criminal Procedure, Sec. 799.

be held incompatible with the nineteenth century arrest law which the Supreme Court has read into the Constitution. There is some basis to expect that the Court by silence or by subtle explanation may back away from some of its earlier statements derogatory to state legislative power, but in the meantime our state legislatures, if they contemplate changes like those I mention, must recognize that there is a serious danger that a federal court will later declare their legislation unconstitutional. If this proves to be the case, the only way to achieve a modernized law of arrest will be to amend the federal Constitution to include one; this in itself would be a tragic departure from our traditions, in which only broad principles are to be found in that document.

This rigidity also affects how we treat criminals. I am a co-reporter for a committee of the State Bar of Michigan which is to draft a new criminal code for ultimate presentation to the Legislature. There have been several instances in which, from the point of view of rehabilitation of the offender, minor penalties only are needed. Examples are shoplifting and joy-riding. But if these offenses, which are now felonies, are reduced to misdemeanors, the police will be able to arrest under the present arrest law only if the crimes are actually committed in their presence, and citizens will not be able to arrest at all. In that event, both criminal statutes will become totally unenforceable. A common sense solution would be to reduce the crimes to misdemeanors and permit officers, and perhaps citizens, to arrest on reasonable grounds to believe that a misdemeanor has been committed by the person arrested. But if the standard for determining the constitutionality of arrests is a federal one based on nineteenth century law, an officer can arrest only for a misdemeanor committed in his presence, and a modernized arrest statute would therefore be unconstitutional. As a result, for the time being we have to use the expedient of leaving these crimes as felonies, but permitting the sentencing judge to reduce the offense in his discretion. A constitutional standard which inhibits modernization of the criminal law hinders, not promotes, control of crime in the community.

A Sense of Complacency About the Solution of the Conflict Between the Community's Interest and the Criminal's Rights

Appellate courts talk as if the key to controlling police "abuses" and promoting the civil liberties of all citizens is an exclusionary rule of evidence which requires elimination of any evidence obtained illegally, or any evidence derived from the matter originally gotten. For example, if police illegally break into a doctor's office and find that a woman he has illegally aborted has just died of an embolism they are prohibited from testifying to what they saw, and the autopsy surgeon is prohibited from giving his report as to the cause of death.[9] The state is then helpless, as a practical matter, to prosecute a crime which everyone knows has been committed. According to judicial theory, however, police will be so struck to heart by this that they will reform their practices.

If the appellate judiciary is wrong about its theory, then the problem of lawless law enforcement remains to be solved. And it may well be wrong. The police may, if they wish, rationalize that it is the courts who have chosen to let the defendant go free; the police arrested the right man and it is not their responsibility what happens later. Furthermore, the judges' decision about whether the officers were

---

[9] *Cf. Killough* v. *United States*, 336 F.2d 929, D.C. Cir. 1964, and *Wayne* v. *United States*, 318 F.2d 205, D.C. Cir. 1963.

"reasonable" in their conduct occurs long after the fact, and the judge is not a trained policeman. In a great many instances, the officer was acting competently and conscientiously. In effect, he is penalized for doing good police work. To tell him he was wrong, without telling him what in detail he should have done which was right, is to leave him utterly confused, a matter I mentioned earlier. Moreover, if the courts' requirements cannot be met unless the community's demands for security against criminals are frustrated, the voice of the community will probably outweigh the courts'. One more element to consider, the exclusionary rule does not touch at all the officer who misuses his office to his own sadistic ends. Events in racial cases in the South and in the North suggest that the brutal police officer gets his "kicks" from the maltreatment itself. He could not care less whether there is ever a prosecution against his victim.

Even if the exclusionary rule operates efficiently in at least some cases, there still remains the problem that the courts, by talking of the "great judicial safeguards" under the Constitution, lull the community into believing that control of police, and at second remove control of crime, are the business of the courts and not of the citizen. It is perhaps this "creeping judicial paternalism," this judicial placebo, more than anything else which threatens the community's role in crime control.

The Solution Is at the State and Local Level

In fact, the operation of judicial rules reaches only a small number of cases so far as the average community is concerned. There are many problems, of much greater magnitude than those with which the courts occupy their time, that we all have to work to solve in each community. Let me suggest a few.

Creating Local Standards for Police Practice

Judicial decisions and state statutes together give only slight guidance to police officers. A lecture on the law by the prosecuting attorney or circuit court judge may be like the traditional army medical officer's lecture to the troops on venereal disease—guaranteed either to scare them to death or put them to sleep. What is needed is perhaps a working committee at the city or county level, which will work out a code of police practices within the broad limits of formal statutes and judicial decisions. Police command officers, the circuit court and juvenile court judges, the prosecuting attorney, school administrators, and concerned members of the community should gather, ready to work and work hard, to identify first the problems which the police face, as they themselves describe them, next the detailed guides which the police feel can help them both in training and in the field, and finally the means by which each policeman can receive adequate training and guidance in trying to comply with both the local code and the more general legal principles. As examples of what needs to be worked out, under what circumstances are citizens on the street to be stopped and questioned? How is the initial approach made? How is the decision to arrest or not to arrest to be made? Is there anyone available for the officer to consult? Is it to be another officer, the prosecutor, or the judge? If a car is stopped for traffic violations, what further steps can be taken with reference to the driver, the occupants, and the car? What statements are to be made or warnings given by the officer before questioning a suspect? What part of the police booking must be done now and what may be done later? When and how does the arrested person contact a lawyer? What can the lawyer do? What notification is made to the family? When can they see the prisoner? When and where is a magistrate to be available to hear applications for warrants or to handle the preliminary appearance of an arrested person? These are only illustrative; the actual planning and drafting will take considerable amounts of both time and goodwill.[10] They are not merely "legal details"; every person in the community ought to be deeply concerned about them, if for no other reason than because he himself might be the one some day on whom they operate. This effort must be made, perhaps in time with financial help under the new Law Enforcement Assistance Act of 1965 signed into law September 22, 1965. The University of Michigan Law School and the Institute of Continuing Legal Education are now exploring a pilot project which could result in a set of local practice rules, hammered out in this way, which can be presented for consideration at the next Judicial Conference of the state judiciary. Similar operations are under way in other states. These, if successful, may encourage widespread use of the method throughout the country. Whatever the specifics, of content or experiment, here is a challenge for everyone in the community.

Deciding What to Do with Those in Need of Protective Care

Judicial decisions often read as if the sole function of the police is to arrest and deliver the arrested person into the hands of a criminal court. This is not in fact so. The police protect the community in a variety of ways, of which arrest and prosecution are only a part. Where many kinds of police activity are concerned, nobody, policeman included, expects a prosection to follow. If, however, police and citizens settle back in the belief that the sum total of police activity is in fact arrest and complaint, and that the Supreme Court is the sole regulating agency over police practices, the result will be a failure on all sides to come to grips with the large areas of police functions which lie totally outside the area of criminal arrest law. Let me offer four brief illustrations of what I have in mind here.

First, every community has its share of chronic alcoholics, from the one or two in Durand, Michigan, to the hundreds in Detroit. Technically speaking, anyone who is drunk in public, whether awake or asleep in a doorway or alley, commits an offense in the officer's presence and can be arrested. It is common knowledge, however, that in most instances men in this condition are taken into custody for their own protection, in what the Detroit police call a "Golden Rule drunk case." In larger cities, judicial proceedings may follow in only a minority of cases, and in these, the primary objective is shelter or hospital treatment for the defendant.[11] In the majority of instances, the arrested person is released when he is sobered up, to return to his job if he has one, or perhaps to be accommodated by a social agency or hospital if he needs that kind of help. This is technically "illegal," since under the law of most states, every arrested person must be formally produced in court, charged, and tried.[12] I doubt, however, that many citizens would consider it "immoral" to try to cope with what is a very real problem in our society by means other than a criminal prosecution. Please note also that judge-made exclusionary rules of evidence are of no help here. The case is never contested either in the trial

---

[10] Rules or standards as such might of course be drafted by a legally-trained consultant and submitted through command channels. I do not recommend this, however. It is the educational process inherent in a group discussion in which all classes of persons engaged in criminal law administration are participants that is of primary value.

[11] See Comment, The law on skid row. 38 CHI. KENT L. REV. 22 1961; Foote: *Vagrancy-type law and its administration,* 104 U. PA. L. REV. 603, 1956.

[12] There are statutory exceptions. *Cf. Mass. Ann. Laws,* ch. 272, § 45, Supp. 1964.

court or in an appellate court, and the police conduct is never attacked. The charge is read, the officer testifies to what he saw, the judge says "guilty," and the defendant goes back to the county jail or city hospital. What these cases present is the problem of what the community is to do with its marginal souls. It must identify the individuals within it who need aid, must decide whether the police or some other class of public officials will have prime responsibility for detaining those who require help, must make up its collective mind whether jails can ever be an effective medium by which medical and other treatment can be afforded the alcoholics who need it, and must decide how far courts are to participate in the protective process to safeguard the civil rights of the people who are its subjects. A preoccupation with federal appellate cases lulls the community and the police to sleep where chronic or vagrant alcoholics are concerned.

Second, narcotics addiction is a major problem which criminal law administration alone can do little to control. If the premises underlying Michigan and federal narcotics-control legislation were applied to the sale of aspirin, many among us might be shoplifting or committing prostitution to combat migraine. This is a problem shot through with fear and irrationality, and the hidebound policies of the federal narcotics authorities are no assistance to a coping with these fears or with the problem of addiction itself. Perhaps the President's recent call for civil commitment legislation will help bring about a rational treatment of that problem.[13] In the meantime, citizens must begin to take steps other than criminal prosecutions to bring narcotics addiction under control and to reduce the tremendous toll in crime and human suffering which it exacts.

Third, there are mentally-ill people at large in every community; certainly many inhabitants of our skid rows are in this category. Police, on occasion, have to take them into custody to protect them from themselves or citizens from them. In most instances, the "arrest" itself is valid, either because what the arrested person is doing fits some definition of crime, or because there is probably a traditional common-law power to arrest one who is dangerous to himself or others because of mental illness. The police are no doubt eager to turn the man over to hospital authorities or the family, but under most circumstances, probate court action is required for either. Circuit judge, probate judge, police commanders, and local hospital administrators must work out policies on which police can rely when they have a mentally-ill person on their hands. They receive no guidance from appellate courts in this respect.[14]

Fourth, most communities have only begun to consider what police are to do when they are dealing with juveniles.[15] Though there are a few cases which provide guides for police if a prosecution of the minor in a regular trial court is in the

---

[13] "The Justice Department will shortly submit proposals for a federal civil commitment statute to the Congress and for limiting the coverage of the mandatory minimum penalty sentences. The proposals will seek, to the fullest extent consistent with the public safety, to give offenders a maximum opportunity for return to a normal life." *Message on Crime, Its Prevalence, and Measures of Prevention*, March 8, 1965, 111 CONG. REC. 4253 (1965). See also Lindesmith, THE ADDICT AND THE LAW, 1965, pp. 269–302; Eldridge, NARCOTICS AND THE LAW, 1962, pp. 116–131; and Rubin, PSYCHIATRY AND CRIMINAL LAW, 1965, pp. 112–138.

[14] Canadian statutes provide a possible pattern for American legislation. See, *e.g.*, Ont. *Rev. Stat.* ch. 236, 28; MacDonald: *The police and the mentally ill*, 1 CRIM. L.Q. 400, 1959.

[15] George: *Juveniles and the police*, 43 MICH. ST. B. J., No. 10, 24, Oct. 1964.

offing, most juvenile problems remain untouched. The broad and general language of the typical state juvenile code itself gives little guidance either. It is therefore imperative that police, probate judge, school administrators, and parents work out ground rules governing when and under what conditions police can question juveniles on school property or during school hours, the conditions under which juveniles are to be held, if at all, in temporary police custody, the probate court personnel to be contacted if detention is necessary, the means to be used to contact parents and other relatives of the juvenile, and the detention facilities which are to be provided until the parents appear or when the probate court authorizes temporary detention. These are the problems which the community must largely solve for itself. It also must undertake to find out why some juveniles become delinquent and what straightens them out. The police may not have all the answers on these points, but they have insights which should be relied on by the rest of the citizenry more than seems to be the case now. And the structure of the courts which decide what to do with neglected and delinquent juveniles must be radically overhauled. This, too, is a decision about which everyone should be vitally concerned.

Developing Fair Machinery to Examine into and Check Police Misconduct

Only a fanatic will claim complete purity for his group. We must recognize that police abuses do occur, and often enough to merit our concern. But it is no answer to make charges of "police brutality" a way of life which creates "we's" and "they's" in our community. Conscientious concern on both sides is necessary. Police command officials ought to find it in their own interest to use their departmental administrative machinery to weed out the few bad actors on the force, and not only when, through police oversight, some prominent citizen or his relative is affected by police misconduct. The body of taxpayers might very well recognize that even bad policemen are there to act in the community because the municipality hired them to be there, and the state or municipality is under a moral duty to compensate those who are injured in person or property because of police misconduct. It might even go further to authorize a standard minimum recovery for anyone whose civil rights have been impaired; a substantial item in a city's or state's annual budget might bring home to all of us the "price" of official misconduct.

Perhaps, however, we need to go further to create some sort of arbiter to investigate and decide the truth underlying charges of police brutality. This might be a citizen's committee, though I hope that such a committee might not be thought of as a speaker's forum for every minority and interest group's position on everything from housing to the American presence in Vietnam. If a committee like this was constituted as most of our human relations commissions are constituted, we might well expect a fair airing of the problem. Police commanders ought not overlook the very real educational function which a presentation of law enforcement problems as viewed by the police serves so far as citizen members of a commission are concerned. Or perhaps the solution lies in the creation of an impartial "inspector-general" at the state level, protected in tenure as a judge might be and paid highly enough to attract outstanding people to the position. The pattern for this is the Scandinavian *ombudsman*. Or it might be that members of the state judiciary should be regularly designated to travel circuit to hold informal nontrial proceedings and report officially on the truth or falsity of charges made against the police. Perhaps other ideas would work more satisfactorily. I hope, however, that responsible police and community leaders will recognize that experimentation along these lines is not an attack on the police, but rather a way of providing guidance for the police and instruction for the community about the problems which the police face. To quote President Johnson's message to Congress of March 8, 1965: "We need to think less . . . about taking sides in such controversies and more about our common objective: law enforcement which is both fair and effective."

Conclusion

Intervention by courts after the fact in cases in which the police have arrested and the arrested person has been prosecuted can provide only a limited guidance to police and the community. The police protective function will continue to exist independent of technical rules of arrest law and unaffected by rules of evidence. The community and the police must direct their joint attention to how they, not the federal government or state judges, are going to identify and process alcoholics, narcotics addicts, mentally-ill persons, the destitute, and neglected or delinquent juveniles. What we require is concern less for judicial abstractions than for our own inescapable responsibility, our community's policing of itself.

Section 2

Psychological and Sociological Aspects of Police–Community Relations

Many students of human behavior have observed that man either learns from those around him, or he perishes. Man is man in large part because of his learning ability, matched by his great *need* to learn.

An important part of the learning process is the way we view ourselves. Who am I? How do I see myself? Each of us answers this in several ways, as a result of our experiences with others. One discovers who he is by what he thinks other people think of him. Understanding others begins by understanding ourselves.

If therefore, concern is evident regarding "the public image of the police," it is logical to inquire as to the status of the police self-image. Some observers define the morale problem of police in terms of a lack of self-respect. But one's self-image is not entirely self-generating; it is governed in part, indeed in large part, by the "feed-back" one gets from others. What the police officer sees, then, when he views himself is a self-portrait based in some measure upon what the community he serves tells him he is — e.g., "splendid chap," "friend to all," "neighbor," "crooked cop," "flat-foot," "professional," "prejudiced punk," "Gestapo," "fuzz," "lazy louse," "kind-hearted simpleton," etc.

The list is long!

Question: if police and community cooperation is to be advanced, how do we *concurrently* improve the police self-image and the police public-image? It seems clear that this process must be concurrent. The answer to this question appears to reside in the professional development of law enforcement personnel.

This "community," telling the policeman what he is, may not — in the functional sense — be a true community at all, if the modern metropolis (where approximately 70% of our population resides) is the case in point. Demographic trends, unprecedented physical and social mobility, the pace of social change, "contracultural conflict," these ramifications of affluence and the sociology of leisure — these and other social phenomena have created a baffling universe for the police. New dimensions in police training and education are one result, with increasing emphasis on matters psychological and sociological.

These are the matters analyzed in the essays in this section.

What Makes Us Behave as People?

G. M. GILBERT

*Chairman, Department of Psychology, Long Island University,
Brooklyn, New York*

MAY 21, 1963

There are several scientific theories of human behavior, which we'll mention later. But for the moment, the main question I wish to raise in your minds is: "How is it possible for men to hate and destroy while they preach brotherly love?"

It is obvious that mankind has two opposing qualities: the constructive, which can create works of art or cooperative achievement, and the destructive, which we have seen in the many evidences of man's inhumanity to man. We have witnessed men being able to order and carry out the extinction of 5,000,000 people in the same age in which man is achieving the conquest of the universe. How does a psychologist view this, scientifically?

Science has thoroughly refuted the pseudoscientific racist theory that we like those who are like ourselves and hate those who are not. This simple statement has been accepted too long as an adequate explanation. But how does the scientist conceive man and his behavior? There are various theories. The first is the idea that man is a machine. This is the idea advanced by Pavlov who, through his experiments on dogs, concluded that man, like other animals, will respond to a certain stimulus in predictable ways. According to this theory, man's emotions develop by conditioned reactions, to which he is exposed in his environment. As the behaviorists put it, man's personality is the result of his cultural stimuli. But there is no room in this theory for the idea that man is any different from other animals. It allows no room for his spiritual and judgmental potentialities that make him different from other animals. This push-button conception makes man a passive object of environmental manipulation. This idea has been rejected by most psychologists today as being inadequate—except in Soviet Russia where their educational system is based entirely on social control to produce the kind of adults the Russians want, indoctrinated in their system.

The second theory is the psychoanalytic notion that man gets along in society by suppressing his primitive instincts. This is a continuously frustrating experience, the theory goes, and creates a reservoir of pent-up aggression which must inevitably erupt into overt actions of hostility. These may take the form of prejudice and convert hostility, or may cause him to resort to acts of violence as in race riots, war and other brutalities. Modern religions, the law, and our moral codes all tend to make us curb our sex impulses, and according to Freud, the best we can hope to do is to contain the aggression which is the price of civilization. This is certainly a hopeless view of human nature.

The third theory of human behavior is what we call the bio-social concept. It is the most recent, and it is the one which I've been helping to develop. This theory, which really goes back to Darwin, considers man as basically a social animal. It explains man's constructive potentialities through his innate social sensitivity and his innate social ego needs, as well as his need for constructive mastery

(Note: Dr. Gilbert was chief psychologist for the United States government at the Nuremberg criminal trials, and as such was a witness at the trial of Adolph Eichmann in Israel.)

of the environment. This theory answers the question as to why man tends to socialize—not because he is forced to, but because he naturally *wants* to. Beginning even as early as the infant functions, we observe that man has a built-in empathy and sympathy with other human beings. This is the foundation stone of the theory. It is biologically innate in his central nervous system. It makes man biologically susceptible to the idea of the brotherhood of man.

If this be true, what about man's hostilities? The very desire of the human organism to be associated with other humans—this innate social sense—gives us the explanation of the extremes to which he will go to achieve it. Man wants to belong—to belong to some group—a family, a social group or even a gang if need be. To win the approval of the members of the group to which he wants to belong, he will do whatever he feels the group wants him to do in order to gain acceptance. If the group happens already to have irrational prejudices, he will adopt these as part of his own thinking. If the group, as such, is frustrated and explodes in some group violence, the new member will often join in, to prove he is worthy of acceptance. The enemies of the group will therefore be his enemies. Thus, he accepts the group's prejudices unwittingly, uncritically.

When I examined the chief exterminator in the war crime trials, Col. Hoess, the man to whom Eichmann shipped trainloads of Jews to be exterminated in Auschwitz—I asked him how an ordinary sane person could possibly bring himself to be a part of such a program. Had he hated the Jews so much himself? Were they guilty of any crime? His answer was the more horrifying because of the casual tone in which he gave it. He simply said, "I never stopped to think about it; it was just something everybody took for granted. No, I never hated the Jews myself. It was just an order." Then he went on to explain that he only believed the racial propaganda because everybody else seemed to believe it, and now everybody was saying it was all propaganda, so he guessed it was all a mistake!

I do not mean to say that Col. Hoess was a normal man, but never underestimate the mild citizen who (to avoid conflicts with his peers) simply "goes along." He is necessarily the victim of the group's prejudices. He doesn't question whether the prevailing attitude is "right." His emotions may be built up along with those of the group, even to the point of joining a lynch mob. The uncritical "good guy" can be a menace. The fact that the group thinks a certain attitude or action is right doesn't make it so.

Then there is such a thing as an institutionalized social discrimination. This further exaggerates intergroup conflicts. It actually creates group differences and its own hostilities. For example, the high incidence of Negro crime is the actual *result* of their treatment by the majority group—the whites—not the cause. Underprivileged in so many senses of the word—economically, politically, socially—they build up resistances against white discrimination to the point where their sustained and truly remarkable group patience is exhausted. Many harbor deep resentments, develop antisocial tendencies, some go in for delinquency and crime. This is not to excuse criminal behavior, but merely to explain why the incidence is often greater among minority groups, as a result of institutionalized discrimination.

The institutionalized discrimination of older generations continues to affect our present-day human relationships by perpetuating old hostilities; yet if given a chance, human nature would allow all men to live in mutual respect.

Now finally we come to "the nut." I have had some intimate experience with the pathological type of prejudice. These are the fanatics, the chronic haters who hate because they have to, because this is a symptom of their sickness. These people are in the minority, but they are dangerous because they can always whip up the emotions of the conforming people into a movement or even a revolution of defiance of law and order. But now let me provide a bit of insight as to what is really involved in fanaticism. Fundamentally, fanatic race hatred is an extension of self-hatred. The fanatic who believes that others are basically inferior, and who thinks that the brotherhood of man is hogwash is a person who is sick with self-hatred. He is using his own prejudice as his own defense against his own inferiority—the well-known "scapegoat" technique.

Now this sounds like a dreamed-up psychological formula or moralistic reasoning, but I'm talking from rather grim experience. The classic example of this pathological fanatic hatred is for all time, as far as I am concerned, Adolf Hitler himself. Lots of people have speculated about Hitler; but I submit to you that I got about as close to him as any psychologist could, because for an entire year, I discussed Hitler with all of his henchmen. These included Hermann Goering, Rudolph Hess, Von Ribbentrop, and all the rest. Especially during the closing months of the trial, and while they were awaiting sentence, they talked about Hitler more than anything else. And one of Hitler's most intimate associates, Hans Frank, who was the governor of Poland and Hitler's lawyer, in his eagerness to make me understand what made an intelligent lawyer act so inhuman, wrote me a little essay about Hitler which ran to 1,000 pages. This is how conscience-stricken he was, and how eager he was, before he died, to help a psychologist understand the problem. I mention this so you'll know that I am speaking from authentic information.

It so happens that Hitler's fanatic hatred of the Jews stemmed, first of all, from a neurotic need to find a scapegoat for his own sense of failure as a young man. This much is generally known. But what is not generally known is that, having committed himself to this fanatic prejudice, he was trapped by it. He found that there was reason to suspect that maybe he had "Jewish blood" himself. In his neurosis, he whipped up his own hostility, his own extension of his inferior self, to such a fanatic hatred that he had to prove to all the world that he was the worst enemy the Jews ever had. This festered in his mind until, when he had power, he determined upon the extermination of all the Jews that could be found. As you know, this culminated in the mass murder of five or six million innocent men, women and children.

Here was a man who was hating a group with whom he had reason to identify, by using them as a scapegoat to divorce himself from them. What was the outcome of this kind of race hatred? Toward the end of the war, it became obvious, even to Hitler himself, that he might not win the war. Having actually precipitated World War II as a test of the fact that he was the leader of the master race, and that Germany would prove this by winning the war, he began to fear that his experiment might end in a negative judgment of history; that Germany would be defeated and could not prove itself to be the master race.

You recall that when General Eisenhower had successfully invaded Europe, suddenly there was a reversal in the Ardennes counter-offensive by the Germans, followed by their scorched earth policy. Here's what happened. Hitler decided that he was going to make one more all-out effort to destroy the Allies because he had to do it to prove that he was a member of the master race.

He called Albert Speer, the Minister of War Production, and said he wanted him to squeeze out all the war production he could for a last-ditch effort. "We're going to smash back the Americans, and Germany will yet rule the world, and the German race will prove its superiority." Speer said he'd do the best he could, but that they were nearing the end of their rope. "But if this fails," he told Hitler, "you must promise me that you will immediately surrender because we will not be able to hold out another week after that."

The counter-offensive was smashed back by Eisenhower and Patton and as I learned later, Speer went back to Hitler and said that they had lost their last effort and asked Hitler to surrender immediately. But the Fuehrer said, "No, we will fight on!" When Speer told him they had nothing left to fight with, Hitler said they would follow a scorched earth policy. Speer warned that this would only help the enemy and lead to the destruction of the entire German race. And Hitler said in effect: "I know that! The Germans have proven that they are an inferior race and they are not fit to survive!" He determined to commit suicide and go down to destruction with the rest of the *inferior German race!*

This is what actually happened behind the scenes of the closing months of the war. Albert Speer told me about it and I have the written testimony he used in the trial. This was the final culmination of this pathological hatred of his fellowman. It shows what happens when fanatic hatred is allowed to run its course. It starts as a projection of self-hatred. It violates the finer instinct of man, which is to regard his fellowman as his brother, and ends logically in mutual self-destruction. To assume that a part of the human race is inferior is a fallacy which can't work in the long run. The Germans themselves realized this, and one of these exterminators even remarked to Eichmann, when receiving Hitler's orders for extermination, "But Herr Eichmann, what happens when one of these other races decides that *we're* the inferior race?"

So you can see that this is a vicious circle. There is no possible way of making it stick because it isn't natural. Even if Germany had won the war, they would have split into mutually exterminating factions. I can tell you that as a fact, because Goering told me how he was going to exterminate Himmler and his gang, since he knew that Himmler already had plans to exterminate Goering and *his* gang. After one nation becomes supreme, then another nation must show that it is supreme, or one faction within the victorious group must vie for survival with another one. This means a constant mutual hostility, which sooner or later must end in complete mutual destruction.

But won't the *majority* survive? If you stop and think about it, there is no majority race or ethnic group in this world. Everybody is a part of a minority. There is no such thing as a superior race, and there is no such thing as any group being able to prove that it is innately superior to any other. It is racist ideology that contains the seeds of its own destruction! Sometimes the cause and effect doesn't work out so neatly as it did in Hitler's case. But I have a suspicion in the back of my mind—and I am not trying to preach theology—that there was a purpose behind all this bit of history. There was a purpose in giving man such a disastrously perfect case of the self-defeating psychology of race hatred. Man had better learn the lesson now, or he won't survive to learn anything more.

We are living now in very troublesome and yet very challenging times. We are living at a time when man's constructive potential is rising to undreamed-of heights, and his destructive potential is reaching undreamed-of depths of self annihilation. It's up to us now to decide whether we can rise above all of the prejudices and the petty bigotries of the past, and face our responsibilities as community leaders, teachers, law enforcement officers, theologians, or whatever we are, to try to meet this threat, because it's now or never. No generation ever had such an opportunity to decide the course of history as we have: you and I.

Let me close with a final challenge that I got from Hermann Goering when he was cursing the Judeo-Christian ideals and democratic brotherhood and all that, saying that the dog-eat-dog law of the jungle is the only rule in history. Here was a member of a dying order, a cynical psychopath going down to his doom, still kicking and cursing, and he wasn't getting a rise out of me until he added one parting shot: "Anyway, Herr Professor," he said. "It isn't you do-good professors who make history—*we're* the ones who make history and don't forget it."

I haven't forgotten it, and I'm telling you that we people of good intentions, people dedicated to constructive work in our society—that it is about time that *we* decided who will write history—whether we'll allow the aggressive psychopaths and fanatics to write history, and allow demogogues to take advantage of pre-existing prejudices, to foment men's hostility into mutual self-destruction, or whether we will call a halt and assert ourselves as leaders in the community, and see to it that men's natural sense of brotherhood is allowed to prevail.

References

Gilbert, G. M. NUREMBERG DIARY, New York: Farrar, Straus, 1950 (paperback, Signet Books, 1961).

Gilbert, G. M. THE PSYCHOLOGY OF DICTATORSHIP, New York: Ronald Press, 1950.

Police and Community—
As Viewed by a Psychologist

MILTON ROKEACH

Professor of Psychology, Michigan State University

MAY 16, 1966

There has been a marked rise in the past ten years in the number and types of protests and demonstrations in the United States. It started with the Negro protests, but now we have those against our role in Viet Nam, draft card burners, pacifists, etc. These activities divert the police from what they once conceived as their normal roles in enforcement. They find themselves playing new roles for which they are ill-prepared emotionally, professionally, and ideologically. Enforcement is based on maintaining law and order. Lawbreaking in the United States is lawbreaking. We have not begun to distinguish between civil and criminal violations as they have in Europe. An article in a recent issue of THE POLICE CHIEF makes no distinctions in its description of recent demonstrations as "law-breaking." The author uses the loaded phrases, "so-called freedom songs," and uses adjectives such as "sinister" and "irresponsible" to describe actions of the protesting groups.

I respect the law, but such editorializing seems to me to picture the conservative view of the police role. It does not take into account the Constitutional guarantees of civil rights, including free speech and free assembly. I think that the social scientist's understand of the nature of civil disobedience may be instructive. We must understand social protests in the context of our times. For example, the Negro protests have been made by middle-class Negroes with a great deal of white support. The Viet Nam protests have been led by college professors in many cases. This is the nature of the age in which we live. We have had self-immolation and protest songs; even committees of the United States Senate are protesting. And these protests are not confined to our country. They are happening in Eastern Europe, too. Various explanations have been offered. Some explain them as the result of communist agitation. Others explain them as the result of "family breakdown."

How is the world different today from what it was but a short time ago, say, in the Thirties? The world of today knows about the civil rights movement (civil disobedience began with Ghandi in India), about Nuremberg and about Eichmann. What, actually, was Eichmann convicted for? He felt completely and sincerely innocent of the charge that he had murdered millions of people and, instead, insisted that he had merely carried out the orders of his superiors. So, we convicted him, in effect, for not having a conscience of his own, for obeying instead the "lawful" orders of his superiors.

A symposium was held recently on "the legitimization of evil" at the annual meetings of the American Psychological Association. The participants at this symposium were exploring the idea that society often encourages evil by "legitimizing" it, by condoning and encouraging evil through norms, laws, and folkways which sanction man's inhumanity to man, as in laws and customs which "legitimize" patterns of racial or religious discrimination. It is such "legitimized evils" which Martin Luther King is concerned with when he advocates new techniques of law breaking. But the great difference between King's lawbreaking and that of others is that King and his followers are prepared to go to jail for their civil disobedience; criminals and the Eichmanns of this world are not.

Suddenly, in our time, the youth of today are protesting as they have never protested before. In what ways are the protesters of today different from those of yesteryear, say, the Thirties? And how can we understand this unprecedented increase in the student protest movement? I would like to offer several reasons which seem to account for it. First, there has been a decline in monolithic communism and along with this a sharp reduction of fear on the part of students that they will be accused of communism. The fear of communism seems to have lost its meaning since the break-up of monolithic communism, and along with this the fear of being accused of communist sympathies has declined, too. There are too many kinds of "communism"—Russian, Chinese, Polish, Rumanian, Albanian—and the term is not quite the bugaboo it was in the early Fifties, or Forties, or Thirties. Second, the student of today lives in an age of bigness—in the multiversity, where he is treated like an IBM card and has thus lost his identity. Third, the student of today knows about Eichmann in Jerusalem and the Nuremberg trials which established the legal basis for disobedience of orders which condone crimes against humanity, and the student of today knows about Ghandi and Martin Luther King's concepts of civil disobedience to socially legitimized evils (actually, it was Thoreau who had originally advanced the idea of civil disobedience as a protest against injustice).

Recently, research was done at the University of California at Berkeley on the differences between the students who demonstrated and those who did not. It found that the former were far less rigid and younger than the latter. There were more girls than boys among the demonstrators. Their parents had had 25% more education, chiefly in the social sciences and the humanities, rather than in engineering. Although their grades were about the same as the average students, they were obviously more brilliant because they had been able to maintain that record despite the fact that much of their time was occupied with demonstrations.

Another experiment which is relevant to the present discussion was carried out at Yale several years ago to test respondents' reactions to authority. The purpose was to discover whether the subjects had an individual conscience, or were merely responding to commands of authority figures, regardless of the morality of such commands. Dr. Stanley Milgram, the researcher, set up the experiment to discover whether a subject would help the experimenter administer electric shocks of increasing severity to a "subject" (really, an accomplice of the experimenter) who failed to memorize certain assigned tasks. With each "mistake" made by the accomplice, the subject who was helping the experimenter was expected to deliver increasingly greater amount of shock. The first button supposedly administered a 30 volt shock, and was succeeded by shocks of 60, 90, etc., volts with each of the following buttons, as more errors were made. The largest amount of shock indicated on the panel was 330 volts and was labelled: "Danger, severe shock." Each time a shock was administered, the subject screamed with increasing apparent pain. The experiment was designed to test whether the subject would continue to obey the experimenter's commands to administer shocks of increasing severity to the "subject." Of course, no electric shocks were actually delivered. The "subject" who was playing the role of "learner" was actually a gifted drama student who screamed as called for. The experimenter's helper—the real subject—had no reason to believe that the shock was *not* being delivered. The real shock of the experiment was that 65% of the subjects, both students and adults, pushed all the buttons, including the final button, obeying orders. These were ordinary college sudents at Yale mostly from good, middle-class families. Similar results were obtained with adults from various walks of life in New Haven, Connecticut.

Eichmann was apparently not unique. We are trained (or in the past we have been) not to challenge authority. And many of us will apparently condone evil when it is socially legitimized. We might speak of this phenomenon as the "Eichmann syndrome." But throughout the world today, resistance to socially legitimized evil is growing, especially here in the United States, among the Negro people and among college students. I don't believe that our demonstrations are ideologically motivated, but are motivated by the search for justice and freedom, for oneself and others.

In the preceding, I am not advocating violence, but I am trying to understand the motivation underlying the protest phenomenon of our time. Martin Luther King was awarded the Nobel prize, not so much for his leadership in the civil rights movement, but for his willingness to risk punishment and jail and perhaps death at the hands of lynch mobs, in order to stand against legally constituted authority for moral principles of justice, and freedom and equality.

Thus, it seems clear to me that the police people of the nation need to re-think and re-examine their attitudes toward the protesters of today, if they are to be able to understand them and to cope with them. And they must also understand our social institutions and the built-in injustices inherent in them, and not automatically assume that everything which is lawful is necessarily good and everything which is unlawful is necessarily bad. Only if we get away from such simplistic, black-white thinking will the police begin to contribute creatively to the further development of a truly free and democratic society.

A Look at Ourselves: Elements of Misunderstanding

MILDRED PETERS

*Professor of Guidance and Counseling, College of Education,
Wayne State University, Detroit, Michigan*

MAY 25, 1959

Mirror, Mirror on the Wall

From the beginning of time, man has shown from his folklore, fables and stories that he is in a continuous struggle with a good self and a bad self. Whether we deal with the villain and hero in fairy stories, or the "good guys" and the "bad guys" of the popular westerns on TV, we find that all fiction is a product of the struggle between the good self and the bad self. The ogres and witches that trouble the dreams of children are also a reflection of the struggle that the young person is enduring because the bad self tries repeatedly to get the upper hand. Even the witch in the fairy tale looks in the mirror and asks, "Mirror, mirror on the wall, who's the fairest of them all?" The reply she expects is that the mirror will tell her that she is beautiful and not ugly. Basically she is no different, except in degree, from the rest of us who want to be pictured only as the good people, the villains being only those who disagree with us.

An ancient Hebrew legend retold by David Rappaport in Robert Knight's PSYCHOANALYTIC PSYCHIATRY AND PSYCHOLOGY, illustrates the point well.

There was an Eastern king who heard about Moses. He heard that Moses was a leader of men, a wise man, and he wished to meet him. But Moses, busy wandering in the desert, couldn't come. So the king sent his painters to Moses, and they brought back a picture of him. The king called his phrenologists and astrologists and asked them, "What kind of man is this?" They went into a huddle and came out with a report which read: "This is a cruel, greedy, self-seeking, dishonest man." The king was puzzled. He said, "Either my painters do not know how to paint or there is no such science as astrology, or phrenology." To decide this dilemma, he went to see Moses and after seeing him he cried out, "There is no such science as astrology or phrenology." When Moses heard this he was surprised and asked the king what he meant. The king explained, but Moses only shook his head and said, "No. Your phrenologists and astrologists are right. That's what I was made of! I fought against it and that's how I became what I am."

This part of the legend makes it sound as if Moses was then the perfect man. However, we know from the Bible that Moses, too, was not without his weaknesses. "When told to touch the rock, he hit it. He acted as if *he* were doing the wonders and not the Lord. When he descended from Mount Sinai, after communing with the Lord, and seeing the golden calf and the erring of his people, he went into a violent rage and broke the Tablets."

This is in keeping with the idea expressed in one television program that, "There is a little larceny in all of us." We know that even the most law-abiding citizens, at times, test the limits of the law by such activities as skinning through on the yellow light or by being litter-bugs. This is not to be interpreted as approval of such transgressions, but merely shows that all of us are struggling with the war between the good self and bad self, in varying degrees, and—fortunately—most of us have established enough controls so that the good self has the upper hand most of the time. In spite of our awareness of the scientific truth in respect to this concept we still ask, "Mirror, mirror on the wall, who's the fairest of them all?" We expect the mirror to give the answer we want.

How Do We Know What We Are?

In trying to establish an image of ourselves, a very necessary activity, we find our identity through the jobs we hold, the possessions we have, where we live, what we do for recreation, what we wear, but most of all through people, some of whom are our love objects and some of whom we feel we have reason to dislike. It is the nature of the human being that he tends to take unto himself the attributes that he considers desirable, and to project on to others those that he cannot accept in himself. This is the result of the process used to make him a social being. The closer his image of himself is to the image that a majority of people hold of him, the nearer he is to excellent mental health. We say that his reality-testing is very good. We say that he is capable of giving and receiving love and affection, of using healthy aggression and recognizing his displaced hostilities. This would be the essence of maturity, a stage that none of us ever reaches completely. Rather, good mental health is the process of becoming increasingly mature.

To understand why we are beset with such diverse polarities, we must go back and ask how our concepts of self came about. At birth, the human infant is a bundle of impulses expecting full satisfaction. It is hard to say "expecting" because this would imply that the human infant was consciously aware of his demands, and this would not be true. Because the human infant at birth is so dependent upon those around him for his nurture, he is very much at the mercy of his parents and others in order to survive. Indeed, at birth he cannot see the face of his beloved mother at all and will not see clearly for some months. In this period, he must allow himself to be cared for by others. We say that he is in the passive stage. Those of you who have young infants at home will be inclined to disagree with me because your pride and joy makes his presence felt with a good deal of noise when he awakens and is hungry. However, if you don't respond to him there is nothing he can do to change the state of affairs. He is incapable of getting up and doing for himself. Even in this early stage, he is getting some signals that will help to make a social being of him in the future. He is learning to bear frustration by having to wait. However, there is a point beyond which he cannot wait without giving up the struggle to live. Through his signal system, he knows results will be forthcoming, and if you watch an infant of several weeks of age, you will discover that he does not cry immediately on awakening, but moves his mouth as if eating. When the delay is too long, he then cannot tolerate the discomfort any longer and cries. Only neglected or ill babies cry immediately on awakening after the first few weeks. Their groundwork for control is laid.

I am sure you are asking yourselves, what in the name of goodness babies have to do with the police profession, other than having to deliver them in emergencies

or rescue them from neglect. In answer, it must be said that understanding ourselves requires knowing how we got the way we are in the first place. Unfortunately,
all of us have amnesia in relation to childhood events that really forecast the kind
of people we become. For example, when you are sitting around socializing with
your parents or brothers and sisters, you will find that all of you tend to either
glamorize your early childhood experiences, or to make them appear more rugged
than they actually were. This is one of the reasons why adults cannot possibly
understand the thinking of very small children. We have been bombarded with
so many experiences in our lives, and had to put so many of them under cover,
we do not understand the directness in the thinking of children.

As soon as the infant can see clearly, at about the third month, he begins to
act and do to others the things they have been doing to him. When his mother
tries to feed him, he then in turn tries to feed her. Many nice mothers think their
small ones are being good hearted, but they are really not; they merely want to
do the same things to you that you do to them. Everything would be fine if the
child accepted giving up the demands for pleasure with no pangs of regret, but
this is not so. Whenever he learns something new, he has to give up one pleasure
—namely, indulgence—for the promise of a future pleasure, the acceptance by
others as illustrated by his mother's response.

From this point forward, his concept of himself is being refined constantly.
The original impulses that he had, the original demands for gratification, have
undergone a considerable degree of modification. He is angry over the demand
to give up pleasurable indulgence, but he represses the anger he feels toward his
parent because of fear of the loss of her love. From then on, throughout his entire
life, he will be ambivalent, varying on a continuum of love and hate. The love
feelings he will readily accept, but the hate feelings are denied. This presupposes
that in his rearing, he has been given an adequate amount of gratification in return
for giving up one of his instinctive demands. It is a well known fact that children
and adults who find it hard to relate to others, or who are unwilling to show respect
for the rights of others, are people who have either been denied love returns for
their withholding of demand, or they are people who have never been helped to
bear frustration.

Each step along the way in the socializing process, the child in a sense leaves
some of his soldiers to hold the fort, so that the old impulses do not get out of
hand. He learns that "good boys do this" and "bad boys do that." He learns that
he must be clean and control his own toilet processes, that he must share the love
of his parents with brothers and sisters. He learns that there are differences between
boys and girls, and that he must control his sexual impulses. Finally, all children
go through the process of first denying that the behavior belongs to them, then
projecting it on to someone else, and finally accepting that the behavior belongs
to them, and that they must internalize the responsibility and put under cover the
old wishes. The capstone of success in this process is the identification with the
parent of the same sex and the formulation of an ideal self. This latter process is
generally completed during the elementary school years and accounts for the great
interest in heroes and heroines. The collection of baseball cards is not just a satisfaction of acquisitiveness, but rather an identification with a hero whom the boy
would like to be like. It also accounts for some of the "us kids" groups of little
boys that sometimes get into trouble when they band together.

The Imperfect Image

It would be a fine thing if every child had two loving parents who were comfortable with their own masculine and feminine roles, if every child had been helped to control and in return received love for the controls, if every child could be helped to some degree to learn to share his parents' love with his brothers and sisters. But even in the best regulated families, it is impossible to avoid the anxieties that beset young people. The peace that must be made between the inner impulses that threaten to get out of hand and the demands of the real world is never complete. All of us have repressed the original wishes, but somehow the feelings that went along with the original experience have a way of sneaking out into the open. As a result, we find ourselves expressing feelings in situations that do not call for so much feeling. We find ourselves reacting to individuals in a manner that has not been invited by the real behavior of those individuals. At other times, we find it impossible to engage in some behavior that is really socially acceptable, and we don't know why. It was mentioned earlier that the child leaves some of his soldiers at each fort of development, in order to control his impulses, but if he leaves too many, he then finds that he does not have a large enough army to face the battles of the day-to-day realities. In spite of the fact that he may leave all these defenders behind, the battle is never completely won. When stresses arise in his daily life that have a tinge of the original problems, he finds that feelings arise that don't seem to belong to his present situation. Although he has tried to create a comfortable image of himself, the society around him and his life events tend to chip away at this image, so that he cannot live in the world of self-love of his babyhood.

His perfect image is impaired through comparisons with others in the family, even if this is not done intentionally by his parents. Just being younger or older puts one in a position of comparison. This process continues in the neighborhood when we come in contact with others outside our families, in the school where we have to compete with other children, and so on, for the rest of our lives. Unfortunately, we don't get much help in the building up of our perfect image. Rather, we find that the folks of our world are more than ready to remind us of our weaknesses. In fact, when we do something well, others will say, "*I* am so proud of you," instead of saying, "How proud you must be." They don't even respect us enough to let us take responsibility for our own acts. They say, "*I'm* so ashamed of you," instead of saying, "How ashamed *you* must be." The latter is really a compliment, because it implies that we think the person is strong enough to take responsibility for his own behavior. In all, though, we know there is no perfect image, but in general, we all go on behaving as if the imperfections were outside ourselves.

Compensations for Imperfections

The old war in ourselves between the "good guys" and the "bad guys" has to be fought on a reality level, and sometimes in the battle, we make it hard for others to hold their "bad guys" in check. The ideal, of course, is to find socially acceptable ways of channeling the old impulses that we no longer recognize. For example, we can release a great deal of hostility in a comfortable way through competitive sports, through watching prize fights, through reading various kinds of literature, and actually through our jobs. Schoolteachers can satisfy their feelings of domination through the leadership of the classroom, or they can satisfy their feeling of rivalry with their own siblings by being the good one that helps the children. This they do through a sublimation of the original impulse, and thereby use their energies in a self-gratifying way while at the same time making a social contribution. Incidentally, both schoolteachers and law enforcement officers are targets for unconscious feelings of people. Both occupations must ally themselves with the controls side of the personality, and as a result, even before people get to know us, they view us as the "forbidding parent," who is against fun and who "won't let you do nuthin."

Every occupation we select, every social activity, every civic activity has within it the possibility of some legal gratification. When we contribute to charity drives we feel wonderfully altruistic, and we can then allay our consciences for some of the hostile impulses we have had. Our political activities make it possible for us to work out some of the "good guy," "bad guy" stuff on our own candidates and on the opposition.

Sometimes the very structure of our society makes it difficult to find adequate compensations. We teach children that it is bad to fight, and then we confront them with a veritable competitive jungle. We try to pretend that it is not necessary to show emotion, when in reality we know that all of us must find outlets for angry as well as good feelings. We give people the impression that there is equal opportunity for all of them, and then we deny people of some groups the right to select their place of living or choice of neighborhood schools. We create images of capacities for certain ages, and deny the employee who is past forty the right to enter a new field of employment. Finally, in our social world, we are always charging people to expand their love feelings for all their brothers, but we give them no help in the handling of their old hates and misplaced hostilities. We don't even offer them the opportunity to bring these feelings out into the open and to examine why they feel the way they do.

This is not to say we must create a therapeutic world, but rather that we deal with realities. These feelings are facts. A climate must be created for examination of the facts and a way in which to help individuals to show that they disadvantage themselves in the misplacement of emotional energy. This energy is like a sum of money. If you spend it all at the races, you have none of it left to pay off the mortgage.

The Error of Being Human

It may sound as if I were blaming some outside "society" for the ills we experience when, in truth, we ourselves make the society in which we live. In the city in which I live, large urban redevelopment projects are going on, and this is good. Funds have been received for clearing the old skid row. We're all happy about this improvement but in a sense, because we are human, we play the ostrich game of hoping that the new development will make the old skid row go away. Truly we know better, but being human, we can't quite get ready for the prevention of a new skid row forming. This is part of feeling that if we do some of these good things, the bad things will go away.

Our very humanness make it very difficult to come to grips with our feelings. But somehow or other, we are stuck with being human, and if this world is to continue, we must come to grips with what humanity means for others as well as for ourselves.

I have a friend who prides herself on her acceptance of others. She gets very angry when some of her uncouth relatives make slurring remarks that are stereotypes about Negroes or Jewish people. She openly expresses disgust with others who will nôt permit people their own religious choices and, in general, she is a humane person. Recently, she phoned me to say that she was just furious because her landlord had rented the apartment under her to a Japanese couple. I was a little shocked. She has lived in the same apartment for twenty years, and she is now looking for another apartment. She says she cannot stand the smell of the cooking. This saddens me very much, because here is a basically good person who cannot see that she, too, holds the same feelings as her relatives, and would deny this couple the opportunity to choose their own place of residence. She wants to accept people as long as they are not on her home base. It isn't enough to be sanctimonious about another person and to feel that we are pure ourselves. We have all helped make the world where such feelings exist, and in spite of her feelings arising out of some old hates that have been put under cover, she is a part of a society that reinforces such feelings.

It is hard for all of us to realize that all of the stereotyped behavior that we attribute to groups in the society is really part of the original impulses that we had to tame in our childhood. We talk of some groups being dirty, but we had to have cleanliness training and at the time we did not like it, but eventually concealed our displeasure. We talk of others grabbing all they can and feel that their acquisitions have somehow or other been acquired at our expense. These are feelings that stem from old rivalries with our own family members. We accuse some groups of being belligerent and hostile. We're sure that they are all fighters. Remember, we too had to have these impulses tamed. The classic accusation is that of being over-sexed or having only one major goal, namely sexual indulgence. Our parents had quite a job in taming these impulses in us. Every stereotype that we attribute to any group on a general level stems from some old impulse that all of us in the society have had trouble taming. But then, we are the "good guys" and those who haven't tamed them are the "bad guys."

Catching Ourselves

A while ago, I was at a dinner party in honor of a man in our profession who was visiting from another city. Later he said to me, "You don't like that young man who sat next to you, do you?" This gave me pause. I hadn't really thought about it but, as a matter of fact, I don't care particularly for this man. I was surprised and said, "How did you know?" He then answered, "All the while we were talking, you kept your shoulder turned away from him and did not really include him in your conversation." This was true, and although not saying anything to indicate that I did not like the gentleman, my posture had indicated the truth. Although I could take this comment from the visitor because we are old and dear friends, I would not advise others to go around watching for such behavior among their friends and colleagues, unless they wish to make themselves very unpopular. Armchair psychiatrists, on the whole, are working their hostilities out on other people.

However, it is hard to catch one's self in the unconscious acting out of some of our old feelings. Just the way we say the name of a person is often indicative of how we feel about him. Calling someone by his first name can be a compliment, or an evidence of disrespect. There was a recent complaint registered in the letters to the editor of one of our metropolitan papers. It was from a young Negro woman who is a schoolteacher. She had been stopped by a police officer for not making a full stop at the entrance to a main street, but instead had made what is called a rolling stop. When she gave her driver's license to the officer he turned to her and said, "Alice, don't you believe in signs?" She felt that he did not know her well enough to call her by her first name, and I would be inclined to agree with her. This story will either amuse you or make you angry, but it does relate to my earlier point. Police officers are not the only ones who do this, because all of us make such slips. We tend to deal with the names of people in terms of some group attitudes we have toward them.

It would be an error if I conveyed the feeling that all of us must examine our every act, or feel guilty over old transgressions, because everyone is guilty of them.

The refinement of our perceptions is a difficult and often a seemingly impossible task. We all know that when someone is caught in an act and asked, "Why did you do that?" and he replies, "I don't know," that he well may not know. We can't always identify the true source of the motivation for a particular act, and it is true that we have to judge the act on its meaning in the society. Nevertheless, it is the obligation of everyone given a public trust, whether he be schoolteacher, police officer, councilman or any other, to make sure that his or her actions are called for in relation to the person and his individual behavior, and not based on some group generalization that we have held as truth. We need to ask ourselves how scientific we are, and on what evidence we base our reactions.

An example of this came out of the research of a man who works as a religious counsellor in an institution for delinquent girls. Because of the arrogance shown by the behavior of many such girls, many people have felt that these girls thought they were "pretty good." This man recorded one hundred interviews that related to the life stories of these girls. These interviews were analyzed to get the attitudes of these girls toward their parents, other adults, authority, their own age mates and themselves. This analysis was put together with other data, such as broken homes, alcoholism in the home, the number of foster home placements, and many other factors in their histories. The data showed that the girls with the most disorganized life experiences, and most of these were the most difficult cases, had the poorest image of themselves. They felt they weren't worth very much and were not capable. Those from the less disorganized lives, and often less severe in terms of transgressions, had better impressions of themselves. The positive feeling about themselves ranged in a continuum from a very poor image to not-too-bad a self image, according to the background of these girls. The danger of dealing with all of these girls in a like manner is readily seen.

We know it would be impossible to check all of our impressions with scientific evidence, but we must be on guard by asking ourselves if the reaction we have is based in the reality circumstances, or whether it stems from some old feelings of our own, even though we cannot find the true source.

Living with Our Feelings

One thing is certain. We all are somewhat the "good guys" and the "bad guys." As was said earlier, we are all the product of the socialization processes that took place in our own homes and in our communities. We have made our own society, and we are products of that society. The obligation we all have is to recognize that both good and bad feelings belong to each of us, and the real task is to use those appropriate to the reality circumstances in which we find ourselves. It is hoped that all of us are equipped with appropriate signal anxiety that helps us to ready ourselves to deal with dangers encountered in all parts of our lives. It is important that we use these feelings in such an economical way that we have enough energy available for all sets of circumstances. Overindulgence or overinvestment is bound to leave us poor in some other areas.

Living with our feelings does not imply that we just say, "Oh well, I'm just human and I can't help what I do." This, in essence, would be to refuse to take the responsibility for our own acts. Everyone who lives with others must take responsibility for his own acts. Part of the difficulty stems from an inability to free ourselves from some frustrations because of reality circumstances, and the pent-up feelings spread to other areas. The man who cannot express some feelings about what he considers unfair or unjust treatment on the job is often likely to take it out on his wife and children, or even kick the dog. It could be likely that he will get into an argument with his neighbor. This, in turn, brings aggression his way, and we go round and round with anger, guilt feelings, more anger and often find ourselves stuck on the merry-go-round. Getting off isn't always the easiest task. The better part of intelligence is not to get on the merry-go-round in the first place. This is easier said than done. Is there no out then? Of course there are ways to help us.

The first step in the modification of any behavior is the recognition that it is our behavior, and that it is not helpful to us, but carried out at our own expense. Overinvestment calls for more overinvestment, and finally results in a depletion of good emotional energy, with none left for the positive things in life. When we catch ourselves in the act, we can often be saved by feeling relieved that we are capable of catching ourselves; somewhat the feeling of, "Now, you rascal, I have you." At these times, a little humor in relation to ourselves is most necessary to relieve the tension. Recognition often leads to freeing one's self of the act.

When an event happens, we need to ask ourselves, "Who pays for this?" We cannot excuse attitudes in ourselves that are paid for by someone else. In the long run, the debt falls back on us. We pay for it with the poorness of our own human relations. In a larger sense, life becomes more difficult for all of us. Because man is so dependent on other people to give him a refined image of himself, the quality of the lives of others around him makes his life better or poorer. The worst punishment we can give anyone is not physical punishment, or even death. The worst punishment for any of us is isolation. When punished physically, one person is relating to another in some way. This is not to say that physical punishment is good. Physical punishment is bodily activity and not based on the transgressor coming to grips with the responsibility for his acts. It throws the emphasis back on the body, an emphasis related to our old impulses that had to be educated. It requires no use of intelligence. The extreme of physical punishment, namely death, changes nothing in the transgressor, but does leave the rest of us with varying degrees of guilt feelings.

A former professor of mine said that when a Chinaman sneezed in China, it affected all of us. This sounds a little extreme, but when we examine the real meaning of this, we see that he is correct.

We can recognize that we are human, but when because of some misplaced feelings, we deny adequate housing, employment, child care or any of the other necessary human needs to any group of individual, we impair his self image, raise his frustration and ultimately his anger—anger that will be turned back on us. In our humanness, we will recognize that all of us harbor some prejudices, but we cannot expect others to pay for our prejudices without ultimately having to pay the large debt ourselves — a debt that comes as the result of increased disease, increased anger and ultimately, increased lawlessness.

We are all in part "good guys," and in part "bad guys." But the judgment of behavior does not belong to groups, but rather in the meaning of the act of the individual in relation to society. Refinement of our own perceptions helps to modify the perceptions others have of us, and ultimately we can have a change in this hostile world of ours. Human relations will have to become more human, or the use of science for destruction may mean that there will be no humans to be human.

Personal and Social Disorganization

JOHN J. KANE

Professor of Sociology, University of Notre Dame

MAY 19, 1958

Man, it has been said, is as vitally dependent upon his society for survival as the fish is upon water. While certain exceptions to this statement may exist, it is definitely true that among the vast majority of mankind, man does depend upon his society, which he has created, for the satisfaction of his social, economic, educational, political and other needs. Perhaps this has never been truer than in the era of urbanism in which we live. In terms of space, we are crowded together in cities or in suburbs; because of rapid communication and travel, we can get to Europe faster than a man in colonial times could travel from Philadelphia to New York, a distance of one hundred miles. Our children attend class in crowded classrooms; our economic system is so tightly knit that a teamsters' strike in New York can threaten the city with starvation. Race disturbances in one American town can lose us essential friends in Asia, the Near East and Africa. The "one world" of Wendell Wilkie is a startling reality today.

This living together in close proximity, as we do in most American cities, even has physiological aspects which influence personality, morbidity and the death rate. Recent reports on an experiment carried on among animals and birds over a period of time in the Philadelphia Zoo indicated that when they were confined closely together, the degree of competition, anxiety and tension increased, as did the cholesterol level in the blood. This, as you know, results in arteriosclerosis, and ultimately in death. It is a disease of the circulatory system. It is not, as previously believed, associated with either diet or age, according to this study, but rather with tension. In the United States today, the highest death rate comes from diseases of the heart, and this, incidentally, increased from 137 per 100,000 persons in 1900 to 355 per 100,000 persons in 1950. In other words, in fifty years, it almost doubled. Some of it is traceable to the increased life span, but undoubtedly some of it stems from the tempo of life, the tensions and anxieties of contemporary living. The incidence of ulcers, hypertensions and allergies, some of which are similarly caused, has also risen.

We face a problem today that man never faced so severely or so extensively in his entire history: how to preserve social and personal organization in a tightly knit nation and world that seems to become increasingly disorganized, both socially and personally? A successful society or person, socially and psychologically, is one that is able to maintain sufficient stability to survive by executing those tasks essential to its existence. Our primary concern here as peace officers is the maintenance of law and order. Of course, all citizens should be dedicated to the same task, but yours is a particular responsibility by reason of your occupational choice. But rapid and cultural change have made your tasks more difficult and have increased the area of knowledge essential to the adequate performance of your duty.

Ultimately, social and personal disorganization occur when value systems are in conflict. It is not merely the prevalence of diverse value systems, for this has characterized both the colonies, and later the United States. Some conflict of values is inevitable. It is the degree and extent of the conflict that is important. This can best be illustrated by some anthropological data on primitive societies. In what the anthropologists term "sacred" societies, there is a common core of values pretty much accepted by all. These are both the traditional and "right" way of doing things. Such societies are invariably small, and for the most part untouched by cultural and social change. What we would consider the deviant is rarely tolerated, unless the mores of the society have made special provision for him. The most fearful punishment is banishment, which usually results in death. Furthermore, in a relatively small society, the individual is constantly under scrutiny. It is difficult, if not impossible, to avoid detection when he violates society's regulations. In addition, the process of socialization, that is, the way in which a child is inducted into his culture, is more thorough and better integrated than it is in our society. The family is a highly important social institution, and while there are some variations which we may consider bizarre, adequate provision is made for the child to acquire both a knowledge of the values of his society and facility in living according to them. When or if social disorganization does occur in such simple societies, it is frequently as a result of contact with what we call "civilization," because it brings in its wake conflicting values and social change.

Now, while the primitive family serves as an excellent illustration of how social and personal organization can be maintained, it is of comparatively little use to us in application. Sometimes the excessively permissive child-rearing of certain primitives has been mistakenly recommended to us. But one cannot take a single culture trait, such as child-rearing, out of one culture and impose it on another, because there is a strain of consistency within a society, and it would not work.

Now I should like to attempt the answer to two questions: what is the reason for social and personal disorganization within our society, and what positive steps can be taken to diminish it? The first and most obvious reason is rapid social and cultural change. Let me explain these terms in some detail. Culture refers to the ways of doing and thinking of a people which have been acquired via the social heritage. In other words, language, customs of dress and diet. Above all, *values* are transmitted from one generation to another.

If you will recall that at the beginning of the twentieth century, the following inventions and discoveries were either nonexistent or just beginning to make their impact, you can better appreciate just how much change has occurred in America.

We did not then have radio and television. The automobile was a novelty, the atomic and hydrogen bombs were yet to be discovered, divorce was relatively rare, woman suffrage was unknown in America, married women seldom worked outside the home, the various electrical home appliances were yet to be invented, and even electric lighting in the home was not common. Many of you will recall oil lamps and gas lighting. Most Americans lived on farms. The impact of such inventions and alterations in human relations pretty much occurred within a period of fifty years. Yet society must adjust to them. How well can some of the traditional values stand up under this impact? Let's look at a few.

On the farm, the American father was and could be a patriarch. He knew more than his sons did about farming, and he could teach them. He was the major breadwinner. Until his sons reached twenty-one, he was the only voter. The status of the father was not one to be challenged lightly. Now, most fathers live in cities; in many cases, their sons have much more formal education than their fathers. Indeed, sometimes sons teach fathers, instead of fathers teaching sons. When mother works full or part-time, she is also the breadwinner, and challenges what was once father's unique status. Mother may also be a voter; in fact she may even be the president of the League of Women Voters, while father is less interested and less aware of politics.

Today, we have a ratio of about one divorce to every four marriages performed within a given year. The economic dependency of women is past, the stability of the home is lessened. Life in large cities provides a certain amount of anonymity. Furthermore, the automobile can whisk a person fifty miles from home within an hour, to another town or city where he may be completely unknown. Thus, the social control exerted in the small town, village or rural area has disappeared.

As a result of such changes, some of the traditional values have been challenged. What is the role of the wife and mother today? What is the role of the husband and father? Even more important perhaps, what are the roles of children? A famous American family sociologist, E. W. Burgess, has called this a period of transition, in which we must undergo some conflicts while we reinterpret, modify or reestablish some of the traditional values. Add to this the pressure groups and vested interests in American society, whose values clash, and it is not difficult to understand the origins of our social disorganization. However, it is most important to note that while we do suffer social disorganization, we have not reached the acute stage of the actual breakdown of society's functions. Some, it is true, have been impaired, and it is certainly possible to express concern about the future in some specific areas, unless directions are altered.

Now, social disorganization inevitably results in personal disorganization. Personal disorganization is perhaps most easily explained by the use of two terms, status and role. We all have various positions within a community: fathers, brothers, husbands, physicians, peace officers, and such. Each of us attempts to portray this position, that is, we try to play the role. How we play the role depends first on how society defines it, and how we ourselves define it, against the background of our own particular values. One of the psychological sources of feelings of insecurity stem from ambiguity in role. If you have ever been in a situation in which you had responsibility but no authority, or where you simply couldn't determine just what your obligations were or how you should behave, you probably have experienced this feeling of insecurity. In various areas of life, some Americans do suffer such feelings of insecurity because they do not know how to play their roles. Part of it is the result of social disorganization, resulting from conflicting values within our society.

Let me provide some instances of what I mean. The northern cities today are facing the problem of the in-migrant. Some are southern Negroes, some are Puerto Ricans and some are poor whites from certain areas of the south. These peoples particularly suffer from ambiguity in their roles. Some of the values of their former cultures conflict with northern urban values; some of the values of their former culture are useless in the new situation. Yet northern urban society does not help them define their roles, in fact it tends to reject them. They are frequently thought of as problems. The result is inevitable—a certain amount of personal disorganization reflected in slum living, delinquency and similar social problems. Yet the very society which has helped render them insecure places the blame on them, and is frequently unwilling even to extend the aid of ordinary social agencies to these people.

There is the conflict in our society between its reputed democracy and its actual practice. Here is an example of social disorganization. This, in turn, filters down to the individual level, where the white urban-born native cannot define his role toward in-migrants, and they obviously have difficulty in determining theirs.

The indices of personal disorganization, at least in its acute stages, are a startling statistical reality. Two out of three hospital beds in this country are occupied by the mentally ill, and the most common mental disease is schizophrenia, which so far as we know, has no organic basis. It is called a functional disease, and is apparently the result of extreme personal disorganization. Generally, it incapacitates the young persons more than older persons who tend to succumb, if they do, to a different type of mental illness. A few years ago, it was estimated that one out of every twenty-two persons in New York state would spend some time in a mental institution as a patient. More recent estimates contend that one out of every twelve persons in the United States will be similarly afflicted at some time in his life. A less extreme reaction to personal disorganization are the neuroses, and no one can even estimate their extent. Finally, we have a psychiatric grab-bag known as the "psychopath," characterized by a lack of social conscience. It is claimed that such persons are responsible for many of the heinous crimes committed in our society, and that punishment for them is no deterrent, since many seem unconsciously to *seek* punishment as a function of their mental aberration.

Social and personal disorganization have something in common with contagious diseases in that they spread throughout a population, and the symptoms are exhibited in what we term social problems. Poverty, a high incidence of physical and mental illness, slum living, prejudice and discrimination toward minorities, the prevalence of vices such as alcoholism and narcotic addiction and adult and juvenile delinquency are all interrelated and interdependent. I am not suggesting that there is one single, simple cause of these problems. All large, complex societies have them, but it is rather the matter of their incidence and their probable increase, which we cannot prove scientifically for lack of adequate statistics in the past. What I am maintaining is that the extent of social disorganization within a society will increase the frequency of personal disorganization, and thus multiply disproportionately some of the social problems mentioned.

How to remedy or improve the situation is an even more complex question. In the course of this Institute, a number of speakers will discuss certain aspects of these problems in more detail, and will be able to handle the question of improvement within certain areas through specific measures. Furthermore, these speakers are highly qualified specialists within some of the areas and can provide more first-hand and minute information than I am able to do. My function is to speak in more general terms, and in these terms, I shall propose certain steps that may be taken.

Basically, it is a matter of developing, reinterpreting or restoring certain values to the culture. Social change is here to stay, and we must therefore learn how to live with it. As the foremost power in the world, a position America never before occupied, our social problems become exhibits to disprove our claims to freedom, democracy, belief in the profit motive, private property and many other values at the core of our society. As an example of this, when Vice-President Nixon recently visited South America, one charge hurled at him, along with the actual rocks, was "Little Rock."

The first step I would propose is a thorough publicizing of our problems in a reasonably scientific way. Americans must be made aware of what is happening and why it is happening. But unless it is done in a calm, dispassionate manner, it is worse than useless; it may even be harmful. The launching of the first Sputnik by the Russians resulted in national discussion of our system of education. Unfortunately, some journals and journalists were far from scientific or objective in their writings and publications. Some leaped into the fray—and this is about the best term by which to describe it—with vengeful glee. Here was an opportunity to become destructively critical of certain educational philosophies and practices which these persons deplored. Now, no one denies that there is room for improvement in American education. But to illustrate, a certain TV show depicted a class in co-educational cookery as a horrible example of what is happening to our youngsters. I asked a class of fifty-five students how many had such a course in their high school. Two said "yes," and added they had not taken it. If one believes that co-educational cookery is a farce, he may well criticize it, but isn't it important to discover just how many schools offer it, and how many students take it? It is the implications and suggestions in such approaches which disturb me. I admit, recently, some effort has been made to publicize some of our better schools.

Next, I believe it is important that Americans realize that one social problem is not entirely disassociated from another. For example, the man who is deeply interested in mental health—may in fact contribute to it—may be the same man who is opposed to slum clearance for economic reasons, because he realizes his income from such a source.

This leads inevitably to the third step, in which we must ask ourselves two questions: first, what values underlie and contribute to our social and personal disorganization; second, to what extent do we ourselves share and contribute to the salient position of such values in our society? This requires some deep, personal soul-searching, and few of us will come out of it unscathed.

Finally, we shall have to exert our personal influence within our own communities on government, education, economic and educational institutions, in an effort to affect the social changes essential to a better way of life. Above all, we can begin within our own families to provide sound values for our children. Admittedly, in a democratic society, there will be no monolithic system of values. We will disagree, and we should disagree at times, but in face of the facts, in a

spirit of true objectivity and zeal and love for our country, we can at least agree
on the basic values essential to the better life. We can, if we wish, in a democracy,
act together to attain them.

The Implications of Population Trends for Urban Communities

PAUL MUNDY

Professor of Sociology, Loyola University, Chicago

MAY 20, 1964

Between 1950 and 1960, the American population increased by 28 million
people, an average of almost 3 million persons per year, as the population grew
from 151 to 179 million. What is especially significant about this increase is that
all of it took place in urban areas, and rural areas lost one-half million people.
That increase of 28 million people in the space of 10 years is one and one-half
of the total population of Canada or almost the total population of Mexico. It is
equal to the entire population of the United States about a century before,
around 1850.

Our population is increasingly concentrated in densely packed clusters. For
example, the *city* of Chicago in 1960 had a population greater than *33* of the 50
states; the Chicago *metropolitan area* (six counties of northeastern Illinois) had
a population greater than that of *43* states. More than 25 million people (or
approximately one in every seven Americans) lived in the New York-Northeastern
New Jersey (14.8 million) and the Chicago-Northwestern Indiana (6.8 million)
Standard Consolidated Areas, to use Census Bureau terminology.

What a tremendous transformation has taken place since the first census of
the U.S. in 1790, when we had less than four million population; when 95 per cent
of that population was rural and 5 per cent was urban! Moreover, this trend
toward an urban population, while it was accumulating over time, did not produce more than 50 per cent of the population in urban places until 1920. Thus
it has been only in the past generation or so that the majority of Americans have
lived in urban areas. The concentration is now so great that in the 212 Standard
Metropolitan Statistical Areas, each of which has a core city of at least 50,000
persons, there is now a concentration of about ⅔ of our population on less than
5 per cent of the land area. The focus of today's police concerns, then, involves
less than 5 per cent of the land area, but 70 per cent of our human population.
This is part of what is meant by "metroplexity" today.

Of equal significance to this, quite obviously, is the new, dramatic shift as far
as racial distribution of our population is concerned. In the first census of the
U.S. in 1790, the Negro population was 19.3 per cent. One in every five persons
in America was a Negro. The proportion of Negroes consistently declined,
although their numbers increased, so that by 1910, Negroes constituted only
10.7 per cent of the population. What is not generally recognized is that in 1910,
and for the past 40 years, the Negro population of the U.S. has held almost
exactly constant, so that in 1960, the Negro proportion of the population was

10.6 per cent, or one-tenth of one per cent *less* than it was 40 years ago. In numbers, however, this amounted to about 20 million people in 1960. And the 20 million people, for obvious reasons, assume a new importance to you in police work, with respect to the problem of trying to maintain social tranquillity in the midst of a developing revolution.

I say a *developing* revolution, in order not to convey the impression that there is anything new about this, for revolution is a continuing part of the American experience. Born in revolution as a nation, we have substantially lost sight of the historical background and continuity that characterize us as a people. We fail, as a consequence, to develop the kind of perspective and self-understanding that would enable us to comprehend the continuing forces that are at work in our society among those who still are not free. Let us look briefly at the changing distribution of non-whites before we pursue this matter of revolution.

The transformation of the urban–rural concentration of Negroes in America is indicated by the following statistics. In 1940, 48 per cent of the non-white population was urban; 57.5 per cent of the white population was urban. By 1950, both the white and non-white population had 59 per cent in urban areas. By 1960, the white population in urban areas was 70 per cent; the non-white population in urban areas was 72 per cent. While there has been a generally dramatic shift of population for all Americans into urban areas, this shift has been particularly significant as far as the non-white population is concerned. (And may I note, parenthetically, that I use these labels "white" and "non-white" as we conventionally understand them, although they are without literal meaning. Anyone knows that there is no such thing as a white man. The closest thing to a white man is an albino. The fact of the matter is that all human beings are colored. We are all colored in various hues and degrees. And if we Caucasians can be wrong about calling ourselves white, how obviously wrong we can be in describing other peoples.)

The migration of Negroes to urban areas has resulted in their making more than half of the population in Washington, D.C.; among the other 24 of the largest 25 cities of the U.S., eight cities now have a non-white concentration of 25 to 49 per cent, as of the 1960 census: Philadelphia, Detroit, Baltimore, Cleveland, St. Louis, New Orleans, Memphis and Atlanta. Nine of the major 25 cities in the U.S., as of 1960, have 10 to 24 per cent non-white populations, including New York, Chicago, Los Angeles, Houston, San Francisco, Dallas, Pittsburgh, Buffalo and Cincinnati. Seven of the largest 25 cities had a non-white population of 2.4 to over 9 per cent: Milwaukee, Boston, San Antonio, San Diego, Seattle, Denver and Minneapolis. To speak of these relatively few cities is to identify the national pattern; it is to indicate that the thrust for full equality and for full participation is nationwide, and primarily focused in the metropolitan areas.

For those of us "whites" who belong to what we mistakenly call "the majority group," we should recall that on a world-wide basis we comprise about one in every three persons. It is good for our humility to understand this — just as I think it is good for the wisdom of Americans to recall that we are only 6 per cent of the world's population. For every one of us, there are 15 other people in the world. We are a minority, in one way or another.

Now let us return to the theme of revolution. The very success of the American Revolution has deluded those of us who have benefited so magnificently from it. Most of us think that for the past 200 years, America has been a haven for the oppressed from every land. This idea is false. Those among us Americans from Africa have not been and are not yet fully free. When a revolution worth fighting for is won, as our American Revolution was, it is altogether proper that our stand should then become conservative—that we should conserve the values that were gained—for perpetual revolution is meaningless and absurd. But when revolution has not, in fact, achieved the full freedom of all citizens in this country, it is inevitable that the revolution should continue. And yet there is a psychological alienation on the part of most of us toward revolutionary currents. It rests, I think, on the basis of the success and authentic freedom that have been achieved by so many of us, and failure to grasp that these have not been achieved by all of us. The source and meaning of this revolution, then, are particularly American.

That revolution is continuing in a circumstance of unique historical and demographic meaning. Our central cities, which grew with extraordinary rapidity, are emptying themselves of great numbers of the white population (who have come to reside in them only recently) as the non-white population grows. The speed with which our cities grew in America is an indication of the complexity of the problem. Most of us do not really understand that on a world-wide basis, the development of urban living, to any considerable extent, is less than 200 years old. It corresponds almost exactly with the industrial revolution. The great cities of the past were extraordinarily rare; the great cities of the present are coming to be the order of the time.

Most of the very largest cities throughout the world grew to one million in size over a period of hundreds and hundreds of years. Some of our major American cities reached this population in 50 to 100 years, made up of European minorities, predominantly rural people, the unskilled, the under-educated, the illiterate, the poor, the adventuresome. These were our parents and grandparents, for the most part. What many of us in middle-class positions today fail to recognize is that when anybody is talking about the illiterate poor, they are talking about our people—my people and yours. They were recently the uneducated and the unskilled. We forget what our historical roots are. We are only two or three generations removed from terrible ignorance and poverty. Our grandparents were basically unprepared to live in urban centers. We white grandchildren, however, often resent it when Americans of darker hue assert their rights as persons and as citizens.

In a single city like Chicago, between 1950 and 1960, about 600,000 whites left the central city and migrated to suburban communities. The total central city white population loss was 400,000, because there was an excess of 200,000 white births over deaths. The Negro population increased by about 330,000 in the same period, from slightly more than 500,000 to almost 850,000. Previously, the Negro population of Chicago, which was 30,000 in 1900, reached 120,000 by 1920. Thus the non-white population quadrupled, as compared with what it was in 1900.

By 1960 Negroes constituted a total of 14 per cent of the population in the six counties of northeastern Illinois; they represented an increase of one in every three persons added to the metropolitan area population between 1950 and 1960. This is truly typical of metropolitan areas across the country. The implications of this are extremely significant because, while Negroes are presently a numerical minority, in Chicago this is a condition that is very likely to change in a few years. At the rates of change of 1950–1960, there is every likelihood that Chicago will become predominantly non-white about 1975. And a few years thereafter, as a consequence of the aging of that population to voting age, there will, in all probability, be a non-white mayor.

I am inclined to think that this strikes some people with some fear and concern. They cannot be sure what the outlook and the mentality of that non-white mayor will be — or non-white mayors in other major cities before and after Chicago. I think they have a lingering suspicion and fear that perhaps Negroes will reciprocate, and treat whites as they have been treated. They are wondering if the Negro mayor will be a statesman or a racist *provocateur*.

If people migrating from the central city could simply write off the central city and be done with it, the problem would be very simple for them. But in 1980, when 60 per cent of the total population of the Chicago metropolitan area will be residing in the suburbs, and 40 per cent in the central city, the most reliable estimates that we have of economic opportunity suggest that 60 per cent of the jobs will be within Chicago, and 40 per cent in the suburbs. Chicago, like every other central city, is the economic heart of the metropolitan area of which it is a part, and the people in the suburbs cannot ignore this meaningful fact. There is a very real danger that if the problems and the denial of rights of non-white citizens are not rectified in the very near future, the white suburban citizens will enter the central city under a virtual state of seige, because all the notions that we have of majority and minority will very likely be reversed.

The real sociological test of *minority* and *majority* relationship is social power and institutional control. In the Union of South Africa, Negroes are a numerical majority but a sociological minority. In the U.S., Negroes are simultaneously a numerical minority and a sociological minority. Negroes are now concentrating in increasing numbers in the 12 states that hold the electoral key vote to a presidential election. The out-migration of Negroes from the South and the suburbanward movement of whites from central cities together constitute a political factor that should not be overlooked.

In the 1940's, a total of 1,547,000 Negroes left the South in a ten-year period. In the 1950's, 1,457,000 Negroes left the South, or 14 per cent of the total nonwhite population of the nation. The patterns of emerging institutional change and the fact that the cities and the suburbs are linked together in an economic and social bond should prompt the nation's public officials to comprehend in truly pragmatic terms the meaning of the change that is occurring, as well as the need for metropolitan vision.

I think that Negroes have come to understand that their appeals to charity and love and the sense of justice of white men have gone largely unheeded. They are realistic enough to understand that what white people increasingly understand is power, and that there is a new power alignment emerging in our metropolitan areas. If on no other grounds — if it is not a sense of decency, or justice or humanity — whites must, in their own self-interest, take now the steps that are necessary.

The urban and rural shifts have other implications as well. We speak about the impact of urbanization on our society. But I think that we should not overlook the fact that there has been a persistent impact of ruralization on our society as well. The meaning of this rural past should be overlooked by no one, including its continuation in our central cities. For one thing, as I noted, our population did not become more than 50 per cent urban until 1920. The overwhelming majority of the people who came from Europe were from intensely rural backgrounds.

They were predominantly from the peasant areas. This was true whether they came in the first waves of immigration from northern and western Europe—from the British Isles and from Germany and Scandanavia before 1880–1890—or whether they came later from the southern and central areas of Europe.

The impact of ruralization is shown in such inconsequential things as the wearing of blue jeans in cities, the setting of the school year—which is a carry-over from the time when children had to be released from school for planting and harvesting the crops—the popularity of the country music in our society, as incomprehensible as the popularity of the Beverly Hillbillies. The impact of the ruralization of our society is further indicated by the fact that in 40 of our 50 states, we now have a concentration of people in urban areas, but that few of these states have willingly reflected this new population distribution in representation in the state legislature. This has brought about a political crisis in re-apportionment, as a consequence of the serious under-representation of the urban centers of the nation.

There is also lingering among us a vigilante tradition of our rural past. This is a carry-over of the casual frontier concept of rough-and-ready justice, a contempt for law that is expressed in "String 'em up, boys; don't wait for the sheriff!"

This contempt for law and justice has its carry-over even into the metropolitan concentrations at the present time. I think if we are to understand something of ourselves and what is taking place, we must also recognize that the mold in which most of our ancestors were produced in Europe was a mold that had a legal system vastly different from our own. The American legal system is rooted in the idea that it is the person who is important. At least this is so in the basic theory of our system of law. This is why Justice is represented as blindfolded, and our group affiliations are believed to be irrelevant. The judge is not —or should not be—interested in our religion, our clubs and affiliations, but in the fact that a person is a citizen. This is the theory. But you and I know that this theory has been contradicted in practice. When group affiliations become important, no system of law is able to operate equitably.

This historical past of our ancestors must be understood if we are to understand our own dilemma. Where Catholics were in power in Europe, Protestants were in peril, and the reverse was true where Protestants were in power. There seemed to be something normal and right about this. A calculus of power was assumed in which you were secure if you belonged to the in-group, the majority. That was the normal power structure. What the American system of law presented to us was a unique and a radical idea—that group affiliations were insignificant. There were compromises, to be sure, in the Constitution itself, as the counting of Negroes at ⅗ of their numbers for representation. And there were compromises in practice in different localities. It was difficult to get people to accept this American doctrine, because it was very comfortable to be a member of a majority in a culture that is cruel to minorities.

This historical ambiguity is represented in our assertion that *all* men are created equal and are endowed by their Creator with certain inalienable rights. The dilemma that it presents to the police officer is an extremely difficult one. In a major city of one of our border states, up until a few years ago, the officer of the law was required, under his oath of office, to uphold the law which forbade Negroes to enter a public library, to go to a zoo or to visit an art gallery. Any

Negro so doing would be arrested for trespass or disturbing the peace. The dilemma for the officer was the obligation to uphold local law, vigorously supported by majority opinion, in defiance of national law. Some years ago this changed. In some communities, the anomaly no longer persists.

If such compromises constitute a dilemma for the police officer, can one comprehend how they would affect the Negro! It would make me strive to correct such a situation with all my heart and spirit. James Baldwin said, "To be a Negro in American society is to spend half of one's life mad." Ponder the emotional waste that is thus represented. And yet no one who is not a Negro in America can really know what it is like. Certainly no white man can. I had some comprehension of this a few years ago when I was doing graduate research in Washington, D.C., on the Negro drop-out. I had to work in some of those despicable slums. Joseph Alsop in a recent column said "Every white American should be compelled to spend one week in the slums of Philadelphia . . . but this would be too impossible to impose upon him." Imagine what it would be like to spend one's entire life in such a place. It is an experience that no human being should ever be subjected to.

Baldwin asks, "What do Negroes want in American society?" and he answers: "Negroes want to be treated like men." Nothing less, nor more. One of my colleagues at Loyola has said, "What this country can be grateful for is that it never tried to impose those indignities upon the Irish."

The emergence of extremist groups like the Black Muslims (I met my first Black Muslim back in 1947) — still fortunately a very small minority of the population — has demonstrated to us the absurdity of some of our ideas, such as the idea that the NAACP and the Urban League were radical and extreme organizations. They have helped us to understand what responsible and moderate leadership now is. We must come to understand that if we do not deal with these responsible groups, then we shall surely have to deal with others. If we don't deal with them across the conference table, we shall have to deal with other groups in the blind and ignorant fury of the streets, to the mutual disaster of all of us.

The year 1919 marked a year of revolution. They took the form of race riots in America. These have been studied, and there are some important lessons to be learned from them. From 25 racial clashes in that year, of which seven were actual riots, three were extremely serious — in Washington, D.C., in Chicago and in Phelps County, Arkansas. Research reports show that:

These three explosions, as different from each other as they seem at first glance, together point some lessons for preventing racial conflicts from turning into riots. In each of them the trigger to violence was the un-neutral action of the local police. And the most important factor in ending the riot was the more neutral intervention of outside force. If any single act is most likely to set off race riots, it is behavior by police that signals to whites that they are free to use violence against Negroes, and signals to Negroes that they will have to defend themselves. If racial demonstrations continue, and there is every reason to believe that they will, and if the police continue to behave as if demonstrators were armed marchers intending to burn down city hall, there will be riots. The thwarting of non-violent protests forces violence upon those who are protesting.

Louis Lomax in an article on what mass protests can't do says:

> We have not lost faith in the law so much as we have lost faith in the
> local officials who have blatantly refused to obey the law. We do not distrust
> the law so much as we distrust those who would make us wage a town by
> town, state by state, costly and lengthy legal fight to get what the Supreme
> Court has already said is our right. We are not out to change the law so much
> as we are out to shock the nation into a complete awareness that the local
> white power structure in the South and the North is committed to defiance
> of the law. It is to be regretted that few white people realize that the law
> has long since been reduced to mockery. The only time the law operates for
> the Negro is when it is being used against him. Otherwise, when it comes to
> voting rights, fair housing and fair employment, the law is little more than a
> glittering unrealized promise. . . . The Negro, through demonstrations, is
> attempting to redeem the law in the eyes of those who know it only as an
> instrument of oppression and denial. What the Negro seeks is law and justice.
> Law without justice is tyranny. Justice without law is anarchy. Justice with
> law is democracy. And that is what all the shouting in the streets is about.

The Negro is asking when will white men affirm their belief in the political
philosophy of the U.S. by demonstrating (not merely pledging) their allegiance
to *one* nation under God, *indivisible,* with liberty and justice for *all*?

The Negro is troubled that many whites do not seem to realize that civil
rights are simply the ratification of every man's human rights and human dignity.
Civil rights are a problem only to the uncivil human being, the lingering barbarian
in us. Education, learning and science shatter all the stupidities of racism. When
all whites in greater numbers grow in reverence and awe before the masterpiece
of God's creation — the human person — and not blaspheme the God of all of
us by hating and insulting the fact of God's variety. When will the white man
come to terms with himself; when will he explore more fully what he means by
those words that he mouths with such frequency: the dignity of the human
person, the free society, the pledge of allegiance, the majesty of law?

These are the questions that are reverberating throughout America. They
cannot be ignored much longer. A reconciliation based upon law and justice must
occur and the police responsibility in this area, it seems to me, is of unparalleled
importance. North and South, East and West, small community or major metropolitan area, the police officer really makes the most meaningful decisions that bear
on the ultimate resolution of this extraordinarily complex and difficult problem.

Contra-Cultural Conflict
in the Metropolitan Community

MEL RAVITZ

Professor, Department of Sociology, Wayne State University, Detroit

MAY 20, 1963

This is not an easy subject to analyze. It will be necessary, first, to outline the
general nature of the urban community, then to note some of the cultural conflicts that exist or may exist, and finally to suggest the role of the police officer
in this kind of situation.

Let me begin by reminding you that cultural conflict is as old as man. When the European colonists first settled in the New World and brought with them their own cultural background: their social system, their laws, their traditions, their values, their religion, there was conflict. The history of the struggle between the Indians and the white men was a struggle for land, and might therefore be deemed an economic conflict, but basically, behind the desire for land was the differential use for which each wanted the land: the Indians for hunting and fishing, the white settlers for farming. Thus, there ensued a long, bitter conflict that cost many lives, that precipitated many injustices on both sides, that developed many prejudices and much discrimination which continues to this day. I note this ancient struggle because I want to underscore that America was born out of cultural conflict, and that it is not a uniquely modern phenomenon.

It is true, of course, that the cultural conflict we witness today is not always as devastating as that of pioneer days. Yet in some instances, it is even more deadly. Surely none will deny that the paramount cultural conflict that holds the world's attention today is that between the two giant power blocs: the Soviet Union and the United States. In essence, this cold war is a cultural conflict between two major cultures with different social, economic, and political philosophies. That presently the conflict is conducted on a more or less nonviolent basis is simply because it is to the advantage of neither side to permit it to erupt into total war. The leadership of both sides knows well that violence to secure the advantage in this cultural conflict may be the last violence anyone now living witnesses.

Important to appreciate in analyzing this world conflict is the fact that there is no strong police force acknowledged and accredited by both sides. Thus the peace is kept uneasily by mutual fear and by mutual recognition of the terrible consequences of war. Were there a strong police force, well equipped and supported by a majority of people of both sides, we would have less fear that the present cold, cultural conflict would become a shooting conflict of annihilation.

Not all cultural conflict today is of this awesome sort that holds the world in balance. Most of the cultural conflict that exists occurs within a more limited framework. Much of it is currently in process in the big cities of America and the world. This is so because the metropolitan community has become the living place of people of many types: racial, religious, ethnic, political, social class. It is a human spectrum of many cross and conflicting cultures. The metropolitan community is a laboratory for the study of cultural conflict.

Let us take a closer look at this metropolitan community and at the principal cultural conflicts raging within it.

In describing some of the major characteristics of the local urban community, we may begin by considering a basic physical feature. The generalized urban community is composed of three main growth areas: the old central core of the city, a large middle-aged area, and the newly developed sections and suburbs. Within the old core area of American cities are dwellings generally built prior to the turn of the century. Many show obvious signs of decay and obsolescence and require clearance and redevelopment. Just outside this core area are the homes in middle-aged neighborhoods. These are the homes and neighborhoods in need of conservation and improvement to prevent them from becoming future slums. Finally, the third area of the city is the newly built portion near the boundaries and in the suburbs. The new homes in these neighborhoods are in good condition at the moment, but they, too, can and will deteriorate if they are neglected.

In recent years, the urban community has grown in almost fantastic fashion. Not only has it increased in population, but this population has redistributed itself in the region. It has spilled over the city boundaries, and there is a rapidly growing population now living in the suburbs and in sprawling fashion beyond. In some metropolitan areas, a majority of the regional population already lives outside the city limits in the surrounding areas.

Another apparent social characteristic of the urban community is the mobility of its population. The city itself is a result of the population movement from the farms and countryside; that movement from rural to urban centers is still continuing, both north and south. It is no secret that people from the rural sections of the south and from Puerto Rico have moved and still are moving to northern industrial points such as Cleveland, Chicago, Pittsburgh, New York, Philadelphia, Detroit. This movement has been especially heavy during periods of war and war preparation, e.g., the early forties and early fifties. Many of the people who have come have stayed to make these cities their home. Because of insecure jobs and generally lower incomes, and because of formal or informal restrictions elsewhere, many of these people were forced to crowd into the oldest and most deteriorated areas of the city.

The presence of vast numbers of these peoples in our cities compels us to consider the real nature of the problem. Actually, the basic problem is not new; it is as old as cultural difference among and between people who meet. It is, however, a problem that comes in a new guise each time it arises. It is the problem of the "culturally different," and of the consequent cultural conflict.

One way to consider this important problem is by pointing out an interesting parallel between American efforts to help different people all over the world, and the efforts now beginning to assist these American migrants who live in what has been variously called "the slums," "blighted areas," "depressed areas," "multiproblem neighborhoods."

There are several similarities worth noting: first, of course, there is the essentially rural character of both peoples; those who come to the city are chiefly from the rural south and Puerto Rico at the present time. Second, both peoples have generally low levels of formal schooling, but they are by no means unintelligent. Third, both peoples are proud of their cultural traditions and are quick to resent any hint of condescension. Fourth, both peoples are willing to learn, but they must be taught on their own terms; they cannot be cajoled, intimidated or embarrassed. They must be dealt with as mature adults. These people cannot be expected to realize their full potential unless they are helped at the point of interest and education they are at. Fifth, and finally, it is very expensive in many ways to try to help either people to modify their traditional values, attitudes and behavior.

These lines of similarity between working with the so-called "under developed" countries (really culturally different countries) and working with rural in-migrants to American cities ought certainly to be understood and appreciated. What has been happening these past several years in many American communities is this: they have been the destination for countless thousands of Negroes, southern whites and Puerto Ricans, individuals and families, who have come mainly in search of jobs. With hope and a general willingness to work, they have come from the isolated portions of the back-country of the south; they have come without money, and they have brought their problems with them.

Most have come to these cities to stay. Large numbers of these people have crowded into the deteriorated interior core of the city to which they have come, there to live until they make some money. After that, if they are white, they may choose either to return to the south, or try to raise their living standard enough to step onto the outward-bound escalator that moves from the core toward the suburbs. If they are Negro or Puerto Rican, they will probably not seek to return south, but will instead try to raise their living standards to board the shorter escalator, to move into the better neighborhoods that beckon beyond the interior core of slums. Not many of these people will easily move upward in the social structure; most will continue to live in the blighted core of the city, trying to raise families without much knowledge of the city and its ways, and remaining there only because it is, in economic terms, worse where they came from.

These are the people, too, who get shifted and shunted around as the processes of expressway construction and urban renewal proceed. The inner core of the central city is being remade, and those who now live there are sooner or later to be displaced. They will be forced out into the present middle-aged or conservative neighborhoods, bringing with them cultural habits that are so often threatening to the lower middle and middle class Negroes and whites who now reside there. Indeed, the gradual influx into these neighborhoods of these lower class rural people of whatever race or birthplace is one of the chief factors prompting the exodus of middle class residents. Middle class whites are moving to the fringes and out of the city; middle class Negroes, of whom there is a growing number, strive desperately to find some opening in the surrounding wall of housing segregation through which they and their families can escape the invading lower class influences.

This, then, is one significant part of the pattern of movement in American cities. Everywhere groups of people are moving away at the approach of other groups with real or fancied differences.

As noted earlier, the problem is an old one, but it is nonetheless critical; the specific issue is essentially: how do those who are middle class and who administer and control the schools, the churches, the government, the social agencies, and all the other organizations of the urban community, learn to relate effectively with those people who have come and who are coming to these cities and who want to remain and be accepted? What do they do?

Obviously, one answer is to have nothing to do with them and hope they will go away; this alternative, however, is naive and ridiculous, even though some people advocate it. These newcomers and some not-so-newcomers cannot be ignored. Their over-all cultural impact on neighborhoods, on schools, on health and welfare agencies, on churches, and on government is tremendous, and will continue to be so. There is no real choice except to recognize the existence of these people, and then seek to integrate them into the community in such a way that they will be able to live in the urban environment with some greater degree of civic-mindedness, convenience and satisfaction, both to themselves and to others around them.

Certainly recognition of these lower class rural people, these presently "culturally different" people, and concern for and with them does not arise simply out of superior urban nobility. Doubtless, most present residents of these cities would breathe a hearty sigh of relief if these people could be persuaded to return to their rural birthplaces. It is only because they cannot be persuaded to return, and because they have a full right to be where they are, that anyone even pretends to be willing to help them. There is a growing awareness, too, that they must be helped to assimilate, because failure to do so threatens the cohesion and stability of the urban community.

When these people come to the city—and some have been here many years—they come principally because they hope that life's circumstances will be better than they were in the agriculturally blighted areas from which they came. They moved to these cities to find jobs and to make their modest contributions to society. They arrive, bringing with them the habits of the world they left: its costume, its speech, its cooking patterns, its standards, its beliefs, its attitudes, its values. Just as a generation or more ago America hosted large numbers of newcomers from western and eastern Europe, so today a domestic population shift is bringing to these cities fresh waves of newcomers who arrive culturally encumbered with the ways of their rural birthplaces.

In those earlier days of this century, Americans marshalled their resources, established day and night schools, developed a comprehensive social work pattern suited to the problems of the European newcomers, and proceeded in a relatively short time to assimilate these people into the mainstream of American life. It was not easy, it was costly, and it was not done overnight, but ultimately there was a reasonably successful assimilation, to the greatest enrichment of the American culture.

This assimilation was achieved without insisting that every newcomer pass through the "melting pot" and emerge with standardized beliefs, customs, or behavior. It was done with a deep appreciation that social diversity—cultural pluralism—was the true basis of heterogeneous American lift. The principle was accepted that assimilation in America does not require that all religious, verbal, culinary, fashion folkways of the sub-group be surrendered. The principle was accepted that people may retain many of their own cultural patterns and still be regarded as loyal, contributing members of the society. It was even implied that American society would face grave danger if this culture pluralism disappeared, and the mass culture of the emerging society smashed all diversity before it, to produce a low level cultural monotony. Indeed, this is a significant threat to the present day!

Here again, in the middle of the twentieth century, American society is confronted with a challenge to its belief in cultural pluralism. Present in our great cities are these newcomers who are different in cultural background, even though for many the root of their language, their religion, and their basic values is similar. Their major differences are these: they are poor, some very poor; they have never known comfort and convenience in material things; they were reared on the hard hearth of country cabins and they knew few of the graces or niceties of urban living; they have many different standards: of health, of sanitation, of law, of education. Although the Puerto Ricans are Catholics, the religion of the southern whites and Negroes is, by middle class urban criteria, pentacostal and primitive, with much appeal to emotion, a frontier religion with emphasis on elementary Christianity. These people speak a language filled with the colloquialisms of their region, and they have various kinds of southern accents that set them apart; the Puerto Ricans are set even further apart by their Spanish language. Finally, most of them have had little formal schooling; they are thus untrained for most work in the industrial community, and if they get work at all, they must accept the menial, the unskilled, the low paying, transient jobs.

These, then, are some of the characteristics of both the southern Negroes and whites and the Puerto Ricans who have come to the city, and who will doubtless continue to come. Though in their northern trek, these people travel by several different routes, one way or another they get to their destination, and when they arrive, they must be assimilated as immediately and as adequately as possible.

In the face of any vexing and sensitive issue, it is particularly essential that people be honest with themselves. The presence of these culturally different people in many American cities poses such an issue. Most of those people already in the city are urbanized, and either already middle class or middle class in their orientation. Most of those who have come recently and who are still coming are neither; they are both rural and lower class. The issue to be considered is simply: how can these two sets of culturally different people relate more effectively and harmoniously with each other? How can the inevitable cultural conflict be reduced in both scope and severity?

At this point it is appropriate to suggest a basic principle of social interaction: if, in any community, two culturally different peoples meet on a continuing basis, community cohesion requires one or the other of these peoples to attempt at least the partial assimilation of the other. An adequately cohesive community cannot remain with two or more significantly diverse cultural groups. In the particular instance under consideration here, this principle may be translated as follows: an adequately cohesive community cannot continue to exist with both large numbers of lower class, rural people and large numbers of middle class, urban people. Either one group or the other will have to try to assimilate the other, or one of them will solve the situation created by withdrawal.

Some of the lower class, rural people will withdraw to their southern birthplaces, when and if the economic conditions become so desperate that things are worse in the city than they were in the country. Some others will withdraw to other cities, especially in the west. Still others will withdraw when and if the various forms of subsistence assistance that are available is reduced, restricted or terminated. On the other hand, some of the middle class residents of the city will withdraw, as many have been doing, when these lower class people begin to move into their neighborhoods. Their withdrawal will be and has been to the fringes of the city or to the suburbs.

As a corollary principle to the one just cited, it may be suggested that the group that is numerically, educationally, politically and economically superior will try to assimilate the other group. It will seek to do this eventually, after it has tried to avoid the issue altogether. It will seek to do this, because it will slowly dawn on its members that they have most to lose by inaction and the most to gain by successful assimilation.

If this larger group proceeds with care and concern in its assimilation attempt, it may well succeed. Indeed, unless it desires to withdraw, there is no reasonable alternative for the urban middle class but to try to change some of the values, attitudes and behavior patterns of its own members and of the rural lower class. The middle class must change its own ideas and ways to be better able to understand and accept these newcomers; the middle class, because it is the dominant category, must take the initiative in helping newcomers shed some of their thornier and no longer functional traits. The issue is not really whether assimilation shall occur, but rather how best can it be accomplished.

Within this context of the metropolitan community and its various patterns of cultural conflict stands the police officer, or more significantly, the peace officer. What is his role? What is expected of him? What should be expected of him? What should he expect of the community he serves?

First, let us appreciate that the police officer is not a teacher, or a social worker or a politician, although to be sure he must be prepared to play all of these roles and others too. Principally, his role is that of keeper of the community peace. As such, he is sworn to uphold the laws of the land and his community, and to do so with efficiency and equality.

In the best of circumstances, where the police officer works in a culturally homogeneous community of which he is a part, law enforcement is not easy. It becomes a truly difficult assignment when he must work in a seething situation of persistent, and somewhat even bitter cultural conflict. This is indeed the situation in most of our metropolitan communities today, as I have indicated.

In such circumstances, the majority of police officers are frequently members of one of the groups engaged in the cultural conflict. Thus, in many of our northern urban centers and in most of the southern ones, police officers are white and urban in background, and members of the lower middle class. This means that their own cultural background influences them; their attitudes, values and behavior are different from that of the Negro, the Puerto Rican, the rural lower class people who have been moving into the cities. This situation today, however, is no different from what it was in the past, when waves of immigrants arrived in America and found that those who were policemen were members of the majority group who were already here. In either instance, then or now, the need is for understanding. Police officers today must understand that the newcomers in our cities, who are culturally different, are neither better nor worse than were our ancestors when they arrived years ago. In a recent speech in Detroit, Dr. Robert C. Weaver noted:

Everything we see today in crowded Negro urban settlements was noted by social workers—and doubtless by policemen too—in the crowded immigrant quarters of our cities at the turn of the century—whether these were Jewish, Italian, Polish or what have you. There was overcrowding; unrelated persons living in the same households; poverty and discouragement; and the observable consequences. And we can go further back, to 17th century England. The rate of illegitimacy then was so disturbing that Sir William Petty . . . proposed a system of government maternity hospitals for pregnant unmarried women, and urged that the illegitimate children born in them become wards of the state.

I mention this in some detail because the police officer, more than others, must understand that crimes, corruption, violence, and other vices he may see among the current urban newcomers belonged also, in all likelihood, to the group from which he emerged. This single bit of understanding may help him more than anything else to perform his critical role with fuller capacity.

Let me be perfectly clear: I am not suggesting that police officers condone or approve or accept the evils they see in the cultural conflict. I am simply saying that if they are truly to fulfill their required professional function of enforcing the law with equality, they would do well to appreciate the cultural background of the people they must deal with. This may help them to overcome their own inclination to participate in the cultural conflict by expressing in word or action their contempt of the culturally different.

Although I certainly believe that police officers would be helped in performing their sensitive community job by additional education about people and their cultural background, I am not advocating a law or soft law enforcement policy. By all means let the policy be firm, but let it be just and equally applied to those on both sides of the cultural conflict. Ours is indeed a society of laws, and they are presumably enacted in order to be enforced for the greater protection of the total community. I recognize also that there are some people who scorn the law and can only be approached and dealt with firmly. Softness will be ridiculed by some, and the officer showing it may be hurt or killed for his reluctance to be firm. What is needed is not a soft approach to law enforcement, but rather a rational policy based on our best knowledge of what makes people behave as they do, and that policy should then be enforced fairly and firmly for all.

If, as a member of one of the groups engaged in the cultural conflict, a police officer allows his own bias to interfere with the professional performance of his duty, not only is he contributing to the conflict, but he is also jeopardizing the community to a greater extent than others by giving the impression to the members of the other cultural group that the law is partial and prejudiced. Once this image of biased law enforcement prevails in a community, the very cohesion of that community is endangered, as people often take the law into their own hands because they don't trust its official custodians.

It is not easy being a police officer in a large urban community crisscrossed by cultural conflict, but it is a job that must be done and done well. As communities across the country come increasingly to appreciate that the police officer position is a vital one, perhaps steps will be taken to fulfill the officer's legitimate expectation of the community. This expectation can be phrased rather simply: the police officer has a right to expect of the community that it will provide him with all the necessary tools to do his job with dignity and dispatch. He has a right to expect proper equipment, adequate associate manpower, qualified leadership, freedom from political interference, and support in the honest discharge of his duties. He has, moreover, the right to expect recognition of his role as one of tremendous significance for the safety and welfare of the community, for such is indeed the case. Correspondingly, he has a right to expect that as the community can afford it, he will be paid a salary commensurate with the respected social position he should hold. All this the police officer has a right to expect and enjoy.

The city has always been a place of human variety; there is no reason to expect that this will change in the years ahead. There is a constant necessity for us to appreciate cultural difference, and the inevitable cultural conflict that accompanies it. But this conflict need not be violent. The question before us as police officers, as teachers, as social workers, as public officials, and as citizens, is: How can we join our knowledge of human behavior with our moral compassion for people, to create an urban community wherein all people may feel and be safe and secure in their persons, on the streets or in their homes?

The Idea of Community

LOUIS A. RADELET

(Then) Director, National Program Development for Community Services, National Conference of Christians and Jews, New York

MAY 24, 1961

What kind of community are we trying to build?

I refer to the idea of community in general, not to any particular community that we think of as "home." The idea of community is surely elusive. When I was a fledgling student of sociology in my undergraduate days, I memorized a definition of community with which I shall not tax you here. It was a standard textbook definition, and it reminds me a little of the Snap, Crackle and Pop of a well-known breakfast cereal. A well-known social psychiatrist has said that "a community is love." This is a definition of community that, perhaps, a police officer finds hard to digest. It is not easy to define community in terms of love and understanding when your job is apt to provide a disproportionate view of the seamy side of human behavior.

My point is simply that our definition of community will depend a good deal upon what we are looking for. Thus, there would probably be some difference between the definition of a commercial artist, and . . . let us say . . . a night watchman in a deserted toy factory. Yet I wonder if their respective definitions of community would differ so much, in essence. I think they might agree, for instance, that the ultimate resource of a community is PEOPLE. They might even agree that the fundamental function of the true community is in what Maritain calls "the nurture of human-ness." You see, I am speaking of community in a functional rather than in a geographic sense. We might profitably pursue this line of reasoning a bit further.

With respect to community in the general sense in our society today, we are hearing a good deal about trends in population, urbanization, suburban flight from the central city, metropolitan planning, urban renewal, etc. Projections are being made for the next fifty years, and I would suppose that these estimates are more or less dependable. However, we note that these predictions deal largely with physical and material phenomena. Little is said about the *human* and *social* dimension of community, about the values implicit in small but crucial options in the day-to-day affairs of free and responsible men and women. Obviously, it is impossible to predict such values; indeed, it is difficult even to define them. Dr. John B. Thompson, dean of Rockefeller Chapel at the University of Chicago, reminds us that because most of today's projections about the community of tomorrow are based upon material and technological advances, there is a certain Utopian quality in these projections. Power will be almost as cheap as air; depressions will no longer occur; weather and climate will be more or less controlled; nuclear energy will provide our heat and light. But when we think about what kind of community we want to build in terms of human relations, we are too sober to set our goals in romantic, Utopian terms. I would prefer that we base them, rather, on a realistic, practical *faith*. Lest you suspect that I am talking jet-propelled gibberish, permit me to dwell on this point for a moment.

All of us in this country have been reared with a faith in democracy and in a free society that is as simple as it is earnest. One aspect of this faith is the notion that the solution to the problems of democracy is to be found in more democracy. The goal in this has been described by Robert Maynard Hutchins as "the civilization of the dialogue"—in which, he points out, "the great crime is to try to prevent people from speaking up, or to say that there are certain things not to be talked about, or certain people not to be talked to. In this view, education and communication are of prime importance—because if I cannot understand others, or if they cannot understand me, there cannot be *dialogue,* there cannot be real discussion or communication, and democracy thereby becomes meaningless."

So it is that the democratic faith may be said to be, basically, faith in man— faith in every man — faith that men, if they are well enough informed and well enough motivated, can solve the problems raised by their own aggregation. One advantage of this faith, Dr. Hutchins says, is that it is practically shockproof. Industrialism can sweep the world. Nationalism and technology can threaten the extinction of the human race. Population can multiply phenomenally. Suburbia can deprive the central city of invaluable human resources. Man can take off from this planet and create new planets to shoot from. Education can be reduced to trivia, almost beyond belief. The media of communcation can become the media of bland entertainment and crass commercialism. The dialogue can almost stop—because people have nothing to say, or if they have something to say, no place to say it. And still it is possible to believe that if democracy and communication can continue, if they can be expanded and deepened, then freedom, justice, equality and peace can, somehow, finally be achieved in the family of mankind.

This, then, is the *faith* of which I speak. It is this faith, by the way, that explains fundamentally why there are Institutes in Police–Community Relations. It is a faith, the very analysis of which helps us to define what kind of community we seek to build. Our dream is not of Utopia. The goal is *ours to make,* in the community that we call Kalamazoo, Covington or Cozy-Corners. The critical test of our time is in whether the possibilities of freedom can be achieved. We dare not think in grandoise, Utopian terms. We can begin to build this better community by thinking of some very practical questions, and undertake to do this rather more self-consciously than we have. For example, this question: what needs are we trying to meet, and toward what ends do we seek to work? Our values in answering such a question must become more *explicit.* How do we do this?

One way is to set out deliberately to make our community a kind of "laboratory of democracy." We try to do this, in a very limited degree, in the microism of the actual community that this Institute represents. There is an attempt here at developing dialogue—better communication across "fences of differences." There is a notion here of the possibilities in a teamwork approach to community problems of common concern. I realize that we make it all sound so much simpler than it really is. So let me complicate it a little by taking a moment to consider what is involved in this matter of the dialogue, so-called.

Far from being the exception, misunderstanding is part and parcel of our daily living. It feeds upon every opposition: differences of sex, age, social environment and profession, differences in character, in our manner of existing, of thinking, in the way we see ourselves, the world and others. There is only one way to overcome misunderstanding. The different viewpoints must be brought face to face, for the very purpose of reconciliation. Yet we know that discussion does not always shed light on problems. Sometimes the deaf talk to the deaf, and misunderstanding is aggravated. Why such difficulties? Ultimately, it boils down to this: each party comes to the discussion "with guns loaded." One says, quite naturally, that experience is on his side. We ask others to "open their eyes to things as they are." We claim to "let the facts speak for themselves." But the unfortunate thing is that facts themselves never speak. So we presume to speak for the facts. It hardly occurs to us that our neighbor might possess the truth. We come to a discussion almost with a prepared statement. Our partner need only accept its terms, capitulate and sign here. In such a "combat" approach, true dialogue is ruled out. The aim is rather to disqualify the other person. Rivalry overrides a concern for truth. The only thing that matters is to attack and to defend oneself. To accomplish this, anything goes: smug statements, pretended indignations, mockery, shrugging of the shoulders, irony, play on words, intended ambiguity and all such things. We even glory in reducing to silence someone with whom we set out to have a discussion. When the battle is over, we must admit, if we are sincere, that what we considered forceful argument was really more force than argument.

In this insightful analysis of the qualities of dialogue, the French scholar, Marcel Deschoux, adds that it is the spirit of peace that is the condition for authentic dialogue. War, attack, violence and diplomacy have no place here. The essential thing is to accept fully the presence of someone else, and to open ourselves to his influence. What makes a dialogue is reciprocal presence and actions based on recognized equality. In both the action and the presence, there is mutual involvement. Dialogue is related to propaganda as love is to rape. For any authentic dialogue, therefore, there is work to be done first within ourselves. It is, after all, truth—as Emerson insisted—that is the third party in true dialogue.[1]

The community that is our goal is a community of COMMON-UNITY. It is a community which dignifies the right to be different. It is a community in which there is no penality or sanction exacted upon those who protest. It is a community disposed in spirit to the dialogue. It is a *decent* society in the sense of Jacques Maritain's emphasis, viz, a society which helps people to be *persons,* i.e., "bearers of values." As Dean Thompson concludes, the root of the idea of community is *participation;* not condescension, not patronage, not rescue, but the dignity and worth that men and women on any level of life experience when they are part of what is important to their fellows.

Perhaps I have been speaking too abstractly. Perhaps you would welcome more "bread-and-butter." Yet I think there is a place for consideration of the somewhat abstract values that are the wellsprings of true community. If these values cannot be translated into activities and relationships in everyday community life, then we are wasting our time here. Who are we, what are we trying to do, and why? It is, I submit, in how we answer this that we answer the related questions, what kind of community do we seek to build? You remember John Donne's admonition: "For I am involved in mankind . . ."

To shift gears slightly, it is obvious that the idea of community implies human relatedness. When people come into contact, certain basic patterns of interaction occur. We call these patterns cooperation, competition, conflict, accommodation, assimilation, stratification, etc.—and the sociologist defines each of these social processes rather precisely. The maintenance of social order, a function in which

[1] Marcel Deschoux, *L'Homme et son prochain;* Presses Universitaires de France; originally, a lecture presented at the Eighth Congress of the Sociétés de Philosophie de Langue Française in Toulouse.

the police are prominent, is ultimately a matter of insuring that these interaction patterns in the society are more positive than negative. It is in this fundamental sense, and quite apart from other salient considerations, that law enforcement not only plays an important role in community relations—law enforcement is, in fact, in the very *metabolism* of community reations.

Working together in community groups for the common good is not a uniquely Western institution. Threshing, haying, barnbuilding and house-building bees, once so common in rural America, have their counterparts in Europe, Africa and Asia. Universally, for example, the harvesting of crops is characterized by mutual aid among neighbors, and formal community gratitude for enough to eat is found where man relies upon power machinery and where he knows only the hoe. People everywhere live under law and within a complicated system of beliefs, customs and traditions. Even the most revolutionary societies depend upon law to keep their system intact. Every community has its rules as to what is good and bad, and these values are transmitted in the cultural heritage, from one generation to another. From the vantage point of our culture, we sometimes think that the way these things are done in other cultures is strange, and indeed "primitive." For instance, the Bambala people of the Western Congo—when involved in litigation— sing allegorical songs which contain proof, they believe, that justice must be on their side, and in these songs they are accompanied by the drummers and friends who are present. This kind of thing strikes us as highly bizarre, and we are apt to be suspicious of people who behave, we say, in such an "uncivilezed" manner. The other side of the same coin is, of course, what they may think of us—a point which we might turn to some humorous possibilities—but I will repress the temptation, and settle simply by saying that we too rarely turn the coin over. This single footnote might be added: the bride-price and ancestor-worship customs of another culture may induce moral astonishment in us, but what we may lose sight of is what is implicit in such customs; affection and love, aspirations, hard work, humor, personal ambition, response to beauty, contemplation and other like values, all of them common to the family of mankind. One of the spare-time activities that I heartily recommend for all students of human relations is some delving into the field of social anthropology. It helps give us perspective.[2]

To do this, one does not need to be a college professor. Recently I read a stimulating monograph on the topic, "Creative Leadership in the Pluralistic Society," written by the director of the IBM Executive School, Mr. Louis R. Mobley. Evidently Mr. Mobley had done some reading in anthropology, from which he drew five simple propositions that he described as axiomatic:

1. Each individual is unique;
2. Creative acts of individuals result from interactions between individuals who are different from each other;
3. Healthy change in individuals and organizations results from creative acts of individuals;
4. Such change is necessary for growth;
5. Growth of individuals and organizations is, in this sequence, healthy.

This brings me to the note with which I want to conclude. There is a good deal being said these days about the plight of the individual and of the society. Witness the non-fiction best sellers: THE LONELY CROWD; INDIVIDUALISM

---

[2] See Papers published by the Council on Economic and Cultural Affairs, Inc., 14 West 49th St., New York.

RECONSIDERED; THE ORGANIZATION MAN; THE POWER ELITE; THE WASTE MAKERS; THE HIDDEN PERSUADERS; THE AFFLUENT SO-CIETY—and there are others, including "the cult of confident living" category. Now I am not critical of such sociological or psychological erudition. But as SATURDAY REVIEW editor Norman Cousins suggests:

> Bleak and dismal portrayals of the plight of the individual and of the society do harm if they tend to reduce the individual's sense of responsibility. They do particular harm if they promote the "conspiracy" or "crisis" theory of history, because of which the individual reacts with self-pity, with despair, with a sense of angry, frustrated helplessness. In our time as in all other times, something new is being fashioned constantly by history, and we cannot escape social and moral responsibility simply by blaming those in positions of power, or by scape-goating what we call "the system." Individually and socially, we pay for what we get. If we prize individuality, we must pay for it by welcoming "difficult" people and "difficult" situations. A reconciliation of the individual with mass society is possible only through a regard for the dignity and worth of the in-dividual person. To have individuality digested by society is to destroy the individual immediately and the society eventually.

One difficulty we have is that each man wants evidence of some visible amelioration of the total problem before he feels justified in his own feeble efforts. Each man tends to underestimate the power of his own example to set others in compassionate motion. Yet, no one man involved in the vast and infinitely mys-terious enterprise of reducing human misery and pain really knows enough about the intangibles of social interaction to be pessimistic about the future. As Editor Cousins puts it, "progress proceeds out of elusive but vital fractions."

Where to begin? Begin with the first man who puts his life into your hands. Reach out and take hold of the man who is nearest to you. To help put mean-ing into one life may not produce universal regeneration, but it represents the basic form of energy in a society. It is also individual responsibility at its best. For as Albert Camus has said: "Each and every man, on the foundation of his own sufferings and joys, builds for all men."

Special Problems of Police–Community Relations

GORDON W. LOVEJOY

Chairman, Department of Sociology, University of Tulsa

MAY 22, 1958

We are gathered to engage in a social ritual more widely observed and more carefully regulated than almost any other in American community life; namely, to listen while a so-called "expert" tells us what to do. The ritual divides experts—like Chinese mandarins—into various classes.

A professional group follows most avidly the words of the "first-hand expert." This is the person who has learned by "practical knowledge." He is essentially a technician of the how-do-you-do-it category. His advice may work well when ap-plied to situations essentially the same as those in which he worked. Thus, for example, driving lessons based upon English rules of the road could produce fantastic traffic jams in an American city. A training course based, however, on the practical knowledge of what makes for safe driving, coupled with an admonition to observe local variations, could be of real significance.

A second class of experts may be labelled the "vicarious experience" authorities. Thus, we have in the United States today an outstanding authority on courtship, a bachelor; the leading counselor on marriage relationships, a divorced man; the principal writer of books on the care of babies, a doctor with no children. These experts, unlike the first group, begin with theory, and then proceed to practical knowledge. I, who have never had the experience of walking a beat, issuing a ticket, meeting a muster, or apprehending a criminal, may be classified as a vicarious expert.

Of course, I am teasing when I divide experts into the categories enumerated above, but at the same time I am serious. There are some people who feel they can learn only from the person who has had experiences identical to their own. This is as erroneous an approach as to believe only theoretical matters are important. True knowledge, however, is a blend of the insights of theory and the hard knocks of experience. My comments will be primarily in the realm of insight.

You may remember Johnny One-Note, that pathetic character who, no matter how hard he tried, could sing only one note. Since my whole professional orientation is in terms of the South, I intend to explore the topic—"Special Problems in Police–Community Relations"—against a Southern background. In my home area, (North Carolina) a far-reaching evolutionary change in the human relations patterns of white and Negro is in process. Screaming newspaper headlines have attempted to simplify the change as one associated solely with school desegregation, but the rivers of change run deeper than this. Because I state so frankly the delimitations of this paper, do not fall into the trap of assuming what I say is unimportant to you who are law enforcement officials in non-Southern communities: the transitions are well on their way to becoming national trends.

Thirdly, I have chosen to place my emphasis in Police–Community Relations upon the first word of that title; namely, "the police." In so doing I would not have you think for a moment I feel the police *need* what I shall say, any more than any other person. Quite the contrary, I feel the police are such key people I want to pay them the tribute of addressing my remarks to them. Every problem I pose and every challenge I make are applicable as well to teachers, social workers, firemen, or just plain citizens, but if I seem to be singling out law enforcement people, it is because of the respect in which I hold them and because of the enormity of the task they face.

I shall consider five problem areas which I feel contain insights needed by all law enforcement officials, non-Southern and Southern.

I. The Problem of Tradition

The English poet Swinburne, in his "Ode to England" writes this magnificent line: "All our past proclaims our future . . . ." If we of today would understand where we are at present, we must begin by examining the heritage of our past. Since you are law enforcement officials, I shall deal with a portion of the past based on law, because there was once a legal basis for many of the things we still believe and even practice.

Late in the 17th century, the legislature of Virginia adopted a special set of laws—the infamous Black Codes—which established a pattern of legal relationships between whites and Negroes. Soon, other colonies where slavery was practiced did likewise. The Negro—through the provision of these laws—was forbidden, for example, to testify in any court of law, or to expect from any court legal redress of injury. He could not be taught to read or write, to own property, or to contract a legal marriage. Human beings, for slaves were human, were given, thereby, the legal status of chattel property, and as such could be bought, sold, mortgaged, or disposed of as we do furniture, cows, or jewelry.

From 1688 until 1865, laws akin to these were on the statute books and were enforced. What did they do to people? The answer should not be too difficult to imagine. Gradually, but persistently, the idea that the Negro was a sub-human without legal rights became the accepted, group-approved belief and practice. A differential pattern of justice for the Negro, and less concern about the safety and security of the Negro's person, was a logical outgrowth of the Black Codes.

In 1865, only 93 years ago, these laws were invalidated. Barely a decade later began the effort to re-establish as many of them as possible. Out of this effort of re-establishment developed the Jim Crow laws of today. Soon, there were laws requiring every Negro to be in the employ of a white. There were laws providing for segregation in trains, boats, in jails, in chain gangs, in schools, for the insane, the blind and the feeble-minded. There were ordinances requiring separate systems of taxicabs, separation of prostitutes in brothels, separate undertakers and separate hearses. In my home state of North Carolina, there remains on the statute books a law requiring that school books studied by Negroes be stored during the summer in a warehouse entirely separate from the warehouse for textbooks white children have used. By 1930, virtually every aspect of white–Negro relationships was regulated by law. Then began the transition, as Jim Crow laws began to be invalidated through repeal or judicial review. Many remain, however, in intrastate force.

What have these Jim Crow laws done to us? First, I would say they have closed most of the basic avenues of communication which exist between people. When this happens, the separated groups develop hosts of fears and suspicions of the motives and practices, each of the other. From the fears spring, secondly, a Pandora's box of repressive tactics, uncomplimentary mental pictures, and rationalizations to prove alleged superiorities.

The heritage and operation of these laws have helped developed a virtual etiquette governing the relationship of white and Negro. The title "Mrs.," for example, is still not granted Negro women by dozens of newspapers, since tradition says the legal status of marriage is reserved for white women. It is proper in terms of socially-inspired etiquette to call an educated Negro man "professor," "doctor," or "Reverend," but never "Mr." Regardless of his age, the Negro is called either "boy" or by his first name.

And so it goes from birth to death—a pattern of relationships in which every aspect of human relationships has its culturally sanctioned way of doing things.

The point I would make from this is a simple one: law enforcement officials are as much a part of the culture, and are as much influenced by its heritage, as any other person. Time after time, the subtle influence emanating from the "dead hand of the past" can make itself felt in the mind of a police official. Unless ever on guard, it is simple for the influence of tradition to creep into law enforcement practices.

II. The Problem of Myth

Second only to the impact of tradition is the effect of racial myths as causative factors for the thinking and behavior of people. Here, as above, we find the law enforcement official fully as likely as the banker, the school teacher, the filling station attendant or the newspaper editor to be influenced by false stories and false ideas. Suppose we look at some of the myths most closely related in their possible impact to police work.

First, there is the myth of the Negroes' mental inferiority. It was Henry Clay who said "Show me a Negro who can decline a Greek noun and conjugate a Latin verb, and I will believe he is human." What Clay was saying is that the Negro is mentally inferior to the white. How many of us, to be blunt, would care to prove our right to be considered human by such a test? Regrettably, for those who accept the stories, we have not one single shred of evidence to support such a viewpoint. Quite the contrary: we know that mental ability is distributed through all of the major racial groups. Environmental factors may stunt the use of the ability, but raw material is there.

Secondly, there is the myth centering around alleged ostentation and agressive behavior. We see a new automobile standing outside a Negro's house and we say, "Uh-huh. He's getting uppity." We seldom stop to realize that a Negro with money can buy an automobile without the slightest difficulty, but more likely than not, he is unable to purchase a decent home. We dwell at length nevertheless, on alleged aggressive behavior. In so doing, we forget that loud talk, flashy clothes, and general aggressiveness are characteristic reactions of any minority group attempting to improve its status, and not something specifically Negroid in its origins.

The third most common myth centers around the belief that any interracial contact, regardless of its nature, leads automatically to intermarriage. Here again, myth flies in the face of fact. The best research studies now available indicate that the number of interracial marriages has been decreasing steadily during the past 30 years. We overlook conveniently a rising middle class morality among Negroes, which opposes intermarriage just as vigorously as the same class group opposes it among the whites. We take every incident we can find and magnify it out of all proportion—usually through front page headlines—as a typical illustration of interracial contact. Here, as elsewhere, the police official can be as guilty as his cousin the baker, the carpenter, or the mechanic.

How many times—as illustrative of another myth—have we heard the Negro condemned as shiftless and lacking in initiative? Do we ever measure this charge against what the inability to secure work commensurate with training can do to the initiative of a person? In one of Washington's better known restaurants is a waiter who has a Ph.D. degree in sociology from an eastern university. He is unable to find a job where he can use his training. Why should he show any tremendous initiative or work efficiently? He is stymied by the myth of *certain* jobs for Negroes.

For some reason or other, there seems to be a persistent myth centered around alleged inborn criminality of the Negro. It is perfectly true that in category after category, crime rates of Negros are above those of whites, but the figures are meaningless until we project them against what a background of ghetto-type living and limited job opportunities does to any group—Negro or non-Negro. Only after the nation has grappled with housing and job opportunities equal to the Negroes' ability can we talk learnedly about Negro crime rates.

These things I have enumerated are not the pleasant, gracious matters we prefer discussing. They affect us, though, and they can affect the administration of justice just as they may affect any other aspect of life. Until we have ridded ourselves of myth's stifling hold, we cannot claim, in honesty, to believe all men are equal.

III. The Problem of Pressure

In any period of social change there is always the cry of "pressure." The situation we face in the changing status of race relations is no exception. Those who oppose change "pressure" to maintain the *status quo*. Those wanting change "pressure" for it. There are many persons, unfortunately, who think it is possible to go through this period of social change without any tensions, turbulence or feelings of pressure. This is neither possible, nor is it cause for hysterical alarm.

It is simple to recognize, and even to delineate clearly, the techniques followed by those who would maintain the *status quo*. Primary among them is the cry "If outside pressure groups would leave us alone, we would have no problem." This device is intended, and succeeds unfortunately in many instances, to discredit the work of sincere people whose basic purpose is to guide change through orderly channels.

When the cry of outside pressure groups fails, smear and intimidation campaigns are tried. Thus, we have the whisper and "did-you-know" charges concerning the "pinkness" of certain organizations and individuals. We have the telephone harrassment campaigns, aimed at disturbing the wife of the individual who is willing to consider the possibility of new human relations patterns. Occasionally there is the distribution of mimeographed or printed materials, often quite scurrilous, and generally as anti-Semitic as it is anti-Negro. When all else fails, those opposing change have been known to resort to economic pressure. The ramifications of this are many-fold, but in its simplest form, it consists in curtailing credit to those whose views are considered detrimental to "our way of life."

It is possible, likewise, to analyze the techniques of those promoting change. Actually since they are techniques of attack, they are usually more obvious. The principle strategy for action designed to alter existing patterns is based upon an appeal to the courts, especially the federal courts, for the redress of grievances. Regardless of the opinion one may have about this technique, or what one may think of the organizations and individuals who have turned to law suits for producing change, it will be a sad day for the Republic if we ever reach the point where citizens may not turn to the federal courts for adjudication of their claims. The fact that these suits run counter to long-established practices is no justification for condemning their use.

A second technique much followed is that of "testing." First, one area of group life, and then another is probed for its weak spots. There may be, for example, a successful suit to desegregate the schools. This can be followed by a move against bus segregation, housing discrimination, or bias in the use of public facilities. The ultimate aim of such testing is the elimination of any discriminating practices based upon racial differences.

A third technique for inducing change is only now beginning to make itself felt. Here the minority group—in this case the Negro—turns to morally based, passive resistance. He walks, rather than ride on segregated buses; he prays for the well-being of those who favor segregation, instead of boycotting or suing in the courts. He appeals to the consciences of his opponents, and in so doing, places himself on an unassailable moral plane. Southerners, with their strong roots of Protestant piety, are troubled by this translation into action of the "other cheek" and "second-mile" concepts. Traditional ways of handling the Negro who forgets his assigned status breaks down before prayer. Since passive resistance as a device for inducing social change is almost unknown in the United States, law enforcement officials might well take note before they meet its manifestations face-to-face.

In the midst of these complicated and conflicting measures, but hearing on every side the cry of "pressure," stands the law enforcement official. As a product of our culture, he may favor the *status quo*, but as a sworn upholder of law, he cannot express his private views publicly. Thus, many who are policemen find themselves, and will continue to find themselves, torn between their personal preferences and their official duties. Only in the stillness of each individual heart can the battle be resolved.

There is, however, one area in which the law enforcement official dare not remain officially neutral—that is, he dare not if he would profit from the lessons taught by the immediate past. When, for example, the real, died-in-the-wool professional agitator appears in a community, the law enforcement official has his work cut out for him. On one hand, as a policeman, he finds himself faced by the necessity of maintaining freedom of speech, of press, and the right of assembly; on the other, he hears the agitator's call for violence, destruction of property and intimidation of people. In those cities where law enforcement officials have attempted to confine themselves to passivity, the results have been disastrous.

If those who work professionally in the field of human relations have any clear-cut lesson for the police official, it centers around "do not take lightly the potential, long-term danger of the professional agitator." Bigotry is contagious, and unfortunately, we have seen in city after city how seemingly harmless mouthings lead to subsequent dynamiting and assaults against the person.

As one who has seen the professional agitator in action, I have been amazed by the seeming confusion of what law enforcement officials think they should do when confronted by the screams of a demagogue. No magical technique is needed, and there is not a city in the country which lacks statutes applicable to such persons and situations. In one well-known illustration from American history, a threat of potential violence was brought to a grinding halt when the police arrested the participants for walking on the grass.

It would not be proper for me to conclude this portion of our consideration without saying something about the relationship which exists, in times of social tension, between the working press and law enforcement officials. It is to be regretted, and I say this kindly and not in condemnation, how avidly the mass media representatives look for and play-up the slightest incident connected with the agitator's public appearances. Invariably, newspapermen ask the police, "what are you going to do?" It is my feeling the law enforcement official should not allow himself to be trapped into either issuing manifestoes, or debating publicly the rights of assembly. Instead, all he needs to do or say is, "I shall enforce the law and maintain order." Nothing more can be demanded from, and nothing less can be expected of the police official than this.

IV. The Problem of Reality

Thus far this discussion has dealt with problem situations which are somewhat theoretical. There is, however, another dimension which must be understood in terms of the present situation. I have called it "reality" since I know no better name. It is a problem with two phases.

I can state the first dimension bluntly and succinctly: whether we as individuals like and approve (or not) of the changing status of the Negro, it will go on. In the years ahead, the movement of the Negro from the south to the north and west will increase, and the problems of change associated with race will become national problems. The Negro is rising in his job status, and as he does so, he will move increasingly from the ghettos where he now lives to the suburbs of every city. Such moves will not be welcomed by all, and the law enforcement officials must be prepared to handle the problems arising from residential mobility.

The second phase is one I have difficulty in phrasing. From one viewpoint, I do not want to give offense to the Negro. From a second stand, I would avoid giving ammunition to those who cry quickly, "I told you so." I refer to what the Rev. Martin Luther King calls the problems within the Negro group itself, upon which the Negro himself must work. No matter how kindly and charitably we discuss causes, nor how graciously we excuse the facts, cold statistics indicate certain things about Negro living patterns. Illegitimate births are inordinately high among Negroes. Disease rates of Negroes exceed those of whites. Criminal statistics are higher in every category for the Negro than for the white.

Remember the story of Achilles? As an infant, he was dipped in a liquid which made every portion of him invincible except the little spot on his heel, by which he had been held. Until the Negro comes to grips with the conditions I have mentioned, he is as vulnerable as was Achilles. Here is unfinished business upon which the non-Negro may assist, but whose complete solution rests more with Negro leadership than with any other.

The Negro should learn, in addition, that he cannot establish arbitrary deadlines, by whose expiration date all barriers will be removed. Nor can the Negro allow himself the luxury of criticizing non-Negroes who believe in gradual change. The processes of inducing modification in human behavior do not run on any fixed time-schedule, and the person who works for gradual change is on firmer, research-verified ground than the one who announces a time limit for reaching a desired goal.

V. Advice to Law Enforcement Officials

I have long cherished the old bromide about advice being free to give and to disregard. I feel I would be guilty of nonfeasance were I not to suggest certain directions, certain guideposts, to be followed by police officials desirous of equipping themselves for the evolutionary changes in human relations characteristic of our era. I intend to list, therefore, seven points. Think of them as a personal, check-off list. Each officer might phrase what I state as the question "Where do I stand on this matter?"

(1) Train yourself to think in terms of similarities between people rather than the dissimilarities separating them. This is childishly simple, but it is amazing what happens to our opinions when we begin wondering how far down the same

road we can walk with an individual before we branch away from him. So many of us begin at the branch and seldom look back at the similarities.

(2) Train yourself to recognize the symptoms of prejudice, and how it affects both you, the giver, and the person who receives its manifestations. I feel there are many of us who have never clarified in our own minds how much of what we believe is based on fact, and how much is founded upon old wives tales learned as a part of the group culture. Frankly, I think the law enforcement official is expected to be an even finer person than Mr. Average Citizen. Somehow the policeman must separate his personal prejudices from his official actions.

(3) Train yourself to recognize rumors and the conditions which produce them. Many of us, regrettably, accept as coin-of-the-realm any wild story related about other people, if it is just said in a loud enough voice, or repeated by a sufficient number of people. A few months ago, I saw a great southern city almost paralyzed by the impact of rumor. The streets were half deserted, business was crippled, the schools reported heavy absences, and all this because "something was supposed to happen." Even the police fell into the trap. Rumor was at work. A week later everyone, the police included, were too shamefaced to talk much about how their credulity had led them "like sheep all astray."

(4) Closely related to what I have said but placed separately for emphasis, learn the techniques needed for handling rumors. I am implying here that some of us need to brush up on the latest research findings about the causes of rumors, and what can be done to allay their vicious sting.

(5) Train yourself to realize that many so-called minority characteristics are actually the reactions of people in protest against the status assigned them by society. Whenever I find myself on the verge of overly critical comment concerning some minority group member, I try to remember that there but for the grace of God, I might be. Would I, I ask myself, be as restrained and as truly long-suffering as they?

(6) Train yourself to see that all trouble between groups who differ is not racially inspired. I have seen sandlot baseball games, in which white and Negro youngsters were playing, erupt into a fight. The easy answer is to say the trouble is caused by bringing two races together, but actually, the dispute may be simply the temper flareup which arises between spirited kids. This same principle holds true in other situations, and law enforcement officials must never forget how seemingly racially-inspired frictions may reflect nothing more serious than aching feet caused by a long day of work.

(7) Train yourself to realize that there is no such condition as a "little bigotry." When prejudice first appears in any community, it often focuses upon only one target. Like measles, however, prejudice never remains attached to a single group. It spreads and it grows until, as a forest fire, it bursts out in every direction. What I am saying amounts to the most sincere of warnings: do not be lulled into the belief that everything is well because so little prejudice is evident at a given moment.

*   *   *   *   *   *

Long centuries ago, a prophet of ancient Israel stated with clarity the goal toward which I have been striving in this paper. Listen to the words of Esdras: "I shall light a candle of understanding in thine heart which shall not be put out."

Police and the Community:
a Law–Medicine View

OLIVER SCHROEDER, JR.

*Professor of Law, Director, The Law–Medicine Center,
Western Reserve University, Cleveland, Ohio*

MAY 17, 1966

I have taken a "scripture" from the publication called NATION'S CITIES, February, 1966, p. 6:

> What lies ahead for law enforcement? Vastly more complicated issues, a greater involvement in crime prevention activities, much more use of *advanced technology* in detection and apprehension, and steady upgrading of administrative competence. Underlying it all, however, is the need to develop a new relationship between the community at large and its duly appointed law enforcement officials. We don't regard civilian review boards as serving much positive purpose. Many other approaches might be more constructive. They can be broadly based committees, dealing with *professional and technical aspects of law enforcement.* They can be neighborhood programs to exchange experiences and outlooks between residents and police. They can be formal information programs to spur civic confidence and participation in law enforcement. As a matter of fact, our survey shows some municipalities are engaged in these and other efforts right now.

Now the law–medicine approach to law enforcement seeks to use the more professional and technical concepts that the quotation mentions. At Western Reserve, we want to give this training to officers in non-credit programs—for the uniformed policeman on the beat. This program has met with tremendous enthusiasm from the police in our area. The program has already mounted to a minimum of 40 hours; this is just a beginning. Involved in the program are faculty from the School of Medicine, the School of Law, the Institute of Pathology, and the Coroner's Office professional staff. We soon eliminated the traditional theory of the classroom and came to the practical daily problems of the policeman. What is most thrilling about it all, to me, is that every officer comes into the program enthusiastic for learning. They are dedicated learners. I think it's the result of their having been out in the world and knowing the value of education. Learning is unending, and the policeman wants to learn.

We began with an idea, in 1953, that the problems of criminal behavior had to be identified. The basic elements of criminal behavior may involve some social, physiological, psychological and psychiatric causes. Each offender requires individual attention. Community relations is just a collection of a lot of little individuals with personal problems. What kind of an individual does the police officer face in any single incident? First he is unique. There is no one else in the world like him. He may have certain elements in common with others, but he is unique deep down inside. The policeman therefore makes an individual personal contact. These individual citizens are the building blocks of the community. Whatever and whoever he is, the individual starts out with basic elements in his mind and body. We try to interpret what these are to the police officer; this identification of the basic elements is the first step. But this individual is not static, he is constantly changing. Human being represent a continuous, shifting spectrum of human behavior. They are not in a fixed classification, though we do classify them in general.

First, we can divide people into two broad groups: abnormal and normal. The policeman identifies some of the abnormal ones as criminals. Who are they? Alcoholics; or individuals addicted to excessive use of alcoholic liquors, without addiction. The officer has to decide whether the individual is abnormal, or a criminal. The administration of criminal justice is a complete failure in the handling of the alcoholic, because society is a complete failure. This is an individual problem, and the manner in which the officer handles the case will go a long way toward improving the law enforcement image in our society. This is important.

There are other categories. Take the narcotic addicts: they are normal, neurotic or psychopathic. The officer must cope with this problem, while the rest of society ignores the terrible condition or at best merely increases the punishment.

Third, we have sex criminals: deviants from sexual norms, or the sexually maladjusted. Here is an area where we are making some progress. Even the Royal Commission of Britain questions whether homosexuality is a crime or not, if it involves two consenting adults. Here again, the officer has an individual situation to confront.

Next, we have the psychopathic personality, characterized by persistent abnormality of character and social conduct. Is he responsible for his criminal acts? In this area, we have perhaps advanced furthest in resolving the problem in the administration of justice. We used to follow the *McNaughten* rule exclusively, but we now know there is a whole gamut of degrees of sanity or insanity. Some individuals we hold criminally responsible; others, we say, are not. The courts are slowly trying to work out a rule of law to identify who is what in this category. But the individual officer must bring the subject into the administration of justice.

For example, recently in the community of Shaker Heights, Ohio, a woman was tried for murder. The police did an excellent job in detection and preparation for trial. She was found "not guilty by reason of insanity." And here is the main point: many people said a lot of police work had been wasted because she was not found "guilty" when she killed the small neighbor boy. This attitude infuriated me. The public thinks that the job of the police is to *convict* somebody. Actually, the role of the police officer is NOT to convict. It is the job of the courts to find a person guilty or not guilty.

The police detect the crime and prepare the case for court. We still have a long way to go in educating the public as to the actual role of the police officer.

Next we consider abnormal *civil* (not criminal) problems. The American Bar Foundation is working on a project called "Commitment of the Mentally Ill." Naturally, this is a real problem for the officer who may be called in the night to a scene where he finds an individual who is obviously not behaving normally. If the person is a threat to himself or to others, detention is in order, and the officer must make the decision. We are trying to train these officers to recognize such cases.

The American Bar Foundation Committee is trying to clarify the officer's role in this situation. It would be a lot more helpful if they had some police officers on the committee—too many people are defining police roles without knowing anything about what the police officer is called upon to do.

We have tried to prepare a directive which would help the officer to determine the condition of the possibly disturbed person: take him to the mental hospital if there is a bed; if not, take him to the police station until a bed can be found. But the psychiatrists originally objected to this directive on the grounds that it was their job to determine the mental condition of a person. In the middle of the night—when the decision has to be made immediately? I finally cooled the good doctors by pointing out that the officer would not charge a fee of $50 an hour!

We prepared a pamphlet which would give the officer a little help in knowing how to identify abnormal behavior, because it is the duty of the officer to remove such people from places where they could harm themselves or others. Thus is a police officer the cutting edge of orderly society.

Now, let's go on to the normal people. We have normal delinquents, both juvenile and adult. And there are the normal people who may be either well or ill, such as the diabetics. We're all delinquents; you know that as well as I, but it is better to call us juvenile and adult.

This police officer is a crucial individual with the juvenile. He makes the immediate contact. He is the imposition of the lawful process on the juvenile. The officer must have the education and training to help him know not only when the juvenile has gone off the beaten path but also how best to get him back. How the young person is handled can turn him back on, or turn him further away. Schoolteachers often have the same opportunity. The police task is to *identify* which category the confronted juvenile represents. The police officer is in that crucial position of authority which the adolescent has to have as a counterpart of love—love and authority are but two sides of the same coin.

Another category is the law-abiding citizen who may be a sick man, instead of a criminal. His behavior may cause the officer to apprehend him, but if this person dies in jail in a diabetic coma, the officer is in real trouble. The International Association of Chiefs of Police has issued a bulletin on this topic to help police—so an officer has to be a bit of a medical doctor, too. In the Law–Medicine Center, we can train him, and we are trying to train the police in such matters.

So the job of the police officer is to try to identify properly any of these types we have mentioned. The skill with which he does it sets the environment for human relations in the community.

Next we try to acquaint the police officers with the *causes* of crime. The Law–Medicine view investigates basic causes of crime, so that prevention can replace the need for detection. The cause may be individual, or between two or more individuals, or between the individual and society.

Social influences are a major factor in crime. In trying to build the Negro community into the American community, we have an opportunity to do something superb. This has never been done before in human history—no nation has ever taken a racial minority of twenty millions and tried to assimilate them into a people of two hundred millions, as full-fledged citizens. It is your privilege and mine to be of the generation that is called upon to do this. We must cease, in our minds, to identify crime and the Negro; that's why we must always come back to the individual! Whatever race, creed or color a person has, he has some good and some evil. It is our job to discover the good and to build it up. We have this problem in northern and southern cities of America. Actually, I think the South is going to solve this perplexity long before we in the North do. Our major problem is to explain all this to white police officers, because until the officer understands that it isn't color, but social factors that produce crime, he will not be able to fill his role as guardian of law and order effectively.

The police of America have come to a major turning point. They are now giving sound advice to the community on police problems. It is pleasant to see that there are law enforcement officers on the President's Commission on Crime. Also, the police are helping the American Law Institute to develop a new penal code on law enforcement. The police are the ones who are going to have to enforce the code; their opinions should be heard. This has not been the situation even up to five years ago.

We now have one remaining major area where we must educate as to the police role. That area is the courts. The courts of America do not sufficiently understand the problems facing the community. The policeman can contribute knowledge from his experience. Judges must contemplate this knowledge thoughtfully, if they are to write the laws and to develop an intelligent criminal procedure. The Model Penal Code suggests some interesting developments in the matter of interrogation. We have other examples, showing that the police officer now is stimulating ideas for developing better criminal laws.

In addition to these changes suggested for judicial consideration we must also make changes in the executive branch of government with respect to the laws. Too often the police officer has been controlled by fear. This condition is a hold-over from the political days, when political forces controlled police work. The police have Civil Service protection now. Let us remember that this not only means security for the police, but it is an obligation for them to speak out—just as the college professor has academic freedom to facilitate his expression of opinion. Both groups must remember that this also means *responsibility* in speaking ideas and expressing opinions.

The Law–Medicine view *instructs* the police, not only to improve police practices, but also to help shape community action. The police must upgrade educational standards and training for their own members. That's the whole purpose of great schools such as the one here at Michigan State. Our task is to make sure we have the money and the men and the facilities to achieve all this—and to do all the things I've been asking you to do will require a lot more education.

What of the future? It is bright! There will be more emphasis on the individual policeman and his contacts with the members of his community. More and more is going to be expected of the policeman's mental ability, and wise judgment. We must have (and are getting) an increasing community involvement in the work of the police — wherein the most intimate human relationships are experienced.

Basically, you improve any profession by building up its *esprit de corps*, by stimulating initiative, by asking people to assume responsibility—more and more, higher and higher. So we are in a great and wonderful time of opportunity. The dignity of man rests pretty much on his daily activities within his home community. In our country, based on freedom, law and order, these are basic projects for the local law enforcement officer. True, our federal–state–local system of government is somewhat inefficient, but if you want an efficient society, you have a society under a single authority and completely in lock-step. We have always thought this to be bad. We must develop the local police officer to the point where, when confronting a citizen, he *identifies* an individual human being with all types of problems and then he *responds* in some meaningful way to do what best be done to and for that citizen. The more times he responds correctly the higher the index of good human relations will go in his local community. Respect will be given, and respect will be received. The road is not easy in a world in turmoil, but the goal is challenging: to achieve human beings with dignified personalities living in a free society. The police are the guardians of all this, and that's a very noble position to fulfill.

I would say that the greatest thing one can get out of an Institute such as this is the inspiration to go back and to do the daily job better and with more imagination and creativity. The world and the future of man will benefit thereby, for each officer will be contributing a major share to the solution of today's most important issue: whether modern man can learn to live with his fellowman.

Reflections on Police–Community Relations

H. G. POPE

Executive Director, Public Administration Service, Chicago, Illinois

MAY 25, 1961

Each of us is, under our system, a member of a number of political communities concerned with law enforcement. We are members of a particular village, town, city, or other community of this type. We are members of the community which, in most of our states, is called the county. We are members of the community of the sovereign state in which we live. We are also, of course, members of the community that is our nation, undoubtedly our most important community in that it provides the foundation and furnishes the protective shield for other governmental arrangements within it. Should the national establishment fail, the effect on state and local institutions could be no less than catastrophic.

In speaking of the governmental structure of the United States, I am always reminded of its scale and complexity. For example, there are many thousands of municipalities charged in some way with law enforcement. There are over 3,000 counties or their equivalents which include law enforcement among their activities, and the 50 states similarly have law enforcement functions with enforcement arms separate from those of the municipalities and counties. In addition, of course, the federal establishment has its FBI, its Secret Service, its treasury, customs, immigration, narcotics and alcoholic control officers, and hosts of officials concerned with the enforcement of laws governing public health, conservation, agriculture, commerce, labor, and the whole range of organized human activity within our society. Paralleling the structure of policing agencies is, of course, an extensive judicial system. Altogether, this is an organization whose size and complexity escapes understanding, not only by foreigners, but by the overwhelming majority of American citizens. And there are times and places where it is a bit creaky in its operations. Certainly basic to continued improvement of this system is the need for continued education of the public to the point where it will insist upon desirable and practical improvements.

What I have just said implies that the range of law enforcement is broader than that suggested by television westerns and who-done-its. Obviously, it is impractical, in a short presentation such as this, to cover the full range. Consequently, practicality suggests that I should arbitrarily exclude large areas. This I shall do by omitting reference to the enforcement of regulatory provisions in such fields as health, commerce, agriculture, labor, taxation, and the like. These may be quite as important to our organized society as the apprehension of a criminal, or the provision of other typical police services. However, in this instance, it may be appropriate for me to confine myself principally to the kind of law enforcement provided by state, county, and particularly, municipal police forces. Within the subject even thus restricted, one can do no more than touch upon a few points, not all of which may be closely interrelated. However, anyone who invites someone to offer his reflections automatically issues him a license to choose his boundaries, and I shall take advantage of it.

Reflection presents me with the clear impression that the standard of law enforcement by police agencies has improved greatly in recent years. One might note also that the conditions of employment of policemen have improved greatly. For example, a Labor Department report indicates that in 1938, city patrolmen received an annual rate of pay ranging from $580 to $3,000 for a work week ranging from as few as 40 hours to continuous duty. Excluding New York City, the average for some 360 cities over 25,000 population was $2,181 for all police department employees, including chiefs and other command officers, for—most commonly—a six-day, 48-hour week. At present, the five-day, 40-hour workweek has become common for municipal policemen, and the average rate of pay has probably been about tripled — as have per capita expenditures for police services. Admittedly, inflation has absorbed part of this seeming advantage, but the fact remains that the lot of policemen has, deservedly, improved a great deal.

Similarly, it is my impression that police officers today are considerably better qualified than they were in 1938. This observation seems valid even though then, with a considerable portion of the labor force unemployed, public jobs were avidly sought, whereas today police and other municipal departments must compete with private industry for desirable personnel. Nevertheless, today's typical requirements, that a police officer be of optimum age, physically fit, a graduate of high school, reasonably intelligent, and have an acceptable personal history, are higher than the requirements of a couple decades ago. In-service training is utilized to a degree uncommon then, and pre-employment training in professional schools is likewise becoming more frequent.

This trend toward the professionalization of police services is strong, but as yet by no means universal. To the extent that this trend continues, I would expect a number of favorable results. Among them would be increased attention to the prevention of crime and the elimination of conditions conducive to crime, improvement in the rehabilitation of criminals, a clearer understanding of human rights and obligations, and professional attitudes and standards which reduce irregularities, including special privilege in law enforcement. Also, as professionalization becomes more widespread and standards more uniform and consistent, it will be possible to have a higher degree of effective cooperation among the almost innumerable units of law enforcement that constitute our system.

My reflections in this connection should also probably include the observation that a high standard of professionalization may never be universal. For example, I live in a small community where we have a town marshal and a handful of deputies. Few of these people could qualify for the post of patrolman under the advanced recruitment and selection procedures of large cities. However, our requirements for police service are modest, and the existing arrangements seem to satisfy the citizens of the community. As is typical in small communities, these locally recruited people have complete familiarity with the community, and some understanding of its young people and a few problem citizens such as every community has. They discourage speeding, tend parking meters, see school children across streets, help crowds at local basketball and football games, do considerable patrol, fight fires, and furnish innumerable little services and accommodations to their neighbors. Lest I appear to belittle these activities, I should add that they do this work at times at unreasonable hours, in unseasonable weather, and sometimes at considerable personal risk. Should we have a problem which the local force is unable to handle, the county sheriff's deputies are available quickly. Should this help be inadequate, we can call on a regional post of the state police a mile or two out of town, and get help in strength of professional caliber. Should all this assistance prove inadequate, a unit of the National Guard is headquartered only a dozen miles away and could, at the Governor's discretion, be employed. And should we still have serious citizen misbehavior, I assume that we could wake up some morning and find an airborne division encamped in our community, displaying the ultimate capacity to see that the law is upheld.

I am not prepared to insist that this system is efficient, but I do believe that it is attractive to many Americans, and that its acceptability is an important ingredient in police–community relations. Not many Americans would find attractive the kind of spectacle that I have seen in some other countries, that of a too evident over-supply of policemen in military garb, perhaps in chromed steel helmets, perhaps with short swords, perhaps with rifles, giving an impression of threat and of detachment from small day-to-day human affairs in which Americans expect their policemen to be interested. Rather, Americans may demand effective patrol and quick response, but otherwise they want their policemen only to the extent that they need them. They do not want to be under constant surveillance by the local municipal policemen, the sheriff's deputies, the state policemen, the national guardsmen, the federal marshals, and the army's divisions. However, they take comfort from the fact that, to the extent these elements in their system may be needed in a particular instance, all are available to assure the stability of the system and that the law will prevail even against considerable opposing forces.

Another reflection on municipal police operations leads to the observation that the men in blue have enlisted only modest help from outside their uniformed ranks. Twenty years ago, about 90 per cent of the average police budget went for personal services costs. Today, this percentage is 85. There are few enterprises today where a trained man can be given full usefulness through the expenditure for equipment and facilities of an amount equal to only one-sixth his personal services costs. As we get even more competent and highly trained police officers, it may be worth while to devote a larger portion of the budget to equipping them with more and better facilities and equipment, and to providing programs and activities that will contribute to the prevention of police incidents. Certainly an increase of 5 per cent over a period of 20 years is modest when one considers the greater increases in other fields to enlarge the productivity of manpower.

In addition to this relatively mild trend toward increased utilization of facilities and equipment, the typical uniformed force is being augmented in several other ways. For example, it is no longer completely unusual for a police department to hire women to perform office work that they can do at less cost and with greater efficiency than can men recruited for qualities wholly unrelated to office work. Sometimes, too, women are now employed for other tasks that contribute to the effectiveness of police service. Also, one should note the increasing interest in this country in experimentation with the use of dogs as a means of contributing to the effectiveness and safety of policemen in particular situations.

One becomes particularly reflective when, after noticing that equipment, women, and dogs are finding their way into police departments, one notices that this spirit of charity toward resources other than uniformed manpower does not, as yet, always include camaraderie with firemen. For example, proposed legislation before the Illinois legislature seeks to prevent policemen from performing firefighting duties in communities between 10,000 and 500,000 population. Another specific example is a large municipal public safety building, divided down the middle by a 12-inch solid wall, with an entrance on one street for firemen and an entrance on another street for policemen. The principle of co-ordination of public safety services has been explored too little. Basically, it remains in a medieval stage of development such as existed when the police represented a king and the fire company a particular insurance company. At the same time that there is widespread insistence on the unification of our armed forces and consolidation of our schools, there are probably no more than a hundred cities on this continent seeking public safety coordination seriously, and applying it in some reasonable measure.

I have no notion when the American taxpayer will tire of financing intra-mural gamesmanship among public safety forces. Probably, it will not be before the general realization that the protection of persons and properties is a responsibility which should be organized to reflect the total public interest rather than being fragmented, with the fragments fenced off from each other by law and allocated to particular special groups.

Reflection on the type of legislation introduced in Illinois, which is illustrative and not unique, makes one wonder, and not only in relation to public safety, whether lobbying standards have improved commensurately with improvements in qualifications, training, salaries, and working conditions of the public service. It has become less fashionable to convert policemen and firemen to bellringers on election day to put over a particular mayor, but in relation to their work, they are still less than completely detached from the political process.

Anyone who doubts that the public safety forces are a powerful political influence should have a quiet talk with a few state legislators. And I am afraid that the level of statesmanship in this area has not risen to the point where we are without examples of demands that a state legislature impose on a municipality a certain standard of working conditions, while at the same time caterwauling about federal interference in state affairs, or acquiescing in denying the municipality the capacity to pay the mandated expense. Also, one can find examples where public safety forces exercise their political influence with greater vigor to improve their working conditions than they do to improve statutes concerned with the substance of protecting persons and property.

Generally, prophecy is a risky business, but not in this case. No realist gets too disturbed over attempts to get an extra dollar of income or hour of leisure. However, to the extent that statutes are adopted that create inflexible organizations, mandate unproductive work practices, and limit the scope of operations of trained men, the value of their training is diminished. And, also, in these circumstances we may expect to see the decline of the sometimes crude but usually vigorous and adaptable public administration developed in this country and the substitution of rigid systems of administrative law such as characterize the older nations, with administration oriented more toward defending yesterday's gains than toward exploring and embracing tomorrow's opportunities.

Another inescapable reflection relates to the extraordinary trend toward urbanization in this country, and its implications for law enforcement. Whereas, at the turn of the century, only 30 million of our population were urban, by 1960 over 125 million lived in urban places. Even more remarkable was the fact that by 1960, 113 million, or almost two-thirds of our total population, lived in 212 metropolitan areas, and it is predicted that this trend will continue.

It is in no way belittling the needs less populous areas have for the protection of persons and properties to say that the big police problem ahead probably lies in the metropolitan areas. It is here, for example, that the great masses of automobiles and the attendant demands for traffic regulation and control are concentrated. It is here that vice and organized crime become most prevalent and their interrelations most apparent. It is here that the problems of minorities become most intense, with the in-migrations of great numbers of persons unaccustomed to living in complex, industrial, urbanized communities. It is here that any large-scale unemployment creates conditions which threaten social order. It is here where political extremists, seeking to impair the basic principles of the American system, can work most effectively toward their ends. Similarly, and parenthetically, it is here, in these great industrial complexes, that there will be found the capacity for the defense of our country from external hazards. It is here that the technical difficulties of police administration are greatest. And last but not least, it's here that the responsibilities for law enforcement are divided among many and, in some instances, hundreds of enforcement agencies, existing side by side, or overlapping in such a way that the highest degree of coordination is necessary in order to achieve even a reasonable standard of law enforcement.

I am particularly inclined to be reflective about this last point, namely, the multiplicity of governmental agencies typically found in major urban areas. The problems this situation poses are by no means peculiar to the function of law enforcement. Obviously, a simple answer to them might seem to be centralization of governmental authority and activity, but in many instances this is no answer at all. Typically, people are reluctant to give up governmental units, even when they may have lost their usefulness, for they are familiar with them and feel they control them. They are reluctant to support the creation of larger units in which the role of the individual citizen appears diminished. This fear is in many instances unfounded, and indeed, democracy and personal liberties depend on many factors quite different from the fragmentization of police forces. Nevertheless, this fear is real, and it is understandable in the light of what has occurred through concentration of power in so-called "police states."

James Bryce, the exceptional British observer and author, sensed this feeling in a broader context over three-quarters of a century ago when he pointed to the satisfaction Americans took in their local government, "which enables them to bear with composure the defects of the higher organs of government, defects which would be less tolerable in a centralized country, where the national government deals directly with local affairs, or where local authorities await an initiative from above."

Woodrow Wilson, also writing in a broader context but with much relevance to law enforcement, probably had much the same thing in mind when he wrote, not as an observation, but as an admonition: "Our duty is to supply the best possible life to a Federal organization, to systems within systems; to make town, city, county, state, and Federal governments to live with a like strength and an equal healthfulness, keeping each unquestionably its own master and yet making all interdependent and cooperative, combining independence with mutual helpfulness."

Similarly today, there are many informed and sincere persons who believe that law enforcement by a local community is, or can be, better for the individual citizen than law enforcement by state and federal agencies. They feel that local police are better equipped with a detailed familiarity with the community, more likely to be characterized by service features, and more likely to get and keep public support, if only because they are more closely accountable to the citizens. The enlightened proponents of these views would, of course, encourage every possible cooperation among all kinds and levels of agencies, and participation by state and federal agencies as needed. Such participation would certainly include, but not be limited to direct enforcement of some laws, and the provision of training facilities, and of laboratory, identification, and records services, and the like. In other words, they would encourage federal and state participation to the extent that they do not endanger the advantages they believe local law enforcement provides for the individual.

A somewhat contrary view, supporting the notion of a greater centralization of police activities, can be advanced on the basis of technical considerations. Certainly, many people could move into a given situation in which there are scores of immediately adjoining or overlapping agencies, and figure out an organization and pattern of administration that would provide more protection for persons and property, for the same number of dollars that is needed for the services of the fragmented departments. However, such a proposed reorganization, no matter what its merits, will not be persuasive if its opponents convince the people that a highly centralized and effective law enforcement arrangement either jeopardizes, or is a step in the direction of jeopardizing, individual rights. My reflections suggest that, generally, Americans will not buy efficiency in law enforcement if they suspect that it involves infringements of personal liberties. And we must not forget that, while a police state is privileged to impose an effective system of law enforcement upon its people, our form of government does not permit such arbitrary action. Here, the system must be acceptable to the people, and you and I alike applaud this difference.

Under our system then, such government reorganizations as occur must leave police, like other functions, with direct responsibility to the people they serve. By and large also, effective local government reorganizations cannot relate exclusively to police, but must extend to the local government structure generally, if only because fragmentization of governmental structure by activities endangers the democratic process and the institution of local government. This general approach to local government improvement need not be disadvantageous to the police function, and in fact should be helpful, for it has been my observation that law enforcement in a particular community is, in the long run, seldom better or worse than the performance of other functions.

At the risk of being repetitious, I probably should state the same reflection in another way. Law enforcement is one of a number of governmental activities and, as such, it does not and cannot stand alone. The law enforcement job can be made harder or easier by what happens in the home, in religious institutions, in schools, in non-governmental, civic, and professional organizations, and in other elements in our total social, economic, and political order, including other facets of government. Until we get to the happy stage where we can speak of law observance instead of law enforcement, we must continue to work toward the improvement of law enforcement. It, in turn, will never be better than the governmental system of which it is a part. This means that anyone who is interested in the imporvement of law enforcement must necessarily work for the maintenance and extension of governmental gains the people of this country have made in other areas.

For example, we must maintain stability in our political institutions, and the will and capacity to protect them from any threat from the outside, since failure on this count would undoubtedly be attended by the loss of many of the things we value most. We must work toward the improvement of our training for citizenship and the consistent responsible practice of it. We must improve the prestige of government service so that it enlists the broadest possible participation by the best qualified citizens. As necessary, we should reorganize local governments in such a way that citizenship can be exercised more intelligently and effectively. We must retain reasonable flexibility in our governmental arrangements so that they may be adapted to new circumstances, with the changes in times. As we have for three hundred years created, abolished, and modified government structures, so we must continue to—so that they do not work at cross purposes, and so that a citizen may sensibly support each of the several levels of government that constitute our system, without feeling that he is financing a contest. We must continue to make our governments and their officials responsive to the needs and wishes of citizens, within the limits that these citizens are willing and able to finance them.

Also, we must not permit ourselves to become preoccupied exclusively with the executive branch. We much also give attention to the legislative branch, in order to insure that it is truly representative of the citizenry and that it is equipped to perform its important functions. And particularly in relation to law enforcement, there must be attention to the judicial branch which, upon reflection, I am inclined to think has not kept pace with the improvements in police administration. Overcrowded dockets, postponements of legal actions for months and even years, court attachés that are political payrollers rather than merit selections, judgeships that are considered parts of political parties rather than of government structures, inadequate reporting on court actions and accounting for court funds, inattention to public requirements and convenience, and inadequate organization and administrative arrangements can still be found. Such circumstances, needless to say, are disadvantageous specifically with respect to law enforcement, and generally with regard to broader public concerns.

To the extent that government in all its branches is improved, there will be increased effectiveness in law enforcement—an effectiveness that must be accomplished without unnecessary infringement of basic individual liberties. Within the general governmental structure, the law enforcement agencies should, of course, continue the development of their field and the improvement of its practices to insure the security of persons and property, to treat effectively with offenders, and to provide reasonable incidental services which are a convenience to people and which leaven any harshness of law enforcement with a human quality.

Within this structure of a Republic based on democratic processes, the rights of the people will be protected, both from criminal and from unwarranted official invasions. Within this structure, the public and the individual interest, as reflected in a system of laws, can be fulfilled with a certainty, equity, and justice that fully satisfies the oft-stated measure that a government is effective to the degree that it affords protection of the liberties of its lowliest citizen.

Group Behavior and Civil Disobedience

NELSON A. WATSON

Project Director, International Association of Chiefs of Police

MAY 23, 1967

Over the radio comes an urgent voice, "Step ladder 3—12th and Main." The dispatcher in the station swings into action relaying the message, "Cars 51, 17, and 30. Step ladder 3—12th and Main." With this code three cars and six men are thus sent to the aid of a fellow officer. The "policeman in trouble" call often is the first indication a police agency receives of an uncontrolled mob action or a riot. It may be nothing more than a minor skirmish or it may be the opening moment of a frightening and devastating upheaval. In any event, it is an electrifying call for help in which the behavior of the people involved may well be the type of behavior we are going to consider today.

Group behavior or, more properly, the behavior of people in groups is a fruitful and important area of study for police. The ways people act when in a group setting often call for police intervention. Crowds may become unruly. Mobs frequently become dangerously violent. A gang of juveniles or of rowdy young adults can cause all kinds of trouble for police ranging from intolerable nuisance or vandalism to murder. Another aspect of group behavior often of interest to police is that which becomes formalized into organizational programs.

A community expects its police to be aware of and prepared to deal with groups whose activities violate the law. It is significant to note at this point that the activities of groups engaged in nonviolent demonstrations and whose members are not violating the law may nevertheless require that the police take action —but, in this case, action to protect them in the legitimate exercise of their rights from violent counteraction by those who are opposed.

It so happens that the kind of group behavior that is of immediate and urgent interest to us in the context of this Institute is a special type called COLLECTIVE BEHAVIOR.

Ordinarily, when we use the term collective behavior the first impression might be that we are simply talking about the way people conduct themselves in groups. Thus, it might be assumed that the things we shall do in the discussion session here would fall within the definition of collective behavior. To the uninitiated, the behavior of a family going on a picnic might be thought of as collective behavior. Or, one might think of the joint efforts of an orchestra or a football team as collective behavior. However, none of these are examples of collective behavior as we shall use the term. True, they are examples of the behavior of people in groups or collectivities, but in the technical sense they are not collective behavior.

What then do we mean by the term? Perhaps it is best to offer some examples before attempting a definition. One example—a highly dramatic one—is the behavior of rioters. Another kind of collective behavior is that which occurs at the scene of a disaster—people in panic. Still another and a very common type, is the relatively uncertain or confused behavior of people who find themselves in any kind of strange situation and, finally, we should cite the kind of behavior that may be observed in connection with fads, crazes, and broad social movements. From these examples, it is apparent that there are certain qualities or characteristics which must be present for the actions of people to fall within the technical definition of collective behavior.

The social scientists who have gone into this matter with great care find it necessary to use the term collective behavior in a rather technical sense and it seems to me that for our purposes, it is necessary to approach the subject with caution in order to avoid many of the pitfalls we would encounter if we used the term in too loose a manner. For purposes of our discussion, then, I would suggest that we limit our understanding of the term to that of emergent, spontaneous and usually emotional behavior that occurs in circumstances where the people are not governed by the ordinary rules of conduct and where the commonly accepted cultural norms are not fully appropriate. Now, that is a rather bothersome mouthful and I think we need to clarify it with a few examples. To illustrate, let me refer again to the kind of behavior which normally occurs within a family situation. A family, as a social institution, is regulated very largely by widely accepted cultural norms and institutionalized patterns of relationships. The father plays his role; the mother, hers. The children have their own distinct and unique roles. Many people would consider certain kinds of behavior as appropriate to the father's role but not to the mother's role, and so on. This is not the kind of behavior we are talking about today. As another illustration, consider the kinds of behavior and relationships which are appropriate during a church service. Here again, we have institutionalized forms of behavior in the nature of rituals and certain role prescriptions which are required of participants as appropriate to the circumstances. In this case, there are definite behavior patterns for the various roles of the participants. There is little uncertainty and great formality. There are other kinds of group behavior which do not fall within the definition of collective behavior. For example, the roles and relationships that exist in a police department are partly institutionalized, but more specifically organizational in nature. Most organizations, including police agencies, develop norms which govern the behavior of most of their members most of the time. These norms have some tradition and utility at their base. They are relatively stable and change rather slowly. However, under special conditions, collective behavior can develop in such organizations. It is possible that untrained and unsupervised police officers in an emergency situation may display collective behavior. Lack of or ambiguity of police may lead to collective behavior. It is possible that sudden and radical changes may produce conditions in which the usual norms governing or regulating the behavior of the members are clearly no longer appropriate. When this occurs, we may have random, confused, emergent behavior of a collective nature.

We can say then that the kinds of behavior existing within social institutions and organizations are not collective behavior in the sense in which we are using the term.

Collective behavior has, typically, a certain degree of novelty and spontaneity about it. It is usually associated with a relatively disorganized or unstructured social situation in which the proper course of conduct is not clearly apparent. People are not sure what specific behavior is appropriate to the circumstances. In their uncertainty, people cast about for guidelines or models which they can follow. They are more than ordinarily subject to suggestion. The uncertainty resulting from the lack of clear structure and the apparent inappropriateness of the ordinary modes of behavior produce a state of imbalance and tension. People feel a need to correct this imbalance and to reduce the tension, but they are uncertain how to go about it.

Under these circumstances, people are vulnerable to suggestion. They are relatively easily led—largely because they don't know what to do. Frequently a leader emerges—one who may not be any better informed than anyone else, but who is more impulsive or in such a state of excitement that he simply must do something. Seeing him take action, the more suggestible individuals follow along and soon there is a general movement following the same pattern. This behavior is emergent, that is, it arises more or less spontaneously out of the momentary situation as perceived by those present. The behavior is collective in the sense that those present collectively engage in it.

Collective behavior is usually observed in relatively unorganized collectivities. The lack of organization is either an inherent property of the collectivity itself, such as a crowd or a mob, or it results from change, emergencies, crises, disasters and panics, or the sudden removal of leadership. There is sometimes a demoralization and deciding what is happening and what to do about it becomes difficult. Those involved may experience anxiety or fear, frustration, or anger and hatred. Of course, there are types of collective behavior in which these strong sentiments and feelings of uncertainty and demoralization are not present. This would be the case in connection with such things as fads and crazes which I mentioned earlier. All types of collective behavior are of interest to social scientists, but the kind we are most interested in in connection with our Police–Community Relations Program is that which produces disorderly and even violent conduct, for collective behavior may involve not just noncompliance with cultural norms, but violation of law as well.

Our community leaders and particularly our police departments are frequently faced with situations in which steps must be taken to prevent violence and disorder. In some cases, the only recourse the police department has is to exert pressures to bring such conduct under control when preventive measures have failed. It is unfortunate but true that there have been situations in which ordinary and routine police activity has been the triggering event which set off collective behavior which rapidly becomes violent. We have seen cases in which a routine arrest of an individual for public intoxication has generated the action on the part of bystanders or companions of the person being arrested. In some of these cases large crowds have gathered in which conduct has assumed a violent character. Thus we may have an event in which the police officers are attacked, in which attempts are made to rescue the prisoner, or a full-blown riot develops.

It is undoubtedly true that there must be some kind of triggering incident to kick off a disorderly event or a riot. Much attention has been paid to this principle in police training. It is not uncommon to hear people, police or otherwise, remark about it. Not so frequently mentioned, are the facts that (1) the trigger is only the initiating device in a train of events and (2) that the spring which the trigger activates can be more or less sensitive. The social situation in which the triggering event occurs must be one that is ripe. In order to have an explosion, there must be a critical mix and the more critical the mix, the more sensitive the trigger. In other words, if the situation is bad enough—sufficiently sensitive— very delicate control is needed to avoid the holocaust. In an extremely delicate case the triggering event can be something entirely innocent or even something totally unrelated to the situation. I think it can be said that the more intense the feelings of the people, the shorter their fuses. A riot could be touched off between two antipathetic groups by such an innocent event as an idle remark which may be regarded as an insult by someone who happens to overhear it. It is also possible for violence to result from the mere presence of a hated figure. For example, if a certain police officer who has made an unpopular arrest or who is believed to be brutal or insensitive, happens to be spotted by someone who wants to get even, bricks may start to fly.

It seems to me that the lesson we can draw from all this is that anyone who has any responsibility for maintaining a just social order must do his share toward keeping the lid on. Since I do not want to be misunderstood on this, let me hasten to add that I do not regard the avoidance of disorder and riots as the sole objective—important as that is. I think we must all be committed to the establishment and maintenance of a social order in which everyone will get a fair shake. I do firmly believe, however, that disorder and violence impedes our progress toward that goal. What I am saying, then, is that police training is not the only avenue of attack. We can and do try to train police officers to maintain their composure and self-control. We do try to impress upon them the importance of avoiding rash or impulsive actions which could trigger violence. We do teach that what they do is important and that how they do it is often more important. I am also saying that, aside from police training, we must take steps at the community level to reduce the sensitivity of the trigger by correcting those situations which lead to expressions of dissatisfaction and perhaps eventual rebellion.

In a very strict sense, there is no such thing as collective or group behavior. Every collectivity or group is made up of individuals and the behaving unit is the person. Thus, what comes out by way of conduct, is always a product of the individual's perception of the momentary stimulus complex, his motivational state, his attitudes and values, and his choice from among the behavioral alternatives he believes available to him. It is certainly true that one's behavior as a member of a group may differ markedly from what it would be were he alone or, perhaps, a member of a different group. Teenagers behave as they do partly because the other members of their teenage groups expect them to. People who participate in demonstrations of protest behave in certain ways because they believe it is the thing to do. Police officers act in certain ways because that is what is expected of them. This matter of perceiving "the thing to do" is very important in collective behavior.

The behavior of police officers, based upon training and controlled by policies and rules, is not collective behavior as we have already indicated. Collective or mass behavior is different in many respects from institutionally or organizationally determined behavior and may depart at times from the conduct normally followed as regulated cultural norms. We should note that collective behavior, emergent and unregulated at first, may well produce norms which gradually gain recognition and acceptance and which become part of the cultural pattern. For example, in some circles, the generally repugnant four-letter words are not considered unacceptable. Whether or not they will gain increasing acceptance remains to be seen. We have witnessed in the recent past the increasing use of such epithets or exclamatories as "hell" and "damn" on television and radio, to say nothing of the movies. There is, we must admit, the possibility that such words may come to be regarded as quite normal. We now think nothing of it when someone says, "Gee, I would like to do—something or other." There was a time when the expletive "Gee" was frowned upon because of its origin. Its etymology reveals it to be euphemistic language for "Jesus."

Going back now to the reference just made about the gradual change in social norms resulting from collective behavior, I believe we have reached a state in which the norms that emerged as part of the collective behavior observed in various kinds of demonstrations and protests have come to assume institutional character. For example, it has now become a common and expected practice for demonstrators to carry placards, to sing, to march. These types of behavior which came about originally as emergent norms in a collective situation have now gained recognition as "the thing to do" when participating in a demonstration. In fact, I fear that we may have reached a state in which brick and bottle tossing, arson, looting, and sniping are looked upon as normal and, therefore, expected behavior on the part of rioters.

Among the important psychological processes which influence the behavior of people in collectivities, there are some which are readily communicated and perceived. When one finds himself in an unstructured or ambiguous mass situation in which the ordinary cultural norms do not seem fully appropriate, he perceives and in turn communicates the emerging mood, the objectives, the leadership and status structure, and the action of others in the crowd or group. The mood, the objectives, the leadership, and the actions are emergent in nature in that, as we have previously noted, they develop to suit the circumstances.

It is from these that the controlling situational norms are derived. The participants strive to structure the disorganized situation in their own minds. Rumor is one of the devices used for this purpose. Symbols also serve as rallying points. The people in a collective situation often react strongly to symbols. These may be objects, persons, or even ideas which have a special meaning for the members of the collectivity. For example, signs on certain business places reading "Blood-brother" have a special meaning. Similarly, the term "Nigger-lover" has a certain symbolic and emotion-laden meaning. Such symbols as swastikas, flags, banners, slogans, songs, and so on, may come to carry a special and powerful significance for persons to identify with the group in question, and a strong negative importance to those opposed to the group.

It is significant that symbols are strongly polarized in a collective behavior event. People are reacting emotionally and not rationally and, consequently, they are strongly for or strongly against whatever the issue in point is. There is no middle ground. If the event involves Negro–white conflict, some Negroes will be strongly committed to "blood brothers" and strongly anti-white—all whites; none are friends. Among the whites there are some who hate all Negroes. Interesting and tragic is the fact that for such people, any white who is not a "Nigger-hater" must therefore be a "Nigger-lover" and thus an enemy. One who does not hate Negroes or who does not believe "They're all the same" is a dangerous radical, un-American, and a Communist. The emotional investment in such symbols becomes costly indeed.

It goes without saying, of course, that the type of collective behavior we have been talking about poses many problems for police. One such aspect is the requirement that police, under the law, must deal with *individuals* and not with groups. When law violations occur, our legal system requires that *individuals* be arrested and that evidence presented in court must apply to that specific individual in connection with that specific event. This makes it difficult for the police when, as a matter of collective behavior, large numbers of people engage in activities which violate the law. Police cannot take into court a whole group and present evidence against them en masse. If the police are unable to identify and arrest individual violators and present evidence of the specific violation, case by individual case, all they can do is suppress the violence. It is inevitable that in a large scale disorder many violations of law will go unpunished. This makes it doubly important to devise preventive programs involving all interested segments of the community.

Another problem aspect of the control of violence and disorder as well as crime is that relating to the proper and most effective methods to be used under varying circumstances and with different kinds of people. It is generally conceded that people may be grouped according to a wide variety of characteristics. Based upon these characteristics, one would expect to find differences in attitude, values, and beliefs. One would also expect that behavior would differ to some extent in line with these differences. There are also certain expectations associated with various positions and roles in society. Social scientists generally agree, for example, that socio-economic status or class differences have associated with them identifiable and significant variations in behavior. Another way of stating the matter, according to some students of the problem, is that we have cultural differences largely identifiable on the basis of socio-economic class. Some have called these identifiable cultural groups subcultures. These differences which are psychological, cultural, class, or whatever one wishes to call them, constitute an environmental and personality field out of which behavior flows.

It would seem reasonable to expect that people of different backgrounds would react differently under conditions in which collective behavior would be forthcoming. For example, one might reasonably expect that a schoolteacher would not react in the same way as a skid-row bum. Similarly, different behavior could be expected from a seventeen-year-old Negro male who has been thoroughly "ghettoized" and a white middle-class bank teller.

According to social psychologists, there are certain modal attitudinal, cognitive, and behavioral constellations that are characteristic of the socio-economic classes. What I mean is that there is a background of experience and a cluster of attitudes associated with class which produce a type of behavior that is in harmony. A white middle-aged environment will produce attitudes and behavior different from those learned in a lower-class ghetto Negro environment. For example, in most middle-class families, white, Negro, or any other, children are taught restraint insofar as resorting to direct physical aggression is concerned. Children from lower-class families, in contrast, are often permitted to vent their feelings in physical aggression without remonstrance from the parents. Another contrast is the middle-class attitude toward achievement. Much greater emphasis, in the main, is placed upon study and intellectual accomplishment in middle-class families.

Perhaps the most significant difference is one which centers about the time orientation. Middle-class families are usually future oriented whereas lower-class families are present oriented. The middle-class child is taught to look to the future. He is expected to plan. He is expected to sacrifice momentary pleasures in order to realize greater gains later on. This sense of orientation in time affects what a person does from day to day. It means, among other things, that a greater proportion of the time of a middle-class person is invested in preparing for life in the future and a smaller proportion is spent in pleasures of the moment. It also means a higher value is placed upon punctuality and getting things done.

It is possible that the momentary time orientation of many lower-class people is an outgrowth of their unremitting struggle for existence. Since many lower-class persons are unskilled and are poorly equipped educationally, the most important fact of life for them is the means of obtaining the necessities. For many, existence is a series of crises or emergencies in which food and shelter are principal concerns. The net result is that satisfying their basic needs for the moment demands such a large proportion of their physical and psychological resources that they are unable to devote adequate time to the development of the symbolic skills so important in today's complex society. Their survival problems are much closer to them than those of the more affluent in our society.

Another highly significant difference concerns the relationships of the two classes to authority. This is a complex matter which time does not allow us to explore extensively. We should note, however, that authority relationships have their roots in parental disciplinary practices, especially those which the child experiences early in life. The disciplinary practices of parents in lower-class families, more frequently than in middle-class families, are based upon corporal punishment. The result frequently is that children for whom discipline is chiefly physical punishment come to feel that physical aggression is the effective and proper way to assert one's will.

The point here is that police approaches to the control of crime, violence, and disorder may have to be designed to match the varying psychological fields of the people involved. Please note that I said "may have to be designed." I am here raising a question more than making an assertion.

Our democratic ethic teaches that everyone is equal under the law. We teach police that they must treat everyone alike. We profess belief in human dignity and the worth of the individual. We jealously protect the rights of even the meanest among us. We pride ourselves in being fair. But, we know that in the real world our performance falls short of our philosophy. In the real world of politics, economics, and social status, people are not equal. Nor are people really equal under the law. We would like to be able to claim that we live up to our philosophy and moral code, but we must confess that we don't. It would be a transparent sham for me to claim otherwise and I have no stomach for reciting a catechism of platitudes.

Now, what I am getting at is this. I have talked to police officials from one end of this country to the other. There are some I would get rid of in a minute if I could, but the vast majority are decent Joes who are trying to do a good job. Some are truly outstanding and they are men who can hold their heads high in any company. The vast majority of these men fully subscribe to the philosophy that everyone must be treated fairly, that everyone must be accorded respect, that excessive force must not be used, and all the other principles of good policing. They will tell you, almost to a man, that in the real world as they experience it, there are many people who through ignorance, fear, or animosity, give the police officer such a bad time that he must do things the rough way even though he would prefer it to be otherwise.

To get down to practicalities, let's consider briefly a situation. Assume that a police officer makes a traffic stop—for running a stop sign, let's say. The driver is resentful and becomes abusive and belligerent. The officer, in line with his training, tries to keep his composure, but as a crowd gathers and takes up "the defense" of the violator, the officer finds himself in a more and more untenable position. He cannot escape by letting the man go. He must issue the citation and, as he sees it, he must protect his own integrity and the dignity of his office or he will not be able to enforce the law in that area again. Under these conditions, many an officer has resorted to harsh language which may well have been considered abusive by the bystanders and the violator even though everyone there heard the abuse the officer took, but which the officer saw as necessary in order to maintain control. If some of the crowd were to step in to give the violator a chance to escape, the officer may have found himself physically threatened and he would then have been justified in using force to protect himself. The bystanders may well have regarded this as brutality.

What we have here is a case in which an officer doing his job meets resistance which should not have been offered. And, whereas resistance from the violator may be understandable even though not justified, resistance by the bystanders is totally wrong. This could be the triggering event in a serious clash.

In relation to what I developed above concerning class differences, it is noteworthy that this kind of verbal and sometimes physical resistance occurs more frequently in slums and ghettos than in other neighborhoods. Now, again I ask the question—and it is truly a question—does this mean that a different approach to law and order is required in these areas as compared to others because of basic psychological and environmental differences? As to an answer, my guess would be that if it is required, it would be true of a relatively small proportion of the people because, fortunately, most people are lined up on the side of law and order. Dr. Lloyd Warner says that socio-economic class is a major determinant of an individual's decisions and social actions. It affects his habits, interests, attitudes, values, and levels of aspiration and adaptation. The person we are talking about here is one who has little education, little marketable skill, small income, the worst of residential areas, perhaps a low opinion of himself, and quite limited verbal skills. He may see himself as getting only the scraps in a dog-eat-dog world where conforming to society's norms is not only beyond his reach, it is also undesirable because he cannot compete on equal terms. In some small number of cases, it may be that the police officer is right when he says that "they don't understand any other kind of talk." I feel that we should acknowledge that there are some people who will not let the officer deal with them in the way that he would like.

We should take a look at the other side of the coin insofar as the triggering and handling of collective behavior is concerned. Those of us who work for and with the police must frankly admit that much remains to be done in order to correct all of our faults. It is unfortunate, but true, that we have police officers who are unable to rid their official behavior of prejudicial taint. There are men in the police service who carry a chip on their shoulders. It is regrettable that some police leaders have not come to grips with the shortcomings of their policies or their men. I can say from personal experience that there are many policemen who are suspicious of community relations programs. I regard it as an ominous sign when the officers in a department derogate and deride their fellow officers who are assigned to a community relations program. It would be my prediction that a community relations program set up as a front would cause more trouble than it would eliminate. If the unstated but true objective is to get people off our backs, we might as well not do it because unless the program moves toward the solution of problems, it will not receive the support it needs. It needs support from many quarters not the least of which is the police department itself. Every officer must understand that his every act, his every contact, is an entry in the ledger of human relations—either as an asset or a liability.

Now a few words about civil disobedience. The relationship between collective behavior and civil disobedience may seem at first glance to be rather obscure. That there is a relationship is the point of this part of the discussion. I would assume that everyone here knows what is meant by civil disobedience—the deliberate violation of a law or a regulation having the force and effect of a law believed to be immoral or unjust. It is a calculated challenge of authority by persons who believe their moral or philosophical convictions require them to follow a contrary commandment of a higher order.

To many people, acts of civil disobedience are repugnant. It is frequently said that people should not be permitted to pick and choose among the laws those they will obey and those they will not. It is believed by many that civil disobedience is akin to anarchy. In a survey which we are conducting among police nationwide, we are asking officers to indicate whether they agree or disagree with certain statements. One of the statements reads, "A person has a right to deliberately disobey a law which he believes to be immoral or unjust." Ninety percent of the fifteen hundred officers who have replied thus far say they disagree. I have no way of knowing whether nine out of ten people in general would also disagree, but I suspect that a large majority would.

Civil disobedience is not just the deliberate violation of some law. It may be a protest against whatever is commanded or prohibited by a law, but it may also be a protest against a court order such as an injunction. It may also be a protest not against the substance of a law, but a protest against the manner in which a law is being enforced.

Take school boycotts as an example. We may regard the act of keeping one's children out of school as an instance of civil disobedience. There are compulsory attendance laws and if parents keep their children out of school for other than a customarily approved reason, they are in violation of the law. But the school boycotts are not based upon a belief that the compulsory attendance laws are unjust or immoral. They are, instead, protests against the way the schools are being administered. In contrast, a boycott against a store accused of discriminatory hiring practices is not civil disobedience for no law compels anyone to buy in that store.

Some police officers feel that civil disobedience is such a serious matter and so potentially destructive of social order that violators should be severely punished. In one group in which this question came up for discussion, the suggestion was made that there should be legislation prohibiting civil disobedience. However, the group quickly arrived at the conclusion that such a statute would be futile because all it could say is that it is illegal to do anything illegal.

In considering civil disobedience, there are certain fallacies of which we must beware. A common misunderstanding arises out of an error in logic. It is proper to equate civil disobedience with illegality; civil disobedience is illegal. It is proper to equate violence with illegality; civil violence is illegal. However, even though civil disobedience and violence are both illegal, it is incorrect to equate civil disobedience with violence. Civil disobedience is not necessarily violence and violence is not necessarily civil disobedience.

I believe that civil disobedience is not a matter of fundamental right, for no one has a right to disobey the law. One may deliberately choose to knowingly disobey a law if its observance violates his conscience and he believes that law commands him to break a higher law. This is a grave matter and it should be undertaken only in issues of great consequence, and only when all reasonable alternatives have failed. Even then, one who chooses civil disobedience to prove his point must do so in full expectation of complying nonviolently with the procedures and sanctions applied to violators.

The relationship between civil disobedience and collective behavior rests upon what might be described as the disorderly fallout. It is practically a truism to say that most of the enforcement of the law is done by the people rather than by the police. This is due to the fact that nearly everyone obeys the law most of the time. Even in cases where civil disobedience is being carried out in public view, most people do not participate. However, collective behavior being what it is, some persons who do not have an understanding of the underlying philosophy and who are not motivated necessarily by the same convictions may engage in the same behavior because they perceive its potential utility. Others may "go along" more as a matter of suggestibility than conviction. They are uncertain as to the proper courses of behavior under the circumstances and, casting about for guidelines they copy the behavior of persons perceived to be sympathetic to their own viewpoints.

Also, some police authorities feel it is not too far-fetched to expect that some persons, many of them children and youths, who do not fully understand the philosophy behind civil disobedience will violate not only laws which are considered morally unjust by the leaders of civil disobedience campaigns, but any laws. Many law enforcement officials feel that one of the tragic results of the employment of civil disobedience tactics is to encourage in large numbers of young people an attitude of general disrespect for the law and for all public authority. While this may be so, there is no empirical evidence of a psychological or sociological nature known to this speaker to prove that attitudes engendered by participating in acts of civil disobedience are transferred to acts of law violation in the criminal field. In other words, I know of no evidence to prove that one who deliberately violates an injunction against a demonstration would carry away with him a generalized disrespect for law resulting in his committing burglaries or robberies. The point made, however, by any law enforcement officials, is that young persons who are still in an immature and formative stage of life may well get from acts of civil disobedience this generalized disrespect for all law.

There is still another aspect of this question which is rather abrasive and a source of irritation to police. The object of civil disobedience is to call attention to a condition which the participants want to have changed. Naturally, the more widely and dramatically the acts are publicized, the better for the purpose. Unfortunately, this publicity often makes the police look bad, especially if violence breaks out. And not only that, it also gives the officers a lot of hard and unpleasant work to do. And not only that, the cases are often dismissed and the officers then feel that their work was all for naught. So I think we can conclude undeniably that civil disobedience is quite unpopular with the police.

In conclusion, I would like to say that collective behavior, in the technical sense in which we have used the term, is fraught with many dangers for society and many difficulties for police. I believe that police and citizens, working together on constructive programs for crime prevention in which progress is made toward minimizing causal factors, can help reduce the likelihood of outbreaks of violence. And that is good, but it is not enough, because the police are not in a position to do anything about many of the factors which may tend to cause people to resort to crime or to run wild in a riot. Other governmental departments and officials, private organizations, and many, many more citizens must do their part toward alleviating bad social conditions over which they have jurisdiction or in which they may have influence. The word "community" in Police–Community Relations means the whole community, just as the word "police" means all officers.

Understanding the Community

JAMES B. McKEE

Professor, Department of Sociology, Michigan State University

MAY 18, 1965

The whole concept of community is fraught with illusions and is, to a very considerable extent, a misleading concept. It's misleading largely because it's a very ancient and honorable word that conveys certain ideas that seem to me to be no longer as applicable as they once were. That is, we have images of what we mean by community. The word tends to imply a sense of organization, a sharing of values, a sharing of a common way of life among that population that inhabits a given locality. But all of this, in the modern world, in the modern urbanized community, is an overstatement, if not an outright illusion. Community is no longer like that, if it ever was.

But if we leave aside the question of what it once was, at least I think we can recognize that the roots of the term are located in the concern of men about the change from a distinctly rural community to an urban one. A rural community largely encompassed the totality of human lives, where men were born, raised, and lived in the same community, and shared a common way of life with the same group of people, and that not a very large group.

Community in that sense meant you knew your neighbor, you knew who belonged there. You could readily distinguish a friend from a stranger on the street. All of this is involved in the notion of community: of people who live together, share a way of life together, have deep understandings about their most basic values and about how they want to live their lives, exist together in a fundamental agreement about what is most significant, about how people should behave.

What I am saying is that none of this applies to the modern community. Yet we still use the term "community" to identify a town, a city, a locality, a geographical area, within which there is some concentration of population—where people live and work. At least some of them work there, for it's no longer necessary, obviously, to work in the same community in which one resides. Indeed, this is one of the significant ways in which community has changed.

At one time, a community encompassed the totality of a human life; it need not do this any longer. It does not, in fact, do this any longer for a large proportion of those who—in fact—have residence in a given community. There are significant implications in this kind of change for the phenomenon we call community, and for the understanding of community, I'm going to pursue this one thread a bit further.

What I am saying is that the community is not the kind of integrated entity that the term itself has long seemed to imply. It's not that at all. This makes it very difficult for us, therefore, to assess the meaning of community as a locality, a place where people reside and work. Thus, our recognition of the simple reality of the urban community of today would be to emphasize, in the language of the sociologist, that it is *segmentalized,* that it is *stratified,* that it is *differentiated,* and that it is *un-integrated.* All I am saying, in about four different ways, is that the community is a lot of different pieces that are not well tied together. There are different patterns of life among the distinct groups that are located in the same boundaries of a city, and there are several different strata, or social ranks, that have the most minimum, if any, social contact or communication with one another.

One basic idea, of course, of community in the older sense was that it was a single system of communication, that people spoke the same language and understood one another. I am saying here that the lines of differentiation that mark groups off from one another, the lines of stratification that separate several different kinds of social ranking and prestige levels, and the ways of life that go with these, inhibit communication—indeed, mark a community in which there are discontinuities in communication, not a continuous flow that reaches every single person within it.

The most common error in trying to understand community, it seems to me, is to jump to the conclusion, to the illusion, really, that community is integrated around a common set of values that are shared by those who make up a community by virtue of living there. This is not so. The concept of community, once one imputes to it the notion of common values, then also leads, as the next logical idea, to the notion of effective social controls in maintaining standards of behavior. Clearly, standards of behavior accepted within the community are easier to maintain when there is a common body of values that animates all members of the community, a common body of values to which they have all been properly socialized in their youth elsewhere. But most important of all, being young and undergoing the processes of socialization in the community today does not introduce one to any single body of values, or any single standard of behavior maintained in that community. In part, the community of old, by its greater approximation, at least, to this ideal sense of what a community was, and the exemplification of certain common values by the most significant members of the community, plus the influence which their positions gave them within the community, made it possible to exercise a somewhat greater control over those less integrated members. So much so was this that it was possible for all of us, in looking at communities of the past, to exaggerate their consensus, and exaggerate the processes of integration, and to admire the effective social controls characteristic of the smaller community of the past.

Indeed, one of the first lessons in sociology that I learned in studying the city was that in the transition from the more rural community of the past to the modern urban community of today, social controls, as they came spontaneously and informally out of a common way of life, broke down, because the newer urban community did not effect one common way of life. For purposes of social control, there was a more necessary reliance on formal controls, on law and on the exercise of authority and law enforcement by police.

The conception of the community of the past was, as I earlier suggested, one in which one was born, raised, and lived one's life within the same community, and largely within the same station of life. It is, if we examine it closely, a conception of a fairly static, relatively unchanging community. That alone, it seems to me, would disqualify it for serious consideration in examining community life today. The contemporary community is not an isolated phenomenon set apart; it is a part of the larger society. It stands, in a sense, in the way of, and therefore gets caught in the wash of the sweeping events of our time. It is not independent of what goes on in the larger society.

The individual today is free, to a very great extent, from local control because he's mobile. We live in a society in which mobility, both vertical and horizontal—moving from one community to another, from one place to another around this large society of ours, as well as moving up and down the social ladder—are common facts of life. But what is significant about this, in examining community, is that community is not the only significant grouping in the life of an individual. For the most important sociological implication of the idea of mobility is that one changes the groups of which one is a member, or in the language of the social psychologist, one changes one's reference group, which may be the group of which one is a part, or the group one desires to be a part. In any case, this is the group to which one refers one's self, in taking cues for behavior and styles of conduct in living one's life. Almost every individual changes his membership groups and his reference groups sometimes in his life. And many of us, as a matter of fact, change them any number of times. We also, therefore, change the human beings we are. For, as we change the groups within which we live, the groups in which we play our roles and act toward others and are some kind of person, we change ourselves.

The older notion that you shape the person in the earliest years of life, and that's what he is from then on, is no longer tenable as a way of perceiving human beings in this kind of society. Individuals change as the circumstances of their life change, and we as Americans are a kind of people who must have personalities that are relatively adaptable to the circumstances of change. We do not find it too difficult to do this. Mobility, then, is a fact that loosens the natural tendency of a community to exert control over its members, for it is no longer the exclusive reference group that defines acceptable standards of conduct, and it no longer defines any *one* standard of conduct.

Sociologists like to point out that you can rather simply, and crudely, in any given community, distinguish between those whose major orientation is to the local community, whose roots are there and who are less likely to be mobile, and whose life is focused around what goes on in the community, from those who have a larger focus, a larger involvement and a larger interest in what goes on elsewhere. These may be, for professional reasons or whatever else, tied into groups that are not distinctively local groups, as against those whose whole life is wrapped up in what goes on within the local community.

"Localites" and "cosmopolites" is a kind of sociological phrasing coined to convey this distinction. Localites are those who have a primary stake in the community. What happens in the community is significant because it happens to them. The local businessmen, which are not all the businessmen but certainly the main street merchants, the men whose property and business is centered in that community, and who will rise and fall with the community, are locally oriented. So are the realtors, who buy and sell or serve as the brokers for buyers and sellers of commercial and residential property that constitutes that community. Those leaders who are leaders in local terms, around local issues, and local concerns, and whose capacity for leadership is effectively exercised only within the community, have a stake in that community. There are those whose relatively higher social status is based upon the organization of the community. It is local status, high only within that community, a status that would be lost if they moved elsewhere.

"Localite" never includes all those who, in fact, are members of the community, for there are some who have no significant stake within it. There are people who have social status that is derived from social groups and collectivities that are not based necessarily in one community, but stretch across communities. We need to recognize that many people are no longer primarily oriented only to community, but that in a great mass society, in a world of bureaucratic association, people are involved in other kinds of networks of human association in which they have status, within which they find significant human association, and within which they find significant experience and attachment to others, as well as significant rewards.

An interest in community is frequently competitive with other interests, so that those who are locally oriented are not all of those one would define as members of the community, but only those whose own rewards in life and whose own status is derived more from the organization of the local community, and who thus have a greater stake in it. These are likely to be less mobile people, and they may be less mobile people because they have less capacity, for one reason or another, to be mobile, or because they have less reason to be mobile. That is, they start out advantaged by the community. The old families, for example, that have both property and status, have a stake in the community. They have less reason to be mobile and more reason to be strongly rooted, and more reason, therefore, to be active participants and to provide some of the local leadership. But this by no means designates all who live in the community, nor all the talent within the community, nor all the capacity for leadership within the community, for some of the talent and leadership may be exercised in organizations and collectivities that reach beyond the community, to wider publics and audiences.

It seems to me that one can never fail to note that in the modern community, the minorities, particularly the Negro, the youth, and the poor, are three categories of people who are sometimes "localites" only because the opportunities to be otherwise are limited, but on the other hand are not integrated into the community in any genuine value-sense. Now these are not three mutually exclusive categories; that, I think, is obvious to you. The minorities, the youth and the poor, as a matter of fact, are somewhat overlapping categories. There are human beings who are all three of these. There are lots of others who are in at least two of these categories. These are significant categories of people in our modern communities, just because they are least touched by the rewards of the status system within the community, just because they have least access to the lines of influence and power within the community, just because they live by values that are perhaps most remote from those whose status and stake make them the natural, advantaged leaders of the community, just because the discontinuities of communication probably exhibit their greatest break between the stable, established leadership of the community and these segments of it. And in all three cases, the people involved are potentially mobilizable, particularly the minorities and the young. They are mobilizable for lines of action that may threaten those who feel they have the strongest stake in the community as it is. They are mobilizable in terms of values, criticism and discontent that may reach beyond a particular community, to be reflected in the sweeping patterns of dissent and protest that run across the country.

The problem of dealing with its least integrated members is not unique to any community. Rather, while the youth find it difficult to communicate with the adult leadership of their own community, they do not find it difficult to communicate with other youth across the whole broad strand of America, and to be involved in communication about social movements, ideals, values, forms of protest, lines of action, bringing youngsters into contact with one another from Maine to California, from North to South. They can talk or they can communicate about values, engage in a meaningful discourse with other youth, when they can't talk across the street to city hall. What this suggests is that there are lots of individuals who do not share in the most dominant values of a community, and as far as I am concerned, this is the most fundamental lesson in understanding community today.

What does attach even the seemingly least attached person to a community? It seems to me the one common denominator that every person who is a member of a community shares is the simple fact of residence. But this means more than the physical fact that your dwelling is located within the boundaries of some community. If that's all it means, then there is no attachment, because there is no reason for attachment. But what common residence more typically means, I think, for adults at least, is a cluster of values about family, home, and children, and about an environment for them. It means a common life style that maintains an aura of congeniality, enabling people to live in some agreement about what makes for a good life. People search for a satisfying basis for residence within a community in terms of these clusters of values. Even the property values that some people invoke when invasion by minorities occurs within their area is not, of course, simply a dollar and cents matter; it is more than that. It is, however mistaken the line of thought, indicative of the terms and conditions under which residence is a symbol for home and family and the raising of children. And thus, it touches upon very deeply held values. This is why the conflict of race and residence is the toughest of the several conflicts about race that a community has to face.

Let me wind up, then, by raising the question that I have touched upon only in passing. What about leadership in this? The quality of leadership in a community that is as fragmented, as segmentalized, as differentiated as the urban community of today becomes a matter of crucial importance. More than that, high social status, long residence in the community, membership in an old family whose grandfather was mayor and whose great-grandfather staked out the boundaries of the community, is no guarantee of effective leadership. It is no guarantee that large numbers of people in the community any longer care what your father or your grandfather was. That may look good in the society pages, for society editors are still concerned with these kinds of things. And there may be small circles in which one is more welcome because of these kinds of status claims, but they are no longer a basis for effective leadership. They no longer integrate the community.

What I am saying is that the integration of a community does not naturally arise any longer out of a common way of life, nor does its leadership come naturally out of those who occupy the positions of high status. Rather, community leadership has to be sought after, and has to be developed. Effective community leadership, for there is such, seems to reside in those who, whatever their positions in the community, or whatever their own kind of social background and set of social experiences, are capable of producing some kind of reasonable political consensus. This is why leadership in the contemporary community is fundamentally *political* leadership. This doesn't necessarily mean seeking political office, though the political offices, it seems to me, become increasingly significant as the forms of effective leadership.

If a community is no longer the kind of value-integrated ideal that it was in the past, which may not have been true anyway, what it is today—if it is a community at all—is politically integrated. This is simply the working out by agreement and compromise of some understandings, not intended to last forever, but simply as of now, for an indefinite period, not only about what the community is, but more importantly, of where the community is going. For the whole difficulty with the conception of the community of the past, the older integrated notion of the community, was that it was a view from the present looking backward, and the only possible sensible view of the community today is from the present looking forward. For every community changes and goes somewhere. It may drift into problems, into chaos, or it may somehow organize what resources it has, what interests it has, what values that are there, even its concerns and anxieties and fears, into some kind of relatively stable, political consensus around which it can move.

This implies, as a corollary, that community leadership needs to carefully cultivate and develop patterns for effective representation in decision making. One of the most significant sociological lessons from an examination of communities of the past, in American life, is in fact, how undemocratic they were, how unrepresented were significant segments of the community. This is no longer viable; it is no longer possible. The political consensus that really makes a locality into a community today requires constant searchings for the means and mechanisms and instrumentalities by which all segments of the population can be effectively represented—not merely symbolically represented—but *effectively* represented. This includes the minorities, and increasingly I think it will require that the poor will be consulted, not merely talked to, as they have been in the past. And, yes, it may even involve youth. For these are the kinds of people that have been left out of representation.

Today, it seems to me, the urban community, if it is a community, can only act on the basis of a political consensus achieved in spite of the fragmentations that characterize its internal life, and the intense pressures and pulls from a larger society around it. It can only act on a political consensus that involves effective representation in decision-making by all those who are in the community. For we no longer live in a day in which there can be sizable numbers of human beings in the community who, for all practical purposes, do not count. We are living through a literal revolution, in which we can all recognize that no longer in any community can one say of Negroes—they don't count. Now they do, and in large part, they count because they insisted on being counted, and every other group in our society, including youth, are going to insist on being counted. Integration is the effective involvement of these people in the achievement of a consensus that enables any community to act in some kind of intelligent fashion, in directing its energies toward action on its numerous problems.

The Police and Minority Groups

Police–citizen interaction is clearly not simply "another human relations problem." There are unique features in the situation, involving—at best—adversary elements. In this general sense, therefore, there is a police–community relations problem, under certain circumstances, inherent in the nature of the social contact. It is often a formidable problem, even when the public is disposed to cooperate with and be sympathetic toward the police.

However, as the President's Commission on Law Enforcement and Administration of Justice points out in its 1967 report (page 99):

> In city slums and ghettos, the very neighborhoods that need and want effective policing the most, the situation is quite different. There is much distrust of the police, especially among boys and young men, among the people the police most often deal with. It is common in those neighborhoods for citizens to fail to report crimes or refuse to cooperate in investigations. Often policemen are sneered at or insulted on the street. Sometimes they are violently assaulted. Indeed, everyday police encounters in such neighborhoods can set off riots, as many police departments have learned.

The Commission goes on to say that the problem that is usually—and politely—referred to as "police–community relations" is overwhelmingly a problem of the relations between the police and the minority-group community — Negroes, Puerto Ricans, Mexican-Americans. The Commission concludes: "It is as serious as any problem the police have today."

The essays in the following section deal with various aspects of police–minority group relations.

A Look at Others: Minority Groups and Police–Community Relations

HAROLD A. LETT

(Then) Assistant Director of the Division Against Discrimination,
New Jersey Department of Education

MAY 28, 1959

During the past three years, it has been my enriching experience and privilege to talk with approximately 3,000 law enforcement officers of state and municipal police forces in my state of New Jersey. They have represented all ranks, from patrolman and highway trooper, to inspector and chief. They have come from the countryside of the farm belt, from the small town and from the large city. Almost without exception, at first, they came with very pronounced suspicions and feelings that any discussion of minority group problems was going to be so much tripe, or some kind of brainwashing experiment to which they would be exposed. However, I think it is safe to say that in every one of the institutes or courses that have been undertaken, most of these officers went away much more thoughtful and questioning, much less suspicious and skeptical, than had been their initial reactions. An explanation could be that they had an opportunity to measure the honesty and sincerity of the presentation in each instance; to question and probe as deeply as they wished; to hold up for examination to themselves their own feelings and opinions; and to apply the yardstick of fairplay which motivates the vast majority of law enforcement officers in the contemplation of their exacting duties. It is within the framework of such factors that objective discussion of the problems of human relations will invariably bring greater understanding.

Basically there are two practical reasons for the promotion of such institutes, and for engaging in this free, searching type of exchange of information and views. First is the short range, immediate, and in some places in the country, almost critical need for attention. The climate created by international tensions and domestic intergroup frictions is making it increasingly necessary that community leadership be sensitive to the subtle manifestations of these tensions, as a means of preventing and controlling disorder and conflict. One of the most feared nightmares of the American community is RIOT — an evil, brutal, costly thing, with longlasting aftermath. It has been proven that it is not a spontaneous phenomenon. Invariably, it is preceded by observable signs, if there be sufficient sensitivity, alertness, understanding and concern through which these signs may be greeted by preventive action. The state of social health in the community is measurable to a degree similar to our ability to diagnose the health of a human being. We are taught, in programs of health protection, to check persistent headaches or other pains, shortness of breath, dizziness, and so forth, if we would prevent more serious manifestations later.

The second basic reason for our presence in such institutes is that of pursuing the quest for knowledge and understanding that will bring law enforcement officers closer to the desirable goal of professional status. This status implies something considerably more than just a job, for which one draws wages for certain hours of directed activity; the term signifies that one's calling is a guarantee of dedicated purpose, of constantly accumulating knowledge, and of a technical proficiency which is possible only through such dedication and accumulation of knowledge.

One of the principal roadblocks to the acquisition of knowledge is the constant temptation to oversimplify, when considering an issue or problem. Particularly is this true when our subject is human nature, one of the most unpredictable and variable elements in creation. In this process of oversimplification, is it not true that many or most of us fall into the habit of dividing the human family into two major groups — "WE," meaning our kind, and "THEY," meaning all others? The "WE" group to which we may refer may be the large, racial group which shares our skin color; or it may be reduced in size and exclusiveness by such limitations as language group, nationality allegiance, religious persuasion, or even occupational choice. "THEY" will fit into any framework which signifies difference or separation from the "WE" group. In the same sense that "WE" share many virtues in common, "THEY" can be identified by the unfavorable qualities attributed to them, which serve to justify the different and separate status to which WE have assigned THEM.

By this process of simplification of a complex situation, our human relations decisions are made easier, and our consciences less troublesome, when entire groups of people can be fitted neatly into simple categories that we refer to as stereotypes. For instance, how many of us unconsciously class Orientals as sly; Mexicans as villainous; Puerto Ricans as dirty and uncontrollable; Negroes as shiftless and sex-crazy; Jews as dishonest; Irish as drunkards; Germans as pig-headed and belligerent; Italians as grafters and racketeers? Are we, as law enforcement officers, inclined to class social workers as fuzzy-minded "do-gooders," and do we resent their frequent characterization of police as thickheaded and brutal? These thoughtless tendencies to create stereotypes in the human family become troublesome when feelings or opinions begin to find expression in our relations with other people. Persons whom we classify as being like ourselves — the "WE" group — will vary in our esteem from those for whom we have deep and abiding affection on the one extreme, to those for whom we have contempt and intense dislike on the other. But we will love or dislike these people as *individuals,* and for what they *personally* have contributed to the relationship. The people whom we have placed in the "THEY" category are judged as a single entity, by the lowest common denominator of our experiences with members of the group, and by the emotional climate existing in our community. This climate, in turn, is influenced by the following six factors, by which the role of a minority in the community is determined:

1. Ease of identification of members of the group enables us to pick them out of the crowd on sight, or through very casual contact. At some one period in our national history, the German, the Irish, the several eastern European groups, and others, were in this easily identified out-group. The loss of an accent in speaking, the shedding of old world habits, dress and customs, or their removal from the ethnic ghetto made it more difficult to identify them as members of the out-group. There are others, of course, like the Negro or Oriental, who retain their badge of identification over many generations.

2. The out-group is defined by the slowness with which it is assimilated in the total population; or, shall we say, the number of years or generations that the group's "difference" persists in the public mind.

3. The minority group's identity is fixed by the degree to which it exists in such numerical strength in a community that they irritate just by constant presence.

4. Their numbers and their demands for recognition place them in position of threatening our notions of our own socially superior status, our prior claim to desirable jobs, and our unchallenged control of political affairs in the community and state.

5. The intensity of our reaction to them can be measured by what may be defined as the emotional history of contact between the respective groups, flowing out of labor strikes, teenage gang outbursts, over-publicized and sensationalized crimes of violence involving minority group members, or even such longer range influences as a carry-over of old world conflicts, and political tragedies like our own Reconstruction period misfortunes.

6. The minority group in our community is marked by the number and kind of rumors which are bandied about, emphasizing the criminality, sexual depravity, or diabolical design upon us, which are supposed to characterize the group under discussion. Rumors of this sort have been known to set off race riots costing many lives.

Any combination of these criteria will disclose the groups in our community who may be classified as "the minorities," and about whom this discussion is centered.

Three persistent questions arise in every discussion of minority group problems with police officers. "Why are_____such oddballs and trouble-makers?" Another: "Why don't they do something to better themselves?" and, "Why do they always cry 'discrimination' whenever they are in trouble?" It is true that these questions are raised by others than police, but rarely as persistently and with as deep feeling. There are at least two reasons for police obsession with these questions, the first of these being the inescapable fact that law enforcement officers spend most of their waking hours dealing with the weak, troublesome, maladjusted, frustrated members of society who, secondly, are represented disproportionately by members of minority groups. Does this disproportion signify an inherent racial or ethnic inferiority? Or is it a product of environment and living experiences? The thoughtless, the intellectually lazy, the emotionally insecure and the misinformed person will insist that it is the former reason; science, and the experience of practitioners in the field of human relations, declare it to be the latter. Open-minded individuals will be curious and fair-minded enough to explore both opinions.

Implicit in the six criteria outlined above, as means of identifying the minorities in our communities, is the demonstrated fact that they are forced to accept different treatment — in their pursuit of education, quest of work, of living quarters, and of recreational outlet. To be denied the right of earning a livelihood for one's family, or to be deprived arbitrarily and capriciously of any of these basic needs, for no other reason than the accident of birth, produces a kind of emotional shock that, in turn, creates a deep, smouldering rage which arises out of blind, helpless frustration. Such emotions are intensified when one's children are made the victims of intolerance, whether at school or at play. But America's easily identified minorities are exposed daily to these experiences, in every section of our great, rich, free country.

For instance, in 1936, in the depths of the depression, when employment on any level was highly competitive, a study was made in New Jersey to determine the degree to which a single minority was numbered among the employed population. In the study of nearly 2,000 businesses in the state, it was found that 55 percent of them were not hiring Negro workers in any capacity, not even in menial jobs. The 45 percent who did hire one or more Negroes, with but few exceptions, confined them to the distasteful and low-paying work assignments. Although representing but 5.5 percent of the state's population, this minority constituted 25 percent of the relief load, costing the state an estimated $28 million per year for subsistence. Since the enactment of the Fair Employment Practices law in this state in 1945, this condition has improved immeasurably, but the agency administering the law can cite some shocking statistics and case histories as to the prevalence of employment discrimination, even in these days of prosperity, high employment and widespread labor organization, nearly a quarter of a century later.

It may be indicative of the seriousness of discriminatory practices when I tell you that in 1958, 38 percent of all employment complaints brought to the Division against Discrimination in New Jersey were found to be justified complaints — that is, that 38 of every 100 situations reported exposed employers and union officials who were permitting their prejudices against identifiable minority group persons to deprive those persons of the basic right to earn a livelihood. Records also disclose that 82 of every 100 complaints made against restaurants, taverns, bowling alleys, skating rinks, etc., were actual incidents in which the accident of birth was considered cause enough to deprive the individual of citizenship rights. In public schools and in all levels of housing, hundreds of thousands of American citizens are being exposed to the humiliating and maddening experience of being turned away because of what others consider to be their stupidity in choosing the kind of parents they did. To several of America's easily identified minorities, such embarrassments accompany them from their first play experiences in early childhood, to the final act of interment in the cemetery burial plot.

Constant exposure to such experience develops in many members of minority groups a lack of assurance, an uncertainty, suspicion, anxiety, anger. Nerve ends become hypersensitive; emotional scars are inflicted upon personality. The American Youth Commission was responsible, in the early forties, for a series of studies bearing upon these reactions. The reports entitled *Color, Class and Personality* by Warner, Junker and Adams*, and *Color and Human Nature* by Sutherland* were among the first serious attempts to measure the effect of such experience. More recently, two psychiatrists, Drs. Kardiner and Ovesey, have published their significant analyses of case histories in their book, *The Mark of Oppression*†.

These studies, and long observations of human relations practitioners, disclose an incidence of certain natural and to-be-expected reactions and attitudes of otherwise normal human beings, who are responding to abnormal experiences and situations to which they are exposed. The crippled, the maimed and the blind undergo many of the same experiences with discrimination, and manifest many of the same reactions, despite the growing concern of society that these minorities be given protection from the painful effects of discrimination. It is likewise true, of the maimed and the blind, as of the ethnic and racial minorities, that perhaps a majority of the group is able to muster reserve strength and an inner sense of security, with which to offset the negative influences. These are able to adjust to conditions, no matter what amount of repression or restraint they must apply to their every thought and action.

To the many who are unable to adjust to these experiences, however, other choices in the process of accommodating oneself to the restrictions society imposes become necessary. The choice may be made quite early in life; it usually is done without conscious effort; it frequently is determined by one's temperament, station in life and the nature of the experiences encountered.

One, therefore, finds himself (1) consciously and studiously *adjusting* to the condition over which he feels he has no control, by the exercise of great self-discipline; or (2) he *submits* to the role in which society has cast him, even though it may mean the sacrifice of his individuality, his incentive, and his ambition; or, (3) he *resists* in one of the several forms which his temperament

---

  * Published by The American Council on Education, Wash. D.C., 1942.
  † Published by W. W. Norton, New York, 1951.

may dictate. The task of adjusting, without relinquishing anything of one's self-respect, is a difficult one, but it is accomplished by many. Despite the complete absence of statistics on the subject, it is my belief that this group, which finds it possible to adjust, constitutes and has constituted the majority of all the minority groups of the past.

But it is impractical to expect that all of the people of any particular group are able to control their emotions and inhibit their actions in times of stress. They who are neither so strong nor self-sufficient will choose to submit to or to resist the influences and pressures to which they are exposed. They who submit take the line of least resistance. They conclude that to oppose is useless; that to yield to the stronger force and the louder voice is the surest way to biological survival. Their submission cannot be partial or temporary; at least, not for long. The act of submission has an eroding effect upon that which is the substance of man's spirit. First, he acts as a matter of expediency; then, again and again, until self-respect has vanished. With this lost self-respect goes his human aspirations, his ambitions and incentives, leaving him only empty hopes and dreams, and the contempt of his contemporaries. Such a person is pointed out by the majority group as the spiritless, ambitionless example of the basic inferiority of the entire group this individual is perceived as representing. In the Negro world, this is the character referred to contemptuously as "Uncle Tom."

The third choice is found in a response to the urge to *resist*. Again, the choice is not consciously made through the process of reasoning; it represents an emotional reaction of the individual, guided by his particular temperament. His glands make the choice for him, but he is as completely committed as though his mental processes were involved. His intellectual capacity, his physical agility or his manual dexterity may help him find gratification, through his response to the urge to excel. His motivations might find expression in such unconscious urgings as, "Study intensively, work industriously, run faster, hit harder; be better than anybody. Prove that you are as good as *they,* if not better. Achieve! Succeed! If you cannot do these things through healthy, constructive channels, show them anyhow by the kind of symbols of success you can accumulate! Make big money, no matter how! Buy a big house, if they'll let you. Own a big car, flashy clothes, fine furs and jewels. Show them — show them you can do anything they can do!" This admittedly is an unhealthy, impractical kind of demonstration — but remember, their glands, their emotions, are making the choice for them, and the choice is being implemented within the limits of their intellectual, physical and spiritual capacities.

Then, there are those who have learned to fear humiliation and insult — they seek to escape contact. These set up physical and psychological barriers between themselves and that part of the world they fear. These are the scholars hidden in their ivory towers, and the so-called "race leaders," who bury themselves in the ghetto, avoiding contact outside as much as possible. Within their insular, protected cubicle, they may make constructive, though limited, contributions toward the rebuilding of the self-esteem of members of their race group, but too frequently, also, they are spreading the contagion of racial fear, suspicion and further estrangement. Among these refugees are found the many religious and social cultists. Primitive religion provides the illusion of escape into "other-worldliness." Zoot-suitism and bebop-ism are other cults arising out of the peculiar needs of those wishing to escape from a threatening social order. Members of these latter groups evolve their peculiar standards, their codes of ethics, their mannerisms, their uniform or dress conformity, even their language symbols. "When you cats can't dig their jive, like a square from nowhere," exclusiveness has been established — *they* belong to something beyond *your* reach. These cults have their roots in the minority groups of our cities, even though — more recently — other types of social refugees, e.g., the Beat Generation, have appropriated most of the cult symbols to their own use.

Finally, there are those whose choice has been a response to the basic, direct urge to resist. Our civilization today — the freedoms we of the Western world enjoy — are the gift of countless generations of dissatisfied persons who elected to resist the forces with which they were dissatisfied. These were and are the rebels, the dissenters, the challengers of all ages. Their value to society depended upon whether their intellect controlled their emotions to the degree that their spirit of revolt could be harnessed constructively. Intelligent, organized, consistent revolt has marked man's every step upward toward the sun, and the original rebels in every culture were the social, economic, religious or political minorities of the day. When they have been successful in the waging of their revolt, history has recorded them as patriots and heroes.

So today, the acid test of the American concepts of democracy and of individual freedom is whether or not the racial and ethnic minorities of the country may effectively defend themselves from exploitation and unfair treatment at the hands of the majority. Through such instruments of organized resistance as the National Association for the Advancement of Colored People (NAACP), each thread of the American mantle of freedom is being tested for its strength and durability, in all kinds of times and circumstances. Through a repetition of these tests, the warp and woof of our system of government is being strengthened. This then is the contribution of minorities whose spirit of rebellion is being harnessed and intelligently directed, within the framework of Western law and culture patterns. However, it is the great number of rebels in the minority group world who have neither restraint, self-discipline nor intelligent direction, who are the police "clients" and constant headaches, and who may help you form a distorted opinion of entire groups of people because of the constant one-sided exposure. These are the people whose frustration and rage bring the primitive response of resisting — directly, impulsively, angrily, blindly, in what they feel is a retaliatory vein.

First of all is the impulse to reject largely or completely the ethics, morals, rules and laws by which the majority presumes to guide its conduct. Whereas in the larger world, conformity is an expression of effective social control, nonconformity, to them, becomes a guiding principle. If quiet speech is the mark of a gentleman, then they show contempt by speaking loudly; if politeness and courtesy are desirable traits, then they have a compulsion to be crude and rude. In such manner do they show their displeasure with their lot — express their rejection of those who have rejected them. Cynicism becomes a way of life, starting with teenagers, because terms like "belief" and "faith" are illusions, and luxuries in which only the strong may indulge. Excessive drinking, gambling and fighting provide momentary release from the frustration and rage which consume them, and their unfortunate encounters with officers of the law cause them to look upon police as oppressors and enemies.

These are manifestations to be observed in the minority group world, to a disproportionate degree. To submit or to resist — and in the course of adopting one of the substitutes for the basic human desire for belongingness — to excel, to repel or to rebel. As stated before and repeated here for emphasis, these are the *natural* expressions of otherwise *normal* people, who have yielded to the impact of *abnormal* conditions and situations. These, too, are the manifestations which are singled out by the critic of the minority, as things representing racial or ethnic characteristics — signs of the supposed innate difference or inferiority of the minority in question.

The picture of law enforcement in minority group communities has not been a pleasant one. We have seen repeatedly the beginning and the perpetuating of a vicious cycle where minority group expressions such as we have reviewed have been misread and misinterpreted by police officials, whose summary and oftentimes impatient treatment of the group members has deepened and broadened their suspicions, fear and hostility; this in turn, bringing even sterner police measures. Intelligence, reason, training and logic are not exhibited in such situations. Confidence is the element so sadly needed, if the cycle ever is to be reversed, and a practical and effective law enforcement procedure be employed. It is we who have the leadership responsibility to seek the establishment of confidence, and the specialists' knowledge with which to meet the challenge. This specialists' knowledge must be a demonstrated, tested knowledge, rather than the beliefs and opinions which come through rumor and the blind acceptance of ill-founded customs and practices. The general public is constantly reminded that ignorance of the law is no excuse, when the law enforcement officer apprehends a naive violator. With equal emphasis it may be said, with respect to the statistical predictability of human reaction, that ignorance of these laws of human behavior is no excuse for the officer who would wish to achieve professional status.

Law enforcement procedures in today's tense world require a knowledge and a sensitivity that permits a feeling of the community pulse; that bestows the ability to note signs of majority group acts of aggression which are sure to invite reprisal; that provides an awareness of minority group motivations and temper. It is this kind of sensitivity that makes it possible for police to assess the meaning of small and isolated incidents which indicate underlying tensions, any one of which may trigger the big explosion. In truth, broader human relations understanding is an assurance of more effective law enforcement in the American community.

Understanding Minority Groups

JOHN A. BUGGS

(Then) Executive Director, Los Angeles County Commission on Human Relations

MAY 18, 1965

I suppose that for most of the geographical areas of our country, understanding minority groups means understanding the Negro. This is not universally true; there is, of course, the Southwest and the West, for a part of this problem, also, is in connection with the Mexican-American or the Spanish-speaking, and in other great metropolitan centers, there are other groups that are equally important in terms of this understanding process—in New York, Puerto Ricans, for example. And there are other minorities that also have problems, but our concern, I suspect, is mainly with those groups that we conceive as being a threat to the established and traditional relations between the subordinate and dominant groups in our society, or who in other ways contribute an element, or constitute an element in the community, that causes some concern at some period in time.

Our discussion will mainly be about Negroes, and I suppose the reason is fairly obvious — I've been one for so long. Someone said yesterday, borrowing from James Baldwin, that "it is difficult, if not impossible, to understand the feelings of other persons of whom one is not a part." I think there is a great deal of truth in this. That is, perhaps, one of the reasons that I shall confine myself to the Negro, for the most part.

While in Los Angeles we have a great deal of involvement with the Mexican-American community, I certainly lay no claim to being a part of the feeling process that goes on in the minds and the hearts of those individuals who are Mexican-American. But I do claim this so far as the Negro is concerned. So it's *feeling,* I think, that is part of understanding, and it is my hope that I may be able in some way to impart some of the feeling out of which there might be the development of an understanding — a real depth of understanding with respect to this whole matter, as it relates primarily to the Negro community throughout the United States.

I think there is no possibility of understanding the Negro, or any other minority group, unless we are aware of at least three things. First, the forces in our historical background, and by "our" I mean all of us, not just the Negro, but the totality of the American community — the forces in our historical background that have been responsible for creating the minority-group status of the Negro in this country; secondly, the impact that American ideals and principles have, and are at present having, on the Negro as he assesses his position in the body politic; and thirdly, an understanding that his actions are, in effect, a reaction to what he believes to be society's conception of him, whether the conception is a real one or an imagined one.

Let us provide a little historical perspective to the position in which we find ourselves today as a nation, *vis-à-vis* the Negro as a part of the community in which we live and in which we operate. These historical forces, as perhaps we will recall from American history, began in 1619, because that was the first date when the Negro set foot upon this new land, and this was, as you may recall, one year prior to the docking of the Mayflower at Plymouth Rock. So he's been here a long time. And he came, as we will again recall, not as a slave but as an indentured servant — as did many people during those early years, not just Negroes.

The important thing to remember and to reflect upon, however, is that some 41 years after 1619, the institution of slavery did develop in this nation, and perhaps the great and unsolved (to some extent) mystery about the advent of that institution was the fact that it could have been established at all. When we recognize the fact that many of the individuals who came here during those early years came for a definite set of principles that involved freedom and liberty and equality — values that they did not have in the countries from which they migrated, and that they traversed 3,000 miles of dangerous and unknown ocean in order to secure these values, it seems something of a dichotomy that they could have — almost at the same time they were searching out these values and creating these values for themselves — also participated in the development of an institution that was the antithesis of the very thing for which they had fought so hard. This, of course, was not universally true. The state from which I come, Georgia, was settled, we all know, by English prisoners, and they certainly did not come looking for freedom. I suppose they hoped to secure it in some way or another, but this was not the driving force initially.

But throughout the early years of our development, there was always, deep in the hearts and in the minds of the persons who were being shaped as Americans, the necessity for the evolving of a free society. There are certain points in American history in which this became much more evident than at other periods.

Who among us could not quote from the beginning of our Declaration of Independence, "We hold these truths to be self-evident; that all men are created equal and are endowed by their Creator with certain inalienable rights, among which are life, liberty and the pursuit of happiness." Thomas Jefferson wrote this, as we all know, and he also wrote something else that never got into the Declaration of Independence in its final form. It was something of a castigation of the King of England for having forced upon the people of these colonies the despicable institution of slavery. This was taken out of the final draft, and seventeen of the signers of the Declaration of Independence were slaveholders at the time they signed it. These were honorable men, men of integrity and men who honestly believed in the principles for which they were about to fight and die.

One tends to wonder what went through their minds as they read those words in the Declaration of Independence, and as they, perhaps, reflected on the fact that they were not living up to, in practice, the principles to which they were ascribing their names and their honor. There was actually not so much of a dichotomy in their thinking as we might suppose; there was not so much of a dilemma as we might believe, with respect to these two widely separated positions that they held. One of the most interesting indications of the process by which men were able to sign their names to that Declaration — to say one thing and to practice something else — might also be discovered in another one of our ancient documents — the Constitution. I don't know how many of you recall what the first article of our Constitution is all about, but it sets forth the manner in which the several states were to be represented in the national Congress. At the Constitutional Convention in Philadelphia, they got "hung-up" on that first article.

The first article set forth the manner in which representation was to be had, and it stated that there was to be one representative in the House of Representatives for every 30,000 people in the population of each of the several states. Immediately a controversy arose as to who was going to be counted for the purpose of that representation. The delegates from the South that had become by that time the agricultural part of our nation wanted as much power in the national Congress as they could get, and they insisted that Negro slaves be counted for the purpose of representation. The delegates from the North objected. They said, in effect, "you've always taken the position that slaves were property, not really people, and that they were property in the sense that any other chattel was property, things to be bought and sold, and you can't, with consistency, expect that they should be counted as people. They should be counted for the purpose of taxation," the argument went on, "as property. But not for the purpose of representation in Congress as people." So a compromise was effected (compromises have always been effected on this problem), and the compromise was that Negroes would be counted both for the purpose of property and for the purpose of representation as people, but that each such individual should be counted as three-fifths of a person. This was the way our Constitution stood until that part of it was, in a sense, outlawed by the 14th Amendment in 1868.

Now this dichotomy on the one hand — the belief in, fighting for, dying for and creating a free society — and on the other hand, the negation of these very principles through participation and development of the institution of slavery, was made possible by what had started relatively early in our country, which might best be described as a "plurality-of-humanity" theory. It was a necessary rationalization, in those days; one would have been schizophrenic if he had been required to believe in the principles of freedom and equality and in the tenets of his religious faith on one hand, and on the other hand, to believe in and to subscribe to the holding in bondage of persons who were as human as he. These two things just couldn't live together. Some rationalization had to be found for it. The rationalization was in the fact, in the assumption, that there were two kinds of human beings: one kind that would be 100 percent human, and they could always be distinguished by the lightness of their skin; and another kind that was perhaps a little less than human, say 60 percent, or three-fifths, and they could always be distinguished by the darkness of their skin.

Slavery in the United States, therefore, took on quite a different aspect than it had, historically, in other places and at other times in our history and in the history of the world. Whereas it originally began in this country as an economic institution, it became much more of a social institution than it was an economic institution.

I would highly recommend for your reading a book written by Milton Konvitz and Theodore Leskes titled A CENTURY OF CIVIL RIGHTS, in which the authors discuss the character of slavery in the United States. I think it has great relevance to the fact that one of the overriding problems that we face in this country today grows out of the character that the institution of slavery took in the later years of its existence. Konvitz and Leskes say that whenever in history slavery has existed, it has always been considered an economic institution; as the result of war or the consequence of extreme poverty, anyone might become a slave. The Israelites in the Promised Land did not consider it a badge of shame that their forefathers had been slaves. On the contrary, they were commanded to hold ever in their consciousness, not only the fact that they had been led out of bondage in Egypt, but also, and with equal importance, that before the exodus, they had been slaves. Slavery served as a bond to humanity in general, because at one time or another, almost every people had been held in bondage. But in our own country, it was different. Calhoun held in 1837 that the maintenance of the existing relations between the races was indispensable to the peace and happiness of the races in the South. And it was believed and maintained that since slavery had come with the Negro, it was a question of race which could not be solved by emancipation. On the contrary, the argument went, slavery had to be continued, for since Negroes were unfit for freedom among whites, slavery was the only reasonable and workable solution, not to the economic problem but to the race problem.

Basic to the concept of slavery in our country, with some exceptions of course, was the firm conviction that the Negro belonged to another and inferior species of humanity. It was claimed that there was scientific and Biblical proof for a plurality-of-humanity theory; that humanity was made up of distinct species that originated from different original pairs of men and women. And it was thought that the Negro was not a man in the same sense that a white individual was a man. He might even be said to be a strong "animal-machine." He was sub-human, not because he was a slave, but rather he was a slave because he was sub-human.

America has always placed a great deal of store in its judiciary, and if the *coup de grace* was ever given to any concept of the basic and inherent equality of humanity in general, it was given in the judicial decision handed down by the highest tribunal in our land in the Dred Scott case in 1857. You may recall what that decision was. It set the stage, so to speak, not only for the hardening and crystallization of the concept throughout this nation with respect to the place and the function of the Negro in the body politic for a long period of time, but it placed the stamp of approval on the attitudes that had been held toward that segment of our population for generations past. That case involved the claim of a Negro that he was a free man because he had left the South and gone into free territory, and then had returned to the South. In effect, it was a test of several laws that had been passed by the Congress during that period — the Fugitive Slave Act, Kansas–Nebraska Bill, the Missouri Compromise — all of these things were tied up in that decision, in some degree. The Supreme Court held that Negroes, slave or free, could not sue in the courts of the United States.

"In the Constitutional sense," said the Chief Justice, "Negroes, even if free, are not a part of 'the people of the United States.' And even when free," he said, "they had for more than a century, before the adoption of the Constitution, been regarded as beings of an inferior race, and altogether unfit to associate with the white race, either in social or political relations, and so far inferior that they had no rights which the white man was bound to respect." Thus, the Negro might justly and lawfully be reduced to slavery for the white man's benefit. "Whether slave or free," the Court continued, "Negroes were subject to the authority of white persons and had no rights or privileges but such as those who held the power might choose to grant them."

By this time, the process of dehumanization was practically complete, and as we look back upon those days, it was not difficult to convince the American people of the basic and inherent inferiority of the Negro, or even to convince the Negro this "fact." We only need to recall that it took Adolph Hitler a little less than five years to take one of the most highly civilized, cultivated, progressive nations on earth — a nation that for many, many years had been almost at the top rung of the ladder in what we are pleased to call the evidences of civilization — technological achievement, cultural achievement — and through the process of constant repetition, convince at least a working minority of the German people that there were two classes of humanity. The Aryans were the superior brand of that humanity, and the Jews were the inferior brand, and to convince them of this fact to the extent that they permitted the atrocities to occur in that land that subsequently did occur.

If it could happen there, in such a short period of time, is it any wonder that over a period of almost 300 years, it was possible to convince Negroes of their inherent inferiority, and to convince Caucasians of their superiority?

But 1863 came, and there was Lincoln's Emancipation Proclamation, which was a war measure. And Wendell Phillips, one of the great abolitionists of that period, who worked with William Lloyd Garrison, said something that was true then, and to some extent is true now, about the Emancipation Proclamation. He said that it freed the slaves, but it ignored the Negro. There was a great difference in freeing the slaves and in freeing the people who were slaves, because the Emancipation Proclamation in no way conferred upon the Negro any of the advantages, privileges and responsibilities of being men in a free, democratic society. The interesting thing, however, is that the Negro *thought* it did. It didn't take very long for him to recognize what really had happened, because in 1865, just two years after the Emancipation, he received a rude awakening, and that rude awakening was in connection with the adoption of the Black Codes in most of the states of the South. The answer to the Black Codes of 1865 was the passage of the Fourteenth and Fifteenth Amendments, and the Civil Rights Act of 1875, which was declared unconstitutional in 1883. If you read the Civil Rights Act of 1875, it is startlingly similar to the Civil Rights Act of 1964. From almost the beginning, of course, many slaves rebelled against bondage. Those who could not accept the plurality-of-humanity theory always existed, and they shared with other Americans the desire to see created in this land an example of a free society that could challenge the rest of the world. They were not unaware of the "freedom-seeking" immigrants who, in an ever increasing stream, were coming to this new land. They saw other men from other lands given the opportunity to become a part of the mainstream of American life. This challenged them and still challenges them to be in that mainstream. There were always leaders of one kind or another who propelled Negroes on, both in terms of thought and action, to the attainment of that goal. Men like Frederick Douglass, Booker Washington, Marcus Garvey in the early twenties, and many others, who in their own way attempted to provide a way for Negroes to become accepted as human beings and as a part of the mainstream. But attitudes developed over a period of more than 240 years are difficult to change.

From 1863 to 1925, the prevailing attitude encompassed in the plurality-of-humanity theory did not materially change. I say until 1925, because if any of us, up to 1925, had wanted to find out what a Negro was, the book we might first have turned to for a definition would have been the ENCYCLOPEDIA BRITANNICA. This is what one would have found in the ENCYCLOPEDIA BRITANNICA, up to 1925, as it defined the Negro:

> In certain of the characteristics mentioned above, the Negro would appear to stand on a lower evolutionary plane than the white man and to be more closely related to the highest anthropoids. The characteristics that demonstrate . . . this are: the length of his arm, the prognathism of the forward projection of his jaw, a heavy, massive cranium with large zygomatic arches, flat nose, depressed base, etc. . . . Mentally the Negro is inferior to the white. Upon viewing them, Negro children appeared to be sharp, intelligent and full of vivacity, but upon approaching the adult period, a gradual change set in. The intellect seemed to become clouded, animation giving place to a sort of lethargy, briskness yielding to indolence. We must necessarily suppose that the development of the Negro and the white proceeds along different lines. . . . While with the

latter, the volume of the brain grows with the expansion of the brain pan, in the former the growth of the brain is, on the contrary, arrested by the premature closing of the cranial sutures and the lateral pressure of the frontal bone.

How were people to get any different concept of the Negro when every index that could be applied to the Negro in our society, to some extent, tended to document precisely what the ENCYCLOPEDIA BRITANNICA said. If one looked at the Negro in terms of his economic status, he was at the bottom; if one looked at his educational achievement, he was at the bottom; if one looked at the character of the housing that he inhabited, he was at the bottom. By every index that one could apply, he was at the bottom. And so we used the effects of segregation and discrimination as the argument for continuing the system.

For many years, therefore, the prevailing mood in the Negro community was that of frustration, and until 1935, no element of government had attempted to implement the promises of citizenship as a means of eliminating the frustration that did exist.

By 1960, Negroes were even more of an urban population than was true of the general population. Sixty-nine percent of all the population of this country in 1960 lived in urban places. Seventy-three percent of Negroes lived in urban places in 1960. But as they moved into these urban places, Negroes found that the city itself had an effect upon them and upon their attitudes and upon their mode of living. I think it is sufficient to say that the city never proved to be, to the Negro (or to other visible minorities), what it had been to the earlier stream of immigrants from Europe. The city, according to Charles Silberman, has always served as the "incubator" of a new middle class. But it did not do this and is still not doing this so far as the Negro is concerned. What we have seen developing in cities throughout our nation, particularly the large northern and western cities, has been a constant growth in the pattern of segregation and ghettoization.

Segregation in the great northern centers has, therefore, become a barrier to communication and a constant vehicle for the re-enforcement of the old stereotypes and old antipathies, by both Negro and white. These antipathies and these prejudices exist with both Negro and white. Negroes are just as prejudiced as anybody else. I have seen Jews who are anti-Semitic; Mexican-Americans who wouldn't be caught dead living next to a Negro; Orientals who find it difficult to communicate with other than Orientals because of the prejudices they hold; and there are Negroes who are anti-Negro! There are some people who are like the cartoon in the NEW YORKER magazine some time ago, showing the picture of a man standing in the middle of the street, wildly waving his hands above his head and shouting, "I hate everybody, regardless of race, color, or creed!"

However, since World War II, America has given more and more voice to its commitment, to what Gunnar Myrdal called "American ideals and principles," and Negroes and other minorities have come, not only to believe that this means them, too, but have given voice and meaning to that belief in an attempt to procure for themselves and their posterity the full meaning of those ideals and those principles.

Here, I suppose, is the point at which my earlier statements with respect to my mixed feelings comes into play, as I talk with police officers. Perhaps more than any other segment of the total body politic, the Negro—and particularly the Southern Negro, as I am—comes to view the police as the symbol of almost all his ills. He views them this way because the policeman is a symbol of the com-

munity's method of control. He is the symbol by which the community imple-
ments what Burtram Doyle, a long time ago, called "the etiquette of race relations." He is the symbol of the community's attempt to re-enforce the *status quo*.
And all of his past experiences as a person, and the vicarious experiences that he
has had as a member of a minority group, come into play whenever the Negro
sees a blue uniform, regardless of where he lives — North, East, South or West.

I can never forget the Sunday morning when I was eleven years old in Brunswick, Georgia, walking through the park after Sunday School with three of my
schoolmates, and sitting down in Brunswick's only park, only to be told by the
man in the blue uniform, with the gun on his hip, that "niggers don't sit in the
public parks." Like every little good Negro, I got up and walked out with my
friends. But as I did so, I stopped by a beautiful artesian fountain that was bub-
bling cool water for a drink, and I can still (psychologically) feel the lick that I
got on my fanny with the policeman's baton as he impressed on me, once and
for all, the fact that Negroes don't drink at a public fountain. I moved to Los
Angeles fifteen years ago, after I was grown and married and had children, and
it took me five years to drink from a public fountain without having the adrenalin
drain into my bloodstream as a means of getting ready for some kind of confrontation which I fully expected emotionally, although I knew intellectually it
wouldn't happen.

It takes a great deal to get over the emotions built up over a period of more
than thirty years by intellectualizing about it. And all it takes in a Harlem, or at
103rd Street and Central Avenue in Los Angeles, or in any of the Negro communities in any of the cities of the nation, is for one police officer—in circumven-
tion of the policies and the principles of his department—such as is true in Los
Angeles occasionally—to say or to do something that reminds the Negro of the
man in blue back home, and all of those antipathies and antagonisms are again
directed toward the police as an institution, and as the instrument of law enforcement. Even though he supports the institution of law enforcement, the Negro sees
in it also a symbol of the control that has historically been exercised over him.

Someone has indicated that there is a sort of cognitive awareness on the part
of the police in Harlem that violence might emanate from a youngster with a
black jacket. There is that same kind of cognitive awareness on the part of the
Negro as he looks at the police, and looks upon him as a threat, an agent of the
process by which the community constantly exercises its control over him.

I suppose that what we are most concerned about is: how do we resolve these
problems between minority groups and the body politic—the rest of the body
politic? There is one reason for wanting to understand minority group people,
that is, in order to determine how best we might resolve the problems that exist
between the minority and the majority.

I think that one of the things that we must recognize in these days is that there
is a particular and peculiar role that Negro leadership must play. Most of the
Negro leadership would like to see progress toward American ideals and principles
without conflict. But if the Negro leader is going to do this, he's got to retain his
reins of leadership, and to do this, he needs help from the white power structure
in the community. Whatever the mood of the Negro today, as he attempts to exercise that role of leadership, it is partially fashioned by what the average Negro
conceives to be the mood of white America toward him. The process of change
is often a difficult one, fraught with tension, and tension is always an ingredient

of social change. But it need not degenerate into conflict and violence, if there is communication and understanding, and if we look upon communication and understanding as a necessary ingredient to change, without which conflict and violence are perhaps the only alternatives.

There is, therefore, a role of the power structure and there is the role of the police authority in effecting change. This role might best be illustrated by recognizing the fact that there is an inherent need in man to conform, and Americans, whether we like to admit it or not, are basically conformists. We like to conform to the standards of behavior the community has set for us. Gordon and Roche have suggested that there are four kinds of people in the United States, with respect to this matter of racial problems: (1) those who might be classified as the all-weather liberals—the people who are way out on the far extreme, and who in all cases and in all places will make their positions known, who believe in the implementation of American principles and American ideals, and who will always say this, some-times with vociferous, loud voices; (2) on the other end of the continuum, there are the all-weather illiberals—the Gerald L. K. Smiths, the Ku Klux Klanners, and the illiberals in the Negro community—the Black Muslims, for example, who will take a position, sometimes in total opposition to any of the concepts we hold when we talk about integration. But these two groups are exceedingly small, and in the middle is represented the vast number of Americans—98 percent who are the (3) fair-weather liberals, or the (4) fair-weather illiberals, and they are the individuals who are the conformists. They will take a position in support of al-most any proposition, if they feel that this is the prevailing standard that the community has set for them. It is the responsibility of the community power structure and the community leadership (and the police are a part of that struc-ture and that leadership), to set these standards of behavior in terms of their own conduct and their own attitudes, if the community is going to conform to such standards of behavior.

I have often heard it said, and I have lamented when I have heard it, that it is not important for the police not to be prejudiced, it is only important that they do not exercise that prejudice in the performance of their duties. I don't think that this is a good philosophy on which to operate. I think that the whole movement, not only with respect to police but to the majority as well as to the minority groups in our society, is the re-creation of society in which each man can be thought of as a part-and-parcel of that society regardless of his race, his religion or his national background. And if we're going to create that society, we are going to do it only when we create a different set of attitudes. It is im-portant what a man *thinks* and *feels*, just as it is important how he behaves.

Stewart Alsop and Oliver Quale, the public opinion expert, reported last year in THE SATURDAY EVENING POST, that the white North is no more ready to accept genuine integration and real racial equality than the deep South. They concluded that for the moment, there is simply no way to reconcile the aspirations of the new generation of Negroes for real integration and true equality, with the resistance to these aspirations by the majority of whites. I believe that this attitude, this mood on the part of white America, constitutes the real problem for all of us today. For what Negroes accept as the solution of their problem is not quite as important as what white America is willing to accept as a solution of its prob-lem. I feel that the solution must be in the constant and ever-increasing tempo of the challenges that all of us, Negro and white alike, make on the barriers that separate us. But I also believe that with dedicated men in the forefront, and the police an important part of that vanguard, any good and true concept can be sold to America.

Our problem at the moment is how to sell those who do the selling to America, and how to do it quickly enough to avoid the fire that James Baldwin talks about and seems so fearful of. In the world in which we are living today, racial bigotry and hatred is folly.

Rousseau wrote in the 18th century, "provided a man is not mad, he can be cured of every folly, save vanity." Rousseau was probably right—that is, of course, unless we all be mad.

Los Angeles: A Case Study

NOEL A. McQUOWN

(Then) Inspector, Assistant Commander, Patrol Bureau,
Los Angeles Police Department

MAY 15, 1956

I would like briefly to analyze the setting in which this case developed. You are well aware that Los Angeles is not a model city. Although it has achieved remarkable success in building intergroup tranquility, it has its intolerant citizens, its incidents of conflict. Beginning with World War II, the nation's westward population migration brought to Los Angeles an increasing number of Negro residents. As in other areas, this has caused some community tensions, as competition for homes and jobs became more acute.

In the southeast sector of Los Angeles, at one particular Junior High School, as late as 1948, the great majority of the students were white. By the fall semester of 1952, this situation had been reversed.

You are well aware of the typical progression of events from there. Briefly stated, changes in neighborhood racial composition brought out latent prejudices which were quickly communicated to the children. Community tensions were intensified. Students engaged in fisticuffs with other students, on and near school grounds. Students and non-students from other areas were found loitering nearby and became involved in incidents of discrimination. The racial lines became clearly defined during these incidents.

The school officials worked very closely with the Police Department. Everything that could be done by the school authorities to prevent disorder was undertaken. The Police Department was aware of the situation and worked closely with community agencies, and action was taken in every incident where there was a violation of the law.

At this point, the problem had not reached a critical point. It was the first simmering of a large pot which could some day boil over. The incidents at this time were similar to the fights that normally occur between students. There was, however, a major difference. Here, there was a definite split between the antagonists on a racial basis.

During the balance of the year, the situation was contained, but a serious potential remained. Radio cars in the area were alerted to intensify patrol around the school, particularly during the hours when classes were dismissed. Juvenile investigators and detectives were alerted and efforts continued to prosecute those who violated the law. The situation might have been contained at this point except for a number of unfortunate incidents.

At about this time, a racial problem developed in an adjoining city. A number of Negro families purchased homes in a formerly all white neighborhood. From this, several near riots developed. The community press and the press of neighboring cities carried many stories on that situation.

A second factor was that an emotionally disturbed boy recently released from an institution was enrolled at the school. During his first two days in school, he was involved in three fights with other students as a result of actual or imaginary racial slurs.

Finally, in an unfortunate accident in the nearby railroad yards, a Negro student from this school was accidentally killed by a freight train. Almost immediately, a rumor developed that this student had been pushed under the train by a white student. This false rumor was believed and passed rapidly through the community. Other rumors spread, new incidents of conflict occurred, leading to still more rumors. The older rumors, nearly forgotten, were recalled and intensified. Other schools in the area were soon rife with wild stories of gang activity, organized fights and retaliatory raids. Solicitations were made to form groups, to gather and do battle.

I think you are aware that the problem was about 95 percent conversation and rumors at this state. But the critical point had been reached. Fantasy was about to be transformed into fact.

The Captain of the concerned Police Division immediately called a meeting which I, as the Area Commander, attended. Here all the facts and rumors were discussed. It was apparent that neither the normal nor intensified patrol could contain the situation. It was also agreed that the problem was not solely that of the police, but of the entire community. However, it was evident that the non-law enforcement groups and organizations would not be able to cope with the situation which could rapidly become a problem in mass disorder.

Following this meeting, I immediately contacted the County Conference on Community Relations and gave their representative a complete story of what had occurred and the potential danger. I requested that their full resources be applied in the area.

They were informed that intensive policing activity had commenced, and that we would hold the situation until they could organize community groups to successfully combat existing tensions. They agreed that although they had for some time been working in the area, the latest developments required an immediate intensification of effort.

Junior High School authorities readily agreed to a staggering of classes so that the entire student body was not released at the same time. Five radio cars were assigned to the immediate area on a full-time basis. As each class was dismissed, they were escorted as far as necessary from the school. This was done for two reasons: (1) that they would not be assaulted by other groups and (2) that they would not form into groups for gang activity themselves.

The radio cars then returned to the school to repeat this activity for each succeeding dismissal of classes.

One team of Juvenile Investigators, who had handled most of the cases resulting from earlier conflicts in the area, was assigned to a full-time task of gathering all information available. They compiled a list of the leaders of the recurring incidents and developed comprehensive dossiers of youth and groups involved.

The problem was discussed at police supervisory meetings and Juvenile Investigators' meetings so that all field personnel would be aware of the situation, the method of handling and the type of occurrences and incidents to watch for, in order to prevent the situation from spreading to other schools.

One of the ways in which this contagion was localized was to list students from other schools who had been observed in the area of tension. Authorities at those schools were contacted and brought into the picture. Principals held locker inspections and removed several baskets of weapons from student lockers. Included were illegal knives, lengths of chain, clubs, sharpened beer can openers, and other weapons. Each student was called in to explain his possession of the weapon and in some instances, due to the nature of the weapon, the parents were also called in for a further discussion at the school.

The Juvenile Officers assigned worked as an intelligence unit. They were very effective in tracing back rumors to their source and locating key persons who were prominent in these incidents. These officers also met with various professional workers in the area, other law enforcement agencies, and referral agencies. Information gathered was freely disseminated, so that appropriate action could be taken on each identified youth by the agency best equipped to handle the particular boy or girl.

At the request of the County Conference on Community Relations, these Juvenile Officers met with citizen groups in the immediate and adjacent area, explaining the problem and the police program to control the situation, soliciting citizens' assistance in the program.

The County Conference organized a Neighborhood Parents' Council from representatives of many existing community groups, including PTA, teachers' organizations and ministers' alliances. Represented in the Council were citizens of divergent backgrounds residing in the area.

During the same time, our field patrol units were able to prevent large groups from meeting near the school and participating in actual riots. Caravans of automobiles containing youths on their way to a prearranged location were intercepted. Arrests were made wherever violations of the law occurred, such as weapons, late hours, traffic violations, etc.

Field interview reports on each persons in these caravans were made. Where a youth was on parole or probation, a report was referred to the concerned parole or probation officer. Juvenile Officers talked to the parents of each boy, and where the same boy had more than one field interview report made as a result of his being at more than one incident, the parents were invited to the Police Station for a more formal discussion. School authorities were notified when any student of their school was found at more than one incident.

We soon found that parents and students from both sides of the controversy were calling the police, notifying us of the time and location of expected trouble. We responded. The very presence of uniformed officers generally prevented disorder.

Within 90 days, it was determined that an acute problem no longer existed in this area. The combined efforts of the Police and community groups had minimized a serious threat to community order.

You will note that a proper evaluation of incidents and rumors by the police and community organizations was the first step toward the solution of the problem.

In the beginning, the Department immediately took police action in each incident observed, and accumulated information which gave us an estimate of the situation.

As the tensions increased to the point that mass disorder appeared imminent, a mobilization of community forces was accomplished while the Department intensified police action. Through joint community effort, we were able to achieve our objective of maintaining community order.

I would like to point out several additional factors that are extremely important in the evaluation of the problem that confronted the community.

First, although the area was in a transitional phase, no incidents of a violent nature involved residents or nonresidents other than the teenage group.

Second, only a small portion of the total student body at the Junior High School, to which I have referred, was involved.

Third, the newspapers were extremely careful in their reporting to avoid any reference or statement that would tend to intensify the problem.

And, finally, the Police Department received the fullest cooperation and support from individual citizens, groups, and organizations.

When you drop a stone into the water ripples form and spread out in concentric circles. In like manner similar incidents spread throughout the city. But as a ripple decreases in size, the farther it moves, so did the incidents reduce in intensity.

Given impetus by this particular problem was the establishment of a city-wide community problems unit. The team of Juvenile Investigators originally assigned to do intelligence work on this particular problem was transferred to the Juvenile Headquarters Division, to become the nucleus of that unit. Today, they carefully analyze every rumor, every conflict that might be based on racial differences, assisting the Department in its work with all groups and agencies to minimize community tensions.

Philadelphia: A Case Study

EDWARD M. PAYNE
(Then) Deputy Police Inspector, Philadelphia Police Department

MAY 15, 1956

Philadelphia, just as any other large city, has a long history of community tensions. For example, as far back as the early 1800's there are records of riots which were directed against the Negro residents of the city during which homes were burned and lives lost, labor disturbances which flared into violence, riots which were instigated by the so-called Native American Association, directed principally against new arrivals from Ireland, and incidents which were focused upon the Roman Catholic Church—which resulted in the destruction of a number of churches by fire.

As population shifts occur, because of changing economic conditions and for a variety of other reasons, we find new people entering our communities. In many instances, such people are of a higher intellectual level than the people among whom they are forced to live, through inadequacy of housing and because of financial conditions, as is the case of the new arrivals to this country from eastern Europe. Others are different from other residents of the communities because of their language or skin color or both, or because of their religion. When such people enter a community, they are not very enthusiastically received. Usually they encounter hostility and are the cause of trouble.

The need for a good community relations program is crucial to all police departments, since the police are usually the first to be called to the scene in the event of friction. Police personnel should have training to prepare them for such emergencies and should be aware of community resources available to aid in improving community relations.

It is a known fact that improper police activity and indiscreet actions on the part of the police will tend to aggravate and inflame situations of this kind. It is generally accepted that the proper professional approach of the well-trained policeman will, in many instances, prevent overt acts in potentially tense situations. However, where such situations develop, a good community relations program, in which police and other organizations which are active in community work, take the concerted action, is most effective in bringing about a satisfactory adjustment.

In September of 1955, such a situation developed in the western section of Philadelphia. In this case, a property at 6427 Lebanon Avenue which is a two-story row house on a dual highway, was listed for sale for several months with the real estate office of Lenert Roberts. William Roberts, of the same firm, subsequently handled all transactions involving the property. The property was sold to Mr. and Mrs. James Whitsett, an established and respected family in the Negro community.

Mr. Whitsett is a veteran of World War II, a graduate of the University of Pittsburgh, and holds a responsible supervisory position with the Department of Public Welfare in the City of Philadelphia.

Settlement of the property was made on Thursday, September 15, 1955. The Police Department and the Philadelphia Commission on Human Relations, in accordance with standing procedure, were notified of the sale, after settlement was completed.

Mr. and Mrs. Whitsett visited the property preparatory to moving in. Police on patrol in the area contacted the Whitsetts in their home on Friday evening. On Saturday, between midnight and 4:00 A.M., windows in the sun porch of the house were smashed with stones. The Whitsetts arrived at the house at approximately 8:00 A.M., Saturday morning, September 17, 1955, and immediately notified the police and the Human Relations' Commission of the damage. A police officer was then assigned to around-the-clock duty to guard the property. The Whitsetts moved a small quantity of furniture into the house in the early afternoon, by way of the rear entrance.

Mr. William Roberts, the real estate agent who had negotiated the sale of the property, arrived at the house in the early afternoon and clashed verbally with a group of onlookers who were standing across the street from the house.

Another window was broken shortly thereafter, and the Police Department and Commission on Human Relations were notified. Police reinforcements arrived and dispersed the growing crowd, which was estimated at 500 persons, and blocked off the street. A police detail remained on duty throughout the evening. There were no additional incidents, as the crowd appeared to be curious rather than antagonistic. The most noticeable members of the crowd appeared to be young men who drove around the area in automobiles. At approximately 7:30 P.M. on Saturday evening, two boys — age 16 and 17 — were removed from the crowd by Juvenile Aid Officers of the Police Department for leading catcalls and yells. At approximately 11:45 P.M., a third boy was apprehended for the same reason. All three boys were subsequently released in the custody of their parents. On Sunday morning at 8:00 A.M. the Commission on Human Relations distributed approximately 500 initial leaflets in a four square block radius of the Lebanon Avenue address. Leaflets were also distributed to police officers on duty. Residents of the area were observed to receive the leaflets with interest. Several were heard to express regret over the incident. On Sunday afternoon, crowds again gathered in the area. A picket line of approximately 75 teenagers paraded in front of the house, making derisive remarks in the direction of the house. The pickets and crowds were warned and dispersed by the police. On Sunday evening at approximately 9:00 P.M., six Negro men came through the street. In accordance with their instructions, police who were keeping all people out of the area instructed the men to keep moving. Two of these men resisted, became involved in an altercation with the police and were arrested. The remaining four complied with police instructions and passed out of the area. On Sunday evening, street barriers were erected by the police to block off the highway front of this residence and, for the time, order and quiet prevailed. A permanent detail of policemen was assigned, made up of 40 policemen per tour of duty which meant a daily complement of 120 policemen, three sergeants, and three lieutenants. Other supervisory officers, including the Commissioner of Police and Deputy Commissioners, made frequent visits to the scene.

On Monday, September 19, 1955, 18 representatives of community organizations and Negro leadership met with the staff of the Commission on Human Relations and representatives of the Police Department to review and discuss the incident. The group agreed unanimously that the authorities had taken sound precautionary measures, and that the results, to date, were highly satisfactory.

It was found that press, radio and television treatment of the incident had been constructive. Positive steps taken by local leadership within the area of the incident included:

1. Overbrook Baptist Church
   a. Invited the Whitsetts to attend services on September 25.
   b. Invited James Whitsett to speak to all classes of the Baptist Theological Seminary on October 12.
   c. Expressed welcome to the Whitsetts through friendly letters and personal visits.
   d. Personal visits to the home by the pastor of this church and other clergy.
2. Addison J. Henry Memorial Presbyterian Church
   a. Sermon from the pulpit by the pastor explaining the incident.
   b. Personal calls on local neighbors by members of the congregation, with the

distribution of informative literature furnished by the Commission on Human Relations.

3. Episcopal Divinity School of Philadelphia
   a. Invited Commission on Human Relations speaker and discussion leader to participate in the Interdenominational Seminary Conference on October 15.
   b. Invited Father Harris (Negro Episcopal clergyman) to address the same group at the afternoon session.

4. Lutheran Theological Seminary
   a. Discussions by the Lutheran clergy and seminaries.
   b. Distribution of informative literature furnished by the Commission on Human Relations on October 25.

5. St. Calistus Parish
   a. Personal calls by Msgr. Pasto on parishioners living in the Lebanon Ave-Society, to counteract misunderstanding and anxiety.

6. St. Donato Parish
   a. Personal calls by Msgr. Pasto on parishioners living in the Lebanon Avenue area.
   b. Attendance at meetings with police officials and Commission on Human Relations representatives by members of the Parish, referred by the pastor.

7. Catholic STANDARD & TIMES (Philadelphia Diocesan Weekly)
   a. Issue of September 23, 1955 carried a digest of the six point neighborhood stabilization program outlined by members of the Catholic Interracial Council.

8. Jewish Community Relations Council
   a. Invitation to the Commission on Human Relations for speakers for several meetings and for the distribution of informative literature.
   b. Attendance by representatives of local chapters at meetings with the police and Commission on Human Relations representatives.

The Whitsett family, encouraged by the many expressions of moral support and friendship, proceeded to renovate their home and make improvements which were apparent to passers-by. From this point, there appeared to be a growing realization on the part of the Lebanon Avenue residents that the Whitsett family had become permanent and peaceful neighbors. The intense feeling of hostility and anxiety subsided, and no further incident of any kind occurred to disturb the peace of the neighborhood.

Although a good police–community relations program is extremely valuable in a situation of tension, such a program is also essential in bringing about an atmosphere of togetherness and mutual effort. Police departments are dependent upon public support, not only for favorable legislation, but also for aid in the developments of projects which have community significance. One such project is the work of the Police Sanitation Unit of the Philadelphia Police Department. This unit was first placed into operation in 1938. Its original function was to enforce regulations concerning the disposition of refuse, which was placed at the curb by householders to be picked up by city trucks for disposal. In the beginning, the principal duty of personnel assigned to this unit was to precede trucks on disposal days and issue summonses to offending householders. However, through the process of evolution, this unit has become a force in the development of good police–community relations.

The major emphasis now is to educate the public rather than to take punitive steps. Mrs. Walter Craig and Mr. C. P. Jarden of the Philadelphia Chamber of Commerce, both of whom have been active in the "Clean-up, Paint-up, Fix-up" movement, work very closely with Police Sergeant Edmont Maines, the present commander of the Sanitation Unit. There are 22 policemen assigned to this duty, all of whom have been carefully selected. One of the functions of this unit is to set up cleaning block areas in the less substantial sections of the city. They are sections which the more fortunate citizens seldom see or want to see. In this phase of the work, the officers make use of the folk leaders in organizing block committees. The officers must sit down with the people who comprise the block units, give them individual attention and encourage them, and provide the assistance they need to get rid of the debris that results from "clean-up" work.

There are more than 300 such block groups in Philadelphia. More are being formed; many of them have carried out small scale reclamations projects. Not a few of them exist in racially mixed neighborhoods and are proof that the various elements of our population can work together on the family level, to mutual advantage.

Where residents have united to form a block group, elect their own officers and carry out a street and home beautification program, one sees the fruits of respect and goodwill.

In May, 1955, which was "Clean-up" month, about a half-million people performed more than 2,750,000 clean-up jobs. A great majority of these same people continued their effort through the year, another evidence that cooperation and mutual respect were well-founded.

Another important evidence of good human relations behind Philadelphia's clean-up effort, is the city's Junior Sanitation Units. They were first founded in 1953, the first of their kind in the nation. Now there are more than 6,000 youngsters from six to thirteen years of age organized through some 300 public and parochial schools. New members are sworn in by members of the Police Sanitation Squad at a regular ceremony in the school assembly. The children keep their classrooms, playgrounds and neigborhoods clean. Their pledge is: "I will do all in my power to make my school, my neighborhood and city a cleaner, healthier and happier place in which to live."

A Rationale for Racial Demonstrations

JOHN A. MORSELL

*Assistant Executive Director, National Association for the
Advancement of Colored People, New York*

MAY 19, 1964

I take it for granted that our concern here is not the abstract, constitutional principle which underlies today's demonstrations, as it has existed in this country since the nation's beginning. The basic guarantees of freedom of speech, assembly and petition for redress of grievances have been exercised by American citizens in one form or another for over 175 years. The parade, the picket line, the mass meeting, the public rally, and the written petition have been commonplace for generations.

Over these generations, abolitionists, suffragettes, temperance propagandists, political religionists, peace advocates, war advocates, trade unionists, partisans, and a host of others have engaged in public demonstration of their viewpoints, seeking thereby to acquire popular support and to enlist adherents. Free silver, the single tax, the income tax, the alien and sedition laws, the draft, Federalism, greenbacks, national banks, civil service reform, 54-40 or fight—have at one time or another been among the subjects opposed by marching throngs and loud-voiced assemblies.

The contemporary racial demonstration appears to be something very different, almost unique; its proportions have caused alarm in some quarters, and rejoicing in others, on a scale unlike anything we have seen in this century. We ought to spend a little while examining why this is so. I think that the reasons are to be found, first, in *who* it is that is demonstrating; second, in the manner of the demonstration, including especially the forms they may assume in the future; and third, in the extraordinary effectiveness of these demonstrations, including the immense impact derived as a by-product of modern mass communications.

The essential fact about today's racial demonstrations is that they *are* racial. Whites are often involved, but, fundamentally, these are demonstrations by Negroes, who are taking this means of demanding an end to the long and bitter second-class road which they have been forced to travel since they came to these shores 350 years ago. The spectacle of these marching hundreds and thousands and tens of thousands of black faces is traumatic to most white Americans. It worries them. It challenges their assumptions. It keeps the wounds of guilt open and fresh. In acting thus, the Negro is behaving out of character—the character which his white fellow citizens fabricated for him, rather than finding out what he really was like.

In this image, the Negro has been the somewhat inferior junior member of the firm, the victim, to be sure, of a certain amount of injustice, but destined eventually to make his way, if he learned to behave himself and to let time take care of everything. As Charles Silberman observes in his book, CRISIS IN BLACK AND WHITE,

> For a hundred years, white Americans have clung tenaciously to the illusion that if everyone would just sit still — if "agitators" would just stop agitating — time alone would solve the problem of race. . . . Myrdal (who believed white Americans were torn between their devotion to the Americans' creed and their actual behavior toward Negroes and called this AN AMERICAN DILEMMA) was wrong. White Americans are not torn and tortured . . . they are upset by the current state of race relations, to be sure. But what troubles them is not that justice is being denied, but that their peace is being shattered and their business interrupted.

In such a circumstance, the surging insistence of the Negro demonstrators and their repeated willingness to risk hardship, arrest, prison, and personal violence rather than desist, has introduced a completely new factor into the national life. Part of the difficulty, of course, lies in the fact that the truth about the Negro's past in the United States has been distorted or obscured by the writers of most of our history books. They bear a large share of the blame for the fallacious image of the Negro as childlike and docile, submitting quietly to enslave-

ment and gratefully accepting his emancipation through the valor and wartime
sacrifices of white soldiers in blue. Few know, therefore, of the endless slave re-
bellions and revolts throughout the years before 1860; and fewer still, perhaps,
know that almost 200,000 black soldiers fought bravely and effectively through
most of the Civil War, receiving at the end the accolade of President Lincoln,
who said that the war could not have been won without them.

Few know to what extent the image of the docile Negro was intentionally
fostered by Negroes themselves as an aid to survival in a racially hostile environment. Thus, generations of Negro children have been taught two kinds of behavior: one for dealing with whites— tell them what they want to hear, behave
the way they want you to behave — and another for their relations within the race.

Few know to what an extent the myth of Negro shiftlessness, carelessness with
property and inability to handle tools was the result of the slaves' subtle and
self-taught effort to sabotage the slave system. By malingering, by waste, by careless handling which led to breakdowns, the slave who could neither rebel nor
escape did what he could to fight the men who owned his body and his wife's
body and his children's bodies.

Because of their failure to learn these lessons, today's whites are puzzled and
frightened. But the real fault goes much deeper than that, as I suggested above.
It is in the basic failure of whites, on the whole, to see Negroes as people — just
like themselves, except for color. This is what Ralph Ellison complained of in
INVISIBLE MAN. This is what DuBois meant 60 years ago when he wrote of
"The Veil" that lies between white and black. This is the essence of much of
James Baldwin's bitter commentary.

This is why you will find many Negroes today unmoved by the evidence that
their demonstrations may be producing a serious "backlash" of resentment among
otherwise neutral northern whites. After all, these Negroes say, it is better to be
actively and positively disliked than to be overlooked or ignored. At least, no
one can continue to be unaware of our existence—we have irritated you, and now
you know we are here.

And they may well be right. It may well be that exposing to the light of day
the latent hostility and fear of white people is a necessary first step to relieving
them of that hostility and fear.

At the same time, it cannot but fascinate the dispassionate observer (if there
be any of these) to note how short-lived are people's memories. For it was only
eight years ago that 50,000 Negroes in Montgomery carried on a unified protest
for 12 months, bringing the local bus line to its knees by a boycott which would
have attained its goal if left up to the company itself. The intransigeance of the
political power was such, however, that federal authority, via an NAACP lawsuit, was required to end bus segregation. Surely here was a clear demonstration
of how black Americans felt about their status.

The second feature of today's racial demonstrations that arouses concern
is the varied form which they have taken and, more than that, speculation as to
the forms they may assume in the future. For the purposes of this discussion, I
am including under the general heading of "demonstration" all the manifestations
of Negro discontent with which we have become familiar in recent years. This
means, in addition to picketing, marching, parading, rallies and the like, such
actions as sit-ins, kneel-ins, freedom rides and other kinds of direct personal

challenge of segregation; and it includes activities which may properly be classified as civil disobedience.

The forms vary as the purposes vary. A picket line, with placards, chanting
and slogans, has as its purpose the focusing of public attention on a grievance,
just as a union picket line seeks to secure public support of a strike or call attention to a labor grievance. Where the racial protest is linked to a boycott against
an establishment being picketed, it—like the union effort—attempts to persuade
the public not to patronize the offending business. (In this category belongs such
an extension of the picket line as the ILGWU is currently conducting against a
blouse manufacturer: three million shopping bags have been distributed free to
shoppers, each bag carrying the union's appeal not to buy the indicated brand
of blouse.)

So, too, a march or parade, or an outdoor rally, is designed to publicize a
grievance, and to enlist the public's support behind efforts to remove it. Mass
meetings serve this purpose also, to the extent that they are reported; but here
the emphasis is on the morale of the troops, on maintaining unity and on keeping
the participants aroused and eager to work in the cause. This is obviously a key
objective in virtually every other kind of demonstration also, and many planners
of demonstrations consider the overall goals well-served if there is no other result
than this one. Not only is this a thoroughly legitimate function for demonstrations, it is very probable that it is of major importance in channelling emotions
which might otherwise be expressed in less controlled ways.

In recent months, civil rights picketing has begun to take a leaf from the trade
union book of the 1930's, when so-called mass picketing was employed as a direct
weapon against employers. In those cases, the pickets physically barred the entrance to plants and businesses, so that employees who wanted to work could not
do so. In Philadelphia last summer, NAACP pickets linked arms and blocked
the entry to construction sites in which the contractors were charged with discriminatory hiring. The variations in this came shortly to include not only attempts
at this kind of blockage, but lying down in front of trucks and other devices. Here,
it is obvious, was a new turn in the civil rights demonstration, a turn to genuine
civil disobedience, with willingness to bear the consequences, including arrest and
imprisonment. The purpose was no longer simply to call public attention to a
wrong; it was, instead, to prevent the continuance of an operation which was being
conducted in a discriminatory manner, and to keep this up until an acceptable ac-
comodation was achieved.

In some instances, these tactics succeeded, in others they failed. Last fall, a
number of civil rights leaders who had been heavily engaged in actions of this
kind, all aimed at job bias, expressed disillusionment with the meager or non-
existent gains produced by their long, arduous and sometimes painful efforts during the summer. This disillusionment was short-lived, as indeed it should have
been. Just as one swallow does not make a summer, so one summer's hard work
at construction sites will not necessarily bring the desired outcome; it may take
several summers.

Perhaps more important than the temporary disillusionment was the realization by civil rights leaders of the necessity for careful assessment of the nature
and focus of demonstrations — for a genuinely strategic calculation, in which the
type of activity is related as accurately as possible to the objective, and in which
people's time, energies and money are not committed without realistic appraisal

of the probable gains and the possible losses. Among the latter, of course, is the chance that white resistance may be engendered to such an extent as to imperil attainment of the ultimate objectives. It is important, however, in touching on this aspect, to make it clear that the possibility that white people will be angered by a demonstration, or series of demonstrations, is not in itself sufficient reason to abandon or reduce them. If this had been the criterion for Negro protest, there would never have been any at all, because very little change can take place in the American racial scene without disturbing or annoying some whites. It is to be expected that efforts by an oppressed minority to change the *status quo* will arouse resentment in the majority and will lead to an increase in tensions. The real question is not the increase in tensions, but how rapidly the majority grasps the necessity of change, for its own sake as much as for the minority's.

Thus, the fundamental error of those who tried to pull off the abortive "stall-in" at the opening of the New York World's Fair was not so much that the maneuver would have irritated large numbers of people. The error was that the stall-in could not be tied clearly or directly to any specific grievance, or to any specific source of redress of the grievance. It was purely and simply a nuisance tactic, one that was resented by many Negroes as well as by whites, and would have demonstrated nothing except that any determined group of people can, if they are willing to face the consequences, create disorder and confusion and inconvenience to large numbers of others who are not in a position to do anything to rectify the situation.

Another lesson of the "stall-in," of course, was that more is needed for success than emotion and appeals; meticulous organization is essential, and of this there was none. Civil rights is, after all, serious business and it must be taken seriously by its advocates, the best of whom know that zeal is no substitute for planning.

I think there is point in making another distinction here with regard to civil disobedience. I do not classify a restaurant sit-in, for example, or a freedom ride, as civil disobedience. These actions are based on the premise that exclusion from a licensed public facility on account of race is a violation of a constitutional right. This was notably true in the case of the freedom rides, which simply sought to implement judicial and other rulings which entitled bus passengers to service at bus station lunch counters and restrooms. If the acts were in violation of local laws, it was the local laws which defied the law of the land, not the freedom riders or the sit-ins. A sit-in to block the entrance to a World's Fair pavilion, or to the office of a government official, a school boycott, or a stall-in, on the other hand, are civil disobedience because no one challenges the validity of the law which is invoked to prevent or punish such actions. Those who engage in acts of this kind understand what they are doing, and they have chosen these methods because they believe they are necessary in the light of the failure of less extreme methods to bring about the needed remedies.

Here lies the most fundamental consideration of all. It goes to the very root of the Negro's involvement in protest activity, and upon it almost certainly hangs the answer to the question of where the demonstration movement will go from here. If the Negro's experience in this country gave him any assurance that traditional courses of action—patient exposure of his wrongs, patient exploitation of judicial remedies, patient pleas to the Congress and other legislative bodies to enact laws to help him — would pay off in a reasonable time, he would confine himself to those courses. God knows they are less difficult, less demanding of personal sacrifice, less dangerous than the kinds of protest to which the Negro has increasingly become committed in recent years.

But as he looks about him, he sees no reason whatsoever to place his trust exclusively in the traditional legal processes. The truth is that he has never felt himself restricted to such methods; the history of the NAACP, for example, despite the predominance of legal and legislative action in the popular image of the Association, is replete with instances of every other form of protest in the book. These did not make the headlines accorded our victories in the United States Supreme Court, but they were always as integral a part of NAACP strategy as was anything else. The sit-in wave of 1960, for example, was preceded by NAACP youth sit-ins in 1958–59 in Oklahoma City, in Wichita, Kansas, and in St. Louis, Missouri, which led to the desegregation of several score restaurants and lunch counters in these cities. Fifteen thousand marched for the NAACP down Fifth Avenue in New York City in 1917, in protest against the lynching abomination, then at a peak of 100 a year. Boycotts, rallies, marches and other forms of direct action were undertaken by NAACP branches throughout the country, almost from the very beginning of its existence in 1909.

The Negro has consistently chosen those methods and instruments which have, from time to time, seemed most likely to be effective in producing change. The 1954 Supreme Court ruling on public schools knocked the props of legality and respectability out from under racial segregation, and became thereby the stepping-stone to new dimensions in protest. The courts then became primarily the vehicle for application and enforcement of the rights, rather than for their definition. The results may not have been predictable, but they are certainly understandable. As the courts have become bogged down in delayed and desultory implementation of the school segregation decision, Negroes have rightly concluded that they might well wait a thousand years for this right to be freely enjoyed by their children. They have determined that other approaches are called for.

As Negroes watch with growing disgust and disillusionment the spectacle of the eleven-week filibuster in the United States Senate, and when they reflect that this so-called debate is taking place in the year 1964 to decide on rights long since granted all Americans by law and morality, they cannot be expected to sit patiently without seizing the initiative and striking their own blows for freedom. If one set of tactics does not appear to work, they will try others. Thus far, with astonishingly few exceptions, the things they have done have remained within the framework of the traditional methods of protest discussed above. It remains to be seen whether this state of affairs can prevail indefinitely.

It is perfectly logical and the height of good sense to hold that more radical measures, more direct confrontations, are doomed to failure because of the sheer numerical inferiority of the Negro population. The Negro cannot take on the white population, solely in terms of relative numbers, to say nothing of the infinite disparity in power and resources, and hope for success thereby. But if enough Negroes are convinced that they are not going to win anyway, many may be tempted to lose in such a way as to inflict the greatest possible loss upon the majority as well. This has happened before in the history of mankind and it can happen again.

Such a development could occur, even in the face of the obvious fact that many demonstrations have been highly successful. The sit-ins opened up hundreds of public eating places across the South; the freedom rides of 1961 led to the ICC ruling on bus station facilities; boycotts in a score of communities have opened up jobs and training opportunities for Negroes. Perhaps the crowning illustration were the Birmingham and Jackson demonstrations of 1963, as a direct result of which the Kennedy administration scrapped its modest plans for civil rights legislation and introduced the present comprehensive package of proposals. The trouble is that it all happens too slowly, however rapid it may appear to white citizens who do not suffer under the deprivations. I do not need to remind you that it is human nature to become ever more impatient the nearer one comes to a cherished goal—which is one explanation for the explosive character of much Negro protest in northern cities which, so far as formal attainments are concerned, had made genuine progress in advancing opportunity for Negroes.

More, even, than in concrete gains, the expanded Negro protest movement has brought the whole issue of race relations to the rank of number one domestic concern for the nation as a whole. It was not too many years ago that so-called "race" news was almost the exclusive property of the Negro weekly press. Getting the daily press to take notice of it was a difficult task. Today, no newspaper, no television or radio news program, is without some item dealing with matters of race. Millions of Americans have been eyewitnesses to Negro children being hissed and cursed and spat upon as they sought to enter white public schools; they have seen the dogs and firehoses of Birmingham; they have viewed beatings in Jackson, Mississippi, and in Plaquemine, Louisiana.

They sense, some vaguely and few with total comprehension, that the country is passing through the mightiest internal convulsion since the Civil War, and I think they will come to understand, in the language of the resolution adopted at the NAACP's 54th annual convention last year in Chicago, that "there will be no relaxation, no tranquility and no rest in this land until Negroes have gained first-class citizenship everywhere, with all the rights, privileges and responsibilities of first-class citizens."

The role of the mass media in this revolution has been noteworthy; indeed, the full dimensions and significance of its role may not be properly assessed for years to come. No one has been able as yet, for example, to record and evaluate what television has meant throughout this period, since television itself is a recent addition to mass communication and is still far from completely understood in its own terms of reference. There is no doubt, however, that the mass media have been far more than recorders of events; they have, unwittingly most of the time, been actors and movers and stimulators of events. It is well known that much of the success of the Montgomery bus boycott was due to the publicizing of it over the week-end in the daily paper; otherwise, few Negroes could have been made aware of it in time to boycott the buses on Monday. Similar instances have since become fairly frequent.

It needs also to be said that the press and television have tended, to a disturbing extent, to see the civil rights issue in terms of sensation and banner headlines. Exceptional indeed have been the instances of sober, informed reporting, and no newspaper that I know of has done so with consistency. A charge of general irresponsibility in covering the greatest domestic issue of these times can be sustained without difficulty. The number of first-rate reporters, armed with the depth of background knowledge prerequisite for the task, can be numbered on the fingers of two hands. Newspapers which would not dream of assigning untried and ignorant reporters to their financial and business news columns think nothing of sending out anyone who can hammer a typewriter to cover the civil rights scene.

Worse than this, they do not confine these race relations novices to straight reporting; they allow them to do so-called "in-depth" reporting, which calls for maturity of judgment, objectivity and basic knowledge, and which would be approached with some circumspection even by persons who have many years in civil rights work. Last week, the New York HERALD-TRIBUNE featured, in the space normally occupied by Walter Lippman, a column of pontifical prose on the topic *Split in the Negro Ranks*. Its author, whose ignorance was liberally illustrated throughout, was the assistant to the real estate editor.

The consequence of this kind of treatment has been a serious absence of perspective in the coverage of events, personalities and, in particular, organizations. Television and radio are equal offenders, and the kinds of questions frequently asked of civil rights participants by the electronic reporter or interviewer often make one flinch. (Of course, we are used to having persons just dragged out of wreckage confronted with the ubiquitous microphone and asked: "How do you feel about being rescued?" or something equally inane.)

The inevitable by-product of the mass media's quest for sensation is that many people have become adept at creating the desired sensation. Wild proclamations, daring announcements of vast (and often impossible) actions to follow at some date in the future, are dear to the heart of the press, and there is no dearth of persons willing and anxious to help. If the whole business were not so serious, and if careful and responsible treatment were not so vital to the general understanding on which ultimate solutions must rest, one could simply enjoy the unconscious humor of this situation and pass on to other matters. But there is a crying need for competent reporting and analysis by the media, and it is little short of tragic that as yet there is so little of it.

In spite of this, the net result has been the placing of the civil rights issue squarely before the American conscience. The prospect is that it will be kept there for the foreseeable future. What means are used to keep it there will depend in large part on how that conscience responds to the insistent challenge of the Negro protest. There is no visible future for any of us if we are irrevocably caught in a collision course between Negro needs and aspirations which will not be silenced, on the one hand, and aroused white intransigence, on the other. The outcome of this would be national disaster. We can and we must exercise discretion and patience where they are needed, but the time has come when these noble qualities will have to be assumed more and more by white Americans; Negroes have exhibited them almost alone for far too long.

The Constitution and the Citizen: The Quest for Balance

GEORGE EDWARDS

(Then) Commissioner, Police Department, Detroit

MAY 23, 1963

The quest for balance that we seek is the quest for balance between freedom and order. This indeed is a quest which pertains to the Constitution and to the citizen, and this indeed is the dilemma with which those concerned with law enforcement have been involved since the founding of this nation, and will be involved so long as it continues to exist. When we think of the task of the police officer in making decisions in the heat of an emergency on the street, and we see that he is required to answer so many profoundly difficult questions in a hurry—that appellate judges and courts may study for literally years before spelling out their carefully wrought opinion—what we really are doing is simply acknowledging that the United States of America, when it was founded, took on quite a task. It was the first nation in the history of the world ever even to assert that it was possible to merge the two principles of individual freedom and societal order, to live side by side, not as opposite forces, but as complimentary forces. From the time our nation was founded, we had imposed upon us as a people the challenge and the task of building a society which one justice described in the simplest and most complicated phrase I've ever heard as "our society of ordered liberty."

Under all circumstances, the balance between individual freedom and order is difficult. It's been so difficult in most of human history that until 1776, no government had ever been inaugurated which asserted that it was possible. Even today, there are many nations which reject that the idea is even conceivable to have a state organized to serve each human being, giving him the fullest possibility for the development of all the creative skills and potentials which lie within him. This, we say our nation is dedicated to do—and at the same time, to establish sufficient order of the whole that each person may live in peace and harmony and with equal privileges. That's quite a challenge!

When as a police officer, you occasionally feel frustrated about what you're dealing with, in a particular episode on the street that involves freedom of speech, or the problem of search and seizure, don't be so surprised about the fact that it's tough. It's the toughest job that's ever been laid down in the history of the world. And so when we find ourselves not wholly satisfied with our answers, or with the answers which somebody else may bring to the same situation, remember that this is built in; it is difficult. But I'm not going to spend much time dealing with the theory of search and seizure, or with the Bill of Rights of the United States Constitution, or with why we have guaranteed certain inalienable rights to our individual citizens which from time to time conflict with what police officers might desire to do.

I believe that the crucial problems of law and order in the mid-part of the 20th century and the quest for balance in serving the purposes of the law have been so heightened by one aspect of our total social problem that it is of overriding importance to all law enforcement officials, whether in the southern portion of this nation or in the north. It is on this that I wish to concentrate.

If it has always been difficult to balance freedom and law and order, and it has been, it's even more so today. We have higher standards in every portion of our land, we have higher expectations, and over and above this fact, we are engaged as a nation in the historic task of seeking to raise 11 per cent of our people from the effects of slavery, segregation and degradation in which they have lived for 200 years in the past. This is no minor challenge, and let's not any of us think that it's going to be easy. The police role in this historic revolution is a crucial one. I don't intend to spend much time on episodes of the nature of Birmingham and Oxford. The use of the police, who should always be the representatives of the law, to defy the Constitution of the United States and the courts is tragic. It requires condemnation by every law-abiding citizen of our country, and perhaps more than that, we should say it is one of the most futile exercises known to man. There isn't any question about whether the rights of equal education and equal voting which are guaranteed by our Constitution are going to be granted to all citizens in this country. It's only a question as to when and under what circumstances and how. Those who are engaged in leading the resistance know this in their own hearts. It is required by the basic religious concepts of the people of this nation, and by every bit of our Constitutional law.

But let's not overlook the fact that if we do not, in our big northern cities, have to deal with orders from political headquarters requiring us to use dogs and fire hoses on citizens who are parading in the effort to eat at public lunch counters, or enter public schools or register to vote, we have enormous aspects of this basic problem on our hands nonetheless. Let me see if I can put it to you succinctly and directly, in terms of a tremendous change which has taken place in this nation, and to some degree, is still taking place. And I'm quoting from an article in FORTUNE magazine, March 1962 entitled *The City and the Negro.* Speaking of the greatest problem of the cities in the mid-part of the 20th century, the author says:

It is not, as so many people have assumed, to bring the wandering middle class back from the suburbs. A large city cannot import a middle class; it must manufacture its own. And indeed most of the huge middle class that dominates American life today was manufactured in the big city slums of yesteryear. Cities have always had to create their own cultivated citizenry out of whatever raw material was the stream of immigrants pouring from Britain, Ireland, Norway, Russia, Germany, Italy and a dozen other lands. The city needed these immigrants to build its streets and offices, to man its factories, to service its homes and hotels and restaurants, and to do all the dirty and menial jobs that older residents disdained. But the city did more than use its newcomers. It equipped them to take their place as fully participating members of United States society. Bringing people from society's backwaters into the main stream of American life has always been the principal business and the principal glory of the American city. It isn't any longer. The city is in trouble today, because it isn't dealing successfully with its newcomers. They're still pouring in — not from County Cork or Bavaria or Sicily or Galicia — but from Jackson, Mississippi and from Memphis, Tennessee. And a whole host of southern towns with names like Sunflower, Rolling Fork and Diresberg. The new immigrants are distinguished from the older residents, not by religion or national origin but by color. Between 1950 and 1960 the twelve largest U.S. cities lost over 2,000,000 white residents and gained nearly 2,000,000 Negro residents. It is the explosive growth of their Negro population which constitutes the greatest concern of the largest cities. When city officials talk about spreading slums, in the main they are talking about physical deterioration in the areas inhabited by Negroes. And when they talk about juvenile delinquency or the burden of welfare payments, or a long list of city problems including the problem of crime, officials are talking about the problem of Negro adjustment to city life, for the large city is not absorbing and urbanizing its new Negro residents rapidly enough; its slums are no longer acting as the incubator of a new middle class.

Some may deduce that I am identifying crime in the big cities of the north as a race problem. I think crime is a problem which is produced by human degradation. I think that if you submit any portion of a population, regardless of its national origin or color, to conditions of poverty, lack of education, lack of culture, lack of employment opportunities, that portion of the population will automatically, in very short order, become productive of children who are known in our cities as delinquents, and adults who grow from those children to careers of crime.

If it is true, and it is, that in most of our big cities, a higher percentage of recorded crimes are committed by Negro citizens than by whites, it also is true that they have, statistically, a far higher percentage residing in slums, a far higher percentage of inhabitants occupying the lowest paid jobs, a far higher percentage of persons who are completely unemployed, of school drop-outs, and a far higher percentage of people who have known degradation, poverty and discrimination through the 300 years which I have cited.

Now in every one of our big cities—and somehow it's overlooked to a tremendous degree—when this problem is discussed, two facts are likewise patent and obvious. The portion of our society with the greatest stake in effective and vigilant and vigorous law enforcement is the Negro portion of our population. As more crimes are committed by Negroes, in the core areas of our cities, so more of the victims are Negroes than is true in relation to the whites. An article in LOOK magazine (June 4, 1963) dealing with Washington, D.C. in very dramatic terms, points out that 84 percent of the assault victims are Negroes.

This is an interesting statistic. I would hardly be prepared to believe it, except that last summer we ran a similar study in Detroit of one of our different precincts, and found that the identification was within 2 percent in that particular precinct in the summer portion of the year which we studied.

One other fact which is widely overlooked. Just as it is true that it is easy to police the better sections of the white-occupied portions of our city, it is also easier to police the better sections which are occupied by Negro residents. We have a neighborhood in Detroit in which, for 40 years, Negro businessmen, lawyers, doctors, and workers in the factory with long seniority have bought land and built homes and reared their youngsters. Conant Gardens is known as one of the quietest neighborhoods in the entire city of Detroit, and it always has been.

These things lead us to conclude that the notion that crime is a race problem is a totally false one. They should *not* lead us to overlook the fact that wherever there has been discrimination, wherever there has been impoverishment, wherever there has been a denial of rights, we have built-in problems in relation to the social order. These are aggravated in our big cities by many additional, emotion-charged problems, many of which do not carry labels of F.O.B. Detroit, or F.O.B. Chicago, or Philadelphia or whatever the northern city may be.

If it is true that crime is not a race problem, it certainly is true that suspicion and hostility between the Negro community of a big city and its police department is a major problem to the forces concerned with law enforcement. This is the major problem that law enforcement deals with in seeking a balance between order and liberty at the present time.

From our leading Negro newspaper in Detroit, in an editorial of recent weeks, I quote: "Two years ago, the relations between the Detroit police department and the Negro community were like a keg of dynamite. Resentment and animosity over the hostile attitude and approach of the police department were prevalent throughout the community. It was an aggrieved and indignant community, still bristling from an infamous crime crack-down which had resulted in mass arrests and a police reign of terror." I do not suggest to you that there is any necessity for endorsing these editorial paragraphs as statements of fact. But we accept that they accurately revealed an attitude of a community, which now represents 29 percent of the people of Detroit, toward its law enforcement agency; when such attitudes exist, problems of law enforcement are indeed formidable ones.

I suppose for a State Supreme Court justice to leave the cloistered halls of an appellate court and accept an assignment as police commissioner of a big city, in the mid-part of the 20th century, is the reasonable equivalent of someone trying to stand an elephant on its head on the steps of the city hall. There must be many who wonder at such information. Perhaps I should share with you a bit of personal history that lies deep in my heart and is always present there. I grew up in a southern city—Dallas, Texas. In 1910, my father's first criminal assignment was to defend an elderly Negro man charged with an assault upon a child. Before he had reached the room to which he was required to go in order to interview the client whose life he was required to defend, a mob broke into the courthouse, into the courtroom, into the jury room, seized the man, tied a rope around his neck, threw him out the third story window, dragged him up the main street of Dallas, and hanged him from an arch built for the Elk's Temple national convention in 1910. That was the last lynching in the history of the city of Dallas.

My father's last case, in 1959, when he was 79 years old, was a defense of the rights of the National Association for the Advancement of Colored People in Texas to continue to exist and function there, against a petition for an injunction filed by the attorney general of Texas. After a three months trial in Tyler, Texas, this case was won. Moreover, I was a member of the city council in the city of Detroit in 1943, in the blackest days of the history of that city, when the great race riot broke out — a race riot stirred by unreasoning animosities and hatreds.

Don't anyone ever think that race hatred is a one-way street. If you do, you delude yourself. Don't ever think that all the extremists have the name Ku Klux Klan. There are extremists who have black faces as well as extremists with white faces, and the extremists took over the streets of Detroit for 24 bloody hours. Although I was a member of the Detroit city government, I never was able to find out how many people died in those 24 hours. I would think upward of two dozen. I want to tell you about two of them.

One was a Doctor de Horatius, of Italian origin, I believe; certainly white skin. Dr. de Horatius had served on the east side of Detroit for many years, and among his patients he had many Negroes. Around 2 A.M. on the morning the riot broke out in the city of Detroit, he was called to respond to a patient on the east side of the city, and in pursuance of his duty, he responded. He was met on the streets by a mob full of anger and full of race hatred. They didn't know Dr. de Horatius from a bale of hay; all they knew about him was that they, the mob, had black faces and that he had a white face. And they stoned him to death, with no more knowledge than that.

Later in that 24 hour period, there was another instance, and this was one that was apparently not recorded. I still don't know the name of the person, although I tried to find out. I know it happened. People of the fire department told me the all-too-gory details. It was a Negro workman going home from his job, driving alone, and he was stopped by a mob with anger and race hatred in their hearts. They didn't know any more about him than that the mob's faces were white and this man's face was black. They turned the car over, and when the gasoline spilled out of the car, they lit a match and set fire to it, and burned up the man inside the car.

Think a little about what we're doing in this America of ours. Think hard about what we're talking about. I say to you, in as earnest terms as I can say it, there is no other road for these United States of America than to make good its promises of equality and freedom to *all* of its people, and to make good its promise of order to all of its people at the same time.

Now, if you say to me, that's tough, I couldn't agree with you more. But I say to you it's possible and it's necessary, and that's the job which we have ahead of us. How do we go about it? Let me indicate what we've tried to do.

On the precinct station walls in the city of Detroit, you'll find a motto, under glass. It's called the program of the Detroit Police Department. It says, "We seek: (1) More law enforcement and more vigorous law enforcement. (2) Equal protection of the law for all law-abiding citizens; equal enforcement of the law against all law violators. (3) The support of law-abiding citizens for law enforcement."

I was at a conference about a month ago, a somewhat historic one, where 14 big city chiefs and police commissioners met for the first time in history, and spent a day talking about their problems. The problem which we're talking about was the one which occupied the greatest amount of time, and to which we gave the greatest amount of attention. When we finished that day, after each had explained what he was seeking to do, the statement put out under the name of the chairman and the convener of the conference, Commissioner Murphy of New York City, adopted the three point program that the Detroit police department has been operating under during these past 16 months.

What do you do to produce equal law enforcement? This is crucial to the task of ending this hostility and conflict and fear and distrust which affect the major portion of the people in our American cities. The first thing you do is to find facts and face them. Now let's not kid about this matter, or we'll never get anywhere. This has not always been the practice. This has not always been what's been done. The suggestion that the police officer is always right is a pretty familiar suggestion, not in the public prints, but in precinct station houses. And the temptation, regardless of the facts, to defend that which violates the book of procedure and the law is a temptation to which many police officers are, by social pressure of their own clan, quite inclined to yield.

This isn't to ignore the facts. The facts can be misstated against the police as well as for them. This is common. The criminal defendant arrested on the street wants to find something on the police officer. The fact that he would lie should surprise nobody. You start out, in fact, with some suspicion in relation to almost anything which such a person is likely to offer in mitigation or expiation of his situation. But there are ways of discovering facts.

Most things that happen on big city streets have been seen by a lot of people. If you ask, and take down what's told you by those who were there on the scene and who saw, and if you look at what's there to be seen, the chances are you can come out with a pretty accurate picture of what actually occurred. Oh, there are some things that you can't figure out. You can't figure out, for example, in the arrest of a belligerent drunk who takes a pass at the arresting officer, exactly how hard he should have been hit in return. This you can't figure out. But I'm not ignoring for one minute the fact that there is, of necessity, a basic discretion vested in the police officer in dealing with this kind of situation. Afterward, no one is going to be asked to judge whether the pounds of pressure exerted by his fist or by his billy were scientifically calculated to be the least amount of physical force needed to subdue this person. The police officer knows that his own life is, perhaps to an important degree, in jeopardy in the conflict in which he is involved.

But there are some things not in this category that I'm talking about. If you have a prisoner with his arms handcuffed behind him and four officers on the scene, it ought to be possible to bring him in to a precinct station reasonably intact. And furthermore, I've often tried to figure out exactly how you would go about it if you were deliberately undertaking to develop a four-inch cut on the top of the head by "falling on the precinct steps." But in the early months of my administration as police commissioner, I saw some reports which literally described this somewhat fantastic feat as having been accomplished by a shackled prisoner.

This doesn't mean that every error made by a police officer is fatal or requires discharge. He deals with difficult and complicated problems. But if he deserves correction, he should have it, as in any other walk of life. As a matter of fact, this kind of situation, where the truth is covered up by official reports, is productive of the greatest amount of hostility and disregard for law. This is a major source of problems in the area in which we're speaking.

As police commissioner, I have found that direct investigation of important community problems is essential. Our Community Relations Bureau has been doing this for some time. We man our Bureau with intelligent officers—officers who have courage enough to face a hostile public as well as some hostility from within the department.

It is important that the administration of the police department make it known that it really means to end the institution best known in police circles as "alley court." Our law never has provided for alley courts. The Constitution doesn't allow for it. But it's been an institution, There are police officers who are sincerely and thoroughly convinced that unless they are allowed to maintain their authority in the street when they feel it necessary, even with their billies, they can't maintain peace and order.

The law prohibits this. Our total society prohibits this. Punishment is not the function of the police. It is the function of the courts. The function of the police is to detect and apprehend, and to bring into court for punishment. Alley courts are ordinarily used against minority groups. If used, it inflames the attitude of that group—in this case the Negro population—inflames everybody in that community who hears about it. And it deprives the police department of the most important ally that it can have—the support of the law-abiding populace residing in the core areas of the city, in the police department's war against crime.

There are relatively few police officers who have this attitude toward alley courts. But they've been successful in perpetuating it as an institution of concern in police circles by two means: by the slogan that no police officer can do wrong, and by skilled write-ups that keep it from getting to the top of police administration. Police commissioners are really not supposed to know what goes on! They call them "boss" because they know they aren't. They're really supposed to be sort of a mouthpiece for the department, and represent it whenever it's in trouble with the community. The law doesn't define the job that way.

Equal law enforcement requires arrest on the basis of a reason for making an arrest. I tried for a long time in our department to talk about "probable cause," and finally gave it up. I just couldn't get the concept of probable cause over. And I ended up by simply saying, "You gotta have a reason to make an arrest." And you know, that's been working. When they listened one sentence longer, I said that there had to be a reason related to a crime, and that *this* was the fellow who did it. There's the whole ball of wax. Last year, as a result of pressing both for more arrests and better arrests, we cut our total arrest picture by around 8,000, and at the same time increased our prosecutions by 5.6 percent and brought more felony prosecutions into Detroit Recorder's Court than had ever been there in the history of that court, and increased its prosecution arrests and felony trials by 7.1 percent, as compared with the preceding year.

What about community support? Can you do anything about that? People told me you couldn't. They told me that the thing you could never do was to get the NAACP, for example, to say a friendly word about a police officer. Nor the Negro press either. Well, that's bunk—it can be done. You just have to try. And you have to ask for support in order to get support. Last year, we were in a bitter battle about whether or not we were going to get pay raises for police officers. I went to the NAACP and asked them, along with a lot of other community groups, extending to every section of the city and every walk of life, to support requests for more policemen and for better pay. The NAACP passed a resolution which helped considerably in getting us the raises that we got. And they supported the request for more officers.

All the way through this year, the editorial position of the Michigan CHRONICLE, our leading Negro newspaper, has been one of staunch support for the program of the Detroit Police Department. You might say that these are just the top figures, these are the educated, these are the ones that you think would have a stake in law enforcement, but what about down on the street? I don't want to gild the lily, or convey the impression that we've reached any millenium—we've got lots of problems—but we have had some changes in attitude there, too. In Precinct 10, our most difficult precinct, we had a community relations meeting just a month ago that was supposed to be a regular quarterly meeting, but it wasn't a very ordinary affair. There were 450 citizens seated in the police garage—the only place we had that was big enough to accommodate them. They are seated on hard folding chairs, and they stayed there for three hours, to talk in detail with the Precinct inspector and the officers in the Precinct about law enforcement in the Precinct. During the course of this three hour meeting, there was not one complaint about discrimination or brutality.

The most popular man at the meeting was the Precinct inspector, who was bringing the most vigorous kind of law enforcement to the 10th Precinct. What they were asking for was more enforcement in their particular block or neighborhood, rather than wanting to have the police removed. They were telling us where stills were, or where "blind pigs" were operating, or who was pushing people around in their neighborhood. This is the kind of information which makes the law enforcement job much easier. We gave out 10 department citations for dramatic work of assistance to the police on the street. For instance, two gunmen had gone into a bar and held it up. Three of the Negro citizens who were at that meeting, when the gunmen left with the "swag," went out the door after them, chased them, caught them, and held them until the police got there.

Now we don't really recommend such tactics for civilians in our town. But after it was done, we couldn't do anything but say that it was an act of considerable courage.

What we do encourage is having people tell us when they see things going on. Most of the other nine citations were given to people who had done that. They'd seen something suspicious that ended up being the commission of a crime. Through this we get help for law enforcement. We've used the technique of community meetings. We've used the policy of treating all offenses, no matter against whom they have been committed, as the same. I'm very familiar with the old attitude in the old southern city—and I trust that it's disappearing now, but it certainly was prevalent in my day as a boy, that if a crime was committed by a Negro citizen against another Negro citizen—"Forget it, boys will be boys." This is not the standard of law enforcement which will take this country anywhere. This is the standard that leads to the idea that the law of the jungle still prevails.

I remember vividly a scout car ride in February of '62, shortly after I'd become police commissioner. The crew told me about an episode of a month earlier. They got a call to a bar—there was a victim slashed with a knife, cutting an artery. Blood was spurting all over the place, and the subject obviously was about to bleed to death. Another scout car arrived, and they loaded the victim on a stretcher and put him into a station wagon, rushed him off to the hospital operating room and a doctor stuck a needle into his heart. He was already unconscious and just about dead. They shot him full of adrenalin to keep the heart beating. They tied bottles of blood to both arms and filled him up and sewed him back up. Ten days later, he walked out of the hospital saying two mutually inconsistent things: (1) "I don't know who did it," and (2) "I'll take care of it myself."

Back at the bar, where there had been 30 people at the time of the assault, none of them had seen a thing. One of them even got off that old saw about, "Officer, I was tying my shoe." Now you see this is where we start. It is against this that we seek to work.

We have meetings with all the ministers in the city of Detroit, urging them to ask their people to report all crimes—asking them to trust the police department as the law enforcement agency, and to give us support in every aspect of enforcement—including, incidentally, a pretty vigorous drive against the numbers operation. This has existed in our town on a boys-will-be-boys basis. There was a hotel in the city that everybody knew was the headquarters of a numbers game. It was also the somewhat elite social headquarters for Negro society during a period when it had felt distinctly unwelcome in downtown hotels.

One of the tests that I had set for myself was whether or not we would end the known use of a known location as headquarters for a numbers racket. I suggested we should do this in January, and we finally accomplished it November 9th. It was simple. That's another story, but I mention it only to say one thing about it. Institutions so deeply imbedded would probably involve a total payroll of four or five hundred people. It had existed for at least 19 years, probably longer. Our action did not produce one single complaint. When it was raided, all the people involved were taken before the local and federal courts.

What is the effect of this, in relation to law enforcement? Can you have more vigorous enforcement? Can you have equal treatment and vigorous enforcement at the same time? In Precinct 10, we're over a thousand crimes lower this year than last year as a result of two things: (1) more vigorous law enforcement, and (2) public support for law enforcement. As of the end of the first quarter of this year, our total crime picture, counting Part One and Part Two crimes, is down 6 percent, and our prosecution arrests, which went up last year over the preceding year, are up 8 percent over last year.

The racists in any community always suggest that if you should apply equal enforcement in the core area of the city, somehow or other this will mean that murder will run rampant. Actually, in 1962, we recorded fewer murders than in 1961, and at the present moment we are seven murders behind last year. In terms of vigorous law enforcement, it might interest you to know that, as of today, we have had 42 murders, and in every single case there has been an arrest and the persons are now before the courts as charged. This is not a picture of a relaxed police department. Our department is going hard all the time. We haven't forgotten about traffic. We are 6,250 traffic tickets over the record of last year. And while Michigan is suffering a 16% rise in traffic deaths, we are holding slightly lower this year than last.

At the end of 1962, the police department of the city of Detroit was honored by the Freedoms Foundation of Valley Forge, the only police department honored by this organization. The citation read: "For their program of people's war on crime, their youth awards and citizens' code, enlisting the cooperation of community and religious leaders, the newspapers and the general public in aiding the police in fighting crime and race prejudice, bringing to the citizens of Detroit a greater awareness and understanding of each individual's responsibility in helping to maintain law and order." This is ultimately how we secure a sound balance between freedom and order, because it is in the search for the support of every law-abiding citizen for law enforcement that we have the greatest amount to gain.

I go back to a recent editorial in the Michigan CHRONICLE. You might say, "If your arrests and prosecutions are up, doesn't this mean that your community relations situation goes to pot?" The CHRONICLE says:

> There have been changes in personnel policies and practices. Greater emphasis has been placed on the importance of good community relations and citizen cooperation. These changes have contributed to a marked change in the relationship between the department and the Negro community. There are still some problems, but the climate of hostility, tension and suspicion has been reduced considerably. Tangible evidence of the effect of these efforts is the report indicating the crime rate in Detroit for the first quarter of 1963 was lower than the same rate in 1961 when the crime crack-down was in effect. The increase in arrests for the first quarter of the year may well indicate the cooperation of citizens in reporting crime.

Finally, yesterday's paper carried some comments which are interesting to a police commissioner. We have in Detroit the assistant attorney-general in charge of the criminal division of the United States Department of Justice, Mr. Herbert J. Miller, and along with him Mr. William G. Huntley, who heads the crime and racketeering section of the Justice Department. The Detroit NEWS of yesterday quoted them as saying, "The crime rate of Detroit is less than most metropolitan areas. . . . The recent raid on numbers operations, especially the raid on the former Gotham Hotel, dealt a crippling blow to the numbers operators in the Detroit area." And the lead sentence of the article is, "Law enforcement officials today complimented the Detroit Police Department." In this same paper, there is a fantastic bit of journalism recording that the American Civil Liberties Union lauded the police superintendent's handling of a police shooting case. That's a man bites dog story, if there ever was one.

We have, in relation to the core areas of our city, the prospect of choosing one of two paths—either the path of equal and vigorous law enforcement, which seeks public cooperation for law enforcement from all law-abiding citizens, or the occupation-army alternative. The occupation-army alternative means that the police officer, in walking his beat, or riding his scout car, sees every person as a hostile figure; doesn't see a friendly face, and when he talks to somebody, the person he talks to "doesn't know nothin'." The occupation-army procedure guarantees a maximum of hostility toward police and guarantees that every episode will be exaggerated out of context and beyond truth—because there is no confidence in the investigative process of the law. It also guarantees that hostility directed toward the police will also be directed toward the total white community — it guarantees that we will travel back down the road to 1943.

There is another way. It is the way of the Constitution; it is the way of our essential morality in America. It is the way of practicality also. It calls for vigorous law enforcement, which is equal and which has the support of all law-abiding people.

Racial Factors in Law Enforcement

THURGOOD MARSHALL

(Then) Director-Counsel, NAACP Legal Defense and Educational Fund, New York

MAY 19, 1960

We all feel that our own problems are the most important. And we constantly are brought up short in realizing the importance of the problems of other people. I spent February in Kenya, drafting a bill of civil rights for their minority group in their new democratic government. It is interesting to note that the minority in that case was the white man.

"We the people" means *all* the people, despite the fact that our Constitution recognized the existence of slavery (although some of the writers tried their best to eliminate its mention from the document). But we must point out that the "States Rights" concept was in large measure eliminated by the 14th Amendment. The fact that the argument persists today illustrates the too frequent lag of reality behind promise in a democracy. For example, the Supreme Court's "separate but equal" pronouncement of 1896 was never really implemented, at least as to the "but equal" part of it. In the South, it is still true that it is not only against the law for a Negro to be buried in a white cemetery, but his dog can't be buried in the white man's pets' cemetery—even if it is a pure white spitz!

The Southern segregation laws are not as old as some people think. They began to be written just before the turn of this century. After some of the states in the South began to write segregation laws, Northern states began to do the opposite, enacting, for example, fair employment laws. Both groups of states have vigorously enforced whichever type of laws they have. It is important to note, too, that segregation in the Armed Forces was not terminated until the middle of the Korean affair. The universities had no trouble until the relatively recent Lucy case, followed closely by incidents in public schools, beginning with schools in White Sulphur Springs. There the trouble started because two Negro football players displaced two white boys on a team, and the mother of one of the white boys got on the telephone and roused the community.

It is said that we should not press things, that we should have waited in the Lucy case, and, in short, that we were "pushing." The Lucy case was four years in the courts, and the Hawkins case was seven years, before the students were actually admitted. That could hardly be called pushing. Our children keep asking us, "When do we get ours?" The Little Rock case reached the Supreme Court twice, and although there was a change of four justices between the hearing of the first and second cases, both decisions were unanimous.

It is said that democracy constantly strives toward an ideal that will never, and can never, be achieved. That may be true, but we must work toward the time when "the son of the poorest Negro in the rural south will really be born with the rights of a baby born to the Rockefellers." I cannot forget the sound of 5,000 Nairobis shouting in unison, "Ahooru, ahooru!" (Freedom, freedom). Let us bring out problems out on the table, recognize them, analyze them, and meet them. For every school case this year, there will be ten next year, and more the next.

It has also been said that it may well be the judgment of history that our governmental authorities in these times faced no more vital issue that the problem of prejudice and racial discrimination. Be that as it may, there is no doubt that recent court decisions and other legal developments, spurred by the activities of private voluntary organizations such as the NAACP, and stimulated, in addition, by the development of human relations as an applied social science, have awakened public interest in these problems. More than that, a large part of the general public and professional police officers, too, have become concerned about the intrusion of racial prejudice and discrimination into the operation of law enforcement agencies and the actions of law enforcement officers.

Before dealing with the variety and extent of discrimination in police work, let us define it. Discrimination, lawyers and scientists agree, is the different treatment of persons classifiable in a particular social group on the basis of race, religion or some other common characteristic. Prejudice, although often confused with discrimination, is a prejudgment of persons who are members of some such social group; it is an attitude or a belief which may or may not be translated into action. Both are symptoms of individual as well as social disorganization, and may infect the whole range of an individual's public and private life. But these phenomena do not always occur together; many people who discriminate are not prejudiced, and not all prejudiced persons express their belief in overt discriminatory action.

Our examination of the evidence demonstrating that discrimination in police work is an un-American and unrewarding experience, paid for by both those who practice it as well as by those who suffer it, will be limited to discrimination against Negroes. I so limit it for two reasons: first, most of the current concern with "the problem" has arisen because of the efforts of Negroes to penetrate the barriers of discrimination erected by law, or in the face of it; and, second, the Negro is today the last large minority yet to win equal treatment in our political, economic and social life. Therefore, in my view, the treatment of the Negro is the common denominator of all discrimination.

Let me make it clear that I recognize and sympathize with the problems of police officials in this so-called sensitive field. I recognize the fact that in many areas of this country, there is a deep gap and lack of understanding between police officials and minority groups. I also recognize that this misunderstanding has brought about actual mistrust and mutual lack of respect between minorities and police. I sympathize with the individual police officer who believes, as I do, in protection of minority civil rights, but who is still the victim of the misunderstanding brought about by police officials who actually suffer from deep-seated racial and religious prejudices. As a lawyer, I am of course aware of the similarity between the distrust that lawyers as a group and the distrust of police as a group suffer solely because of the willingness of many members of a community to blame all for the sins of a few.

Some years ago in a city in the deep South, I was staying at the home of a Negro who lived in a block predominantly settled by Negroes and one adjoining a white community. Sitting on the porch of that home, I noticed a policeman coming through the white block, patting the white children on the head, saying nice things to them with an obvious exhibition of good feeling on both sides. The same policeman, when he reached the Negro block, yelled at the Negro children, told them to get out of his way, and brushed by them, with antagonism exhibited on both sides. Similarly, in many northern cities, we have found that there is complete mistrust and suspicion between minority groups and the police.

It seems to me that we have to face this issue squarely. It exists in differing degrees from one end of the country to the other. There will be those who say that it is not a policeman's duty to change laws, or to change community attitudes, mores, and customs. There are also those who take the position that the police, as an arm of the government, have an equal responsibility in bringing about changes in customs and mores, especially now, because such changes are dictated by law, either statutory or judicial. Regardless of how one approaches this problem, it cannot be denied that a forward-looking, efficient police official must be aware of the problem and the so-called delicate lines between one's individual prejudices and enforcement of the law of the land.

Let us look at the law itself — the law as to civil rights, civil liberties and human rights. In this country, a constitutional democracy, we have a government of laws, and not of men. This is particularly pertinent for police officials. You will remember that, under Article Six of the United States Constitution, all state officials are required to take an oath to support the Constitution of the United States as well as the constitutions of their particular states. The same Article of our Constitution makes it crystal clear, in unmistakable language, that the federal Constitution is the Supreme Law of the land, state constitutions and laws to the contrary notwithstanding. While there have been variations in detail as to particular rights or provisions, the federal Constitution is recognized as having been grounded in the theory that all men are created equal and stand equal before the law.

While, in the past, court decisions have upheld state-imposed racial segregation in public facilities, recent decisions of the United States Supreme Court have made it clear that segregation in public facilities is unconstitutional; and this is true regardless of the state law. The decision in the school segregation cases holds specifically that state laws requiring segregation must yield to the federal Constitution. Thus, as the law now stands, every citizen of the United States should enjoy rights equal to those of any other citizen, regardless of the color of his skin, his ancestry, or previous condition.

If your personal belief is that there is such a thing as inherent racial superiority or inferiority, you might consider that scientists throughout this country have exposed that belief as a myth. And the law has made clear that such notions must be disregarded in any official action of any official of any state. Therefore, crime prevention, arrest of criminals, treatment of criminals, and all other phases of police activity must be carried on with this basic understanding.

I would like to touch on one other point. It is usually not difficult for a police official to enforce a law against a citizen of the same race or religion, and even a neighbor or close friend, where the crime is one of violence, lust or violation of trust. However, where the incident or alleged collision with, or disobedience of, the law comes about as a result of a court decision involving segregation in schools, recreational centers, or any other situation involving a change of mores and customs, the same police official finds it more difficult to set aside his own personal prejudice and enforce the law without regard to these feelings.

There are, of course, many beautiful exceptions to this thesis. I can remember, for example, the action of the late police chief of Little Rock, Arkansas, who last year urged the white mob objecting to Negroes attending Central High to disperse, and when they refused to do so, used normal police tactics to disperse the crowd—no doubt including many of his friends—and to arrest those guilty of rioting.

Many individuals in this country still believe that Negroes as a group are either criminals or potential criminals, liars or potential liars or, at any rate, not as good citizens as others. Indeed, I think many of you are familiar with the fact that at some state conventions of police and law enforcement officials, the Negro is used as the brunt of the worst jokes—all involving the libelous beliefs just mentioned. While it is difficult to cope with the inner mind and the actions which it impels, the least the police official can do is to try and separate his personal belief from his official actions. As one police official put it:

> We don't have to look at a racial minority group to make that point. We can just think about ourselves. I run into far too many people who think of a policeman as an ignorant, flat-footed, stupid fellow that any private detective or layman can outwit. This stereotype of us has been developed in detective stories, in the movies, in cartoons, and on the stage. We know there are as many different kinds of people in police work as there are patterns of fingerprints. Yet some of us have the stereotyped idea that a Negro is lazy, indolent, lustful, and carries a razor. And that thinking doesn't work for us as policemen. Until we realize that there are just as many different kinds of Negroes as there are different kinds of policemen, we shan't be able to make intelligent and creditable decisions.

An even more difficult problem is presented when the governor, the mayor and other officials are openly opposed to the democratic principle of equality of all citizens without regard to race. In such instances, the police official, convinced in his own mind of the theory I am advocating, finds himself in the middle. The answer to such a problem is a simple one; you merely face the problem of separating the men from the boys. If there is any question as to the right and wrong of the position the policeman should take, perhaps it would be wise to quote from the Hon. J. Edgar Hoover, Director of the Federal Bureau of Investigation. He has stated:

> Law enforcement is a career service. Each officer should dedicate his life to the service and protection of others. A successful police officer must put aside his personal opinions in the line of duty, renounce pursuit of wealth, and seek only the highest good for the organization he represents so that the community may live in peace and security. The badge of a law enforcement officer is a sacred trust which must be guarded with his whole mind and his whole body, for it is his to hold only while he lives a life beyond all reproach and censure.
>
> The law enforcement officer is the guardian of civil rights, the protector of the weak, and the defender of the innocent. The community recognizes his training in public service and his loyal devotion to duty. He is the friend of every child and the ally of each law-abiding adult. By far the greater portion of his work is the removing of the ugly finger of suspicion from innocent persons.
>
> A modern law enforcement officer is a well-bred gentleman of clean habits, high morals, clear mind, and sound body. Well trained in his profession, he treats all with respect without deference to anyone. . . .

I am not just talking about theory. I am talking about what is perhaps the most important factor in bringing about the unity of this country, so necessary in these trying times. Consider that, while Negroes are in the minority in this country, darker people form from two-thirds to three-fourths of the population of the world today. This country can no longer preach democracy to Asia and Africa and practice racial discrimination at home. The world picture today, with short wave radio, supersonic transportation, and the like, is such that we can no longer sweep racial discrimination and other problems under the rug and dispose of them that way. Even more important, from a strictly moral position, human beings must be recognized as human beings and the policeman must treat all in the community as such. The first thing one must understand is that people vary infinitely; they range from good to bad and from stalwart citizens to vicious criminals, yet all without regard to race, color or religion. One must also realize that each person must be treated as an individual, not as a stereotype.

How shall this be done? First of all, a policeman must convince himself that, under the law, this government requires non-discrimination in terms of race or religion. He must convince himself that this is the law of the land and that he cannot overrule nor disregard it. Next, he must realize that, when he is on duty, his every action must be on that basis. He cannot make a practice of calling one citizen "Mr." and another "boy." He must recognize that a Negro in the eyes of the law is innocent until proved guilty, the same as anyone else. He must realize that he has no more right, unlawfully and without provocation, on the pretense of protecting himself, to beat the poor defenseless Negro, any more than to take his billy to the leading white citizen of the city. In other words, it is my thesis that the police official in the United States has a tremendous responsibility, on the one hand, to recognize the quality of man without regard to race, and on the other, to do his part to destroy the image that the policeman is the oppressor of the civil rights of minority groups.

In recognizing this as more than theory, but as a belief to be put into practice, I fully recognize the concurrent responsibility of minority groups to recognize this change, and to do all in their power to break down resentment against police as a whole. It is a two-way street but if each side waits for the other to move, there may well be no movement at all. Because the police have the full authority of the state behind them and the gun and nightstick to support them, it would be well for police to make the first move, by demonstrating in clear and unmistakable action their recognition of Negroes as people, as citizens with rights to be respected to the same degree as those of any other citizen.

In closing, I commend to you the words of the Chief Justice of the United States, who — speaking recently at the Centennial Celebration of Northwestern University's Law School — said: "We must recognize — that justice, equality and freedom under law are the basic right of every person — and can be denied to none except at peril to the rights of all."

Understanding the Community: Community Change as it Affects Police–Community Relations

HERBERT JENKINS

Chief of Police, Atlanta, Georgia

MAY 23, 1961

Henry W. Grady, Editor of the Atlanta CONSTITUTION, was a spokesman for the new South in 1890. He visited Boston, Massachusetts, and spoke to the Chamber of Commerce. He told them all about the suffering, the hardships and the handicaps of all the people living in the rural South, following the Civil War and Reconstruction. He told them of the great need for working capital and asked their assistance. He spoke of the discriminatory freight rates that had been imposed upon the South. He told them about the death of a Georgia farmer, who was buried in a suit made in Cincinnati — and in a casket that was made in Pittsburg — and the marker that was put at the head of the grave came from Vermont. Georgia possesses an abundance of raw material to produce such commodities, but the only thing that Georgia could furnish for this funeral was the hole in the ground and the corpse. He also told them of the new South's determination to establish schools, plants, and to provide jobs for all of the people. He spoke of the efforts being made to remove the hatred, the prejudice, and the Ku Klux Klan from the South, and to provide equal opportunities and justice for all, regardless of race, creed, or color. Little did Mr. Grady realize at that time, the great effect of police–community relations in achieving these goals today.

Today, we are most furtunate in Atlanta in having Ralph McGill, publisher of the Atlanta CONSTITUTION, as a spokesman for the new South. Mr. McGill has a complete understanding of all the problems involved. He is setting the pace and pointing the way to achieve the goals outlined by Mr. Grady, and I am happy to be on his team. It has been my experience that many of the problems that we are confronted with today are caused by misunderstanding — first, by the leaders of the community — second, by the police — and third, by the press. Certainly we are all striving for the same thing, and that is to make our community a better place in which to live and raise children. Every community has the undisciplined few who will create all the misunderstanding and confusion that they possibly can, to conceal their selfish and unlawful motives. The only way to deal with these individuals is to identify them, and focus attention on their motives.

The police have the responsibility of getting public support. We can't do the job without it. We must first have public confidence before we can expect public support and cooperation. I recall many years ago, we had a very effective traffic control program in Atlanta. Traffic fatalities were reduced from 85 to 30 per year, in just a few years. But the enforcement program was so far ahead, or so far out of step with public support, that a man ran for Mayor and was elected on a platform to eliminate "hiding" police. This was no reflection on the man who was elected. He simply developed a program and a slogan that had public support and was elected, but his election caused the traffic enforcement index to drop from 33 to 3 almost overnight, and traffic accidents and fatalities increased by leaps and bounds. Then it was the public who demanded a strict traffic enforcement program.

In 1948, when we first employed Negro police in Atlanta, generally we had public support for that project. Ninety percent of the police personnel were much opposed to it, because they did not understand the purpose and the need for Negro police. After the Negro police were properly selected, screened and trained, they were accepted, and today they are unanimously accepted in Atlanta — not because they are Negroes, but because they are good policemen and doing a good job. We are continually adding more.

We are witnessing great changes all over the world today. Conditions change and even people change — especially young people. The police must be trained and disciplined to meet these changing conditions quickly, or we will be left behind. About a year ago, we had the first sit-in, lunch counter demonstrations in Atlanta. I served on Mayor William B. Hartsfield's committee to try to solve the "segregated–integrated" question between the Negro students and the merchants. A solution was not possible at that time, and the demonstrations and boycotts continued for almost a year, placing a terrific strain on the police. At one time we had students carrying signs and the Ku Klux Klan element, wearing robes, picketing the same places at the same time. If you don't think that will turn your hair grey and develop stomach ulcers, you should try it sometime. We did not have a single instance of disturbance or fighting, nor was it necessary to make a single arrest, because the police were there in force. They were trained and disciplined to respect the rights of everyone, and to maintain peace and order at all costs. We had public support. A solution has now been reached. It was very much like a labor strike. Both sides had to wear themselves out and try the patience of the police, and see what they would do. The demonstrations have stopped, and the lunch counters will be integrated on a given date in accordance with the agreement.

The United States Supreme Court handed down its much-debated school integration decision in 1954. The Georgia political leaders, at the State Capitol, immediately denounced the Court, and proclaimed to the world that the decision would never be accepted. The Legislature started passing laws to protect segregation in public schools, and to cut off all public funds to any white school that admitted even one Negro. This went on for seven years, while most of us knew that the decisions of the Supreme Court were the law of the land—that this was a country governed by law and not by man, and that the decisions would eventually be obeyed.

We must continue to develop a better understanding of the law and its application. Blackstone defined the law as "a signal rule for human action, commending what is right and forbidding what is wrong." That is a fine definition, but its great weakness is that men of goodwill simply cannot agree on what is right and what is wrong. For instance, in the last 20 years, the U.S. Supreme Court has handed down decisions in thirty cases that originated from police action, usually cases of "searches and seizures." Not a single one of these decisions received unanimous support from the Court, and most of the cases were decided by a five to four decision. In January, 1961, two Negro students were admitted to the University of Georgia. This caused a demonstration and a disturbance, but in less than a week, the Legislature met and repealed all of the laws that would interfere in any way with the two Negroes attending the University, and then changed the subject by raising their own pay.

All of this goes to prove that all problems are caused by people—and people are funny.

A Sense of Responsibility

HAROLD A. LETT

Consultant, National Program Development,
National Conference of Christians and Jews

MAY 21, 1963

In approaching this topic, I have had a feeling of compulsion to resort to definition of terms as an opening gambit. This I am resisting, yielding only to the degree that I may provide a simple frame of reference for the discussion to follow. I shall attempt to emphasize the thesis that there is in the theme, THE ADMINISTRATION OF JUSTICE AS A COMMUNITY RESPONSIBILITY, the recognition of an interdependence between all segments of the American community, in the administration of justice and in other phases of community development which contribute constructively to democratic living.

The extension and guarantee of justice is not alone a function of law enforcement agencies. It embraces nearly every aspect of man's relation to his fellowman: the granting of another's right to dignity, to self respect, to growth and development, to participation in the benefits of a free society, giving assurance of his right to dream and to have those dreams come true. Justice cannot be seen and measured in a vacuum, nor as an absolute. In all human affairs, it is a relative concept, whose definition in a particular time and place is an index of the maturity of a culture and of the people who have fashioned the culture. It is a measure of the integrity with which the rules of interpersonal and intergroup relations are defined and observed. It is the yardstick by which a society determines its present stature, its rate of growth and its expectations in terms of safety, security, stability and strength. Like such concepts as "Freedom" and "Democracy," it is a goal toward which men constantly work; a dream, a hope; not ever fully attainable because of ever advancing demands, expectations, aspirations. Yet, in its attainment to the highest level and the widest application, lies the only hope of this civilization. Surely this imposes a tremendous burden of responsibility upon a society, even in the single interest of self-preservation.

The maintenance of law and order, and the administration of justice as broadly defined, have a high degree of correlation. In a community where justice operates in a capricious, prejudicial fashion, there will be found serious problems in the maintenance of law and order. In like measure, where the peace and tranquility of a community are threatened, deeply within those areas of rebellion or of ir-responsibility may be found evidence—or a deeply-seated belief—that justice does not prevail.

Wherever irresponsibility or rebellion have threatened or interrupted the peace of a community, invariably it has been traceable to the shirking of duty by many elements in that community. Religious leadership may charge it to public apathy; citizens generally may blame the political leadership; police will cite a condition of general lawlessness chargeable to abdication of parental authority, or general cussedness of particular groups in the population; the press will point to inefficiency in the police force. Full circle of charge and counter-charge will have been drawn; all may be right in terms of identifying *some* of the important factors in the decline of community pride; but all are wrong in pursuing efforts to fix blame *elsewhere* than within their own realm of responsibility and competence.

Each is wrong, too, in criticizing others in the community, on the basis of their own unrealistic levels of expectation of others. The clergy may expect much higher levels of civic participation from the general public; the public always expects and demands higher performance from poltical leaders than its own apathy can justify; the press forever seeks news of deviations from perfection, the sensational, the unfavorable side of socio-political developments and of police performance; and all seem to expect highly motivated, middle-class, urban-oriented performance from that part of the public least exposed to these values, to which are attached the more disturbing statistics of arrests, violations and convictions. This segment of the population, whose needs, experiences, fears and desires are of least importance to the whole community, turn their frustrations and dissatisfactions upon the police who, to them, are the highly visible representatives of an invisible and hostile society.

Two eminent Americans have commented upon unrealistic levels of expectations generally, though unconsciously accepted in our nation. Just a year ago at the annual Texas A & M Police Community Relations Institute, Chief Bernard Garmire of the Tucson (Ariz.) Police Department, said of public expectations of police:

> . . . [A] police officer must have the mind of a lawyer — the soul of a clergy-man—the heart of a social worker—the discipline of a Marine sergeant—the integrity of a saint. He must believe in a community of law, while seeing little but lawlessness; believe in the goodness of man, while seeing man most often at his worst—work in a community of men who resent his presence but depend on his faithfulness—know his city like a sociologist, and he must understand people like a psychologist—take the long view of life like a philosopher, and yet never lose his common touch.

The noted author, John Steinbeck, was quoted in the SATURDAY REVIEW a few years ago, in a comment upon the Negro segment of our population. Under the title *The Black Man's Ironic Burden,* Mr. Steinbeck also listed a great number of high expectations imposed by society upon this group; I quote just a few:

> We expect Negroes to be wiser than we are, more tolerant than we are, braver, more dignified, more self-controlled and self-disciplined; they must be ten times as gifted to receive equal recognition; have more endurance than we in athletics, more courage in defeat, more rhythm and versatility in music and dancing, more controlled emotion in theater. We expect them to obey rules of conduct we flout, to be more courteous, more gallant, more proud, more steadfast.

You who are police, and I, happen to be members of two highly visible "minority" groups. Each of us has developed a high degree of sensitivity to, and rejection of, these unrealistic levels of expectation, of which we have been made victims. Nevertheless, each of us, by our own hypercritical assessment of the other in most test areas, unconsciously express the expectations we *demand* of the other—whether or not we really *expect* high level performance. As a result of this mutually critical attitude, each is much more easily irritated by the lapses of the other; our impatience shows more easily; we voice our dissatisfactions more readily; and we can engage in recrimination and conflict on slight provocation. Just like cousins, if you'll forgive the expression. Meantime, the rest of the "family," which is the community around us, urges us on in our perennial disagreements with a "Let's you and him fight" kind of encouragement.

At this point, I should like to bring this discussion to the level of the specific problem of police and the Negro segment of the American community — not to plead a cause on the racial front, as such—but that I may be in position to relate particular examples and examine particular problems in concrete form, as distinct from discussing some of these issues in the abstract. I think this is a legitimate approach if my earlier references to justice and to law and order are valid. It just happens that I have been a Negro longer than anything else, so my experiences have been more varied in this area. I believe there would be the same degree of validity to this approach if we were to use the example of Indians in reservation country, Spanish-speaking people in the Southwest or the eastern seaboard, or other highly visible minorities in other parts of the country. This is so because it is in the living experiences of these peoples of high visibility that we find the more pronounced examples of dislocation, of separation, of deprivation or lack of belongingness. It is here that unemployment is highest, and where underemployment reduces annual income to 50 percent or less of that of the so-called majority group worker; it is here that housing discrimination is greater, and the otherwise routine task of finding decent shelter for a family becomes a maddening experience. It is here that things most of us take for granted—availability of reasonably good schools for our children, of ordinary recreational facilities, of convenient stations in which to secure food, drink and shelter—are withheld for no other reason than one's racial or ethnic identification. And it is in such groups that we find reflected the highest rates of arrest in any metropolitan center in America.

In your community, and mine, unless it is a very exceptional community with respect to the meeting of responsibitlity on many levels, we presently are concerned about delinquency and crime rates. The more the police and the press and the political leaders and the clergy pass the buck around the circle, the more directly implicated minority group elements in the community become. The characteristic defensiveness of those of minority group status becomes accentuated; the nature of contact between them and the police, individually and collectively, creates more sensitivity and more defensiveness, and again we have completely rounded out the vicious cycle of charge and counter-charge, of action and reaction.

In an Eastern city which shall be nameless, a new Chief of Police—in one of his early public statements—announced his intention of "cracking down on Black Muslims." There had been no public demonstrations by Muslims warranting a line of type in local newspapers; whatever number of Muslims may currently be residing in the community, there have been no group actions that would justify a crusade against the sect. The announcement, however, did serve to suggest, from the background of a long, painful history, that *any* Negro coming into the toils of the law would be subject to different and harsher treatment. The Chief's next pronouncement was of his intention to put police dogs into service. Even before occurrence of the recent Alabama and Mississippi incidents, Negroes had learned that police dogs represent a particular threat to them and their civil liberties. It must be remembered that dogs have played a dramatic, if not tragic, role in the South's oppression of the Negro throughout the slave regime and since, and all the Negro world has been touched by this history. The inhuman use of vicious dogs against nonviolent demonstrators certainly has not lessened fears and suspicions.

It was not surprising, then, that Negroes in this community and their allies increased the volume of complaints of "police brutality," induced, perhaps, as much by fear as by any particular incidents, and they began pressing for creation of a Civilian Review Board. An official Human Relations Commission, which had come into being a number of years ago in answer to similar political pressures of disadvantaged minorities, supported the petition for a Review Board. This official position was taken because of the inability of the director, appointed several years earlier by the Mayor, to establish any satisfactory communication with the police in meeting just such situations.

The reaction of the police has been an interesting study of the need for, and almost complete absence of channels of communication between police and the minority community. It also provided a rather frightening demonstration of cynical disregard for basic democratic practices, values and ethical standards. Day after day, the press was provided by the police with hysterical charges of Communist and criminal influence being responsible for the civil rights movement, with blistering personal attacks upon the individuals associated with the petition for a Review Board. A federal government official felt job pressures from above because of his advocacy of a Review Board given in his capacity as a private citizen and individual civic worker in his home community; respected clergymen found themselves blanketed by a general accusation that "only the criminal element is seeking this means of destroying police effectiveness." The director of the Mayor's Human Relations Commission, himself a respected professional who had given many years of effective service to the community, was the target of a concerted attack by the Chief of Police, the PBA, the Superior Officers' Association, the Fraternal Order of Police, and two or three other satellite organizations—all demanding summary dismissal from city service and a rescinding of the ordinance that had created the Commission.

Nowhere had there been any proposal or move toward resolving differences through conference or conciliation; there was no presenting of logical and reasonable arguments by police leadership against the petition, or in meeting the fears which prompted the movement; no inclination was shown to search out the motivations of so many responsible citizens who had expressed a need for some form of central clearance of police–community problems. The one idea disclosed by every public move by department leaders was that of eliminating the opposition, intimidating the protestors, applying power politics through threat of loss of job or of respectability in the eyes of the larger community. They who demanded liberty for themselves resorted to calumny and intimidation of others, and urged denial of their freedom of speech, as a contribution to the state of human relations in that particular community. Situations of this kind bring to mind a statement made by President Kennedy in a speech to Latin America in 1962, when he said: "Those who make peaceful revolution impossible, make violent revolution inevitable."

Please understand that this reference to a Civilian Review Board in no way is intended as a pitch for or against such an instrumentality. Personally, I am quite ambivalent on the subject, because I've never heard anything in many discussions of the topic that suggested a consensus of *what is* a Review Board — what would be its duties, responsibilities, limitations, authority. If it is intended to mean a body of civilians who, publicly or privately and through application of hindsight, would have authority to pass judgment upon an act of an officer who has been accused of misuse of police authority, while working under pressure in a tense, demanding situation—then I would be vigorously opposed to such procedure. I have too high regard for the manly, courageous, efficient way the average police officer faces up to the severe demands society places upon him to see him exposed to this experience. If on the other hand, it is intended to mean a body of civilians and officers serving together to provide a medium of communication and interpretation, through which confidence of the minority group community could be regained, then I can say that I wish some such reasonable machinery were available in the community from which I have drawn the example above.

The foregoing recitation refers to an actual situation, but I admit that it may be out of the ordinary. It does serve to highlight some of the natural elements of conflict which characterize problems of law enforcement in American cities. The minority community, with its serious social, economic and political disadvantages, is confronted by uniformed symbols of society—a society that has reduced the minority to its level of dissatisfaction. This uniformed symbol, the police, possesses a power and an authority that historically are interpreted as having been used *against,* rather than *for* the minority group's interest. It is not necessary for this power to be misused regularly or constantly, to have reinforced the suspicion and fear that memory of other times and other places has created. Only one unfortunate incident will supply this reinforcement; that is—if there is no positive, constructive effort being given toward the building of confidence to offset the suspicion that prevails.

Repeatedly we see enacted the drama growing out of natural conflict to be found in this confrontation. At the core of each conflict situation is the human tendency to equate "my rights" with "his responsibilities." A rational approach is that of consideration of "our respective rights," then on to the natural next step of "our respective responsibilities" in achieving our mutual rights. Constructive implementation of a sense of our respective responsibilities is that which develops the concept of "community," involving as it must, the interdependence of all, for the common good. Essential to this development is mutual respect for the rights of others, assured only where there is healthy communication.

In contrast to the foregoing example, I know of a number of police departments in different parts of the country which have begun to recognize human relations to be as important an area of study for their personnel as are the more technical aspects of police work. Among these, too, are the departments which have employed specialists in human relations, under whose leadership a closer communion with citizens of the community may be developed. That these departments stand out as the exception rather than the rule, throughout America, indicates that still there are those in police work who look upon this kind of emphasis as a lot of "do-gooder" hogwash, firmly believing that police should be exposed only to sterner stuff. Not long ago, two highly competent social scientists and I were engaged by a large municipal police department to present a series of lectures on human relations, in a long-deferred, in-service refresher course for all personnel. Sessions were chaired by a Deputy Chief of Police who was approaching retirement age. At the close of each session, when the three specialists had given their very best accumulation of knowledge on the subject, the Deputy Chief closed the session with his own interpretations, all of which served to deny, refute, and dispose of every bit of valid information that had been presented by the specialists—his premise being that the practical experience *he* had acquired in years of police work gave *him* the best knowledge of human relations problems— at least as much as police are required to know.

In the case of the increasing number of departments that are working constructively in developing human relations understandings, there is evidence of a desire to learn from authoritative sources, in order that through the understanding that may be acquired, they may cope more effectively with the complex problems of tension in today's metropolitan areas. These efforts too, are resulting in the training of an impressive number of police who themselves are providing competent human relations skills to department training and administrative operations. But there also are those police who insist upon judging the phenomena of this trying period with a singularly harsh standard of values, which conveniently ignores the abnormal conditions out of which problems have sprung, and with equal harshness seek to abandon to oblivion those human beings who spiritually and physically have succumbed to the forces which have caused them to be out of step with society. In which of these reactions is to be found evidence of the greater, the more realistic, sense of responsibility?

In indicated earlier that my preoccupation with so-called minority groups is due to the high incidence of anti-social behavior in minority group ghettos, as disclosed by statistics on delinquency and crime, and as seen in the day-to-day experience of police officers. What of these minority groups? Where do they stand with respect to recognizing and accepting a sense of responsibility?

In scores of police–community relations conferences which I have been privileged to attend over the past fifteen or more years, an inevitable question has been, "What is the Negro doing to improve himself?" The question serves, first of all, to disclose the grave need for communication between police and the Negro minority, in some other relationship than that of arresting officer and Negro violator or suspect. Certainly the question is an implied confession of ignorance of what *is* transpiring behind the ghetto walls; and it implies also that minority group leadership is possessed of some magic quality to soothe its angry people, heal deep psychological wounds, provide sustenance and inspiration for its marginal rebels, preach away dissatisfaction, no matter how deep-seated— something that society has been unable to do, for the whole population, even when it possesses the necessary tools, facilities and means for aiding the healing process. Lest I appear to you to be defensive in answering my own question, I wish to assert that the more fortunate members of any society bear great responsibility for aiding the less fortunate members of that society, and this applies to minorities as well as to the community generally.

But this assertion still does not answer the question. What, then, *is* the responsibility of Negro leadership—that amorphous segment of a mysterious world that exists apart from everything we know? Is it to aid the group to become more economically independent and self-sustaining? But they don't own nor control the factories, banks and commercial establishments, nor direct the policies of labor unions. Even if a racially separated economy were possible or desirable, they have not the means of employing all workers, building their own housing, supplying their own needs. It is their responsibility to see that more of the group secure education adequate enough for competitive purposes? But they do not own the schools and academies and colleges, nor have they even been able to gain admission to such institutions in parts of the country where the group need is greatest.

Perhaps they can work for development of higher standards of group morality and social behavior? This question intrigues many whose acquaintance with minority group life is limited to sensational articles, or as with the police, to contact only with the lower socio-economic levels in conflict situations. My interest was caught by a comment by Dr. L. D. Savitz of Temple University in an article *Factors Influencing Crime Rates of Negroes*, as follows:

> Even assuming that every arrest in a given year involves a different person, and that every arrest results in conviction, it is clear that well over 90% of the Negro population are law-abiding citizens. Since these assumptions are unwarranted (that is, every arrest does *not* involve different persons and every arrest does *not* lead to conviction), the estimate of 90% is decidedly conservative.

The logic of this statement does not pretend to ignore the disproportionate rate of Negro involvement with police, but it does serve to attack the validity of existing stereotypes that would place the Negro group as a whole (or the Mexican or the Puerto Rican or the Indian) in the criminal class. Nevertheless, in 65 Urban League local offices, and in hundreds of NAACP branches, youth group activities are being promoted, toward the difficult task of lifting the sights of Negro youth above the sordid, mean, unpromising horizon which greets their eyes from the limits of the racial ghetto and its *de facto* segregated school. Through various other community activities, the Urban League is reaching the reachable, with programs designed to accelerate the adjustment to independent city life of many Negroes who have come out of a feudal, rural slum society in recent years. Negro churches are struggling, as churches in all groups and denominations must struggle, to hold attention and do constructive work; fraternities and sororities are making their contributions through scholarships and other aids, however limited and unsatisfactory. Those who are doing these humble tasks, under difficult circumstances and against a rising tide of youthful cynicism, themselves must fight against terrific odds in order to retain their own faith.

A recent television program brought this out very sharply. A public affairs discussion program presented the noted Malcolm X, youthful and fiery spokesman for the Black Muslims, in an exchange of views with a well-educated Brooklyn Negro clergyman. On the panel were two white men and a Negro former college professor and a high New York State official. Malcolm X, in his usual emotional tirade, repeated and reemphasized the endless story of white exploitation of black people, particularly in America. According to Malcolm X, there is no meeting ground between the races, nothing in common, no hope for cooperation and peace. The two university-trained Negroes sharing the program were in violent disagreement with the Muslim philosophy, expectations and conclusions; yet in analyzing what was being said throughout the hour-long program, one was brought to a realization that neither of the college-trained, conciliatory, "reasonable" men was able to deny the truth of Malcolm X's assertions, refute his recitation of wrongs or offer any concrete promise of change. The one single thing which separated them in their views and conclusions was the word "Hope." Malcolm and his sect have lost theirs; the others still retain theirs—the experiences, study, and faith of all three Negroes had undergone the same traumatic assault upon their own lives. Each has known, during his entire lifetime, the effect of deprivation of simple human dignity, whether by thoughtless act or studied deed; each is required to walk in that shadowy world in which move those who are less than men.

But I repeat—what then is the responsibility of Negro leadership? In the days of the slave regime, the Negro clergyman who preached his other-world doctrine of passive endurance *here* for assurance of reward hereafter, did what he thought was good. But this in no way contributed to the elimination of slavery; it helped only to make it more endurable. The unceasing work of abolitionists, of dedicated people of deep religious conviction, and of people who truly believed in the dignity of the human personality, by their joint efforts made it feasible for President Lincoln to issue the Emancipation Proclamation just 100 years ago. Then, the fight was the one important task of eliminating the blot of human slavery from the Western world.

Over 50 years ago, two different organizations were formed in the Negro world by the joining of hands of dedicated white people and colored people, for separate attacks upon injustice. The National Urban League came into being for the purpose of improving employment opportunities, housing, health and recreational facilities; and to secure the privileges of full citizenship for Negroes in urban centers. Theirs was the chosen role of providing calm, dispassionate, persuasive spokesmanship for the Negro race in America, as their way of gaining recognition and opportunity. For over 50 years, this organization has struggled along with seriously restricted budgets, with painfully inadequate staff, with polite but contemptuous disregard by the majority community, for the human problems embraced in League program proposals. I know, because I spent 16 years of my life in the discouraging, disheartening effort to gain the sympathetic ear and the cooperation of businessmen, labor leaders, clergy, educators, police and the whole range of officials, great and small, who represented the outreach of the power-structure of the community. It is extremely difficult to keep Hope alive, when encountering this kind of experience. It is even more difficult for those whose lives are confined physically and spiritually to the lowly, unpromising, sordid limits of the ghetto.

Over 50 years ago, the National Association for the Advancement of Colored People came into being, for the purpose of employing the tools fashioned by the architects of this great country, as means of forever protecting Americans from the tyranny to which their forebears had been exposed. Unique in the history of mankind, this organization has ceaselessly waged a war for human liberty without ever resorting to violence; always expressing hope in the rightness of man-made law and its ability, concretely and objectively, to resolve problems associated with the tyranny of racism. Where else in the world has there been this kind of consistent, tireless but intelligently restrained expression of impatience and hope, manifested by a people who historically, here in the Western world, have been classed with the beasts of the field?

For over 50 years, these two organizations — through their leadership — have had the task of trying to hold the faith and respect of their followers, while pounding on the doors of the conscience of America; and for this period of time, they have had to live with the futility of it all, as they watched the tiny, grudging concessions made in response to their pleadings. I know, because more than 40 years ago I became an ardent member of the NAACP, which fought for years for passage of a civil rights law in my native state, Michigan, and in my native city, Lansing, where I was not permitted to enter the ground floor of a movie picture theatre, or buy a sandwich in a restaurant. I know, because then and since, I have had the soul-searching task of trying to earn and to receive the respect, the sympathetic hearing, the cooperative action from public officials, from police, and from employers that a spokesman for a disadvantaged group should have, in a free and just society.

Today, we are living increasingly with immediate by-products of the indifference, opposition and contempt with which the efforts of these two organizations have been greeted. Many Negroes, whose anger has reached an irreconcilable level, find the Black Muslim movement to be a satisfying vehicle for their spirit of revolt; many others, without guidance, discipline or restraint, strike out blindly against any symbol of society. They who still retain some modicum of Hope, despite discouragement and disillusionment, are stepping up the pace and volume of protest action. Here again, if we will but analyze that which is happening, these demonstrations are unique and highly significant of the role being played by Negro leadership in its attempt to meet its responsibility.

In all parts of the world, the vanguard of protest movements fighting for human betterment has been composed largely of university youth groups. In America, for whatever combination of reasons, this is rarely true. Identification with social, economic and political issues of the day has been limited largely to organized forum discussions, with social action being almost non-existent. Youthful spirits have been content with "high jinks" expressions, such as panty-raids, phone booth pile-ups, and other such mentally elevating exercises. The college youth from whom the least was expected, who had the most to lose and the least hope of gain, are they who have lately given the world inspiring demonstrations of purpose, self-discipline, love of fellowman and faith in the ultimate triumph of decency. Negro youth who have never known the real meaning of freedom, or the inner meaning of a sense of human dignity, have been the ones who have given demonstration of the heights human dignity can attain, even in the face of unbelievable provocation to cause loss of dignity. A profound sense of responsibility, manifested by minority group leadership, has made these demonstrations possible. My mind is brought back to a statement made by Dr. Franklin Littell of Chicago Theological Seminary in a speech delivered at the recent National Conference on Religion and Race. Said Dr. Littell: "What would our situation be in America today, facing our most important internal crisis, if the Negro leadership were at the level of Ross Barnett, Orville Faubus, Jimmy Davis and Edwin Walker?"

I could have countered with references to Malcolm X and Elijah Muhammad, but fortunately, neither of these is in position to determine the course of the entire machinery of law enforcement or operation of a complete educational system—nor have they been so effective as to sway the emotions of many persons in many strategic places—at least, not yet!

World events are placing greater responsibilities upon the shoulders of the many levels of minority group leadership, particularly the Negro. The grievances with which he must deal are part of the ferment of a world which has been taught to revolt in violence. Yet his choice is and has been the alternative of relying upon a system of law, which in national perspective is idealistic in the abstract, but which on the local, operational plane frequently is coarse, biased and arbitrary, reflecting the character of administrators of such caliber. His patience is tried, not only by the insistent pleas and demands of the group he would lead, and by the constant assaults by the outside world upon the dignity of his own personality, but also by the calloused or thoughtless admonitions of well-meaning majority group persons who, without patience of their own, counsel patience to him who has been the epitome of forbearance and patience.

In our chronic preoccupation with each other, as the "aggressor" group, we, the police and the Negro (again as a symbol and example of minority status and aspirations) may feel that neither is in position fully and perceptibly to change community positions or attitudes. In time and with consistent effort, we may influence and mold these attitudes, but this is not done by wishing. Neither of us had much voice in the making of the rules, but both of us can help reshape them, if reshaping is called for. Chief Herbert Jenkins of Atlanta has stated what he expects of his police force, and of the community, if confronted by this or any similar issues. He planned and trained his men for such eventuality, and when the test came, he carried his community with him in meeting the test. Whatever may have been the mores of the community— its fears and traditions—they yielded to the influence of a government and its police force, which truly believed in the role of preserving law and order, and implemented this belief by being prepared to restrain those who would be perpetrators of disorder.

The third area of responsibility therefore is that of the community, its leadership, its organizations, its "power structure." This "community" can be, and frequently is, as cruel in its indifference to its police as it is to its minorities. Only constant vigilance on the part of citizens' groups can keep the "community" on course with respect to its responsibilities. These citizens' groups are frequently referred to as "pressure groups." The term is one of opprobrium if applied to some other group with which we are not in sympathy—but all of us, even police, at one time or another find ourselves in the position of being "pressure groups." It is in this way that the checks and balances of a free, democratic society operate.

And it is in this area that both of us, or all of us representing group interests, bear a double responsibility; the first to ourselves and our interests (in terms of compelling need), and the second, to the conscience and awareness of the larger community. If our society, or "community" if you will, is able to preserve its integrity, fulfill its guarantees of freedom for its citizens, maintain its strength and resiliency and build greater unity for the difficult days ahead, it will be only because there are enough concerned citizens who will be willing to inform, educate, challenge, prod, even shock the community into a sense of its responsibility.

What I have hoped to convey is that a sense of responsibility is essential to any man who would be free, but that the measure of the effectiveness of that responsibility, to a considerable degree, is found in the role each of us plays. I have presented the minority group world as Exhibit A in the police task of preserving law and order, first as evidence of society's neglect of its responsibilities, and secondly, as the sternest challenge to police in their need to recognize human relations training and active community relations, as an essential part of professional preparation and action. I intended to provide a factual but believable interpretation of the weight of responsibility resting upon the police, upon minority group leadership, and upon society as a whole. I should like to close with the thought that has been uppermost in my mind. Communication represents our greatest single need, as between police and minority groups: as between police and the community. This needs to be emphasized over and over again. Where communication has failed, there the darkness of suspicion and distrust prevails.

Challenges in Contemporary Law Enforcement

THOMAS J. CAHILL

Chief of Police, San Francisco, California

MAY 21, 1964

We find ourselves today in the most crucial, critical era of modern American history. The civil rights and racial problems are nationwide, and extremely explosive. The principal speaker at the University of San Francisco graduation exercises last year stated, amongst other things, that people in every field of endeavor are finding "that it worked up until now, but now it doesn't work any more." We in the field of law enforcement certainly are realizing this more and more every day. Concepts of law enforcement, of necessity, have had to change. We have to go far beyond the concepts of law *enforcement, per se.* We now find ourselves reaching deep into the social service sphere. The whole social order of the United States is changing. In most of our communities, the social structure is completely changed; and in many areas we find a restless, moving, ever-growing population, resulting in new tensions, new conflicts, and new demands for service. They cannot be met by the controls we used in the past, because the attitudes of people have changed so much. We ourselves have to develop new attitudes and new techniques. Old methods that proved so successful in the past would today set off a riot.

The disrespect for authority about which we complained so bitterly a few years ago now has become even more general, and assumes the characteristics of outright defiance—a rebellion against authority at every level. Outright violations of the law are rationalized and justified on the basis of resentment against centuries of oppression by the white man. Let's face it—the minorities' fight for civil rights centers almost exclusively around the Negro of today. We are no longer confronted with a Negro revolt—it is now a Negro revolution. The Negro is demanding equal rights *now*. He is demanding better housing *now*. He is demanding better education *now*. He is demanding work *now*. He is not going to be stopped. They are admittedly going to continue to make demands and more demands. They will be supported more and more by federal legislation, as well as state and local legislation. The tensions, the conflicts, the confusion, and sometimes the bewilderment, are not going to go away tomorrow, or next month, or next year. They are going to be with us for a long time.

When speaking at the International Association of Chiefs of Police Conference in Washington, D.C. in 1960, as Chairman of their Crime Prevention Committee, I made the statement that we were entering the most difficult decade ever to confront American law enforcement. I know that many old-time police officials raised their eyebrows in skepticism, but I am sure they would agree with me now. Of all the groups, of all the agencies caught in the middle of this great conflict, law enforcement must bear the real brunt of it. It is, therefore, necessary for us to be realistic, and men of positive action—action carefully studied and particularly suited to occasions at hand.

We must select and bring into the fields of law enforcement men of the character, caliber and intelligence capable of meeting the challenges of our time. We must train these men, not only in the basics of law enforcement as we know them, but we must give them a thorough foundation in the field of human relations, and provide them with the leadership, supervision, and direction necessary to enable them to perform their difficult role in society with efficiency and effectiveness.

In my own department, our standards are now at a level which allows only approximately 5 percent of those who apply to qualify for entrance into the San Francisco Police Department. They are then given an intensive course of training at our police academy. Included in the curriculum is comprehensive training in the field of mental health so that the officer will be equipped to handle the mentally disturbed with whom he will come in contact. He is also given intensive training in the field of human relations. Eight hours of this course are conducted by experts brought in from our nearby universities, and include such subjects as "Race and Ethnic Factors in San Francisco," "Prejudice and Discrimination," and "Law Enforcement and the Ethnic Group." Six hours of the course are conducted by members of the police department, discussing our own Community Relations program, the work of our Intelligence Unit, and all other units in the department directly affected by the civil rights situation.

Recently we brought in our captains, lieutenants, and the greater percentage of our sergeants for a brief, concentrated course of instruction, to update their information and knowledge in connection with racial problems today. This month we instituted an in-service training course for *all* members of the department, dealing with the regular routine police problems and operations, and dealing specifically and very directly with the civil rights question and racial problem.

(This will include: "The Policeman Looks at Himself"—behavior, habits, what is expected of him, tendency to become personal, etc.; "Minority Groups—particularly the Negro, the minority group problems in the community; "Mob Behavior and Psychology"—background, types of people and factors involved, *rumors and rumor control*, desegregation, resistance, police action; "Juvenile Delinquency" — behavior at public functions, antisocial behavior, walk-outs from schools, etc.; "The Importance of Advance Knowledge and Planning.") In any progressive police department today, it has to be recognized that these steps are necessary, to update our own training and information in light of the many changes that have developed so rapidly and that have made hardcore crime a secondary consideration, despite the fact that crime has reached a new high at this time.

San Francisco is a cosmopolitan city, and always has been. In the past, we have never had racial problems. But in the last few years, the social structure of our city has completely changed. We have many people in San Francisco from many parts of the country and the world—many who have never lived in a city before—many who have no knowledge of the city's past and not too much interest in its future—merely concerned about their own existence and welfare at this moment. Some, however, are sincerely attempting to make a place for themselves and their children in the world of the future. Before World War II, we had a little over 3,000 Negroes in San Francisco; today, we have between 80,000 and 100,000. We are the hub of the nine Bay Counties, with a population of some four and half million people, many of whom are Negro. They visit San Francisco, and as you know, problems gravitate to the hub. All of this has brought new and ever increasing problems to the doorstep of the police department.

Encouraged, and I might say urged, by the National Conference of Christians and Jews, and seeing the rising tide of trouble in early 1961, I established the Police–Community Relations Unit in the San Francisco Police Department. In January of that year, we had participated in the Third Annual Police–Community Relations Institute, co-sponsored by the NCCJ and the University of San Francisco. Our Police–Community Relations Unit works exclusively on matters of human relations, and it is presently staffed by a lieutenant and four patrolmen. One of the latter is a Negro. One of the other officers will shortly become a sergeant and will remain in the Unit. Another member is assigned on a full-time basis at the Youth Opportunities Center in our Hunters Point area, spending his entire time as liaison officer between that Center and the Police Department. His efforts in this field, I might say, have been most successful and most rewarding.

Since the inception of the Unit, we have had in excess of 100 demonstrations in San Francisco — not one of them resulting in violence. True, emotions ran high, and verbal clashes and tumultuous, unruly conduct have taken place, particularly in the more recent demonstrations, but were held under control without serious incident. This control does not just happen. It is the result of endless hours of organization, planning, and preparation.

The Police–Community Relations Unit in San Francisco today is in full operation in the three most crucial of the nine police districts in the city. Each police district is divided into geographical areas, and each area is supervised by a district citizen known as a section chairman. He is assisted in carrying out the purposes of the program by a number of other district citizens known as assistant section chairmen. They operate under the direction of a general chairman, vice-chairman, and secretary in each police district. Each section chairman holds a meeting with his assistants in his own area during the month, to discuss community affairs and problems as they see them, and as they are affected by them. These section chairmen in turn meet during the same month with the chairman and vice-chairman, together with the commanding officer of the police district, and the members of the Police–Community Relations Unit, comprising an executive committee. Pertinent matters involving district problems are fully discussed, and appropriate action taken. At times, these problems are not necessarily police problems; they may involve another agency, either public or private. However, the police give advice and guidance as to how to contact these agencies, or how the matter may best be handled. There is a third and final meeting in the district during the month, which is a general public meeting. This meeting may be held in the police building in the district, in a school, in a church, or a recreation center. It's held in different locations so that no one residing in the district will feel that it is inconvenient for them to attend. The public is invited, and they are given full opportunity to take the floor, state their opinions, their problems, or their suggestions. On many occasions, and particularly when a really controversial issue is involved pertaining to the police, I personally am present, so the antagonisms are not directed only at the men under me. Those who are disturbed thus have an opportunity to talk to me personally and directly. This we have found has opened up channels of communication and understanding that have had the most beneficial results. Citizens have an opportunity to meet and understand the head of the police department. This has brought about a widespread change in the thinking and the attitude of many people who previously were openly hostile. They feel that they have an opportunity to express themselves, an opportunity to tell not only members of the police department, but the head of the department himself how they feel, and why. They develop a feeling that the Chief himself is interested in their problems, and therefore the entire department is interested, and that no longer is the police department an agency set up to protect the well-to-do, and to control and suppress the underprivileged, but rather a group of human beings just like themselves, interested in solving the problems of all the people in the community, and sincerely seeking their assistance.

This general friendly feeling is very evident, particularly during demonstrations. However, there are other factors which I must touch on, necessarily as a part of this overall picture of good will and understanding. Demonstrations must be anticipated. The leaders of the participants must be identified, sought out and conferred with. When the demonstration is carefully planned and organized through as great a degree of cooperation as possible between the leaders and the police, the policeman's task is much easier.

On May 26, 1963, for example, we had 20,000 persons, largely Negro, parade through our main street in San Francisco to the Civic Center Plaza. For approximately ten days prior to the demonstration, members of the Police–Community Relations Unit and the Intelligence Unit of the Department worked very closely with the leaders, advised them as to the necessity for a monitor who would be identified by an arm band to be assigned to approximately every 100 participants, and in this way police themselves. Arrangements were made to enable the participants to move in an orderly manner along Market Street, and to assemble in the Plaza without interference. There were very few uniformed officers in sight. There were, however, a number of plain clothes officers in sufficient numbers to handle any situation that might arise. Uniformed officers on solo motorcycles, three-wheel motorcycles, and in radio cars were stationed on the perimeter of the area at all times, so that—had it become necessary—they were only minutes away, and yet they were not in sight to create antagonism that might result from over-policing. It was one of the most orderly demonstrations that I have ever seen. The leaders paid tribute from the platform, not only to the participants, but also to the police department for their cooperation and assistance. This expression in itself created a great deal of good will for the department amongst the Negro population of the community and their friends.

I must hasten to point out, however, that there are some types of demonstrations where it is necessary to make a clear show of force, in order to prevent violence or to prevent clashes between conflicting groups. This again requires advance knowledge and information regarding the type of participants who are going to take part in a particular demonstration. For example, when groups connected with CURT—the Committee to Uphold the Right to Travel, meaning to Cuba—and other, anti-Castro groups gathered in the Civic Center Plaza simultaneously, it was necessary to separate them with an almost solid line of uniformed officers.

On Saturday, September 14, 1963, we had our first sit-in demonstrations in San Francisco. They were no surprise to us, because the leaders of the sit-in (Negroes) came to my office and fully informed me of the action they intended to take. They did in fact sit-in and they were taken into custody without any problems whatsoever. In fact, in this first case, they submitted some twelve representatives to be arrested, and the rest of the group went their way, thereby proving their point by forcing the arrest of some of their group, and yet not making it an issue between themselves and the police.

However, that was only the beginning. Since those days in 1963, the demonstrations and sit-ins have become far more militant and more explosive than anything we previously experienced. Recent demonstrations have been carried out by white youths from our nearby colleges and universities. During our roughest demonstration at the Palace Hotel, 167 of the 171 arrested on that occasion were white persons. They are now being tried in the criminal courts for various violations of law, including trespassing, disturbing the peace, resisting arrest, and in some instances, battery and assault. The minority groups are now employing new tactics to exert pressure on what they term the power-structure of the community in order to open up more jobs, better housing, and better education. We are confronted with mass picketing, mass sit-ins, and mass shop-ins that go far beyond the peaceful stage, and are referred to as civil disobedience. Some claim that while their rights are being violated, they have no qualms of conscience about violating other people's property rights. Penal statutes are deliberately violated, to force arrests. In fact, a demonstration is usually considered a failure if it does not culminate in arrests. We, the police, find ourselves in a position of attempting to maintain that delicate balance between the rights of the individuals, and the rights of society and the persons demonstrated against. The many weapons and tactics that we can use against the regular violator of law—the criminal—are not applicable here, in many instances. All of this has made it necessary to have special in-service training programs, to provide the nucleus of a force to be used at the scene of this new type of demonstration. The men have to be carefully selected, from both the physical and mental standpoint, because they are going to be required to carry individuals who go "limp," and also they are going to have to be able to withstand the jeers and ridicule of those with whom they deal. Plans must be carefully made for the transportation of these prisoners by a sufficient number of patrol wagons. There must be an orderly system of transportation, from the scene of arrest to the prison. Additional men must be provided, for an orderly system of booking, handling of property, fingerprinting and identification processing, providing for the compliance with law in allowing the required telephone calls, attorney interviews, arrangements for bail, and the many other problems attendant to mass arrests. Many problems must be worked out with the management of the business being demonstrated against, as to how far they wish to allow the sit-ins to go, and their attitude as far as prosecution is concerned. The proper legal sections of the Penal Code must be invoked, and these must be made clear to the leaders of the demonstrations in particular, and to all the demonstrators in general. We have made use of portable tape recorders to record warnings, orders, and notification of pending arrests to the demonstrators. Proper crowd control must be exercised, including the use of ropes to hold back those who merely wish to demonstrate and not sit-in for arrest purposes.

Where demonstrators have locked arms and feet, it became necessary to have officers trained as "separators," who are skilled in using pressure on the sensitive area under the jawbone, or a bending pressure on the fingers and thumbs, in order to bring about the voluntary release of holds, without using violent or cruel methods which might bring injury both to the arrested person and to the arresting officer in the struggle. The officers effecting the separation are actually the arresting officers, and will have to testify in court. It is, therefore, very important that with each person arrested, a police photographer takes a photograph of the arresting officers and the person arrested. Great care must be taken to establish a proper system of identification of each arrested person, with the arresting officer, for the purpose of the orderly presentation of evidence in court. This is an absolute necessity if the proper dispositions are to be expected in our courts.

There must be overall teamwork among all divisions of the department in handling the many phases of a demonstration. Command posts at the scene must keep in constant contact with central communications, to provide a clear picture of the situation for top command at all times.

In some cases, juveniles have been involved in these demonstrations. They have been taken directly to the Police Juvenile Bureau, cited, and turned over to their parents. Speaking of juveniles, this opens up a whole new field, which I do not intend to go into, other than to point out the fact that it is an absolute necessity to maintain the closest liaison and working relationship with the school departments — public, parochial, and private — as well as parent–teacher associations and all groups, public and private, connected with youth programs and problems.

In conclusion, let me say that if we are to achieve a satisfactory degree of success in meeting the multiplicity of complex problem confronting law enforcement today, it calls for constant, extensive and untiring efforts on our part, and continued study, evaluation and reappraisal of our program and plans. We are either going to adapt and carry out this kind of intelligent, aggressive approach in order to meet the challenges of change of our times, or we are going to be confronted with greater problems, perhaps violence and bloodshed, that will not reflect credit on any of us in our demanding profession. However, it is my confirmed opinion that law enforcement throughout the world, and particularly in the United States, is putting forth outstanding effort and demonstrating great initiative and leadership, to meet the many and the rapidly changing challenges confronting law enforcement today.

Section 4
Social Change and Law Enforcement

Few students of law enforcement and criminal justice processes today would deny that social change has forced a total reassessment of traditional notions as to the role and functions of the police. Yet, as so often is the case, agreement in general becomes widespread disagreement in specifics. Police officers testify to their grudging assent to the generalization (if assent it is!), by such expressions as: "What are ya' trying to do — make social workers out of us?"— and assorted variations on this theme.

We have concluded, consequently, that the common generalizations and platitudes regarding the effects of social change upon law enforcement and criminal justice processes are not very helpful to the growing profession. Specification is necessary. Indeed, it may be argued that one mark of the true profession is in the relative degree of consensus reached, among those functioning in the particular field, as to the specifications of professional status in the field, in and of itself. The medical profession may be cited as an illustration.

In any case, the essays in the following section focus upon some of the specifications of social change in our time, and its effects or implications for police activities.

Defining Police–Community Relations

MANUEL LOPEZ-REY

(Then) Chief, Social Defense Section, United Nations

MAY 19, 1955

What I am going to say should not be considered as a criticism of the police system of any country, or as something addressed to any particular person or body. My comments should be considered as a series of general considerations which may be used anywhere, either as a basis for further discussion, or as comments on a subject in which all those dealing with social questions are, in principle, interested. Also, I should like to point out that my considerations are purely personal, and do not represent in any way the point of view of the Secretariat of the United Nations.

The problem of community relations is not a new one. Actually, if we look back into the past, we can see that in one way or another the study of such relations has always been considered as deserving careful attention by those in charge of public institutions or agencies. Although historically these precedents may be interesting, the question of community relations has nowadays acquired greater significance, and as a result of the increasing importance attached to the larger question of public relations, is receiving more and more attention. Public relations and community relations, although different in certain respects, are closely related to one another, and therefore it would be rather difficult to say anything about community relations without having some idea of the main aspects of public relations.

In a general way, it has been said that the purpose of "Public Relations" is the study of the techniques enabling an individual or an institution to get along satisfactorily with other individuals or other institutions or agencies. According to another widespread opinion, the purpose of "Public Relations" is to gain the goodwill of those individuals or institutions with which the institution concerned is directly dealing. In support of this point of view, it has been said that such goodwill is essential for the adequate performance of certain functions, and that goodwill can be increased if certain public relations policies are applied. The implication of such an assertion would be that certain public functions, in our case the police function, should be revised and accommodated to public goodwill, or perhaps to the broad aim of satisfying people or public opinion.

Without denying that public opinion, and for that matter public goodwill, are important and even necessary in certain circumstances, it seems to me that none of them should be considered as being the main scope of "Public Relations," especially as far as public functions are concerned. Among other reasons which will be later examined, public opinion or the goodwill of the public are by their very nature matters which cannot easily be measured. Very often what we call public opinion is no more than the reaction of certain individuals which, although representative of certain classes or groups, cannot be considered as reliable samples on which a public relations policy should be built. Secondly, even assuming that public opinion is measurable, in some cases, besides being easily misled, the measurements may be at fault, and consequently may not offer a safe ground for the formulation of a "Public Relations" program. At the best of times, public opinion and related goodwill may be interesting, but are not very safe points of departure. As we very well know, public opinion more often than not is based on impulses, or on generalized personal experiences. The resulting changes in public opinion, occasionally considered as unpredictable, prove again the instability of public opinion as a basis for publc relations policies. In this respect, may I refer to Mr. G. Douglas Gourley who, in commenting on a survey about police–community relations in Los Angeles, concluded that the lack of information on the part of the public about the police was appalling.*

In view of the foregoing, it is my belief that the purpose of "Public Relations" is not to get along with people or to obtain their goodwill or support. Such aims, although having a certain value, are not the most important. The real purpose of public relations should be to convey to the public the idea that in performing certain functions, especially those performed by public agencies, the responsibility rest, not only on the shoulders of those in charge of the institutions concerned, but to a certain extent also on the shoulders of individuals and the community as a whole. This idea of *indirect co-partnership* should be the guiding principle in all policies and programs of "Public Relations." In other words, what

---

* See *Police Public Relations* by G. Douglas Gourley, in THE ANNALS OF THE AMERICAN ACADEMY OF POLITICAL AND SOCIAL SCIENCE, January 1955.

is important is not to start from the assumption that two separate entities are facing each other: one, the institution or agency, and the other, the public or the community, and that the former should do its utmost to ingratiate itself with the latter. No, the essential thing is to assume from the beginning that both the institution and the people are closely related parts of the same structure, i.e., of the community, and secondly, that the acceptance by the community of an institution or agency, in our case the police, does not rest on the goodwill of a rather changeable public opinion which may be misled or unacquainted with the problem, but on the *correct performance* of the function entrusted to the institution or agency concerned.

To what extent are the foregoing considerations applicable to police–community relations? What are the main aspects of such relations? The answers to these questions are determined by the purpose of police functions, and by the nature of the community concerned.

Generally speaking, it can be said that since the beginning of the nineteenth century the police, as an institution, has made great progress in its organization and professional training. The fact that the extent of such progress varies from one country to another does not reduce, for our purpose, the value of the preceding conclusion. On the other hand, and for reasons which cannot be examined here, social problems have become more and more acute, and very often the police have been affected in many ways by their impact, and have therefore occasionally been called upon to participate in the solution of some of those problems. Such a trend, which is quite noticeable in certain countries, has been reinforced by the increasing impetus given to preventive activities in all social programs and policies. In this general movement, the services of the police, as an agency, have also been enlisted. As a result of such participation, new social functions or activities have been either suggested or assigned to the police, especially in the prevention of juvenile delinquency and other forms of social disorganization. This development has raised the question whether policemen should be entrusted with some of the tasks mainly assigned, until now, to social workers?

In favor of such an extension of functions, it has been said that the police are entrusted with a *preventive* function, especially with respect to crime, and that participation of the police in the general preventive movement of crime increases police prestige and improves police–community relations. Against this point of view, it has been stated that the police have already a very definite function which should not be identified with that assigned to social work or similar activities; that the police are still not professionally well-equipped everywhere to perform the duties they have already, and that the enlargement of these duties and the consequent increase in responsibilities would seriously impair the performance of police functions and eventually harm police–community relations.

Let us, briefly, examine the preceding considerations. There is no doubt that the functions assigned to the police, like any other functions, are in constant evolution, and therefore duties and responsibilities may change accordingly. On the other hand, correctly understood, evolution means development or evolvement of what is inherent in a certain thing, in our case the function assigned to the police. Consequently, evolution of police functions should mean the unfolding and perfecting of what is intrinsic to such functions, and not the addition of extraneous tasks or duties normally entrusted to other agencies or institutions. What are the natural functions assigned to the police? Fundamentally, they are:

the maintenance of peace and order; the protection of persons and property, not only against accidents, but also against any attack, especially by offenders. To protect means not only to arrest the culprit, but also to detect crime and to prevent offenses. Apparently, it is this preventive function of the police which those in favor of assigning to the police some social worker functions are trying to enlarge.

There is no doubt, either, that in the performance of the described police activities, there has clearly already been an evolution and progress. Detection of crime is becoming more and more scientific, but as we shall point out later, such progress has not suppressed certain more or less lawful police practices. On the other hand, progress is a dynamic concept, and what is considered as an advanced technique today may very soon become obsolete. The functions of the police are constantly evolving, and the progress achieved at a certain stage does not necessarily mean that new functions, rather foreign to normal police ones, should be added to those they have already.

With respect to the prevention of crime, it can be said that crime can be prevented in different ways, provided that there is adequate coordination among the programs directed toward such prevention. One of the most effective ways of preventing crime is rapid detection and investigation. In spite of modern police techniques, a large number of criminal offenses still remain undetected, and others —though detected—are not properly investigated. The conclusion is that a certain number of delinquents remain at large. In spite of all the efforts made and means employed, the results obtained are not always satisfactory. The reasonable conclusion would be that rather than deal with pre-delinquent people in order to prevent crime, the police should concentrate on prompt detection as an effective preventive measure. In my opinion, police–community relations would considerably improve if that fundamental preventive activity were more effective. Such conclusions need not, of course, preclude effective cooperation between the police and those agencies or institutions directly dealing with other aspects of the prevention of crime.

The second element which should be briefly considered here is the community. On the basis of what I have already said, the police as an agency are not something separate, but are part of the community itself. Actually, the police should be considered as an expression of the community. This explains why the way in which the community behaves necessarily influences the behavior of the police. The existence of some exceptions to this general rule does not alter the principle that a certain kind of community will sooner or later have the corresponding police. In fact, in this question of police–community relations, the stronger element—as far as mutual influence is concerned—is usually the community, and not the police. As we shall see, this preponderance has a definite bearing on the relations between community and police.

For our purpose, community means a more or less definite group of people living — in a certain area — in accordance with a more or less general system of social values. In principle, every member of the group, including the policeman, participates in one way or another in the community system of values. The community as such, and all its members, are supposed to be bound by that system of social values. These are important because they govern or should govern to a great extent police–community relations. The fact that in some areas of large cities, especially in the less privileged districts, the scale of values may be somewhat different from the general one, and even occasionally partially opposed to it, does not invalidate the preceding conclusion. While there may be such occasional differences between the social values of different scales or systems of social values within the same community, police–community relations should be governed by the system of values as represented by law and related regulations. For example, if some of the locally accepted social values in a more or less delinquent area differ from those generally accepted by the community as a whole, police–community relations in that area should be guided by the latter, and not by the system of values locally accepted by a more or less anti-social group.

From the foregoing, the conclusion would be that in dealing with police–community relations, it is important to take into account the different interests of the community, which occasionally may run in opposite or even antagonistic directions. Examples of such opposed interests occur when certain groups discriminate against others, or in the appreciation of the methods which should be applied to juvenile offenders.

Actually, police–community relations are mostly based on individual contacts with different members of a group. These individuals belong not only to different classes, but they are also of different sex, age, profession, education, etc., and very often, in certain countries, of a different ethnic origin. The conclusion would be that from an individual point of view, police–community relations are concerned directly with individual attitudes, habits and sentiments deeply rooted and expressing, more often than not, indifferent or hostile reactions. If such is the case, it seems rather difficult to expect significant changes under the impact of police–community relations, programs or policies, based on tournaments, clubs, teaching boxing or the organization of similar social activities and entertainments. While such efforts may be of some value, none of them can yield what an intelligent and impartial performance of police functions may achieve.

From the foregoing, we may summarize our final considerations on the main aspects of police–community relations, as follows:

1. The building-up of such relations depends for more on human, impartial and effective performance of police functions than on the formulations of specific programs for the improvement of these relations;

2. It would be inadvisable to consider that in the building-up of police–community relations, the principles and techniques used for managerial purposes in private enterprises can be applied. The reason for such a distinction is that the function assigned to the police has a public character, and as such it does not need to be "sold." What is important is an appropriate performance of the function, taking into account its purpose and the rights and interests of the individual and of the community.

3. In carrying out their functions, the police should consider themselves as part of the community, and not as something outside it.

As you can see, police–community relations is not, according to my belief, a question of programs or policies, but primarily a question of *performance* — and by this I mean the *right* performance of police duties and tasks. These are not at all easy, especially when the police must face situations like those resulting from a legal or social recognition of discrimination against certain ethnic groups or classes. But it is in these and similar situations that a *correct* performance of police duties may serve to build a good relationship between the police and the community.

The manner in which police duties are carried out is very important for the improvement of such relations. In some countries, we still see a rather curious phenomenon: the co-existence within the same police department of scientific methods for the detection of crime, and the application of irregular and even unlawful practices in dealing, not only with offenders, but also with innocent or honest citizens. We still read far too often that a person has been interrogated for twelve or more hours, or a confession extracted or violence employed. As long as the "third degree" is applied, it would be rather a delusion to think of special programs of police–community relations. Individuals may, perhaps, participate in them, and give the impression of support that actually does not exist. Honesty, fairness and courtesy are tools for any kind of human relations.

As a concluding consideration, I wish to state that I believe in good police–community relations. They are essential in any well-organized community, but these relations, like many others deriving from the exercise of a public function, will prosper only if the ground has been prepared by the honest and efficient performance of a function in which every person should be directly interested.

Changing Attitudes Toward Crime

ROBERT H. SCOTT

(Then) Director, Youth Division, Michigan Department of Corrections

MAY 21, 1962

I. Introduction

Attitudes toward crime have undergone considerable modification in certain quarters. These changes are not universal, and sharp disagreement may be expected among proponents of differing ideas. These attitudes toward crime also differ in their degree of objectivity and reliability. They range from untested popular opinion to verified professional knowledge (always remembering that popular ideas are not always unscientific, nor do scientists or professionals always deal in objective certainties).

The following explanation suggests the differing degrees of scientific accuracy upon which the discussion of this subject is based. The order is incidental. There is the basic scientific discipline which undertakes to classify and verify the concepts held and methods practiced. (Examples: psychology, sociology, law, medicine, economics, etc.) There are the professional fields which draw upon those basic disciplines. Many professions look to the same disciplines; for example, social work and corrections look to psychology and sociology, among others. These professions are more aware than police of this reliance, because of the degree to which practitioners are expected to utilize specific knowledge and acquire formal education. Clearly, the application of these abstract principles differs in each of the three fields—law enforcement, social work, and corrections. Within each professional area, there are often sub-groups or specialties, and few are equally proficient in all of these specialties. For example, traffic police are not specialists in scientific criminal investigation, etc.

Then there is the problem which arises where two or more professions or skills are engaged in the same general area, such as social work, law enforcement, law, and corrections. These interprofessional concepts give rise to competition, misunderstanding, and scapegoating. Examples, unfortunately, are not scarce. Police lament the legal technicalities which often frustrate their task of apprehension and conviction of the known guilty; social workers decry the confinement of juveniles in jail; corrections administrators observe the financial lack which limits treatment programs; police complain that parole practices are too lax, and that probation is permitted to the wrong persons—and so it goes.

Popular opinion further clouds these issues. Public anxiety and indignation are aroused by the threat of delinquency and crime. From many angles, the general public is made to feel that it causes crime and delinquency. Parents "rare back" when the home is spotlighted as part of the cause, and lash out against TV and obscene literature. Single causes are selected for concentrated attack and become "cure-alls" in the popular mind. Thus, slum clearance and recreation programs—to mention only two of many—assume well-nigh universal appeal as *the answer*.

Finally, the sensitive and prickly questions of philosophy, politics, and religion enter the picture in ways that could and should be creative and dynamic, but often inflame rather than inspire. Current controversies range around problems of social welfare where cries of "creeping socialism" rend the air, and proponents of "no work—no pay" programs urge stringent regulation of relief, with special reference to illegitimacy. And of course, the whole area of intergroup relations raises problems that affect all professions. Important social issues weigh heavily upon social work, law enforcement, and corrections, since we are called upon to aid the distressed and regulate the socially deviant. Theories of social relations express themselves in painful and critical ways in the parts of society which we are called upon to aid, to police, and to correct.

Thus suggested are some current changes in attitudes toward crime. These do not represent attitudes about which there is universal agreement, but let us risk some specification.

II. Some Major Changes in Attitude Toward Crime

(a) Crime Now Seen as Caused Behavior

More attention is being paid nowadays to the underlying causes of crime, rather than considering it as isolated behavior. We tend to look more at the roots than the fruits. If criminal behavior is to be treated and diagnosed for treatment and prevention, the underlying reasons for this behavior need to be understood.

(b) Tendency to Differentiate Among Types of Criminal Behavior

Along with the attitude toward crime as caused behavior has come an awareness that different persons may commit the same type of crime for quite different reasons. The legal definition of crime does not always reveal the attitudes and problems which prompt it. For example, some people shoplift for profit; others, because of peculiar inner drives or problems. Apprehension and threat of punishment may be good reason for motivating the compulsive offender to seek treatment, but punishment, as such, will not accomplish much by way of treatment. Quite apart from the types of crimes committed, there appear to be different categories of offenders. Many classifications of offenders may be used. The ones suggested here are:

(1) *The accidental or situational offender*—The person who commits a crime largely because of special circumstances. Examples:

the hit and run driver;

the wronged husband who seeks revenge;

the teen-age boy charged with statutory rape of the just-under 16-year-old girl with whom he has been having a love affair;

the trusted employee who "borrows" money from his employer to meet a grave crisis.

The crimes committed by the above persons are not a reliable index to their normal behavior.

(2) *Adjustive crime*—This describes behavior which is occasioned or expected by the group (or sub-culture) of which the offender is a part, but which conduct is an offense against social standards. Examples:

the gang member who gets involved in a "rumble";

the kid who steals cars;

college kids on a "beer bust";

drunk driving on way home from New Year's party.

(3) *Abnormal behavior*—Criminal conduct which manifests emotional disturbances, but not mental illness. Examples:

the alcoholic check-writer;

the kleptomaniac;

the deviated sex offender.

(4) *The professional criminal*—one whose basic business is unlawful.

III. Changes in Treatment of Offenders

The theory which views crime as caused behavior has produced corresponding changes in attitudes toward the treatment of criminals.

(a) Prevention

Considerable attention is being paid to the background conditions which appear to encourage the development of crime and delinquency. A long catalog of these efforts could be listed, but a few examples of the principal efforts will suffice:

Slum clearance	Character-building programs
Recreation programs	Community efforts toward prevention
Prevention of school drop-outs	Elimination of obscene literature
Mental health programs	Reduction of violence on TV
Child guidance clinics	

Each attack upon crime and delinquency has its weaknesses, and the chief weakness to be noted here is the "one cause—one cure" theory; that is, the answer to crime is to be found in the elimination of slums or, if kids are kept sufficiently busy by recreation programs, they will be less apt to commit crimes. Generally speaking, these efforts at prevention are, first of all, aimed at the conditions which seem likely to produce crime and, secondly, at the early identification of the probable offender, and getting help to him before the damage becomes chronic or serious.

(b) Special Programs for Delinquents

The development of the Juvenile Court movement in the United States has provided a method for the legal handling of delinquent children in ways that minimize the negative effect of the criminal process and treatment—eliminate the lifelong criminal record—and reduce the likelihood of contamination and abuse by association with hardened, older offenders. New methods of classification and treatment have been developed. Police administrators have increasingly recognized the importance of special juvenile procedures within police departments and recent years have seen the considerable development of this movement.

A deficiency claimed in this field is the inability, in certain jurisdictions, to provide treatment considered adequate for psychically disturbed or dangerous persons who are nearing the upper limits of Juvenile Court jurisdiction. (This varies from state to state, but in Michigan, one legal category—delinquency—covers all crime, from the most trivial to the most serious, for those who have not passed the 15th birthday. But after the 15th birthday, the law provides too few effective means for handling immature youth, other than the conventional criminal code.)

Furthermore, the separate staff and facilities required for juveniles often do not keep pace with the law. For example, juveniles under the age of 16 cannot be confined in a county jail in Michigan; yet there are virtually no detention homes in the northern half of the state. By contrast, there is a county jail in each county of Michigan.

(c) Inadequate Procedures for Youthful Offenders

The most seriously neglected group of offenders today is the youthful offender. In a majority of the jurisdictions in this country, no satisfactory legal provision exists for the handling of youthful offenders (about 16–21 years) other than those provided by the Criminal Code.

This discrepancy or deficiency has contributed to the hue and cry against young criminals who account for such a large percent of auto thefts, larceny, and burglaries. Certain law enforcement bodies urge more stringent means for restricting this group, when in reality they are talking about the juvenile delinquent. The situation might be compared to the husband and wife who bought an electric blanket with dual controls, because the husband liked less bedcovering than his wife. The first night they used the blanket, the wife got colder and colder and turned her blanket control higher and higher. The husband, on the other hand, got warmer and warmer and turned his blanket control lower and lower. When the indignant couple returned the blanket to the store the next day, the clerk pointed out that the controls were reversed; that is, the wife had the husband's controls, and vice versa. Greater care and accuracy needs to be exercised among those concerned with these problems to be sure that we are talking about the same question, before legitimate differences in philosophy and treatment are seriously considered.

IV. Differences in Correctional Treatment

Several important changes have also occurred within the Corrections field (both adult and juvenile). These grow out of the tendency to regard crime as caused behavior referred to above. These changes may be briefly described as follows:

(a) Probation

Courts are making extensive use of this treatment device for the casework and supervision of offenders likely to succeed in the community, without the major dislocation of a prison sentence upon the offender and his family. In

Michigan, for example, about 50 percent of those convicted of offenses for which they could receive a prison sentence are placed on probation. Only about 35 percent of the total convicted go to prison. The cost of keeping a man on probation is about 1/10th of what it costs to confine him to prison—quite apart from his inability to support his dependents, and without regard to the $15,000 that it costs to construct one maximum security cell.

Obviously, a thorough pre-sentence investigation is essential to a sound disposition by the sentencing court.

This enlightened and effective procedure may give rise to several criticisms on the part of other professions and the public, in general. The first dissatisfaction is with the inequity of the sentence. Certain individuals violate important trusts or commit grave crimes against the public interest. The matter of the offender and his circumstances might be such that public exposure and condemnation would be a greater punishment than anticlimactic imprisonment. Furthermore, the resources for treatment of the offender, and the likelihood of his repeating the offense, make probation a preferable alternative to prison. Yet the gravity of his offense may give rise to a sense of unfairness where someone who commits a much lesser offense receives a prison sentence. This discrepancy can give rise to the statement by an offender, "He stole 1,000 bucks and got probation—I took a measly 10 bucks to feed my family and got five years." Furthermore, the process of "copping a plea" can result in a serious offender receiving a comparatively light sentence.

(b) Institutional Treatment

The current trend is toward smaller, specialized institutions which can provide a program and a setting conducive to treatment more appropriate to individuals. Thus, more promising offenders can benefit by programs (example, forestry camps) which could not be granted to more dangerous men. This presupposes adequate diagnosis and treatment—a strong tendency in current Corrections.

Unfortunately, this change can give rise to the criticism of mollycoddling and the cry of "country clubs for criminals." The public forgets that people are sent to prison *as* punishment, not *for* punishment.

(c) Parole and the Indeterminate Sentence

Many jurisdictions use some form of indeterminate sentence (in Michigan, the maximum is specified by law, the minimum is imposed by the sentencing judge). Some form of early release, usually through parole, is well-nigh universally available throughout the United States. Theoretically, this permits release at a more favorable time, depending upon progress, than would be the case with a flat or fixed sentence, which would require a degree of predictability virtually unattainable. Normally, parole is granted only after a hearing which, in turn, is based upon a report of progress. The goals of parole are casework and supervision of released offenders so as to provide greater protection for the community and greater assistance to the offender in successfully returning to society. In some jurisdictions, parole is for a fixed period of time—example, two to four years (which can be extended on application by the paroling authority). In others, the parole is for the balance of the sentence. (A man paroled on a life sentence would be on parole for the rest of his life.)

Some jurisdictions use conditional release to designate those cases not deemed desirable parole risks, but for whom supervision is necessary. Other jurisdictions - -like Michigan—use the designation of parole to cover both types of cases.

The problem sometimes encountered is twofold. First, law enforcement agencies often regard the "ex-convict" as a poor social risk, since he belongs to that class of persons more apt to commit crimes in the future. Having gone to considerable trouble to investigate the crime and apprehend the criminal, some police officers have been critical of what seems to them to be improper or premature release on parole. Allowing for human error that does sometimes result in premature parole and for the unpredictability of human behavior which results in apparently good risks getting into trouble (and vice versa), the fact still remains that it is often better to release an offender with some time remaining, under parole super-vision, than to wait for discharge at which point the offender is free from any supervision.

To all of this must be added the problem of the "copped plea," in which an individual who has committed a serious crime is convicted of a relatively less serious one or, on the other hand, where a person convicted of a serious crime for technical reasons may actually be less dangerous than others with less serious convictions.

Further complications arise in the juvenile field when the juvenile institution can refuse a delinquent committed to it, if space is lacking. The delinquent may be placed on probation when all agree that institutional treatment is indicated.

V. Philosophical Conflicts

From the foregoing, it might appear that there was consensus of opinion among Corrections workers as to the most effective methods of prevention and treatment. Actually, this is not the case, and any survey of the national scene would reveal many disagreements within the profession. The same comment might be made about police administration and social work. The main point about such profes-sional differences is that an objective attitude is needed which differentiates between fact and opinion, and is willing to test conclusions.

To this fact of disagreement in principle must be added the problem of in-sufficient services in programs, about which there is substantial agreement. Many times we are able to supply only token services, with resulting public misunder-standing. This is the old manpower problem so familiar to police and social workers.

But apart from these professional differences, we are also confronted with philosophical differences which color and confuse and clash. One of the most common of such philosophical differences is that between free will and determi-nism. The punishment theory of crime depends heavily upon an assumption of free will—this is, all individuals are equally free to engage in criminal conduct, because they choose to do so. This freedom of choice is often coupled with re-ligious concepts. Recent trends within the behavioral sciences have emphasized the degree to which an individual's choices are dependent upon the circumstances, his background, and his personal idiosyncrasies. These insights and opinions have heavily influenced theories of treatment as against punishment. By some pro-ponents of the behavioral sciences, these ideas have been carried to the point where it has been made to appear that all criminals are sick, are not accountable for their actions, and that they should, in effect, be treated as mentally ill. This is a very extreme position. Other practitioners in the Corrections field would de-emphasize the psychological or psychiatric dimensions of criminal behavior, its prevention and treatment, and some would exclude them altogether.

There is popular confusion and apprehension at this point, and some segments of popular opinion regard the insights of the behavioral sciences as incompatible with a religious approach to the problem. This apprehension results from a possible combination of intellectual confusion and fear of psychology. The persons holding this view equate the insights of the behavioral sciences with the faulty notion that this implies a mechanistic determinism excluding religion and freedom of choice. These two points of view are not necessarily inconsistent. A person may have the wideness of his choices severely restricted by his personality and/or his circumstances, and still be free to make some degree of choice, and for this choice be legally, morally, and spiritually responsible. The interests and insights of the theologians have great validity at this point, and it is hoped that they will join in the dialogue to give clarity to the professional and to reduce the confusion and anxiety of the popular mind.

VI. Age of Interdisciplinary Cooperation

The efforts of the past decade have been more toward generalization than specialization. There is an increasing awareness that human behavior has more than one dimension and the efforts of many professions are needed. The Police and Community Relations Institute is eloquent testimony of this principle.

VII. Age of Experimentation and Evaluation

More recently observers in the field of antisocial behavior have looked to practitioners for promising experiments in reducing crime and delinquency. New programs are originating in the field and are being measured by researchers to determine their effectiveness. Vast sums are being appropriated by the federal government and by private foundations, as seed money to encourage and evaluate these projects.

VIII. Conclusion

Attitudes toward criminal behavior are complex and are modified in part by a process of change and growth. Many of our unfavorable comparisons are based upon defensiveness and lack of information. We compare the best of our own methods with the worst of our rivals. Police–Community Relations programs provide us with an opportunity to see the whole process of our relationship to the community and our cooperation with our colleagues.

Community Development for Better Police and Community Relations

NELSON A. WATSON

Director, Research and Development Division, International Association of Chiefs of Police

MAY 22, 1963

I have been asked to discuss the general idea of community development as it touches upon improving police and community relations. This is a fairly large order in these days of social smog and cultural collision, and I realize that I am proceeding on the basis of certain assumptions which are, to say the least, suspect. For example, the unwary may uncritically accept the assumption that there exists a functional set of protocols governing interaction between the police and some monolithic entity called the community. Corollary to this assumption, one may carelessly conceive of the police as an independent or "extra-community" body, thus setting up a false premise—false because it ignores the reciprocal nature of the relationship. Further, there is the implicit assumption that police and community relations need to be and can be improved—and that this transformation may to some degree be effected through "community development." Unless we are careful, we may assume that "community development" means the way to better police and community relations is through a program aimed at changes in the community and not the police. Moreover, is it safe to assume that the real wielders of social power are interested in establishing better police and community relations? Finally, and most important, is it legitimate and are we justified in specifying improved police and community relations as *the* objective?

We must, by all means, approach such assumptions with reservation. I think that in police work, when making policy or procedural decisions, we are obligated to assess critically the validity of all underlying assumptions. In these days of profound social change, failure to do so almost surely results in failure to adapt to new conditions. Stubborn adherence to time-honored tradition and value systems is a state of comfortable complacency which a public agency that is supposed to serve all of the people cannot afford. It would be time well spent to examine some of these assumptions.

Let us, first, direct our attention to the concept of the community. I mentioned that "community" is often erroneously thought of as a monolithic entity. This is a dangerous misconception relative to practically every so-called community. It is conceptually misleading to look upon a political collectivity as an organic whole, because we are then apt to overlook its inevitable heterogeneity. And it is this very heterogeneity that is, at once, the essence of its vitality and the source of its restlessness. To the policeman, as a social practitioner, such an error is serious. It means that he is attempting to deal with a public he assumes is homogeneous, instead of the conglomerate populace which is actually there. In no jurisdiction can there be one simple and most effective program, because of the widely varied interests and viewpoints of distinct and often conflicting "publics."

A policeman, because of his legalistic orientation, is likely to think of his community as a political system existing within legally defined boundaries. He thinks of it as a territory within which he has police power. Now so far as the exercise of that power is concerned, in making arrests and performing related police functions, that is all right. It is not a realistic approach, though, to human relations. In terms of effectively interacting social systems, the concept of community seldom coincides with political boundaries. Social and psychological boundaries, such as "the wrong side of the tracks" and "separate but equal facilities," are very real and functionally significant. There are people in whose concept of community the welfare office, police station, and jail are far more important than are the church, school, library, or city hall. They may live their lives in vermin-ridden, cold-water flats, streets, and taverns instead of clean, warm homes, steady jobs, and country clubs.

From the point of view of police and community relations then, we must sharpen our social awareness and realize that a program aimed at a nonexistent, monolithic community is misdirected. There will be many for whom it will hold no appeal, for whom its objectives will have no meaning.

At this point, since it is a concept subject to similar misinterpretation, I think it would be well to mention the so-called police stereotype. Again, I suggest that there is not *a* police stereotype. The image of the police held by our varied "publics" differs from one to another. I am sure you are familiar with them — the dull-witted flat-foot, the smart-alecky ticket writer who throws his weight around, the political leech who picks the pocket of the public treasury, and the outright crook who exacts graft as the price of not doing his job. However, while these highly uncomplimentary images are all too familiar and irritating to police, there is another stereotype of wide currency which is more directly related to our context here. It is one which, we must admit with shame, like the others, has some basis in fact. I refer to the image in which the officer of the law is looked upon as an agent of repression. He is seen not as a protector, but as a persecutor; not as a friend, but as a foe. He is regarded as using his police power as an instrument of oppression, not of justice. The law and its machinery, including the police, are perceived to function in a manner designed to perpetuate second-class citizenship. The police, far from being impartial, are looked upon as agents whose job it is to enforce not only the law, but also the mores, conventions, and taboos of an intolerable social caste system.

In these days of rapid social change and (let us not hide our heads in the sand) even revolution, this stereotype assumes an operational significance that cannot be overestimated. The police executive who expects to achieve better police and community relations through a program which ignores this stereotype is in for a rude awakening. Bear in mind that is makes little difference whether or not the image is based upon truth. Psychologically, it is the beliefs and feelings, and not the facts which count. People who hold stereotypes react to police on the basis of their beliefs. They do not stop to inquire as to the truth of those beliefs, but treat them as facts. The only counter to this kind of stereotype is absolutely fair and impartial police work.

What is right and just and good depends upon the judge and in matters of this kind, each of us is his own judge. Probably many of you know the story of three umpires who were discussing their profession. The first said, "I call them as I see them." The second said, "I call them as they are." The third said, "You're both wrong. They ain't nothing until I call them."

Any realistic program which attempts to reach out into the community, for better police–community relations, must take cognizance of this socio-psychological reality. At the same time, we must be prepared for the reaction of others who would unhesitatingly support the police in fighting crime, but who would not do so relative to improving race relations.

We acknowledge that many people do subscribe to unfavorable and derogatory stereotypes of the police. Are we forthright and honest in admitting it, when there is a factual basis for the bad image? Are we intellectually strong enough to appraise ourselves in a realistic way? Are we wise enough to discover our own faults as the ground from which the weeds of bad relations spring?

Most people willingly subscribe to the ideology expressed as the American ethic or creed. Few Americans would deny that all men are created equal—not physically or intellectually, of course, but in the eyes of God and the law. There are few who debate that all men are endowed with certain inalienable rights and that life, liberty, and the pursuit of happiness are the heritage of all Americans. That every man has a right to try to better himself, that he is entitled to participate in governing himself through the ballot are basic tenets of our American philosophy. Be he ever so depraved, every man has a right to a fair and speedy trial, to be secure from false arrest, from unreasonable search, from confiscation of his property, and from cruel and unusual punishment. Certainly we believe in and cherish these ideals. It is not their philosophical purity that concerns us. It is their application. Like the joke translated from one language to another, these principles often seem to lose something in the translation from philosophy to action.

We cannot assume that everyone subscribes to these principles. Nor can we assume that everyone defines them in the same way. Persons who feel deprived may be painfully conscious of a gap between philosophy and reality. They may protest, and take steps demanding the very rights supposedly guaranteed by the ideology so widely and loyally supported by nearly all American citizens.

The groups or "publics" constituting our communities naturally will view these matters differently. To some, the privilege of buying a lunch in a place where it is for sale to the public is nothing more than the exercise of a fundamental right. To some, the privilege of attending institutions of public education, without consideration being given to the color of their skin is simple justice under the American creed. To others, granting of these privileges constitutes an unhappy and foreboding change in a cherished way of life. To still others, any concession is nothing but appeasement and cowardly retreat.

In situations like these which, like earthquakes, rock the very foundations of established social systems, the police are often in the middle. We are charged with enforcing the law and maintaining the peace. If violence occurs, people on both sides blame us. Such people are frequently guilty—(and so are the police, sometimes, in their planning)—guilty of another false assumption, namely, that everyone is against violence—that all want harmony and peace. Obviously, this is not true. There are vested interests with much to lose. There are youths in revolt against threatening changes in social values. There are minority groups with much to gain. There are the demagogs and agitators who fatten on conflict. Police planning which fails to tackle these problems, head-on, in attempting community development will not produce better police and community relations.

Once more looking critically at ourselves, I think we must reappraise our social role. I think we must adapt to a realigned society by broadening our social perspective of the police function. I think traditional concepts are rapidly becoming outmoded and inadequate. The established and orthodox view of the police function as one of enforcing the law, preventing crime and protecting life, limb, and property has been instrumental in restricting police activity to patrol, investigation, gathering evidence, making arrests, and employing other negative or repressive techniques of behavior control. Such a conception of the police function is a narrow one, unsuited to the complexities of today's world. It has already been modified by many urban police departments. Police executives today are rapidly coming to the view that police departments have broad social responsibilities, and not merely legal ones.

For instance, in crime prevention, police planning looking toward reduction in the number of robberies, burglaries, rapes, assaults, and the like, only through

conventional, repressive police measures, such as increased patrol, is a relatively
sterile approach, and one which often has not worked. We all know that crime
causation is multidimensional, and that there are no simple and sovereign solutions. At the risk of oversimplification, I would like to suggest that, for police in
some localities, improving communication with certain groups in the community
has helped materially.

The bulk of offenses involve persons at the low end of the socio-economic
scale, most of whom are already community burdens in one way or another.
These people are problems for the schools, for the welfare agencies, for the police,
and for the courts. They are the ones who are most often unemployed and who
have the most pressing housing and health problems. In short, they are problems
for the entire community. It is apparent that the un-coordinated efforts of numerous agencies in meeting these problems will be wasteful and ineffective. They
will often be working at cross purposes. Each agency has its special job to do, of
course, and its jurisdiction and powers are limited in various ways. But there is
no reason why they should not exchange information of interest to others. Such
an exchange would be helpful in unifying a multi-pronged attack on an area problem. It would prevent wasteful overlapping of effort. It would avoid having one
agency played against another. But most important of all, it would provide an
inter-disciplinary attack upon situations that are complex—requiring legal, sociological, educational and other treatments.

I would not suggest that police officers should take over the functions of social
caseworkers, but I would assert, and strongly, that police and social workers
should not be at odds. Probation is not a police function, and I would not suggest
that police officers undertake even "informal" probation duties. But progress could
be made in reducing crime through coordination of effort between the police and
probation services.

I would not suggest that police abandon patrol as a crime prevention technique, even though the manner in which it is carried on in some places is expensive and inefficient. I would suggest that a re-examination and re-orientation of the
police role as social practitioners could, in the long run, produce more effective
crime-reducing techniques. Police and community relations undoubtedly would
profit from police participation in coordinated community development programs,
aimed at improving the status of people in the crime-breeding areas. Certainly,
the detection and arrest of criminals must continue, but this is an essentially negative approach to crime prevention. Why not join hands with people who are trying to provide jobs, better housing, family care, etc., and add crime prevention
to the list? I believe this is an intelligent, forward-looking, promising approach to
community development, and to better police and community relations.

The police do not exist and function in isolation. In their social relationships,
the police are faced with other than legal problems. There are intergroup or ethnic
problems, economic problems, and political problems to be solved. The development of the community — for the purpose of bettering the police and community
relations — is not a task which the police can handle alone. Intergroup and interagency communication must be made meaningful on the practical operational
level. There must be a clear understanding of function, operational procedure,
and limitations. We cannot afford friction between the police and the schools,
any more than we can afford friction between the detectives and the patrol. We
cannot afford bad feeling between the police and the juvenile court, any more

than we can between the vice squad and the juvenile officers within the department. In the interest of effective police and community relations, we cannot afford
to be at swords point with minority groups, any more than we can afford to fight
with labor or the press. Meaningful communication is indispensable. We cannot
solve our problems by giving the police department an unlisted phone number.

Students of social problems have pointed out that population mobility and
urbanization are among the sources of unrest today. Our urban centers are experiencing great changes. We have seen the exodus of middle-class white and the
influx of poverty-stricken Negroes and other minorities. There is overcrowding,
economic want, and squalor. With little to hope for, they lack ideals and ambition — a fertile breeding ground for discontent, friction, violence, and crime.
The police must not be guilty of compounding the difficulty by insisting upon a
traditional, repressive, legalistic approach to what is essentially a complex of
serious social maladjustments. As a matter of fact, lack of communication and
understanding between the police and the people, coupled with heavy-handed treatment, aggravates the problem — not only for the police, but for all community
agencies. Development in police circles of a broader social perspective, accompanied by development in the community of channels of communication with responsible and respected leaders of ethnic groups, is an indispensable element in
bettering police and community relations. The broader the representation and
the deeper the commitment to democratic ideals and social justice, the more likely
are the programs to be successful.

Preserving order and promoting a hospitable social climate in the community
are among the responsibilities of the police. The stability which characterized
many a community, even a generation ago, has been largely dissipated today by
the transience and mobility which the past few years have witnessed. Social responsibility has been diluted by large numbers of rootless and aimless newcomers
in our big cities. The cracking of the segregation barriers has raised the hopes of
the Negro minority and has shortened its patience with those barriers that remain.
Young Negroes, in particular, feel this very keenly, and they want to get on with
the job. For the police, maintaining order and stability under these circumstances
has become increasingly difficult. I think that part of the problem arises out of
the mistaken notion that stability means *status quo*. Moreover, while I certainly
deplore violence as a technique in seeking social change, I feel impelled to emphasize that the absence of violence is not a reliable measure of healthy social order.

Community development for better police and community relations is a job
for men of good will, understanding, and keen social awareness. A policeman
trying to establish a good working relationship with a neighborhood group surely
would not begin by announcing, "We want to establish better relations with you
niggers." The atmosphere of the ensuing forum would hardly be conducive to
better relations. Police employ dogs, tear gas, and riot guns only as a last expedient in a desperate situation. Such measures are not expected to win friends
— though they certainly influence people. The better course is for men who can
mutually respect each other to meet and calmly deliberate regarding problems
and grievances.

Chief Brostron of St. Louis describes the operation of his citizen–police committees. At meetings in the district police stations, problems relating to law enforcement are aired. The Chief has said, "Some of these meetings turn into
'gripe' sessions, both ways. This can be painful, especially when complaints against

the department are based on misinformation, half-truths, and on occasion, are obvious prejudice against policemen. There is only one thing more unpleasant than this, and that is listening to complaints that have a good basis in fact. We have had some of those, too. In both cases, this is a necessary pain. Unless police and citizens get their mutual complaints on the table, there is no way to correct false impressions or to rectify the trouble." Chief Brostron went on to say that the griping and the emotion accompanying it soon disappear, and the committees have gone on to do some really constructive work.

I think this is a courageous and intelligent approach to the problem of community development for improved Police–Community Relations. It is not the only one, of course. There are many other approaches in other parts of the country and, growing out of them, will be community development programs at the local level which, I am sure, will be all the richer as a result.

I want to close on this thought. If our sole objective is a police–community relations program is to smooth the way for the police, to make the police job easier, to make the policeman's lot a happier one, we are missing the boat, and we will fail. The only way to better relations is through better police service. Our objective should be an improved offering to the people — more effective police work, impartial enforcement of the law, better community service — and better police and community relations will follow as a by-product.

I would say that community development for better police and community relations requires that we critically examine our underlying assumptions in order that our program may be in tune with social reality. Objective and critical self-examination is essential, so that our house may be put in order before inviting guests. We must open-mindedly broaden our perspective as to the rapidly changing social conditions with which we are faced. We may then proceed to fashion programs that will fit into today's new order.

New Frontiers for the Police

A. F. BRANDSTATTER

*Director, School of Police Administration and Public Safety,
Michigan State University*

MAY 21, 1962

From the beginning of our civilization, it has been recognized that conflict begins with individuals or small groups of people, and may ultimately spread to nations and engulf the entire universe in a holocaust that could erase mankind from this planet. When we find conflict and social disorder in their incipient stage at the community and state levels, the police can play a significant role in creating a local climate in which social order prevails. However, the community must participate actively, if law and order are to be preserved as a way of life.

It is of considerable interest to note that whenever the community has actively supported the police function, and the police, in turn, have actively participated in community affairs in both a professional and nonprofessional sense, the individual and the community have profited, as well as the police. It is from this type of relationship that respect for the law of the land has emerged.

The British police system was designed with the full approval of the English people, and has been molded by experience into the outstanding police service it represents today. Prominent from the earliest history of the British police was the close relationship of its personnel to the community, out of which grew its prestige. Another characteristic is the degree of decentralization and elements of control by the central government that permit a greater uniformity and standard of operation than in any other democracy in the world. The British system permits an effective inspection program without violating, seriously, the "home rule" principle.

To adopt a system similar to the British is not being proposed but it is essential for the American police service to re-examine management concepts as they presently exist. If this occurs, perhaps the nation can recapture the sense of community enjoyed in the early history of the American police service. Before we achieved the high degree of mobility and communication we enjoy today, the police responsibility was an integral part of the community and shared by individuals and groups throughout it. The police officer was respected and frequently consulted about many problems confronting the family, as well as the community. This condition prevailed until the early days of the enactment of the Volstead Act. In the 1920's, beginning with the prohibition era and with the increased use of the motor vehicle and the trend toward specialization, we began to witness a slow, but steady loss of respect for the law enforcement arm of government. Perhaps it has now reached its peak. If not, I fear for the future of law enforcement, as we know it today. Public resentment is revealed by the fact that today, more police officers are attacked than at any other time in our history. Many of these attacks occur for no apparent reason, and in New York City last year, none of the attacks upon police originated from racial conflicts; they occurred throughout the five boroughs and in all sections of the city. In 1960, a total of 9,621 assaults on American policemen were reported to the FBI.[1] We should be alarmed by this manifestation of hostility toward an arm of government whose principal function is to preserve the peace and to prevent crime, but instead finds itself creating disorder by discharging its responsibility to the community.

What has brought about this reaction at the community level? Certainly the many investigations by Congress, as well as those by state and local groups since 1931, have had their effect. In 1931, the National Commission on Law Observance and Enforcement, known as the Wickersham Committee, was the first Congressional committee in our time to invite the attention of the public and students of government to the abuses of power by law enforcement officials as "inefficient and delinquent officials," and the shortcomings of other agencies involved in the administration of criminal justice. Other reports having a similar effect are:

1. President Truman's Committee on Civil Rights;

2. The Special Senate Committee chaired by Senator Estes Kefauver to Investigate Organized Crime in Interstate Commerce;

3. The 1952 report of the American Bar Association Commission on Organized Crime, which stated that the basic contributing factor to the growth and development of organized crime is inefficiency of local law enforcement agencies; and

4. More recently, the United States Commission on Civil Rights released its report entitled, JUSTICE, and offered both praise and criticism of local law en-

forcement agencies, and urged federal agencies to pursue civil rights violations more vigorously.

In the meantime, state commissions in several states (California, Massachusetts, New York) have conducted investigations concerned with alleged corruption in municipalities and the inroads made by organized crime in our society.

In 1958, the State of New York created, by statute, the Commission of Investigation. Its responsibilities are to "keep the public informed as to the operations of organized crime and problems of criminal law enforcement in the state." The Commission's first report, released last year following an investigation of crime in one of New York's major cities, said:

> Claimed ignorance of criminal conditions, professed lack of knowledge of rules defining responsibilities, failure of direction and leadership, absence of rudimentary investigative and intelligence programs, minimal coordination between headquarters and precincts, ineffective and wasteful use of manpower, gross disregard for accurate and meaningful investigative reporting, poor quality and quantity of gambling arrests, and a general indifference in attitude toward dealing effectively with organized gambling, all clearly demonstrated at both the public and private hearings, were the principal existing aspects of the department's incompetence in gambling enforcement.

All of these conditions reported by various boards and commissions prompted one writer, in an article appearing in the July 6, 1961, issue of THE REPORTER, to state that corruption is practically the normal condition of American municipal police forces.

Of course, this indictment of the American community and its police service is not valid, but there are many who accept it as fact, while others will allow the seeds of doubt to be sown and wonder how many American communities not yet exposed allow corruption, civil rights violations, and organized crime to flourish. In recent days, three police scandals involving municipal operations in three different states have been reported by the press. Compounding this picture is the fact that crime has increased four times faster than our population explosion. It is a grim picture when we examine these reports in their totality. The image American law enforcement projects to the nation and the world is negative. Some are saying that our society is the most lawless in the world.

It seems incredible that the indictments made and scandals reported have occurred in a period during which American law enforcement has made its greatest advancements. In 1954, the late Bruce Smith wrote that "advances made by American police during the past thirty years are certain to be recorded in the history of our time. The brilliant record of the Federal Bureau of Investigation, the emergence of a dozen or more state police offices of outstanding quality, and the striking reversal of old police patterns in many cities and villages — these are the physical evidence of a radical change in police thought and action that has exercised an influence in many ways."[2] There is no question about the advancements made, but they were made primarily in technical facets of police work.

The advances made have not been uniform. The most important areas have received less attention, some none at all. We still have the sheriff–constable system, which is centuries old and was abolished by the British many years ago. We cling to patterns of police organization and personnel practices that are inadequate for the 20th century. The advent of the metropolitan community only serves to increase the number of small police forces, creating a fragmentation of services that increases duplication of effort. We seek to resolve the ensuing aggravated problems of law enforcement by adding new police equipment and developing new techniques for its use, instead of consolidating our fragmented jurisdictions, recruiting superior personnel, and improving existing staff and operational practices in all jurisdictions, not just a few.

We find federal authority creeping ever closer, to assume additional enforcement responsibility for local crime problems. The most recent legislation proposed seeks authority for federal agencies to have jurisdiction over football pools that corrupt university and college football players. Are local agencies admitting they are unable to cope with this problem and relinquishing their authority to federal agencies? If this type of legislation continues, we will, in fact have a national police agency.

In the meantime, the crime problem looms larger on the horizon and in the public mind. Except for recent efforts taken on the Federal level, there seems to be no long-range solution to crime being advanced at the local level of government. Yet, this is where the roots of crime are deeply embedded. In my judgment, the only significant movement occurring throughout the nation has been the work of the National Conference of Christians and Jews, through the support and leadership it has given to the development of programs at the community level patterned after this Institute. NCCJ is to be highly commended for its pioneering effort in alerting the American community and its police forces to the need for a concerted and united effort to alleviate social disorder and to promote the good will present in all our communities.

There is an increasing need for all public service agencies to understand that crime is related to the social conditions existing in the changing community, particularly the metropolitan city. The urbanization caused by the increased mobility of our people has created problems for our schools, housing shortages, and competition for jobs by inadequately-trained men and women from low economic groups. We find ourselves with the disadvantaged citizen who tends to regard the police, not as the protector of law and order, but as an armed enemy.[3]

Dr. James Conant, in his book SLUMS AND SUBURBS, describes the all-white slum areas in these terms: "The only possession most of these families have is children — In such an environment all forms of evil flourish — the peddling of dope, drunkenness, disease, accidents, truancies, physical, mental and moral handicaps, sex perversions involving children . . ."[4] He adds this about other areas: "The building up of a mass of unemployed and frustrated Negro youth in congested areas of a city is a social phenomenon that may be compared to the piling up of inflammable material in an empty building in a city block. Potentialities for trouble — indeed possibilities of disaster — are surely there."[5]

In addition, the cleavage between the police and the community is no longer confined to the criminal elements, minority groups, and slum areas. It seems to have expanded to the great middle class, for reasons that are not clear. This is significant because the middle class tends to set the standards for the community.

These conditions indicate clearly, in my opinion, that the problem confronting the American community and its law enforcement agencies is critical. We face a crisis, and as we look to the future, we must seek remedies which will project a new and positive image of law enforcement to the American public. Several ideas suggest themselves, but each proposal will require courage, complete community support, and aggressive and unselfish leadership — and I underscore the latter.

Let us explore a few "new frontiers" for the police. Police functions that need review and radical change are police personnel management, police patrol practices, organizational patterns, the concept of crime prevention, and activities which have been scrutinized by every Congressional and state investigating agency, namely, questionable practices in the interrogation, custody, and treatment of police prisoners, which adversely affect the relationship of the police with the community. Unless substantial progress is made in these areas by the great majority of American communities, progress towards continued improvement and police professionalization is threatened. The fear of police must be erased from the minds of all elements of our society.

To provide perspective, let us examine for a moment the principal responsibilities of municipal police service in America. Order has been the theme of organized society since the dawn of history. Yet in trying to achieve order, the police are frequently accused of violating the freedom of the individual. This is a serious charge when we consider that our political and social system is rooted in the Judaeo-Christian concept of the dignity of the individual.

This has been the preoccupation of our society from its earliest history. When Thomas Jefferson and his associates were drafting the Declaration of Independence, they chose their words carefully. In saying that all men are created equal, they meant equal before God and before the law. They spurned the thought that there was any natural distinction between individuals by reason of their parents' station in life. They spurned the notion that some men were born to rule and others to obey; that one class should have the benefits and protection of the law, while another should be at a disadvantage because of the law's very existence. Thus, the U. S. Supreme Court continues to reverse convictions where due process of law has been violated, regardless of whether it involves the derelict of society or the most socially prominent. And America continues to pay tribute to liberty by preserving the dignity and freedom of the individual.

Our belief is that the wealth of America lies in its people more than in its material things; and if given equal opportunity, our nation will prosper.

The equality of opportunity in past history has given America its great men in every field of endeavor. It is perhaps appropriate to mention two distinguished and great Americans during the year in which we celebrate the centennial of the Emancipation Proclamation — Abraham Lincoln, who rose to the presidency from the humble surroundings of a log cabin, and George Washington Carver, born of slave parentage, who became a great scientist and made significant contributions to scientific agriculture.

It is within this framework of freedom that police officers pursue their work. It is these freedoms that made possible the mechanical advantages they possess. Are these advantages enough to create the conditions necessary for developing popular support for police restrictions and enforcement practices? I don't think so.

In one sense, the advancement made in police technology is not as substantial as we are led to believe, primarily because it has materially assisted the police to withdraw from the community, to become isolated. The contemporary police officer's contact with the public is distant—if it exists at all—and the friendly, personal relationship is lost or obscure. The contact currently made is the result of a complaint requiring an interrogation, or an interview conducted on an official level. Thus, the concept of patrol has reverted from a positive to a negative function.

The patrol function is basic to effective police work, yet it continues in the traditional pattern with little regard to the results obtained. Patrol activity should be developed on the basis of scientific study; otherwise, police service continues to be dissipated in unproductive and meaningless tasks, some of which serve only to antagonize the community.

By careful manipulation and experimentation with patrol methods and utilization of personnel, the police can develop a positive service to the community by working cooperatively with others, and developing a relationship that wins respect and builds prestige for the entire department. This is crime prevention at its best. If the results justify it, the assignment of patrol officers on a permanent basis to schools and other interested community agencies should be considered, instead of a routine patrol assignment. Thus, police work can become an exciting challenge, rather than a routine activity, and can take its place with other professional activities offering a humane service to mankind.

When a boy is a thief at six, a hardened criminal at twelve, quits school at fifteen without knowing how to read and write, becomes a father at seventeen and a husband a few weeks later, and has never held a job in his life, he has never had a chance since the day he was born.

When a girl is raped at the age of twelve by a gang of neighborhood boys and seduced at thirteen by an elderly man, is a prostitute at fourteen, and a ward of the courts at fifteen, she hasn't had a chance either. [6]

These are case histories of young people who come from so-called disadvantaged, culturally deprived, and underprivileged families.

The most humane police service we can offer is to identify, with the assistance of other agencies, the conditions described in their earliest stages, and attempt to salvage these youngsters before it is too late. This is one of the objectives of the Police–School Liaison Program in Flint, Michigan, an example of official agencies and parents working together to resolve difficult situations involving teenage crime. Prior to the development of this program, one child for every thirty-six public school students was involved in a crime in a certain area of the city. After the program was in effect one year, only one child in every 280 students was involved in crime. The results in one year were convincing enough to continue the program and extend it to other parts of the city. It consists of the assignment of a police officer to the junior high schools on a full-time basis. He becomes an integral part of the school personnel and works with the teaching staff, the school administrators, the students, and the parents. The officer also serves as a member of a Regional Counseling Team, consisting of a registered nurse, a qualified teacher, the junior high school dean of students, and the elementary school principal. Their function is to identify a juvenile problem at the pre-delinquent or early delinquent stage, and to make a proper referral. This type of enlightened, constructive crime prevention activity is a challenge to a police administrator and his department.

The application of the crime prevention principle through the patrol force has never been fully exploited in American law enforcement. The potential is limited only by our lack of ingenuity and imagination.

The capacity of a person to perform the increasingly complex police task in a difficult and mobile society; to begin to understand the social, economic, political, and cultural impact upon segments of the community in the metropolitan complex, and the potential hazards that may erupt into disorder and conflict, require — indeed demand — that communities hire men for police service who have the greater capacity to understand and work with these tensions in the community.

The Wickersham report of 1931 stated: "Many surveys of the American police systems point out that they are far from satisfactory in either methods, personnel or organization. This report cannot examine in detail such defects. It can merely note that these defects are frequently attributed to inadequate methods of selection and training, to the lack of permanent, responsible and trained leadership, and to a continual shifting and uncertainty in administrative policies."[7] Although there are notable exceptions to this statement, in general it applies today, also.

In 1954, Superintendent O. W. Wilson stated: "The nature of police service imposes unusual demands on the individual policeman . . . To assure success, all policemen must have above-average intelligence."[8]

Others have written in the same vein, but in spite of these suggestions by writers and police leaders, men are still being recruited for police service whose educational qualifications are limited to the high school diploma or its equivalent. The college graduate, and other resources of our great institutions of higher learning, are virtually ignored by American law enforcement. Only a few bold and visionary police administrators have sought the services of these institutions and their graduates.

Those who would ignore or discredit the role of our educational institutions in serving law enforcement should be reminded that America is great because of her educational institutions. The public university, in particular, is committed to the service of all mankind. There is a growing acceptance by many educators that all human activities, not just a selected few, are worthy of the most serious, scholarly attention.

In our institutions of higher learning, emphasis is placed on nuturing and developing conceptual skills, creativity, judgment, and the desire to continue to learn. It is not feasible to teach everything, because what is taught today may be obsolete tomorrow. When this nation was new, knowledge was doubling once in 150 years; now, new knowledge is doubling once in eight years.

Colleges and universities continue to be an instrument through which society acts to improve itself. These institutions can serve, also, as intsruments for screening applicants for law enforcement service. One of the important objectives of a selection process is not merely to screen out those who are less able, but to screen out those who are less highly motivated. Therefore, those persons who are finally accepted are not only men of outstanding ability and potential, but men whose character is commensurate with their ability. The young student who elects to study in a four-year law enforcement curriculum is usually highly motivated. Too often, intellectual capacity is not the critical factor in the police selection process. Sometimes, and perhaps too often, young men of capacity are eliminated solely because of their physical stature or the inability to perform, fully, some non-validated physical agility requirement.

Colleges and universities continue to be the avenue of opportunity for able young men and women. If police service is to continue to progress at a faster pace, it must get its share of the bright, young graduates from our higher educational institutions. However, it cannot at the same time fail to maximize the potential of the vast majority of officers who comprise its personnel, who have not had the good fortune to obtain a higher education.

Three barriers exist which cause capable people to seek opportunities elsewhere. First is the pre-employment residential requirement, which has a double-barrelled effect, working against the best interests of the community and against those of the interested applicant. This requirement should be eliminated completely, and applicants selected on the basis of their qualifications, as determined by competitive examinations.

The second barrier is the lack of opportunity for police personnel. Upon entry into police service, everyone is required to wait a minimum number of years — ranging from about three to seven — before he becomes eligible for promotion. There is no scientific basis for this rule; it represents an arbitrary decision by city officials or administrators which should be discarded. The present requirement assumes that the quality and quantity of each person's experience is relatively the same, and that each individual acquires knowledge, develops judgment, and matures at the same pace. This does not happen. Each person is different. Some are ready for advancement very early in their careers, others are not; the problem is to distinguish one individual from the other. The present system for promotion is inflexible, stifles initiative, and denies opportunity.

In 1960, the Commissioner of the New York City Police Department emphasized the shortcomings of the promotion system in his department. He argued that five years was too long to wait for an attempt to achieve the first advancement for any ambitious young man; that the system was discriminatory; that it did not promote the best man; that examinations were held too infrequently; that the system did not develop individual potential for leadership as fast as the department needed it; and that in terms of skill, experience, judgment, and maturity, many men were ready for promotion long before the cumbersome promotion system permitted them to achieve it. He stated "that dynamic leadership in the police force depends on catching these men young, at the height of their abilities, when they are technically and psychologically ready and eager to take the step toward greater responsibilities. If they are to be allowed at this point to languish in a lower rank, the keen edge is lost. The dead hand of routine and the sterility of inertia set in, driving out initiative and imagination."[9]

A third barrier is lack of competition for positions of responsibility. A competitive climate should be created in police service, designed to promote the most capable men who are willing to rise to the challenge confronting them. This can be accomplished by permitting any officer, after his probationary period is over and he is tenured, to be eligible for advancement to any vacany occurring in the department.

The challenge in present day police service is so great that the search for leadership potential should have no limits or boundaries, and should extend to every nook and cranny of our society.

The proposal to eliminate the pre-employment residential requirement and improve the promotional climate can be accomplished, if the community will actively support and urge the police to adopt these concepts. In many cases, the authority to act rests with the civilian who serves on civil service commissions and similar agencies, or legislative bodies.

Under the law, we find ourselves as citizens held to a high degree of responsibility. An eminent clergyman reminds us that "all human law of honest purpose is an extension of Divine Law and, hence by right, can command our respect and obedience. When the majesty of the law is lightly regarded, it means that the citizenry has become forgetful of the Divine Lawgiver Himself, whose sanction attends upon all reasonable human laws."[10]

Those who enter public life take on great responsibilities. The good of all the people within their authority and the perfection of the total society should take precedence over every partisan or individual interest.

The courts have supported this principle and have held that police officers act in their public capacity, and not as agents or servants of the municipality.

In our form of government, it is fundamental that public offices are a public trust. We are reminded dramatically of our trust and responsibility by the proclamation issued in 1919 by Governor Coolidge following the Boston police strike. It reads in part as follows:

> There is an obligation, inescapable, no less solemn to resist all those who do not support the government. The authority of the Commonwealth cannot be intimidated or coerced. It cannot be compromised. To place the maintenance of the public security in the hands of a body of men who have attempted to destroy it would be to flout the sovereignty of the laws the people have made. It is my duty to resist any such proposal. Those who would counsel it join hands with those whose acts have threatened to destroy the government. There is no middle ground. Every attempt to prevent the formation of a new police force is a blow at the government. That way treason lies. No man has a right to place his own ease or convenience or the opportunity of making money above his duty to the State.
>
> This is the cause of all the people. I call on every citizen to stand by me in executing the oath of my office by supporting the authority of the government and resisting all assaults upon it. [11]

The statement, "This is the cause of all the people," is as valid today as it was in 1919, whether we are concerned with a police strike, or the problem of crime, or social equality in our communities.

If a community is stricken with the cancer of corruption, if law is ignored and enforcement is neglected, a fearful judgment rests on the people whose apathy and inaction amount to silent approval.

The community cannot ignore or neglect its responsibility to the agencies which serve the public. Too frequently, the police have had to assume, alone, the full responsibility for attempting to alleviate crime in our society. The high incidence of crime in the U. S. is an indictment of our society, not of the police, and can only be resolved by fixing a share of the responsibility with the community, and seeking its assistance in the resolution of the crime problem.

Thus, when the police seek bold and imaginative changes in administrative practices, discard the mantle of defensiveness, and erase the aura of mystery surrounding their operations, and actively solicit the community's support, it should not be withheld.

Police Commissioner Michael J. Murphy of New York City reminds the community that "the responsibility for maintaining law and order does not devolve on police alone. Without the cooperation of the public, law enforcement cannot be an effective instrument of democracy."[12]

The U. S. Attorney General, in a Law Day address made in 1961, emphatically adds:

> In too many major communities of our country, organized crime has become big business. . . . it is not the gangster himself who is of concern. It is what

he is doing to our cities, our communities, our moral fiber. Ninety percent of the major racketeers would be out of business by the end of this year if the ordinary citizen, the businessman, the union officials and the public authority stood up to be counted and refused to be corrupted.

This is a problem for all America, not just the FBI or the Department of Justice; but all the high rhetoric on Law Day about the noble mansions of the law, all the high sounding speeches about liberty and justice, are meaningless unless people — you and I — breathe meaning and force into it. For our liberties depend upon our respect for the law.[13]

In my belief, the alarm bells are tolling, asking us to look at ourselves as a people, and determine whether we will perish or survive as a free nation, if we embrace a value system that supports organized crime on a scale unknown in history, and a moral decay in the public service and business community resulting in conspiracies to fix prices, to defraud the customers, to cheat the government, and an appalling apathy toward the less fortunate in our society.

The re-examination of ourselves must begin at the community level, and be developed on a person-to-person and group-to-group basis. We must have respect for each other, recognizing that differences of opinion exist which may tend to drive us apart, but this tendency must be resisted.

The fundamental, and perhaps most important, step to be taken is to establish a means of keeping the public informed regarding the magnitude of the crime problem in the community. It is perhaps as important to continuously remind the public, through whatever media are established, that crime is the problem of the entire community, and the police are only one of the agencies involved in the process of administering justice in our society. The prosecuting officials, the courts, and the corrections officials have an equally grave and important responsibility. The negative actions of one agency can thwart or minimize the efforts of the others.

The police are the first target of the perennial critics and of others who honestly and sincerely believe the police are inefficient, and have the courage to voice their opinion.

It is only natural for the police to resent this criticism and to respond in kind, or to be defensive. But, neither approach — arrogance or hypersensitivity — is the answer to the problems confronting the community and the police. These attitudes merely drive them farther apart.

What is needed is some common ground on which to meet and begin to explore common problems in an atmosphere of mutual trust. Both sides have their point of view and will defend it vigorously. However, there is a need to be united, and it seems to me this can be achieved best at the level of government where the problems exist; namely, the state and local governmental level. There is need for citizen support at the federal level, also, but that is another story, and I leave that aspect to the U. S. Attorney General. I hope that the Federal Crime Commission proposal will be resurrected and implemented.

The tendency of local and state government agencies to increase the distance between themselves and the communities they serve must be reversed. I am convinced, therefore, that in the future, we will witness an increasing number of metropolitan communities and states organizing citizens' groups or commissions which will direct their attention to assisting the agencies administering justice.

The concept of a citizens' group to develop public support for law enforcement is not new. The police have strongly endorsed public support in the traffic safety movement, as a primary requisite for success. I am certain their resistance to citizen group activity in the area of civil rights will subside as they gain more experience with these groups and realize their potential for good.

These groups or commissions will take the form of official or quasi-official agencies created by statute or by executive authority. They will have authority to "observe the criminal law in action," but will not have any statutory authority pertaining to any of the existing duties of agencies responsible for administering justice in their respective jurisdictions. Their principal duties will be to strengthen the cause of criminal justice by evaluating the criminal law as an instrument of social control.

Two states have adopted legislation providing for advisory bodies at the state level. Utah, for instance, has passed a bill without a dissenting vote in the Legislature creating a State Council on Criminal Justice Administration.

The action in Utah followed a report dealing with increased crime, delinquency, an inadequate court system to cope with juvenile delinquency, lack of coordination between law enforcement and other agencies, and inadequacies in the corrections program.[14]

New York has its Commission on Investigation, whose actions in one community I have described. Its responsibilities are to "keep the public informed as to the operations of organized crime and problems of criminal law enforcement in the state.[15]

The states and cities mentioned are on the forward edge of reform, and their programs reflect a new frontier emerging. Others will follow their example. As these additional programs emerge at metropolitan and state levels, they will focus attention on the need for a federal agency with similar responsibilities. When the federal agency is established, it will forge the bond of civilian public support from local to state to the federal levels of government. When this occurs, the chain of criminal justice will be completed at the citizens' level, and the burden of developing an effective and enlightened criminal justice program will be lessened.

The police must have public support and the public must have police service — one is dependent upon the other; each will fail without the other.

There is one remaining "frontier" I want to develop. There are countless law enforcement associations in the United States. Their membership rosters include the names of officers from municipal police departments, federal law enforcement agencies, sheriffs' departments, constables, and many others. These organizations seem to have wandered aimlessly. Because of the diverse interests represented among their membership, perhaps this is understandable. Few have taken a public position, through their elected representatives, on the problems confronting municipal law enforcement, or have developed a program designed as a guidepost to assist local police officials. No measures have been taken in advance to prevent scandals in our communities. In many cases, if not most, the police administrators of indicted departments are members of these organizations. What their status is after indictments are returned is not clear.

Nevertheless, what is needed in American law enforcement is an organization exclusively for the American municipal police officer, organized in such a way that its board of officers would comprise the senior police administrators of municipal police service. Chapters of this organization should be developed by region or by state throughout the United States, in order to serve more effectively the vast, complex enterprise that characterizes American municipal police service. Its membership should be comprised of municipal police officials who represent communities where the highest standards of ethics and municipal police service are observed. This organization would be comprised of and limited to dedicated police administrators whose principal concern would be the vigorous advancement of the cause of police professionalization at the municipal level of government. It could ally itself appropriately with the resources of this country that share with equal vigor and dedication that basic goal. It would give material and moral support to these resources, wherever they may exist.

The critical need, from an organizational point of view, is to bring together, regularly, the most able administrators; the keenest minds; the most visionary, bold, and courageous men in municipal police service to direct the destiny and to shape the future of municipal police service, before we are embarrassed further by scandals and corruption at the local level of government. It is not enough to send, "after the fact," the most able police officials to communities where there has been police corruption, in an attempt to heal the wounds and right the wrongs. This process is not the answer to crime, corruption, or social unrest. It is merely another way to dissipate our resources, our talents, our intelligence, and our skills, at the expense of the communities which share these men with the organizations that seek their services.

I am not implying any criticism whatever of the fine, able, and dedicated administrators who respond to the call for help. However, I deplore the situation that often exists, wherein no action is taken to prevent the conditions from developing in the first place.

Individual citizens or police officers cannot function as effective members of the community, if they remain ignorant or silent about a local problem, whether it is crime, welfare, education, or some other activity that is at issue.

To the police and the community, I direct these questions: Should we remain silent in the face of the indictment contained in the reports I cited at the beginning of this address? Should we permit the weakest among us to establish our reputation in a world audience? Should we remain silent and permit the ebb and flow of the tide of criticism and indictment to wash back and forth over us, until we are weakened to the point where the American dream of individual responsibility and the courage to govern ourselves is dissipated?

Ella Wheeler Cox offers this comment about silence:

To sin by silence, when we should protest, makes cowards out of men. The human race has climbed on protest. Had no voice been raised against injustice, ignorance, and lust, the inquisition yet would serve the law, and guillotines decide our least disputes.

The few who dare must speak and speak again to right the wrongs of many. Speech, thank God, no vested power in this great day and land, can gag or throttle!

Let us speak out. Our society is a bank in which all of us must make a deposit for good citizenship—we cannot continue to appear before the withdrawal window only.

References

1. Federal Bureau of Investigation, UNIFORM CRIME RE-PORT, 1960, p. 106.
2. Smith, Bruce. *A Preface to Law Enforcement,* ANNALS OF THE AMERICAN ACADEMY OF POLITICAL AND SOCIAL SCIENCE, (January 1954), pp. 1–4.
3. *School Changes Urged to Prevent City "Jungles,"* Detroit FREE PRESS, April 1, 1962. (Excerpts from a report titled *Education and the Disadvantaged American,* National Education Association, Washington, D.C.)
4. Conant, James B. SLUMS AND SUBURBS. New York: McGraw-Hill, 1961. 147 pp.
5. *Ibid.,* p. 18.
6. Hodenfield, G. K. *Underprivileged Children Posing Terrific Challenge to United States Schools,* THE STATE JOUR-NAL, Lansing, Mich. March 8, 1962. p. 19.
7. National Commission on Law Enforcement and Observation REPORTS, Vol. VI, *The Causes of Crime.*
8. Wilson, O. W. *Toward a Better Merit System,* ANNALS OF THE AMERICAN ACADEMY OF POLITICAL AND SOCIAL SCIENCE, (January 1954), pp. 87–96.
9. Press Release No. 80, New York City Police Department, November 29, 1960. 4 pp.
10. Cushing, Archbishop Richard Cardinal. *The Christian and the Community,* Pastoral letter, 1960. 60 pp.
11. Sheehan, Robert. *Lest We Forget,* POLICE Magazine (September-October, 1959), pp. 8–14.
12. Press Release No. 65, New York City Police Department, September 5, 1961. One page.
13. Address by Hon. Robert F. Kennedy, Attorney General of the United States, prepared for delivery at the Law Day Exercises at the University of Georgia Law School, Athens, May 6, 1961.
14. *Criminal Justice Administration in Utah.* Report by the Criminal Justice Advisory Committee of the Utah Legislative Council, October, 1960. 33 pp.
15. *An Investigation of Law Enforcement in Buffalo.* Report by the New York State Commission of Investigation, 1961.

Professionalization of the Police

ALBERT J. REISS, JR.

*Professor, Department of Sociology, University of Michigan,
Ann Arbor*

MAY 22, 1967

Readers, listeners and viewers are confronted daily with reports of crime and with what seems like increasing frequency, reports of civil violence. There are two recurrent themes. There is more crime, more crimes of violence, and more criminals in the United States than ever before, and our civil order is threatened by mass disobedience. Underlying themes are that Americans are losing their respect for law and order, that they have lost the code of the good Samaritan, and that they do not support their local police.

But anyone familiar with the history of policing for the past 150 years is aware of the fact that these themes are far from new. What is more, although the dilemmas and contradictions between the public and the police from the past are still apparent today, it is equally clear that waves of crime and public protest have made for substantial changes in police organization, strategy, and tactics.

Changes in police organization and operations have been sporadic, however, tending to follow upon periods of organized public protest and violence, upon a scandal within the department, or on the genesis of a "crime wave" that leads to public investigation and political debate about the police. While local police departments have undergone organizational change as a consequence of police scandals and waves of reform, major changes in policing across the country generally have followed public definition of crime or policing as a national problem of political, legal, and moral scope. We are in such a national wave now.

I do not propose to discuss the nature of past changes, nor most of the dimensions of the present problems. Insofar as past changes are concerned, it should be apparent that their effect on the police has been an increasing reliance on the centralization and specialization of command functions in the processing of complaints and violators. In short, the changes in police departments are those we ordinarily associate with bureaucracy. Our larger police departments, at least, have become major bureaucratic organizations. Many of their problems are less often uniquely problems of a police department than they are the problems of any bureaucratic organization. Failure to recognize this fact has led to some muddled thinking about police departments, a matter I shall have more to say about shortly.

There has risen on the horizon during the past few decades a major movement —not uncommon for bureaucratic organizations—a movement to professionalize the police. The occupational and organizational attempts to make a profession of police work is my major concern in what follows. I shall begin with a conclusion and then discuss it, drawing some references for police and community relations.

The conclusion is that most attempts to make a profession of police work have led to a professionalization of the police department, to a lesser extent a professionalization of those in staff positions, and only to a relatively minor extent to professionalization of the rank and file officer in the line. In stating the evidence for this conclusion, two arguments will be advanced: First, that the nature of changes within police departments work against the professionalization of the line officer; rather the department is professionalized through bureaucratization and the line officer becomes, at most, a technician, at the least a person who is commanded. Second, that changes in the Great Society work against professionalization of the line, primarily through redefinition and monitoring of the police role and work. I shall then move to the argument that the nature of police work coerces discretionary decision-making in social situations, and that both the ends and means valued by our society require that in the long run at least part of the line must be "professional."

Before turning to these arguments, I shall need to make clear what it is I mean by "a profession" or "becoming a professional." It is common to think of a profession as a special kind of occupation, where the job of the professional is technical, the technical knowledge generally having been acquired through long prescribed training, and the knowledge itself being systematic in nature. Furthermore, it is assumed that the professional man follows a set of professional norms that may include a code of ethics that binds the professional to behave ethically toward his clients.[1] Both the training and norms generally fall under legal or professional organizational control, specifying who can practice.

Now all of these things may characterize persons who are called professionals. But they miss a central feature that characterizes any profession. At the core of any profession is a relationship with clients. Professions are based on practice, and a major element in all practice is the relationship with clients.

What is crucial in defining any professional in the nature of this relationship with clients? We can say that it is technical in nature, where the specialized knowledge is utilized in practice, as when the physician calls upon his specialized knowledge to diagnose illness. We can say that it is moral or ethical, as when the lawyer treats information from his client as privileged or confidential. But a core feature of the relationship with any client is a *decision* about the client—a decision in which the professional person decides something about the client that *relates to his future*. In some professions, this decision is given largely in the form of advice. The client presumably is free to ignore or follow the advice. But in some professions and in certain roles within other professions, it is a decision over which the client can exercise little if any choice. In that case, we speak of this decision as a coerced decision, an evaluation, a judgment, or a determination. The teacher decides whether the pupil shall pass or fail. The social worker decides whether the applicant is eligible for additional welfare rewards. The judge decides whether or not the defendant is guilty, and what disposition shall be made for the case. Jurors who render verdicts, by the way, are not professionals, and some of the conflict in the criminal trial procedure today arises over the very question of competence of jurors to decide what have come to be called technical questions.

To return to the point under discussion, I shall base the discussion of professionalization of the police on the presumption that the core feature in professional practice is a decision that involves technical and moral judgment affecting the clinets' future. In the jargon of the professions, this is called "professional judgment," or a "discretionary decision." Though there invariably are boundaries that surround the freedom of choice, a professional decision presumes both latitude in choice and responsibility for making the decision.

---

[1] See, for example, Harold Wilensky, *The Professionalization of Everyone?*, THE AMERICAN JOURNAL OF SOCIOLOGY, LXX (September, 1964), p. 138.

The Department and Professionalization of the Line

I said that changes within modern police departments have led to professionalization of the department through bureaucratization. These changes, it was stated, work against professionalization of the line officer, particularly the patrol where initial contact is made with the public. Let us examine three main changes within police departments that support this conclusion.

First, there is the increasing centralization of both command and control in departments—a centralization of decision-making. Some police departments have been reorganized so that most of the command and control functions are essentially removed from the precinct level of organization. The precinct functions, then, primarily to allocate men to assignments and supervise them in their work roles. The core of many modern police departments is the centralized communications center, where allocative decisions are made under centralized command. The line officer on patrol is commanded from a central headquarters and reports directly to them by radio, with reports in some cases being made directly to central headquarters by radio or telephone. Furthermore, the bounds of decision-making by the line are officially narrowed, so that the officer is left without functions of investigation or, at most, a preliminary report. It should be clear, however, that such moves toward a centralized bureaucratic system have not necessarily limited the discretionary decision in practice, but simply to point out that they have not been consistent with a model of professionalization of *those* decisions by the line. *A bureaucratic system where decision-making is decentralized to the line would be more consistent with professionalization of the line.* The discretion exercised by command personnel often is more bureaucratic than professional. The decision is not more "professional"; only authority is more firmly fixed in a bureaucratic sense.

Second, most modern police departments have moved toward specialization of functions in particular units. Generally, such organizational specialization of functions is seen as more "professional." They could be, but more often than not, they become more in the nature of "technical specialities"—more the province of technicians than the province of professionals who make decisions on professional grounds. The centralization of the investigative function in a "technical" elite of the department—the detective bureau—may serve as a case in point. Much overrated in its capacity to investigate and certainly to "solve" most crimes, it nonetheless increasingly bears the "professional" label. Though there is much evidence of increasing bureaucratization of the investigative functions within police departments, leading to a large number of special investigation units over and above that of the detective division, there is much less evidence that the requirements of technical knowledge and training are consistent with professionalization of the personnel in these units. It is in this sense that we speak of the professionalization of the organizational system, leaving the corollary development of professional role specialization relatively untouched.

A recent study by John Gardiner that accounts for differences in traffic ticket-writing among police departments, shows that high ticket-writing for moving violations is related almost entirely to specialization of traffic enforcement.[2] But the

---

[2] John A. Gardiner, *Police Discretion: The Case of Traffic Law Enforcement,* Unpublished Ph.D. dissertation, Harvard University, 1966.

significance of this specialization was not in any sense that related to the high
training of officers, but almost entirely to the fact of specialization in and of
itself. When writing traffic tickets is the only function of a policeman, the number
of tickets written becomes the sole measure of his "work"; hence to be seen as
productive, he *must* write tickets. Again, here, we clearly find an effect of bureaucratization. Bureaucracy means specialization of function, to more effectively get
a job done.

But in traffic, we find specialization in the sense of "work-assignment," not of
"professionalization." Indeed, interviews with police officers assigned to special
traffic enforcement indicates these sharp differences. Only a small proportion of
officers see themselves as specialists in even a highly technical sense. An officer
of this kind described his job erroneously in professional terms, but correctly in
specialist terms when he said: "In medicine, you don't have general practitioners
any more—you have obstetricians, heart men, brain men, and so forth. It's the
same way in police work. No officer can know *all* the laws. It's a full-time job
just knowing when you can arrest a man or when you have to have a search
warrant. So, when I was put on enforcement, I started out reading Chapter 90
(the motor vehicle laws) from cover to cover. Whenever the newspaper reported
a change in traffic laws, I cut it out. You have to know what laws to enforce.
You have to be a specialist."[3]

But most men came closer to the point in describing the job as they saw it:
"Since our only job was going to be ticketing, we knew we could stay on days
as long as we produced; the Chief might put us back on nights if we didn't produce." Or, "Nobody is pushing to get tickets written; men write tickets when
that is their only job." Or, yet another, "I don't care what happens to my tickets.
If I write up the violations I've seen, I can sleep nights—I've done my day's
work."[4] Such comments show that it is difficult to say whether traffic men write
traffic tickets because they are "pushed." They do show, however, that writing
tickets is what superior officers expect enforcement specialists to do, and that
men enjoy the enforcement assignments, if only because of the hours and the
freedom from (direct) supervision. So—they write tickets. It's their job, not a
profession.

Third, there is a growing tendency to make decisions at the staff rather than
the operating levels of the department, and to introduce professional specialists
at the staff rather than the operating level. This is partly due to the fact that
increased bureaucratization and introduction of a complex technology necessitate
the utilization of other professions within the police system. But such professionals are generally introduced at the staff level, or as special consultants inserted
for a special reason into operating units. Thus, a department employs medical
internists and psychiatrists to perform certain applicant or promotion-screening
functions. The planning or analysis sections may include professional statisticians,
programmers, or analysts. These professional specialists are generally referred to
as "civilians" within the department, separating them not only from the line, but
in many cases from the "sworn" staff as well.

The tendency to make decisions at staff rather than operating levels is readily
apparent when one examines the staff units of a department. There is considerable

³ *Ibid.,* Chapter VII.
⁴ *Ibid.,* Chapter VII.

evidence that the handling of "human relations" within police departments is largely a staff function. Despite a spate of human relations training for the line, it is the staff units that are regarded as "professional" in human relations work. The training division and the human relations unit of the department are more "professionalized." There is, in fact, little provision for actual implementation of "human relations" in the line, except by "central order" and some training of the line in the classroom of the academy. Without explicit provision for professional *implementation* in the line, there is little opportunity for professional treatment of clients in what is bureaucratically referred to as human relations.

Some studies we have done of actual contacts between police officers and citizens in several major metropolitan police departments may serve to make this point clearer, with respect to human relations in police departments. We examined 14,679 encounters between police and citizens in dispatched and on-view mobilizations of the police. Time does not permit me to tell you most of what we found out about how the police and citizens relate to one another in such transactions.[5] But I want to tell you about two paradoxes that are suggested by our findings.

The first paradox arises from our findings about the dominant mode of conduct that police and citizens take toward one another. The dominant mode of behavior of the police toward citizens is to treat them in a "businesslike," "routinized," or "impersonal" fashion. Seventy-four percent of all citizens in encounters were treated by the police in this way. Such conduct is often termed "bureaucratic" or "civil," and attributed to officials in civil service systems. At the same time, we find that the dominant mode of behavior of citizens toward officers is to respond in a "civil" fashion. Seventy-six percent of all citizens were observed as behaving with civility toward the police. And as one might expect, more often than not, civil behavior by the police occurs with civil behavior by the citizen.

Herein lies the paradox, however. *The citizen who treats the officer with civility often regards civility in the officer as a sign of disrespect—and the officer who meets civility in the citizen often perceives it as a sign of disrespect.* The paradox arises because of differences in their expectations of one another. Our interviews with citizens show that the citizen wants the officer to behave with more than civility; he wants to be treated as a "person," what has come to be termed, a "human relations" perspective. Our interviews with officers show that they want the citizen to behave with more than civility, to show deference toward their authority. It is striking that in a civil society, for neither the police nor the citizens is behavior with civility enough. Yet, expectations for deference and for personal treatment lie outside a system of civil, bureaucratic treatment. To be sure, the problem of differences in expectations arises in part because the police continue to operate within a "traditional bureaucracy," where *legitimate* authority is at the center, while the citizen increasingly operates in civil rights-oriented democracy where "human relations" or the "person" is at the center. Clearly these problems lie in the structure and operation of organizations.

The second paradox arises from the differential treatment officers give citizens according to their race, and the responses citizens make to such treatment. When

---

[5] See *Crime and Law Enforcement in Major Metropolitan Areas,* Field Studies III for President's Commission on Law Enforcement and Administration of Justice, Washington, D.C., U.S. Government Printing Office, 1967, Vol. 2.

the police officer departs from the model of civil treatment of citizens in a *positive* fashion by good humored or jovial treatment of citizens, he is more likely to do so toward white than Negro citizens; 21 percent of the white citizens were treated in this way, as contrasted with 12 percent of Negroes. Correctively, when the officer departs from the model of civil treatment in a *negative* fashion, with hostile, authoritarian, or belittling behavior, he also is more likely to do so toward white than Negro citizens; roughly twice as many whites as Negro citizens were treated with aggressive behavior by the police. Furthermore, the police act more harshly toward antagonistic white than they do toward antagonistic Negro citizens. The differences in treatment of whites and Negroes are largely accounted for by the fact the police are more likely to treat Negro citizens with civility; 80 percent of all Negro citizens were treated in this way, as contrasted with 66 percent of all white citizens.

This suggests that when the police depart from the model of "civil treatment" of citizens, they are more likely to treat white than Negro citizens with both "traditional human relations" and "traditional punitive" perspectives. Indeed, there is somewhat of a paradox; why should the police treat white citizens both more positively and negatively than Negro citizens? The answer may lie both in the expectations of the police about white as contrasted with Negro citizens, and in the structure of modern police systems. The structure of the modern police system, despite many changes, still supports traditional behavior of officers toward citizens. Despite the police academy and its human relations training, police line culture supports traditional ways of handling citizens, ways that the classroom has not overcome. The traditional human relations perspective of the line was to use humor and joviality toward citizens as a means of obtaining conformity, or of relating to them. At the same time, if the citizen failed to conform, sanctions were generally punitive. These are the traditional ways of behaving toward persons in terms of their conduct, or the "face" they present to the police.

It should be apparent that given these traditional expectations and ways the line handled citizens, police officers are more likely to respond to a white citizen's behavior in this traditional fashion, since whites are expected to behave toward the officer in the prescribed traditional ways.

Negroes present somewhat of a different problem, however, given the strong pressures both within and without police systems to have the officers behave positively toward the Negro citizen. The outcome is not a human relations approach (often presumed to be taught to police officers), but increased civility in conduct toward them. The officer has an obligation to treat them with civility, but hardly as "persons" in the traditional sense. Indeed, they may not regard Negroes as "persons" at all in the traditional sense.

What is lacking, it seems, is not only a "human relations" approach toward Negro citizens, but an approach to *both* white and Negro citizens that is based on the rights and dignity of individuals and a recognition of them as *persons* rather than as *clients*. But again, paradoxically, that problem is at the center of all civil service bureaucracies, not only large police departments but larger hospitals, universities, or government agencies.

External Organizations and Professionalization of the Line

A metropolitan police organizational system faces considerable penetration of its organizational environment from organizations and interest groups that lie outside its boundaries. This is so for a number of reasons. Legally charged with responsibility for law enforcement, it nonetheless faces problems of overlapping jurisdiction with county, state, and national enforcement agencies. Law enforcement likewise is intricately linked with a larger organizational system of criminal justice, such that its output is an input into the criminal justice system where it is evaluated. Furthermore, it is directly linked to a municipal, county, or state organizational system that controls at least its budget, and it also maintains a host of transactions with other municipal and community organizations in providing "police service." A police system thus engages in transactions not only with its clients who are *citizens* demanding a service, and with victims and their violators, but with a multiplicity of organizations where problems of service, its assessment, resource allocation, and jurisdiction are paramount.

We can only illustrate how these relationships tend, on the whole, to militate against the professionalization of the line, and to suggest how they militate against the professionalization of the staff as well. The recent decisions of criminal and appellate courts defining the limits of interrogation, search of the person and property and the seizure of evidence, and of the use of force have been defined by the police and the courts as limits on discretionary decision-making. Some segments of the general public and the higher courts view the police as having exercised too much discretion in their relationships with the public, and hold that decision as to method is to be defined on *legal professional* rather than police professional grounds. In short, the prevailing view is that the police must be controlled by more legitimate authority—authority that is invested in either the law, the public prosecutor and the courts, or in a civil procedure.

Apart from the emphasis on civil review procedures, this dilemma faced by the police is a classic case of dispute over jurisdiction; indeed, of professional jurisdiction. A group of professionals—in this case largely made up of lawyers and jurists—seeks to restrict the powers of "would-be-professionals"—in this case the police. This conflict is not unlike that between medical doctors and nurses, or prosecutors and judges. What is generally characteristic of such conflicts are questions of jurisdiction. But over and above that is an equally important consideration: such conflicts generally arise where one group of professionals controls the fate of another group of professionals (or aspirants to professional status) in an intricately balanced organizational system. Much of the conflict between the courts and the police is, in this sense, inevitable, given our system of law enforcement and criminal justice. For in that system, we have on the one hand institutionalized the introduction of clients into the larger system in the hands of the police, since operationally at least, it is they who largely exercise the power of arrest. Yet on the other hand, we have institutionalized the power of assessing outcome of arrest of the client and assessment of police procedure in the prosecutor and the court. When the ultimate fate of clients rests in another group of professionals, and particularly when they are removed from the situation that precipitated the client relationship—conflict is endemic in the system.

We could, by analogy, show that the relationship between the police and the courts is not unlike that which might prevail in a university where the determination of the grade a student gets rests not with the professor but with someone else. To force the analogy, most professors in the American system probably would object strongly to someone else not only grading their students, but requiring the professor to take back into his classroom students whom he regards as failures. Such conflicts, also, by the way, tend to arise in professional training, where the experienced professional regards the trainee with distrust and severely restricts his opportunity to make discretionary decisions, or to gain the requisite experience. Howard Becker has pointed out that this is an essential ingredient in the production of student subcultures in professional schools. Policing as a subculture in the larger society may arise for somewhat similar reasons.

Civil review boards are an organizational mechanism for penetrating the police organizational system. Apart from general questions of jurisdiction and legitimacy of authority to make decisions, the organizational arrangement introduces important questions about professional control of professional practice. What the civil review board does, in effect, is to monitor practice by setting itself up to review client complaints about practice. The monitoring of professional practice is zealously guarded by professional groups, the norm being that a "professional" group is able to police its own professional practice. Though no professional group is entirely free from an external monitor, since there are at least some conditions for judicial proceedings charging malpractice, the traditional professions have tried to retain virtually complete control of standards of practice, arguing essentially that professionals are the most competent to judge their own professionals. Even where professionals are employees of public organizations such as public hospitals, civil service review has generally been restricted to complaints of the organization against the employee (or vice versa), and of client against the organization.

Civil review boards thus pose some barrier to professionalization of the police, attenuating the latitude an occupation or an organization based on an occupation has to "police" itself. That the police have not been altogether ineffective in preventing the creation of civil review boards in the United States is apparent. Much of their success probably is due to the effective organizational effort of the line organizations of police officers, backed by legitimacy of their claims from the police chief. Locally organized, they bring local pressures. Yet, lacking effective organization on "professional grounds" across local departments, their long-run effectiveness may be more restricted. Unlike trade unions that increased their bargaining power through extra-local organization, the only extra-local police organization of consequence is the International Association of Chiefs of Police. The line, therefore, is without national power.

The issue for professionalization of the police is one of whether civic accountability will take the form of an inquiry into an individual's work within an organization, whether it will take the form of accountability of an occupational organization of police, or whether accountability rests with a local police organizational system headed by a chief as the "accountable officer." Traditionally, line organizations of police have "protected" the rights of the officer in charges involving the local organization. Traditionally, the local police organization has been held accountable through control by the mayor, the occasional appointment of "civilian" chiefs, and the sporadic investigations of the department under charges of scandal by "blue-ribbon" committees. Traditionally, the organization of the line has failed to develop standards for control of practice by members of the occupation. The dilemma that exists for the line, then, is that the police occupation exists within a local, formally organized police department that controls practice, rather than with a professional organization of the police.

To shift the balance of review and control to an external review system, however, creates problems both for the operating departmental organization and the occupational association. This is particularly the case when there is external review of an individual's performance within an organization. For this form of accountability interferes with both institutionalized forms of professional control of practice in the United States, and with organizational forms of control to protect its boundaries. The same kind of dilemma was presented to public school teachers. Historically, they were under review from both a school organization and a civil review agency—respectively, the school administration and the school board. Increasingly, the professional organization of teachers has resisted school board review on "professional grounds," thereby coercing the relationship of public school teachers to organizations, employers, and clients more along the lines of traditional professional organizations. It is obvious that police now lack the effective extra-local organization developed among public school teachers.

In the United States, then, professional organization has resisted client review by external organizations. The professions also have tended to resist accountability to the organizations within which they are employed. Accountability has generally fallen within the province of the professional association, and where a profession has been relatively weak in its formative period, it has tended to rely upon the employing organization to resist client claims on practice.

There are, of course, major issues of accountability of public employees and organizations to civic authority in any democratic society. The Scandanavian countries and New Zealand, among other democratic countries have created a special role, the ombudsman, to protect the individual citizen against abuse by public employees. The ombudsman generally is distinguished in these societies by the fact that no public official, including public prosecutors and judges, are exempt from inquiry. Moreover the ombudsman has enormous powers to investigate and order sanctions against offenders.

Without doubt, attempts to institutionalize the role of ombudsman in American society would encounter considerable resistance, particularly from lawyers and judges, who perhaps have been most exempt from public scrutiny among the professionals in the United States (unless it be physicians). Quite clearly also, their resistance would be stipulated on "professional" grounds of competence to control practice. Since police in the United States are inextricably linked to the system of criminal justice, they are inclined to regard with cynicism a civic accountability system of their organization that exempts the office of public prosecutor and jurist. But they are more vulnerable to client claims. Unlike the lawyers and social workers in the criminal justice system, their claim is based primarily on local police organizational control of police malpractice, rather than on professional association control of malpractice.

Discretionary Decision-Making and Professionalization of the Police

The third argument was that discretionary decision-making not only is institutionalized in the police role, but that the nature of police work requires discretion in making decisions. The open question is whether the decision-making is generally of a kind that is "open to professionalization."

To discuss this question, it seems worthwhile to call attention to the obvious distinction between the organization of an occupation, and the organization of work for persons in an occupation. Police are members of an occupation and an organization, an organization that historically was composed almost exclusively of members of the occupation. We already have noted the tendency to professionalize police organization rather than police practice. The failure to separate the two facets of organization poses certain additional problems for police professionalization, as an analogy may make clear.

Police organizations often formulate the problem of professionalization as one of developing a single profession of employees of the organization. The analogy between craft and trade unions immediately comes to mind. But perhaps analogy with a university may make the point more obvious. A police department, like a university, is an organization that deals with clients. There are many kinds of work roles in the organization; only some of its members deal directly with the clients. Furthermore, not all who deal with clients in a university are professionals. A large state university today may have over 10,000 employees, many of whom are clerks and technicians, others are managers or administrators, some are skilled craftsmen, and some are unskilled laborers. Indeed, the professors comprise fewer than 50 per cent of the work force.

But to think of a university as made up of professors who are professionals is also misleading, despite the organization of the American Association of University Professors. Professional competence largely rests with other criteria. There are professors who are medical doctors, others are lawyers or social workers, or economists, or physicists. Even within these groups, there are professional distinctions. One is a psychiatrist, a pediatrician, or a surgeon as well as a medical doctor, and these are the professional specialties. Not all professionals in universities are teachers. Some are professional librarians—even professional law, or medical reference librarians. Claims to professional competence, then, rest in a specialization of a task, or a kind of practice, as well as in a "general practice" or occupation of common practitioners.

And so it is with police departments. Police work itself is many different occupations, and a police department is comprised of an even greater range of occupational specialties, specialties that range from professional and technical through clerical and maintenance. That all should be regarded as bound by more than an allegiance to an organization—the police department—and by a common identity as "involved" in a common task—police work—seems doubtful. Professionalization of police rests, therefore, in determining tasks that lend themselves to professionalization. The occupational organization of a police department rests, then, in a number of professions, in numbers of technical specialties, and in occupations with more limited skills.

No attempt is made here to delineate those skills within police work, as currently organized, that lend themselves to professionalization, or to examine those niches in the organization that are already occupied by professionals from other specialties. Nor will I examine the way that selection into police roles may be defined in terms of prior professional training, such as the limiting of investigative roles in the FBI to persons with law training.

Rather the question that will be addressed is whether the basic discretionary role in the police department—what often is regarded as the heart of police work — the patrol — is a task requiring professional competence. To provide some answer to this question leads us to examine the nature of this particular police role, bearing in mind, as already noted, that there are other police roles, some of which appear to lend themselves to professionalization.

Superficial examination of police patrol work suggests that while it has features common to technical work roles, it also has some that are more characteristic of roles that have been professionalized. Since we have suggested that the core of the professional role is the relationship with clients, we shall examine the patrolman–client relationship in some detail, indicating how professional ideology and practice might relate to it.

Patrol work, first of all, is characterized by the fact that — unlike most professional or technical roles — a police officer must *expect both physical violence and verbal aggression directed against him in the performance of his work.* In the absence of a "professionalized" public that will not resort to such means, police officers always will have to deal with aggression directed specifically against them as they perform their work role.

Though there is considerable evidence that homicide where the police officer is the victim is less common today than ever before, physical aggression against the police still is high. There are no reliable data on physical aggression against officers, since in many cases the officer suffers no physical harm of consequence. Yet the number of work days lost in any police department due to physical injury in line of duty is higher than in most occupations. Even assuming that the rate of physical aggression is fairly low, the fact remains that it is not easy to forecast the situations where it will occur. For that reasons, officers must *always* expect physical aggression, including that which threatens their very life. And further, it is expected that an officer will use no more force than is necessary to deal with aggression directed against him.

Verbal aggression against the police is far more common than physical aggression. It is there, too, where major changes in expectations concerning police behavior have occurred in recent years. The police officer today, in modernizing departments, is expected to accept verbal aggression without responding with counter-aggression. In brief, what is expected of him is that he respond to verbal aggression with what is commonly referred to in the professions as "affective disengagement," or neutrality. He must not allow verbal aggression to influence his judgment other than in a professional sense.

To cope with aggression, then, the police officer is expected to respond with judgment as to the amount of force necessary to meet the situation of physical aggression, and to respond with affective neutrality to verbal and physical aggression, i.e., it is not "personal." Indeed, the police officer is in something of a dilemma in that both forms of aggression can be defined as offenses against an officer (as they would against any citizen), justifying in many cases formal charges involving arrest. Yet it is also apparent that almost all sectors outside the law enforcement field "expect" the police officer to respond to such aggression without pressing formal charges. It is suggested here that such dilemmas and matters of judgment involving affective neutrality and discretion in using coercion in "unpredictable" situations are most easily dealt with in a system by professional ideology, norms and practice.

That line officers at the present time lack the kind of professionalization that permits them to deal with these dilemmas is clear from our study of the police and citizen transactions. Antagonism and verbal aggression from citizens quite often led the officers to behave in an unprofessional way toward citizens. When citizens behave antogonistically toward the police, they were far more likely, than when they behaved civilly or deferentially, to be treated in a hostile, authoritarian, or belittling manner by the police. Furthermore, though a majority of any kind of police behavior is directed at citizens who are civil toward them, a disproportionate part of unprofessional or negative police conduct is directed at citizens who do not show deference toward them. Quite clearly, police officers on the average are unable to gauge their behavior on the basis of professional police norms; rather, they respond to client norms and behavior.

The social setting for police work generally takes place when the *police go to the client and his "stage" or to clients on a "public stage."* There is considerable variability in these social settings, and the patrol officer must be prepared to act in *any* setting. Almost no other professional operates in a comparable setting, since characteristically, professionals eliminate this necessity by bringing the client to an office or a bureaucratic setting where the client is "not at home." The house call of the physician is almost gone; their clients even are preprocessed by semi-professionals, clerks and technicians; their setting is an office, a clinic, a hospital room, or a laboratory. Even social workers have made considerable strides toward bringing the client into their office. So much so, that the most progressive programs today in social work are billed as "detached worker" programs, or "reaching out to the unreachables." Police officers need not be reminded that this is precisely what they are expected to do, twenty-four hours a day, rather than from nine to five. Even when social workers move into the community, they are more likely to operate in a public state over which they exercise some degree of control over time. The police, by contrast, must move continually from "stage" to "stage" — stages where the scenery, the plot and the actors are at most defined in general terms like "family trouble," "prowler," or "B & E."

It is incumbent upon a police officer, then, to enter upon a variety of social scenes, encounter the actors and their roles, and figure out the plot. Indeed, the main task of the police often is to discover the "plot," and to learn more about the actors. This is true in emergency situations where an officer is expected to assess the situation almost momentarily, and make judgments as to what he has to do. For the fate of the actors and the situation in such cases may lie with the police. Perhaps it need not be pointed out that quite comparable forms of assessment and judgment are treated as professional matters in our society.

Though police officers ordinarily deal with only a relatively small number of actors in a social setting, they must be prepared to deal with *large numbers as well.* There may be large numbers in picket lines, sit-ins, an unruly crowd or mob, drivers in traffic, or an audience at a mass event. Though superficially, their role is to preserve the peace and cope with any individuals in the large aggregate who violate the law, they must be prepared to deal with large numbers of persons to either preserve the peace or enforce the law. The major emphasis in such settings falls on "teamwork," and the work may be para-military. While "professional" judgment on the part of individual officers is less important in such settings, clearly the command function is facilitated by a "professional orientation," and the outcome will vary considerably depending upon the degree of professionalization of police work.

Police officers must deal, not only with actors on stage, whether large or small in number, but often with an audience as well. The audience may range from members of a family to strangers in the street, or a large gathering. This poses for the police the *problem of control of audience as well as client*. The officers must assess their audience as well as their immediate actors, since the audience may have an important effect on their work. Are they cooperative or hostile? Can they supply information? How can they be utilized in the situation? Involved then are matters of judgment and control of the audience.

The feature of police work most commonly emphasized is the necessity *to assert authority*. This is closely related to two other facets of the work situation — the willingness of the client to cooperate with the police, and the necessity to utilize force to control the client. Police must be prepared to assert authority when the client is unwilling; if necessary, to use coercive authority as in physical force.

Clients of professionals are not always cooperative. The teacher is faced with unwilling pupils, the psychiatrist with a resistant patient, and the judge with a hostile witness or defendant. Yet the situation is different for the police. When any practicing professional is faced with a particularly violent client, he can call the police. The police must cope with any and all clients, regardless of their willingness to be processed.

A striking feature of police work is that, not infrequently, the officer is confronted with a dual set of clients — those who call the police, and those who are to be "policed." Those who call are prepared to accept his authority; those who are to be policed often do not. The major form of control open to the officer in such a situation is to assert "authority." It is not surprising, therefore, that on entering a situation, an officer typically takes command by asserting authority. Unlike most other professionals who deal with clients who are preprocessed to accept the authority of the professional when he enters the situation, the police officer must establish his authority. The uniform, badge, baton, and arms all may play a role in asserting authority. Yet it appears that the police exercise command in most situations largely through the exercise of the person in the role. The more "professional" the person in that role, the more likely authority will be regarded as "legitimate" by the public, and the more likely the officer will exercise authority legitimately.

One often hears these days complaints from segments of the public that the police use illegal means and exercise undue coercion in their dealing with the public. From the police, one hears another set of arguments—that a police officer must take more abuse from the public than ever before, that the power to enforce the law is gradually being eroded, and that the public is uncooperative in helping the police perform their role. These complaints from both the police and the public undoubtedly stem from common sources of change, changes by the way that affect both public and police behavior. And despite often expressed views, the changes reflect that perhaps more, rather than less, orderly relations are in prospect for both the public and the police.

Despite dissatisfaction with the "new" role emerging for the police officer, it seems clear that the changes underway involve a reinterpretation of client role and behavior in terms of a more "professional" ideology and practice. The dilemma for the police is to somehow balance traditional moral and quasi-legal concerns with enforcing the law and catching criminals who are to be "punished," with the emerging concerns for civil rights and legal requirements on police methods. "Professionalization" of police work appears to be one "legitimate" way to deal with the dilemma.

As professional work in our society is bureaucratized, the professional deals largely with clients that are preprocessed in a bureaucratic setting. There is a preparation of the client for professional practice. The more common situation for the police is to encounter a client whom they must begin to process.[6] It is not surprising, therefore, that police officers often begin by getting a "case history," as well as an account of events that led up to the immediate situation. An interesting question surrounding the professionalization of police work is that regarding the quality and quantity of information necessary to judgment, and the manner in which it is obtained. In recent years, the manner that information is obtained by the police has been given priority over the quantity and quality of information. It should be apparent that both are essential ingredients in the exercise of judgment, particularly in what is regarded as professional judgment.

The police officer, like all professionals when faced with a client, must make a decision — a decision that determines the fate of the client. Only some of his decisions will be evaluated by others, both in and outside the department. And with some decisions rest not only the fate of the client, but the fate of the public as well. Often, too, the decision involves not only the fate of an individual, but the fate of a social relationship or a family unit. Each decision is potentially a decision of consequence.

There are, of course, many decisions that must be made to arrive at the decision of "fate." These involve not only technical questions of whether this is a civil or criminal matter, whether to detain or arrest, but of what information is necessary to arrive at a decision, what other units might be mobilized to provide that information, what is needed for testimony, and so on. Unlike the physician, who may take a long time gathering information to make a diagnosis that leads up to a decision, an officer often must make a "quick" decision. In many ways, this creates a paradoxical situation for the police. To be professional about the decision requires more information and more time; to obtain the information lawfully, and to protect the interest of the client and the public coerces a quick decision.

Police decisions, furthermore, are complicated not only by professional standards and judgment, but by a sense of justice. To be sure, more "professional" advice is available to the patrolman from his superiors, but most decisions must be his. They must be not only correct, but disregarding legal fiction, both the police and the public sense that they must be just.

To complicate matters further, some decisions by the officer will be evaluated by others, both within and outside the department. These "superiors" will regard it as their prerogative to solicit information from the officer, and most certainly to withhold a decision for indefinite periods of time while they exercise the "professional" judgment. Inevitably then, an officer who makes a decision that will be processed within and outside the department, makes a decision that later is subject to review.

---

[6] The increasing bureaucratization of police work means that officers can treat some clients as preprocessed by calling upon the organization to supply information on the client, securing (as is now the case) a quick response to their inquiry for information. It should also be clear that police officers at the district station or the lock-up receive clients that have been preprocessed by the department. Their role and behavioral response to clients differs as a consequence of this fact.

This pivotal decision position of the patrol officer, controlling as he does subsequent organizational processing, poses a dilemma both for the officer and the organizations that later process the case. The position of the decision, in a sequence of decisions, presses toward control of the decision by persons who process it later in the sequence. Those who will process the case within the police department, e.g., the detectives, make the claim they are "more professional," thereby coercing the patrol officer to the role of a technician. Those who lie outside the organization, e.g., public prosecutors and judges, press toward a decision on technical grounds, regarding the "professional" decisions as falling within the province of the law, to be made by lawyers.

Whenever a number of roles are involved in making decisions about the *same* case, problems of overlapping jurisdiction and rights to make the decision arise. Where professionals are involved, there will be competing claims to professional competence to make the decision. The role of the patrol officer, occurring as it does at the lowest rank order in the decision-making system, makes his role most vulnerable to counterclaims to competence, and least defensible. Paradoxically, however, it is the officer's original decision that controls whether law enforcement and criminal justice agents can process the decision at all. He has the broadcast potential range of discretion and jurisdiction and therefore, of possibilities for the exercise of "professional" judgment, but the most vulnerable position in the system of law enforcement and criminal justice for restricting his jurisdiction.

This paradox exists not only for the individual officer, but lies within the organizational system itself. For the system of law enforcement and criminal justice is organized such that the output of the police organization is constantly evaluated by the courts, both as to the substantial nature of the case and the manner in which the law enforcement occurred. This is the case again where one group of professionals controls the fate of another group of professionals. In this case, the lawyers — through the courts — will set the ground rules and the basis for decision within the broad interpretative powers granted within and under the law. Regarding their position as the more professional one, providing the greater amount of discretion, they will resist claims by the police to provide more definite ground rules. Indeed, the public prosecutor will insist upon his right of "choice" among the charges that the police will bring against an individual, and the courts will insist upon their view of "justice." Yet the police, in the nature of the case, insist upon broader jurisdiction, greater discretion, and they are engaged in the doing of justice. In a sense, when the police are denied professional autonomy in discretionary decision, they seek more definitive rules to make technical ones. But the prosecutor and the courts insist, even here, upon the discretion to decide in each individual case.

Paradoxically, then, what the police want clear, the courts want to leave open. And what the courts want clear, the police want to leave open. Thus, the courts want police procedures to be clear, definite, and unambiguously defined. The police want to be left with broad discretion in enforcing the law, obtaining information, and in procedures for handling clients. But what the police want clear — (How is substance to be applied in this case? What evidence must be available in this case? How can we have a *bona fide* case?) — the courts want to leave open to argument and decision, even to new interpretation and precedent. For them, precedent governs, but does not rule.

This organizational arrangement then inevitably poses problems for the professionalization of the police. For the prosecutor and the courts, to say nothing of outside agencies, will insist upon prior claims to competence in these matters. A colleague of mine once summarized this dilemma by remarking that in our system of law and order, everyone seems to have the law, and the police get stuck with the orders.

Understanding Others: Police and the Citizen

BERNARD L. GARMIRE

Chief of Police, Tucson, Arizona

MAY 25, 1961

I begin with a quotation from Abbe Raynal:

> Government owes its birth to the necessity of preventing and repressing the injuries which associated individuals have to fear from one another. It is the sentinel who watches in order that the common laborer is not disturbed.

A government cannot function and a people cannot live amid chaos and disorder; consequently, all governments must recognize that their fundamental duty is to preserve the peace and protect their constituents' life and property. To do this, government employs police. Analyzed in fundamental objectives and duties, the police is the most important of all divisions of government, for it has a graver obligation to its constituents than any other division.

The magnitude of the police responsibility becomes awesome when analyzed objectively. It is truly a sword of Damocles, hanging by virtue of the frequently frayed and tattered sash of a constituency's halfhearted support, apathetic attitude toward regulation, ignorance of the power and potential damage which can accrue to their personal liberty if police authority is ineptly, ignorantly or deliberately misused.

Unfortunately, in every section of our land and in every community, there exists a segment of the population which has no respect for its police, and has a hatred developed by a complete misunderstanding or lack of understanding. A member of this segment has no desire to come in contact with police officers, either socially or officially. Members are usually those individuals who are loathe to participate in any phase of governmental affairs — too busy to protect their God-given freedom and pursuit of happiness by even spending a few minutes to exercise their franchise, or in any way attempting to familiarize themselves with the functions of their local political subdivision of government, much less the federal government. In spite of this, they are quick and prone to vociferously condemn any act of government which fails to meet with their uninformed, warped concepts. This becomes especially true when challenged by a police officer.

This type of citizen is, to me, the most difficult and potentially dangerous of our country. It is this individual who, armed with little, if any, information, makes snap decisions, and by so doing frequently becomes a part of movements which become radical in their thinking and violent in their actions. They are the dupes which must be contended with almost daily by police officers throughout our country. They are the ones who parrot those who fleetingly appeal to a passing fancy, and they unthinkingly partake of harrassing so-called minority groups — groups who may subscribe to doctrines, dogmas or traditions (superficially thought to be in contrast to their own), or groups having a different-colored pigment in their skin. They are that segment of our population who are constantly admonishing others in the familiar, cowardly statement, "Let's you and him fight."

Unfortunately, this facet of our population, because of their vociferous, sophomoric lamentations, frequently — temporarily — sway the thinking of a majority of our solid and substantial citizens. This results in emergencies with which police are confronted — situations which must be handled in a manner commensurate with the American way, and consistent with precious personal rights and liberties. The police administrator must be calm, forthright and, above all, morally and legally correct. He must recognize that, as a police administrator, there exists no such thing as a minority group in his jurisdiction; that each citizen, regardless of his race, color or creed, is first, last and always still a citizen. That regardless of his degree of affluence or his politics, he is entitled to no more nor less than any other person. Each citizen must be treated with the respect due the dignity of man and the freedom of each individual as guaranteed him by our Constitution, structure of laws and system of justice. He must realize that justice is not social, economic or political. It is all of them. Justice is justice, plain and unqualified. It cannot be qualified. If limited to a class, it is no longer justice. Every citizen, not merely a class, is entitled to justice. To do other than this renders the police administrator derelict of duty and unworthy of being called a police officer.

Police of yesteryear were not placed in a similar, potentially volcanic scheme of things. Life was, by comparison in most areas, a rather routine existence. Incidents involving police action were quite infrequent, and it was not unusual for the night police blotters to have "No hits, no runs, no errors" boldly scrawled upon them in comparatively large communities. It was the era of the rugged individual, who exercised his prerogative in a positive sort of way and took care of his own pretty well. He was not prone to call the police to settle family or neighborhood disputes, and if an adolescent became unruly, he usually dispatched the trend of thought or action in his own inimicable way — usually in the woodshed. His word was his bond, and he needed no one to determine where black is ended and white began. He was not inclined toward hypocrisy and conformity was a matter of personal desire. The modern concept of the "organization man" was practically non-existent. The primary cell — the family — was closely knit and America was, for the most part, composed of homogeneous communities.

It was this era that prompted Alexis De Toqueville to observe that "America is great because America is good." To further observe:

In no country in the world has the principle of association been more successfully used or applied to a greater multitude of objects than in America. Besides the permanent associations which are established by law under the names of townships, cities, and countries, a vast number of others are formed and maintained by the agency of private individuals.

The citizen of the United States is taught from infancy to rely upon his own exertions in order to resist the evils and the difficulties of life; he looks upon the social authority with an eye of mistrust and anxiety, and he claims its assistance only when he is unable to do without it. This habit may be traced even in the schools, where the children in their games are wont to submit to rules which they have themselves established, and to punish misdemeanors which they have themselves defined. The same spirit pervades every act of social life. If a stoppage occurs in the thoroughfare and the circulation of vehicles is hindered, the neighbors immediately form themselves into a deliberate body; and this extemporaneous assembly gives rise to an executive power which remedies the inconvenience before anybody has thought of referring to a pre-existing authority superior to that of the persons immediately concerned. If some public pleasure is concerned, an association is formed to give more splendor and regularity to the entertainment. Societies are formed to resist evils that are exclusively of a moral nature. In the United States associations are established to promote the public safety, commerce, industry, morality, and religion. There is no end which the human will despairs of attaining through the combined power of individuals united into a society.

Inefficient police departments, if not desirable, were perhaps tolerable in this semi-geoponic society. But there were those who noted the paradox presented by governments operating under these conditions, conditions which provided a fertile field for the Jacksonian type of spoils system. It had caused James Russell Lowell to once observe, "We trust a man with making a constitution on much less proof of competence than we should demand before we give him our shoe to patch." At the turn of the century, the condition of municipal government was a disgrace. A revolution in American attitudes and behavior was inevitable.

In retrospect, it is evident that the swiftly changing forces of a technological age made the old concept of indifferent government obsolete. Large scale shifts of population, urbanization, motorization, and profound changes in citizen attitude took place. With these changes, more demands were made upon local government, and it soon became obvious that the local governments were not sufficient to meet these demands. Changes designed to streamline and increase efficiency of local governments were adopted, and emphasis was placed upon getting things done — particularly those things which were of aesthetical and convenience value, things which could be seen, used and admired.

Unfortunately, those intangible but fundamental responsibilities of local government were given just passing, if any, consideration. Consequently, while cities were being materially improved, they were tending to decay morally. Police were generally overlooked or if noted at all, were provided basement quarters and starvation budgets. Even to this day in many localities of our country, one finds police headquarters located in the most undesirable quarters to be found among the municipality's buildings.

It was during this era that organized crime was spawned and allowed to grow to adulthood — yes, even to proportions of a Frankenstein's monster — so great, in fact, that today we are seeking solace from it from the federal government. Traffic has outstripped all reasonable control devices. Juvenile delinquency has become a tragic blot on our once almost unblemished countenance. The bold figure of the organization man has become deeply etched into the American way of life, and the body politic appears to be casting its whole dependency upon one or more facets of government. At times it appears that the only well-adjusted persons are those whose intake of pep pills overbalances their consumption of tranquillizers just enough to leave them sufficient energy for a weekly trip to their psychiatrist.

That facet of government having the most frequent contact with the citizen is the police. The public's comparatively recent development of a dependency philosophy has in many ways overwhelmed us. We are eager to assist and respond to the best of our ability. However, in our zeal to fulfill our responsibilities, some of us, I fear, have gone overboard and have encroached upon territory and activities clearly within the realm of sociologists, recreationists and others.

I believe we should confine our efforts and activities to those areas which are clearly indicated as police functions:

1. Preservation of peace.
2. Protection of life and property.
3. Enforcing the yardsticks of human behavior, i.e., laws.
4. Detecting and apprehending law violators.

This must be done intelligently, forthrightly, uniformly and with constancy in every community of our country. Our citizens have a right to expect that the same brand of justice prevails throughout our country; that it will be administered by efficient, honorable and dedicated police officers.

Some progress has been made in isolated areas of our country. Unfortunately, there is yet a long, rough and rugged road to travel, beset by ruffans such as partisan politics, guildism, ingrowth, false senses of loyalty and probably worst of all — gross and incorrigible incompetence. Partisan politics has a habit of taking the very heart out of conscientious law enforcement, for efficient, competent law enforcement never lends itself to political longevity. Hence, wherever we find police officers being used as political pawns, we find a blemish upon the integrity of law enforcement.

Guildism runs rampant, with its sister evil — ingrowth — throughout American · municipal law enforcement. While a moderate amount is desirable in any professional group, too much tends to warp its perspicuity, and the ideal of service is lost. Ingrowth is readily discernible in many of our departments. New concepts, theories and practices are frowned upon, and members have gradually come to assume that "connections" are the only means of prospering within the organization. In some areas, this philosophy has so thoroughly permeated the thinking that unless one belongs to a certain church or certain fraternal organization, he has no chance for advancement.

False senses of loyalty are frequently found in all walks of American life, but nowhere can they wreak havoc as in law enforcement. Abraham Lincoln once observed:

> I am not bound to win, but I am bound to be true. I am not bound to succeed, but I am bound to live up to what light I have. I must stand with anybody who stands right; stand with him while he stands right; and part company with him when he goes wrong.

As inconceivable as it may seem, gross and almost incorrigible incompetence occupies several berths in American municipal policing. Some of it is the result of yesterday's concept of a police officer, and some because of obsolete and even archaic devices still used in selecting those who are to attempt to fulfill the complex requisites of a modern day police officer.

Those incompetents who are superannuates should be pensioned off. Others should be eliminated from the service, thereby vacating positions for those who possess desirable prerequisites and are adequately examined and screened.

This cannot come to pass, and every citizen cannot hope to secure equal protection, so long as there exists a single community relegating its police service to a status equal to garbage men, truck drivers, painters and other semi or unskilled laborers. There exists within a comparatively few miles from here a great city which has traditionally required its police recruits to have only the ability to read and write. Another I know of, still closer, requires only an eighth grade education. Several of the larger communities of this midwest area make and break commanding officers on the strength of political party affiliations.

There will be no understanding of police by our nomadic and heterogenous American public until a unanimity of thinking by police administrators on fundamental issues is adopted — until each administrator is given reasonable tenure, and at least once a year is required to render a full and complete accounting of his stewardship of this most vital activity of government to the people he serves; until each state of our nation recognizes that the uniform enforcement of the criminal law is a matter of general concern, and not merely local concern — as is the elimination of organized crime from *any* community; further, that each state has a responsibility in this vital matter.

This can and should be done as soon as practicable. California and New York have started by requiring that all recruits for municipal police departments possess certain minimum prerequisites and receive prescribed pre-service training; however, not until it has been ascertained that these aspirants possess integrity and character so necessary in our chosen pursuit. There appears little or no excuse for each state not to follow this admirable lead in assuring our people of quality and desirable municipal law enforcement practitioners.

It is sincerely hoped that this is but a harbinger of greater things to come — that one day, in the not too distant future, the various states will as rigidly control the practice of law enforcement as they do medicine, law, barbering, nursing and a multitude of others. Many of those now licensed assure only the quality of material things, guaranteeing only comfort or aesthetics. Is it being too much of a maverick, too much of a dreamer to fervently hope — yes, pray — that those empowered to administer the first process of criminal justice be licensed? Too much to hope that we soon will see fit to provide our people with qualified practitioners in the entire administration of justice? To demand that a person, literally provided with the power of life and death, with the legal ability to deprive our citizens of their liberty — and the privilege of personifying law and order — first prove his worthiness before he is licensed to ply his chosen profession? I think not!

I think such a program would be the most constructive, most positive development in the history of American municipal policing. It would eventually provide for lateral entrances or transfers, thereby proliferating uniform thinking, and hence uniform approaches to all police problems — at least those of fundamental importance. Police administrators would be prone to co-operate fully, for they would know of the competence and capabilities of another department's personnel. The epitome of professional intercourse would transcend petty differences and misunderstandings. All of these things would ultimately prove beneficial to the American public, for each is designed to improve the administration of criminal justice. Each is designed to combat the selfish and vicious attempts of some lay groups and uninformed quasi-professional groups, who are frequently harassing the police administrator with such pusillanimous paradoxes as citizen disciplinary review boards; public condemnation of the equitable use of laws concerning the activities of social parasites, and even provoking public dubiousness of qualified, studied approaches to the traffic problems of many cities. Paraphrasing Shakespeare — at times "Me thinketh they protesteth too much."

If I am correct in my prognostication, the innovation of licensing would almost immediately develop an *esprit de corps* within the ranks of municipal law enforcement that would produce ethics and canons without peer in modern professional annals. A cherished dream come true would produce unprecedented uniform civil liberties and mutual undertanding so long sought.

> Justice is the great interest of man on earth. It is the ligament which holds civilized beings and civilized nations together. Wherever her temple stands, and so long as it is duly honored, there is a foundation for social security, general happiness, and the improvement and progress of our race. And whoever labors on this edifice with usefulness and distinction, whoever clears its foundations, strengthens its pillars, adorns its entablatures, or contributes to raise its august dome still higher in the skies, connects himself, in name, and fame, and character, with that which is and must be as durable as the frame of human society.
>
> Daniel Webster

Social Change, the Law and the Common Good

FRANK J. REMINGTON

Professor, The Law School, University of Wisconsin

MAY 19, 1964

The title covers a broad area of human affairs. Perhaps there has never, in the history of this country, been a time when so many people in government and in the community generally have been so much concerned about the relationship of one group of citizens to another. Nor has there probably ever been a time when so much reliance has been placed upon the legal system to effect the kind of change that is desired. The situation is a particularly difficult one for governmental agencies which find themselves caught between those who desire change and those who resist change. And, of all of the governmental agencies, perhaps the police are in the least enviable position, because they must often deal quickly with unanticipated crises which arise. Even when there are no crises, police still come in contact more frequently with people, particularly with members of minority groups, than any other representative of government. As a consequence, many citizens know their government and its policies primarily through the practices of individual police officers whom they meet on a day-to-day basis.

There seems little doubt that the way police conduct themselves will have a major impact upon social change and the common good. Knowing this, what should the policy of police be?

It is sometimes said that all police need to do is remain neutral. But it may not be apparent what neutrality is, when confronted with a bulldozer moving ahead and a human being lying in its path to stop it. The objective of neutrality seems clearly to be a proper one, but not easy to define in particular circumstances. If, for example, certain types of assaults are viewed as less serious by one segment of the community than by another segment, does neutrality require equally strict enforcement throughout the entire community, or may enforcement remain neutral and at the same time reflect differences in group attitude?

It is also said that all police need to do is to enforce the law fully and fearlessly, leaving it to other governmental agencies to decide whether policies should be continued or changed. The objective of full enforcement of the criminal law is one of the traditions of the American system of government. This is probably what we mean when we say, with pride, that ours is a government of law and not of men. But the objective of full enforcement, if taken literally, is not possible, and even if it were possible, it would result in a clearly intolerable situation. Whatever we say about our traditions, we do not in fact want an automatic, mechanical enforcement of our criminal law. Rather we want an intelligent and responsible exercise of discretion in the development and implementation of a law enforcement policy which is effective and consistent with the requirements of law, and with the traditions of a democratic society.

These are objectives difficult to achieve. They are doubly difficult during a period of rapid social change. To some extent, responsibility for the development of law enforcement policy at the local level falls upon mayors and other officials, trial courts and prosecutors. But it is apparent that much is left to the police agency.

While the focus of public attention today is upon the racial demonstration, there are many other points of contact between the police and the individual member of a minority group. And I would guess that in the long run, these individual contacts between the police and the citizen will have a greater impact upon social change and the common good than will the more infrequent but more publicized demonstrations.

In a period of rapid social change, it is important to ask how an officer can steer a course of neutrality if he cannot rely upon the principle of full enforcement of the law against all citizens, regardless of social or racial status? The difficulty of the task makes it tempting for police to pretend that the problem does not exist, or that the responsibility is not theirs, a common and understandable public attitude of many police officials today. But I have long been convinced that police agencies have as important, perhaps more important, social, policy-making responsibility as many local, state or federal administrative agencies. And the common denial by police of this fact has had an adverse effect upon police themselves, and upon the communities which they serve.

It may be worthwhile to digress at this point to recount for you a case in which I was involved in Wisconsin some fifteen years ago. The case did not involve a police problem, although it does have a relevance to police responsibility which I will try to point out. The case involved a Milwaukee Negro who had applied, and been denied, a policy of state life insurance. In Wisconsin, during the LaFollette era, the state legislature enacted a provision authorizing the state to sell life insurance, up to the amount of $5,000, to residents of Wisconsin. In doing so, the legislature provided that applicants could only be insured as "standard risks," according to the "American Table of Expectancy." In denying the Negro's application, the Insurance Commissioner pointed out that the life expectancy of Negroes as a group is less than is the life expectancy of whites as a group, and therefore that he could not, by law, insure Negroes as standard risks. The "American Table of Expectancy" was, in fact, based upon white mortality experience. This action of the Insurance Commissioner was challenged.

In the testimony, it was pointed out that Negroes as a group do have a lower life expectancy than do whites as a group. However, there was also uncontradicted expert testimony that racial factors were not causal, that is, that the difference in the life expectancy of the two groups reflected social, cultural and economic rather than racial factors. Following this kind of testimony, an able and experienced member of the life insurance profession was on the witness stand and was asked this question, which seems to me to have relevance to the problem with which police are confronted today. He was asked whether it was possible for insurance companies to classify insurance risks so as to reflect the actual environmental factors which affect longevity, rather than classifying on the basis of race. The witness answered that this probably could be done, but that it would be very difficult to do so, and it would take a very imaginative insurance company to undertake such a program. It is, in other words, much easier to classify on the basis of race, because it provides a significantly different statistical picture, and it is a classification which is so obvious that it can be understood and administered by even the least qualified insurance man.

Like the Wisconsin Insurance Commissioner, police must classify the people with whom they deal. The Insurance Commissioner cannot insure all applicants. Nor can the police investigate all suspects, arrest all criminals, or even cause to be prosecuted all persons who are arrested. Neither "push button" insurance nor "push button" law enforcement is possible or desirable. The task is to devise a policy which will fairly differentiate between individuals. The objective should be neutrality in dealing with the matter of race. But a racial classification is so obvious, so easy, in fact, seemingly so significant, that it is difficult to resist race as a basis for differences in law enforcement policy. As a consequence, there are de facto racial classifications in law enforcement, even where there is no desire to treat one race more or less severely than another. What often appears to be a discriminatory enforcement practice may often be a consequence of administrative convenience, rather than an administrative desire to treat one race differently than others. In saying this I do not, of course, mean to assert that there is never discrimination in law enforcement. Rather the point is that the treatment of the various races presents a very difficult problem, even for the enforcement agency which desires to follow a nondiscriminatory policy. And my basic assumption, influenced in part, no doubt, by the professional bias of the lawyer, is that it is better to make this fact explicit and to try — difficult though it may be — to fashion defensible enforcement policies, than it is to continue to represent that police are ministerial officers who really have nothing to do with, and thus no responsibility for, important law enforcement policy decisions.

Perhaps it will be helpful to try to clarify what I have in mind by citing several illustrations:

1. It is common today for many enforcement agencies to treat assaults between Negroes less seriously than assaults between whites. It is said that assaultive conduct is more common among Negroes, and that there is a greater group toleration for this form of behavior. If one were to measure the seriousness of individual behavior by the degree to which it deviates from the group norm, one could probably demonstrate statistically that an assault by an individual Negro upon another Negro is no more common than an assault by an individual white upon another white. And, is in the insurance case, race is a most con-

venient basis for classifying the statistical incidence of assaultive behavior, even though it is apparent that race itself is not the causal factor, but rather that social and cultural factors are. If this is true, some whites share the social and cultural factors which cause assaultive conduct, and some Negroes undoubtedly do not. However, merely stating the issue this way demonstrates the difficulty of the task. If a law enforcement agency is to have differential policy in the enforcement of the law prohibiting assaultive conduct, what factors other than race are sufficiently identifiable to make the classification workable? As in the insurance situation, a classification reflecting the actual social and cultural factors which are causal would be immensely difficult to work out, and it will take a most able and imaginative law enforcement agency to embark upon such a program. But it seems to me that there are only two defensible alternatives: (a) treat all persons alike, or (b) base differences upon those factors which actually account for individual behavioral differences.

Police deal with assaultive conduct every day. They probably know more about the incidence of assaultive conduct and its social causes than any other group in the nation. If genuine progress is to be made in law enforcement, it seems to me that police ought to take advantage of the unique knowledge which they have to fashion an enforcement policy that does distinguish between serious and non-serious assault, but does so on the basis of factors other than race. This will obviously be difficult. It will take a great deal more public support and understanding by the community of the importance and difficulty of the police task; it will take research and experimentation; and it will no doubt involve some failures and inevitable criticism from some in the community. But trying is certainly better for the community and, in the long run, for the police than is falling back on the easy alternative of claiming full enforcement, and administratively relying upon race as a simple, readily available indication of behavioral differences.

Police frequently talk about professionalization, and sometimes point with some envy at the correctional field, which seems to have acquired a professional status more quickly and more easily than have police. Issues at the correctional stage are, in my judgment, quite similar to many which exist at the enforcement stage of the criminal justice process. In sentencing and in making correctional decisions, there has long been a commitment to the position that it is desirable to make distinctions between classes of offenses and classes of offenders. The difficulty has been in knowing what distinctions are significant for sentencing and correctional purposes. And it has been apparent that this issue is important enough and difficult enough to merit the sustained attention of qualified persons in practice and in the universities. There probably was a time when it was assumed that sentencing was a relatively mechanical task — that of making the punishment fit the crime. But that proved as unrealistic in the correctional field as the principle of full enforcement is in the police field. The difference is that while the corrections has confronted the actual problem, the police field continues, too often, to rely upon the myth that it does not have a major policy-making responsibility.

This is not to say that imitation of the correctional field is the solution. There are obvious differences in responsibility. But there are similarities also. The important similarity is that both agencies must make distinctions between individuals with whom they deal. I have no doubt that a statistical study of sentences according to race would show that Negroes as a group are treated differently than whites as a group. This is an inevitable consequence of individualization in the correctional process. To conclude that current correctional practices are wrong would, however, grossly oversimplify the issue. It would be the same as assuming a bias for or against marriage because of a statistical showing that married offenders are treated more or less severely than unmarried offenders. The objective is not statistical equality, but rather a system which takes account of causal factors other than race on the assumption, which seems to me clearly accurate, that race itself does not bear a causal relationship to critical conduct. How much progress has been made in corrections may be debated. But it is evident that efforts are being made to articulate sentencing and correctional policies; to subject them to critical re-examination; and to change them when experience demonstrates that they are without factual basis. In contrast, police policy in assault cases is seldom made explicit, seldom debated, and probably never studied to determine whether the effect of current policy is a constructive or destructive one.

2. There are other illustrations. In some large cities, a law enforcement practice is used which is called aggressive, preventive patrol. Sometimes the objective of this practice is to find and confiscate as many dangerous weapons as possible. This is done by stopping and searching persons on the street or in vehicles. The practice is usually confined to those police precincts or districts which have the highest crime rate. These are commonly districts in which the vast majority of persons are members of minority groups. As a consequence, preventive patrol tends to be used only against members of the minority group. Here again I think the insurance case analogy is relevant. No doubt police are convinced that statistically there are more dangerous weapons possessed by minority group members in the particular precincts or districts than by other groups in the community. And as with the Insurance Commissioner, the objective of the law enforcement agency is a laudable one. It is to concentrate police effort where they believe the greatest danger exists. Unfortunately, the most practical, easy classification is a geographical–racial one. To devise an alternative policy would be immensely difficult.

Aggressive, preventive patrol is said to be essential for the protection of the community against seriously assaultive conduct. It is also said that this kind of protection is expected, indeed demanded, by a majority of law-abiding citizens. Even so, practices like aggressive, preventive patrol raise some serious long-run problems which ought to be of great concern to police.

In many situations, street searches which are part of the aggressive patrol program are without legal justification. For police to engage in illegal practices which seem, at the time, to have the support of a majority inevitably casts police in the role of an opponent of the minority for whose protection rights, like the right not to be illegally searched, are primarily designed. For me, the concept of neutral, police illegality is a practical impossibility.

There are other reasons why such programs are self-defeating from the police point of view. So long as police are willing to make do with what they believe to be inadequate police authority, they will never get additional authority, because there is no practical necessity for increasing the authority of police, and it will be generally assumed, as it is today, that giving police greater authority will result in even greater abuse by police of that authority. The common assumption, for which police are largely responsible, that police will deliberately abuse whatever power they are given, places police in a most unenviable position.

In being critical of some current police practices, I hope I am not understood to be saying, as is so often said, that the problem is a simple one, which can be solved if only police will have a due respect for the law and the rights of the individual. Quite the contrary. Issues like the handling of assault cases and the maintenance of adequate preventive patrol are among the most difficult social problems facing us today. They admit to no easy solution. Indeed, the basic need, as I see it, is for police to give greater recognition to the difficulty of the issues which they confront, and to the important responsibility which they have for aiding in the solution of these issues.

The objective of an intelligent neutralism in law enforcement, with respect to race, is obviously difficult to achieve. As with so many important social problems, we lack adequate knowledge about the effect of current governmental programs upon individual and group behavior. But it is important that a start be made. It seems to me that there are some available guidelines for constructive action.

(1) Police insistence that police illegality is essential for adequate law enforcement is self-defeating; inevitably it places police in conflict with minority groups, and it perpetuates the common belief that police authority should be drastically limited because they will abuse whatever authority they are given.

(2) Police insistence that their responsibility is to fully enforce the law is to perpetuate a myth which is impossible of achievement, and would be undesirable if it could be achieved. At times, this may be an understandable public relations position, but it has seriously adverse consequences for police if they fail to recognize that theirs is a responsibility for the development of an adequate and fair law enforcement program within legal rights.

(3) In the development of law enforcement policy, race ought, wherever possible, to be rejected as a proper basis for classification. The factors which cause crime are nonracial. Difficult as these other factors are to identify and to make a basis for a workable law enforcement program, this is the proper objective; a start needs to be made; and police have experience which ought to make it possible for them to make a meaningful contribution to the objective of adequate law enforcement, which is neutral with respect to race.

All of this suggests that the very substantial social changes which are occurring in American communities need to be reflected in equally substantial changes in the conception by police and by the community of the nature of the police function. In closing, I would like, by way of illustration, to indicate some specific changes which seem to me to be important:

(1) The concept of police professionalism must be much more clearly identified with social science, rather than with the conception of the police professional as a laboratory technician. As important as scientific methods of detection are, the difficult task for police is to develop law enforcement policies which are adequate to deal with the complex social and behavior problems which exist in American communities today.

(2) Universities must do more than they now do in research to try to furnish the knowledge necessary for the adequate evaluation of alternative law enforcement practices, and also in teaching, to more adequately prepare law enforcement personnel, and to more adequately acquaint the average citizen with the complexity and importance of the law enforcement responsibility.

(3) There is need for the constructive participation of legally trained persons in the development of more adequate law enforcement policies. Too often lawyers, whether they be judges or prosecutors, assume that good law enforcement can be accomplished by the creation of restrictions upon police authority which are designed to prevent abuse. This kind of negative approach is more likely to create a sense of frustration in police than it is constructive action, unless there is also forthcoming, from legally trained personnel, assistance in the development of a law enforcement program which is both effective and consistent with democratic principles.

Police and the Community: Probing for Mutual Understanding

PATRICK V. MURPHY

Assistant Director, Law Enforcement, Office of Law Enforcement Assistance, U.S. Department of Justice

MAY 21, 1967

Dr. Al Germann, of Long Beach State College in California, pointed out in a recent speech to a conference of policewomen that conservatives are urging support for local police and that liberals have countered by urging control of local police. He urges that citizens attempt to *understand* their local police.

Support for the police is very necessary. I urge all police departments and policemen to win it. Support does not come automatically. As many police administrators have pointed out, it must be earned by eliminating poor practices and by improving performance. Police must deserve support of young people, the poor, Negroes, even the "criminal element."

It seems to me that too many police officers deceive themselves by thinking of people as divided into two general classes: the first group is responsible, respectable, law-abiding or good. The second group is the criminal element, irresponsible, bad. The National Crime Commission has pointed out that people cannot be easily classified. A patrol officer who cannot distinguish between the vicious, corrupting, well-heeled organized crime overlord and the deprived, uneducated, poverty stricken, emotionally disturbed youth who steals an automobile is not qualified to make the decisions facing them in a large city in 1967.

A policeman should understand that he greatly needs the support of citizens. He cannot perform his basic functions of maintaining the peace and preventing crime without such support. This is especially true in high crime areas.

It is obvious that police in some cities are not receiving sufficient support from poverty neighborhood residents. It is obvious too that many police departments and individual officers are not doing enough to obtain support. Some seem not to know the first step to be taken in seeking support. Unfortunately, none of us knows nearly enough about the best methods for obtaining support in 1967. However, it is likely that

— officers assigned permanently to the same beat become better known;

— friendly officers are better supported and informed by citizens concerning problems and problem people; and

— officers who are sympathetic to the problems of the people whom they are policing will find their work easier and their efforts more rewarding.

New techniques must be found and applied. The billboard signs and bumper stickers which read "support your local police" will not suffice. In fact, they may do more harm than good. The chief of police needs wide-based citizen support. If he is losing it, he is failing. Deputy chiefs or other would-be-chiefs can start counting the days!

Better control of our police is also a worthy goal, in my view. It is not a goal that is easily achieved. Because the police have great power (which can be easily misused) and because each police officer exercises broad discretion, sound, effective control is essential if we are to have the kind of democratic society that we say we believe in. The police should not be independent of outside inspection and evaluation; yet there are departments with too much independence. Many departments function in unnecessary secrecy, which may be a cause of misunderstanding and lack of support for police budgetary needs. It probably has something to do with the persistent doubt and suspicion in many minds concerning the "terrible" things that occur in police buildings.

Of course, many police departments have been controlled, and some may continue to be controlled, improperly. Too many mayors overcontrol their departments. Too many councilmen annoy chiefs of police by asking for favors and preferential treatment. Too many politicians interfere. And too many corrupt political–underworld alliances are effective in "handcuffing the police."

Every city in this nation has an influential group of people sometimes referred to as the "power-structure." Its members sometimes dictate to the police — openly or surreptitiously through a political party. The power structure has money. Political parties need money. So "money talks."

Unfortunately, the powerful people in our society have frequently used the police unjustly against the powerless. Too often the police have been a tool of the strong against the weak. It is difficult for me to think of the New York City Police Department as being anything but Irish. In fact, during the past year, some New York newspapers referred to the high-ranking group that served under former Commissioner Mike Murphy as the "Irish Mafia." But the department was not always predominantly Irish. In fact, about a hundred years ago, the police refused to wear uniforms in the poor Irish neighborhoods of New York because the gangs would attack them on sight. In today's jargon, I suppose we would call those youth gangs "hard core," "militants" or advocates of "Irish power" or maybe "Catholic power." Those Irish and some others were good rioters, too. They stormed police stations. I am sure all of you recall why they rioted — to protest the draft. It seems that some of the young fellows in the "power structure" were avoiding the draft, for it was legally possible to be excused from the draft by paying a sum of money.

Of course, the Irish were newcomers then. Within a hundred years an Irish Catholic was in the White House. Negroes were here for well over a hundred years before the Irish. I wonder how much longer it will take them to acquire the political power to elect a President. I often think how patient and understanding our Negro citizens are, and how blessed this nation is for having them.

We hear much and read much about "taking the handcuffs off the police." This is a reference to the alleged unwarranted control of police methods imposed by the Supreme Court in its *Miranda, Escobedo, Gideon, Mapp* and other recent decisions. Perhaps some of these decisions have gone too far. It is difficult to know, because there is a lack of sufficient data on which to make a rational judgment. However, it is clear that even if all these decisions could be reversed, the effect upon the crime problem would be minimal. Before and since *Mapp,* too many crimes have been unreported, too many unsolved, too few of those arrested convicted and too few of those sentenced reformed.

Police departments throughout the nation and the police systems in the United States must be improved tremendously if they are to meet the challenge of crime in the years ahead. It may well be that an improved understanding of the police by citizens would result in greater control of the police. Understanding might also effectively contribute to the upgrading of police personnel and service.

Many of the problems of poor relationships between police departments and their communities result from misunderstanding. It is not only true that citizens not only do not understand police problems, authority, and limitations, but police themselves generally do not clearly understand their role. Too many police officers see themselves as "thief catchers," even though many studies have indicated that only a small percentage of a patrol officer's time is spent in enforcing the law. As O. W. Wilson pointed out many years ago, "Patrolmen should be practical social workers and encourage persons to come to them for assistance and advice when in trouble. Distress situations are frequently symptoms of deep-rooted social ills that, if not corrected, may result in criminal or other antisocial conduct, and thus adversely affect the remainder of the life of the individual. By giving assistance, advice and sympathy to those in distress, patrolmen help prevent wasted lives, and also win friendship and cooperation for the department."[1]

A necessary ingredient of improved understanding between police and citizens is improved communication. The motorized patrolman, with all of his advantages over the foot officer, functions with the difficult handicap of fewer opportunities for person-to-person communication with individual citizens. While keeping his automobile, the patrolman *must* leave it frequently in order to communicate with citizens. Police administrators must devise ways of bringing the patrol officer into closer contact with the people on his beat.

Since the time of its inception, the federal law enforcement assistance program has supported a substantial number of projects dealing with police and community relations and has taken a close look (or in some instances a distant look) at programs being conducted in various parts of the nation.

Basic to all these programs were two survey efforts funded under the Law Enforcement Assistance Act and contributory to the National Crime Commission's efforts. One of these was conducted by the National Center at Michigan State. It ranged over many cities and a representative number of non-urban law enforcement agencies to determine and evaluate practices in police–community relations throughout the nation. A second study, conducted by the School of Criminology at the University of California at Berkeley, took an in-depth view of two cities.

I think it is fair to sum up the findings of the Michigan State study in this way: There are individual cities here and there in the nation whose police departments conduct police–community relations programs with varying elements

---

[1] Wilson, O. W. POLICE ADMINISTRATION, 1st Ed. New York: McGraw-Hill, 1950.

of excellence and strength. There is no single program to which one could point and say, "Here is how it should be done; here are all the techniques and answers executed with skill and wisdom."

However, there are a number of programs whose elements are very much worth examining, both for their successes and the hard lessons learned the hard way. Some of these have been supported by our Office; some have been supported by other federal programs or private agencies. In virtually no case that we know of has a police department outside the nation's largest cities been able to conduct an innovative program in police–community relations without outside financial assistance.

Let me note that there have been several broad-based training programs supported by the Office of Law Enforcement Assistance, interesting in themselves, but interesting also as an indication of the type of activity that should be considered for the future. First, at Michigan State there has been conducted a series of training conferences in police and community relations. The first was for community relations police officers (with a few civilian community relations persons); the second was for training officers, and the third was for personnel officers.

Second, under a grant to the IACP, chiefs of some thirty cities attended a June conference dealing with human relations techniques and problems. As a follow-up effort throughout the past ten months, an IACP consulting service in police–community relations has been available to police departments who requested such assistance. Similar service is available through the Michigan State Center.

Third, a totally different effort was a one-month institute in Puerto Rican culture and social problems. For key police personnel in nine major American cities, the institute was conducted in the Spanish language at the Inter-American Center of the Catholic University of Puerto Rico. I understand that the 30-odd officers who attended this program responded very favorably to their experience.

There are at least two key problems which the Office of Law Enforcement Assistance has tried to address in our decision of support. The first of these is the need to reach the policy-and-decision-makers in police departments. You can sensitize a patrolman and send him back to duty with a genuine enthusiasm toward more effective human relations, but if his commanding officers and the upper echelon of the department are not thoroughly aware of, and thoroughly committed to, the concepts behind the training, the effort with the patrolman might better be left untried. Better to let a man do the best he can within the system than to show him what appears to be the better way and then frustrate him by not permitting it.

Our second concern was with developing techniques for studying human relations problems beyond the conventional lecture method, where so frequently the reaction of the trainee was that he had no opportunity to respond to or defend himself against people he perceived as critics, propagandizers or do-gooders.

The genesis of a series of training programs using a discussion leader is a complicated one. Originally it was developed in Philadelphia. A textbook on the technique was published thereafter, and in the summer of 1965, the city of Detroit and Lake County, Indiana, both used adaptations of this technique for in-service training programs. By and large, the experience was an encouraging one. I think both programs pointed up the great need for skillful direction of the discussion group and indeed, for leadership in general.

Various adaptations of the program have been LEA supported. The New Orleans police department program embraced the entire department, including sweeper and janitor. The technique here was to use lectures, with subsequent discussion groups under the direction of professionally trained leaders of non-police background. The key to this particular program was very clearly the competence of the lecturers themselves. An effective lecturer could set up the group for a useful discussion, but a hostile or ineffective speaker could leave chaos in his wake.

In Newark, New Jersey, an interesting sort of program provided training for groups of 30 police and 30 citizens together, again in a lecture-and-discussion format, with a field work element added toward the latter part of the schedule. No results have been officially reported, but observers and participants in the program generally feel that the method is a promising one.

A very promising program has been conducted in the District of Columbia for groups of 25 patrolmen, and here there is essentially no lecture element whatsoever. The leaders of the program are industrial relation specialists (or leadership training specialists), and the input consists of simply setting up the ground rules for discussion of problem areas in groups of 25 patrolmen, who in turn break down to task groups of six or seven men.

Similar sorts of programs have been tried or are under way in Grand Rapids, Michigan, and Covina, California. Boston, Massachusetts, under the leadership of the Human Relations Center at Boston University, ran a pilot experiment under tightly controlled circumstances, using discussion groups of seven citizens and six patrolmen, with no agenda whatsoever.

All these programs have elements of promise; all have produced new knowledge. I think none would pretend to have achieved perfection, but the people who have been associated with them are excited about the potential they have revealed. Perhaps the area in which the least progress has been made is the development of training techniques for top echelon police personnel.

Very briefly I should also like to sum up the 25-odd grants made to police departments all over the country to initiate or expand efforts in police and community relations under one of our special (or package) grant programs. This effort was also conceived as an extension of the training program for Chiefs of Police conducted last year, and most of the resultant programs have been rather primary efforts to establish police–community relations units and to find an effective way to operate them. Many of the programs have involved visits to other cities' departments for exchange of ideas. In addition, research and investigation have been conducted in their own communities to discover attitudes and causes and to uncover resources at all levels: from the neighborhood, the service agencies, the business community and the academic institutions.

Several of the programs have involved an actual training element within the allowable $15,000 maximum. Several have tried an innovative operational program:

—St. Louis is using special store-front police–community relations units for community contact.

—San Jose, California, has a special multifold effort concentrated on a disadvantaged neighborhood.

—Rochester, New York, is, among other things, conducting Spanish classes and using a well-known athlete as a liaison person with ghetto youth.

—Pontiac, Michigan, will attempt a variant of the junior cadet program developed in Detroit.

Other interesting approaches which either have been developed or are pending are: (1) the use of subprofessional police assistants in the Richmond, California, police department; (2) the development of a community service unit within a police department in Winston-Salem, North Carolina; and (3) the proposed development of police–civilian three-man neighborhood teams, with intense special training in Charlotte, North Carolina.

Last October Vice-President Humphrey suggested to the Chiefs of Police of the nation, assembled at their annual conference in Philadelphia, that they "get the monkey off their backs." He said that the police were unjustly bearing the blame for crime whose root causes they could not control. These root causes are poverty, discrimination, unemployment, poor housing and other social ills. The Vice-President advised the chiefs to tell their mayors, city councils and their citizens to do more in curing the social ills of their communities, if they want law and order. While such ills exist, even the best police departments can do little to control crime. I hope that more police chiefs and more policemen will accept this thesis and speak out against the root causes of the problems they face every day. Frankly, I know nothing the police can do that will better demonstrate their understanding of the community.

Unfortunately, the police chiefs of this nation fail to provide the kind of community leadership they should. We are better able to understand this fact when we realize that the chiefs are not part of the power structure. The bar associations are part of the power structure. Judges, prosecutors and defense attorneys are members of the bar. As our police become professional and articulate, they will better exercise their opinion-molding responsibility. Yet police chiefs, police organizations and spokesmen for law enforcement do provide leadership for our people in their thinking about the crime problem. Much of it, in my view, is false leadership, for it effectively directs the concern of our citizens toward the wrong targets: the Supreme Court, bleeding-heart judges, the parole and probation systems, do-gooders, soft prisons, etc.

It is my conviction that many Americans of good will, who now accept the erroneous views so commonly held in the police world simply because they come from those closest to the problems, would strongly support with words and deeds and dollars an effort directed at the correct targets: inadequate police salaries, qualifications, training and education; so-called correctional systems that can't correct because they lack the funds; poverty; unemployment; bad housing and racial discrimination.

But how many police leaders are ready to become involved in such an effort —the most important part of the fight on crime?

Some may feel that I have been unfair to the police in my comments and unsympathetic in my point of view. In response, I can say only that our police have been and are handcuffed by a refusal to face the truth and honestly discuss the issues. "The truth shall make you free."

In fact, the problems of the police are, always have been and always will be my very deep concern. I'm sure some of you are familiar with that University of North Carolina cheer, "I'm a tar heel born, I'm a tar heel bred, and when I die, I'll be tar heel dead." Well, I'm a policeman born, policeman bred, and when I die, I'll be a policeman dead.

I accept the proposition presented by Reith in his writings on the British police: The role of the police officer in a free society is the essence of the concept of democratic government. If the people can successfully govern themselves, they must be able to police themselves through their police. To maintain the individual freedom that is so sacred to us, while maintaining peace and order, is the great challenge facing every police officer, especially the man on patrol. He deserves much better treatment than our communities have given him. As the President's Crime Commission report points out, his decisions are as complex as those made by people who today are truly professional. He deals every hour with the most complex problem facing man—human behavior. He should be a true professional. He should receive a salary equivalent to that of an FBI Special Agent and should enjoy the same prestige.

Obviously, our communities have not understood or properly supported our police. They fulfill the noble calling of keeping the peace and protecting the people, especially the weak, the sick, the old, the young. They deserve much better.

As community leaders improve their understanding of the police, they will vow to increase their support. And in accordance with their great tradition of service and as their perception of the community improves, the police will serve every citizen even better than before.

The Police as Community Leaders

WAYNE E. THOMPSON

(Then) City Manager, Oakland, California

MAY 16, 1965

In the spring of 1957, a youth lay dying in the streets of our city. He had been shot by a roving gang from a neighboring community. When he died the following morning, "war" was declared. His own gang promised immediate revenge and threatened to "get" two Berkeley youths for every Oakland boy attacked. Tension and fear gripped the neighborhood. Yet it was only one of many incidents that brought Oakland face to face with the ugliness of street violence in 1957.

Where does a community turn for leadership in such crises? In Oakland, it was a policeman who provided the leadership. He knew that we could not solve our problems by racing police cars up and down the streets of the city. He stated clearly, and with conviction, that these were "not just police problems." They were "community problems." In this approach he demonstrated his own wisdom and depth of understanding about the "people problems" of the central city, and the police responsibility to help find basic solutions.

He was convinced that governmental agencies, working unilaterally and often in conflict, actually contribute to the continuing disorganization of our urban life. His proposal to cope with this situation was simple, yet feasible. He argued that the problems of the central city demanded the concerted and coordinated action of all public agencies concerned with youth. As a starting point, he suggested that we appeal to our friends in the public schools, in recreation and in probation and parole.

These agencies had the "know-how" and legal resources to contain explosive neighborhood situations long enough to give this new team time to develop more effective controls over serious community problems.

The Multi-Agency Approach

The response to the police call for joint action was gratifying. Five agency heads, from four levels of government, met at the request of the City Manager, and agreed that the community could not afford fragmented and conflicting services.

New, multi-agency channels of communication and action were quickly developed to identify and contain juveniles typically at the core of neighborhood tensions. Success in North Oakland led to similar success in East Oakland. The operating manual for the delinquency control program we now call "The Associated Agencies" was developed within a few short months.

In the process, we broke down many of the barriers that separate agency groups. For example, the recreation director in Oakland no longer attempts to "protect" the delinquent from the "bullying" and "heartless" police; and our police no longer regard the recreation director as a "bleeding-heart" and a "coddler" of vicious juveniles.

Prior to the Associated Agencies, our police complained that they had been "locked out" of the public schools. Today, principals welcome them and depend on them for help with critical school problems. They have learned to trust and respect each other, and to work as a team.

Our Police Chief was right. Central city police cannot do the job alone. They must work in partnership with the rest of the community and its service agencies.

The Ford Project in Oakland

It was this teamwork approach that focused the attention of the Ford Foundation on Oakland. We are just now completing three years of experience with a two-million-dollar Ford Foundation grant. We have learned a valuable lesson. Yet I can remember being told by a beat policeman, at the outset of the Ford Project, that "we are spending all of our time cleaning up after society's neglect." He wanted to know why we were planning new projects that attacked only the symptoms of community failure. We are convinced now, in Oakland, that we must direct our future attacks at the root causes of the social and racial unrest that has created so much turmoil in the central cities of our nation.

The significance of the Ford Project in Oakland, then, is the fact that it allowed us to build the organization and staff necessary for a comprehensive assault on the most critical problems of our city: crime, poverty and racial unrest.

Note that all this was begun by an enlightened and concerned policeman.

A New Department of Human Resources

By 1964 Oakland was ready to place planning for human development on a par with physical and economic planning. New programs proposed under the Ford grant, as well as those developed in response to the federally-financed "anti-poverty" program were so broad and varied that we soon recognized our need for a new department of city government, to control and coordinate all of our "people" programs. We have created a new structure and call it the Department of Human Resources. Its task is to provide central direction to the efforts of some twenty governmental, voluntary and citizen organizations that are now working together to attack crime and poverty at the grass roots.

A brief description of several of them should suggest the extent to which we have gone in Oakland to find solutions to the problems of a central city. The more significant ones are:

1. *Adult Minority Employment Project:* The purpose of this project is to find employment for unemployed and underemployment adult minority males. Subsidiary projects include establishment of an inventory of job skills among unemployed adult minority group males, and training and retraining of these people to aid them in becoming employable. This project is supported by grants totaling $1,250,000. It was conceived and fostered by a group of leading Oakland businessmen and industrialists.

2. *Youth Employment Project:* Here the purpose is to train unemployed school drop-outs in usable skills and to place them in jobs, or to channel them back into the school system. Grants of about $1,000,000 support this project.

3. *Compensatory Education Project:* This project was designed to give special remedial instruction in language development to those students who need help in overcoming their deficiencies.

4. *Health Maintenance Project:* Directed at newcomers, this project attempts to discover, treat or refer health conditions which prevent adults from earning a livelihood, or children from performing satisfactorily in school.

5. *Leadership Development Project:* Effective citizen groups are essential to the life of every city. This project was directed at selected representatives of indigenous neighborhood organizations. It was designed to encourage their broader participation in community affairs.

Several new Oakland projects that were recently approved by the Federal Office of Economic Opportunity include the following:

1. Preschool classes aimed at improving the academic readiness of youth nearing school age;

2. Family planning clinics and other health services for those unable to afford them;

3. In-service training programs designed to prepare teachers to work more effectively in low income areas;

4. Extended language development and remedial reading programs;

5. Preventive health services for school drop-outs, selective service rejectees and newcomer nonresident families; and

6. Compensatory education programs to be conducted by our parochial schools.

The need for a high caliber staff to plan, direct and evaluate such a comprehensive program was apparent. Fortunately, the Ford Project made it possible for us to attract outstanding people. They are the senior staff members of our new Department of Human Resources.

Social Research: An Integral Part of Central City Government

The new Research and Evaluation Division of the Department of Human Resources also represented a significant breakthrough at the municipal level. Not only are central cities confronted with the necessity of pioneering in the area of human development, but the problems emerging from our rapidly changing social scene made it imperative that research be conducted in the area of "people problems" as well. Our Research and Evaluation Division provides us with our single most important protective device that we will spend our money wisely in the social area.

Our own police department is assisting with the current research efforts. For example, the commander of the Police Department's Planning and Research Division played a major role in the development and evaluating of our present delinquency prevention program at the elementary school level. That program has been an integral part of the Ford Foundation program in Oakland.

The Oakland Economic Development Council

One other important addition to city government was our new 30-man Economic Development Council, recently created by the Oakland Mayor and City Council. This new citizens' group will be looked to for leadership in determining how an anticipated five million dollars in federal and foundation grants will be spent in Oakland during the next two years.

Who are the Economic Development Council members? They are top Negro, Mexican-American, Oriental and American Indian leaders, plus a capable group of business and industrial leaders. The Chairman is a Superior Court Judge and a prominent Negro. The Vice-Chairman is a vice-president of the Kaiser Corporation. Through such groups as this Council, we are beginning to get the help of citizens at all levels in finding solutions to our poverty and crime problems.

The New Phase: "Free Oakland Now!"

It was during our early planning for the Department of Human Resources that a new kind of call came to City Hall. The University of California wanted us to rush 250 policemen to the campus to help control student demonstrators. The request came after several days of student demonstrations against a new University policy restricting their political activities. In the course of the demonstrations, the students—at times numbering 3,000—literally captured and held a police car for over 24 hours.

The "Free Speech Movement"

Negotiations between the University administration and student leaders followed. A tentative agreement was reached. It did not last long. Within a few weeks, the student demonstrators, under the leadership of the "Free Speech Movement," gathered in force and staged a massive sit-in, sleep-in demonstration in Sproul Hall. At three in the morning, Governor Brown ordered the demonstrators removed, noting that near-anarchy prevailed.

As a result, we ordered out over 250 Oakland policemen to help remove students from the building. The atmosphere in Berkeley and Oakland was immediately charged with new outcries — about "freedom of speech," about "police brutality" and about civil disobedience.

"Free Oakland Now"

The dust of the Sproul Hall sit-in had barely settled when a newly-formed Oakland Direct Action Committee marched on Oakland's Police Administration Building. The charge was "police brutality." A new lapel button appeared in Berkeley and Oakland. It read: "Free Oakland Now."

During this same period, the University and Oakland chapters of CORE launched a series of demonstrations directed at alleged discriminatory hiring practices by Oakland and Berkeley restaurants. Our police worked closely with demonstration leaders to set the ground rules for "peaceful" picketing.

During a series of pre-planning sessions, arrangements were worked out for motorcycle escorts, for reserved parking for picket leaders and for electrical power for microphones. Police also indicated what streets they planned to rope off and what their general plans were for crowd control, if needed.

During the demonstrations themselves, the major news networks stood by, recording the action in minute detail. Few actual incidents resulted, but the potential was ever present. Police again played a sensitive and critical role in the maintenance of law and order, indicating again what police leadership can mean to the economic health and welfare of a city. The willingness of police to get involved with the people leading the demonstrations has been a critical factor. Intelligent and enlightened police handling of such community problems has maintained social peace so far in Oakland.

A New Role for Law Enforcement

At the same time that our police were learning to handle demonstrations more effectively, they began to look for means of combating citizen apathy in the neighborhoods. Beat patrolmen reported repeated incidents in which citizens not only failed to exercise their responsibilities as citizens, but actually interfered with officers as they attempted to carry out their duties. These incidents led the police department to conclude that they would have to *go out and teach* citizenship and community responsibility. That conclusion has resulted in a new concept in police work. In certain instances and to a degree, the policeman is finding the blackboard to be a more effective weapon than the blackjack.

The Oakland Police Citizenship Program

For example, we all recognize that one of the causes of crime is a lack of understanding of why we have laws and how laws can help people. Our present Police Citizenship program was developed to help elementary-school-age youngsters realize this fact before they got involved in serious difficulties. It has been so popular that classes are now held four nights a week, and often involve whole families.

At the request of the Superintendent of Schools, we have expanded the program to all of our junior high schools. It is now a part of the regular school curriculum and reaches over 4,500 youngsters a year.

Consider for a moment the significance of uniformed officers teaching citizenship responsibility, as instructors in the junior high school classrooms of our city. An entirely different kind of relationship is being established, and both sides benefit from the pleasant, friendly atmosphere. Even "old line" officers developed new attitudes toward their work as a result. What a change for them, to find themselves handing out citizenship certificates instead of citations.

The Police Citizenship program has convinced us that we must enlarge the opportunities for officers to meet citizens under positive conditions. Without such personal contact, it is doubtful whether we will ever be able to reduce the suspicion that separates citizens and police in our central cities. We are frankly looking for new ideas in this area. For example, we are considering a scholarship program for selected "gang" leaders. Ways must be found to send them to our state colleges, not state prisons.

The Need for a New Image

It seems clear, then, that the policeman of the central city will need a deeper knowledge of people and their problems, particularly those of the ethnic groups in our communities. The professional curriculum for law enforcement officers will need to be heavily oriented toward the social sciences. In addition, the peculiarities of the core-city police job will require intensive and special training. Who knows—the title "human affairs officer" may designate the policeman of tomorrow.

Research and Development

The carry-over of the new police image to research and development activities is equally important. In the past, police have been asked to assume responsibilities for patrolling freeways and other facilities after they have been completed.

In the future, police must get involved in the preliminary planning of freeways, colosseums, subways, and other physical structures that must be policed. For example, a new billion-dollar rapid transit system is already on the drawing boards in Oakland, which will soon become the first subway in the West. Police must play a decisive role in the design of the public safety features of that system. To accomplish that goal, police must become aware of technological developments that can contribute to public safety.

An Urban Intelligence Center for the Central Cities

Our search for efficiency must also capitalize on daily advances in space and science technology. In fact, the technology of the space age has added an entirely new dimension to police responsibilities. They must participate in the development of urban intelligence and data centers that will make possible the systematic application of space and science technology to our urban problems. New computer techniques such as "matching and searching" should be used extensively, if we are to maximize the spin-off from man's venture into space.

Oakland-East

"Oakland-East" is another concept worth considering. We are proposing to build a new satellite-city that will be part of Oakland. This new community will serve as a laboratory for the solution of urban problems. Our Police Chief is interested in this idea, because he sees an opportunity to test crime prevention theories under experimental conditions.

The Need for Improved Communications

As exciting as some of these ideas are, we are not going to be successful unless we can reach our citizens more directly. In Oakland, we have failed to get the mass media facilities to do the job. For example, we have only limited access to radio and television in our community. Yet in times of great social change, it is imperative that local radio and television stations cooperate to the greatest extent in providing public service time. This is not being done in Oakland. We believe that the Federal Communications Commission can help us to measure up to our responsibilities in this area. FCC regulations clearly state that locally franchised radio and television stations are licensed to serve their local communities first.

Modifying Attitudes and Institutions

All of us recognize that police are confronted daily with shocking examples of citizen apathy or outright hostility. Oakland is no different. A cab driver was recently robbed and then brutally beaten while over a hundred persons watched from their windows and doorways. No one interfered. No one even called police. Such incidents have led police across the nation to conclude that there is a need for a change in community attitudes.

Recently, we met with a representative of the United States Attorney General's office to discuss ways of changing community attitudes. The statement made by our Police Chief has significance. He said, "We will also have to change the attitudes of the police."

A municipal court judge has pointed out to us how an untrained police officer provoked a serious and unnecessary riot, just by the manner and tone of voice with which he apprehended a Negro male.

Disturbing, too, was a recent research report prepared by the University of California. It suggested that we in the public service needed to look, once again, at ourselves. The report quoted the following as typical of police views toward minority persons. I quote:

> They have no regard for the law or for the police. They just don't seem to give a damn. Few of them are interested in school or getting ahead. The girls start having illegitimate kids before they are sixteen years old, and the boys are always out for kicks. Furthermore, many of these kids try to run you down. They say the damnedest things to you and they seem to have absolutely no respect for you as an adult. I admit I am prejudiced now; but frankly, I don't think I was when I began police work.

That statement brings us face to face with the important question: How do we effect the change?

We now realize that only as we change our own attitudes, within the city "family," will we begin to achieve the results we need so badly: a change in community attitudes. There appear to be no shortcuts to attitude change. We cannot, for example, build a new police image if we tolerate negative social attitudes, no matter how well those attitudes seem to be "justified" by our real life experiences.

Where, then, can we find leadership wise enough, objective enough and diplomatic enough to persuade each element of the community that we are living in rapidly changing times which require that both individuals and institutions modify long-held attitudes and values.

With the caliber of men we have been recruiting from Michigan State University, from the University of California and from other fine universities, we have today in our police department one of the greatest resources in our community. Our men are carefully selected, well trained, dedicated, courageous and knowledgeable about our city problems at the best level.

It appears that once again it is the police department to whom we must turn for leadership.

Guidelines in Seeing Ourselves

C. G. CONNER

Inspector, Highway Patrol, Texas Department of Public Safety

MAY 22, 1961

I shall bring to bear upon the subject my experience in the field of police service, and the experience and writings of other people who identify some guidelines for seeing ourselves as police officers. I am being presumptuous, perhaps, in calling these ideas "guidelines," for in reality they are situations or conditions that exist in police service, for which the officer can compensate in some degree.

To begin with, I shall have to accept certain presumptions or premises. They are as follows: (1) Many segments, or groups, exist in the community. These are groups based on racial, vocational, social and other distinctions; (2) It is desirable for the welfare of the community that harmonious relations exist between these segments or groups in the community; (3) The police can contribute to harmonious relations between the various segments of the community by the way they perform their basic task and by the leadership they give in the community; (4) A police officer who sees himself and his position properly is better adjusted, has fewer frustrations, and can perform his work and give leadership more effectively; and (5) There are guidelines that will help the police officer to see himself properly.

Based upon these premises, I shall try to identify some of the guidelines the officer can use for seeing himself and his position in the proper light.

I shall present four things an officer can do that will serve as guidelines for seeing himself and his position. They are as follows: (1) The officer can define and understand the police product — what he produces. (2) He can understand and accept the position of police service in this Republic. (3) He can identify inevitable conflicts within himself resulting from police work. (4) He can recognize and understand that there is a spiritual meaning in the affairs of men.

Let us now examine these four points. In relation to the first point, a definition and understanding of the police product, I should like to ask a question. What do the police produce that is essential to the community, the state and the nation? Were I to have you write these answers down, I should probably get as many different answers as there are people in the audience. This fact highlights a significant point: our society has not developed a clear and concise philosophy of police work. This I think is tragic, because it has handicapped the quality of the product produced and has produced frustrations, misunderstandings and conflicts among the practitioners in police service.

What is this police product? I should like to give you some qualities it must possess. It must be positive. It must be a desirable condition of society, not a number of activities to achieve the condition. I fear that too many times, police themselves have described the activities they perform, such as hours worked, miles traveled, investigations made, arrests made, convictions, etc., as their product. These are not the product; they are merely the means by which the product is obtained.

Let me supply an example. Suppose you employed a contractor to build a home for you. This man, for a fixed price, will produce for you a completed home. This is his product. To produce this home he will have to excavate, run concrete, saw, hammer, paint and carry out many activities. You will not necessarily be interested in any difficulties that he has regarding materials, excavation, water, labor or anything else. Your prime concern in the thing in which you will live will be the finished product, the house. When you ask a contractor what he produces, he will tell you it is houses. You ask a man who operates a factory and he can name his product, or give a list of his products. I say to you it is bad that the police and society have never fully agreed upon what is the product of the police.

I should like to give you what I believe is the police product. I believe that it is large enough to encompass all of the activities of the police, and I know that it is a condition that is absolutely essential to any organized society. That condition is social order.

A great political philosopher once said, "Mankind's two most precious possessions are individual freedom and order in his society. It is the essence of the problem of government to maintain one without destroying the other." When this man equated *order* in a society with personal freedom, I believe he identified the importance of the product of police service, social order. In our society, the police are the principal instruments for maintaining social order.

Perhaps in our day we have forgotten the prime importance of order in our society. By taking a high point in time, we can see better the importance of social order. You remember that in 476 A.D., Rome fell. Her legions no longer preserved *Pax Romana,* all over the Western world. As a consequence, chaos descended upon the Western world. And you will remember that the institution of feudalism arose. What happened? Because of total disorder, where men's persons and property were constantly subject to attack, people went to strong, unscrupulous, powerful local men and bound themselves and their children into serfdom, virtual slavery, to receive one thing: order in the society in which they lived. Yes, history records that men in Western Europe sold their freedom in order to have social order, this condition so necessary for their existence.

A review of the frontier in our own country will reveal the same thing. When remote frontier settlements began to build, disorder was constantly present. As soon as there was any semblance of organized government, you will remember that they employed men of the Bat Masterson, Wyatt Earp, Bill Hickok variety. They put up with brutality, even lawlessness, on the part of these men because they, and they only, could produce social order in the community in which they were employed. Perhaps we have forgotten the precious quality of social order, but the need for it still exists to the same extent in our society. I repeat, the police are the principal instruments for the preservation of social order. This is the product they produce. This is the product that our society must have.

When a police officer sees what is his product, it will serve as a guiding philosophy for all of his activities. This will allow him to see himself and his work in the proper light and will reduce, in my opinion, many of the frustrations and conflicts that handicap the successful performance of his task.

The second point I mentioned was a clear understanding and acceptance of the position of a police officer in this Republic. It would seem that in our country, with our ideal of a democratic society, that we stand always on the thin edge of anarchy. Perhaps this is desirable. Perhaps the nearer one can come to anarchy and still preserve social order, the greater is individual freedom. In a society with this concept and this philosophy, it is inevitable that the work of police must be difficult. It should be. Now when difficulties begin to impede the officer in achieving his own satisfactions, when they become time-consuming, when they reduce the approbation of the community for his activity, it is almost inevitable that he grows cynical, disillusioned and frustrated, unless he clearly sees and understands the position of the police. These conditions reduce his ability to perform his task so as to promote harmonious relations between various groups in the community, and they impede his giving leadership in the achievement of satisfactory relations.

The remedy, perhaps, comes from a recognition of the basic concepts of which this government is founded. The police officer must see that the preservation of the Constitution, with all of its guarantees, is his prime objective. Some officers will, I fear, in their zeal to enforce statutory enactments, sometimes violate Constitutional provisions, which take precedence over any statutory enactment. When the provisions of the Constitution interfere with the efficient enforcement of statutory law, it is easy for the officer to grow resentful. This resentment and disillusionment can only be cured by careful study and understanding of the position of police in this country. It could be greatly helped by a better recognition on the part of the public, particularly the public information media, of the position and work of the police as well as their contribution to this society.

The third point I made was that the officer should identify the conflicts produced in himself by the nature of police work. I call them inevitable conflicts, and I believe that they are. In my discussion of this topic, I shall lean very heavily upon the writings of Dr. Richard H. Blum. Dr. Blum wrote an article entitled *The Problems of Being a Police Officer,* which was published in two parts in the November–December, 1960, and the January–February, 1961, copies of the magazine POLICE. I shall be quoting extensively from these articles, as well as drawing upon my own experience in discussing these conflicts.

The first conflict which I believe to be inevitable in police service, I call the conflict of the policeman's duties with his Christian concepts. Of course this would apply only to men who are Christians; however, other great religions have similar concepts. Jesus in His dealing with criminals was forgiving, as in the case of the harlot; he taught the philosophy of turning the other cheek. A police officer who does his duty must arrest violators of the law, and it is sometimes necessary for him to use force. Many times the mind of the police officer is disturbed in trying to reconcile these two opposing concepts.

Another typical conflict Dr. Blum calls the "conflict of loyalties." Policemen want to be loyal to brother officers in order to win their friendship and approval. Like men in any other work group, friendship ties and loyalty help people work together, and make a man confident that he can count on another's help should danger or trouble arise. The policeman's problem is that conflict can arise when loyalty runs afoul of administrative directives, or the law itself.

Take for example the case of the two-man patrol car, called to investigate a burglary in a liquor store. One man observes his partner taking a fifth of whiskey off the shelf and putting it in his pocket. Here is the conflict. Should the observing officer be loyal to his thieving partner by saying nothing about the matter? Should he apply differential standards of law enforcement by merely saying to his partner, "You better put that back or you could get into trouble," or should the observing officer enforce the law by turning his brother officer in? There is no happy solution. The conflict of loyalty versus lawfulness is always with the officer as he is faced with wanting trust, friendship and reliability on one hand, while wanting to be lawful on the other hand. The conflict can lead to mental health problems in policemen shown by nervousness, sleeplessness, self-doubt or a guilt feeling.

Another conflict mentioned by Dr. Blum is the conflict over human misery and evil. A policeman in his job is forced to deal with human pain, misery and evil. At a scene of an accident, he must face death and gruesome injury without giving in to his own inclinations to get sick or run away. He may be called to a scene where a drunken father has terribly beaten a little child. He many times sees innocent victims of criminals horribly mutilated. A policeman must do his duty without indulging in his personal urge to punish these vicious criminals. His first human reaction is an emotional one; to be sickened by gruesome injury, to want to run from a mangled body, to want to assault the person who has killed or injured the victim. The problem for the policeman is that unlike other human beings, he cannot allow his real emotions to be expressed. He cannot show what he feels when faced with misery or evil. His job and his personal pride require that he maintain control of himself and of others, that he act with calm efficiency to help the injured, to protect the public safety and arrest the felon. Under these conditions the police officer learns ways of controlling himself. He gets used to horror by paying less attention to it. He puts on the protective armor of being hardboiled. No matter what he does, a policeman does not escape the fact that he daily is faced with human tragedy which he can do little to prevent or alleviate. It is one of the great emotional burdens of police work. As long as policemen are faced with these conditions, there is no real solution. The most common solution is to become somewhat "hardboiled." In doing so, however, the police-man must also try to be sure he does not lose his inner human tenderness and sensitivity.

Dr. Blum also mentions conflicts over decisions. The police officer, in his daily occupation, is faced with the task of making very difficult decisions, and making them in a split second. In many of these situations, there is no desirable alternative. All are bad. Take, for example, the instance when a foot patrolman is pursuing a felon on a crowded street. The felon begins to fire at him. The officer's decision is whether to fire back and risk killing or injuring an innocent bystander. If he does not shoot, he may be shot himself, or he may be criticized for his failure to apprehend the felon. Either alternative is undesirable.

Faced with these conflicts, police officers frequently grow resentful about persons with whom they must work who do not have to make such decisions. The psychiatrist, the attorney, the judge, the social worker may draw the police-man's resentment because of *what appears to him* their "easy" way of operating.

The fourth guideline I mentioned was for the police officer to recognize that there is a spiritual meaning in the affairs of men. The materialist and the positivist have influenced our thinking to the point that many of us, though professing Christians, or professing other religious beliefs, have come to think that there is no meaning or significance to anything that cannot be measured, analyzed or otherwise evaluated in a physical way. I do not believe this is true. I believe that there is a spiritual force at work in the affairs of men; that there is a moral law in the moral universe, just as there is physical law in the physical universe that has meaning and significance in the work of men, especially the work of the police officer. I think when we believe that nothing has meaning in our existence unless it can be measured, defined, analyzed or evaluated, it tends to produce cynicism and disillusionment. The falsity of the assumption that nothing has meaning that cannot be physically measured can be illustrated by the example of a man writing on a piece of paper. Now it is possible to measure the paper in all of its dimensions, to analyze the ink, measure the size of the pen, analyze its elements, even to measure the energy expended in the muscular movements of the arm. Yes, all of these can be concisely measured and analyzed. But none of them reveal the meaning of the writing. The writing may have deep significance in human affairs. It may be a judge signing a death warrant, it may be a person leaving a great inheritance to somebody which ought to mean happiness. It might be any other thing that would bring joy, sorrow, grief, regret, pleasure or in other ways have meaning in the life of a human being.

I believe that a recognition by the police officer that his work is constructive, that it has meaning, spiritual meaning if you will, in the affairs of men will assist him to see himself in proper perspective.

In closing, let us summarize. I stated that we began with some assumptions or premises. Those premises were that there are many segments or groups in the community, that harmonious relations between these groups are desirable, that police can contribute to harmonious relations between segments in the community by the way they perform their basic police task and by giving leadership in the community in the formulation of programs designed to stimulate harmonious relations, that a police officer who sees himself in his position in proper perspective is better adjusted and can contribute to good relations existing between segments in the community, and last, that there are guidelines that will help the police officer to see himself in the proper perspective.

I have covered four of those guidelines. An officer who can clearly define and understand the product of his work, the police product, is better fitted to perform his task satisfactorily, and accomplish the objective of harmonious community relations. If he sees that the sum total of his activities is designed to produce social order, it will assist him in seeing activities in proper perspective, and will give him guidance in making important decisions. To see himself properly, he must understand and accept the position of police service and police officers in this Republic. He must recognize that the work of police in this country, by its very nature, must be difficult. That, in essence, it is a contradiction of freedom. If he can identify and understand that there are certain conflicts that are inevitable in police work, he can adjust himself to them. By the formulation of a personal code of ethics, by high level training and broad understanding of the whole philosophy of police service, he will be able to adjust to these conflicts and see himself in the proper light. And lastly, he must recognize that there is a spiritual meaning in the affairs of men. If he realizes that the work he does, the contacts he has with people, have meaning that goes deeper than the mere material, then he will have a staunch support that will serve as a guide in all of his activities.

Following these guidelines, I believe that the police officer can see himself and his position more clearly than without this knowledge. If he faces up to these honestly and sincerely, he will be a better adjusted human being. Because he is better adjusted in his basic work of police service in the community, and in his opportunities to afford leadership, he will be able to develop more harmonious relationships with and among the various segments of the community.

Police and Community Relations as a Political Issue

DAN W. DODSON

Director, Center for Human Relations and Community Studies, New York University

MAY 24, 1967

All large cities of America look forward to this summer with trepidation. "The Long Hot Summer," borrowed from a popular play, has come to express the dread of race riots and other public disturbances occasioned by civil disobedience of minorities in concentrated ghettoes within these inner cities. Almost invariably, these riots and other disturbances are touched off by police attempting to deal with some aspect of disturbance of the peace. In some instances, the disturbances reflect an almost total lack of support for the policeman in the enforcement of the law. Unhappily, in a few instances, the policeman is looked upon as a member of an army of occupation within the ghetto, maintained there by the dominant power of the community to keep the powerless in their servile position.

How does it happen that this situation could come to pass? The average city has half as many policemen as it has schoolteachers. The qualifications for becoming a policeman have steadily risen, and police training programs have steadily improved. Salaries, while nothing to boast of, are not out of line with other comparable lines of work. Modern technology has placed at the disposal of police departments equipment never before available for the detection and solving of crimes. Yet safety on the streets has reached such a point that social activities of the inner cities have become severely curtailed at night because of fear of bodily harm. The difficulties which are of major significance for police departments reside in the issue of power and political relations. It is to this problem that the remainder of this paper will be devoted.

If the community were ethnically and socio-economically homogeneous, and there were a high degree of consensus concerning norms of behavior, policing would be relatively simple. Its tasks would be to perform the service functions such as traffic direction and safety, and to apprehend the occasional deviant who broke the law. This is not the situation in the modern city. It is tremendously heterogeneous. There is not a great degree of consensus as to norms. It is often possible for underworld organizations to have such power that they stand above the law. In some communities, organized crime is believed to be the largest single industry.

In addition, the inner cities of America have undergone great transformations within the past three decades. The inner cities have been abandoned by the white middle class, and their places have been taken by the lower socio-economic background, ethnically identifiable populations. We have just finished a small study of Brooklyn, N.Y. In 1960, this Borough of New York City had 2,627,329 population. This is the largest single political aggregation in America, except the remainder of New York itself, Chicago and Los Angeles. Of all these two million six hundred thousand odd persons, 71.6 percent were either foreign born, children of foreign born, Negro or Puerto Rican. It almost staggers the imagination to realize that this great aggregation of population could be concentrated in that space, and more than 70 percent of them with less than three generations experience, living in the most complex urban environment the world affords.

Brooklyn could be replicated to a lesser degree in every large city of the country. As a result of these concentrations of the powerless within the inner cities, the political complexion of the cities is changing. The changing complexion of the cities, it might be added, is changing the political organization of the total country. These encapsulated poor in the inner cities have, now, what they have never had before. They have suffrage. In addition, the city has awakened in them new hopes and aspirations, and has given them sophistication in the use of the ballot in order to get what they want.

In fact the civil rights revolution was spawned out of this change in the population composition of these large cities. Thedore White, in his MAKING OF THE PRESIDENT, 1960 says:

> Just how much the Democratic Party owed to men like Dawson and the Negro vote did not become apparent until 1948. But when in 1948 Harry Truman squeezed ahead of Thomas E. Dewey by 66,612 votes in Illinois, by 17,685 votes in California, by 7,107 votes in Ohio, no practicing politician could remain ignorant of how critical was the Negro vote in the Northern big city in a close election (Page 233).

The Democrats are learning that this minority vote is not monogamously married to their party. In New York City, the incumbent mayor owes his election in no small measure to the splitting of the vote on the part of the Negroes in Bedford-Stuyvesant in Brooklyn. Negroes are 90 percent registered as Democrats. But the Republican mayoralty candidate was elected because they split ballots and defeated the candidate of their party — although electing a Democratic city council.

In other ways, this sophistication with the ballot is showing itself. In Virginia where all-Negro districts went 90 per cent for Johnson in the past Presidential election, they reversed themselves and went 90 per cent against the Byrd machine in the primaries, to form a coalition with the suburbanites of Washington, D.C., to achieve reform.

What does this portend for police departments in these cities? It indicates that a redistribution of power is taking place within the city. Police departments were beholden to the power structure of the city in years gone by. In fact, it is usually the instrument of force to coerce minorities, in most communities. The cattle prods and other types of harassment could be used by the police in instances of civil disobedience in Southern communities. This will be no more.

In the past, the poor had few rights the police departments were bound to respect. They had little status before the law. The law was often in the end of the nightstick. Today, the Supreme Court has sensed the changed power base of these encapsulated poor. It has made a number of landmark rulings which shore up the rights of the poor. In addition, public money to provide legal services for the poor is rapidly becoming a part of the response to this inner city political pressure. The result is that law enforcement is taking on a different hue.

In these years ahead, this citizen participation among the poor will grow. There is an insistent demand on their part that this power arrangement be altered. They have the votes with which to do it. In community services, there is an insistent demand that the consumers of the services be allowed to participate in policy decision-making — rather than that the power arrangement provide decisions for them. This is reflected in education where the principal of Northern

High School in Detroit was removed by community boycott and pressure. At Intermediate School 201 in Harlem they said, "If racism is such that you cannot desegregate the schools, then isn't it logical that it is such that white teachers cannot get creativeness out of Negro children? Hence, the community, not the school system, should decide who the principal should be."

In the poverty program they have contended, and the government has backed them up in the demand, that a stated percentage of the poor themselves should be on the poverty boards. In welfare, the poor are pressing for the end to midnight raids, trying to catch a man in the house of women on welfare, so they can take her off the relief rolls. They are pressuring for legal services. On the Lower East Side, in a review of 100 cases of applications which were denied relief, it was found that 80 would have been eligible for relief had they been adequately represented by counsel. In New York City schools recently, the courts held that a child could not be expelled without being represented in a hearing by an attorney.

In the near future, these encapsulated poor of the inner cities are going to alter the economic structure through which relief is provided — unless I miss my guess. After the depression, we socialized the risk of poverty in old age through the Social Security system. More recently, we have socialized the risk of prolonged and serious illness in old age through Medicare. It would not surprise me to see the socialization of poverty itself through a guaranteed annual income. If this should happen, it would be an indication that people in these inner cities are not going to accept the position that they are second-class citizens simply because they are poor. They are not going to have a social worker put on them to rehabilitate them (as if they had been dishabilitated) because they are poor. They are going to bring the economic system to heel sufficiently that this second-class treatment will not be attached to economic limitations. One's status will reside in his citizenship, not in the size of his purse. Those of the poor will stand as did the Apostle Paul in the dignity of their citizenship and say as did he: "I was born free. I am a citizen of no mean city."

An illustration of what this difference may mean is indicated in a North Carolina community I visited recently. The poverty board was trying to get the mayor to allow them to use a vacant building in the town. He said, "Well, I will take it up with the Council and see if they think this is the way the taxpayers want their money used." In the new order which I see emerging, this mayor will say instead, "I will see if this is the way they think the *voters* want the money spent."

What does this say to police departments? This great bureaucracy of government is caught in the throes of this same revolution which suffrage is bringing. In the first place, the representatives of the law tend to be second and third generation persons of the groups just ahead of the bottom group of new arrivals. They tend to be led by those who are about another migration ahead of that. In New York City, for instance, it was no secret that the appointment of the present Police Commissioner was resisted because it meant loss of control of the leadership of the department by the Irish-American group. It takes some time and a lot of effort to recruit from the new group sufficiently fast to meet the demand that they be part of the force itself. This is particularly true with the Negro and Puerto Rican communities, for the rising standards of recruitment means few can pass qualifying examinations. Hence, police are suspect first, because they represent the arm of force of the power structure of the community, and second, because they are often represented by persons whose ethnic backgrounds are identified as those of the group with whom they are most in competition — namely the group just ahead of them. It is going to mean pressure in the years ahead for departments to recruit and upgrade minority persons as policemen. If civil service standards are not to be swept away, there is going to have to be a lot of recruitment in selective places to get more and better qualified minority youths to seek policing as a career.

A second implication for police departments is that their work is going to be under more review than in the past. There is emerging what is called accountability. There is the demand, for instance, that educators be more accountable. If a teacher teaches a class through a year and children do not improve their performance, while another teacher with a comparable group does get performance, why shouldn't the first teacher be held accountable? In a like measure, policemen are going to be held more accountable. Now this gets to be a touchy subject with us all. School people are yelling and saying "Oh! These parents do not have the competency to judge how we are doing our work." Policemen try to say the same thing. All of us who are high priests of the profession in which we are involved would like to be excused from being held accountable for our work. We would like to develop the mystique that only we, or people of our occupation, can pass judgment on our competencies. The poor are not going to buy this in the future, just as the middle class communities have never bought it.

In our community, a Civilian Review Board was created by the mayor. The police department raised "holy hell." Through a referendum, they were able to overrule the administrative action of the mayor. In this the department demonstrated sophistication, in that it knew that if it were to protect itself from the growling of the poor, it would have to mobilize power to counteract the new pressure. In a well-oiled campaign, they scared the community into voting in their way overwhelmingly. The analysts are split over what was the significance of the vote. On one side people are aghast that an arm of government would have enough power to prevent itself from having to face this type of evaluation. Mayor Wagner was quoted as saying, before he left office, that he could not set up such a Board, for there were too many people with too many relatives and friends on the force. For some of the liberals who have always distrusted the policeman as a symbol of authority, this smacks of the beginning of a police state. This group is also very concerned about the type of campaign which the Police Benevolent Association held. It was full of racial smears, appeals to fear and panic, and reaction. They point to the support they got from the Conservative Party and the white backlash groups. They contend that it further reinforces the stereotype that the police department is usually identified with conservatism, and particularly with reactionary elements of the society. In other words, it is but another indication of the Christian Front, Birchite connections which from time to time, they would contend, have been evidenced in the police department.

On the other hand, many saw the Review Board issue as but the foreshadowing of things to come in the urban milieu. If a group is to protect itself from other groups, it must mobilize, take power, and come to communal decision-making as peers or equals. Police officials felt that they could not get the support necessary to shore up the perimeters of authority in their precincts. If they were to enforce law fairly and fearlessly, they must have such support individually and collectively. Politically, the mayor could not give it to them. The only way they could protect themselves, and the public, they felt, was to organize and take it to the voters. Here it should be pointed out that the vote was overwhelmingly in their support. Even in the minority communities, the police department's viewpoint was upheld surprisingly — again, indicating the sophistication of the minority in the use of that ballot.

The Review Board issue indicated two things. In the first place, it indicated that people in the minority areas want good policing like everyone else. They are willing to support the police department if given half a chance. In the second place, it indicated that the minority community was not all of one kind. There was no bloc vote. Self-annointed leaders who had spoken for "My people" found that they were not speaking for as many as they had thought. Some had marched as if they had an army back of them, when in fact they did not have a corporal's guard. Again, the ballot box was a place, *par excellence,* to test out the legitimacy of the leadership of the minority community.

There was also another aspect of the issue which is worth indicating. We all have great fear of what a group will do with newfound power. We are afraid such groups will abuse such power, because they have not had experience in its use. Here in the Review Board issue was an illustration that the minority community with the ballot behaved about as responsibly with it as did the remainder. It also indicated that when leadership tries to go too far in the use of its power, the society has a way of checking its abuses.

It would be a serious mistake, however, for police departments to assume from this experience that they will escape being held to high levels of accountability. A strong Police Benevolent Association can serve as a pressure group to shield the department from criticism, but it cannot shield it too long from mediocrity. If there is one lesson to be learned from the past controversy through which we have gone, it is that unless the department does its own monitoring from within, it is going to be monitored from without.

If there is to be adequate policing in these years ahead in these inner cities, the police departments must come to terms with these new, marginal, ethnically diverse populations. They are going to have to recognize the fact that in a democracy, politics is the major way through which power is redistributed. If there is not democracy, and the redistribution cannot be done through the ballot, the alternative is to "take it to the street." In this latter, we are dealing with a different phenomenon to that of criminal deviancy. This becomes *sub-cultural* deviancy. The policeman finds himself in a compromised position, for he must uphold the power arrangement of the society. He must enforce the law, which is to say the rules laid down by the powerful. This always militates against those who are less powerful, for the rules were made to enhance the entrenched position of those on top. How do policemen behave when the power order on which their authority rests becomes threatened? Can they be so trained that their private and personal prejudices do not get in the way of impartial law enforcement?

Let us look at the prospect in these months ahead. There is a growing nationalism in the Negro community. Increasingly, there is political alienation from the mainstream of community life. To this point, the protest has been civil disobedience, as in the case of Martin Luther King, or sporadic violence, as in the case of Los Angeles. There has been little evidence that violence has been planned and professionally agitated. Suppose, however, that group undertook to utilize the insurgency tactics, such as were used in Algiers or as used by the North

Vietnamese? Indeed, as may already be happening in the Hough District of Cleveland, where a school has already been burned and other acts of arson have been rampant.

In these instances, unless police can build real bridges to a substantial part of the community, they are in fact an army of occupation, sent into an area to control it. In this latter circumstance, killing a policeman or getting killed is not considered murder. It is merely the casualties resulting from a kind of warfare. The police did not create the condition which relegates Negroes in Cleveland to ghettoes — especially Hough, with 50,000 people. The police did not ring these ghettoes, as described by Paul Hofmann (NEW YORK TIMES, May 20, 1967), with low income "unsympathetic neighborhoods of Poles and Italians," who I dare say, constitute a major portion of the police force. They, the police, are however, the instrumentality of force which must be called on to quell any disturbance.

In these situations, the police departments of the future must understand the role of power. They must create a power bloc themselves, to protect their own equities in the family of community services. They have to be able to challenge the appointment of the Review Board, as was done in New York City. Let no one be misled, however, when this is done, other groups are going to be mobilizing power also. This means, then, that groups come to conference as peers in power, to negotiate between their separate equities in situations. It also means that those who abuse power are going to get slapped down by the wider society. If the liberals were right in New York City, and the Benevolent Association did win by fear, smear, and bloc-interest tactics, it will only be a matter of time until this will generate enough counter resistance to sweep away the protections which the police have built in. Now I do not believe this to have been the case. I must admit, however, that with the power which the department demonstrated it had in the community, there is a consequent responsibility that goes with its use. It is now in position to negotiate from strength. What will it do? It should move forthwith to a pacification of the minority community leadership. Unless it does this, it will have missed a golden opportunity to build very much needed bridges between itself and people on whom it must rely for support in the years ahead.

This foray into these matters suggests the emerging pattern of policing in the years ahead. Max Weber, in his discussion of a true Bureaucracy, indicates that such establishments do not set policy themselves. These are politically set, and the bureaucracy only carries out the mandates of the politicians. This has been the pattern of policing in the past. It is still true today. Which laws are enforced is a matter of policies expressed or implied by the political leadership of the community. Polly Adler indicated that Mayor LaGuardia was easier on the prostitutes of New York City when he assumed office than was his predecessor. He was determined, however, to break up organized vice rings. In a like manner, it is being publicized now that Mayor Lindsay — in trying to develop the stance that New York is "fun city" — may be easing up on vice. Be that as it may, no one in the large city really wants a completely clean city. If it were completely clean, there would be no excitement to it, and no one would want to go there. The problem is to keep it clean enough to not get embarrassed, and at the same time leave the excitement about it. In these years ahead, police departments may be able to solve the old problem of how to keep themselves from being the fall guys in this dilemma. The old newspaper reporters used to say that in this situation in the large cities, either the politicians controlled the vice, or else the police did.

In this latter instance, there have been periodic investigations of departments, and occasionally heads have rolled.

The civil rights revolution may have suggested to departments that the way to deal with these issues is to organize, take power, and move to create a profession of law enforcement. In other words, if the politicians will not stand behind the policemen, as usually they do not in these political situations, the policemen will organize and find mutual support in each other to stand for fairness, honesty, firmness and sympathetic treatment of all. They will not be the handmaidens of the power arrangement of the community used as an instrumentality of coercion, but rather as impartial arbiters of justice, without regard to social status of those served. They will make their arrangements politically with groups, and they will foster alignments between themselves and other groups, to the end that justice will prevail.

If this professionalization is to come about, police departments must understand that they begin by disciplining themselves. To be professional means, in part, to be able to discipline those within the ranks to agree on standards.

I realize that what I am saying is dangerous doctrine. We are too near wars in which we have fought police states to be talking about police departments taking power, setting policies for themselves, and organizing to put themselves in preferred positions. The raw realism of it is, however, that inner city life is political. It is direct and overt confrontation. Parents are organizing and pushing Boards of Education around. Teachers are mobilizing and refusing to work under conditions which they contend imperil their lives. Nurses walk off the job in city hospitals saying they cannot be professional and work under the conditions which prevail. White backlash mobilizes, and neutralizes the minority efforts to desegregate schools. The poor mobilize and demand a voice in communal decision making.

There is a sense in which this is not bad. It means people are sloughing off their apathy and demanding a voice in the control of their collective destiny. Where do the police fit in this picture?

It is to be observed that in all the history of policing, we have not learned to work with the community. We have not developed a sense of partnership in law enforcement matters. We have often been afraid to meet the community in free and open encounter as equals. I believe where this has happened openly and honestly, it has been rewarding. I was impressed that one of the men with the short-lived Review Board in New York City came away with a tremendous admiration for the department, based on his short experience. Our unwillingness to take the community in our confidence belied a lack of confidence in either our programs, or else the intelligence of the community. The only way to make sure that we are forced to take these community people into account is to frankly acknowledge the political nature of policing, and seek support for it through political means.

A simple illustration will indicate what I mean. Several years ago, Floyd Hunter did a study called COMMUNITY POWER STRUCTURE. It was a study of Atlanta, Georgia, in the years before the present transformation took place. He indicated that about 27 men at the top of the power pyramid called the tunes to which the whole community danced. He described how the "man at the bank" controlled the Negro community. Those who were elected to office beat a trail to the door of these men, to get the word as to what policy would be. In this circumstance, it is no wonder that police are a constabulary for the status arrangement of the community. As the order is changing, political power is breaking up this cozy arrangement. The Negroes are taking power, and forcing the white community to make policies at City Hall through free and open debate, rather than through consensus of the informal power structure. It means, increasingly, the police department will not be mortgaged to one segment of the community, but will have the base of its authority broadened to take in more of the community. As this takes place, unless it is able to organize and look after its interest for itself, it is likely to become the floor mat for contending groups.

In this new role, the police must stand for the equities of the community which represent fairness and justice to all people. It must be able to keep itself from being used by any group to bludgeon others. It must come to realize that the poor are taking power too, and that policing will have to revalidate its methodologies against this new power arrangement of the community. It will have to have enough muscle to say to the erstwhile power arrangement that it has to respect the rights and perogatives of the least of these who are citizens. It will stand as a bulwark against tyranny and injustice of whatever sort.

If this it can do, policing will emerge as a profession which will draw from all segments of the community for its personnel. It will imbue all with such a sense of dedication to professional conduct that it will be able to stand above the controversies of civil rights and other contests in which groups vie with each other for prestige and status, and will discipline itself to enforce the law with such fairness and justice and efficiency that these great cities will be able to take these newcomers — these 2,000,000 souls in the Brooklyns of the cities — and bring them into full stream participation, without the social disorganization which has been so characteristic of the ghettoes.

Police organizations have demonstrated they have muscle enough to beat down review boards, require that their interests be considered in communal decision-making, and in other ways indicated they have a self-protection society going for themselves. In this they have been political. There is nothing wrong with this. It is the way things are done in the large city. The issue is whether they will now rise to the greater task of also using this power to discipline themselves, and go forward to making a real law enforcement profession. Perhaps there will be no better test of that ability than the long hot summer which is predicted just ahead of us.

Police Conduct and the Public

MONRAD G. PAULSEN

Professor of Law, Columbia University, New York

MAY 25, 1967

I would like to begin by giving you some impressions of mine as to the sources of the difficulties which the police face in their relationship with the public. They were captured up for me by a picture that a colleague of mine has shown me. It is an enlarged photograph of a policeman, his back can be seen with a large pistol hanging on his hip, his right hand is reaching for the gun. A little bit away there is a young man, dressed in a jacket. He is going away, maybe running. From the photograph you cannot tell whether it is a white boy or a Negro. This bitter picture bears a legend: "Save Court Costs." The photograph somehow captures the heart of the problem with which we concern ourselves.

Your problem and mine it is. It is the problem which mankind has been struggling with ever since he found some way to organize himself into a community which requires limit on authority of force. How can we control the use of authority? How can we control the use of the community's monopoly of force exercised through the police and the armed forces? It is a perennial problem and we face a little part of it. But it is a principal problem of government everywhere. It should be some small comfort to know that we here are not trying to solve a unique, discrete problem, but a general issue about which Plato and Aristotle and all the great political philosophers of our common heritage have had something to tell us.

We confront a crisis of confidence respecting law enforcement in the United States today. Perhaps some of you would deny that we have it and others would assert we should not have it. As to the first, I'm in disagreement and the second, I believe, is irrelevant. It is a fact with which we must deal.

A primary difficulty in the United States is that there is, I sense, a deep anarchistic strain in all of us. I think, in general, American young people have not been taught to respect authority. It's not in the bones to do it. My father held and, I think, still holds, as far as I know, the firm view that all public officials, from police to President, are personal failures. If they were men of quality they would create a living in private life instead of consuming the contribution of taxpayers. Many in this country hold that true excellence in man comes from personal achievement in the private sector of life while the public sector is the refuge for those security conscious and the timid.

We have often not respected authority nor supported it. We experience a great deal of fun when officials are frustrated. Obviously I can't prove these assertions. I must rest content to ask you whether you don't find essential agreement based on your own experience. We Americans manipulate law and legal roles relatively easily. Often we don't play the game fairly. Time and time again we are perfectly willing to smirk, wink, and point to a literal conformity to rules. If you doubt this proposition I invite you to stay up late and to watch the late, late show on television. The old movies about police and law enforcement are all full of "wink situations." We are shown scenes of officers, not only policemen but other public officials, who say, "We know what the rules are, but we'll do it this other way, and it will be all right." Our habit of manipulation, of not playing the game honestly, of following the rules only when a policeman is looking over our shoulder, has contributed to mistrust of authority and mistrust of legal process. We see it most starkly in the South when, in the desire to stop the wave of integration, Southern officials, over and over again, have manipulated the system in order to frustraate the ends which the rules demand. We make a profound mistake, however, if we believe such conduct is regional. It is a deeply ingrained habit throughout all of American society.

Another source of community problems is the stereotype of the policemen. This stereotype has derived from the day when policemen were generally untrained persons, when attempts at police education were rare. The stereotype of the tough bully-boy is still very much with us.

Another source of trouble for us is found in the law. We have given the police a job to do, but we haven't told them what the rules are. The Anglo-American law has never provided a clear guide for police action beginning at the time the police identify a suspect. The rules respecting "threshhold" investigations, searches without warrant, and the scope of interrogation, have never been very clear. We have very detailed rules when the formal charge is lodged. But, in regard to the time prior to this relatively late stage our legislation has been spotty and sometimes contradictory. I take it, this very day, none can answer the question whether it is lawful for a policeman to stop a "suspicious" person in the city of Detroit at 4 A.M. on a dark block and ask him what he is doing and where he is going and search him lightly. I think most police officers and police administrators believe they can do that, but it is precisely such an issue which is pending before the Supreme Court of the United States at this very moment. We do not know whether electronics eavesdropping may be done constitutionally. We cannot tell you whether a suspect has, in given circumstances, "waived" his Fifth Amendment rights respecting silence in the face of questioning.

There is an instructive story told by a lawyer from the city of Buffalo who had been engaged to defend a person who had given a statement after a brief stop and frisk. "I was working on this case and I couldn't sleep, arose and decided to go get a paper about 4 A.M. I went outside my hotel in a raincoat and stood at a lamp post, apparently looking very suspicious. A policeman came up to me and said, 'What are you doing there buddy?' I took a long time to answer and then said, 'I'm thinking whether you have the right to ask me that question.' "

We have learned within the year, that when a person suspected of a crime is in custody he must be told of his right to remain silent. He must be told of his right to have a lawyer present at the questioning. He must be told that if he has no funds a lawyer will be provided for him and the questioning will stop until such a lawyer is provided. Nobody knew that two years ago today. It is not surprising, then, that the police didn't know.

In general it has been extraordinarily difficult for the police (and everyone else) to find out what the rules which govern the police are. Everytime the Supreme Court makes a change in the rules, the police are put in the posture of having been the law breakers. By the very nature of things, a court decision which alters the law is always retrospective in the case where the new rule is announced. The new rule will then seem to govern police conduct which could not have complied with an undiscoverable regulation. As a consequence the Supreme Court decisions have put the police in a bad light over and over again, because the Court upsets convictions based upon police work that is now held to be unconstitutional, but no one, with any sure-footedness, could have held the issues as constitutional some time before.

There is another fact in respect to police conduct which creates tension between the police and the public. Whatever rules we have call for judgment. Police work requires, does it not, the use of force and split-second judgments? It is very easy to sit back a few months later and sort things out, but man must act and judgment may be exceedingly difficult. Very recently, one of my colleagues was my host at Sunday dinner. During an after dinner stroll in his neighborhood two huge dogs started a terrible fight. Soon one dog had the other by the throat. My friend was carrying a large walking stick and after a moment of agony, he decided to do something lest those two dogs tear each other apart. He hit one of the dogs with great force and the two parted. As we walked home, we reviewed the event and concluded that he had beaten the wrong dog. He had hit the dog whose throat was being caught, not the other one.

Surely, any list of tensions between police and public are made more complicated today by America's extraordinary difficult race problem. Racial tensions exist in every corner of urban America and a good deal of rural America. Policemen and the members of the minorities involved are indeed human and the interchange between them is sometimes bitter. The police, caught in the midst of social unrest, lose some support as they act.

The strident and discourteous ways of making a point in the 1960's cause additional trouble. Students are never satisfied to send a letter to the college administration. Those who protest today haven't "been heard" until they arrange a huge rally with fiery oratory. It seems that meaningful communication begins only when ordinary routine is disrupted by a sit-in in administrative offices blocking ingress and egress for a number of hours. Then they feel they have been heard. Again, the police are expected to sort out a difficult situation. To what extent is picketing and demonstration justified because no other avenue of communication is fairly open? To what extent are they justified because even if other avenues are open, political authority does not listen until the most extreme protest action is taken? The police, having the duty to maintain public order, find themselves thrust into highly tense situations; here, once more, I put it to you, the rules are not very clear.

So far we have discussed problems which arise because of deep-rooted social issues — problems which have been thrust upon the police. There is, in addition, a source of trouble which follows from a failure on the part of police establishments and police leadership. It is the failure, in instructing police, to take into account the many values of the democratic order. Far too often, in the past, the leadership in law enforcement has tended to focus on questions of police efficiency: how can we do this best? how shall we deploy the police? should we have squad cars or should we have patrolmen? how can we use this electronic device or that one? — without, at the same time, considering the total value system of a democratic society? To these democratic values (free speech, petition, protection of the accused) the police must inevitably respond. It is obviously important that they be inevitably tuned to them. I hasten to say that this is in my opinion rapidly being rectified with conferences and institutes such as this one.

Let us make one final point. Police may feel that too much legalism and too much formality has been injected into police work. Police have less and less discretion and must deal with more and more lawyers. It is true but let me tell you that you are not alone. The phenomenon is a general trend in our society. When you return home inquire of any juvenile probation officer or juvenile court judge and ask about the growth of legalism in that area. To take an example, in the city of New York recently, Judge Constance Baker Motley of the Federal District Court in Manhattan has decided that a youngster who was involved in a school suspension hearing was entitled to counsel at the hearing. The opinion overturned a long-standing regulation of the Board of Education of New York that forbade lawyers to appear.

You are not alone in experiencing the trend. Why is it that we find a greater intrusion of law, legalism, legal norms into areas that hitherto have been discretionary? The lawyers are not moving in for money for there isn't much money to be had. We are too wise to ask "Why?" "What's happening?" To some extent, I think the answer is — that we have become aware of the great gap between what we do and what we say. We have greater sensitivity to the tension between our stated ideals, the words of the Bill of Rights, the speeches that are made on formal occasions, and what happens out on the streets, night after night. We are also learning more facts about what happens out on the streets. There is more research money available; we know more. The enhanced sensitivity to the reality has disclosed a chasm between promise and the performance of our institutions.

What is it that this crisis in law enforcement requires? We might say we wish it would go away. We might say that it shouldn't be there, it's just a few agitators, there isn't any such crisis. I believe such notions are profoundly mistaken. The crisis is real and whether or not it ought to exist is rather beside the point. One has to deal with the walls of the room in which one lives.

What, then, are corrective measures which can be taken? First of all and of first rank importance, we can see to it that an effective and honest system is established to correct complaints which are made.

We would all agree that, for major breaches of discipline and the law, the criminal law should be invoked. Yet, we all know that to apply criminal sanctions to policemen presents enormous problems. We need not dwell upon the difficulty of obtaining a conviction, or the difficulty of persuading the prosecutor that he should press the case. It is more important to say that it's kind of the wrong solution to the problem in all but the most aggravated case. We do not want a police force that is so timid that it is fearful to act. The easiest thing in the world is for policemen to keep out of trouble simply by looking the other way. As a citizen who lives where I do, on the West Side of Manhattan, I say that is a poor option. The criminal law is too rough, even if we could use it. So also is the tort law (suits for damages). It can hit the policeman much too hard.

Another trouble with the law of civil wrongs, is that the damages — the penalty, if you please — are open-ended. They are not awarded in proportion to the seriousness of the conduct. An officer can be liable for $30,000 of damage yet be guilty only of 30 cents of fault. We could soften the blow by providing that policemen do not have to pay. Suits involving police misconduct can result in liability on the part of the political unit which hires the policeman. The taxpayer's representatives, anxious to balance budgets, presumably will see to it that the men who cost the money will be forced off the role. It might mean that one or two mistakes would not end an officer's career, but the habitual offender will prove just too expensive to retain.

The familiar rule or sanction against the police is, of course, the exclusionary evidence rule. Sometime try and explain the meat of that rule to a European. I tried it once, in the summer of 1964, and just barely missed being committed as a lunatic. The rule obviously seeks to discourage police misconduct by the method of failing to convict persons who have been the object of such misconduct. It also frees the malfactor to continue his career in respect to some innocent person. The rule does not compensate the victim of police misconduct. If one were to sit down and imagine the kind of remedy which had almost none of the advantages of ordinary measures for redress, you might come up with the exclusionary evidence principle. It has little to commend it except that it is a sanction that has had an impact on police procedures.

Is the exclusionary rule the best we can do? What about the more direct method of a complaint system inside the police department itself? This involves the most sensitive issue today because such a proposal immediately raises the question of whether there should be civilian participation or civilian domination in complaint review boards. The plea for civilian participation is grounded in several arguments. One is that the civilian participation is necessary to keep the system honest. Inside the police department, officer-board members are likely to be overprotective of their own, so the story goes. They are likely to find ways of making it inconvenient for the complainant. If the complainant owns a little candy store the officer charged but feeling protected by his brother officers might take a lively interest in all the rules that that candy store is required to obey; lighting requirements, space requirements, fire prevention rules, etc. The hope is that a civilian complaint review board would simplify complaint-making and prevent subsequent harassment.

We have not had a wide experience in this country with civilian complaint review boards. Generally speaking, they have been agencies which have received complaints and have caused investigations to be made, though not typically under their own auspices. The few that have existed have been under-financed and the disciplinary function itself remains within the police department. The boards have functioned to sort out complaints and make recommendations to the police department. They have operated somewhat like a grand jury does in making formal charges. After the charge the police structure itself hands out some appropriate response.

Any review board, whether it has civilian participation or not would require an adequate budget. It ought to have its own independent investigative services. There should be provision in the system for lawyers on both sides, in any adversary proceeding, with an opportunity also to call witnesses under the subpoena power.

Let us address ourselves to two questions. First, should there be a strong police review board, and second, should there be civilian participation? The arguments against civilian participation are many. Such a board with civilians judging police conduct is harmful to the morale of the police. We don't have such bodies for other officials in the community; to single out the police for such special administrative attention assumes that police misconduct presents a special problem of requiring a special tribunal. The police structure loses control of its disciplinary proceedings and, just as the Army would resent bitterly civilian tribunals at the trial level, so also do the police. Civilians understand very little about police work. It is a highly specialized task which civilians can only serve to disadvantage by imposing sanctions in situations which require not penalty but praise.

In my view, the case against a civilian review board has not been as strongly stated as it might be. There is, in my view, a better system for processing complaints. Here I lean heavily upon the work of my talented colleague, Walter Gellhorn, who has recently published important studies of complaint procedures throughout the world. He urges us to consider the adaption of the ombudsman.

The ombudsman, conceived in Scandanavia, is an official who is somewhat like the Inspector General in the Army. The ombudsman has different powers in different parts of the world but in general, the notion is that he is an official outside the structure of any administrative department. He is an outside eye. He offers a fresh look from a different stance. He receives complaints about government from anyone. He may or may not have the power to right wrongs. In some places he has only the power to recommend administrative change to government. He is, in the last analysis, an official who makes it his business to inquire into complaints and to seek improvement if the complaint lays bare a situation which requires improvement.

A great advantage of the ombudsman over a complaint review board is that he can make improvements without the use of contention, without the adversary system, without putting the complainant and officialdom into a polar stance. Professor Gellhorn perceives a great many advantages to this point. He believes, for example, that the stance of contention is not a happy one. Furthermore, not all problems are resolved by a single case. Indeed, there may be no "case."

For example, there may be problems about which an individual officer can do little. Correction of a difficulty may require the adaptation of a new practice with respect to records or with respect to the keeping of fingerprints. Discourtesy, disrespect, and loose use of words in incendiary situations may not yield itself to improvement through the filing of charges in certain cases. The ombudsman, on the other hand, could, if he received a large number of similar complaints, recommend to the police department that they embark on a special program of education directed at courtesy.

To take another point, administrative change at a high level doesn't always take place as a result of a single complaint. The significance of series of complaints is often lost because no one has the duty to pay attention to the cumulation. The ombudsman would keep a careful watch over the kinds of complaints and take appropriate action.

Furthermore, there are many situations in which one may not be able to find out who the perpetrator of a certain outrage is. For example, in the confusion of a riot, police work may be poor and yet it may not be possible to pinpoint the blame on individual officers.

Finally, let me say this. If the suggestions for a civilian participation review board are unacceptable, and if one rejects the ombudsman idea, it is fair to ask the police among you for their answer to our problem. What is an acceptable plan to restore confidence in the police, given this tragically divided and explosive society of ours?

As I look at America today, I no longer see the melting pot, but a society with deep divisions not easily papered over by singing patriotic songs and pledging allegiance to the United States. The society in which I grew up seemed to me to be a society consisting of members and pledges of the fraternity. Everybody wanted to join. Is it still true? Are we growing closer together as a people? Or must we now conceive of America as something different? Something not so unified, but still a country which must foster peace and harmony?

Confidence in law enforcement in any conception of the United States, I put it to you, is a necessity. If the measures we have described do not appeal to you, then I have the right to put the question to you, "What would you do to restore confidence in law enforcement in the United States?"

Police and Community Partnership in Crime Prevention — as Related to Poverty and Unequal Justice Under the Law

WILLIAM T. DOWNS

(Then) Deputy-Director, Midwest Region, Office of Economic Opportunity, Chicago, Illinois

MAY 18, 1966

In approaching this formidable topic, I thought first, that I was asked to consider poverty and unequal justice under the law. I proceeded to draft remarks in that conception of the assignment. It was during that exercise that I came to understand that the topic must be dealt with in context of *police* and *community relations.* So I drafted a second set of comments in which I expanded the focus, rather than addressing what had primarily been a consideration of the judicial process. In the process of revising those remarks I was reminded further of the theme of *partnership in crime prevention.* It was then that I realized that I must deal with each of three topics in a way which would harmonize and integrate some thoughts on each of the three approaches. I mention this because I think it important that we are all thinking within the same limits — by the same ground rules. Only in this way can there be some promise of communication and understanding.

If we look first, then, at the question of poverty and unequal justice, and specifically that segment of the administration of justice which is the judicial assignment, we ask ourselves the question: what does *not* cost the individual money? What does not cost the accused money? The answer is that it does not cost him money to stay in jail, or to plead guilty, or to throw himself on the mercy of the court. It does not cost him money to be sentenced to prison. Everything else does cost the accused money, in the out-of-pocket sense.

If he is not to go to jail, it is likely to cost him money. If he is to plead "not guilty" and present a defense, it will cost him money. If he is to persuade the court that he should be released to the community, it will cost him money. If he is to present reasonable alternatives to imprisonment, it will cost him money. Consequently, since this economic factor is ever present through the judicial process, it must be obvious that the one who has money has an advantage over the one who has not. It is as simple as that. Poverty means unequal justice; poverty means unequal application of the law — unless something is done to balance the scales.

We as a society, in our quest for more equal justice, have developed a number of efforts to equalize the opportunity of the indigent for justice. We have developed, in the last couple of years, a bail release process which is designed to make it possible for the defendant to be released without bail.[1] We have developed, in some States, a defender system, an attempt to provide a defense for the indigent defendant.[2] And, more recently, we have developed, under the Office of Economic Opportunity, a legal services program, which may or may

---

[1]National Conference on Bail and Criminal Justice, May 27–29, 1964.
[2]See National Legal Aid Defender Society.

not include bail for the defendant.[3] The OEO legal services projects are the first to recognize that it costs a great deal of money to *even the chances* for equal opportunity for the indigent defendant. It costs more than *counsel*. Money is needed to bring in expert witnesses, if they are needed. Money is needed to investigate, to discover and to evaluate facts. It's necessary to have money for court costs. All of these things are given legal and budget recognition in OEO legal services. I suspect when the results of these projects are tabulated, it will be a revelation to the citizen to realize just how much money is involved.

But we have spoken here only of out-of-pocket costs. There are other tremendous human costs in the procedures of bringing an accused through the judicial process. I am sure you are aware that the impact of the criminal process on the poverty person is, in no wise, similar to the impact upon the affluent. The indigent defendant is continuously on the borderline of bankruptcy. *Any* interruption to his income triggers a number of other economic problems. His situation is so precarious that such economic problems frequently become other legal problems.

Until now, I have been speaking of only one part of the process of administration of criminal justice; namely, the judicial part. You might ask what this has to do with the police and specifically with police–community relations. The police are the forepart, the front line of the process of criminal justice. The police initiate the judicial process. In one sense of the word, the police are the suppliers of the criminal courts. When we speak then of the burden of the judicial proceeding upon the indigent defendant, we are at the same time pointing out that this places a burden upon the police to be certain that no person is wrongfully accused, and that each person subject to the criminal process be rightfully there and fairly and properly handled. The great economic and human costs involved in criminal proceedings should be a caution against impetuous police actions of any kind.

The great economic cost which is involved in providing adequate defense for the indigent in our present system has caused me to think that perhaps we are taking the wrong approach. Our approach has been one of attempting to provide the same protection and services which are available to the affluent offender. From the point of view of equalizing the process between rich and poor, this may be sound. However, it has its weakness in that it does not challenge the system itself nor is it likely to reveal defects or costly appurtenances which are not really necessary. In other words, I am suggesting that perhaps we should take an opposite approach, to reverse our thinking. Instead of providing similar services for the indigent, we should analyze what is necessary for the administration of criminal justice and eliminate all that is not necessary. We should analyze and query what extras and additions have been made to the process simply because there have been affluent defenders. Such products of affluence should be eliminated.

We should inquire into the additional cost of maintaining current institutional arrangements. In my judgment, such institutional costs are not a necessary cost of criminal justice. We should then see what is necessary to change institutions and procedures and thereby reduce the cost for all. I am saying that while it is laudable to be concerned about the fact that the indigent does not have $500 to

---

[3]Guidelines for Legal Service, Office of Economic Opportunity, 1966.

bear the cost of a preliminary examination, the real question is why it should cost $500 for any defendant to receive a proper preliminary examination. In this direction, I would suggest a drastic decentralization of courts to bring them closer to the people, more readily available, and to reduce time and cost of attendance. I would suggest a system of lower courts, "community courts," if you will, where minor offenses would be heard and where no lawyers would practice, either for the prosecution or for the offense. Some people would consider this to be regression, and will say that we are only just now getting rid of the justice of the peace courts. I question the whole movement away from the justice of the peace. In my opinion, it is being done for the wrong reasons. The problems with the justice courts arose out of the manner of the selection of the justices in many instances, and out of the unnecessary complication of the criminal proceedings. The penalty we are paying for the elimination of these lower courts is much more costly than the proper correction of the abuses which have admittedly existed but did not require the elimination of the system. In connection with the establishment of "community courts," we should also redefine a whole class of acts currently called criminal into a category of noncriminal social misconduct. Decisions with reference to such matters should not impose any criminal penalties. This is not a radical idea, and I am sure that most of you realize that I am talking about such things as alcoholism, drug offenses, and sexual offenses. Time does not permit further elaboration.

Having looked, then, first at the question of poverty in the judicial process, and having said that the police really trigger this process, I think we come naturally to the police and community, the police and the *poor* community. I think that we must recognize that the police are of a number of different kinds of community, particularly in our urban areas. I have noted a tendency for the police to think of themselves as separate from the community. But they are of and by the community, and must never forget this. The police enforce the community's interpretation of law. If their interpretation does not conform to the judgment of the community, there will be friction, if not outright hostility. I think that over a long period of time, the police have responded to one segment of the community — in many instances, this was the most conservative and affluent segment of the community, or the politically powerful segment. In no instance has it included the interpretation of the poor segment of the community. In fact, in many instances, it has excluded consideration of minority groups.

Don't misunderstand me; I am not saying that this is exclusively the fault of the police. The poor and the minority groups simply have not had a voice — they have not had channels of communication with the police. This situation has obtained too long, and we have not progressed to a maturity in community relations where the police should have the confidence to reflect the needs of all segments of the community. In the last two years of civil rights demonstrations, the mere suggestion that the poor be given recognition has been looked upon as radical — as an assault on law and order. Nothing could be further from the truth.

The poor are now beginning to raise their voice in community affairs. They will, and should, be heard. In police–community relations, this means that the police must develop arrangements which provide for broadly representative groups to influence police policy.

I am reminded of a situation. For the last several months, I have lived on the South Side of Chicago. I, who am not a member of the poor community, feel oppressed and coerced by the presence of the police in that area. I think that I have some feeling of what people must feel. I think that when stop-and-question procedures are instituted in a city (and by some mystical decision, it is only applied in the slum areas of that city), this conveys an image of an army of occupation. I think that when stop-and-detention procedures are instituted in a city — but only in the slum areas of the city — that they convey discrimination. So, I think it should be no surprise that the poor in our cities appear to be growing hostile toward the police. Whatever the justification may be, I think the police must be aware of the kind of image they project. I think that when they define an area as one of high criminal activity, by implication they define everyone in that area as a criminal — when, in fact, we know that even in the highest criminal area, the greater number of people are not criminals.

I suggest that by these practices, the police are stimulating much more serious problems than the criminal actions which they are trying to control. What, then, do I suggest? If we look at the process of defense of criminals, and the problem of police communication to the 20 or 30 percent of the population which is poor, what can we do to make the police and community partners in crime prevention?

We must have visible evidence of equal administration of justice in the neighborhood, and equality of treatment, and mechanisms for citizen participation as partners in crime prevention. If the police are to respond to the poverty segment of the population, we must develop an institutional arrangement which will provide the mechanisms for communication. I suggest that each precinct station should have a citizen's advisory committee, drawn from that neighborhood, and that this committee should deal with policies and practices, and they should convey an interpretation of those policies to their segment of the community. This would be evidence that the police and the community were indeed partners in crime prevention. This should not be a typical committee which *listens* to the police and advises about community problems. The police should listen to it, and it should advise about police problems and practices. The committee should have a neighborhood person as staff for it, on a part-time basis at first—more as needed.

It is frequently said that crime prevention is everyone's business—let us make it just that, by giving all an equal opportunity to participate and contribute.

The Police Role in a Democratic Society

FREDERICK ROUTH

Executive Director, National Association of Inter-Group Relations Officials, Washington, D.C.

MAY 20, 1966

Let us talk about the police role in a democratic society, and about how the police are viewed. Part of this should be focused in such a way that professional law enforcement officers can examine (in their own communities, or from the perspective or the focus of their own community) how their force is regarded, and how the force and its members regard themselves. In the long run, in a democratic society, there is no more important professional group than law enforcement officers. If this is properly understood by the various sectors and segments of government and of the public, we can proceed with the task of developing a more democratic society, with the full participation of the police as one of the instrumentalities of government.

It is important to understand that the image of the police ultimately depends upon performance. This is true, I would guess, of any professional group, but it is particularly true of the police departments, of the law enforcement agencies of this country. In terms of performance there seem to be certain things that are absolutely essential:

1. The most important is the equal administration of law, the equal administration of justice. If our police departments across the nation can practice the equal administration of justice, they will have come a long way along the road toward securing for themselves and for society the type of image that they should have, and in many cases, indeed, deserve.

2. There must be a professional attitude toward law enforcement itself, that it is a career, that it is not just walking a beat or riding a squad car, but it is a professional career, and it calls for integrity and professionalism and dedication. I believe that a police force must be both well-disciplined and good-mannered. There has to be, too, an awareness on the part of the police in any community of the various changes that are taking place in their community; they must be sensitive to those changes; knowledgeable about them; and must understand that in a democratic society, there is a dynamic of change. The one certain thing in a democratic society is change; hopefully, part of the role of the police department is to see that change remains orderly, and to see, too, that there is no interference with orderly change as it takes place.

3. Another crucial determinant in how a police department is regarded is professional leadership, not only the professional attitude of the man on the force, but professional leadership at the top level. This means the command officer, it means the police commissioner, and it also means the mayor or the city council, and their regard for the role of the police.

4. Finally, there is real need on the part of police departments across the nation to interpret the role of the police to the community. I do not mean a Madison Avenue, P-R type of approach. There is a real need for public information about the role of the police department, how the police department functions, and the knowledge that the police department is a part of city government (for the most part), county government (in some cases), or state government, etc. (in other cases). There is a need for the police *themselves* to play this urgent and important role of public interpretation and public information, not simply public relations.

The good police officer has certain attributes. One of these is the desire and the capacity to grow, the desire and the capacity to learn, the desire and the capacity to become more professional. There has to be, among the police of the nation, a high degree of intelligence. The day when we could entrust a badge, a billy and a side arm to the unintelligent is past. We need intelligent police; and increasingly across the nation the standards are rising; increasingly across the nation we are getting men with higher intelligence than we have had in the past. If you look at police forces across the country today and compare them with, say, thirty years ago (the period before World War II), there is a marked rise in the caliber of men being attracted to the police department.

Moral courage is another attribute of the good police officer. There has to be complete honesty and integrity, both personal honesty and integrity and professional honesty and integrity. There must be a high degree of emotional stability. I'm reminded of the young officer in Texas who was in a squad car one afternoon when a great white Lincoln Continental went roaring by. He looked at it, took out after it, pulled it over to the side of the road, came back and looked in and said, "Mr. President, my God!" The President looked at him and said, "And don't you ever forget it, son." Now, that man had moral courage.

There has to be social awareness and social intelligence in an increasing degree among the police; again, I think I see this developing among the forces of the country. There is more sensitivity to the needs of society among law enforcement officers today than ever before in our history.

There has to be adaptability on the part of the individual, a flexibility, a possibility of recognizing sometimes that all of us are subject to making errors, and the moral courage to admit it. But this flexibility is important: the ability to grow and to change.

And finally, I'd say, one of the most important attributes is a sense of pride, pride in the profession of law enforcement, pride in the force for which the man works, and pride in himself as a man who has chosen this career, and intends to develop increasingly as a professional law enforcement officer. There, I think, are the attributes of good policemen.

In terms of how the force is regarded, another very important thing is the *esprit de corps*, the sense of belonging, the sense of the importance of the work. I have noticed, as I've traveled around the country that this tends to be more true of state police than of municipal police; there is more sense of *esprit de corps* among the state police. In some of the city departments I have seen, there is a sense of *esprit* among certain groups—often among the motorcycle corps there is this special sense of belonging and of significance—but this must be developed across the board in each of the departments, not a phony sense of *esprit de corps*, but the real thing. This counts; this is important, that there be this pride.

There needs to be the careful selection of capable men; and again; in the recruiting that is going on in the country, in the standards that have been established, I believe we have made great strides. But there needs to be still further gains in this area. I would submit that there is nothing more important that police departments can do than to raise the salaries of beginning police officers. The police officers of the country are badly underpaid, and I don't think there is anything more important that you can do than to convince City Hall that this is so. If you want to continue to attract high caliber people, you must pay them adequately. And this is something that a police department legitimately can work for. It is not self-seeking; rather, it is a professional attitude of seeking sufficient community support to attract and retain professional people.

There needs to be more thorough professional training than there has been in the past; roll-call training alone is inadequate. There needs to be, in every force, an opportunity for everybody in the department to receive additional professional training. I think we will find increasingly, universities and colleges offering graduate work and offering undergraduate degrees in police administration and law enforcement. California is leading the way in this at the present time, with something like 30 different colleges offering specialized classes in police administration and police work. Michigan State University has led the nation in establishing a center in police training. I predict that this will spread, and more and more such opportunities will be made available across the country. I hold that it is the responsibility of the police departments to insist that this be so. I think you have a responsibility to go to the colleges and universities in your community, and ask that specialized courses be set up at these centers of education. There is no reason why something like this shouldn't exist in every major city in the United States.

Finally, in this area of *esprit de corps,* it seems to me there is one other thing that is absolutely essential, and that is the question of the "climate," if you will, on the force; the feeling that people have about being part of an organization; and whether or not those who belong to it feel that this is important, that there is leadership that is knowledgeable and professional, and there is regard and respect, both up and down the chain of command within the department.

Another area that has concerned me recently is the lack of recognition in many cases of the differing norms of behavior of people of different ethnic, racial or nationality backgrounds. I think, for instance, of the Puerto Rican in New York who has recently come up from San Juan or from Ponce who, when he was home, often stood out on a beautiful balmy evening, on the street corner and watched people go by and chatted with his friends—this was perfectly acceptable behavior. But he comes to New York, or to Buffalo, or to Washington or to Philadelphia or Detroit, and too many police officers think of him as loitering, when he does exactly what he did down home in a very acceptable way. We need to be more sensitive to the differing norms of behavior, or acceptable behavior among people of different backgrounds and groups.

There is a question often asked recently about the role of Negro police officers, and there have been occasions when Negro police officers have been accused by some of the more militant people in a given community of "enforcing the white man's law." I talked with one Negro police officer who has been in one of these situations, who had stepped up to a young Negro (who was in a group that was about to change from a crowd to a mob) and asked the young man to give him a hand—give the police officer a hand—in dispersing the crowd before it became a mob; and the Negro police officer said to him, "Now look, I know the problems. I'm Negro." And the young man looked at his blue uniform, looked him up and down very carefully, looked him straight in the face and said, "Baby, you ain't colored. You're blue." Now, we have to get away from this type of thinking, both out in the community and on the force. What we need to do is develop the professionalism that is called for, and the type of sensitivity that comes with being a real professional.

There are some specifics that I would mention which I feel are important, and I would list them this way:

First of all, we are falling behind the times in our geographical jurisdictions. We have city police departments, and county sheriff's offices (or police departments), and state police departments. What has happened in many situations is a jurisdictional limitation on necessary police activity. If you look at the early stages of the Watts situation, for instance, two police forces were in the area, but only one of them really was involved; and the question of jurisdiction became crucial. We must get over the idea of narrowly defined jurisdictions, and not just when we're in "hot pursuit" of a criminal. More than that, the basic concept should be of a peace officer who is on duty within his state to maintain law and order and peace. Now police departments cannot do this by themselves, but there is need for this type of re-examination on the part of municipal government, county government and state government; and the building of the concept of metro-governments, and particularly of metro-police departments, to cover a much larger jurisdiction than they currently do.

There is also a need for the development of a police code of ethics that is known or made known to the community, as well as to the men in the department. The International Association of Chiefs of Police has such a code of ethics; it's an excellent one. But probably it needs adaptation for any given community because of the unique nature of each of our communities. The promulgation of such a code, rather than restricting and limiting the power of the police, would make known the professional level and the integrity, if you will, of ethics in the department.

There must be, continually now, relationship and liaison with leadership out in the community, both the majority community and the minority community. It is not enough to say there is an open door at the precinct house or at the Chief's office; this must be done with intelligence and done with consistency, so that liaison is established on a regular basis; the police will then better know what is the leadership and what are the goals of the community; and the leaders, in turn, will know the responsibility of the police departments.

There must be further involvement of citizens, and I'm not talking about the citizen review board at the moment. I believe that's a question that must be resolved, community by community. There are areas where I feel it would be completely impractical, and there are other areas where I think it would work very well. But I don't think one can hand down any flat rule on whether this is good, bad, or indifferent—too many things affect it. There does need to be increased involvement between the department and the citizenry. Take for example the situation in Chicago, with Crime-Stop; but it shouldn't *only* be on the level of crime prevention; it should go well beyond this. It should go into the whole question of a lawful and orderly society. There should be recognition on the part of the police department, and on the citizenry together, of the differences between protest movements, of redress for grievances (real or imagined), of civil disobedience, and of lawlessness. Police departments must recognize that protest movements — protest demonstrations — are attempts at redress for grievances to bring notice to the community of grievances (either real or imagined). And the whole concept of the right to seek redress for grievance is as old as English Common Law itself, and older than our own Republic.

Civil disobedience is another matter. When groups engage in civil disobedience, it will often be the responsibility of law enforcement agents to arrest them; the purpose, often, of civil disobedience is to secure arrest and to challenge laws that are considered to be unfair. If there is good liaison between the police and the community, this can usually be accomplished without great difficulty. I think of Atlanta, Georgia, for instance (where I lived for five years), where, when a law was to be tested, the police department was notified in advance. The people did perform the civil disobedience, they were arrested, charged with that specific violation of law, and were released on bond. But then, they went to court to change the law.

Lawlessness, however, is another matter. Lawlessness cannot be tolerated in a democratic society, and we must distinguish between these three levels of activity. Police departments must be particularly sensitive to the three different levels.

Finally, there is one other major area that I want to mention. This is the question of how police officers see themselves. I have done some consultant work with departments around the country; very often, in talking with police officers, I find they think of themselves as a minority group, and they display in some ways the same attitudes as any minority group that has been isolated from the mainstream of society. There is a sense that they are not understood; there is a sense that they are unfairly regarded, both by the community and by the government. There is a sense that they are discriminated against. There is a sense that out in the community, they are not liked. I think that we need to examine — almost individual by individual, and certainly police force by police force — how the force and how the individuals see themselves; what role concept, what role perception police officers have. I suspect that this type of examinination will lead to vastly increased efficiency and ability among the forces. I believe that with that type of insight, with professional training, with a proper regard for Constitutional rights, the police departments of this nation will gain the respect which they must have if they are to be successful.

This is a big order, but I point out to you there is not another group that should be quite so interested in it as the law enforcement profession itself. I point out to you that the time to start and move ahead rapidly is *now,* not in the future. This should not be the education of one or two or a team of men from a force alone, but it should be the bringing into the force of new leaven, the bringing into the department of a new understanding that should be shared across the board.

The Police as Community Leaders*

E. WILSON PURDY

(Then) Commissioner, Pennsylvania State Police

MAY 20, 1965

The American community and its police administrators today are faced with the greatest challenge of all time in meeting the responsibility of the preservation of law and order.

We are witnessing increased crime rates, a mounting traffic death toll, and a reduction of police powers as a result of Supreme Court decisions. We see a wave of public apathy and tolerance toward criminal offenses in general, and organized crime, specifically, which society has failed to recognize.

The increased workload which has been heaped upon the police service agencies of our nation has dramatically pointed out the need for the professionalization of law enforcement.

---

* Reprinted with permission from POLICE Magazine, Volume 10, No. 5, May–June, 1966, pp. 57–63; Charles C Thomas, Publisher, Springfield, Illinois.

This can be accomplished only through the establishment of an entirely new set of standards in selection, training, and education of not only the police administrator, himself, but of the most important member of the law enforcement agency—the officer on the street and highway, whose responsibility it is to preserve law and order on a daily basis.

Understanding, through education, must come to the police family, if we are to fill that important position of "Community Leader," fully prepared to lead society through today's social upheaval into a better community of tomorrow, one in which we can feel confident that we may raise our families in the traditional American way of life.

One of the major problems which we have been witnessing in recent years is the social revolution sweeping our nation in connection with equal rights for all citizens.

In addition to its successes, this revolution has at times led to riots, demonstrations, vandalism, and even murder. Along with this and with equal regularity have come the allegations of "Police Brutality."

As community leaders, we cannot hide the fact that these events are caused by ignorance, hatred, fear and prejudice . . . but we must recognize that these are problems which must be faced and that the full energy of the community will be needed.

These problems will test the moral stamina of American communities for many years to come; however, we shall see no abatement of the widespread destruction of mankind through crime and highway slaughter, or the establishment of equal rights and opportunities for all persons so long as we accept, as a part of our community's way of life, the wholesale disrespect for traffic laws, for criminal laws, and for the rights of others.

It is a basic responsibility of our law enforcement agencies to meet every emergency situation. Yet, when civil disorders began to occur throughout this country, few police agencies found themselves equipped, either psychologically or physically, to cope with the serious problems resulting from such demonstrations and disturbances.

Shortly after being appointed Commissioner of the Pennsylvania State Police in 1963, it became apparent to me that this condition existed in many communities throughout our state, and that state and local police agencies were not fully prepared to cope with this problem.

An early incident involving the move-in of a Negro family into a previously all-white community in the suburbs of Philadelphia clearly demonstrated that this community, and many other communities throughout the Commonwealth, had made no preparation to meet such a problem, and had for the most part, refused to recognize that such a problem could occur.

Although this incident resulted in riotous action for several hours, we were fortunate to be able to control it without injury or loss of life, and with very little property damage.

There was small consolation, however, to be gained from this, when we realized that the entire problem could probably have been met without incident, had a proper police and community relation program been previously established.

Considerable criticism resulted from this incident. A group of ministers was extremely critical of our procedures; however, they also admitted they had made no attempt to prepare the neighborhood, and that they knew of no other segment of the community that had made any effort to do so.

As usual, the police wound up in the middle.

To fill the vacuum created by a lack of community planning throughout the state, the Pennsylvania State Police immediately launched a leadership program in Police–Community Relations on a state-wide basis . . . in an all-out effort to wake up all Pennsylvanians to the shadow of tragedy which hangs over any community or state which chooses to sleep or attempts to sleep through a social revolution involving man's basic rights, and fails to take action to meet the problems of rising crime rates, highway slaughter, vice, corruption, and organized crime's effort to jeopardize the American way of life.

Through the joint sponsorship of the Pennsylvania State Police, the Pennsylvania Chiefs of Police Association, the Pennsylvania Human Relations Commission, and with the all-out support of the National Conference of Christians and Jews, a conference was held on May 8th and 9th, 1964, at the Pennsylvania State Police Academy in Hershey.

More than one hundred Chiefs of Police and all Troop Commanders of the Pennsylvania State Police attended this two-day conference on "Police Responsibility in Racial Tension and Conflict." The participating Chiefs of Police and command personnel had been carefully selected from throughout the State, in order that full geographic representation would be present.

Enthusiasm generated by this conference led to the establishment of nine similar conferences throughout Pennsylvania, attended by more than 1,200 top police administrators, who were privileged to hear the story of the civil rights movement from outstanding Negro leaders.

The next step in this state-wide Police–Community Relations program was to present a similar program to a conference of more than 250 mayors and city officials, held at the Pennsylvania State Police Academy.

The outstanding reception and the tremendous interest displayed in these Racial Tension Conferences clearly demonstrated to us that community leaders were vitally interested in police and community problems.

The next phase of this program was the presentation by the Pennsylvania State Police of a skill program, at the fifteen State Police Troop Headquarters throughout the Commonwealth. These programs were attended by more than 2,200 policemen, representing many police departments, who received a training program in the basic skills and techniques of handling social disorders before, during, and after such demonstrations.

This intensive program has resulted in the establishment of a very close relationship between State and local police and Negro leaders, which may have prevented the development of potentially dangerous situations.

State Police now establish immediate liaison with local police, Negro leaders, and Human Relations Commissions, when any information is received indicating a problem may develop.

We all agree to the importance of the racial problem, and we must be fully in support of the civil rights movement. We must understand and believe within ourselves that there is no moral, legal, or religious justification or basis for segregation. We must be willing to stand up and be counted as community leaders in this field.

It is tough to stand up and be counted, and it is even tougher to stand up after you have been counted. We have all experienced that . . . but take a stand, we must!

This does not mean that we always have to agree fully with the tactics being used, but we must be alert to the problems which are growing out of the civil rights movement, and must assume a leadership role in the community effort to overcome these problems.

One problem which I am sure we recognize is that the civil rights movement may be contributing to other problems, such as the further development of a crime tolerance. In many of the civil disturbances, we find young people taking an active part. They are being encouraged and taught to violate the law, and thus perhaps, civil disturbances are becoming a way of life . . . which they, as future adults, will pass on to their children. Thus, we may have a situation developing for which our nation will pay for generations to come.

This may be a far more serious by-product of the civil disobedience today than the civil disobedience itself . . . the actual teaching of disobedience and disrespect of law and order, which may be with us long after the main issues have been either solved or programmed for successful solution.

We are responsible, as law enforcement officers, to see that each member of the community is held accountable for his behavior, in accordance with the type of behavior that is acceptable for the community as a whole.

The police administrator and the police officer of today are faced with the major personal problem of prejudice, and how to keep our personal prejudices out of our performance of duty. We all understand that we must be absolutely impartial, regardless of race, color or creed, with those with whom we deal on a daily basis.

Let us be honest enough with ourselves to admit that each of us is prejudiced on almost every subject we consider.

One of the most obvious prejudices is that of racial prejudice. Our problem is to learn to live above this prejudice in the performance of our official duties.

So it is important that in our Police and Community Relations programs at municipal, state, and national levels, we recognize and put forth full effort in working toward a solution of civil rights problems.

But let us not believe that this issue . . . important as it may be . . . is the only police–community relations problem we have . . . nor is it necessarily the most important community problem facing us.

There are, perhaps, more basic problems of the grass-roots type, which face us on a day-to-day basis, at the hometown level.

We are much concerned today with the Communist threat to the free world. This is the enemy from without; however, there is a far more serious threat to the American way of life, and that is the enemy from within . . . organized crime and corruption . . . which is eating away the very foundation of our government.

It must be emphasized there can be no coexistence with crime, and there can be no appeasement with the criminal, and there can be no compromise of good law enforcement . . . because if and when organized crime completes its take-over of the American way of life, all other efforts to help society will have failed.

Historians relate that no civilization has ever fallen to an enemy from without until it has first succumbed to a moral deterioration, to a rotting and crumbling, from within.

This indicates the very real Police and Community Relations problems in which all members of the community must be interested . . . those problems which today make the greatest contribution to the decay, corrosion, and deterioration of moral standards; which result in an unhealthy political climate of greed, vice and corruption, which exist in thousands of American communities . . . a climate which prohibits the establishment of a professional law enforcement agency.

It is these problems which we are attempting to bring to the attention of Pennsylvania communities.

Inspired by the success of the Racial Tensions Conference, the Pennsylvania State Police have recently launched an expanded program.

Plato said, "The penalty of wise men who fail to participate in government is to live under the government of unwise men."

Based upon this statement, we hope to interest wise men of our communities in the affairs of their own hometown.

Our next step was to hold a conference of some 250 clergymen of all faiths at the State Police Academy in Hershey, at which time an open and frank discussion of police and community problems was held.

"No holds barred" discussions were conducted regarding racial problems, traffic enforcement (the problem of slaughter on the highways, where neighbor kills neighbor), the tremendous rise in crime rates, and the true picture of the inside story regarding organized crime involving gambling, narcotics, prostitution, liquor law violations, and the corruption resulting from these activities.

The problem of youthful criminality was also discussed. For the first time, members of the clergy were given an opportunity to see these matters as police *and* community problems, in which they have a grave responsibility and a vital personal concern.

This first State Police conference for clergymen was followed by fifteen Regional Conferences throughout the State, reaching nearly 3,000 clergymen.

The same program has also been presented to the membership of the Pennsylvania Broadcasters Association, and to all District Attorneys of the 67 counties of Pennsylvania.

In the planning stages for presentation of this same vital program in the months ahead are the Pennsylvania Newspaper Association, County Superintendents of Schools and their staffs, labor leaders, Chamber of Commerce representatives, industrialists, business and Negro leaders.

Such programs will also be presented to other interested groups.

The subject may be of interest to you.

Traffic

In the field of traffic, it is pointed out that during the year 1964, 96,300,000 drivers driving 86,200,000 automobiles a distance of 900 billion miles killed 47,900 people.

This causes us to wonder if we are fulfilling the Biblical prophecy as set forth in Nahum II:4 . . .

The chariots shall rage in the streets,
they shall jostle one against another in the broad ways:
they shall seem like torches,
they shall run like the lightnings.

Is this a picture of Main Street, Hometown, USA?

This presents a truly serious police–community problem, one which calls for a new philosophy of enforcement, in which the American public must accept the fact that violations of the traffic law are violations against society and not against the police; that traffic enforcement is not a sporting proposition; and that the device known as the automobile . . . the greatest mechanical killer of our society today . . . must be controlled by the community as a matter of self-preservation.

Juvenile Delinquency

Today, we are dealing with the most intelligent and best educated group of young people that the world has ever known, and yet, we have failed to fulfill our community responsibilities to them.

The State Police have established a Youth Aid and Crime Prevention Bureau on a state-wide basis, designed to assist in the coordination of efforts of the existing social service agencies in the various communities, and designed to help them meet the problem of youthful criminality.

Central Juvenile Index

The Central Juvenile Index is a central depository for information on juvenile arrests and contacts by local and state police. This information will be made available exclusively to law enforcement agencies and juvenile court authorities. It is the first state-wide central juvenile index to be established in the United States, and is designed to help communities help themselves, with the Pennsylvania State Police serving as the coordinating agency.

We are also approaching the young man through other than police channels . . . for example—

Explorer Scout Program

The Pennsylvania State Police currently has upwards of sixty-five men engaged, on their own time, in police-oriented Explorer Scout programs in eleven of our fifteen troops throughout the State.

When we recognize that our young people of today are our hope for the future, we must agree that they deserve an all-out police and community effort.

Narcotics

The ever-growing problem of narcotics is presented in our conferences, supported by a dramatic film presentation which enables the various community leaders to view, personally, for the first time in their lives, the actual narcotics problem. They see hopped-up kids, needle scars of the main-liners, and the torture of withdrawal.

Prostitution

The problem of organized, commercial prostitution, which is flourishing in sections of our nation today, is presented to these community leaders in a cold, white light of day manner . . . along with the tragic effects, such as wide-spread venereal disease, dope addiction, and other types of criminal activities resulting therefrom.

Nearly 400 prostitution arrests by the Pennsylvania State Police were made during the past year and a half, clearly illustrating that this is not a problem that went out of style in the 1890's.

The rise and existence of powerful organized crime groups or syndicates have been made possible through weaknesses in federal, state, and local laws, and through the corruption of public officials.

This lawless army infiltrates through every loophole to appease their illegal and selfish demands upon society.

Their plundering is an infinite shame to the countless law-abiding national, state, and local leaders and every honorable citizen across the nation.

A major reason for the increase in crime rates is public apathy toward crime, due primarily to society's development of a tolerance for crime.

One of the areas in which tolerance for crime has shown the greatest development is in the field of gambling. Society closes its eyes to gambling; yet, gambling provides the bankroll of organized crime.

When gambling plays an important part in our daily community, as it does in so many communities, it is easy to see why people in general, and younger people in particular, learn a tolerance for one type of criminal activity—gambling —and thus, develop a tolerance toward many types of criminal activity.

Two major types of gambling activities pose the greatest problem . . . a so-called "Hard Type" of gambling, such as bookmaking, numbers operation, slot machines . . . and that type which is usually referred to as "Charity Gambling."

There is little public protest over the enforcement of gambling laws in connection with bookmaking and numbers operation; however, political insulation has, in many instances, provided immunity to these major gambling operations.

The field of so-called "Charity Gambling" is making a tremendous contribution to organized crime, first, because a major portion of charity gambling is actually controlled by organized crime, and, secondly, because charity gambling (which is frequently considered socially acceptable) provides a daily community training program in the development of tolerance and public apathy toward all gambling and toward other criminal violations. (Examples: numbers racket, pinball machines, 50–50 pools, Lucky Seven, punchboards, bingo, veterans' clubs, fraternal groups, churches.)

It has been estimated that the profit to organized crime from gambling alone is greater than the total gross of the automobile industry.

The steady flow of money in small sums from the masses to the heads of crime syndicates actually amounts to a vicious and unofficial taxation extracted from the weekly income of the wage earner. These sums are then used to establish a sinister government within our government, through influence-buying, corruption of public officials, and investments in legitimate businesses . . . and where does the money come from? Thousands upon thousands of wage earners from the plant, the mill, and the mine.

Consider the typical working family's contribution to gambling. Dad plays the numbers, and bets on the horses at work; stops at a local bar or fraternal club on the way home, where he purchases a few drinks, plays the punchboard, buys a treasury ticket, or pulls a few tickets out of the fishbowl.

Mom plays her favorite charity game a couple of nights a week at $5.00 a night . . . representing, as a family, a loss from total income of $25 to $30 per week . . . most of which flows to organized gambling interests . . . and we ask ourselves, "Is gambling designed to support the charities, or do we have charities as an excuse for gambling?" . . . when we see professional bingo operators make $25,000 in a week, off one midway bingo game; when we see a veterans' club donate $10,000 in a year to a local charity through these gambling devices, by which — by their own admission — they take in $180,000 ... where the $75-a-week club steward drives an expensive airconditioned car.

Organized crime cannot flourish unless there is corruption and public apathy, but again, the police receive the blame.

Seldom do we find a policeman who is dishonest, but frequently we find one who is not permitted to do his job. He is prevented because of the political climate in which he must operate. I have never seen a policeman working at an intersection, in the rain, the sleet, and the snow, who enjoyed watching the local gambler drive by in his Cadillac.

This is a very real police and community problem ... one which is basic to the preservation of the American way of life.

I am afraid, too often, we think of police and community relations from the philosophical or idealistic approach, instead of bringing it down to the cold, hard facts of day-to-day realities—basic, grass-roots, dirty facts, that we would rather not face up to. All too often, the idealistic, the proud, the enthusiastic rookie policeman, who is usually from the middle to lower economic class himself, soon has to face up to the reality that there is a double standard of law enforcement, which he must observe if he is to get along.

There can be no real Police and Community Relations program until it is led by professional police, who have been released from under the thumb of corrupt political tyranny. The hometown police department must be supported by interested citizens' groups.

Unhealthy political control is law enforcement's most serious problem and greatest handicap today.

A lack of citizen support will defeat any program, and to those of you who are not members of the police family, may we say, "We recognize that it is easy to be part of a popular movement, but do you have the courage to support your police in the enforcement of the gambling and traffic laws, and set up a really meaningful Police and Community Relations Program?"

Yes, it is a strange society indeed that will rise up in righteous indignation of youthful criminality, vandalism and other types of criminal acts, and yet, deliberately set out to develop a generation of law violators with total disrespect for law and order — a generation that daily sees and experiences a hometown community where the fraternal groups and churches openly operate the biggest gambling establishments in town, with no fear of the law.

It's a strange society in which the police are expected to enforce school crossing regulations, jaywalking, parking notices, vandalism, petty larcencies, worthless checks, anti-noise and barking dog ordinances, and yet, the same police are not permitted to enforce the gambling laws.

A society where if a local Chief has the courage to attempt to enforce the gambling laws, he is subjected to ridicule by press, public, the official family, and runs the very real threat of losing his job ... and he must look the other way.

Can we afford the luxury of paving the road for organized crime?

Yes, it is a strange society where traffic law observance is considered a "Sporting Proposition" ... a game where the members of the community try to outsmart the police; where the drunk driver appears in court with the best lawyer, before his friend, the judge; where the policeman is put on trial, supported only by the weakest lawyer in town . . . the city prosecutor, who is a kid starting out or a broken-down has-been; convictions are few and far between, although the cases are iron-clad.

Yes, it is a strange society, where the news media continually downgrade police through public ridicule; where false charges of "police brutality" are levelled to serve selfish interests; where such television shows as PERRY MASON, THE FUGITIVE, CAR 54 — WHERE ARE YOU?, BRANDED, etc., ridicule the police, and where justice is proven false every week.

A society where police are relegated to second-class citizenship, under-paid, under-equipped, low man on the city budget totem pole. The same police are expected to possess expert legal minds and to be qualified social scientists.

A society where the political climate results in the "fix" for persons of stature in the community, but we fill the jails with poor folks.

Where the legislatures and city councils pass laws and ordinances which the police must enforce, and then, those same governing bodies demand a "double standard" of enforcement by the police.

A society where gambling is a way of life, and yet, it is the policeman who is guilty because he is forced to look the other way.

Where the policeman must daily watch the combination of organized crime leaders and politicians grow more powerful and corrupt.

Where court decisions which are overly protective to the criminal make it increasingly more difficult for the police to protect society.

Where we have established a governmental system, properly designed to protect society against executive tyranny, but where we now find society rapidly falling under the control of judicial tyranny, which has left the police family completely confused in its realization that today there is virtually no such thing as a technically legal arrest or search and seizure, and where the art of reasonable interrogation has been abolished.

A society where the court system was designed to try cases for the purposes of "determining the truth about a matter," but which has now deterioriated to a system which ignores truth and evidence, and merely engages in a long series of legal gymnastics for the purpose of guaranteeing that the criminal is set free and society remains unprotected.

Yes—it's a strange society we live in . . . and . . . while the police and community problems may appear to be insurmountable, I firmly believe that an all-out leadership effort by police in a community relations program can bring about a tremendous breakthrough, resulting in an all-out community effort by an aroused, interested citizenry, which, if enlightened, will readily see that their efforts are needed to prevent this great American society from slipping into the obscurity of history.

Police and Community —
Probing for Mutual Understanding

LAWRENCE W. PIERCE

Chairman, New York State Narcotic Addiction Control Commission

MAY 26, 1967

This past February, the President's Commission on Law Enforcement and Administration of Justice published its monumental report.

I am sure many of you are familiar with this document. It filled more than 300 pages, and it covered in depth and detail the problem of crime in America — those who commit it — those who are its victims — and what can be done to reduce it.

It was my privilege to have served as a consultant to that Commission.

One of the matters studied was relations between the police and the community, more specifically, the community of the urban poor. This means, almost inevitably, those parts of urban America where there are substantial concentrations of minority group people — Negroes, Puerto Ricans, Mexican-Americans and others.

The Commission's summary report states:

Despite the seriousness of the problem today, and the increasing challenge in the years ahead, the central conclusion of the Commission is that a significant reduction in crime is possible if seven objectives are vigorously pursued.

I call your particular attention to the third of these objectives, which reads as follows:

The objective is to eliminate injustices so that the system of criminal justice can *win* the respect and cooperation of *all* citizens.

And it continues:

Our society must give the police, the courts and correctional agencies, the resources and mandate to provide fair and dignified treatment for all.

The declaration goes still further:

. . . Fair treatment for *every* individual—fair in fact, and also *perceived* to be fair by those affected—is an essential element of justice, and a principal objective of the American criminal justice system.

We should consider with care the deliberate language of the Commission's statement. The American system of criminal justice is called upon to *win* the respect and cooperation of all citizens.

On the other hand, society must *give* the authorities the powers they need to carry out their assignments fairly and effectively. Although fair treatment is mandated for *every* individual, that person must perceive that the treatment accorded him is indeed fair.

These, then, are among the essentials in the American criminal justice system according to the National Crime Commission. And I share that view.

The point I make here is scarcely a new one. The effort to achieve good, sound, fair relations between the authorities and the communities they serve is one which has concerned those charged with regulating human behavior for many years.

In England, for example, the responsibility for policing communities was in the hands of private citizens as early as the 9th century, and a man was paid a few shillings for making an arrest.

Every man was responsible for his own actions and those of his neighbors as well. It was each citizen's duty to raise a "hue and cry" when a crime was committed, and to gather his neighbors and run the perpetrator down.

Obviously, this rather casual approach to law enforcement was fraught with great potential for corruption and injustice.

In France, the establishment of professional police organizations dates back to the 17th century. And the history of those times contains abundant reports of oppression and maltreatment by the authorities, who were far more responsible to the regime in power than to the people.

However, with the coming of the Industrial Revolution to England in the 1700's, when families began moving to factory towns to find jobs, police work took on the character of an organized, authoritative function of government.

It was to be expected that the colonies in America would inherit some of the problems which had troubled the people—and the police—in Europe.

As early as the mid and late 1600's, Boston, Philadelphia and York had established their equivalents of the British "rattlewatch" system.

These were modest forces of eight or ten men, patrolling the streets of the larger towns at night. They carried rattles to let the citizenry know they were being watched over—and to put potential offenders on notice.

The colonies' first uniformed policemen were appointed in the former Dutch colony of New Amsterdam—under an edict promulgated by the mayor. Their job was to maintain a watch in the city, from sunset to sunrise.

In 1844, the New York State legislature abolished the old "rattlewatch" system and created regular round-the-clock forces. Other state governments followed, and by the turn of the century, there were organized police dpartments in virtually all large American urban centers.

The history of growth in this country has been such as to have made law enforcement considerably more encompassing than merely shaking the rattle to let offenders know of a police presence. And clearly, the policeman's responsibility is a good deal broader than simply keeping the watch while the citizenry sleeps.

The National Crime Commission's Task Force on police puts it this way:

> It is when it attempts to solve problems that arise from a community's social and economic failures that policing is least effective, and most frustrating. For while charged with deterrence, the police can do little to prevent crime in the broader sense by removing its cause. On the whole, they must accept society as it is — a society in which parents fail to raise their children as law-abiding citizens, in which schools fail to educate them to assume adult roles, and in which the economy is not geared to provide them with jobs.

Nonetheless, the American people have entrusted the police with the tasks of preventing crime, keeping the peace, insuring the public safety, and arresting offenders, no matter how difficult these staggering assignments may be.

The citizen is no longer expected to gather his townsmen, when a crime is committed, to run the perpetrator down. But he's still called upon to raise an appropriate "hue and cry." And when the police respond to his call for assistance, he is expected to cooperate with them and to support their actions.

Yet clearly, increases in population, differences in population make-up, shifting centers of population, the greater mobility of the American people — all these, and more — have engendered strains and tensions between the police and the community. Yet the interdependence of one on the other remains constant.

Citizens cannot survive in a society without the climate of law and order which police provide. Nor can police survive in a climate in which their very presence and authority are challenged.

In seeking to resolve these problems, it may be of some help if we address ourselves to fundamentals, i.e., to the basic principles applicable to the police and their relationship to society.

What does society seek to achieve through the existence of a system which society created, which it maintains, and which it calls "law enforcement?"

Although self-evident, it seems to me appropriate to restate that society created mechanisms such as courts, prosecutors and law enforcement agencies in order to promote the existence of an orderly and peaceful climate in which the individual members of society could go about their business undisturbed, with the opportunity to function at their maximum potential in a manner consistent with the laws of the land.

Just as in the days of the "rattlewatch," society has designated a selected few of its members it calls "police," and has vested them with the power to do certain things to attain these goals.

Thus, police are given the power and the responsibility of protecting life and property, preventing crime, detecting and arresting offenders, preserving the public peace, and enforcing the law.

How highly society regards its police depends upon how effectively the police meet these responsibilities.

Thus, it should be emphasized that the first and foremost responsibility of any police agency is to perform well the job society has assigned to it in the first place, namely, to promote the existence of a climate or law and order.

Nevertheless, it must be noted that a police agency can be spectacularly effective in achieving this overall goal, and yet be guilty of creating monumental distrust, unrest and public disorder as a result of the *manner* in which it carries out its work.

For example, a small contingent of policemen can restore order by plowing into an unruly crowd with nightsticks swinging. This might well preserve public order at a particular location. Yet the riot and disorder which could result on a community-wide level, based on resentment of such action, suggest very clearly that the *manner* in which police do their work bears a direct relationship to the attainment of normal police goals.

As the Task Force report on police indicates, "poor police–community relations adversely affect the ability of the police to prevent crime and apprehend criminals."

It still further reports "no lasting improvement in law enforcement is likely in this country unless police–community relations are substantially improved."

I have suggested that the best way the authorities can perform their job is to carry out the basic role given to them, i.e., to provide a climate of law and order. I have also submitted that one cannot be oblivious to the fact that if police seek to attain this goal through unreasonable means, that is, in an unprofessional fashion, such methods can become dysfunctional.

Few would dispute that the effectiveness of the police has a direct relationship to the degree of their professionalism. Micheal J. Murphy, former police commissioner in the city of New York, often put it this way:

> It is just as easy to take a person into custody by saying "Won't you step this way, sir," as it is to handle him roughly and uncivilly. Either way he gets to the stationhouse.

But in the civil, courteous, dispassionate approach, not only does it speak well of the arresting officer — it speaks, perhaps even better, of the quality of his training and of the police agency he represents.

Even more important than the image such an officer presents to the community is the fact that his conduct, if professional, is less likely to leave a residue of bitterness and resentment. It is less likely to engender widespread hostility.

The police Task Force report to which I have referred declares that most police departments are keenly aware of serious community relations problems. The report, at the same time, bemoans the fact that most departments have been slow to do anything about the dilemma. A 1964 survey found, for example, that only 46 of 165 cities studied had extensive community relations programs. And of these, only 37 cities had a community relations unit within the department.

A 1966 Michigan State survey for the National Crime Commission showed that only 38 percent of the cities over 100,000 population had a community-relations unit.

In short, as the Task Force report indicates, most of the smaller departments still have no community-relations unit or program.

Sensitive to the difficulties between police and community, and seeking to meet responsibilities which are broader than conventional public roles, some police departments have sponsored police athletic leagues, for two or more decades. And in recent years, I've read where police in one New York City precinct invited a dozen or so Puerto Rican youngsters to visit the city and stay in the homes of policemen.

Are these proper roles for police in their efforts to promote good police–community relations?

As for the sponsorship of PAL's I'd say the answer is a definite "yes." It is important to develop in the minds of youngsters, as early as possible, that police are interested in them, and such interest can well be demonstrated in the sponsorship of athletic and recreational programs designed to develop young minds and bodies.

Ideally, such programs as PAL are best handled if operated by non-police personnel though under police sponsorship, although there is room for exceptions to this rule.

I do question the appropriateness of inviting youngsters into a policeman's home for a two weeks stay. It strikes me that, however admirable the motivation, this is not what is reasonably expected of police, and in any event it seems to be far afield from the basic responsibilities vested by society in a police agency.

One method by which many of these "friendly acts" might be accomplished is through the use of *precinct community councils.*

These are the groups of interested citizens from the local community who unite under police auspices to assist the police in many different ways in the local community.

As I've indicated, there are roles which are proper for police, and others which are not. For example, while it is not the proper role of policemen to produce variety shows, run summer job programs for teenagers, operate day camps, and the like, police can—and in some cities do—sponsor precinct community councils, whereby interested local citizens offer such programs under police auspices.

Some cities have sponsored such programs for the past 25 years. There are lessons to be learned from their experience.

For example, in the New York City Police Department in which I served, our experience indicated the following:

1. A precinct community council can not develop into an effective organization without involvement and support of the precinct commanding officer.

2. Nor can such a council program be effective for very long without the visible interest and support of the police chief or commissioner.

As the Task Force report indicates, if community relations units are to be successful, they must clearly have prestige and authority.

3. A carefully selected police officer should be assigned to work with the council.

4. Where possible, a liaison should be worked out with a lay organization such as NCCJ, and training programs for council members should be sponsored jointly by the police and NCCJ's division of police–community relations.

As the Task Force report indicates, without a central unit to plan overall programs, conduct training, represent the force with citywide citizen groups, and supervise precinct community relations efforts, the job will either not get done, or will lack the expertise, coordination and leadership which are needed.

5. The sponsoring police department should write the constitution and by-laws which govern council affairs, and the precinct commander should have the authority to approve all nominees for office in the council.

6. Fund-raising by council members should be permitted, but all such projects should receive prior approval by the precinct commander, and no police officer should be permitted to assist in ticket sales.

7. A name check should be made on each applicant for membership, not primarily for the purpose of excluding anyone but to avoid embarrassment of not knowing the background of members, in particular cases.

8. Although a liaison between various precinct councils is desirable, especially among councils in a particular community, a citywide structure is not necessarily desirable.

The Task Force report indicates: "Citywide advisory committees serve a different function. They bring together the police leadership and the city's civic leaders, so that the department can discuss with the community leaders citywide issues involving departmental practices or policies and allied problems." The report also goes on to say that such committees can also coordinate the activities of local precinct councils.

While I agree with the report with respect to the need for city-wide advisory committees, I do not agree with the observation that they should be used to coordinate the activities of local precinct councils.

There is a particular dimension to police–community relations which is broader than relationships with minority groups—about which I would like to comment. It pertains to the matter of relationships with the whole of society.

While minority groups present particular challenges to police agencies, the general population presents its own set of problems for police.

It has been stated many times that the police themselves are a minority group, often estranged from the general public. They are frequently misunderstood, criticized, excoriated, and pilloried.

I submit that this situation is aggravated by the public posture of law enforcement in response to recent Supreme Court decisions.

While it is certainly the right and responsibility of representatives of law enforcement to engage in critical comment with respect to laws and court decisions which affect their work, I submit that it is extremely important that such comment be both temperate and restrained.

To do otherwise is to set a poor example for others in the community, especially young people, who are constantly urged to be law-abiding and respectful of police and others in positions of authority.

To be specific, law enforcement cannot, on the one hand, verbally abuse the United States Supreme Court, while on the other hand calling for the public to support lawfully constituted authority.

It must be borne in mind that from the point of view of political science, a *court* has only so much power and authority as citizens choose to give it; a *prosecutor* has only so much power and authority as citizens choose to give him; and *police* have only so much power and authority as citizens choose to give them.

Society must weigh granting to the police whatever lawful authority they require in order to effectively do their job of providing a climate of law and order, against the liberties and rights which thereby must be limited or surrendered.

When society, through its elected or appointed officials, chooses to withhold or withdraw such authority, it must be assumed to be society's deliberate choice.

In conclusion, let me say that I believe important to the resolution of many of the problems of police–community relations is the reconceptualization of the role and function of police in a free society.

From this vantage point, one can judge with greater clarity of thought the efficacy of various proposals which are designed to improve relations with the public.

I am optimistic that we can resolve all of these problems which are our concern, because I know of no group of citizens who are more committed to serving the commonweal of the American people than those who represent progressive thinking in our police agencies today.

As the Task Force report indicates, and contrary to the belief of many policemen, the overwhelming majority of the public has a high opinion of the work of the police. A national survey conducted by the National Opinion Research Center for the National Crime Commission showed that 67 percent of those queried indicated that they felt the police were doing a good-to-excellent job in enforcing the law.

Section 5
Principles of Programming in Police and Community Relations

Convinced as they are that police–community relations programs are important today, most police executives are interested in the WHAT and the HOW of such programs. They are interested in practical ideas that *work*. They are interested in the experiences of other police agencies, with multiple and varied types of programs. If a given program seems to work, they are interested in knowing why it works; similarly, they are interested in knowing why, if a given program fails.

For the most part, police–community relations programming is still experimental, trial-and-error, and even willy-nilly in some instances. The criteria by which success is measured are nebulous, and sometimes largely "in the eye of the beholder." The evaluator often finds himself in the position of attempting to respond to questions akin to: "How much delinquency has this program prevented?"

There are, however, certain emerging, fairly clear-cut *principles* that apply to programming in the police and community relations field. As with all principles in social and behavioral science, cause-and-effect relationships cannot be indicated with absolute certitude or unanimity. But with due allowance, even for strong differences of opinion on some points, not unwelcome in any scholarly field, there are certain ideas which are rather widely recognized as having the force of program principles.

It is with some of these ideas that the essays in this section are concerned.

A Police Administrator Looks at Police–Community Relations

HOWARD R. LEARY

(Then) Deputy Commissioner, Philadelphia Police Department

MAY 28, 1959

Community Relations should function as a radar scope scanning the community and detecting the comments, criticisms, and feelings of the people.

This must be done with a sensitivity that records and reports this information in a way that the police administrator receives it untarnished and undistorted.

These truths are utilized as a barometer of necessary adjustment.

The police administrator must recognize the truisms of criticism of deplorable customs and practices of the past, when unbridled force and threats held sway. Such practices must today be replaced with suggestion and persuasion.

Our every word and deed must be aimed at molding public opinion. Every work spoken, every act performed must be planned in anticipation of the criticism of tomorrow.

The more complex our society, the closer we are together; the more important it is that we do and say the right thing. Our decisions must be based on what the public deserves and wants. It is not only to our advantage that the public be reliably informed, but it is our obligation and duty to see to it that they are.

The apparent apathy, indifference, hostility, and disfavor that we too often find within our public today is the result of our indifference of yesterday.

It is not enough that we say to the public that we do not practice the "third degree method," that we no longer advocate or condone duress, or intimidation, or violation of civil rights. We must be ready and willing to show positive proof that such practices are not only forbidden, but when indulged in, result in quick and certain exposure, and disciplined results.

> There is not a crime, not a dodge, not a trick, not a swindle, not a vice, which does not live by secrecy. Get these things out in the open, describe them, attack them, ridicule them in the press, and sooner or later public opinion will sweep them away.

These words of Joseph Pulitzer were spoken over three-quarters of a century ago, and there is no greater way to insure public security than public confidence.

Cannot Pulitzer's words serve us as the very beacon by which we guide ourselves in answering the demands for police leadership?

This is the key by which we can turn criticism into effective cooperation, and mistrust into confidence.

A "public be damned" attitude on the part of the police has its basis in two injustices: the first is actual wrongdoing by police; the second is an ignorance or a lack of appreciation of human feelings and dignity.

The degree of permissiveness which creates and sustains such an attitude will be exactly what the leader of the organization, and every person from the very top to the lower levels allows it to be.

The determinant factor in the entire zone of the organization is the chief police administrator himself; for the organization reflects, with an amazing degree of fidelity, the attitudes and leadership displayed by him.

It is true that injustices such as these are the causes for criticisms directed towards us, and it is even more true that the only antidote for these poisonous substances in the police body is TRUTH.

Critics and criticism must be viewed by police as a much-needed warning device to signalize that the department may be suffering from a minor or serious illness.

Contained in the persons of the critics themselves, and in the criticisms to which they give voice, very often is the necessary element of truth which supplies us with the remedy to cure our lack of public consciousness.

Police–Community Relations must not, and dare not be hyphenated by today's progressive police administrator.

No longer is the police department *apart* from the community, but rather it is *a part of* the community.

The objectives of the police department are absolutely identical with the objectives of the community. Any effort on the part of the community which falls short of recognition of this fact is, essentially, a vital contributory factor in any deterioration of what we have chosen to call Police–Community Relations.

The quality of the police department's philosophies, objectives, services and performances offered any community, is ultimately governed by what that community demands, and supports.

Such support must be forthcoming from the individual, as well as from any militant group, not sporadically, but on a continuing basis, with the confidence of the community apparent at every bend of the road. It is not unusual to determine, after proper examination, that the failures or weaknesses of a police department are really the shortcomings of the community itself. In general, we find that the wrong answers to the following questions may provide the key to this situation. For example, might not the shortcomings of the community most likely occur in failing to supply an adequate budget or in its lack of intelligent support of a progressive program of recruitment, selection and training of its police personnel?

Is the political administration supporting its police department?

Is support forthcoming from the District Attorney? From the Courts? Are they in sympathy with the remedies for the community's problems?

This only shows that what, perhaps, might indicate — upon first glance — a breakdown in the police department is really a breakdown of the community's support of its own welfare. The community and the individuals who comprise it, alone, can supply the answer to these questions.

The distance that lies between what the people say they expect from their police department, and what they receive merits very close scrutiny. In line with this, I submit that you must ask yourselves this question:

What is your community's "GAP QUOTIENT?" — I repeat, "WHAT IS YOUR COMMUNITY'S GAP QUOTIENT?"

How wide is the gap separating the standards of police performance set by the public, and the actual police performance which the community is willing to tolerate?

Does the community attend mass meetings, and write burning letters to the editor, full of indignation on traffic injuries and fatalities, and then accept, without a murmur of protest, a system of ticket-fixing or haphazard traffic enforcement?

Does the community parade in righteous indignation on the evils of a particular taproom or roadhouse, but permit private clubs freedom from inspection and enforcement?

Does the community complain about inefficiency of patrolmen or of their lack of the "will-to-do"?

We must recognize that lack of community understanding and support of proper police policy and practice in areas such as this only widen the "gap quotient."

Now it has often been said that efficient law enforcement depends upon public support, and we can all agree on this. We must, however, say in all truthfulness, that the welfare of the community requires the support of its police department. We, as police administrators, dare not constantly point our finger toward others while closing our eyes to ourselves.

Why must we, as police, always keep pace with the turtle? Is this not the time to hasten our pace towards assuming the leadership which is ours by virtue of our position in the community? Can we not meet the standards and the ideals set for us by society?

Such things cannot be accomplished singly or independently, without uniting the community's agencies and gaining its militant support—and *all* of that is ours for the *earning.*

We must be ready to *stop* and *listen,* without suspicion, to the suggestions, and more important, to the criticisms of others.

The goodwill of the community must be our most important objective.

It matters not from whom the criticism may come—the first test is its validity. We should not be concerned with the motivation underlying a valid criticism—this is of little or no consequence.

Valid criticism should be solicited and welcomed—*yes, even made comfortable!*

This does not mean that we blindly accept, without proper evaluation, all criticism, but upon due objective examination, all criticism which is found to be valid must be admitted by us with proferred regret that such circumstances ever became a reality. Immediate steps must be taken to rectify the situation.

In this way we build up our defenses against *baseless* and *unwarranted* criticism.

The unwarranted criticism is far more difficult to cope with because of its very lack of substance, and too often we must deal with it in an atmosphere of misunderstanding.

I submit that this atmosphere of misunderstanding can well be eliminated by the department's proving to the public that it is ever-willing and eager to spotlight its own shortcomings.

This criticism should not be looked upon by us as undesirable and unnecessary. Without it we grow blind to our faults, unmindful of the needs of others, and calloused in our disregard of ordinary decency.

Defensive thinking and obstructionist tactics by us defeat our very reason for existence, and the first strong wind of public opinion will strip us of community support and understanding.

How does this work out in actual practice?

For the past two years at the Greenfield Center for Human Relations at the University of Pennsylvania, classes in human relations are taught for police.

Two types of classes are conducted: one composed of policemen who would be the first assigned to tension situations, and who would be confronted with the necessity of recognizing and adequately dealing with the problems inherent in such cases. The other is composed of selected personnel of varying ranks in the department—some of whom, having completed the course, and having demonstrated sufficient interest, insight and skill, with added training, would be capable of assuming an active part in any departmental educational program in intergroup relations.

The first group which started had a very high anti-democratic score on the adaptation of the Authoritarian Attitudes Tests, but showed a marked increase in the tendency toward democratic attitudes by the end of the term.

The second group started with less initial hostility and a lower anti-democratic score. Its final score showed an increase in democratic tendencies.

Some of the remarks made by all participants were:

"Our supervisors should sit in on these discussions."

"The course made me think about and analyze things I never did before."

"It gave me some doubts about ideas I always took for granted."

Role playing, problem stories, rumor clinics, case studies, etc., were a part of the course.

In addition, one of our Negro Inspectors is giving a course in Intergroup Relations to Police Captains and Inspectors of the department.

This type of training is presently in operation and, as planned, it will continue and expand until it reaches *every* man.

These two developments are comparatively recent — our story does not begin there —

Too much credit cannot be given to the helpful role played by the Philadelphia Fellowship Commission. If anyone could be called the friendly critic, counsellor, and guiding light — it is this organization, because they first brought to the attention of the Philadelphia police the need for developing a human relations squad for activating Police–Community Relations officers, and in addition, they formed a Committee on Community Tensions in which the police play a real part.

We also have in our city the Mayor's Commission on Human Relations, which is an agency of city government. They have aided and assisted us in our racial tension problems—not in the office at the time of crisis—but on the street in the midst of turmoil, or in the house when the windows were being broken.

We must better attune ourselves to our community's needs and desires and understand that the people we work for have the right to makes the rules by which we serve.

Daily we strive to be more progressive in the technical know-how, but we also must strive to be as progressive in our thinking and relationships as applied to humanity.

No longer may we remain defensive in our relations with the community; as police we must be as aggressive in creating good relations with the public as we are aggressive in our patrol and apprehension of criminal offenders.

Regularly our thoughts, techniques and practices should be exposed to the laboratory for tests — the laboratory of public opinion for inspection, examination, and recommendation. We must fervently follow the recommendations found from that laboratory analysis.

Police must more fully integrate themselves with the community, toward the end that there is a mutual responsiveness to the common good.

Let us think and perform in glass houses. The community will strenuously support what it sees.

There is no better way to mold public opinion than by saying "Do you have a better way?"

Public opinion, freely expressed, is one of the factors that balances governmental action and public welfare.

We must better prepare our policemen to perform their tasks in a far more complex society than that of even five years ago.

Every day there is less need and justification for the gun and the stick, and a greater need for knowing and understanding people.

These facts tell us that the professional law enforcement officer needs more training in Sociology, Psychology, and United States History, with emphasis on the Constitution and the Bill of Rights. These subjects are equally as important as Criminal Law, Evidence, Firearms instructions and the Motor Vehicle Code.

Equally significant is the crying need for a well-documented analysis of the needs of the individual community for police training in Intergroup Relations.

This is far too delicate and a too important facet of police operations to be approached with naive assumptions and foggy concepts. The Philadelphia Police Department, in concert with the Commission on Human Relations, has a committee on Police Community Relations Training to grapple with this problem.

At the present time, a highly qualified firm of consultants is conducting extensive research and study, with the objective of developing a course, specifically for the Philadelphia Police, in Intergroup Relations. In addition, they will train selected police personnel for the task of conducting this course for every member of the Department.

Summary

In closing, all police administrators, and every person engaged in police work or closely associated with it, must develop the means whereby the inspiration, philosophy and human understanding can be communicated to, and applied by, every police officer throughout the length and breadth of this country.
THIS IS OUR CHALLENGE!

Professional Development of Law Enforcement Personnel

BERNARD C. BRANNON

Professor of Police Science, University of Missouri
(Former Chief of Police, Kansas City, Missouri)

MAY 16, 1960

All of the talk about police law enforcement personnel becoming professional is useless chatter unless we know what is meant by the term "profession," and understand what it is we are seeking in our drive to become a profession practiced by truly professional men and women.

We must, then, first ask, "What is a profession?" Following this, we logically ask, "Why do the policemen of America aspire to a professional status?" I want to answer these questions truthfully and accurately, from my viewpoint of course, which is that of a police officer whose connection with some phase of law enforcement extends over a period longer than a quarter of a century. And I ask that you weigh my remarks in light of the fact that I have served as a patrolman in early youth with but a bare minimum of formal education, and conversely, I have served as a police officer after acquiring a college education, and later a degree from a graduate school. I say this because you are entitled to know the background from which I approach the subject of police professionalization.

It would also be well to add that I have served as a police officer on a department infested with partisan politics; a department where original employment was more often than not the result of an affirmative pat on the back of a ward leader, and promotion was gained by sheer favoritism of political and personal nature. In another era, blessed by an awakening of the citizenry to the deplorable and dangerous environment of a police department writhing under the unconscionable heel of partisan and evil political control, I have served as a police officer where political considerations were divorced from employment, and promotion came only through merit.

Therefore, I do not speak in the professional tone of idealism unaccompanied by practicality (which a few have suggested, perhaps because I once occupied the position of associate professor of police science and administration at one of our large universities); neither do I speak in the undertone of an old line police officer, spitting on progress and new ideas because he is afraid of change, and because he silently doubts his ability to compete.

A Look at the Professions of America

What is a Profession?

There are many definitions, all of which seek to include the many aspects of meaning of the term, but somehow fall a little short. This is to be expected, because minds differ on the subject. But if we would consider that a "profession" is more of a class concept of certain services which are performed for others only by those who are well educated and trained in particular techniques, we will basically comprehend the term.

A service which can be adequately performed only after the acquisition of knowledge, training, skill, techniques of a specialized nature, and which requires intellectual more than physical accomplishments, sounds of a profession. WEBSTER'S NEW INTERNATIONAL DICTIONARY puts it this way: "A profession is the occupation, if not purely commercial, mechanical, agricultural, or the like, to which one devotes oneself; a calling in which one professes to have acquired some special knowledge used by way either of instructing, guiding, or advising others, or of serving them in some art."

In FUNK AND WAGNALL'S NEW STANDARD DICTIONARY OF THE ENGLISH LANGUAGE, a profession is defined as "an occupation that properly involves a liberal education or its equivalent, and mental rather than manual labor; especially one of the three so-called learned professions. Hence any calling or occupation involving special mental and other attainments or special discipline, as editing, acting, engineering, authorship, etc."

The United States Employment Service, through its DICTIONARY OF OCCUPATIONAL TITLES, stated that the group of professional occupations "includes occupations that predominantly require a high degree of mental activity by the worker and are concerned with theoretical or practical aspects of complex fields of human endeavor. Such occupations require for the performance of the work, either extensive and comprehensive academic study, or experience of such scope and character as to provide an equivalent background, or a combination of such education and experience."

Reporting on the occupational groups of the nation, the United States Census Bureau employs this definition: "A professional worker is (1) one who performs advisory, administrative, or research work which is based upon the established principles of a profession or science, and which requires professional, scientific or technical training equivalent to that represented by graduation from a college or university of recognized standing, or (2) one who performs work which is based upon established facts, or principles, or methods, gained through academic study or through extensive practical experience, one or both."

Historically, the "three learned professions" were law, medicine, and theology, perhaps so named because they were taught in the universities. Since this early concept, many other vocations have acquired professional status, and still others (we hope our police law enforcement is one), are in the stages of being elevated to this high shelf of social recognition. Why are there more today, with the promise of even more tomorrow?

Influencing factors.

Obviously, the simplicity of our American society of early days did not require the specialty services of today. There were fewer people and their needs were less. There were also fewer facilities for turning out even the members of the "three learned professions."

Population change. It is sufficiently accurate to say that since the establishment of the first uniformed, civilian police in America, a little more than a century ago, the population of the world has more than doubled, while that of the continental United States has increased more than seven and a half times.

In 1800, every important European country, including Spain and Turkey, had more people than we. Thus, with the growing complexity of the social and economic order existing in the United States, we naturally have increasing need for services which can be rendered only by persons who are highly educated and trained in particular techniques.

It is worthwhile to dwell a moment on the change taking place in America and the vast growth of our country within the span of approximately a century. In doing so we can comprehend the overall professional evolution which has taken place, and better determine whether we deserve a contender's role for such status. When the first uniformed, civilian American police department came into being, there were approximately 26 cities in the United States with populations over 25,000 persons, one with more than 500,000 and only five with more than 100,000. A century later, 18 of our cities exceeded the half-million mark.

Again, in 1790 most of young America was entirely rural. Collective living was limited and needs were necessarily less. Then, slowly at first, came a gradual increase in urban living. It was the 1940 Census which established the acuteness of the trend away from the farm—a condition which has now become chronic. At that time, 60.4 percent of the population was urban. And the movement to the city has increased.

The progress of science, of medicine, of civilization as a whole has led to the switch of many "luxury" items into the category of necessities. Even in my lifetime, the automobile, which was once the exceptional mode of travel reserved for those in the higher income brackets, has become an item for all, even a necessity. It is understandable that new professions have therefore arisen, although the acceptance of many remains for the test of time.

In 1950, the United States Census listed the following professional occupational groups without attempting a current definition of a profession:

Accountants and auditors	Editors and reporters
Architects	Engineers, technical
Authors	Farm and home management
Chiropractors	advisers
Clergymen	Foresters and conservationists
College presidents and teachers	Lawyers and judges
Dentists	Librarians ·
Dietitians and nutritionists	Musicians and music teachers

Nurses, professional

Optometrists

Osteopaths

Pharmacists

Physicians and surgeons

Social workers, except religious workers

Teachers (below college level)

Veterinarians

The engineer listing included metallurgists and aeronautical, chemical, civil, electrical, industrial, mechanical, metallurgical and mining engineers. At that time in 1950, the total labor force in the United States was 59,642,990, which counted all persons in the labor force over the age of 14 years. The number of professional people in this working force was 3,813,770, including male and female. Our population was then listed at 150,697,361. So the percentage of professional workers was about 6.4 per cent of the total working force. The comparable per cent in 1850 was 1.8 per cent, and in 1900, 3.8 per cent.

That the professional man is on the rise is indicated by the fact that from 1850 to 1950, the working force as a whole increased about eightfold, while during the same period, the professional personnel increased almost twenty-sixfold. Some students of history view this as remarkable since the period covers a large part of the Industrial Revolution in the United States, a time when it might be expected that the greatest increase would have been among craftsmen and machine operators, but this industrial group increased only about ten times.

As a reflection of the changing times, the development of the professions varied greatly, rapid in such new professions as engineering and nursing, and slower in the older fields of law and medicine. With the atomic age upon us, the need for scientists in new fields has become urgent, urgent to the point of concern to the federal government, which has stepped in to encourage new blood for new professional undertakings.

And so the time is here for a new count of professional categories, and for the admission of new professions which have, or promise to attain, the qualifications necessary for admittance. Is our police law enforcement one of these? We shall hold an answer to this question until later. Right now, I would like to trace the evolution of the accepted professions, and point out some factors which influenced or retarded their development.

Turning away for a moment from the United States and to an earlier period in man's history, we learn that the original professions had their origin in the church, which might be expected in a society then dominated by ecclesiastical organization of nearly all matters. Later, in the Middle Ages, the professions more and more escaped the church, and through the organization of guilds became secular in outlook and organization.

The State. In one instance, however, the state appears responsible for the creation and growth of a profession—civil engineering—which came out of military engineering, involving the construction of military roads and engines of war. But on the whole, our professions seem to be the result of individual initiative, the dreams and plans and achievements of single individuals who sought new techniques and new accomplishments, who did the most under the free enterprise system. Yet, as time passed, the progress of nearly every profession impelled some relationship with the state, these to take various and different forms.

One relationship of the professions with the state is that of regulation or licensure of a profession, but we shall defer a discussion of this for the moment. Perhaps the biggest boost to the professions has been the relationship of government with the professions in the form of employer and employee. The state employs a large number of professional personnel, especially at war time, or in the periods of critical preparation for self-defense. Many of these are civilian employees; thousands are part of the military, such as doctors, dentists, engineers, and others. Through increasing the demands for professional services, the state has encouraged more and more individual entrance into professional fields and has helped to establish and enforce professional standards. The lawyer of today is not only a private practitioner, he has a career in government available to him, perhaps as a judge, prosecutor, a counselor, a referee, or even in the police law enforcement of the Federal Bureau of Investigation. Then there is the growth of the public schools, government controlled, where teachers may find employment, where, in fact, there is a plea for more and more teachers today. In higher education, the government at various levels has contributed to or built the buildings which house our state universities and colleges, where over half of our supply of specialist personnel are educated. There have been federal scholarships awarded, fellowships, and other financial aids and inducements to students who prepare for professional service.

Research is another method by which government exerts a strong beneficial influence on the growth of the professions. Billions of dollars have been granted for research into fields such as atomic energy, health problems, agriculture and the like. Research produces the findings of advancement upon which the professions feed and grow.

Licensure. Licensure is the process of the state giving authority to do certain acts. Following the Revolutionary War, laws were enacted in some states requiring physicians to obtain licenses to practice their profession. These were issued by medical societies or by state examination. But as time slipped away into the Civil War days, the idea of nonintervention by the state (laissez-faire philosophy) crept in. States gave up their attempts to regulate medicine, and some other professions, and professionalism in America slipped badly.

Soon after the Civil War, professional associations sprang up within the professions themselves, and the move was on for a return to state intervention and regulation. Protection against incompetent and unscrupulous practitioners was lacking without state licensure. Initial licensing acts in a state usually provided for licensing without question or examination for those who had practiced in the state prior to the enactment of the law. Thereafter, all who desired to practice a profession were required to be successful graduates of a professional school, or to pass a technical examination. There was much corruption in this era, with college diplomas being sold for a price which did not include study, which led to an abandonment of the diploma privilege and a dependence on the examination as a test of professional ability to practice.

Different from the license to carry on business, the professional license serves as a public declaration of the competency of the practitioner, and is issued for the welfare and safety of the public. The business license is more a means of taxation. Licenses issued to trades people usually attempt to insure integrity and serve as possible aids to police in regulatory matters, without a guarantee of technical ability.

Earmarks of a Profession.

It may prove helpful to summarize the essential features found in those occupations which have risen to the status of a profession, and this we shall proceed to do by selecting three "earmarks of a profession".

Special knowledge and skills. The first of the earmarks of a profession is the possession by the practitioner of special knowledge and skills which permit him to render the particular service identified with his profession. Usually this involves an extended period of specialized study and training, now largely provided by our colleges and universities, although formerly by means of apprenticeship or preceptorship (which we shall touch on later). During this preparatory stage, the individual acquires a body of knowledge, a group of skills and a professional attitude all of which become the technique of his particular professional service.

Manual dexterity is often an important part of the training, such as found in medicine (particularly surgery) and dentistry; but primarily associated with the professions is the concept of intellectual achievement and operations.

Objective is not pecuniary. Here we may have differences of opinion, but another really necessary earmark of a true profession is that financial reward is not the primary objective of rendering the service involved.

While the professional man may receive either fees or salary for his services, his primary objective is the rendition of service and the degree of skill attained in this performance. Perhaps I speak too idealistically when I maintain that the truly professional man is a dedicated individual, a devoted advocate of his art and one who does not sacrifice his integrity through the substitution of money-making for his finest efforts at service. Of course, many professional men are well-to-do, for the objective of earning a living in keeping with their status in life and expecting, where possible, renumeration commensurate with the service rendered is human and honorable. One incentive in our free land for the development of keen skills and talents is the ability to be compensated higher for greater achievement. But this does not mean the primary objective of the practice of a profession becomes commercial and essentially pecuniary.

Whereas in industry and commerce, the prime purpose is profit-making, an expected and helpful motive in our free-enterprise, capitalistic society, the American people frown upon this motive when adopted by the professional man. In this vein, we cannot but suspect that our professions need a little soul-searching to determine whether American professionalism has been adversely infected by the commercial spirit of the times.

I have been asked to distinguish the actor, the athlete and other occupational groups who lay claim to professional status, from the practitioner of the true profession. Of course, the concept is different; the word "professional" is used in another sense. But this earmark, the objectivity of performance being primarily not for personal gain, is the distinquishing characteristic. Lacking this earmark, the activity or occupation is not deserving of professional status regardless of whether the term "professional", such as professional actor, professional golfer, or professional ball player is attached to the highly skilled undertaking. Paradoxically, the athlete who becomes a "pro" announces that he is no longer performing merely for the sake of his sport and the love of doing it, but has moved into the money class, where his motive is pecuniary.

Associations. Another earmark of a profession is the association of members into organizations within their profession for the purpose of collectively regulating and improving the service they render. Acting together in these professional groups, the practitioner contributes his ideas and receives the thoughts of others. These associations also distinguish the qualified from the unqualified by admitting to membership only the individual who possesses the necessary professional qualities.

From these professional associations, such as the medical and bar associations, come standards of professional conduct, called codes of ethics, which members agree to abide by, and which are enforced by means often so drastic as expulsion from the profession.

Growth of Police Law Enforcement as a Profession

The history of our American system of uniformed, organized, civilian police seems to be rooted in England, where Sir Robert Peel, in 1829, successfully advocated the Metropolitan Police Act, a measure designed to bring some order among the people of that land who were in the economic throes of the Industrial Revolution. A few years later, the idea was adopted in America and first took hold in some of our larger eastern cities. The ensuing years saw it spread westward as the best means of enforcing law and preserving peace in the rapidly growing towns.

As a legal instrument of physical force and power in local government, the politicians coveted control of the police department of their community. The ward boss had much to say as to police jobs. He was allocated so many jobs and filled them from among his precinct workers and their friends, all a part of maintaining his voting strength and, hence, his personal niche in the political machine. It is reported that one large eastern city, in its embryo days of establishing its municipal police department, went through the ludicrous stage of allowing its ward bosses to dress their policemen in uniforms of their own design and color. They were uniformed, but not uniform policemen.

Of course, in these earlier days, very few governmental positions were independent of political influence; it was a natural result of our democratic processes of government. There were not the large number of specialists in government which we have today, and perhaps, the demand for special skills was decidedly less. However, as America grew in size and numbers, as our civilization became more complicated, professional people were called into government employment for services only they could perform. Gradually the people came to demand more of their governments than the sloppy efforts of untrained political jobholders.

This demand for professional type services by the public slowly made its impression within the law enforcement arm of government. Standards of employment for police officers were established and raised in many of our municipalities. Age limitations were applied; minimum educational requirements were established, and training courses for recruits were installed. The politician's grasp on police jobs was weakened by laws enacted to protect the police officer from political retaliation and control in the performance of impartial and honest police services. We are still in this phase of improvement, and there is much left to be done.

As the population grew and shifted to urban areas, crime increased along with the need for police regulatory activities. The advancement of transportation, the motor car, the airplane, and other means of getting around the country faster and easier, merged the population into a homologous exposure to all types of criminal abuse. Science, in contributing to the advancement of our American civilization, provided the lawless as well as the lawful with more efficient means of operating. The corollary of the more efficient effective criminal was the more efficient and effective police officer, who began to emerge as a specialist in his own right. A new profession was calling!

Men such as the late and distinguished August Vollmer introduced college to the cop. Other police educators followed in advocating higher education in police science and administration, and a number (far too small a number even today) of our institutions of higher education established police law enforcement curricula. We are pioneering this phase of police advancement at this time.

Qualifying Police Work as a Profession.

In light of what a profession means, do we qualify for such a status? Do we have the capacity to demand a true professional recognition? How do we tell: One basic measurement would be the three earmarks of a profession. Let's apply them to our police occupation.

Does police work require special knowledge and skills? I would first like to point out that the term "law enforcement" is not relegated in meaning to police work alone. Of course, it denotes other activities, those with placement in the judicial and even legislative branches of government. Police law enforcement is largely a part of the executive function of our democratic process. But the prosecuting officials and the courts are needed to complete the meaning of "law enforcement." I say this because even the legislative branch is now part of law enforcement, because it supplies the laws to be enforced and the permissible means for that enforcement. Further, in current times at least, legislative committees, almost like grand juries, have ferreted out unlawful activity by means of the power of subpoena, administration of oaths, and the right to examine the witness.

Police work, therefore, is a component and vital part of law enforcement, but does not include all aspects of it. In discussing whether police work requires special knowledge and skills in the professional sense, we have to define our work and separate it from its kindred occupations. In this way, we will be completely candid with ourselves, as well as accurate. For this reason I have repeatedly referred to *police* law enforcement, and not to the term law enforcement, alone, to indicate our activities.

It is said that there are approximately 40,000 police jurisdictions in the United States, represented by the Federal government, the states, the 3,000 counties and 20,000 townships. These include the FBI and various other federal agencies, state police, municipal police, sheriffs, and constables. In the late 1950's the total numerical strength of all full-time and part-time police in these many jurisdictions was estimated at 295,000.

The extent of the duties of these individuals varies according to the nature of their place of performance, with its population problems and environmental conditions, and the limitations imposed by law. Thus, the rural police officer and the urban officer may represent a wide divergence in the realm of police activities. Local police agencies range in size from one or two part-time employees to highly developed forces of thousands in New York City and other large metropolitan areas. We know that the ratio of police to population is generally higher in the larger cities and declines by graduated steps as we move to smaller areas. Thus, in the cities of more than 250,000 population, the average number of police per thousand in the latter 1950's was 2.4; while in places of less than 10,000 population the ratio was only 1.4. And I should add that of the total number of police employed in about 3,700 urban places, more than half were concentrated in less than 50 cities with populations exceeding 250,000.

Undoubtedly the degree of specialization in police departments of large cities with hundreds and thousands of officers is higher and greater than in smaller departments of less population. But does this change our concept of police work as a profession? Does the fact that a police force of one or two men performing all of the police duties, as compared to a highly specialized force where the individual officer is limited to specified duties, affect our right to professional standing, insofar as special knowledge and skills are concerned?

Obviously not. If anything, it demonstrates that, like other professions, policing can require general knowledge and skills in some instances, while requiring specialist training and study in others. It might indicate the need for diversified police studies, but it does not affect the basic knowledge needed by all police, whether federal, state, municipal, county or township officers.

Nearly all of the arts and sciences are called upon by the police officer as aids in helping him do his work successfully. Law, medicine, psychiatry, psychology, engineering, teaching and social sciences apply to law enforcement efforts of the police officer. Mathematics, chemistry, physics — simply look through the college and university courses of today to see how much of each the policeman borrows.

Because our calling is unique in its application of such a wide variety of the arts and sciences, it deserves its own classification; especially is this logical when we consider that within our field are areas of knowledge and skill not used in any others. It is not my purpose to go into the detailed list of subjects deserving attention as proper courses for police education and training. Suffice to say, without doubt or reservation, our police law enforcement fits fully and squarely the meaning of the earmark of a profession which requires special knowledge and skills.

Is the primary objective of police work to make money? This earmark of a profession is badly abused — but not by the police profession! Of course, everyone is concerned with making money. We have to be, if we would avoid the status of being charges of society. And certainly we continually push for higher compensation for police officers, largely because it is much, much too low. But essentially, and in full conformity with the meaning of this earmark of a profession, the police officer is or should be an individual dedicated to the rendition of a service to the public. This is truly our primary purpose, for which our very lives are often risked. We ask adequate compensation for the rendition of this service, but we do not substitute it for the primary object of our endeavors.

Associations. We have said that the third earmark of a profession is the association of its members into organizations whereby collective action may be taken in regulatory matters and toward the improvement of the service rendered. And from these associations arise standards of admission to practice the profession, together with the creation and enforcement of codes of ethics.

Here, probably more than any other place, we are deficient. Our deficiency lies in the fact, not that we lack associations of various kinds, such as the International Association of Chiefs of Police, state police associations, county associations and the like, but in the strength and control of the organizations. Used largely as forums for the exchange of ideas and advancement of police knowledge and skills, membership is not mandatory, nor is there any control over those who are members. An officer may be ejected from such associations, I suppose, but it does not affect his right to hold down law enforcement jobs.

Codes of ethics have been advanced by various police groups, and all are very good, and pointed at the self-curtailment of unprofessional police conduct. But there are no enforcement means available. If there is an American code of ethics for policemen, it is to be found in the laws of the various states, and in the city ordinances; yet they are not what we mean by collective and professional rules of individual conduct.

As a government employee, the police officer has limitations placed upon his formation of associations which possess real power; and the fact that a police department is entirely a part of government and the only place where the police-man can practice his profession must be considered.

The lawyer, doctor, engineer, accountant and others can practice their pro-fessions privately, on their own, so to speak, and they may also serve private or governmental employers on a salaried basis with accompanying supervision. Even if the police officer has no choice in the matter of private practice, being required to render a professional service entirely within the field of government is not necessarily a handicap — not, that is, unless the restraint against individual initia-tion of progress within the profession is the result. Stifling of individuality through excessive supervisory mechanisms can affect the speed with which a true professional status is attained.

Police law enforcement qualifies. I believe our police law enforcement work fully qualifies as a true professional undertaking, and deserves this status in American society. We meet the tests of a profession insofar as our kind of service is concerned, but — and we must be honest about this — do we as indi-viduals meet the tests of professional people qualified to practice the policing profession?

In other words, the body of knowledge and skills employed in police work is deserving of professional characterization and status, but are we as practitioners of the profession equally qualified to be accepted as professional men and women? I pose this question because it may be the crux of our problem. We have done well in a short time; we are advancing our service and ourselves, as best we can, under present restrictions. These limitations include the lack of sufficient forums for in-service and preservice police education and training; working conditions which are often discouraging to newcomers as well as to veteran personnel, and the absence of a basic, concrete plan for professional guidance and advancement on a national plane.

Yet these obstacles will be overcome. The passage of time is needed to achieve most worthwhile objectives, but time well marked by hard, intelligent effort and organized planning. But you might well ask, what can we do now — today? The development of a professional attitude by the individual police officer is a current project we should assume.

Acquiring the Professional Attitude in Policing

The word "attitude" may be defined as a feeling or mood. A proper attitude toward life itself and those many things which make up life is the key to happi-ness and attainment. Among the various attitudes we, as policemen, should find worth developing is the correct one toward our daily activity, our police work. Police executive or patrolman on the street, there is a proper attitude for each, one which helps not only the individual but the whole profession. Here are a few factors which help us to gain that proper attitude toward true professionalization.

Know what a profession is. There is or ought to be, according to our tenets of a true profession, a difference between purely commercial occupations and professional undertakings. The essential difference might well be said to be the *attitude* of the worker. If you do not grasp the meaning of a profession (which I have taken some time to discuss), and grasp the importance of acquiring the *feeling* of a professional man or woman, you cannot hope personally to attain a professional status.

Study the growth of other professions. It will do us good to study the hard climb of other professions, to see what they went through to reach their present status and degree of refinement. Here we discover a pattern of rise and progress, one which the police profession will probably have to copy in its push upward. Look back many years in America's growth, to the colonial period. We see that during this period, nine colleges were founded, but in all of these except one in Philadelphia, the religious purpose was dominant. Turning out ministers was the main purpose. When did the turn to other professional training come? The first break was toward medicine, when in 1765 medicine, in addition to theology, was taught at the College, Academy, and Charitable School of Philadelphia (now the University of Pennsylvania); at King's College (now Columbia University) in 1767; at Harvard University in 1782, and at Dartmouth College in 1798.

Why is this important to observe? Because it reveals how even the oldest professions struggled to take hold in America. It is said that there were approximately 300 physicians practicing in America at the close of the Revolutionary War, but only 51 had taken degrees in America, and less than 250 elsewhere. Were they practicing by ear? Perhaps so in many cases, but most had learned through apprenticeship.

During this colonial period and Revolutionary era, the profession of law attempted to enter the colleges, but little came of it. In other words, preparation for the practice of a profession in these very early pioneer days of American growth, other than the ministry, was largely through apprenticeship or preceptorship. The ambitious young man desiring to learn the profession sought out a practitioner in his chosen field, who became his preceptor, or teacher. He read what he could find, he watched, he assisted the preceptor in his practice; in this manner, he acquired such knowledge and skill as he could. With no established standards of professional attainment, he went out on his own to practice his profession when his conscience permitted or, perhaps, when his preceptor gave him the nod.

Is this not much the same as the situation facing us today? A policeman becomes a policeman through a kind of apprenticeship. In our larger departments, he is exposed to the offerings of a police academy or recruit school, but then he really learns his profession from an experienced officer, his preceptor.

It was not until the present century that the apprenticeship route for learning a profession was closed in the case of most true professions. This should indeed be revealing to us. Interest yourself in studying the history of other professions and you will appreciate the sacrifice, the effort ahead for us in establishing our new profession.

Know your police work. Comprehending the meaning and extent of a true profession, learn everything you can of your own profession. Study the police growth in America and elsewhere; learn every fiber of the police structure, the federal, state and local aspects of it; dwell upon the basic law creating your department, its internal organization, its rules and regulations, its policies and attitudes. You will then have a blueprint of the house in which you work, and steppingstone to a more confident attitude toward your profession.

Then, and of vast importance, work harder than ever to acquire the finest knowledge of the Constitutional provisions, the statutes, and the ordinances which you are called upon to enforce. This is the substantive law of your profession.

Avail yourself of every opportunity to acquire the techniques and skills of as many phases of police duty as you can. Learn not only what to do, but how to do it.

To accomplish these things, you will have to have help; not only all of the self-discipline and dedication you can muster, but such external help as you can muster. Since basic academic knowledge of a general nature, English, history, sciences and the like, make for a stronger background for speciality learning, if lacking in such studies, you should seek this necessary background. You will be pleasantly surprised at the avenues open for adult education when you look around for it. Extension courses from our universities and colleges reach into the farthest pockets of our land and are yours for the asking. A small investment of money and time in strengthening your basic education will pay surprisingly large dividends.

Personal conduct and demeanor. A man proud of his occupation respects it and shows his respect by his personal conduct, by what he says and does. Speak well of your police profession, and you will find your attitude undergoing a beneficial change. You can both create a professional attitude and demonstrate it by your individual words and deeds.

The value of words. Not only what you say, but how you say it is important. Perhaps it is much more important than we realize, for if there were a recognition of great value of effectively and properly using the English language, more attention would be given to acquiring some of its fundamentals. One businessman I know maintains that he can listen for five minutes to a prospective employee, and tell quite accurately the extent of the job applicant's education.

There is a great deal of truth in this. While some college graduates still "butcher" English with blissful unawareness, it is rare to find an average grade-making student with a college diploma who does. If this is a test of education, why do we allow ourselves to be so easily detected as uneducated? And it is inconsistent with our premise that professional people are educated men and women to openly profess and demonstrate our lack of it.

Simple grammar is not difficult. Learning the fundamentals of correct English is easy — making the use of them a habit is the difficult part. One of our officers dresses meticulously; he is a walking picture of a sharp, alert policeman. But when he accompanies his video assets with his audio — wow! Why he feels that the manner in which he speaks is less important than how he appears to the eye, I shall never know. A plural verb with a singular subject, an auxiliary verb with the past tense and other very common blunders are all skillfully committed by him.

Can we reconcile a lack of even high school level English with a professional man? I don't think it is a risk we have to take, and certainly it is one we can very easily do something about. Avoid profanity; it accomplishes nothing but a bad impression. Be respectful and courteous even when hard-pressed to the point of exploding. Josh Billings has said, "one of the greatest victories you can gain over a man is to beat him at politeness." Self-discipline is a mark of strength; it indicates a strong man, a trained man, one with hard-earned self-control. Few persons have it by nature; most must acquire it. The doctor, the lawyer, the teacher, the minister, all of the professional people who meet life with their services, have to acquire and work at retaining a professional attitude. So do you.

Community affairs. Take part in community affairs. Learn to speak before groups — you can, if you will try. The professional man is generally looked upon for participation in worthwhile endeavors of a civic or charitable nature, and, if you would assume that status, you must do your bit. Every police officer is a leader. You are looked upon in times of emergency for leadership and guidance, and almost daily your job calls for the exercise of leadership principles. Transfer this activity to off-the-job leadership needs of your community, and see what strides you make in building a reputation for yourself and in creating a favorable atmosphere for the public reception of police work as a high level activity — a profession.

Urge new courses of study. If your department does not have needed in-service courses for its officers who want to learn, and to learn more and more, work toward establishing them. Stir up interest through contact with your fellow officers. Make it a popular subject, one that the men want, and your commanding officers, your administrators and your governmental leaders will get the picture.

Share your interest. Keep your family informed of your work. You can do this without revealing confidential matters. If they know you are proud of the police service, they will rapidly share that pride; they will become effective advocates of the profession. Pride in one's work and enthusiasm are contagious — spread them.

Police associations. With a knowledge of the professions and how they grew and prospered, you will understand that associations within the police profession are necessary. Join such as you feel are worthy, then work to make them better. Exchange your ideas and accept those offered for what they are worth. It has been said that if you have a dollar and I have a dollar, and we swap; now you still have a dollar and I have a dollar, and we are no better off. But if you have an idea, and I have an idea, and we swap; now you have two ideas and I have two ideas, and that's the difference. A dollar does only so much; but an idea may serve you well the rest of your days.

The development of a code of ethics for all American police officers must be preceded by the *desire* to conduct ourselves according to personal ethics of equal strength, morality and value. When the day comes that the American police officer is bound by nationally advocated conduct and demeanor, you will probably have brought it on by making it your code today.

What professional status means to American policing. Now to go back to a question I propounded at the very outset of this discussion: Why do the policemen of America aspire to professional status? Perhaps all of them don't; perhaps most of them might say they aren't too concerned. But all of them would unhesitatingly say that they want the things that professionalization of their work would bring.

It is only that many do not understand the effect of attaining a truly professional status for their choice of service.

Professional status not only means a big boost in the police service to the public, and therefore the achievement of the primary purpose of our entire efforts; it means tremendous personal gain for the policeman. It means higher salaries, better hours, finer equipment and means of doing the job. It is the only means of proclaiming our work a special, highly trained service, deserving of compensation and treatment of equal dignity.

With all of the material benefits of a higher public opinion of policing, there comes something more valuable — a deep, personal gain; a feeling of accomplishment, of satisfaction, of knowing we are members of an honorable and distinguished calling. Impelled to open our minds to the golden reward of acquiring knowledge and more knowledge, we as professional men and women will store away insurance against a narrow and lonely existence in our later years. Charles Evans Hughes once said, "A man has to live with himself, and he should see to it that he always has good company."

Neither should you part with your ideals and hopes for the police profession if progress seems slow, if others do not share your zeal and efforts, for you know the work that lies ahead. I like Mark Twain's words, "Don't part with your illusions. When they are gone, you may still exist, but you have ceased to live." But our future climb to accepted professional status is not an illusion — it is a foregone fact, needing only our work and vision of today to make it a certainty tomorrow.

Planning for Tomorrow's Professional Status

I have just a few more thoughts, thoughts verified and reinforced by test and study in other professions, and which must apply to ours.

Need for an accrediting agency. If we close our eyes to the need for college and university treatment of our police profession, we need not worry about an accrediting agency. But no one does who focuses clearly on our need. We must have pre-service curricula for our profession, and in order to get them and to maintain them in an acceptable condition, we need an accrediting body to operate nationwide.

Perhaps the greatest stride made in other professions was the origin and growth of the practice of setting up standards for educational institutions and according recognition to those which conform to the standards. We call this accreditation, and it is now used in all forms of professional education.

The accrediting process in professional education came from various associations, councils, boards and committees connected with the professions. Perhaps one of the earliest was the Council on Medical Education of the American Medical Association, established in 1904. Then there came others. For law, the American Bar Association; for the pharmacist, the American Council on Pharmaceutical Education; for the dentist, the Council on Dental Education of the American Dental Association, and for the engineer, the Engineers' Council for Professional Development.

It is part and parcel of true professional growth, yet we have thus far ignored the need. In an address before the International Association of Chiefs of Police in 1954, I proposed such an idea, urging the formation of an Association of American Schools of Criminology. The plan was not only to regulate schools teaching law enforcement courses by establishing standards to be met for accreditation, but also to assist in establishing the curricula in those colleges and universities that had not yet gone into this field of professional education. I am still hopeful that my advocacy of the plan will take root somewhere. In any event, I am still plugging away at it.

A uniform law enforcement examination act. In a later address before the IACP, I advocated a Uniform Law Enforcement Examination Act, to be used in the various states on a purely voluntary basis. This obvious necessity in the path toward true professionalization of our work is but a revelation of what the history of other professional progress beams out. To make sure there was enough candlepower in the beam, and to back up my theory with practicality, I wrote and presented to the IACP the following year, which was in 1957, my idea of such an Act. I am still hopeful the light will penetrate and our police leaders will support it. The proposed legislation will be presented to the next session of my own state legislature.

Every profession of recognized status has linked itself with the state in its efforts to uplift standards and protect the public. There is no reason this cannot eventually be done by the police profession — certainly it will have to be done before we reach our goal.

Admiral Ben Morell proclaimed, "Morale is when your hands and feet keep on working when your head says it can't be done." My morale in the fight for police professionalization is high — not because my head says it can't be done, however; and I shall keep my hands and feet working . . . and my voice. . . . But let me conclude before I suffer the plight of the long-winded political speaker who shouted: "What I want is reform. I want tax reform. I want judicial reform. I want high price reform. I want — — —" and who was interrupted by a tired listener with, "What you want is chloroform!"

Why Human Relations Training for Police?

JOSEPH D. LOHMAN

(Then) Sheriff, Cook County, Chicago, Illinois

MAY 17, 1955

In discussing with you the matter of training police officials and law enforcement officials in the problems of human relations, I want to make, in the beginning, a clear-cut distinction between the emphasis which I have made and continue to make in this field, and what characterizes the general concern about the human relations approach to law enforcement in the country at large.

Let me say categorically that I do not believe it is the function of the police department to take on the task of the church or the school or the general concern of citizens of goodwill to promote fraternity and general respect on the part of one portion of the community for the other. I say this not because I am against that objective. I'm very much for it, and applaud such efforts on the part of human relations commissions, both private and public. But I do think it is important to make a distinction between what it is that is the specific task and responsibility of the law enforcement official in this area, and the more general problem of promoting better relations and goodwill within the community at large. I would not go so far as to suggest that I think police officers should refrain from promoting better attitudes, but insofar as they do this, I think they should do it, not as a charge upon them as police officers, but as citizens with a conscience and a sense of personal responsibility — such as may be the case with any other citizen of the community. My emphasis is upon developing a specific initiative, a specific competence, a specific responsibility, that corresponds to that which a police officer must have in conducting a criminal investigation.

In other words, to emphasize here what has already been emphasized in so many other places, the need for understanding, knowledge, insight beyond that of the general public with reference to this problem, and to equip the police with skills and techniques which make it possible for them to employ adequate and correct procedure in handling situations involving contacts between racial and national groups. This problem — for good or for bad — has come to rest in our time in a very special sense on the doorstep of the police department — not because the police have sought out the problem, nor because the police have, in any greater degree than any other section of the community, created the problem or aggravated it, but simply because the problem has become of such a nature in our time as to require, at some critical points, the maintenance of the peace of the community through the agency which is available to bring it about; namely, the police department. It is on that score, because incidents and problems have become chronic, North, South, East and West in the United States, that there is hardly a week which passes in the major metropolitan areas of the United States where a police department does not have occasion to take action with reference to a situation aggravated by racial tension or conflict.

Because of these chronic states of racial tension, it becomes incumbent upon police departments to prepare themselves to cope with this situation more effectively than has been the case in the past. My attention first was directed toward this field some ten years ago in a number of police departments with which I had been working, particularly in the field of juvenile delinquency and with reference to the general problem of how to relate the activities of the police departments to other agencies, which in turn might accept responsibilities which could not be discharged by the police departments. A number of police officials called to my attention a new, and to them vexing, problem. In most cases it was a question of finding an answer to such questions as: "How can we get rid of the problem? Why does it come to us? Why can't we give it to somebody else? Why in the world does it come to us at all? Why don't these people who are specialists in housing take care of the problem themselves? Why don't the people in recreation who report an incident on a playground take care of it themselves? Or why can't someone prevent these new groups which are 'on the make' from getting out of hand?" In any event, the general picture was one of the appearance of a problem which, to be sure, had existed in the past, but existed only in terms of an occasional incident, and which only came to the police as it escalated to such proportions as to require some ultimate action on the part of the police department. The time had arrived for us to do on this front what previously had been regarded as unnecessary — to prepare the policeman to deal effectively with a new condition and problem.

Now, in so doing, police departments will make a contribution to our democratic society and to that for which it stands. If a police officer is correct in his procedure, if he does in fact master his own feelings and sentiments, brings them under control in this area as he has occasion to bring them under control in removing himself from a partisan role in a dispute of any other kind, then in that fact alone he will have made a major contribution to the development of the democratic ideal. However, I do not find it necessary for the police officer to preach, I do not find it necessary for him to take on the function of the minister, or any of these other elements in the community.

I wish not to be misinterpreted. I am not arguing against a police officer as an individual citizen, fighting the good fight for a truly democratic society; every citizen of the community ought to have some sense of responsibility in this respect. But I challenge the idea that it is a special concern of *police officers* to gather people together to instruct them with reference to their obligations ethically. These are matters which I think are appropriately considered by other agencies and institutions, and by personnel trained to accept this as their primary responsibility.

I say all this because it has made a great deal of difference in the willingness to accept what I have had to say in police circles and outside of police circles. I want to say, here and now, that the training program that I have recommended in this area has been equally acceptable in the North and the South. It has been acceptable everywhere in the United States, for I have insisted that the point of departure with reference to training in this area is *the law,* and the law with reference to the particular community in which the officer finds himself. I may have a different view than some of you about what the State of Texas should write into its fundamental law concerning the relations between racial groups. I may quarrel with you with reference to the appropriateness of the law of Louisiana or of Michigan or Illinois or New York — as all of us are free to do as citizens of this country. We may think one state is right and another state is wrong, and we may as individuals, whether we are police officers or not, have differences of opinion on this score. But as a police officer, a man accepts the oath of office under a particular jurisdiction or authority, and it is incumbent upon him that he accept that law as his point of departure. So it is on that score that I suggest that we must have a formula for addressing the problem of critical tension and conflict in human relationships which is governed, for police officers, by the body of law under which those officers operate. This would hold true for an officer in the South, in the North, the East or the West.

To make myself more clear, if I may, I would add that every citizen, including a police officer, may work toward change in the laws of the commonwealth under which he functions or where he lives. And indeed, as a citizen of the society, he has a responosibility in this respect, but in discharging his duties and responsibilities as a police officer, he must take the law as it is written, else there would be anarchy. This applies equally to this area, as it applies to any other.

There are two concerns that I have about this problem, and I want to share them with you. First, I want to suggest the necessity — given the chronic condition of tension in race relations in this country — the necessity for the average police officer — not a special detail, but the *average* police officer — to have some understanding of what confronts him when he is confronted by racial tension and conflict. What is there about the population that he ought to know?

What are the conditions of the population that he ought to know? The purpose of this is to remove him, impartially if you please and in a sense of strict neutrality, from the conflict that rages between the contending parties. To do this will create a performance on the part of the officer which will be salutary in its effect upon the parties and upon the general situation.

Secondly, I want to indicate, on the basis of these insights and on the basis of techniques which have been employed in this area and in related areas, actions that should be avoided by policemen, so that in discharging their law enforcement responsibilities they do not further aggravate an already difficult situation. There are notable instances of racial disturbance in recent years where the really serious blunder stems from failure on the part of the law enforcement agency to step in early enough, to recognize and accept its responsibility when it did step in, and in some cases, from its actually going astray and becoming partisan under such conditions as to aggravate the situation beyond control.

These are matters that can be avoided if we will examine critically the role of the police. Furthermore, there are things that we can do which can minimize and prevent the conflicts from becoming a threat to the community and resulting in serious loss of life and property. There is in fact no legitimate excuse for any racial disturbances or, to put it another way, for any racial incident to take on such proportions, with the knowledge we possess, as to be a threat to life and property in these United States today. If this be true, you can see how important it is that we use this knowledge and insight. This, notwithstanding the fact that I do not call upon the police department to eliminate the cause of the discontent, or the ill feeling or the hostility which characterize the community where these incidents arise. In fact, by preventing them from becoming public disturbances, police departments are in a position to give us the time which is the *sine qua non* without which we cannot solve the problems that we need to solve. The civil disturbances which confront us could indeed so disrupt the society as to make us easy victims for the blandishments and/or the overt attack of our enemies from without. Race disturbances find their origin in situations involving an inadequacy of shelter, or inadequacy of education, or the prevalence of false myths and notions. We need the time to enlighten the population, and to minimize the conditions under which pent-up emotions and feeling are released. This is the only ultimate solution for all of these problems.

We witness the movement of the Negro in great numbers out of the rural South into a situation in the urban North where our population is mixed up in factories, elevated trains, residential districts and playgrounds in nearly every major city in the country. The explosive force which brought about the religious and racial wars of the 18th, 19th and early 20th centuries now has the potential for bringing about a revolution, particularly when that revolution can be fomented by the subversive force of ideological doctrine. Let me give you an instance of this.

In 1953, I was privileged to represent this country in Korea for the United Nations Command Repatriation group. We had the problem of the exchange of prisoners of war. There were twenty-three Americans whom the Communists said they did not want to return. One day in September of 1953, I was interviewing a Chinese Communist near Pusan who spoke good English. He suddenly said to me contemptuously, "Tell me, you — you and your great democracy — how can you explain that racial riot that is taking place even now on the South Side of

Chicago — the Trumbull Park blacks!?" Now, I had gone to Korea before this riot broke out and I did not know about it. I learned about it for the first time from this Chinese Communist prisoner of war.

Let us not deceive ourselves; either we solve our human relations problems, or we shall perish. But a small incident which originally has no racial aspects, if it eventually crosses into such an affair without being checked at the outset, has the potential for mobilizing countless numbers of people. There has been no race conflict in the United States in a generation which could not have been checked at its inception, whether it was initiated by an automobile accident, or on an island in Detroit, or in a housing project in Chicago, or in a swimming pool in Washington. No matter how bigoted or ill informed or excited a gathering of people may be, if they are removed from one another the social consequence of riots need not develop. To understand this is to have at hand the means for bringing such problems under control. Such hysterical people must be removed from the scene to a court of law, where due process can calmly be effected. Such handling of incidents will warrant the confidence of all elements of the community.

There are many police authorities and members of the community who say that the public is not ready for the concepts already set forth by law. You've heard people say, "You can't legislate morals or feelings," that you can't, by law, get people to change what they have believed in for a hundred years or more. I want to say that those who talk this way are advocating a permissive tolerance of law violation; the acceptance of the notion that violence is inevitable when racial changes take place. They say, "If you bring Negro children into this school or park, blood will run in the streets!" I say that by creating the expectancy that it will happen, you encourage it to happen. If you say to people, "We have to wait on your change of mind," you give them the license to carry out what is in their minds, without fear of any consequences from the law. But when it is announced with authority and determination that this, like any other violation of the law, will not be tolerated, it does not take place. This is the lesson we should have learned.

The capacity of the public to act in new ways is much greater than is ordinarily assumed. We must decide in our own minds whether we will discharge our responsibility as law enforcement officers. We can. We are learning the facts, and we are receiving training, in this whole area today. More and more departments are training their men in the area of human relations.

The policeman must be recognized and regarded as symbolic beyond the individual man. He must be possessed of skills, training and information which make him act and feel, not like any other citizen of the community, but like a policeman, with police authority and responsibility. Not only must he have these qualities, he must be recognized by others as having them. He must have the confidence and known skill which make it possible for the rest of the community to say that what this man does is correct, and in the interests of the community. He must be professional. When we speak of professional people we usually think of lawyers, doctors, teachers, clergymen. In a sense these are different from other people. Professional people, through their training, have knowledge and skills in which the average person admits a deficiency and therefore employs professional people for their services. The professional person is presumed to have high ideals and to operate under a superior code of ethics. He is thought of as being impartial, unprejudiced, objective, unemotional.

The ideals of the police profession are based on the law. With the growth of large cities, the development of modern methods of production, transportation and communication, our laws and the problems of their enforcement have become vastly more complex. Police techniques and standards must be continuously revised to keep pace. New, specialized police details are being instituted, such as arson squads, narcotic units, juvenile detachments, traffic patrols, and the members of each such complement become experts in their fields. All policemen, specialist or not, and all levels of command are expected to know more and more about the vast array of specialized knowledge and technique that make up the totality of police work. They are compelled to become professionals in this sense.

Now, what does a police training program in this area consist of? It is not mere indoctrination. The properly trained officer must understand the effects and implications of his skills and techniques — this in order that he may be able to decide which skills and techniques to apply in a given case. This is the fundamental distinction between a professional person and just another technician. For example, a police officer does a different thing if he comes to the scene of an incident *before* people have gathered in what is called a condition of social contagion, than if he comes to a scene which already is inflamed.

Our knowledge today makes it possible to cast a profile of racial tension and conflict. For one thing, we know that every major racial disturbance takes place in the context of the maximum opportunity for the gathering of people. For example, disturbances in the United States most often take place on weekends, in the summer, and on holidays. We know this, though we are not sure why. Furthermore, it is possible for us to plot geographically, in any community, the places where tensions are likely to arise and the kinds of tensions to expect in such places. It is possible to know the places that are under change, and those that are threatened. By knowing these places, we can prevent a situation from becoming explosive, even with limited personnel.

We know, too, the significance of rumor. Students have studied its effects on a community. It is high time police departments learn that they are one of the important agencies for detecting rumors, since they cover the whole community. How many of you realize that a policeman who passes on a rumor himself is doing something almost suicidal? He gives others reason for passing it along, for in the minds of the public, if a rumor comes from a policeman, it comes from the highest authority. There was a situation in Washington when there was to have been a march on the White House, and rumors spread that a great demonstration was going to take place. A meeting of certain officers was called, and they were informed that there was not going to be any trouble, but that this meeting was simply to alert these individuals. That evening, the telephone company reported an unusual number of telephone calls: the wives of police officers were calling their friends, and telling them to stay away from such a place because something very bad was going to happen. The Chief called the officers back and said, "Look, you are policemen. This information is police information. Look how we have used it to create a problem for ourselves!" I might add that, in this case, an informed and intelligent Chief partially remedied what could otherwise have been a very serious incident.

What are the procedures by which a policeman can legally remove people from an area of potential tension to a court of law, where effective solutions can be sought? The answer to this is to know the law, and to study its applications. Not only local and state law, but federal law which is playing an increasing role in local affairs, as people more and more seek help of federal law where local law has proved inadequate to their needs. The U. S. Civil Code, the Civil Rights statutes designed to implement the 14th Amendment, are more and more in the courts as the basis for action. This is a good sign; it is an alternative to violence in the streets.

In summary, I believe it is possible to outline the terms and conditions of racial tension, its incidence and distribution, the way in which it presents itself to the community, and correspondingly, to outline appropriate techniques for dealing with the problem at its various stages of development. It is possible, therefore, to train the police officer so that he can act in ways that win the respect of the community, and thus bring under control a problem which threatens the peace of the community more than any other single one at the present time. There will be many more incidents involving residential tension and overt conflict. But I believe that it is even possible to experience economic duress and unemployment, and still not have racial tension. We have a long way to go before we can possibly satisfy the appetites of the millions of members of minority groups in this country who are becoming effective competitors for the services of our society, such as residence, swimming pools, playgrounds, theatres, schools and a better life in general. It is not likely, under the present exigencies of the situation, that we will produce the means of satisfying these needs as rapidly as the appetite will grow. This may very well prove to be the Achilles' heel of our democracy, except as we are prepared as law enforcement officers to keep the situation in hand, and give our society the time in which to solve these problems.

The Police and Community Conflict*

WILLIAM P. BROWN

Professor, School of Criminal Justice, State University of New York, Albany

MAY 23, 1962

This paper is concerned with the police task arising from those emergency community situations involving overt conflict between groups within a community. In our society, at this time, such conflicts are most frequently seen or anticipated in the area of Negro–white relationships.

It does seem important, though, that before we go into a discussion of these problems and possible solutions, we consider some of the basic premises upon which our plans for action must be structured. Any prescription for police action in regard to community disorder must be based upon the balancing and the ordering of a series of value judgments. These deal with the police relationship

* Reprinted with permission from THE POLICE CHIEF, May–June, 1964, pp. 51–59. Published by the International Association of Chiefs of Police, Washington, D.C.

to the law, to the people we serve considerd both as communities and as individuals, and to the process of social conflict within our communities. The complex of action called forth by disorder within the community can only approach consistency and propriety when it is frequently checked back against these fine balancings of value judgments which constitute our basic premises.

In addition to serving as a beacon towards clearer thinking, our stated premises help to ease the understanding of police action by the representatives of those other disciplines which have so much to offer in dealing with critical social issues. We need the insights to our problems that can be supplied by the sociologists, the psychologists, the cultural anthropologists. Unfortunately, in working with us, they face a major problem of seeking police work in terms of the problem definitions and ideas with which they are familiar. To a visitor from another field of study, our premises are more intelligible than our tactics. Premises stand and may be judged by themselves. Tactics always leave the suspicion that they have been adopted on the basis of unstated facts or beliefs unknown to any but· the experienced practitioner.

1. *Equal service to all.* The first and most important of our premises is one we have heard so often that each of us must consciously rescue it from that limbolike state of the things that are so familiar that we say them or hear them without any longer giving thought to what they mean. Moral and constitutional law alike have affirmed it; no recognized student has even disputed it. Still, most police problems in intergroup relations spring from its violation or the belief or the accusation that it has been violated. This premise, then, is that the police owe all persons in the community equal and effective service, including an equal interpretation of the law.

2. *Police enforce only the law.* The second premise is less familiar and deserves some explanation, for it deals with the police relationship to many of those emotionally charged issues about which group conflicts seem to arise. Conflict among groups is a natural and ordinarily most acceptable part of life — when it is carried out in a legal manner and one consistent with the beliefs of the community. As long as we have legality and acceptability, we get along very well with our differences of opinion. In business or social life, channeled conflict adds zest, pattern and motivation to our lives.

In a rapidly changing society such as ours, it is also natural — though it is usually most unacceptable to many of those involved — that some groups will change the rules of the conflict to give themselves more advantage. Thus — again looking specifically at our Negro–white interrelationship — minority group members have in recent years adopted the economic boycott, the sit-in and other similar tactics. Pro-segregationist forces, for their part, have devoted much ingenuity and effort to delaying tactics that have removed many of the immediate and sweetest fruits of the legal victories the anti-segregationists have won. Invariably, when either group resorts to the tactics which are available to it, there is a cry of "foul" from the other. Each side becomes excessively legalistic — or illegalistic, where its purpose is suited. Economic or political leverage is used whenever possible. The pro-segregationists, since they profess to represent the largest segment (the white 90 percent) of our society, use social or community pressure to enforce their demands. In turn, the minority group undergirds its position by constantly referring to its more clearly documented legal and moral position and to its support from the intellectual strata of our society.

The police problem is to view this complex and strongly emotional scene and to impose on these frequently conflicting demands an order which can be translated into professionally proper action. In particular, we must develop the ability to pick out the legal and professional determinants of our action from the pressures for action based on the unqualified acceptance of what is demanded by the leaders of either our community or of our intelligentsia. It should be stated that we recognize clearly our obligation to both of these groups. We are not anti-community or anti-intellectual. All we ask is that their demands be taken from the arena of partisanship and made legal and professional guidelines for our conduct. *We enforce the law, not truth or social custom or good intentions.*

3. *Disorder planning is based on a combination of conventional police mobilization tactics and an understanding of the community.* The violence in our communities stemming from the inability of some to adjust in a lawful manner to new situations can be considered as a malfunction of the process of community life. It is of great importance to the police. It must be thought about and plans for meeting it must be made. It is important to remember, however, that our plans for dealing with this malfunction must be understood as part of all the rest of the police–community relationship. They cannot be considered as something entirely apart, in which all of our previous understandings do not apply. If that were so, the police acting in the emergency would be in the position of a strange force rushed in to deal with a strange situation by the use of mysterious rituals rather than objectively determined methods. The plans we make for dealing with an emergency situation are based on composites of two sets of principles. We utilize first those rules which have been developed for assembling police strength and using it effectively in the time of any emergncy, and, secondly, the general rules that apply for all police–community relations work.

4. *Communication and interpretation are the basic processes of police–community relations work.* Good community relations work is based upon communication and interpretation. The police must strive to establish the possibility of communication with all persons who are interested in a lawfully ordered community. They must do all within their power to increase communication with groups having important police problems, or affecting important police problems, or affected by police problems. Then the police can learn from the community, and the police executive is given an opportunity to interpret police problems to the community. The tasks of interpretation of information available from the public, or of the police role in the community, merit far more attention than they have been given.

5. *The prevention of intergroup violence is an important goal.* Disorder of the character that is involved when there is serious overt conflict between groups within the community is a scarring process making criminals out of many ordinarily legal persons and leaving bitter memories which are difficult to heal or overcome. It helps no one unless it is by way of lancing a festering situation which has developed to a point where it is not amenable to self-help. In such a case, it is equivalent to major surgery and harms most of those involved as participants. The police owe the community protection from violence regardless of the cost. When violent men rise, they must be crushed with all necessary and proper force. However, to the extent that the community can be saved by preventing violence without sacrificing legality, ethical position, or the proper police function, this benefit should be earnestly sought. In community situations of the

type under discussion, a good statement or a wise police executive action can be worth a platoon of men in accomplishing the police tasks. At the same time, it spares the community the scars which make future progress toward community amity so difficult.

6. *A major disorder is the culmination of a building-up process.* Major disorder usually is the culmination of an observable building-up process brought on by some strong precipitating factor. Where this developing process is under way, the police executive is seriously at fault if he does not make an earnest attempt to observe and understand it. He is doomed to ineffectiveness if his interpretation is not reasonably correct.

7. *There is a serious and complex area of police–community relations work.* If the preceding premises have validity, it follows then that there is an area for police work in the community at a considerably more sophisticated level than "making people like us." We must develop sensitivity to conditions which are the indications of potential lawlessness or conflict in our jurisdictions. We must be prepared to point out these signs and to help our authorities and our publics to do something about them. Particularly important, we must keep this broad view of our community in mind in our administration of our departments so that police actions do not in themselves constitute an unnecessary irritant in the development of a community problem.

It is against these basic premises that I should like to discuss the emergency community situations involved with the outbursts of violence, and with the techniques of nonviolence. I should also like to spend some time in developing the very important themes of disorder prevention, and the preparation for these emergencies insofar as a police agency is concerned.

The Situations Involving Violence

The pattern of group interracial violence has changed very little in recent years.[1] At least since the first World War, disorders have generally occurred because of Negro restlessness under constraint, or because of white fears of the Negro "getting out of his place." The most common form has been that taken by groups of whites reacting with violence to force the Negroes to retain a subordinate position. It has been alleged that the most serious incidents of interracial violence have occurred where members of the white community have felt that the law enforcement services would not interfere with their efforts to impose their wishes on the members of the minority.[2]

One type of violence not frequently encountered in former days was that noted in New York City's Harlem riots of 1943. In that riot, the members of the minority group were numerous and sufficiently uninhibited so that they engaged in a violent foray against the restrictions they felt imposed on them by their situation. This fury was directed mainly against local business and the police.

Violence against the police appears to be on the increase. Incidents of angry attacks by groups of five to fifty members of a minority segment of a community upon law enforcement officers arresting a member of a minority group have been

[1] Grimshaw, Allen D., *Urban Racial Violence in the United States: Changing Ecological Considerations* in THE AMERICAN JOURNAL OF SOCIOLOGY, September 1960, 66:2:109–119.

[2] See Curry, J. E. and Glen D. King, RACE TENSIONS AND THE POLICE, Charles C Thomas, Springfield, Ill., 1962, pp. 105–108.

observed with reasonable frequency. The growth in this type of disorder seems to have coincided with a general increase in the number of assaults by groups from the majority or white segments of the community upon law enforcement officers carrying out some unpopular mandate.[3] It should be noted, however, that there appear to be no recent reported incidents involving large segments or responsible groups in the minority communities. The situation seems to be that the absolute size of these communities has increased to such degree that even a small percentage of the minority population can create something resembling a mob situation.

Action with regard to interracial violence must stress speed and adequacy of the police forces responding to handle the situation. Generally, the removal of the inciting factor by, for example, bringing an arrested member of a minority group away from the scene to a station house or to a hospital, should be given high priority. It becomes extremely important that the police not aggravate the situation by being unnecessarily jittery or by prejudicial or rough handling of the persons involved. Where the disorder becomes large-scale in proportion, the standard riot control prescriptions apply, and it becomes necessary to engage in such activity as breaking up of mobs, dispersing their members, arresting those inciting to riot, imposing cordons, "frozen areas" or other barriers between hostile groups, and possibly establishing necessary precautions against looting.

The detailed prescriptions for handling disorders of a very large scale can be found in any of those extremely comprehensive orders issued by many of the major departments throughout the country.[4] The one problem that I find with those monumental prescriptions is that they tend to give an impression that, merely by their adoption, the racial violence situation has been disposed of.

It should be made crystal clear that almost anything we say about what the police can do is based on the assumption that they can operate in reasonable freedom from improper political interference in their intergroup policing task, and that the political authorities have the willingness and the capacity to do their part in maintaining a climate of law. If the community has not done its part, a department may need plans for an all-out emergency. However, if the local government has fulfilled its obligations, it is almost inconceivable with the size and social structuring of the minority groups that exist today, that entire communities will become no-man's lands. It is almost equally inconceivable that great mobs of pro-segregationists will assemble and move against the minority quarters if they know the police will not tolerate them or allow them to build up such an illegal force.

It is quite conceivable, however, that groups of persons within a minority group will engage in violence when there is an arrest or some other strongly resented action against one of their members. It is also conceivable that gangs of hoodlums will make sallies into minority areas. If such incidents have occurred,

---

[3] Deputy Police Commissioner Walter Arm, New York City Police Department, noted that there were 223 group attacks against New York City Police in 1961. These attacks were not confined to minority or depressed areas. Speech before The National Conference of Christians and Jews Institute, *Violence Against the Police—Its Community Implications,* New York City, March 6, 1962.

[4] See also Curry, J. E. and Glen D. King, *op. cit.,* Chap. 17, *Police Tactics.*

as recent Chicago experience has demonstrated, minority group members can be expected to retaliate in kind.[5]

The point is that the type of violence which is likely today can usually be controlled by well-executed conventional procedures, rather than by resorting to an unfamiliar major disorder plan. Emphasis should be on the adoption of standard operating procedures and on the training to insure rapid assemblage of personnel and proper police action at the scene. Then, assuming that the community has done its part, it can be said that if the police know their communities, if they will give proper attention to good information-gathering, adequate communication, speedy assemblage and proper handling; if, with their action directives, they combine a sound community relations program and adequate training, a major disorder is almost impossible.

Prior to 1955, the police concern with interracial disputes was primarily in connection with incidents involving violence. On December 1, 1955, a Negro woman refused to vacate her seat in a segregated bus in Montgomery, Alabama. She was jailed and a new era of strong minority protest action had been launched.

The Montgomery action was certainly the most widely publicized, but the economic boycott was also used by the Negro residents of the city of Orangeburg, South Carolina, in a school desegregation matter. A similar boycott developed in 1957 in connection with the Tuskegee, Alabama, gerrymander case. These incidents were only rather visible indications of a complex and extremely important change of mood and tactics on the part of the Southern Negro population.

Now it is quite obvious that boycotts, "sit-ins" and other protest actions have been taken before. What was new here was the pattern and the times. The World War II changes in our society, the emergence of the non-white world populations to a new dignity and power, the Supreme Court removal during these years of one after another of the legal supports of the practice of segregation — all these and many other factors entered into the creation of what appears to have been a restless and tension-dominated interracial situation in which something was due to happen.

On February 1, 1960, four Negro college students in Greensboro, North Carolina, staged what they described as an impromptu "sit-in" because they had been refused lunch counter service at a Woolworth store. That action opened a floodgate and since that date, "sit-ins," "kneel-ins" and a hundred other varieties of pressure have been engaged in by members of the Southern Negro community and sympathizers with their cause. Invariably, the demonstrations have been characterized by a serious attempt on the part of the participants to avoid violence and in most cases by the assumption of the demonstrators that their action was based on the highest moral principles, including love of their opponents. This attitude of moral superiority has been at once a source of great reinforcement to the demonstrators and of great annoyance to those opposed to them. The related practice of civil disobedience, that is, a deliberate, public violation of a law believed to be seriously unjust with a full anticipation of being arrested, has also been extensively used. It has been claimed, however, that only those laws regarded by competent legal observers as obviously unconstitutional — in particular those enforcing segregation — have been violated by the protest

---

[5] Chicago Urban League, *Reported Incidents of Racial Violence* in Chicago, 1956 and 1957, November 1958, Mimeographed, p. 11.

organizations.[6] A situation where the demonstrators challenge, on reasonably solid grounds, the constitutionality of a law has many more different legal implications for the police than the situation where — as with the pacifist demonstrations — the demonstrators challenge the morality rather than the legality of a law.

These non-violent techniques will be continued because they have been successful. Undoubtedly these incidents will increase in number and in the numbers of those involved. They pose special problems for the police. In addition to whatver is actually involved by way of illegality or interference with the normal peace and order of the community, there is often a pronounced objection by the "best" people in the community. Also, although there is seldom, if ever, a danger of actual violence by the demonstrators, there is frequently a very serious danger of violence from less restrained members of the white community. This has been a particular problem where the police have not made it clear that they will use all necessary force to protect all persons involved. When those who oppose the demonstrators feel that the police will countenance their "putting the agitators in their place," it can be anticipated that violence will result.

Generally speaking, the accounts of police action in the incidents involving the nonviolent demonstrations have been reasonably commendatory of the police tactics involved. In fact, the Southern police appear to have gained greatly in prestige and recognition as a result of their handling of these incidents. There have been some notable exceptions, and where they have occurred the police prestige and the community welfare appear to have suffered greatly.[7] The police pattern that seems to have been most widely acclaimed is one of strict enforcement with all parties being equally treated under the law. Attempts at violence must be effectively discouraged.

We should stress here the importance of making a sincere effort to establish courteous, honest communication with the leaders of the demonstrators, and with the leaders of any organization prone to action against the demonstrators — before the demonstrations take place. The mistake should not be made of believing that the protest leaders will necessarily be the established representatives of the minority groups in the community. Ordinarily they will be students or representatives of protest organizations.

The plans for any demonstration should be requested and ordinarily will be fully given. Official policy and the pertinent laws should be explained carefully, and care should be exercised that no unusual policy or interpretation of the law is adopted. *The rule of thumb should be that no law will be invoked against a member of a group representing a majority in the community, if he were embarked on any project of his choosing.*[8]

The demonstrators should be given every possible physical protection from the moment of their arrival in the jurisdiction until their departure. If arrests are to be made, they should be made legally, quickly, and with particular atten-

---

[6] Response by members of a panel representing the Commission on Racial Equality, the National Association for the Advancement of Colored People, and the Student Non-Violent Coordinating Committee at the New York University Conference, *The Challenge of Desegregation for the American Police Executive,* New York, February 5, 1962.

[7] Anti-Defamation League of B'nai B'rith, *The High Cost of Conflict,* New York, 1961 44 pp., *passim.*

[8] Introduction, *Statement of Recommended Police Policy* adopted by participants in previously cited (footnote 6) conference. The entire statement is attached as an Appendix to this paper.

tion that no unnecessary force or commentary by the police is allowed. There is no need for the police officer to debate the issues of segregation versus desegregation with a person who is being arrested for a violation of a valid and well-understood ordinance. Just as with the issuance of a traffic summons, the idea is to do the job without imposing any additional element into the situation other than that of violation, violator, correct enforcement and correction of the condition.

The record is always important, and it may be desirable to have police photographers in uniform to film any arrests or any provocative or "staged" action by the demonstrators, their sympathizers or their opponents. Accredited newsmen should be given reasonable cooperation and full and careful reports of police policy and action. Any complaints of improper police action should be accepted and thoroughly investigated.

Before the Crisis

Obviously, our preparations must begin well before the time of violence, or even of the brittle tension which appears when disorder may break out at any moment. Long before the problem becomes acute, the police executive should be assessing the possibilities for outbreaks of violence or for nonviolent demonstrations, making the plans that are indicated and concerning himself with the prevention activities that might prove profitable to his department and his community. He will be involved with the creation and development of a sound community relations program, the necessary planning for emergencies, the adoption and carrying out of a relatively few important administrative policies, and the development of a sound training program. We should touch briefly on each of these points, because a limited number of these precautions are vital to our preparation for these emergency community situations.

The Fire Watch

Let's speak first about the problem of maintaining the "fire watch," that is, the vigil against the possibilities of violence erupting in your town. Invariably, there is ample warning of potential interracial violence long before any large-scale incident occurs. Possibly before we say "ample warning," we should add a special note of caution to those governmental officials and local powers who believe that the events occurring elsewhere are strictly the work of outside agitators and are impossible in their city where "a fine relationship has always existed between the races."

The signs of the approaching storm follow a definite pattern. Tension grows rapidly; responsible leaders on both sides realize that trouble is brewing; the police will find increasing minority hate directed towards them. Incidents between Negroes and whites or between Puerto Ricans and "continentals" are blown up out of all proportion. In short, there is plenty of warning before the pot boils over.

Nonviolent demonstrations, on the other hand, may be anticipated almost anywhere. Where legal or unofficial segregation practices are observed, they will be undertaken in an effort to force change. Elsewhere they are quite possible as moral reinforcement for other desegregationists, or in boycott actions against organizations which condone segregation in their Southern branches. Well-ordered communities, where violence is extremely unlikely to occur, may well be chosen for nonviolent demonstrations. An important consideration is, of course, that a nonviolent demonstration may be so unsettling to a community that the possibility of violent outbreak, particularly on a small and unplanned scale, is greatly increased.

Community Relations

At this point, it seems that a few comments on the police–community relations work may be indicated. I have had the experience of trying to establish such a program as a precinct commander, and also of trying to see that other precinct commanders established effective community relationships when I was in charge of a patrol division. I know the reality of such activity is often much more thorny than the rosy picture which we sometimes paint in our discussions. But I am convinced that there exists the possibility as well as the need for this work.

Possibly the first requisites to good community relations are the very obvious needs for good police work and a strong, clear and enforced policy of equal treatment for all members of the community. These are the fundamentals. They represent professional goals of high quality, and when they are achieved, it is much easier to get the community cooperation and understanding that must be added if good police work is to result in an effective job of policing.

Then there should be a reasonably clear understanding of what the department is trying to do in its work with the community. This work is not being done just to reduce complaints, or to develop youth programs, even though these may be very desirable results of our efforts. Basically, an effective community relations program involves the opening and maintenance of a series of channels through which communication can be maintained with all members of the community who are interested in its lawful development. Through these channels, the police can keep informed about conditions in the community which will affect the need for their services as well as indications of the citizen reaction to police problems, techniques, policies, emphases, etc.

It is, of course, a two-way channel. It allows the department to give information to the community as to police problems, crime prevention, safety, and about its needs and the job it is doing. Citizen support for needed legislative action can be marshalled. Increased cooperation in crime control is made more possible. We can get volunteer assistance for our civilian defense work or our school crossing guards. There is even an insurance factor included, for a department which has its community solidly behind it is not likely to be a target for unmerited attack by publicity seekers. The department estranged from the people it serves is a most inviting subject for an "exposé" whenever newspaper circulation needs boosting. The latter side of that particular coin, of course, explains many of the police problems with minority newspapers.

So much for our goals in community relations work. Perhaps, at this point, we should note in rather hurried fashion a few of the factors which are important in establishing such a relationship.

The department must reach all elements of the community who are concerned in this conflict picture. Usually the task is more difficult and more errors are made in establishing contacts with the minority group members. Frequently, calls for volunteer cooperation with the police go almost unanswered by members of these groups. Yet, particular effort must be taken to enlist their services. Generally, such people must be recruited on an almost individual basis, right at the locations where they are particularly needed. Often a serious mistake is made by designating an inexperienced, or publicity or status-seeking member of the minority as the civilian leader, and expecting him to establish an effective organization.

Liaison should be established not with people who like us, in particular, but rather with people who have the liking and respect of their minority associates. We want contact with the people who are the champions of the groups they represent, not our champions to them. We do not need self-seekers or persons of questionable background, and while we are grateful for the "police buff," we cannot afford the luxury of accepting his generously prejudiced view of our problems. Along these same lines, we must make a serious attempt to develop, at least, attitudes of respect for groups which we sometimes feel are unnecessarily hostile to the police. We should consider the possibility that their position may be based upon honest and, at least sometimes, accurate belief. In short, we must make very serious attempts to convince the members of the minority that not only do we do a good job, but that we are *their* police as well as the police of all other members of the community.

In this program, it is well to involve the working members of the local police units, rather than have the contacts handled exclusively by headquarters specialists. It is the local beat officer who is "the law" on his post, and the positive associations we are discussing here are most valuable to the department when he is part of them. It is also important to consider that these positive contacts increase his prestige, broaden his job and are valuable human relations training experiences to him.

Finally, it seems that such a relationship must be founded on a reasonable sophistication about the facts of life where intergroup relations are concerned. We must understand that there will always be individuals and groups in the minorities who will not treat us fairly, because the cry of prejudice has come to have political, economic or even psychological value to them. We will recognize that people do not adjust with perfection to a new, even a fair and new relationship overnight. We will understand that there is still much truth in that observation so often made that the police represent government and the established order to people who feel that they are severely ground under by that established order. Much of the resentment that is directed at the police is so directed because the police are more the visible and possible targets than are the vague concepts of government or social system.

Planning

Planning should include the establishing of procedures for rapidly assembling personnel at any situation, including those involving interracial incidents. Since rapid mobilization is required for any serious incident, it is better if such assembly orders are not given any label or connotation that specifically connects them with interracial problems.

The planning should also, of course, include more detailed outlines for dealing with incidents of disorder or with nonviolent demonstrations. Policies as to action should be carefully established and completely understood throughout the department. Detailed planning should include physical surveys of the areas of potential disorder. Records should be kept of locations particularly subject to attack or looting because of their content, e.g., stores in the minority area owned by whites.

Administration Policy

Administrative regulations are also important. It probably does not need re-emphasis here that a policy of equal treatment for all means very little if it is not strictly enforced by the administration. Departmental personnel should understand that complaints of improper action by police officers are to be carefully investigated, and it seems that good practice dictates the possibility of other answers to such complaints than either a whitewash or a crucifixion. The most recent report of the Philadelphia Police Advisory Board[9] shows the refreshing usage of such determinations as a directed apology, or the correction of a departmental policy to prevent a future incident. It is unfortunate that, in many departments, either the complainant is entirely wrong and the officer blameless, or the complaint is justified and charges must be prepared. Often such all-or-nothing conclusions are merited, but sometimes a less drastic finding would seem possible.

Public statements and actions by the chief and other departmental personnel should reflect a position of propriety. No unnecessary involvement in the background issues is necessary. I recall seeing a copy of a speech by the chief of one department in which he devoted a large part of a lengthy address to giving statistics showing the different rates of crime, venereal disease, and public assistance in the white and Negro segments of his community. He then went on to make the rather tired point "would you want your child playing with another child who had — — — times the possibility of having venereal disease, etc., as he did?" It would seem to me almost impossible that this official could establish a satisfactory relationship with the minority members of his community in those inevitable future times when such statements are going to appear somewhat less than wise. It is not up to the police to defend segregation or integration. The policeman's job is to defend the law and legality, and he should stick to that.

Such a policy by the executive is essential for its internal as well as its external implications. You cannot have the members of a department sincerely believing that their executives want unprejudiced policing when they have the example of biased public statements to prove that the request for equal rights is strictly window-dressing.

Equality of treatment implies also that there will be one standard of law enforcement in all areas within the community. Respectable members of a minority group do not appreciate the fact that minor criminals in their areas are sometimes treated like children, or are laughed at, when their violations are the type that run down the minority community, but do not seriously annoy the police or vocal complainants. It becomes particularly galling to them when, on the other hand, they feel that excessive police attention is given to other violations by their members. They sometimes allege the police make or fail to make arrests of their members to suit police convenience rather than the ends of justice.

Much the same argument applies with regard to standards of administrative control for personnel within the department. I believe that there cannot be equality of service unless all personnel within the department are subject to the same standards of administrative control. There are great dangers implicit in those classic tales about the minority group policeman who is "the law in his area,"

---

[9] Police Advisory Board of the City of Philadelphia, THIRD ANNUAL REPORT, 1962, 9 pp., mimeographed.

"can square anything," is "real tough on the members of his race and they never complain." The minority group officer should not be allowed to be the law unto himself. He should be a respected and supported bridge to his community, not a back door for removing administrative problems by methods that are largely extra-legal. A police administration that casts its minority group officers as back doors rather than as bridges almost forces them into being Uncle Toms, or politicians, or free lance opportunists making the most out of a privileged position. A temporary gain can sometimes be won by "back-door" personnel usage. A complaint can be "cooled" or an annoying local condition removed, but each such instance is another irritant in the police–community relationship — all the worse because it is temporarily buried.

Training

Training is a big subject, but there are a few guidelines which seem to have considerable importance in relation to the problem of preparing a department for emergency community situations:

1. "Human Relations" training and the basic precept of equal, effective and legal treatment for all should be woven throughout all training. Care should be taken that the value of these messages is not lost by those unauthorized, but always fascinating-to-recruit, discussions of "practical" police tactics which are based on entirely different premises. Even more important, the training messages will be reinforced or vitiated by administrative policy governing the practical operation of the department. Reward and discipline — the ancient carrot and stick — can make these pious sentiments either guiding precepts or objects of derision.

2. All personnel should be taught the facts about mob disorder and non-violent demonstrations. It is dangerous to have men expecting violence momentarily when — as with a pacifist demonstration — it is most unlikely to be occasioned. It is also dangerous when they do not realize from where, in a complicated situation, the violence is most likely to come. In those desegregation incidents where violence has occurred, it has not been initiated by the desegregationists.

3. Training in crowd control should not be patterned exclusively in terms of riot control. Particularly in dealing with nonviolent demonstrations, unnecessarily aggressive police tactics can inflame a relatively quiet situation and leave much to be answered for long after the incident has passed.

4. Training should emphasize fast response and proper action in the relatively few typical situations which are particularly likely to result in trouble.

5. There should be considerable training of first-line supervisor and of the supervisors and men working in small teams. Disorder situations tend to become extremely fluid, and direction is needed in many locations at the same time.

In Conclusion

Mob disorder in a city is much like an iceberg in a busy shipping lane. In a few minutes it can cause irreparable damage. Also like that iceberg, the highly visible and much discussed disorder represents only a small percentage of the total related police problem which must be faced. It is the police who must guard against this danger. Each day the task grows more difficult, the stakes become higher. Fortunately, it seems that the challenge can be met if we pay enough enlightened attention so that the potential for violence takes on a different aspect.

We must view cultural conflict as possessing, for the police of America, not an unmitigated potential for evil, but rather an unusual opportunity for community and professional growth.

Appendix

A STATEMENT OF RECOMMENDED POLICE POLICY RESULTING FROM THE NEW YORK UNIVERSITY GRADUATE SCHOOL OF PUBLIC ADMINISTRATION CONFERENCE ON: "THE CHALLENGE OF DESEGREGATION FOR THE AMERICAN POLICE EXECUTIVE"*

It is the obligation of the law enforcement officer lawfully to protect life and property, peace and order in his community. He should extend to all a consistent interpretation of the law and equal treatment and protection under the law. Every person acting in the community has an obligation to assist in this function and to shape his conduct so as to minimize unnecessary interference with the achievement of his obligation.

GUIDELINES FOR POLICE EXECUTIVE CONDUCT REGARDING DESEGREGATION PROBLEMS

1. In matters relating to desegregation the police executive should assert leadership towards, and accept responsibility for, a consistent and proper policy and its execution.

2. The police executive should attempt to maintain full and honest communication with leaders of organizations acting for or against segregation in his community. Complaints of improper police conduct from any group should be freely accepted and fully investigated.

3. Non-violent demonstrators should be expected to establish communication with law enforcement to determine what are the pertinent laws and administrative regulations and to clearly state their immediate anticipated course of action. They should follow agreements mutually made with the police and at least those police regulations which would be considered reasonable for any group engaging in a similar, though not desegregation-related activity.

4. Mass demonstrations have long been held as subject to reasonable police regulations. When there is a rejection of such regulation as would be considered proper for any other group using the same roadways, it should be recognized that there is an element of illegality not present in many desegregation tactics which may or may not be illegal on other grounds.

5. The public and public information media should be given the maximum possible information about desegregation-related events with particular emphasis on clarifying police policy and action.

6. Police personnel should be of high quality, well trained, adequately directed and supervised strictly to enable them to carry out actions consistent with the general provisions previously enumerated.

7. Police executives should — within the bounds of proper police conduct — cooperate with lawful and reputable agencies or institutions working to maintain or establish the peace of the community and should expect similar cooperation in return.

8. Unlawful force or violence by any person or group is seriously prejudicial to the welfare of the community and the professional reputation of its law enforcement agency. It should be clearly and unequivocally forbidden and, if it does arise, met with all proper force.

---

* Held in New York City, February 4–9, 1962, under a grant from the Robert Marshall Civil Liberties Trust. Dr. Brown developed and directed this Institute.

The Police Role in Community Relations

WILLIAM H. PARKER

(Then) Chief of Police, Los Angeles, California

MAY 19, 1955

Within a few hundred miles of this point, a group of scientists are devising what they call "an improved nuclear device." We do not know its range of total destruction or its date of completion. But this much we do know — its power is such that its designers live in dread and apprehension of the forces they have created. And across the seas, other scientists, using other languages, race to surpass our weapons. The power of total destruction may lie within our immediate future. Each second which passes brings man nearer the moment of awesome and irrevocable decision.

As this moment of supreme crisis draws near, we have gathered to discuss community affairs. And I think it is only right to ask whether our subject is rendered meaningless by the uncertain future; whether our preoccupation with simple day-to-day matters is really very important.

In answering this question, I believe we approach the true import of this Institute. The small problems, the seemingly petty issues we discuss today, are in reality neither small nor petty. Our subject is *not* overshadowed by the great international disputes and their deadly consequences. *Rather, the reverse is true.* The great crisis which compels our attention was born in the inequities, the blind passions, and the senseless conflicts which furnish our subject. Conflicts begin not between nations or blocs of nations, but between men. If there is an absolute and enduring solution to conflict, it will not be found at levels where ministers of state propound compromises. It will be found at the everyday level of social intercourse — in our homes, or on our streets, and in our individual consciences.

Controlling Human Weakness

My initial premise, then, is that community relations problems are not an unrealistic and relatively unimportant concern, but a vital issue — a question of human weakness and society's failure to *control* that weakness.

You will note I did not say "correct" human weakness. Let me repeat. Community relations is a question of human weakness and society's failure to *control* that weakness. If social equity and tranquility were dependent upon perfection of the species, then despair might well keynote this conference. If our discussions are to produce results, there is one fact which must dominate all our thinking — *we have not solved the human equation.* Lacking a solution to human imperfection, we must learn to live with it. The only way I know of safely living with it is to control it.

When one man assaults another, or one group violently flouts the rights of another group, the immediate and pressing issue is the conflict, not the beliefs which incited it. We have not yet learned to control what men believe, but we can control what men do. I do not deny for a moment that the final solution is the perfection of human conscience. But in the interim, and it may be a long interim, we must have order.

Social Order — First Concern

My second premise, then, is that social order is the first concern of those interested in improved community relations. It provides, not a perfectly equitable pattern of life, but at least a peaceful arena in which those inequities can ultimately be solved. Community order works another advantage which, to my mind, has never been properly assessed. Man is a creature of habit, not of hate. Order, even though it is *enforced* order — nonviolent conduct, *despite* intolerant and discriminatory beliefs — creates among the peoples of the community habitual patterns of conduct. I suspect that this habit of order, like any other habit, can be so ingrained into the human mind that it will displace baser instincts.

Let me make it abundantly clear at this point, I do not recommend and will never support a police state. My interest is not in more regulation or tighter restrictions on human liberty. I have no interest in broadening police powers. I am concerned that existing police responsibilities, those vital to the peaceful productive society, be professionally and effectively discharged.

Our laws are far from perfect, but even so they are sufficient for the maintenance of human intercourse without violent conflict. That these laws have not prevented violence is not the fault of the laws, but of the manner in which they are construed and enforced. I intend to outline here a realistic and immediately practical program for securing and maintaining social order within the limits of existing legislation.

Some will question the confinement of the discussion to the bare limits of legal propriety. I would like to dispose of those questions now. What of freedom of economic opportunity? What of effective desegregation in businesses and professions, as well as in schools? What of the multitude of "gentlemen's agreements," the harmful, though not actually illegal actions, which relegate some groups to second-class citizenship? Are these not also important questions, some of them as damaging and painful as actual physical violence? The answer must be in the affirmative. But these evils will never be eliminated, so long as conflict keeps alive the beliefs that created them. In the ruins of mob action, in the pain of physical assault, and in the renewed and intensified hates and fears which follow violence — there are no solutions. Conflict does not beget peace. But where people can walk together and live together and do business together without violence, an affirmative step has been taken.

Security Provided by Local Police

Under our system of government, any discussion of enforced order is necessarily a discussion of local police agencies. We have no national police; legislative and judicial branches of government are prohibited from usurping police powers; our armed forces can be used civilly only under the gravest and most extraordinary emergencies. Our rich and complex economic system, our political freedom, the very conduct of our way of life, are made possible because of the security provided by local police agencies. Indeed, the entire social structure is balanced upon patterns of order created by community law enforcement.

This is quite a balancing act. Historically, it is a rare concept; few nations have rested so much on so slender a foundation. Recognizing this, it would appear that excellence of the police would be a principal and constant concern of community leaders. Their selection, their training, their morale would seem to be of critical importance. Understanding all this, certainly our leaders should have provided the police with the finest young men, the most capable leaders, the wisest counsel. That we have not done these things is as obvious as it is regrettable. The disorder and violence which troubles us as we meet here today, is part of the price we pay for our neglect.

Los Angeles — Case in Point

There is in existence today a community which has decided that the price is too high. It is a case study in the successful application of enforced order to the problem of community relations. I have had the good fortune of taking an active part in the experiment. I have watched it mature during twenty-eight years of service as a professional police officer.

I refer your attention to Los Angeles. That city is, today, characterized by a quality of intergroup cooperation which renders it almost unique among our great cities. It is not a model city. It has intolerant citizens; it has incidents of conflict. But those factors have not been permitted to accumulate into mass disorder. *Los Angeles has not experienced an instance of organized group violence in the past twelve years.*

If organized violence occurred anywhere, it should, by all socio-economic standards, have been in Los Angeles. In the last decade, the city has nearly doubled in size; it suffered the intense dislocation of adjustment to an industrial economy; it has been and still is the focus of one of the greatest migrations in this nation's history. Its two million, two hundred thousand people, the hub of a five million person metropolitan area, is a melting pot of races, colors, creeds, and ideas.

Let me cite some examples. Los Angeles is the home of nearly one-quarter million Negroes, an increase of 168 percent since World War II. It has the largest Mexican descent population outside Mexico City. It has the largest Japanese group in the nation; the third largest Chinese group. The number of persons of the Jewish faith at least equals the urban average. The city is a cross-section of the races, colors, and creeds which make up our nation. And, for reasons no one has ever explained to my satisfaction, we are somehow a Mecca for not only strange religious cults, but also for every brand of zealot, bigot and fanatic our society breeds.

This is Los Angeles, not the city colorfully depicted on travel posters — but the one which interests us here today. It has, like other great metropolitan centers, nearly every element which creates community tensions. But its peoples of different background are learning to live together.

Professionalization

The story of that city's freedom from strife is largely the story of the professionalization of its police department. In this respect, I do not discount the efforts of other agencies, particularly those working for community and group betterment. Their progress in the fields of human understanding, education, and welfare, has been remarkable. It holds great promise for the future. But they made one additional contribution. They recognized that there was one thing which would make social tranquility immediately possible. They gave dynamic and unflagging support to police improvement.

I want to approach the subject of police improvement in a bluntly realistic manner.

As I left Los Angeles yesterday, I was introduced to a feature writer from another city's metropolitan newspaper. A capable man. His task — analyze the Los Angeles Police Department, study its techniques and procedures, and take the story back home. Good journalism — the type which justifies our faith in the Fourth Estate. I hope he won't make the error I'm concerned about. If he doesn't, it will be a rare instance. Since Los Angeles has achieved its eminence in law enforcement, dozens of citizen groups, city officials, and journalists have studied our methods. The usual result is a storm of bitter criticism of their department, and demand that their police adopt Los Angeles' professionalism.

Public Responsibility

How simple that sounds. And how dangerous it is to assume that a city's so-called police problem stems from the police themselves. These people who demand that their police be more efficient, more honest, more impartial — I invite them to join me in an exercise in realism. Who actually runs a police department? The mayor, the police commission, the chief? The people do! They set its policies, establish its standards, furnish its manpower, and supply its budget. The police department is not a private endeavor; it has no funds of its own. It is not a legal entity; it has no rights, no vested interests. It is merely a group of citizens employed to exercise certain functions. It is created by the public, shaped by the public, and operated by the public. *And if it operates badly, the responsibility cannot be disowned by the public.*

I have often heard the complaint that the police organization is all right, but the officers just are not producing. And if an employee isn't producing — whose fault is it? The public selected that man — did they select the wrong man? The public furnished the training — was it bad training — or did they neglect to provide funds for training of any sort? What about the supervisors and commanders? Were they selected by competitive examination on a merit basis — or were they promoted on a political basis? If so, whose politics? If there is a machine in town — a few police votes don't keep it running. But the public vote does!

Shrewd Bargain?

A recent news report tells of widespread police graft in a Southern city. Officers are "squeezing" merchandise from businessmen, parking fees from truckers, gratuities from other citizens. The good citizens there, horrified at the exposé, might do well to accept some personal responsibility. The basic salary of their police officer is two hundred twenty dollars per month. On the six-day week, that runs about a dollar per hour. Carpenter's helpers in the same town earn nearly double that scale. What kind of policemen do they expect to get for a dollar an hour? Their police department costs less than a million dollars per year. Of course, the crime bill, the disorder, the under-the-table pay-offs run fifteen million dollars per year. A shrewd bargain these good citizens have driven. Of course, they are going to solve their problem. They're replacing the chief, the seventh in six years.

If a journalist or a citizens' group from that city calls upon Los Angeles for assistance, what should we tell them? They'll want to study our organization, inspect our Planning and Research and Intelligence Divisions, our strong disciplinary program, observe our cadet school, our continuous in-service training. There are no secrets about these things. They are merely adaptions of sound administrative techniques. They are available and understandable to qualified police officials everywhere. But they cannot be put into effect until competent personnel are attracted by decent job benefits, until an adequate operating budget is furnished; until public cooperation replaces disinterest, shallow interest, and special interest. Professional police work will come into being only when the public takes a long, hard look at their police, and instead of disowning what they themselves have created, accept full responsibility for the errors of generations.

Public Acceptance of Basic Facts

Returning, then, to the Los Angeles experiment — the thing which made police progress and social order there a reality was a public acceptance of these very basic facts. At first, it was understood by only a small group — community leaders such as those represented at this conference. The job of selling this concept was a difficult one. Not that it was a particularly new concept — but at some community levels it is an ugly one. Los Angeles members of the groups represented at this Institute were key factors in that sales job.

Assuming a community is ready to support the professionalism of its police agency, there are certain techniques which the Los Angeles experiment has proved necessary. The first step is the attracting of proper recruits. Los Angeles policemen draw $440.00 monthly at the end of three years' service. This is probably a minimum figure. Below that, the possibility of attracting sufficiently educated and capable persons is almost nil. I am of the opinion that the base salary for an experienced line officer should be in the neighborhood of $600.00 monthly at present living costs. The first city to adopt such a scale will attract high quality personnel who now select other professions. At the present time, I am trying to convince Los Angeles that we would save money by paying more. Our attrition rate among the most qualified officers is too high.

Recruitment

There must be minimum recruiting standards — and these minimums must be held even though the Department operates below strength. Far better to have to increase unit output than to corrupt your police future with sub-standard men. In Los Angeles, less than 4 percent of all applicants meet our rigid police standards. We have been considerably under authorized strength for five years, at one time 10 percent under an allowed figure which was itself nearly 40 percent under the recommended population, square mile ratio. We have managed to do the job only because personnel quality allowed us to steadily improve efficiency. We were told by administrative experts we might improve 2 percent per year with much planning and labor. We upped work output 15 percent last year and we are going to do better in 1955.

Recruit selection must be made solely on a merit basis, preferably by an independent civil service department. If a ward boss, an alderman or a councilman can influence selection in any manner, tear up your plans and start over. As a matter of fact, if he can interfere in any way other than through official channels, the police improvement plan is doomed. Categorically, professional police work and politics do not mix — and there are no shades of gray to that philosophy.

A psychiatric test must be included in the recruit selection program. This bears directly on the problem of community relations. The finest training, direction and discipline cannot correct or control serious emotional defects.

Training

Our Cadet Training School runs thirteen weeks at present. Again, this should be considered a minimum and then only if the recruit has an educational equivalent of two college years. I am personally in favor of a six-month training period, plus a six-months' additional field probation under strict supervision. This should be followed up with in-service and advanced officers' schools, specialist and command schools such as are given in Los Angeles. This is, of course, only a sketch of recruiting and training considerations. With it in mind, I would like to consider in more detail some of the training which bears directly on the subject of community relations.

Once the police cadet has received basic technical information, the direction of training pivots to the consideration of human relations. The cadet must be taught to translate his technical background into solutions of field situations — problems which involve people.

Applied Human Relations

In these courses, sociology is stressed more than ethnology. Applied human relations is stressed more than theoretical psychology. The purpose of the training is to provide immediate, usable knowledge. Training schedules do not allow time for building the broad base of theoretical knowledge necessary in university training. The police administrators should not attempt that impossible task under present training time minimums. The advantage of a college education requirement for police applicants is readily apparent here. Lacking this, colleges do provide upper-level courses, and officers should be encouraged to take advantage of these facilities. In a recent survey, we found that 40 percent of our officers were engaged in such training.

The cadet learns that people differ — by race, religion, politics, economic status, occupation, and in a thousand other ways. He learns they have a *right* to be different. He learns that we are all minority group members — that each of us belongs to many groups, any one of which can be, and often has been, discriminated against.

Correcting Stereotyped Impressions

In other classes, statistical diagrams of the composition of the city are studied. The various peoples are discussed, the movements of groups are traced, the tensions resulting from these movements are pinpointed and analyzed in detail. The racial composition of police districts is an important lesson here because it must be made clear that there are no "Jim Crow" areas, no "ghettos." Every police division has everything found in all other divisions, differing only in proportion. The aim here is to correct stereotyped impressions that the city is divided into clearly defined groups and areas, and that law enforcement differs accordingly. The police department's policy of one class of citizenship, one standard of police technique, becomes readily understandable.

Another class expands this policy. The officer now understands the composition of the community, he has learned how people differ. He is now taught that these variations cannot influence him in the discharge of his duties. His department handles the people involved in incidents *only* according to the degree of their involvement. There is no other measurement. Existing laws are enforced and nothing else. We do not enforce beliefs or prejudices — *including the officer's!* During his hours of duty, he is a composite of the entire community.

Typical course titles are *Police Sociological Problems, Human Relations, Ethics, Professionalism, Civil Disturbances,* and *Public Relations.* Course titles do not reveal the full scope of the 520-hour program. For example, although the *Human Relations* class lasts two hours, that subject is a principal concern in courses such as *Interrogation, Patrol Tactics,* and *Investigation.* The firearms class gives more time to "When *not* to shoot" than it does to "How to shoot." The entire training staff is constantly alert in the classroom, on the exercise field, and in the locker room to discover signs of disabling prejudice which might make the cadet a poor risk. Conditions of tension are artificially created so that the man's reaction can be studied — and he may never know that the situation was contrived to test him. At this point, let us consider the subject of racial and religious prejudice. The cadets, of course, reflect a broad cross-section of society and bring to us the intolerant attitudes to which they have previously been exposed. The question — What to do about these beliefs?

Defending Against Unjust Attacks

Recently, a chief of police from a midwestern city made an inspection tour of our Department. He was particularly interested in the extremely low percentage of citizen complaints received alleging prejudicial treatment of minority group members. He was also interested in case studies where so-called minority group organizations defended the Police Department against accusations of such misconduct. One of the instances involved a metropolitan Los Angeles daily newspaper which began a series of articles with the caption: "Cops Lay Heavy Hands on Minorities." You have all seen such articles and, in many cases, they represent good journalism — accurate coverage. In this instance, the facts were patently incorrect. The writer, a new resident, was securing information from old newspaper clippings and from certain special-interest groups. He was committing the cardinal reportorial sin of not checking current facts. The article shook police morale and police confidence. Assuming the facts had been true, it offered no solutions other than a vague recommendation that the police ought to do something about this mess! Fortunately, certain community organizations recognized where the "mess" really was. A coordinating group representing sixty social service agencies contacted the publisher of that paper. He was told, and in no uncertain terms, that the story was untrue, that it was inciting lunatic-fringe elements into disorderly conduct, and was playing directly into the hands of subversive groups. The result — that particular series was discontinued and, to the credit of that publisher, a new series of articles underscoring police–public cooperation was instituted.

Compliance with Policy a Must

The visiting chief of police was understandably impressed. In most jurisdictions the police fight lonely battles. He assumed that such overwhelming public support meant we had somehow erased prejudicial and intolerant beliefs held by police officers. He was wrong. Those of you who work in the field of education recognize we *do* not and *can* not accomplish this miracle. Of course, we will not accept an applicant whose intolerance is so high it is a disabling factor. Where it is not too deep-seated, we can erase it, or at least diminish it. In the majority of cases, we must learn to operate equitably despite it. We do that by controlling the results of these beliefs. With policemen, as with society in general, our immediate concern is not what the man thinks but what he does. Los Angeles police policy recognizes only one class of citizenship — first class citizenship. Any incident of police action which deviates from this policy is met with swift and certain discipline.

For those who question whether that degree of discipline is possible, I have an example. I am thinking of a certain Los Angeles police officer who walks a foot beat in the old section of the city. The street is a racial melting pot. I know the officer personally, he is one of the "old school," recruited long before psychiatric examinations were instituted. If there is a maximum number of racial and religious prejudices one mind can hold, I am certain he represents it. This officer has been exposed to the complete range of police human relations training. He has memorized every maxim, every scientific fact, every theory relating to human equality. He knows all the accepted answers. Of course, he doesn't believe a word of it.

This may surprise you — the officer's eight-hour duty tour is characterized by tolerance, applied human relations, and equitable treatment of all persons. Both his division commander and myself have watched his work closely, a little wary that his deep-seated convictions might win him over discipline in moments of stress.

This has not happened during the five years he has patrolled this highly critical district. We are very near an opinion that his intolerance has become a victim of enforced order — habit has won out over belief.

Discipline, enforced compliance with police policy, is a key which is available to every police administrator. If it works in Los Angeles it will work elsewhere. The entire community relations program is at stake in every officer in the field. It is here that the police department proves itself, or is found wanting.

Specialized Units — Community Relations Detail

The second-line community relations effort is handled by specialized police units. One of the most successful of these is our Community Relations Detail working out of the Public Information office. Its mission is to establish and maintain communications between police and the so-called minority segments of the community press serving them, and key individuals in the human relations field. These officers are members of sixty organizations representing a cross-section of specialized community interests. Few police details pierce so deeply into the stratifications of our complex society or maintain so many privileged sources of information.

Their first task was at the community press level. Certain of these newspapers were parlaying instances of law enforcement against minority group members into sensational accounts of police prejudice and brutality. Many of these articles were written solely from the unsubstantiated account given by the arrestee. The accumulated result was the fomenting of an hysterical "cop-hating" attitude which rendered suspect every police action involving non-Caucasian persons.

The Community Relations officers went to these publishers and laid their cards on the table. Sensationalism was selling newspapers, but it was hurting the community. They pointed out that sensationalism was actually manufacturing new incidents — feeding upon itself. They offered, with the full backing of the Office of the Chief, to provide the publisher with exact and complete facts on every inquiry, whether the police action was right or wrong; whether the facts helped us or hurt us.

The confidence I have in the men who publish the nation's newspapers was justified. Community interest won out over self interest.

Community Relations Detail in Operation

The Community Relations detail is *first,* a public information activity, acquainting community groups with police policies, procedures and tactics. Where necessary, it interprets specific actions, explaining why they were necessary and how they were taken. *Secondly,* the Detail transmits information in the other direction, keeping the police staff informed about minority and intergroup problems and activities. We have found the police are sometimes overly suspicious of a group's militant efforts, seeing in them a threat to order which does not actually exist. The two-way communication furnished by the Detail brings the facts to both sides. *Thirdly,* the Detail reports any police activities which are discriminatory, or may appear to the community to be discriminatory. The police staff does not operate under the assumption that it is infallible. Critical comment from this specialized unit often prevents more dangerous and expensive criticism from the public at large. *Lastly,* the Detail operates as an advance listening post, alert for rumors which might prelude violent conflict. In a recent instance, these officers were informed that racial violence was brewing at a school. A quick investigation indicated the situation was critical. The Detail flashed the word to citizen groups organized to combat just such emergencies. Affected police field units were placed on a standby basis. The result — this Detail, working with citizen groups, contained the situation.

It is profitable to assign to these specialized units officers belonging to minority groups. They are often more sensitive to the problem, have previously established contacts in those communities, and encounter fewer barriers. However, it must be emphasized that the officer's competency, and not his ancestry, is the overriding consideration in making the assignment. Community relations details are not "window-dressing" — they are not publicity gags designed to display non-Caucasians in key positions.

No Mass Juvenile Disorder

A similar detail works out in the Juvenile Division. In this case, the principal concern is with actual offenders. One of this unit's primary values is its detailed knowledge of gang members, leaders and methods. They know their homes, their meeting places, their territories. They deal with what the law recognizes as children, but do not be mistaken — this is intelligent activity of the highest order. The disheartening message of our crime statistics is all too clear — today's delinquent is often a dangerous criminal — an immediate threat to community order. He is sometimes the innocent tool of intolerant adults, but he can also be a moving force behind community violence. We are sympathetic with the ideals of juvenile correction — of rehabilitation over punishment. Here, as with other community problems, we invite welfare agencies to work to eliminate causes. Meanwhile, we ask them to remember that *we* are not a social agency. We are bound to read the message in police records and employ protective tactics accordingly. In Los Angeles, as in other cities, we have a juvenile problem. We do *not* have a problem in mass juvenile disorder, because we face facts, and on the basis of these facts, employ units such as the ones I have described.

Key Factors in Community Relations

Three factors compose the Los Angeles Police Department's community relations program: Training of officers—including training through discipline, *public information* activity, and *efficient* line police work. Unless they are all in existence and *inter-working,* a community relations program does not exist. Training provides a base, but public information and line officers must forward to training that information which keys it to current needs. Public information is a useless activity unless it is backed up with competent line officers who are enforcing the laws equitably. And the most dedicated line commanders can accomplish little unless training provides well-schooled personnel and public information creates a cooperative public.

I would rather have brought to this Institute a simple and revolutionary device — some easy way to an effective program. I know of no such device. I *can* promise that to a mutually cooperative public and police department, no problem in community order is beyond solution. The methods are known, they are proving themselves in the Los Angeles experiment — all that is needed is dedicated citizens who will put them into effect.

To this point, this has been a progress report. The Los Angeles experiment seems to justify the philosophy of enforced order as the first step toward improved community relations. Progress of this type can be reported objectively, without seeming to seek praise, because law enforcement is absolutely dependent upon the public for any successes it may have. The credit for Los Angeles progress must go primarily to Los Angeles citizens.

I would not want to close, however, leaving the impression that the experiment is concluded. It does not represent the ultimate in community equity and tranquility. Certain factors now at work could bring all the progress crashing down into rubble and violence. I have pledged forthrightness and honesty in this report, and it requires some critical comments, perhaps touching upon activities and attitudes of organizations represented here.

Police Deployment Concerned with Effect, Not Cause

The first comment concerns minority discrimination against the public as a whole. Reaction to police deployment furnishes a good example of this danger. Every department worth its salt deploys field forces on the basis of crime experience. Deployment is often heaviest in so-called minority sections of the city. The reason is statistical — it is a fact that certain racial groups at the present time, commit a disproportionate share of the total crime. Let me make one point clear in that regard — a competent police administrator is fully aware of the multiple conditions which create this problem. There is no inherent physical or mental weakness in any racial stock which tends it toward crime. But — and this is a "but" which must be borne constantly in mind — *police field deployment is not social agency activity*. In deploying to suppress crime, we are not interested in *why* a certain group tends toward crime, we are interested in maintaining order. The fact that the group would not be a crime problem under different socio-economic conditions and might not be a crime problem tomorrow, does not alter today's tactical necessities. Police deployment is concerned with *effect*, not cause.

When I am told that intense police activity in a given area is psychologically disturbing to its residents, I am forced to agree. And I agree that it can add weight to discriminatory beliefs held by some who witness it, and that it can create a sense of persecution among those who receive it. Is the police administrator, then, to discard crime occurrence statistics and deploy his men on the basis of social inoffensiveness? This would be discrimination indeed!

Every citizen has the right to police protection, and of employing whatever legal devices are necessary to accomplish it. At the present time, race, color and creed are useful statistical and tactical devices. So are age groupings, sex, and employment. If persons of one occupation, for some reason, commit more theft than average, then increased police attention is given to persons of that occupation. Discrimination is not a factor there. If persons of Mexican, Negro, or Anglo-Saxon ancestry, for some reason contribute heavily to other forms of crime, police deployment must take that into account. From an ethnological point of view, Negro, Mexican, and Anglo-Saxon are unscientific breakdowns; they are a fiction. From a police point of view, they are a useful fiction and should be used as long as they remain useful.

Group Identification a Police Tool — Not an Attitude

The demand that the police cease to consider race, color, and creed is an unrealistic demand. *Identification is a police tool, not a police attitude*. If traffic violations run heavily in favor of lavender colored automobiles, you may be certain, whatever the sociological reasons for that condition, we would give lavender automobiles more than average attention. And if those vehicles were predominantly found in one area of the city, we would give that area more than average attention. You may be certain that any pressure brought to bear by the lavender manufacturer's association would not alter our professional stand — it would only react to their disadvantage by making the police job more difficult. *Such demands are a form of discrimination against the public as a whole.*

For a moment, let us consider this entire problem of group identification. It is one thing for the police to employ it for statistical and descriptive purposes; it is quite another if it is employed to set a group apart from the rest of society. The question must be brought out into the open and discussed because it represents a conflict of opinion within the physically identifiable minority groups.

Some of these citizens object strenuously to being identified with their background. Others publicly announce it by joining organizations bearing that stamp of identity. Either attitude can be supported by argument. But I humbly submit that the man, or the group which changes identification at different times and under different conditions, confuses and impedes the social assimilation process. There is no place for dual status in our society, and it is incongruous that the groups with the keenest interest in eliminating dual status should create conditions which perpetuate it. Organizations which publicly identify themselves with a certain racial group are keeping alive the fantasy that the group is different. By setting it apart from the whole, they help keep it apart. We need such organizations; they fill a vital role in our changing system; I heartily endorse their good works, I suggest that if a single class of citizenship is the key to social assimilation, then practices and titles which contradict it, must be examined and resolved.

Group Identification No Criterion for Promotions

Another problem which plagues the police administrator is organized group pressure to promote officers and make command assignments on the basis of race, color or creed. Before a recent Los Angeles election, I encountered tremendous pressure to replace an Anglo-Saxon commander of a detective division with another commander belonging to a certain minority group. I refused to engage in racial discrimination against the Anglo-Saxon commander. He was the most qualified man for the job and, as such, he retained the job. Neither do I consider ancestry a factor in making promotional appointments. The Los Angeles policy is to take the top man from the list. Racial background should not hinder advancement; neither should it help it. Shortly before I left Los Angeles, I had the pleasure of pinning a Lieutenant's badge on a young officer born in Mexico. He got that badge because he was the top man, not because accidents of conquest created a national border between our places of birth.

No one is more critical of the American police service than myself. For 28 years I have outspokenly expressed that criticism and have sat in meetings and applauded others who have criticized constructively. Certainly, few other organizations in history have been so unanimously castigated. I have no complaints to make — it is part of the painful process of growth and improvement. There is one danger inherent in this process — a point of group masochism is reached where all other groups become wise and faultless and self-reproach becomes the total answer. I caution the police against this danger.

Discrimination a Two-Way Street

I have made the point that discrimination is a two-way street. Those who are most active in combating it are sometimes guilty of advocating that the police practice it. There is nothing shocking in this critical observation — no group is characterized by omniscience. The fact that minorities have received intolerant and discriminatory treatment does not automatically lend justice to all of their demands. They are as prone to error as majority groups, and the wiser and calmer citizens within those groups recognize it. Thoughtful citizens expect the police to stand their ground when they believe they are right. They expect the police to criticize as well as be criticized.

Summing Up

I have tried to steer a course between these extremes tonight. I have assessed the situation as forthrightly as I know how. There is always a temptation when speaking on a subject so emotion-laden as this, to skirt issues, to woo friends, rather than court truth. In my experience with the National Conference of Christians and Jews, I have never felt it necessary to compromise my honest convictions, and I did not intend to dishonor this Institute by so doing tonight.

I would like to close by expressing my philosophy of citizenship, a philosophy which I humbly believe embodies the convictions of all persons and groups represented at this gathering.

Good citizenship is expressed in many ways. It consists not only of bearing arms for one's country, but also of bearing truth for it. It consists not only of facing physical enemies, but also of facing spiritual enemies: Intolerance, Bigotry, and Hate. It consists not only of holding high the banners of Duty, Faith, and Love. Although not all citizens can prove themselves on a battlefield, all can do it by the quiet and devoted living of the spirit of our country. It is sometimes more difficult to *live* ideals than to shed blood for them.

Tale of Two Cities — The Crucial Role of the Police in Community Change

JESSE E. CURRY

(Then) Chief of Police, Dallas, Texas

MAY 23, 1962

The City of Dallas has enjoyed uninterrupted growth since the first log cabin was built on the banks of the Trinity River in 1841. We have had problems, of course. Any rapidly growing city is bound to have them. But we have been fortunate in having city administrators who were dedicated to the growth of Dallas, and who were willing to subordinate their personal opinions to the welfare of the city as a whole.

Dallas was a raw, prairie town of approximately 2,000 persons when the clouds of Civil War began to gather. It had been an incorporated city only five years when an election was held to determine whether it was to remain a part of the Union, or was to secede. It had never been primarily a slave-holding community, but most of Dallas' people had come from the Old South, and when the War Between the States loomed, Dallas sentiment was fiercely and overwhelmingly Southern. In January, 1861, the county voted 741 to 237 for secession from the Union.

Following the War Between the States, 1,260 of Dallas' citizens took the oath of amnesty, and faced the future with hope. They hoped too soon, for then another struggle—Reconstruction—began. Dallas also endured this period, and from the time of Reconstruction to World War II enjoyed a period of prosperity and growth known to few cities.

During this time, racial tension was at a minimum. The white citizens lived in a segregated society, and the pressure from the Negro minority against the color line was slight. Racial incidents were scattered and minor, and were easily dealt with within the framework of existing law and procedure.

With World War II the pattern began to change, and with the change came the necessity for a different approach to race relations. This change was prompted by several factors. During the war, many persons moved into Dallas from integrated areas to work in defense plants. This in-migration from other areas where segregation was no longer actively practiced continued after the war and contributed to the changing picture.

Another prominent factor was the service in military organizations of many Negroes from the Dallas area. After having seen a society that was not founded on segregation, many Negroes returning to Dallas were unwilling to maintain the *status quo*.

At any rate, following World War II, the Dallas Police Department was faced with the necessity for changing its approach to race relationships. Immediately following the war, our department included human relations in its program of training.

With the Supreme Court decision of 1954, declaring that separate but equal facilities were not legal within the framework of the Constitution, came the realization that Dallas must prepare for greater change. Dallas, like many cities, used the interim period between the ruling and the actual date of desegregation to prepare for this far-reaching step.

One of the first things done to prepare the Dallas Police Department for integration was the assignment of a man to prepare a manual for the training of departmental officers. The administration realized that most of the officers of the department had been reared in a segregated society, and had absorbed the culture which had surrounded them. It was unrealistic to presume that donning a uniform and wearing a badge would remove from a man all the prejudices to which he had been exposed all of his life.

The man assigned to the task of preparing the manual had been educated in the schools of journalism of the University of Texas and Southern Methodist University, and was a reporter for the Dallas MORNING NEWS at the time he applied for membership in the department.

It was believed that an appeal to the officers to accept desegregation on moral ground would be risky, and likely to fail. It was then decided that a superordinate goal of good law enforcement should be set up, and the intermediate goal of desegregation set up in front of it. Then, as the department worked toward the proper fulfillment of its responsibility, it would pass through the problem of desegregation enroute.

No attempt was made to change the personal opinions of members of the department. They were told that their opinions were their own, but that in the event their personal opinions conflicted with the law, they would be expected to subordinate those opinions in a professional manner.

In the belief that timing was of great importance, the manual was not used as soon as it was completed. The department waited until the desegregation of public schools was imminent before any training program based on the manual was undertaken.

In 1960 the Federal Court of Appeals indicated that the time for integration was near, and every member of the department was given 16 hours of instruction from the manual. Then, in 1961, just a month before schools were to integrate, an additional eight hours of instruction was provided.

Due in part to the professional qualities of the officers, and in part to the manner in which the problem was approached, Dallas desegregated its public schools without major incident. The members of the department knew what was expected of them, and knew further that no deviation from the established policy of the department would be tolerated.

The preparation of the manual served a further purpose. It gave notice to extremists who might have attempted to take the law into their own hands that such action would not be tolerated, but would be met swiftly and decisively.

Realizing that the desegregation of public schools was one of the most crucial problems in the integrative process, special attention was given to it by the department. As soon as we were able to obtain from the school board a list of the schools to be desegregated, we prepared scale drawings of the areas surrounding each of the eight affected schools. Briefings were given men who would be assigned to the schools — ostensibly to work traffic — and the desires of the department were explained to them in detail.

A command officer of the rank of either Inspector or Captain was assigned to each school, and was made responsible for the activities of the officers around each school, within the framework of overall departmental policy. On the eve of desegregation, signs prohibiting loitering and citing the applicable ordinance number were posted at each site. The normal "No Parking" areas around the schools were expanded.

Prior to the set date, the Criminal Intelligence Section of the department prepared brochures containing pictures and descriptive information on known racists and extremists, not only in the Dallas area, but also those who had been active at the scene of other desegregation procedures. The news media publicized the fact that such a brochure had been prepared, and announced the department's plans for handling such persons should they become active. This advance warning is believed to have been valuable in keeping extremists away from the schools.

In addition, the Criminal Intelligence Section developed and maintained advantageous liaison with the minority groups. Through this liaison, the department was able to learn of contemplated activities of the groups, and was able to explain the department's position.

As an example, on one occasion the department learned that a Negro group was planning a mass prayer meeting on the steps of the City Hall. Such a meeting would have been in violation of long-standing ordinances.

A representative of the Criminal Intelligence Unit called on the minority group leaders, explained that the proposed plans would be in violation, and offered the assistance of the department in finding an alternate location where the prayer meeting could be held legally.

The minority group leaders said that they did not know that what they contemplated was illegal, and that certainly they had no desire to violate the law. Through the combined efforts of the department and the group, another location was found, and the prayer meeting was held in conformance with the law.

The department had worked closely with the press prior to desegregation. Several meetings of the school administration, departmental administration and news media were held, and ground rules were worked out so that each faction might know what could be expected from the others. These ground rules were strictly adhered to by all groups, and provided a common ground of understanding. Our experience with the press, both local and national, left nothing to be desired. Special passes were provided for bonafide news representatives, and printed information sheets were given to newsmen when they registered for passes.

Realizing that they would probably not be needed, but also realizing that the experience of other jurisdictions indicated their desirability, a special group of officers was trained in riot control work. Using military procedures, a group comprised of one Lieutenant, three Sergeants and fifty men were trained in crowd control. They practiced maneuvers designed to break up an unruly crowd, and were placed on a standby basis in the event they were needed.

They did not report to the schools during the desegregation procedure, but rode four men to a car in the areas of the schools, so they would be immediately available in the event disorder developed. I am happy to report they were never used.

Many other preparatory steps were made, and by the time of desegregation, the Dallas Police Department was ready.

I do not want to sound like the credit for the successful desegregation of Dallas schools belongs entirely, or even primarily, to the Dallas Police Department. Certainly such is not true.

We were fortunate that in Dallas, the civic leaders were anxious that nothing should happen to mar Dallas' good name. Perhaps most active, and deserving of greatest credit, is the Dallas Citizens Council, not to be confused with the White Citizens Councils which are active in some areas of the South.

The Dallas Citizens Council is a group of 250 business leaders whose aim is to aid the growth of the City. To be a member of the group, a man must be either the owner or president of the business for which he works. There are no professional people in the Council, only businessmen. This group has been active in Dallas for many years, and has contributed materially to Dallas' growth.

Aware of the bad efforts of desegregation problems in other areas, the Council decided to attempt to forestall such problems in Dallas. Theirs was primarily an economic motivation, for they were primarily interested in the business health of Dallas. They realized, however, that to protect Dallas' business interests, they must become involved in the desegregation procedure.

A biracial committee was formed within the Council, with seven Council members appointed to the committee. The Negro community was then asked to appoint a like number of representatives to work on the committee, and these 14 men met often and fruitfully.

To aid in the coordination of the Council's activities with those of other groups, a public relations counsel was employed, to devote his full time to the problem. A program, covering many points, was devised.

The committee first worked at convincing the businessmen of Dallas of the undesirability, from an economic point of view, of racial friction. They appealed to the general public with the theme "Dallas is a law-abiding city, composed of law-abiding people. Dallas will not resort to violence, but will seek redress of real or imagined wrongs through legal and lawful channels." Programs aimed at the clergy, the medical profession, the legal profession, the labor unions, and the students were prepared and executed. There is no way to measure the value of the activities of this group to the City of Dallas.

The department frequently served as liaison between the biracial committee and other organizations. Members of the department appeared before civic groups many times, stressing that Dallas is a law-abiding city, which could not tolerate violence. The work of the Citizens Council was highly effective in relieving the department of a great deal of pressure, and provided us with the support we had to have.

Another outstanding contribution of the Council was the preparation of a movie *Dallas at the Crossroads*. This movie depicted Dallas as a community of law-abiding citizens, and urged that an attitude of tolerance be adopted. Many Dallas leaders, from most of the professions, appeared in the movie, urging that law and order be maintained. This film was shown widely before civic groups and business organizations. Thirty-five copies were made, and at times, all copies were being shown on the same day. Frequently, a member of the department would appear before the group to explain the department's position.

Another benefit of the Council came from its work with the news media. In meetings with media leaders, it was decided that peaceful sit-ins and picketing were not news, and that publicity would be given the racial issue only if violence developed. This discouraged the publicity-seekers who might have been willing to create trouble for their personal advantage.

Not all of the work of the Council was carried on in full view of the public. It frequently, and successfully, worked behind the scene. One example of this hidden activity was the desegregation of 39 restaurants and lunch counters a short time before school desegregation. In the belief that the adult population should experience integration before it was extended to the youth, representatives of the Council quietly called on owners of restaurants throughout the downtown area, and persuaded them to desegregate. This was done with a minimum of fanfare and publicity, and as a result, was completely without incident.

Following school desegregation, the Citizens Council devoted its time and energy to securing admittance of Negro patrons to the major Dallas hotels. The Council realized that many conventions which might come to the city were scheduled elsewhere because some of the members of the convention group were Negro, who would not be accepted by the major hotels.

Due largely to the activities of the Council many of the hotels agreed to accept colored patrons. This process has been undertaken gradually, with the first Negroes accepted being members of convention groups.

We have learned many things from our attempts to dispel our minority group tensions. We have learned the absolute necessity of a proper attitude on the part of all governmental officials. Without this proper attitude, a climate conducive to proper law enforcement cannot be established.

Of equal importance is the attitude of the civic leaders. Without public support, any program of any department has small chance of success. The police agency can frequently, through contacts with civic leaders, bring this desirable attitude into being.

Following the establishment of the proper attitude within the department should come a clear, concise statement of departmental policy. Each member has a right to know, without ambiguity, what the department expects of him. Equally, each member of the public has a right to know what to expect from his police agency. Frequently, this statement of policy will prevent persons who might resort to violence from challenging law and order, for notice is thereby served in advance what the consequences of such action will be.

Departmental policy must be followed by adequate training. The administrator who thinks that prepared material can be presented to his men, and then left to individual initiative, is doomed to a minimum of success. Adequate training is necessary, not only to acquaint the officer with what is expected of him, but also to mold opinion.

Adequate liaison must be established with all groups, so that each faction may know what to expect from all others. The police must frequently initiate this liaison, for efforts to establish communication will seldom be repulsed.

An appeal should be made to the fair-mindedness of the people. The police agency must presume that the majority of the citizens want to do the right thing. This does not relieve the department from preparing for the activities of the small minority who do not, but nevertheless, the department must trust in the good intentions of the majority. Frequently, a man will perform in a specific way merely because it is what is expected of him.

There must be coordination of the efforts of all groups. Without this necessary coordination the efforts of well-meaning groups can work at cross purposes with each other. Perhaps the most logical coordinating agency is the police department, for the police administrator is usually able to speak with authority. This does not imply that the police chief should attempt to dictate the activities of other organizations, but merely that he should call to the attention of each interested group the work of the others.

Certainly not all of Dallas' problems so far as race relations are concerned have been met. We still have problems to face, but we are confident that, in the light of past experience, we will meet them without violence.

Tale of Two Cities — The Crucial Role of the Police in Community Change

LAWRENCE W. FULTZ

(Then) Inspector of Police Department, Houston, Texas

MAY 23, 1962

"Houston," some perceptive soul once remarked, "is the city that had to be."

And judging from its sky-rocketing growth, from a sleepy little village on the banks of a weed-choked, muddy bayou to the nation's sixth largest city in a scant 125 years, the observer had more than a little insight into the potential of Houston.

Today, Houston has turned that muddy stream into a ship channel and become the second largest seaport in the nation. The superabundance of mineral resources in the area has made this "Baghdad-on-the-Bayou." The world's petroleum capital, the headquarters of international oil tool trade, the natural gas pipeline capital of the nation, the home of America's greatest petrochemical industry complex and — more recently — Space Center, U.S.A., for the National Aeronautics and Space Administration is constructing a 60-million dollar manned spacecraft center 22 miles from Houston at Clear Lake, Texas.

Houston is, indeed, a fabulous town. Oil derricks stand out against a skyline where new skyscrapers are emerging almost daily.

Sir John Barbirolli conducts the Houston Symphony. Fashion models and Houston housewives are so much alike, it takes a program to tell them apart at style shows. Fine hotels extend Houston hospitality to movie queens and visiting firemen alike.

But Houston is much more than fabulous; it's friendly. It's historically interesting. It's gay. It's exciting. It's the most air-conditioned city in the country. Houston scored nationally in a recent Gallup poll as one of the nation's leading cities in four categories of excellence: handsomest women; best year-round climate; gayest night life; and best place to make a living.

Those weren't Texas Brags, either. They were selected from a cross-section of people from all over the U. S. In contests, Houston has been named The Most Beautiful City in the Nation.

In its headlong rush to greatness, Houston's million-plus citizens have not forgotten the finer things of life. The city is rapidly becoming the cultural center of the Southwest, with its many fine musical organizations, its Museum of Fine Arts, its legitimate theatres, its Contemporary Arts Museum and many art galleries.

But perhaps Houston's greatest monument — bespeaking the humanitarian conviction of its citizens — is the ever-expanding Texas Medical Center, a 120-million dollar complex of medical institutions for Research, Training, and Treatment. Intensive pioneering in heart and cancer research have earned the Texas Medical Center a still-growing international reputation.

Houston's ideal year-round temperature (annual average in 1960 was 69 degrees) makes the city and surrounding area a true sportsman's paradise.

As Texans, and more especially Houstonians, we are proud of Houston and very proud also of our achievements in presenting a truly professional police profile to our citizens.

We make claim for national recognition in the manner and method of guiding the South's leading metropolis into a kind of spirited acquiescence in the matter of racial assimilation.

Houston, with its sprawl and exploding and dynamic growth was — to say the least — unpredictable. If we seek a key to explain the successes enjoyed, it is probably that of "intelligence," which is to be correlated with preparedness and concern.

We police a city of a million people with just over 1,100 police officers. This demanding disparity made it necessary to carefully calculate all strategies and tactics.

We, like most Southern cities, experienced the usual acts of public display, wherein Negro citizens engaged in random acts of "sit-in," "stand-in," and protestations of the variety routinely reported across the South.

We could well date our active entry into the field of community conflict based upon racial tensions on or about April, 1953, when a bomb of sorts was exploded on the steps of a Negro home, newly purchased, in an all-white residential area. We fondly recall the precise police action instituted, which resulted in a felony conviction of the "white bomber" by an all-white jury.

To this day, it is felt that we in the department created, in the minds of our citizens, an image that has enabled us to successfully carry out the necessary police action in the nine years that have followed.

Since the initial "move-in" back in 1953, others have been routinely made without incident or report.

From those early days, it was concluded that a new and challenging task had confronted us. In the years that followed, we have availed ourselves of the existing devices for preparation. We have been well represented here at Michigan State yearly. We were represented at the forerunning seminar held at the University of Chicago Law School in the early 1950's. Probably of more closely-measured worth was the injection into our Police Academy of a program of instruction in the field of Community Relations. This has been augmented by yearly seminars held at Texas A & M on Police and Community Relations. The need was so evident and the cry so spontaneous that regional institutes were conducted in the more populated areas across Texas.

We speak boastfully of our program of school integration that most sorely disappointed the national news media insofar as recordable and pictorialized violence. Nothing of a newsworthy nature happened, other than the fact that "nothing happened." The federally-mandated program of integration was commenced in the nation's largest segregated school system in September, 1960. Negro youngsters are now at the third grade level, with yet a documented incident of violence to occur. Here again we feel that proper attitude and respect for law enforcement was established down through the years, enabling us to present a professional front to our various publics.

Honeycombed and spiraling through this operational effort was the work of a little-publicized intelligence group who peered, queried, and pondered upon the pulse of the community daily.

The demonstrations that seemed destined were all anticipated and geared for ofttimes many days in advance. Some protestations were cancelled because of our prior knowledge, which led to a kind of arbitration of effort on the part of the leaders of the student group passively engaged in protest.

Some arrests have necessarily been made. Some convictions have been had. Even in the face of conflict between federal, state and local laws, there have been no capricious or inequitable prosecutions. We have insisted that under the unlawful assembly statutes and ordinances of our state and city, the aggrieved party must make an official outcry, by affidavit, in order to effect police action.

The succeeding city administrations have conscientiously adhered to a policy of awareness based on moderation which has undoubtedly smoothed our path of action. We have employed the talents of a very young police department, 90 percent of whom are native Texans. We have countered on occasion with administrative dilemma insofar as employing a "show of force" or resorting to reserve mobilization of police strength. We have been very successful in the deployment of "intelligence units," in true undercover style into the heart of actual incidents, making valuable use of selected Negro officers.

May I stress the value of information exchange between our local school officials and the department. This one item of effort contributed most heavily to our preparedness.

In returning to the actual processes employed by our department, let me stress, the somewhat uncompromising situation in which we have labored the last nine years.

It is not at all a simple task to bring a degree of unity of purpose to a semi-military group such as a police department wherein there is lacking a thing so necessary and vital to successful management. I speak of "administrative morality." The operational agents of any striking force must respect the wisdom, the skill and the integrity of its leaders. A police department is generally endowed with some degree of collective pride. It is the mandate of those who would command to curry and nurture this "cohesive crust of dedication" into a spirit of excellence and a desire to accomplish the most difficult of tasks.

Could it be that the full impact of transition and mandated evolution could not strike our city until, and regretfully so, tragic failing had taken place in other Southern cities? There were many of us who could recall the spectacle of the Little Rock officer who, for the benefit of national newsreel cameramen, publicly tore his badge from his uniform and stalked off in a protest against his assignment. This act of sedition gained little favor for him or others of questionable loyalty in the eyes of the great majority of Southern police officers.

It may well be, then, that any degree of success in our police effort must be predicated upon the fact that the personnel of the department at all levels were psychologically prepared to engage in a professional police performance, using the tragedies of those departments elsewhere with "too little, too late," as graphic examples.

The demonstrations, as carried out within our jurisdiction, were typical of other protests across the South. The Negro participants, bolstered by a scattering of white sympathizers, were students who were banded together into a group known as the Progressive Youth Organization. The group was by no means a secret organization, and welcomed recruits from among young Negroes and whites alike. Under its leadership, "sit-ins" were conducted periodically across the city. Boycotts of private businesses were conducted simultaneously. The conduct of the lunch counter protestors was completely passive, and no breach of the peace was ever recorded. We withheld a show of force in all these incidents, relying upon undercover intelligence to filter the events to a central command post, which could immediately mobilize a necessary show of force to move in and take appropriate police action. This mobilization has never been needed.

Today, Houston, in a calculation of its accomplishments would spell out these: a concerned and responsive group of City Fathers who cherish the continued growth of the South's greatest city, above all else; a young, but well-oriented police department, demanding the best in leadership and properly qualified for recognition as one of the nation's better departments; and, of greatest significance, a citizenry that has responded to the challenges of these trying times with a cosmopolitan and sophisticated show of pride and optimism for the future.

Police Working in the Neighborhood

ALLEN B. BALLARD

*(Then) Chief Inspector, Community Relations Unit,
Philadelphia Police Department*

MAY 23, 1962

Over the years, institutes, seminars and conferences have been held in all sections of the country, with diversified groups, in an effort to develop programs in police and community relations that will establish lines of communication between the police and the community, and to attempt to interpret the role of the police to the community in a frame of reference which the community understands.

Generally, these conferences have brought together leaders of the community in the fields of religion, education, social work and law enforcement. Over the years, good lines of communication have been established, an atmosphere of understanding in relation to each other's role in the community has developed, and in many instances, efforts have been made to solve community problems cooperatively, with some degree of success. These leaders have usually been in the religious field: rabbis, priests and ministers, recognized as leaders within their groups in the field of intergroup understanding and community problems.

In education: sociologists, psychologists, psychiatrists, superintendents of school districts, principals and even teachers who are recognized authorities in their various fields and communities, have been included in these various conferences, seminars and institutes.

Also involved have been administrative and operational police personnel, usually with the rank of captain or higher. If a graph or picture could be developed, showing the interdependency of the police and the community, it would indicate the following:

COMMUNITY PRESSURES

The above figure indicates, in my opinion, the interdependence and areas of strength in terms of a good Police–Community Relations Program.

It also indicates the direction of community pressures and the community leadership that reflects the first impact of these pressures. If lines of communication are good in area (2), additional pressures can be absorbed.

However, the real strength of this relationship lies in area (3). If, in all three areas, there is strength and good lines of communication, such a community will have a good police–community relation experience.

Good police–community relations is a two-way street of mutual understanding and of mutual respect. This *must* be developed on the part of the police and on the part of the community. There must be *lines* of communication established, where a positive attitude toward law enforcement is evident in the community. This can be done only when there is personal, day-to-day contact between the people in the community and the police who work in that community. The role of a community relations division in a police department is to initiate, develop, motivate, and create *through programming* an environment in which police at all levels, and the community at all levels, can meet and discuss problems within a common frame of reference, in terms of community involvement and police involvement. The atmosphere must be such that there is common respect for, and recognition of, each other's points of view and each other's problems.

The whole gamut of good police–community relations is a philosophy. It has to be — a philosophy of living and working together for the common good. To approach this problem otherwise is unrealistic and frustrating.

It is within this *new* frame of reference that the Philadelphia Police Department has approached the problem. For many years, there has been good communication at the top level of administration; for example, the police commission, heads of city-wide organizations, chairmen of boards, etc. Communications at this level, is, and has been, excellent. However, this is *not* the level at which problems have developed. Lack of communication and lack of understanding has developed at *lower* levels.

What we are now attempting to do, and with some measure of success, is to develop lines of communication and areas of understanding at the level where the problem really lies: the Divisional Inspector, the District Captain, the Lieutenant, the Sergeant and the Patrolman.

As one of the tools for achieving this goal, we are using the "Getting To Know You" program. This program is geared to the divisional and district level — programs designed to bring together the inspector, the captain, the lieutenant, other police personnel and the community with its key leaders, on a person-to-person basis. In this kind of a situation, the community leader feels that he has a direct line to the boss. As one community leader put it in a recent meeting, "We had a petition drawn up to take to the Mayor, but since we've met tonight, we can give it to you, and we're glad to know that we can contact you direct." This statement is indicative of statements made by leaders all over the city during meetings of this kind. This is Phase Two of our program.

Phase Three involves participation at an even lower level, the level of execution: where the person (citizen) who is *directly* involved in the problems of the community meets the policeman who is *directly* involved in the problem of the community from the point of view of law enforcement. It is amazing what can be done in the area of understanding when the community "John Doe" meets the policeman under these circumstances. In the coming months, more and more emphasis will be placed on small group meetings as the most important phase of the whole program.

After eight years as a commander in an area of less than four square miles and 200,000 people, I am convinced that rapport and communication can be established between the police and community that is absolutely essential if we are to do anything positively about the growing crime problem, both in our urban and our rural areas. There are techniques and methods that can be used which are conducive to the creation and the development of the kind of an environment to which we have referred.

Good police–community relations means, "good police, good community;" all "good police," and all "good community" is a utopia we will never reach — of this, I am aware. But this is the goal, this is the objective for which we must constantly strive.

Human relations training is a must in every police department, both large and small.

About seven years ago, we were faced with a problem around a junior high school, after dismissal, when youngsters were on their way home from school. Acts of vandalism occurred to properties in the adjoining areas, and it was necessary for us to detail additional police personnel. Resentment developed among the youngsters, and additional police problems were created.

In conference with the principal, I suggested that he allow one of our policemen, who worked the sector car, and whom the youngsters saw everyday, to participate in one of the classes in "Civics." Here the policeman met the youngsters on their "home grounds" and in their own environment, and discussed problems common to both. Here the youngsters had a chance to ask the policeman why certain things were necessary and why he chased them off the corners, etc. These sessions were most fruitful, and now, when the policeman was patrolling his sector, the youngsters were waving to him in friendly fashion rather than thumbing their noses at him.

One of the most effective means of getting the youngster close to police has been the practice of joint participation in school assemblies, not necessarily by members of special units, but by run-of-the-mill policemen who now and then do a good job.

In our department, official commendations are given to policemen quite often for "service and action" beyond the call of duty. I have made it a practice of accumulating a number of these commendations and then, in cooperation with a local high school principal, setting up a special school assembly at which these policemen are given these commendations. Usually, the president of the school council will read the citation, and then personally present the commendation to the policeman. This does two things. It makes the youngster aware of the fact that, like themselves, policemen are rewarded when they do exceptional deeds, and it gives the lowly policeman a sense of status and importance in the community which he serves. Also, he sees the youngster in a different light. After this, at times, the police have been guests of the student council and some of the parents in the lunch room of the school where they have talked informally with the parents, teachers and the youngsters themselves.

I don't want you to think that this is the general practice of division and district commanders, for this would be far from the truth. We have in our police department men in supervisory positions who believe that this kind of approach is a lot of "hogwash" and "for the birds." I am in no way indicating that these are "the" ways to develop good police–community relations; for there is no *one* way. I am saying, however, that these are *some* of the ways that I know, from experience, have helped to make our burden of policing a little easier.

Unfortunately, we can have all of these very fine community-related programs and approaches, but unless we have policemen that are professionally oriented, and unless we have a continuing in-service training program that at least exposes all echelons of the department to the need for training, and unless the motivation, direction and guidance comes from the top — any kind of program is doomed to failure and is a waste of the taxpayer's money. I am sure that the success of some city administrations in facing the problems of school desegregation in some of our cities was due primarily to the professional attitude assumed by police administrators and their supervisory subordinates in these cities.

Over two years ago, the police department, in conjunction with the Philadelphia Commission on Human Relations, contracted for a survey by Applied Psychological Services of Wayne, Pa., to make a detailed study of the need of the Philadelphia Police Academy in the human relations area, and to develop a training program that would be sufficient to meet the needs.

The *Preface* to this study by Dr. Siegel and his associates states, and I quote, "One of the characteristics common to all large, industrial, urban areas in the United States today is the growing concentration of Negroes, Puerto Ricans and/or other Spanish Americans in the central, older neighborhoods, with gradual and general movement of the white, non-Spanish population toward the widening fringe of the city."

The expanding numbers of the colored and Spanish-speaking minorities have generated widening tensions and conflict and ever-increasing contact between these minority citizens and the local police forces. The growing numbers have also nurtured increased political awareness and power within the minority groups, with corresponding challenge to the traditional patterns of discrimination, segregation and differential treatment.

It is a truism that when intergroup tensions and conflict emerge in any community, the police take the brunt of, and may sometimes add fuel to, the smoldering fires. The rest of the citizenry and of officialdom can withdraw from the conflict, but the police cannot. When other institutions for education, persuasion and order fail, the police take over. They may not always perform their job with finesse, but they are not permitted to fail their function of establishing order, by force if necessary.

It is no accident and no rare phenomenon, therefore, that the local police force is the target of complaint and criticism from all sides with respect to intergroup relations. The more prejudiced elements of the dominant white community complain that the police are "soft" on the minority people. The minority press, legal defense organizations and civic leadership complain that the police fail to distinguish between individuals within the minority population, look upon all minority citizens as subjects of suspicion, are discourteous and often use excessive force.

The term "police brutality" has become a cliché in the discussion of police–community relations.

The police themselves tend to reflect the attitudes of the general population, and often react negatively to the hostility of those citizens who see the officers' color as different from their own.

Human relations training for police officers has been a plank in nearly every recommended program for interracial or intergroup community relations that has been recorded in the past forty years or so. Governors, commissions, mayor's committees, and civic councils have made such recommendations at least since the race riots which occurred in Washington, D. C., East St. Louis and Chicago during and immediately following World War I. They were renewed again after the World War II riots in Detroit, Beaumont, Philadelphia and Harlem. Dr. Gordon Allport of Harvard University published a report on an experiment in police training with a group of Boston police officers in 1942. Joseph Kluchesky, former Police Chief in Milwaukee, wrote a pamphlet on the subject in 1945, after several years work with the American Council on Race Relations. Dr. Joseph Lohman, then Professor of Sociology at the University of Chicago, developed a training course in intergroup relations for the Chicago Park District Police, which was later adopted for use by the Southern Police Institute.

The need of concern for training in this area, and the need for a better understanding, both by the police and the public of each other's problems were forcefully brought to our attention some 18 months ago, when a group of ministers indicated to the mayor of our city and the police commissioner their growing concern about the rising tension against alleged police brutality, alleged police discourtesies and alleged disrespect for human dignity on the part of some of our police officers. The one bright spot in the cloud of community unrest was the admission by this group that the community *itself* was not blameless and could well look into its own attitude concerning its disrespect for authority.

Complaints submitted were thoroughly investigated to the satisfaction of all concerned, and the proper actions were taken.

These experiences pointed up more than ever the need for some kind of continuing, day-to-day program that would have as its purpose the interpretation of the "role of the police in community life."

Using these very same ministers, who now seemed to have been convinced that police were not always wrong, and did not always act with malice and bad judgment, as key persons, we embarked on a program called "Getting To Know You." Originally, we concentrated on church groups. This is how it worked. A minister called together a group of his parishioners, and we brought in top police officials who explained to the people police administration policy. The inspector of the division and the captain and the shift lieutenant of the precinct or district involved were brought in, and each introduced to the audience and each asked to explain his role in the enforcement of law in the community.

Ofttimes we had a small police "combo" that entertained before and after the session. This in itself established an atmosphere where communication was made easier.

After all of the police officials had been introduced and had an opportunity to express themselves, color slides of police activity were shown. Slides ofttimes related to activities within the community itself.

After this, the crowd was usually divided into small groups, and the lieutenant or the captain or one of the police–community relations officers acted as resource persons for discussions.

Here the "little person" had a chance to get his problem off his chest, talk back to the policeman, so to speak, without fear of reprisal. Never is there enough time for these buzz sessions, and they just have to be broken off. More often than not, we were asked to come back again.

You might ask, "What about the size of these groups?" We will go to any group, no matter what the size, as long as we have an opportunity to *sell* the Philadelphia Police Department.

There has been a continuing complaint about the "good old days," when the beat man was constantly on the scene. Mechanization has, in large measure, replaced the beat man with motorized patrol, and motorized patrol is here to stay. Ways and means must be found to develop lines of communication between the car patrolmen and the community in which they work.

One of the most effective tools in developing a good community spirit has been the emergence in recent years of the block committees. We have found that it has been extremely helpful and well worth the time in man hours lost on patrol to have the sergeant and the car crew or crews working a particular sector meet with these block committees so that they may hear firsthand the police problems of a particular sector. Whenever possible, we have insisted on the captain of the precinct or district being present. Thus, the people who are directly involved meet with the captain, who is responsible for the police administration of the district, the sergeant who is responsible for the direct supervision, and the policeman who is responsible for the "doing."

We feel that we must embark on, and push forward an ambitious program of this kind, if we are to offset the attacks made against police by some individuals and some groups who are motivated, not by a desire to help positively in the development of good law enforcement, but to prey on the ignorance, fear, and prejudices of a few who have not been able to understand the role of the police officer in developing a good community.

On the other hand, this kind of program gives some of our police officers, who because of their ignorance, their lack of understanding, and in some cases their bigotry, an opportunity to see that there are some people in *all* communities who have the desire, the ambition, and the vision to see the need for a good community, and who gladly accept the responsibilities that are integral parts of citizenship in this great democracy.

Good police–community relations is a two-way street of *mutual* understanding and of mutual respect.

The St. Louis Story

JAMES T. McCRORY

(Then) Director of Community Relations, St. Louis Police Department

MAY 23, 1958

Tomorrow, the 24th of May, the St. Louis Police–Community Relations program will be three years old.

If we were to dedicate the candles on its birthday cake, the first would have to go to this very Institute, where the idea originated; the second to the St. Louis staff of the National Conference of Christians and Jews, who carried it back and put it into action; and the third to hundreds of citizens and professionals in St. Louis who have volunteered thousands of hours of their time since then to make it work.

I think the Board of Police Commissioners and the St. Louis Police Department deserve a candle too, but we'll wait until next year and claim candle number four for them.

It was May 24, 1955, when the local NCCJ office convened a conference of 60 top leaders in the fields of business, law enforcement, welfare and community organization, to hear a team report on the first Police–Community Relations Institute held at Michigan State a few weeks earlier.

In the discussion that followed this report session, it was agreed that concrete steps had to be taken to improve cooperation between the police and citizens of St. Louis, and between the Police Department and other community agencies in the city.

The question was: How? To come up with a plan of action, the NCCJ formed a steering group representing a wide range of community agencies, including the Police Department. The plan worked out by this steering group was approved in July by the Board of Police Commissioners, and publicly announced in October, 1955.

The first St. Louis plan called for the organization of citizen Police–Community Relations Committees at the grass roots level in each of the 12 Police Districts, beginning in the three highest crime-rate districts.

Staff to organize and get these first three district committees underway was provided on a part-time basis by the NCCJ, and on a voluntary basis by members of the steering group, which included representatives of the school board, the local universities, the Urban League, the Jewish Community Relations Council and the Police Department, among others.

The emphasis, then, was on the involvement of citizens at the grass roots level.

We have learned, for example, that to keep any volunteer program going, full-time staff to coordinate and service the district committees is an absolute necessity.

We have learned that police–citizen relationships are neither the only ones in need of repair, nor the most difficult to work with. There is just as much disorder on the interprofessional playing field, and it often seems harder to unravel interagency wrangles exactly because we professionals are so well equipped, professionally, to defend our own positions—whatever they may be and however, in the peculiar histories of our own community agencies, we may have got into them.

We have learned that merely setting up channels of communication is far from enough, and that mutual understanding between police and citizens, between the Police Department and other community agencies, is no guarantee of better relations. All too often, poor relations are based on a very good understanding indeed, by each one of us, of how the *other* fellow or the *other* department is falling down on the job.

One thing that has not changed, however, is the initial focus of the program — the decision to begin by involving citizens at the district and neighborhood level in problems of law enforcement.

This first involving was anything but an easy job. We began in the three highest crime rate districts — and the districts where the gap between police and citizens seemed greatest.

At first glance, these districts seemed very much alike. They were all overcrowded, they were predominantly Negro, and they were for the most part blighted housing areas — the central city slum areas.

Between October, 1955 and February, 1956, these first three District Police–Community Relations Committees were organized. The first step was making the rounds of settlement houses and churches in the district, explaining the program and asking for the names and addresses of good, solid citizens who lived in the district, as candidates for committee membership.

I wasn't around yet to witness these first meetings, but they must have been harrowing — to the citizens, many of them in a police station for the first time, to the District Police Commander, who had seldom met a large group of citizens in his station before, and for the volunteers from the initial steering group who had to explain a brand-new program, and break some exceedingly sturdy ice on both sides of the fence.

The hope was that by getting representative citizens and District Police Commanders to sit down together and let down their hair, we might begin to break down some stereotypes each had about the other, and begin paving the way for some realistic two-way cooperation.

The success of this process varied from district to district, from time to time, and to be perfectly honest, according to who was "on" at the district and which citizens turned up at the monthly meetings.

The approach of some citizens confirmed the darkest police suspicions that "those are a bunch of cranks who are trying to tell us how to run the Department."

The approach of some police officers confirmed an even darker citizen suspicion that the real purpose of the program was to recruit more "snitchers" for the police.

Even when rapport was best, when police and citizens concluded an evening's discussion with a sincere appreciation of each other's concerns and each other's problems, the question remained: Where do we go from here? So we understand that law enforcement is a joint responsibility — what do we do about it?

One committee, sparked by an energetic chairman and an interested high school principal, sponsored a public panel discussion on juvenile delinquency, with local experts, representative parents and high school students as participants.

It was a great success. Nearly 300 people from the district attended and both the daily newspapers and the Negro weekly press carried stories about it.

But that was that. The principal had an overcrowded high school to administer. The chairman, a YWCA executive in the district, got married, moved away and the district committee collapsed.

Another district committee undertook a project to distribute leaflets on how citizens could help prevent home burglaries. The Police Department and the operating director of the St. Louis Crime Commission helped to prepare the copy. The St. Louis Housing Authority, which had the bulk of its low income housing projects in the district, took care of the printing.

But then we decided it would be best to organize the committee formally, and let the members elect their own officers to carry out the distribution. We tried it too fast, without enough preparation.

Attendance at the monthly meeting when the "election" was held was sparse. The committee members elected as their chairman a man who had no occupation, no income, no phone and, apparently, no ambition other than being chairman, for he never called another meeting. Before it could be patched up, the mission pastor who had steered this group since is origin was called to a church in Cincinnati, and that was the end of that committee.

Our third committee collapsed all by itself, without benefit of a project. The secretary got sick, the chairman lost interest, and the members simply stopped coming after the first year and one-half.

None of this experience was wasted. We were learning.

On questionnaires circulated to participants at the end of the first two years, police officers — almost to a man — gave us one big answer: "Too much talk and not enough action."

A young Jesuit at St. Louis University did his master's thesis on the program and suggested two more answers to our early distress: inadequate programming and lack of full-time staff services for the district committees.

Then in May, 1957, the present Board of Police Commissioners granted funds to bring in three top consultants to review the entire St. Louis program to that date. These were Bob Scott, the assistant director in charge of youth programs of the Michigan Department of Corrections; George Schermer, executive director of the Philadelphia Commission on Human Relations; and Robert Mangum, deputy commissioner of the New York City Police Department.

All three recommended that the first need of the program was for full-time staff to service the district committees. That's how I got into the program — first as staff consultant on a grant from the Police Board, then as director of community relations on the civilian staff of the Police Board, beginning in December, 1957.

The consultants also agreed that the purpose of the district committees needed clarifying. Were these to be small planning groups to carry out projects and take educational programs out into the district? Or were we trying to reach out with educational programs by getting big attendance at the monthly district committees?

Attendance had been running from as high as 60 and 70 persons to as low as 7 or 8. You can't plan a project with 70 people in on the discussion—and even 70 people is a minute slice of the thousands we were trying to reach in an average police district.

We decided to keep the district committees small—30 to 35 members—but to make them as representative as possible, with a representative of every conceivable group in the district: block units, PTA's, service clubs, church groups, and the like.

Our members would carry the police–citizen cooperation message back to their own groups, we hoped, and we would rely on the organizations represented by district committee members to gather the audience for panel discussions, films and other education programs.

We began the third year of the program last fall with one committee reorganized but not yet functioning, two district committees in need of reorganization, with a full-time staff director, a secretary to mimeograph, get out mailings and handle correspondence, and—now—a Police Board not only going along with the program, but fully committed to it.

We began the year with something else I've not mentioned yet — the real accomplishment of the first two years.

I have mentioned that the first three districts committees were started in the highest crime-rate districts. All three were predominantly Negro, but they were not, except in disorganization, really alike.

The worst of these, the Ninth District, had been a slum for years; its police problem was white before it was Negro, and its resources were few: Urban League block units with thin membership, struggling against waves of newcomers from the South and the fact that most of the property was absentee-owned, tenement and poorly maintained; a YMCA, most of whose clientele — like members of most of the established Negro churches — had moved westward to better housing; and one settlement house run on a shoestring in a dilapidated mansion.

These are not many community leaders for a district with 65,000 people in it. Yet before the district Police–Community Relations Committee was started, few of them had ever met each other, much less the district Police Commander.

I think it would be fair to say that it was the district Police–Community Relations Committee that brought them all together. If those first two years did nothing else, they changed many attitudes that key professionals in the Ninth Police District had held about each other, and it led to the development of a working relationship among the police, agency professionals and block unit leaders in the District that had never existed before.

The same thing occurred in the other two districts. The first two years of the program broke down barriers that had stood too long between the police, the agency professionals and the natural leaders of these neighborhoods.

To borrow a phrase from Dr. Lohman, "people met who never met before" — and who should have, because the police commander, the school principal, the settlement house director, and the welfare worker all have a direct stake in each other's work.

By the beginning of the third year, the St. Louis program had as a nucleus a hundred or so leadership people in three police districts who realized their joint stake. The channels of communication had been opened.

Now we had a new problem to work with: communication for what?

The first to ask this question were the citizen members of the District Police–Community Relations Committees. It was not difficult then — and it is not now — to bring neighborhood leaders out to the first few meeting, for an exchange of concerns with the police commander and other professionals in a district.

But after a few meetings like this, the citizens get restive and begin to ask "What are we going to do about this? When are we going to move?" If they don't get an answer, they move themselves — right out of the district committee meetings.

During the past year, the program began to move. The channels of communication we had set up began to be used to work on specific, concrete problems.

In the Ninth Police District, the problem the committee chose to attack was sanitation. There was good reason for this. The Ninth District in the central city was also the dirtiest; sanitation and enforcement of the sanitation laws was a major headache for the police, the Urban League block units, the settlement house, the health division and, needless to add, the city street-cleaners.

A subcommittee looked up the city's sanitation laws, met with the police sanitation officers who must enforce them, and went to court to watch the handling of sanitation violation cases.

This subcommittee decided that educational campaigns by block units, lecturing, and finally, the summoning to court of hardened offenders by police sanitation officers all were being nullified by long-standing practice in the courts of "nolle prossing" most cases on abatement and neither fining nor assessing court costs against offenders.

At this point the project outgrew the Police–Community Relations program, but it is worth sketching what has happened since then.

The district committee members took their report to four of the biggest neighborhood rehabilitation organizations in St. Louis, and found they had encountered the same problem. Representatives of these five groups then met with the Municipal Court judges and asked that in the future, sanitation law violators at least be assessed court costs in order to put teeth into the law.

When this was unsuccessful, these five groups went on to form a city-wide Citizens Committee on Sanitation. At last count, there were 29 neighborhood organizations in this citizens committee. The group has secured a study, by a special committee of the Bar Association, of court handling of sanitation cases, and plans, I understand, to follow this up by seeking better supervision of rubbish collection crews, eradication of nuisances on city-owned property and an expanded sanitation inspection force.

The Police–Community Relations Committee in the Fourth Police District, where the bulk of our low-income housing projects are concentrated, focused its attention on juvenile delinquency—a logical concern in a district with thousands of children, too few recreation facilities, and too many broken or disorganized homes.

Wisely, the committee narrowed its concern to one small, but very important segment of the delinquency problem — truancy, one of the first indicators of delinquency. Again, a subcommittee was appointed which quite literally made the rounds of every agency concerned with truancy law enforcement — the schools, the Police Department, the Juvenile Court and the City Prosecuting Attorney.

The committee found that every agency had its problems — shortage of staff, lack of facilities, lack of supervision. But at the same time, the committee found that perhaps the biggest immediate problem was a lack of interagency cooperation, and a real dispute over who should do what, where and when in cases of truancy.

Just three weeks ago, representatives of the Fourth District Committee took their concern to the new, full-time Juvenile Court Judge in St. Louis, and asked if he might take leadership in bringing all agencies involved in truancy control together, and outlining a clear set of responsibilities and procedures.

The judge agreed to do this. He has a 16-hour a day job on his hands already, reorganizing our Juvenile Court. But he indicated that by the time the schools reopen in fall, he hoped to have the additional court administrative and supervisory staff he needs, and would be free then to take leadership in an area in which he is very concerned.

The concern, of course, is that truancy is one of the first indicators of delinquency. Handled quickly and effectively, many casual school truants in the first four grades would not go on to become chronic truants, school behavior problems and — all too often — delinquents who pose much more difficult problems for the police, the courts and the community.

The members of the Fourth District Police–Community Relations Committee feel they have done something concrete toward a solution of St. Louis' truancy problem in helping to bring together the agencies involved in it. Next year, with the Judge of the Juvenile Court taking leadership in getting closer interagency cooperation, the district committee looks forward to carrying out a second job: publicizing, to the citizens of their own district and to citizen groups throughout the city, the staff and the facilities these agencies need to do their jobs effectively.

The third of our original district committees, the Tenth District group, has had the most difficult time in finding a focus, in terms of a specific survey, action or information project.

Yet at the same time, this group has perhaps the most promising potential of any of our district committees. Nearly half its members are professional people who live in the district — doctors, lawyers, educators, businessmen. In its membership is represented virtually every important organization, field and institution in the district. This committee, in structure, comes closer than any other to being the perfect liaison group between the district police command and the inhabitants of the district.

The problem the group is wrestling with today is "What do we want to use this liaison for?" besides the regular monthly discussion of district problems with the district commander.

Dozens of community problems and needs directly related to law and order have been pointed out in district committee meetings, all the way from inadequate street lighting to a lack of supervised recreation or even adequate playgrounds for youngsters in the district.

Two months ago, the committee laid half its problem — that dealing with juvenile delinquency — in the lap of an interprofessional subcommittee called the Educational Committee on Youth.

This new outgrowth is composed of public and parochial school principals in the district, the district commander and the juvenile officers attached to the district. Its chairman is the district director of elementary education for the public schools.

In just two meetings, this professional subcommittee has come up with a list of potential trouble spots in the district, helped to improve liaison between schools and police in anticipating teenage gang "rumbles," and is making a survey of youth resources in the district with specific recommendations on what else is needed.

This is a pretty wise division of labor. Few people are better equipped than school principals and police officers to tell community leaders why a district's children are getting into trouble.

Once these needs have been specified, the lay committee leaders in the district Police–Community Relations Committee can act to see that they are met with much more vigor and independence than any professional would find it was to display.

Two more district committees have been organized this year, and since they are new, the directions they seem to be taking can only be indicated; but in both cases, the direction stems from the character of the individual district.

Our Third District Committee has been operating since the first of the year under the leadership of a settlement house director. The district is the scene of large-scale in-migration of poor whites from the rural south, and the district committee's first project, appropriately, was a mimeographed pamphlet listing both family counselling and recreation facilities available in the district.

Two months ago, the first of our district committees was organized in the 12th Police District — a so-called transition district in St. Louis' west end. More than half this district is already organized into neighborhood improvement groups, all trying to keep house standards up in a neighborhood of large, but old homes.

Some of these improvement groups are white, some Negro. One — the strongest and best-organized of them all — is integrated. Representatives of these existing neighborhood improvement groups, plus representatives of PTA's and School Patrons Alliances from the one unorganized section, formed the nucleus of the district committee.

The Districe Police–Community Relations Committee has already provided more than a liaison with the police command in the Twelfth District. It has served to bring together leaders of neighborhood improvement organizations who had never met before and who were unaware, in many cases, that other groups were tackling the same problems in neighborhood deterioration with which they were faced.

This group has also come up with plans for a project of unusual interest: a handbook on laws relating to neighborhood rehabilitation and improvement, covering everything from anti-noise ordinances to sanitation and zoning laws. The handbook would list laws by problem, state what can and cannot be done, who is charged with enforcement and what citizens themselves can do about it.

The last week of June, the chairmen of the five district committees will make their year-end report at a meeting of the St. Louis Council on Police–Community Relations, the city-wide coordinating group which has replaced the original steering committee of three years ago.

I cannot speak for the chairmen, but I suspect that the burden of their reports will be that the channels of communication set up district by district and slowly strengthened these past three years are beginning to be used — by citizens, by police and by other professionals, to work out together solutions to specific, concrete problems in law enforcement.

I don't think we can yet claim more than a beginning. At the outside, the Police–Community Relations program in St. Louis has involved perhaps a thousand persons. There are still hundreds of thousands of citizens to be reached, dozens of interagency problems to be solved, many changes we in the Police Department want to make. Most of the doing still remains to be done.

But we are beginning to move.

I believe the thousands persons who have been involved to date are important — perhaps the most active and articulate citizen and professional leaders in the five districts we have covered.

Requests for organization of police–community relations committees in other districts are now ahead of our ability to provide staff services for them.

And, perhaps most important, we have a few modest successes under our belt now.

By orienting themselves to specific problems, the district committees have begun to break down a staggering problem into manageable tasks.

By succeeding at the first few of these, they have helped convince even more people that the job is not only important — but *possible*.

Preparing for Police Leadership in Community Relations

HARRY G. FOX

Chief Inspector, Philadelphia Police Department

MAY 25, 1967

Are community relations programs needed? Who shall lead the way?

A recent study by the International Association of Chiefs of Police, in collaboration with the United States Conference of Mayors, covered cities with 30,000 and up.

They discovered the chiefs of over one-half of the police departments participating in the study admitted freely their departments have been under fire from citizens groups. Charges of biased and preferential treatment, plus accusations of "police brutality" have been leveled by citizens again and again. Yet, less than one-third of these police chiefs have even attempted to develop a formal police–community relations program.

The need for police leadership in community relations is rapidly becoming the number one administrative challenge to law enforcement officials. Just as the Allies were losing the war in 1918 and 1941, until the full support and military power of America was rushed into the breach, so we, in 1967, are losing the war against crime and delinquency and will continue to lose until the police are reinforced by the full support and interest of the American citizenry.

This support, like an acre of diamonds is available in the backyards of all police departments, who are willing to search for and uncover it.

There are four basic tasks which must be performed in preparing to lead and develop any police–community relations programs worthy of citizen support. The first is the selection of obtainable goals.

A. Selecting Goals

The Police Chief who wants his department to grasp the reins of leadership in the field of community relations has a Herculean task facing him. Unlike Mr. Applegate in the show, DAMN YANKEES, who with a wave of his hand, transformed the aged Washington Senator fan into the young superstar, Joe Hardie, a police chief is not a magician.

He must take a department with decades of the "closed corporation" tradition and mold it into one of progressive, dynamic, open-door leadership in the community. This calls for new dimensions in police administration.

The Chief and his staff must pinpoint problems, develop plans, offer training and change attitudes. These are necessary for a firm foundation on which to build a strong police–community relations program.

The first question he must answer is what do I want to accomplish — what are my basic goals? A progressive Chief would consider the following:

1. To firmly establish in every member of the entire community the belief that their *police department* is the most important factor of government, *essential* to their *safety and welfare*.

2. To win the wholehearted *support* of all citizens in *fighting* the forces that breed, nurture and produce *crime* and *delinquency*.

3. To keep the *community informed* of the police department's operations, policies, and problems, prepared to *correct misunderstandings, answer critics,* and *repel attacks.*

4. To stimulate the individual *police officer* to *learn more about his own department* and to influence him to *tell his family, friends and neighbors* what he has learned.

5. To open and keep *open police channels of communication* with *local leaders,* groups, schools, churches and all other persons or organizations who help mold public opinion.

6. To *cooperate* with all *other law enforcement units,* as well as *public and private agencies* in *promoting* a unified *attack* on the problems of juvenile delinquency, adult crime and crime-breeding hazards and influences.

The key words of these goals are *belief, support, inform, stimulate, communicate* and *cooperate.* They're a fomidable array of action words that need plans, decisions and dedication to make them realities.

The next task to be performed is in the field of training.

B. Training for Leadership

The second question a chief must ask is the who and what of training for leadership in community relations.

We often hear the phrase — he's a born leader. Perhaps Caesar, Napoleon and George Washington were born to fulfill leadership challenges destined to change the lives of millions. But, unfortunately, average police officials or men on the beat aren't born with the native qualities of earth-shaking leadership. They must study, overcome reluctances, devote free time, persuade and convince themselves that the police occupation is synonymous with community relations leadership. This takes personal decision, dedication and sacrifice.

The enlightened police chief will provide voluntary and compulsory opportunities for his men to develop their latent talent in this field.

Basic leadership qualities of *intelligence, maturity, confidence, experience, loyalty, strength,* and *resourcefulness* must now be supplemented with new *knowledge, tolerance, enthusiasm* and *vision.*

In Philadelphia, the preparation and training for community relations leadership is given to police officers, both formally and informally, from varied sources. Here are several examples:

On a weekly basis, the police commanders, from Captain to Commissioner, gather in the auditorium of Police Headquarters. A program is presented, designed to promote understanding, provoke questions, and broaden horizons. The guest leaders come from various disciplines. They offer viewpoints that police rarely encounter and often resist. A run-down of program leaders, representing all segments of the total community who appeared in recent months, would include:

The Mayor of Philadelphia
President of Philadelphia Chapter, Urban League
Director of Philadelphia Chapter,
     American Civil Liberties Union
North City Congress Staff
Philadelphia Fellowship Commission,
     Executive Director

Commanding Officer, Salvation Army
Executive Director,
    Philadelphia Antipoverty Action Program
Commissioner of Human Relations
Staff Psychiatrists,
    Temple University Mental Health Clinic
City Beautiful, Clean-Up, Fix-Up,
    Block Committee Leaders
Police Athletic League Board of Directors
Philadelphia Scout Executive,
    Boy Scouts of America
Executive Director, Police Advisory Board
Members of the Northeast Chamber of Commerce

plus many other talented people, representing the various publics, who have daily contact with police. As a result of these conferences, police have become more knowledgeable about new aspects of the area and people they serve. Civil rights, poverty, business, youth, education, religion, mental health, traffic, sanitation, recreation, cultural differences and community services are just a few of the ingredients contained in this "soft sell" training vehicle.

Another approach is through the North City Congress. This is a federation of civic organizations, business organizations, and community leaders, whose territory covers the area of Philadelphia's 1964 riot. North City Congress received a sizeable federal grant to explore new ways of improving police–community relations in their difficult area.

After months of planning, preparing and breaking down barriers, a joint program of police and citizens got under way. Over six hundred policemen, drawn from the patrol cars and footbeats of the area in which hostility toward police is an accepted norm, have participated in a two-day workshop. They resist at times, argue at times, disagree at times, but the sessions always conclude with the police doing new thinking and taking a sharp look at their own attitudes toward the community in general and citizens in particular. The most unusual part of this program is the climax. After both citizens and policemen have experienced workshops and conferences in their own "leagues," they are then placed together for the "world series."

Detailed and on duty, these men, in groups of three or four, are instructed to report to a specific location. Here they sit in living rooms and kitchens of tiny homes, church parlors, and back rooms of stores in the area of their regular assignments. In a relaxed social setting, the citizens, who also act as hosts and neighbors, exchange views and attitudes with the police. Crime, delinquency, sanitation, inspection, traffic, truancy, vandalism, vacant houses, abandoned cars, courtesy, and mutual respect are discussed in depth, over a cup of coffee. It's police–community relations at the grass roots level.

Dean Joseph Lohman of the University of California, advisor to Presidential committees in this field, personally made a trip to Philadelphia to observe this program in action. After sitting in the parlors and kitchens, he commented that the "dialogue" between a policeman and a private citizen, who are both interested in improving the same area, is an exciting pioneer program in the field of police–community relations.

Many other training programs, designed to help police become community leaders, are under way in the City of Brotherly Love. Police officials sit shoulder to shoulder on the Fellowship Commission's committee on community tensions, discussing pertinent community problems. The Board of Education offers special courses to policemen on public speaking and conference techniques, to help them become more verbal and convincing in dealing with citizens groups. Young police officers on their own time and at their own expense are studying psychology and sociology at Temple University. The courses emphasize training for leadership, both in the police department and in the general community.

Many of these training opportunities are geared to the police supervisor on division, precinct, and district level. But supervisors can't do the community relations tasks alone. Much of their time is spent in basic command duties. "Door Openers" or "legmen" on the patrolmen level are urgently needed. This is the third step of preparedness.

C. Selecting and Training Community Relations Specialists

Specialization in the field of community relations has developed in the larger police departments in recent years. These policemen are selected for their background, training, experience and aptitude in the public relations and social fields. Ability to communicate, win confidence and develop new programs are prime requisites. Knowledge of public relations tools, speaking, writing, and visual aids are necessary skills.

Competent men, selected and trained for full-time work in police–community relations, are rapidly becoming as necessary as traffic, juvenile and vice specialists to the police administrator.

The farsighted chief will prepare now. He will use the knowledge and support of community leaders in developing plans and making selections for specialization. An illustration of this technique was utilized by the Philadelphia Police Department when it initiated the Police–Community Relations Unit in May, 1956.

The Police Commissioner stated that, although the Juvenile Division had been working closely with community groups and private citizens, he wanted the program to expand and encompass the entire Police Department. The Commissioner was willing to assign police manpower to this project. The Commanding Inspector of the Juvenile Division was directed to implement this plan of personnel selection and transfer. A Planning and Personnel Selection Committee was chosen. It consisted of:

Police Inspector, Commanding Juvenile Aid Division

Superintendent of Police Academy

Citizen Leader of Philadelphia Block Committees

Head of the Board of Education Visual Aid Division

The Superintendent of Public Schools

These four men and one woman met together with leaders of community organizations. They recommended the following:

1. A selected police officer be designated in each of the police districts as a police–community relations officer.

2. A comprehensive and lengthy training course, designed to prepare these police officers for effective public relations work, be developed.

3. Each community relations officer detailed to a district would work under the direction and guidance of a district captain.

4. The Juvenile Aid Command would be the program coordinator.

5. Visual aids and other tools should be developed, starting with a sound film of citizen–police cooperation.

The Planning and Selection Board next turned to manpower selection. Personnel records were checked for education, police experience, and prior work in the social field. Actions of police who were serving as officers and committee chairman in religious, fraternal, business, educational, youth and civic groups were noted. Police commanders and supervisors, who observed men on a day-to-day basis, interacting with the general public, were asked to make recommendations.

From this pool of men, a series of interviews were held, first, by the Selection Board, and then, by the coordinator, who knew the general problems and differences of individual police districts. Every effort was made to select the men with the best potential and fit the "square peg to the square hole." Twenty-three men were designated police–community relations officers.

Appropriate publicity through press conferences by the Police Commissioner kept the public apprised of the new plans and the progress made.

A five-week training course was designated, first, to help the new police-community relations officer become an expert on the operations of his own police district; secondly, to expose him to the many publics that make up the total community.

Field trips, lectures, demonstrations, and discussions with public, private, religious, civic, educational and business agencies were on the training agenda. The men were ready to begin their apprenticeship, with training continuing one day a week.

The strength of this simple plan was the foundation that included representative of the public. These interested citizens gave their time and talent, without remuneration, to plan, select, train, advise, and evaluate the police–community relations specialists. This method insured door opening to many cloistered sections of the community, because it was a citizen-oriented and police cooperative venture.

The police specialist, chosen under these conditions, can easily engage in a program designed to achieve departmental goals and increase citizen support. He becomes a respected professional segment of both the department and the community. But the job can't end here, for one important factor in preparing for police leadership in community relations is still lacking — the convictions and attitude of the chief.

D. Attitude of Chief

Preachers say, "Do as I say, not as I do," but if a doctor had the same illness as I have, and he prescribes one treatment for me and a different one for himself, would he inspire confidence in his patients?

A police chief can issue orders, directives and memoranda to his men. He can devise plans, procedures, tests, demonstrations and models of perfect police–community relations achievements. But if he isn't unequivocally convinced that the primary police responsibilities of law enforcement can be made easier by an active police–community relations program, all the orders, plans and goals are useless.

A community that fully believes their chief is sincere in preparing for leadership in that community will give him additional respect and consideration. He must convince both the men of his department and the citizens of his jurisdiction that he will work with devotion and dedication to achieve his community relations goals.

He can demonstrate his convictions by performing some of the following recommendations:

1. *Select* a high-ranking police officer from the top staff to command, develop and report on a day-to-day basis the total community relations efforts.

2. *Support* his community relations commander, supervisors and specialists with the full resources of the entire department, including budgeting, for equipment and training.

3. *Encourage* members of minority groups to become members of the police department.

4. *Develop* procedures to accept, investigate, and fairly process citizen complaints concerning the actions, words, and official conduct of police.

5. Develop guidelines and *policies* for the individual policeman to follow, particularly in judgment areas concerning incidents and nonpunitive contacts with citizen groups.

6. Personally inform his men, by word, action, and appearance at the scene of community problems, of his *deep desire* to maintain a professional and cooperative community relations program at all times.

7. Set up an "open door" policy for community leaders to allow and encourage *direct contact* with the chief on major community problems.

8. Make numerous *personal appearances* at community functions and *verbally express* the need for joint citizen-police cooperation to achieve goals.

The chief who follows these recommendations will become known as an enlightened administrator, interested in the welfare both of his men and the citizens they protect.

E. Conclusion

Preparing for police leadership in community relations is not an easy task. It cannot be done quickly. It cannot be done routinely. It must be done with planning, direction, control and dedication.

Like going to heaven, it can be approached in many ways. But one thing is certain. The four factors set forth above may be hidden or disguised. Other words may be substituted, but the meaning will always be present.

To a police chief who wants to prepare for his rightful leadership role in the drama of day-to-day community relations, he must:

1. Select his goals.
2. Train for leadership.
3. Commit his men and department to work in this area.
4. Demonstrate, by words and actions, his firm personal belief in the importance of good community relations.

As the chief studies these four pillars, which act as the foundation for successful community support, he suddenly realizes that the old order, the closed corporation, the "open in the name of the law" dynasty has passed away. In its place is a partnership with the public, citizen leaders, and the neighbor across the street. It is the enlisting of the support of the individual citizen, through well-planned and executed community relations programs, that the police chief will earn his rightful place as a respected and honored community leader.

Oscar Wilde once said, "The longer I live, the more keenly I feel that what was good enough for our fathers *is not* good enough for us."

The police chief who applies this epigram to his department and prepares to lead it in this changing society, will produce a brand of law enforcement that is good enough for every citizen of his community.

Understanding the Police

QUINN TAMM

Executive Director, International Association of Chiefs of Police, Washington, D.C.

MAY 18, 1965

I could not think of a more appropriate title for my presentation than the one assigned to me: "Understanding the Police." I think I can say that seeking to bring about understanding of the police is a pursuit which occupies the majority of my waking hours, and I can assure you that it is a full-time task.

We are constantly searching for the keys to public understanding of our mission and the duties which we are compelled to carry out. Recently, we conducted a survey with the United States Conference of Mayors to gather information from police executives on their problems and programs relating to today's most explosive issue, the racial situation.

The survey attempted to put together a picture of the problems associated with police handling of racial tensions and disturbances by requesting information concerning complaints being made against the police, complaints being made by police officers, and programs and plans for meeting the challenge. Needless to say, demonstrators and other persons deeply involved in civil rights movements or civil disobedience campaigns are not going to see things from the same point of view as the police. There are marked contrasts, and to some extent, adversary attitudes. Demonstrators and civil rights workers, as we all know, have been very critical of police actions in many places. On the other hand, the police have been critical of the tactics employed by demonstrators. The very actions which police consider necessary and proper for preserving public peace and order are the things about which bitter complains are often made. Sometimes the complaints concern methods used by the police rather than the tactics per se, and sometimes it is the tactics themselves that are considered objectionable.

We have carefully scrutinized the responses to our survey questions, and I am gratified by the restraint and reasonableness which characterize the comments made by police executives across the country. From these observations, we have distilled what I believe to be the essence of police attitudes and philosophies which reveal the majority of our colleagues to be truly professionals.

They have neither lamented their role in society, nor have they endeavored to cloak themselves in the raiment of martyrs. Because their observations, in my estimation, constitute a rare insight for persons outside the police profession, I believe we have been provided with important guideposts for an area in which work can be done to smooth out discordant situations. It will be well, I think, for us to examine a few of them, for what concerns the police must inevitably be of concern to the community at large.

As I have analyzed the complaints, I believe they can be attributed to one phenomenon: the growing lack of belief in and respect for the law.

That this is so is indicated by the many complaints made by police relative to the increase in the number and frequency of assaults on police officers, the men who symbolize the law. Our survey indicates that the police today are suffering verbal abuse, provocation, defiance and interference with lawful arrests and other police functions more than they ever have before. Many of our police executives have noted with much uneasiness an increasing belligerence and arrogance on the part of the general public and the persons with whom the police come in contact.

At the same time, they are concerned by the lack of manpower and the attendant fear of unwarranted attacks against lone officers by Negro groups when they are making routine traffic stops or other normal enforcement activities. Another growing and galling situation is the false accusations made against police. In connection with these accusations, we have noted that the purpose behind them frequently seems to be nothing more than harassment of the police. We are also deeply chagrined that in many cases, the lack of prosecution for false accusations has encouraged more of the same.

One of the most frequent millstones hung about the neck of the police professional is the charge that Negroes are discriminated against, as a general practice, in the hiring of policemen. Needless to say, I would be the last to deny that discrimination does exist in some communities, but at the same time, it is unfortunate that all police have to be tarred with he same brush.

Despite the fact that many police departments would gladly employ qualified Negroes as police officers, they are sometimes unable to do so because Negroes will not apply. Some of our members attribute this to the fact the police are looked upon with such disfavor by the Negro community that young men who would make good policemen are unwilling to face the disapproval they fear would result.

This same atmosphere also causes what we have detected to be a growing resistance to overtures at friendly communication on police beats in minority areas. Some of our police executives have pointed out that even though police officers have tried to establish friendly relationships in the interest of harmony and good police service, they have been unable to do so, because the people react to them with coldness and remain aloof.

While minority leaders decry alleged excesses in the application of police authority to Negroes, there is another side to the coin. Many police have complained that the law is being applied unequally, with preferential treatment being given to minority groups. They feel that pressure groups have succeeded in preventing police from fully enforcing the law where minority individuals are concerned. Officers feel that they are sometimes compelled to assume a "kid gloves" attitude, in order not to appear to overstep their authority and to avoid criticism, against which they have no adequate defense. Many officers feel that no amount of "bending over backwards to be fair" can satisfy what they regard as the unreasonable expectations of the more militant leaders and, at the same time, allow for effective enforcement of the law.

There is no question that there is extreme apathy among the public and lack of support in enforcing the law. Police sometimes feel that they are being asked to do an impossible job. They are expected to maintain order and to arrest violators and, having done so, find that when the "heat is turned on," they are "left holding the bag." In this connection, our profession finds it particularly discouraging when support is given by some public officials to acts of civil disobedience and other pressure tactics. We see in this kind of encouragement, and especially in situations where politically motivated officials actively participate in the pressure tactics, a situation in which the official is "feathering his political nest."

Other dissatisfaction among our ranks stems from the leniency of the courts and their hesitancy to convict when the race issue is raised as a defense.

Meanwhile, minority group members seem increasingly ready to complain about minor matters, routine methods and police actions that are essential and unavoidable in the enforcement of the law. Some officers feel that undue emphasis is being placed on the racial aspects of many questions affecting police performance, at the expense of successful enforcement against criminals.

These are but a few of the grievances among police, but it can readily be seen from a study of these comments that there remains a serious communications gap. As one police official has remarked, there seems to be a communications block between law enforcement administrators and police officers on the one hand and minority group leaders and the minority group "man on the street" on the other, and this block appears to be growing. He expressed the opinion that the minority group leaders seem to have an increasing fear of an "Uncle Tom" label, which militant leaders place upon those who do communicate. He declared that he fears that the average minority group citizen is being unduly influenced by what he calls the propaganda of the militant leaders, which labels law enforcement as a tool of the white power structure. The differences in viewpoint illustrated by these statements point out the difficulties involved in impartially and impersonally enforcing the law, and the importance of reaching an effective method of communicating.

I am convinced, based upon the sincere and conscientious responses to our survey, that many police executives believe in fair and equal treatment of all people as a measure for controlling discontent. Contrary to the views of some who are prone to stereotype police, it would appear that law enforcement officers, by and large, do strive for impartiality in the application of legal sanctions.

I cannot believe that the police, as a group, regard as part of their job the suppression of legitimate demonstrations and peaceful protests. It is necessary for them to be present to maintain order, to prevent violence by anyone — demonstrators or onlookers. It is unavoidable that heavy concentrations of officers are required at times, but some of our more progressive police executives follow a policy of committing as few officers as adequate control will permit. This intelligent policy arises not solely out of manpower considerations, but largely to avoid the appearance of police harassment.

On the other hand, when arrests must be made for violations of the law, it is essential that this action be taken promptly and decisively. Our critics to the contrary, the fact that demonstrators or anti-demonstrators have to be arrested is no source of satisfaction to police. It is their general feeling, with few exceptions, that police should exercise restraint, and arrest only when the cause is clear-cut and perhaps even aggravated.

Of great concern to many police is the sometimes unfair treatment by the news media. Many feel that the police are portrayed unfavorably and are being used as whipping boys. Of course, the most repetitious charge against police is that of "police brutality."

As Superintendent O. W. Wilson of the Chicago Police Department has stated, however, "We have a duty and a responsibility to maintain law and order. If people throw themselves in front of trucks or climb poles or otherwise engage in obstructionist tactics in violation of the law, we have to arrest them. If they kick and bite and struggle, we have to use reasonable force to subdue them. This is *not* brutality; this is the law. The law requires us to use whatever force is necessary to effect a lawful arrest. We have not and will not interfere with peaceful picketing. However, we will meet force with force, and I want everyone to understand that."

News media have greatly distressed and angered some police by their coverage of police actions at riot and demonstration scenes, and the picture of police brutality has thereby been grossly over-exaggerated. Many police authorities feel that the press has been at times unduly critical and unfair. Instances of distortion in text and misleading captions or photographs have often been cited as examples. Many of my colleagues feel as I do that they are sometimes unfairly criticized when they are doing the best they could under very trying conditions. It is hard to put into a picture the circumstances which made the use of the night stick necessary, and the only thing the public sees is the policeman beating someone. This disturbs police because they feel that often they have little choice but to use these tactics under the stressful conditions of civil violence.

Another aspect of the publicity problem that is bothersome is a tendency to exaggerate or overplay the importance of the demonstrations. Naturally, the occurrence of a demonstration, and especially a riot, is newsworthy. However, inflammatory coverage involving advance publicity, citing threatening statements made by various parties and publication of rumors, can convert a relatively harmless protest into a serious disorder. Furthermore, the practice of the news media indicating that additional actions of violence are expected "this weekend" or "Friday night," etc., can themselves incite or inspire certain individuals to "come downtown looking for trouble." Police know all too well that when people who "carry a short fuse" go looking for trouble, they can easily find it. Police feel that publicity is often a prime objective of some of the demonstrators.

This points up that the news media have a vital responsibility in connection with today's social upheavals, and I believe that it is time some news executives pause and reevaluate their duty to their readers, to their community, and to themselves.

Civil rights leaders, and indeed, the entire community should also reexamine their views relative to the traditional role of the police service.

In the matter of making arrests, the police have no choice in the face of violence and threats to public welfare and safety. It must be understood that police cannot wink at breaches of the peace, for the potential victims of violence have a right to protection also.

The police know their responsibility under the law, but it is important for city authorities to issue a timely and unequivocal pronouncement when demonstrations are imminent, demanding compliance with the law and making clear the action to be taken should citizens persist in the prohibited conduct. Where outright breaches of the peace occur, arrests are definitely indicated. To do less would be to betray our solemn oath as defenders of the law.

It is abundantly clear that city authorities, including police, must exercise a great deal of thoughtful discretion when the cloud of civil strife appears upon the horizon. The course of action chosen can have a significant influence on the outcome. Obviously, the affair can be overplayed and thus blown out of proportion to its original potential. If adequate preparation has been made, and if the general public has been properly conditioned, demonstrations can be held without great excitement and public furor. If the city authorities are weak or inept, have not adequately planned in advance and if they do or say things that are legally or ethically out of line, the actions of the demonstrators and the general public will be harder to control.

In any event, one must not get the impression that these problems are only police problems; they are problems for the whole community, and until the citizens in the affected communities come to this realization, the police will continue to be the unwarranted scapegoats in these situations. There must be recognition of the fact that the elected officials of the community, i.e., the political power structure, are even more deeply involved than the police.

When police action is aimed at the protection of the rights, life, limb and property of all citizens, and when police officers do their job impartially and competently, they should receive the full support of city officials and all citizens. Police officers are not expendable, and when they are assigned to tasks exposing them to injury or death they must be allowed to defend themselves. The people must understand and accept this in the interest of an effective police service.

All must realize that the general nature of the police job produces conflict. The people are paying officers to enforce the laws. If they do their job, there will be complaints about what they do and how they do it. When they act properly and within the law, they must be supported.

The racial situation is without a doubt one of the most troublesome, difficult and complicated problems ever to confront American law enforcement. The comment has been made so often that it is now trite to say, that the police have been squarely in the middle in relation to the contending forces in this controversy. This quandary makes it even more imperative that the police and the community plunge ahead together to see what we can do toward helping each other, by exchanging useful information based on the experience each has had, and by airing the differences and the various goals on one side and the other, in order that conflict may be avoided.

I am firmly convinced that the police establishment, by and large, is doing what it can to bring about new techniques, and to adapt old methods to the modern concepts utilized by today's demonstrators in seeking to dramatize real and imagined grievances. At the same time, the police are receiving generous support from some conscientious organizations.

As many of you know, for example, last year the IACP conducted a conference for more than 130 police executives from all parts of the country, to discuss the Civil Rights Act of 1964 and its implications for police. Its sponsors included the Southwest Center for Human Relations Studies and the Southwest Center for Law Enforcement Education of the University of Oklahoma, the National Anti-Defamation League of B'nai B'rith, and the Potomac Institute of Washington, D.C.

Since that time, working very closely with the Potomac Institute, we have summarized the highlights of that two-day conference into a concise and meaningful study, and published it in a booklet entitled THE POLICE AND THE CIVIL RIGHTS ACT. Copies of this booklet are available, without cost, from IACP headquarters. It is our desire to give this booklet as wide a dissemination as we can, since we believe it constitutes an excellent guideline for police who will be confronted with certain ramifications of this act. The law is primarily one over which federal authorities have jurisdiction, but as we all know, any new law must inevitably, in some manner, involve local police.

There are many other ways in which we are doing our part to maintain, as much as possible, the public peace in a time of trouble. We are going to be faced more and more with perplexing, demanding and stressful situations, but we know we cannot carry out our mission unless we have the complete and wholehearted support of the citizens we serve.

I believe that the police service, on the whole, is reaching out its hand to society, and I am hopeful that society will grasp that hand, so that we might, as one, solve the problems besetting us.

Section 6
Special Considerations

Any book of this type should enjoy the luxury of a "miscellaneous" section. This is especially appropriate in a field of study such as police relationships with the community. It is, by its nature, multidimensional — interdisciplinary, to use the academic term — a complex of interlocking issues and problems.

Thus, we are left, still with a number of intriguing facets of the field not thoroughly enough considered in the essays comprising the preceding sections. For example, there is the substantial question of discretionary use of police power. In the criminal justice process, what are some of the important community relations problems affecting the role of the prosecutor? The role of corrections and so-called treatment agencies? How do these relate to problems affecting the police role? What problems are there in the relationships among the police, prosecution, the courts and corrections?

These are among the questions considered by the authors of the essays appearing in this, the final section.

Full Enforcement vs. Police Discretion Not to Invoke Criminal Process*

HERMAN GOLDSTEIN

(Then) Executive Assistant to the Superintendent, Chicago Police Department

MAY 22, 1963

Parking meters are a common source of irritation to both the public and the police. They were a particular source of annoyance to a city manager friend of mine whose council membership included one man whose sole concern in life appeared to be those vehicles parked alongside meters on which the time had expired. After repeated criticism of the police department for its failure to achieve a greater degree of compliance and enforcement, the city manager was moved to speak on the issue. He offered the councilman a choice from among what he referred to as levels of enforcement. He suggested that the city would assign one police officer to enforcing all of the meters throughout the city. If this

* Reprinted by permission from PUBLIC ADMINISTRATION REVIEW, Vol. XXIII, No. 3, September, 1963, quarterly journal of the American Society for Public Administration, 1329 Eighteenth Street, N.W., Washington, D.C. 20036.

were done, he anticipated that the frequency of checks would be low and the number of overtime violations and red flags would increase. On the other hand, he could assign one police officer to each parking meter in the city. With such extensive coverage, there would be reasonable assurance that a summons would be issued at the moment the meter expired. The city manager then suggested that the council determine through its appropriation, just how many police officers were to be provided and what level of enforcement was desired as between the two extremes. The point was well made.

Without full recognition on his part, the city manager was addressing himself to one of the very basic problems in law enforcement today. We need only substitute people for parking meters and the broader categories of crime for red overtime flags. Given the total amount of criminality in a community and the resources with which to cope with it, what is the position or policy of the local law enforcement agency? Is the agency committed to a concept of "full enforcement" of all laws, or is it committed to something less than full enforcement?

A policy of "full enforcement" implies that the police are required and expected to enforce all criminal statutes and city ordinances at all times against all offenders. It suggests that the police are without authority to ignore violations, to warn offenders when a violation has in fact occurred, or to do anything short of arresting the offender and placing a charge against him for the specific crime committed. It views the police function to be that of relating the provisions of the law to a fine measurement of the quantum of evidence. Out of this cold and somewhat mechanical calculation evolves an answer which provides the basis for police action.

The exercise of discretion, on the other hand, suggests that the police are required, because of a variety of factors, to decide overtly how much of an effort is to be made to enforce specific laws. It recognizes that actions short of arrest may achieve the desired goal. It implies that a police officer may decide not to make an arrest even in those situations in which an offense has been committed and both the offender and the evidence are at hand. It tends to portray police officers as something other than automatons—as reasonable men whose judgment is essential in determining whether or not to invoke the criminal process.

To date, this dilemma has been of principal concern to those interested in the total system for the administration of criminal justice—those interested in the workings of the prosecution, the courts, and the correctional agencies as well as the police. To understand how the system functions in its entirety, these students of criminal law have necessarily focused their attention at that point where it is most commonly determined whether or not a person is to be subject to the system — on the initial screening function performed by the police. If a person is arrested, he enters the system and the path which he takes, in large measure, is established. If he is not arrested, the action of the police terminates the case before the person enters the system and the action is not subject to further review.

The bibliography of thinking of this subject is rapidly increasing. This body of thought and analysis is of more than academic interest to the police. It has some very practical implications.

What is the position of the average police administrator in these deliberations? He is most likely to support the view — somewhat hesitatingly — that he is committed to a policy of full enforcement. It is, after all, the policy most commonly enunciated by police agencies. In contrast, the mere suggestion that a police administrator exercises discretion in fulfilling his job may be taken as an affront—an attack upon the objective and sacrosanct nature of his job—that of enforcing the law without fear or favor. Here too, there is a little heisitation—an awareness that discretion must be and is exercised. But like planned parenthood, it may be something you practice; it is not something you admit or even discuss.

This awkward position, in my opinion, places the average police official in a most embarrassing situation. What are the facts?

Do we have full enforcement, as the term is defined here? Obviously, we do not. How often have law enforcement personnel released a drunk and disorderly person without charging him? released a juvenile offender to his parents? warned a driver who had clearly committed a violation? ignored the enforcement of some city ordinances? arrested an individual known to have committed fornication or adultery? arranged for the release of a narcotic addict in exchange for information? dropped charges against an assailant when the victim failed to cooperate in the prosecution? ignored Sunday blue laws or simply been instructed not to enforce a specific law?

And yet, in acknowledging that some or all of these practices exist, police officials feel a sense of guilt; that these actions were not quite proper; and that they had no basis in law. Why, then, do police officials do these things? Because they are, consciously or unconsciously, acknowledging what they do not wish to proclaim—that the police must exercise discretion.

The Exercise of Discretion

Why must discretion be exercised? Let us take a look at some of the laws under which the police operate, some of the procedures which must be followed, and some of the pressures which exist in the typical community which the police serve.

Examine, for example, the criminal code of any one of our states. By its action, the legislature has attempted to establish those forms of conduct which its members desire to be declared criminal. But this action, as reflected in the statement of the criminal law, is often expressed in such broad terms as to render a clear interpretation of the legislature's intentions most difficult. Ambiguity may be intentional so as to provide greater flexibility in enforcement; it may result from a failure to envisage the day-to-day problems encountered by the police; or it may simply be a result of language limitations. Whatever the basis for the broad statement of the law, the need for resolving these ambiguities frequently places the police in the position of having to determine the forms of conduct which are to be subject to the criminal process.

The State of Illinois has a typically broad statute defining gambling. Under its provisions, the flip of a coin to determine who shall purchase coffee or the playing of penny-ante poker must be considered a violation. As a general policy, the Chicago Police Department devotes its efforts to seeking out gambling activities which are part of an organized operation. We do not devote manpower to ferreting out social card games conducted in the privacy of a home. But, upon complaint, we have an obligation to conduct an investigation of any alleged gambling activity.

In March of this year, the department received a complaint of gambling in the basement of an American Legion Post. Three police officers were sent to investigate. They quickly established that the affair was being run by the post auxiliary as a benefit and that a variation of bingo was to be played with the proceeds going to the men at a veterans' hospital. The officers politely warned against any activity which would be considered gambling and left. The patrons of the social, however, got panicky, grabbed their hats and coats and fled. The expected flurry of letters and newspaper articles followed. One such article concluded with this statement addressed to the Superintendent: "Most of the people of Chicago don't want you or your men to raid a women's social. They want you to go chase some crooks and leave the good people alone."

Both state statutes and city ordinances may be explicit in defining conduct to be considered criminal, but there may be little expectation on the part of those who enacted the laws that they be enforced to the letter. The statute or ordinance may be stating the ideals of the community; that adulterous activity, for example, will not be tolerated. Through this action, the community is placed on record as opposing a form of conduct considered morally wrong. Lawmakers and citizens alike derive a certain degree of comfort from having legislated against such activity. Should this false sense of comfort be a source of concern to the conscience of a legislator, he is faced with a dilemma: he might more easily choose to seek full enforcement than to be caught supporting the repeal of such a prohibition. Since few legislative consciences are upset, it falls to the police agency to live with the law without enforcing it.

The problem does not always stem from a double standard in matters of morality. Often it stems from mere obsolescence. Earlier this year, the Chicago Police Department was subject to the wrath of the community for having arrested a driver of a jeep, equipped with a snow plow, which was used in the plowing of neighborhood sidewalks as a friendly gesture and without charge. The young officer who made the arrest had been confronted with a complaint. The benevolent driver had piled snow in a driveway to the displeasure of its owner. The officer was unable to find an ordinance that prohibited piling snow in driveways, but he did find an ordinance which prohibited four-wheel vehicles from being driven on sidewalks. The public became enraged as news of this action spread and we were once again asked if we had run out of honest-to-goodness crooks in need of apprehension. Members of the department no longer arrest the drivers of four-wheel sidewalk plows; the ordinance, however, remains on the books. We have just decided not to enforce it.

Another major factor which forces the exercise of discretion is the limitation on manpower and other resources — a factor to which previous reference was made. Few police agencies have the number of personnel that would be required to detect the total amount of criminality which exists in a community and to prosecute all offenders. Rarely is consideration given to the relationship between the volume of what can be termed criminal acts and the resources available to deal with them. New legislation declaring a form of conduct to be criminal is rarely accompanied by an appropriation to support the resources for its enforcement. The average municipal administrator who has budget responsibilities brings a different orientation to the problem than does the police chief: his determination as to the size of the police force is based more directly upon a value judgment as to what the tax structure can afford rather than upon a determination of the degree to which the community wishes to enforce the criminal laws; he is more concerned with efficiency, production, and quality of service in handling the routine tasks which accrue to the police and which are so important to the citizenry; he has only a slight interest in or knowledge of the provisions of the criminal law.

Since there are no established priorities for the enforcement of laws prohibiting one type of conduct as against another, the police official must determine the manner in which available manpower and equipment will be used. The daily assignment of manpower is, therefore, perhaps the most easily identifiable exercise of discretion on the part of the police.

This need for discretion was acknowledged in at least one case adjudicated in 1909 in the State of Michigan. The Michigan Supreme Court held:

> (T)he (police) commissioner is bound to use the discretion with which the State within the city of Detroit, but he is likewise charged with the suppression of all crime and the conservation of the peace. To enable him to perform the duties imposed upon him by law, he is supplied with certain limited means. It is entirely obvious that he must exercise a sound discretion as to how those means shall be applied for the good of the community.[1]

In establishing priorities of enforcement, greater attention is ordinarily given to more serious crimes. A determination not to arrest is most common at the level of the petty offender — and especially if the offender is an otherwise law-abiding citizen. Policies — albeit unwritten — begin to evolve. Just as social gamblers may be arrested only if their activities become organized and move into public places, so drunkards may be arrested only if they are belligerent and homeless as distinct from those who are cooperative and long-established residents.

Discretion may be exercised on the basis of a police officer's particular assignment. Many police agencies have officers assigned to specific types of investigations, such as those relating to homicide, burglaries, or narcotics. Officers so assigned understandably consider their respective specialized function as being of greatest importance to the department. The generalization can be made that police officers frequently refrain from invoking the criminal process for conduct which is considered of less seriousness than that which they are primarily responsible for investigating. A group of officers, intent on solving a homicide, for example, will complain bitterly of the lack of prostitutes on the streets from whom they may obtain information. Narcotic detectives will likewise make frequent use of gamblers and may even tolerate petty larcenies and minor drug violations on the part of their informants. Whatever the merits of the practice, the goal is an acceptable one: that of solving the more serious crime.

Where the volume of criminal activity is high, it is common to observe police policies which result in the dropping of charges against minor assailants when the victim is unwilling to testify. Without a complainant, the case cannot usually be prosecuted successfully. While an effort can be made to prosecute in the name of the state, the mere volume of work demanding attention ordinarily rules out a decision to do so. The determination not to proceed is clearly an exercise of discretion and terminates at this early stage in the process a case in which an offense has clearly occurred and an offender was identified and apprehended.

---

[1] *Gowan* v. *Smith,* 157 Mich. 443, 473, 122 NW 286, 297 (1909).

Discretion is often exercised by the police in a sincere effort to accomplish a social good. This is a sort of humanitarian gesture in which the police achieve the desired objective without full imposition of the coldness and harshness of the criminal process. The drunk may be ushered home; the juveniles turned over to their parents; the new woman driver warned of being found headed in the wrong direction on a one-way street. It is the exercise of discretion such as this to accomplish a desired goal to which others refer when they exhort the police to enforce the "spirit" rather than the "letter" of the law.

These are some of the reasons why the police do, in fact, exercise discretion not to invoke the criminal process in many cases. These same considerations provide ample indication that the police do not, in fact, engage in full time enforcement. Why then are the police so reluctant to acknowledge that discretion is exercised?

Reasons for Not Acknowledging the Exercise of Discretion

To acknowledge that law enforcement officials do exercise discretion requires an overt act—the articulation of a position—an action which is rare among those in the police field. Most law enforcement officials long ago resigned themselves to the role of the underdog upon whom the unsolved problems of society were piled high. Having developed what might best be termed a defensive posture, the police have, for example widely accepted responsibility for all that is criminal despite the fact that crimes are not committed by the police, but rather by the citizens of the community they serve. How often do we hear a police official admonish a community for a rise in crime? How often does a police official point an accusing finger at conditions which produce crime and criminals? Instead, whenever the publication of crime statistics indicates a rise in crime, he feels that he has in some way failed and that his department has failed. In carrying such a burden, the average police official sees nothing especially strange about having to carry responsibility for a type of enforcement he is unable to fulfill. He has learned two characteristics of his job: he must bear this burden well and he must refrain from discussing it lest it be a source of embarrassment to him and the community.

If he should have the urge to discuss his problem of achieving full enforcement, the average police official would not wish to do so in public. To acknowledge the exercise of discretion belies the very image in which he takes such pride and which he strives so hard to achieve. This is the image of total objectivity — of impartiality — and of enforcement without fear nor favor. A cursory examination of the typical oath of office administered to police officers, the rules and regulations of police departments, and the several codes governing police conduct give the general impression that strict adherence to the "letter of the law," has come to be the ideal toward which all well-intentioned police officers should strive. There is great difficulty in recognizing that discretion can be exercised without being partial. It is, of course, extremely important that police officers be impartial in their enforcement policies, but it is possible for them to be so and still exercise discretion.

Impartiality requires the establishment of criteria for uniform action — a difficult task and one which perhaps constitutes the most valid objection to acknowledging discretionary powers. It is easy, from an administrative standpoint, to support a program of full enforcement. Instructions and training are simple. One need only teach the difference between black and white. If discretion is to be exercised, criteria become essential. And here the problems begin: (1) there is a general reluctance to spell out criteria as to those conditions under which an arrest is to take place lest this written modification of existing laws be attacked as presumptuous on the part of an administrative agency and contemptuous of the legislative body; (2) in the absence of written instructions, it is extremely difficult to communicate to large numbers of policemen the bounds of the discretion to be exercised; (3) an officer cannot be forced to exercise discretion, since the broad oath which he takes places him under obligation to enforce all laws and he can maintain that he is adhering to this higher authority; and (4) if a written document is desired, the preparation of criteria for the exercise of discretion requires an expert draftsman — one more skilled than the legislative draftsman who may have tried and failed. Is it any wonder that the typical reaction of the police administrator to the mere suggestion that discretion be acknowledged is likely to be: "It isn't worth the trouble!"?

Broadly-stated laws are, after all, one of the lesser concerns of the police. Most attention of law enforcement officers in recent years has focused upon legal provisions which are too narrow. The average police official is not very concerned about having the authority to enforce adultery statutes and not having the manpower or the community support necessary to do so. He is much more concerned because of his inability to attack organized crime effectively. And there may be an occasion upon which he can use an obscure or otherwise unenforced law to launch an oblique attack against a situation or activity which he feels warrants action on his part. His attitude is often that the law should be left on the books; it may come in handy sometime. Why impose self-limitations on police authority beyond those established by the legislature?

Another contention is that discretion breeds corruption and for this reason should be denied. This constitutes another strong administrative argument against acknowledging its existence. The average police administrator spends a considerable portion of his time worrying about the integrity of his force. Corruption, when it does exist, usually stems from the misuse of authority in order to attain selfish ends or from restraint from exerting authority in exchange for personal gain. It is always difficult to investigate. But, it is easier to do so if policemen are expected to function on a black or white basis. If regulations require that an officer make an arrest when a violation occurs, the officer who does not do so is suspect. If, on the other hand, an officer is told that his decision to arrest should weigh a number of factors, it is difficult to determine if his failure to act was an exercise of good judgment or in exchange for a favor or a bribe. If the exercise of discretion is sanctioned by a department's administration, it becomes known both to the violator and the officer and creates the atmosphere and bargaining power for a corrupt act. It is the fear of this possible consequence that constitutes another strong reason that open acknowledgment of discretionary authority is frowned upon by most police administrators.

To the several arguments already stated, the police will usually add the contention that whatever their practice, they are required by law to subscribe to full enforcement. Indeed, in response to a suggestion that discretion in the area of traffic enforcement be acknowledged, the objection was raised that such an assumption on the part of a police department would be "unconstitutional."

Some jurisdictions do go so far as to impose a penalty upon police officers who fail to take action upon learning of a crime, but there is no indication that such jurisdictions provide a higher level of enforcement than do those without such provisions.

There is, among police officers, a healthy respect for "the law" in its generic form whatever the attitude may be toward specific provisions of either the substantive or procedural codes. It is one thing to ignore a law; it is much more serious to acknowledge publicly that it is being ignored.

One of the factors that results in a healthy respect for the law is the knowledge on the part of every police officer that he may personally be held accountable in a legal suit for actions which he takes as a police officer. Should he be subject to legal action, he knows that a literal interpretation of his authority and his actions will determine the outcome; and that any exercise of discretion on his part is, in the eyes of the court, clearly outside the law. Concern for legal actions fosters support for a concept of full enforcement.

There is some basis to share the concern expressed for the legal obligation to enforce all laws without the exercise of discretion. In 1960, the then Police Commissioner of Philadelphia asserted that for lack of funds and personnel, he would limit initial enforcement of the Sunday closing law to large retail establishments. When a Pennsylvania court reviewed this action, they ruled in favor of one of the large retail merchants and stated that

> The admitted discrimination in enforcement is a calculated result of a definite policy on the part of a public official and thus results in a denial to the plaintiff of the equal protection of the law to which it is entitled by virtue of the fourteenth amendment of the United States Constitution.[2]

Strong as is the fear of legal entanglements, the fear of public reaction to an announced policy of selective enforcement is even greater. Since the police know how difficult it is to meet accusations of nonenforcement when they profess full enforcement, they fear that acknowledging a policy of nonenforcement is even less defensible. The average police official recognizes that no amount of explanation will placate the citizen who, for example, is obsessed with·the need for strict enforcement of an ordinance requiring that bicycles not be ridden on sidewalks. He must simply be politely "brushed off." But, what does one tell the citizen who feels that too much effort is going into traffic enforcement and not enough into apprehending burglars; what is said to the citizen who demands additional manpower to apprehend disorderly youths congregating in park areas; and what does one tell the citizen who argues in favor of tripling the effort presently directed toward apprehending narcotic peddlers?

To answer such questions intelligently, the police official must have a defensible formula for the distribution of his manpower. Such a formula rarely exists because of the reluctance of the average police official to make value judgments. He, understandably, is unwilling to decide what should be of greatest concern to the community. The whole thought of trying to defend a policy of selective enforcement is a bit frightening. It is asking for trouble. So, he often concludes that it is, in his opinion, much safer to maintain he has no discretion in these matters.

---

[2] *Bargain City U.S.A. Inc.* v. *Dilworth,* 29 U.S. Law Week 2002 (Pa.C.P. June 10, 1960).

The Advantages Inherent in a Policy of Recognizing the Exercise of Discretion

Some of the arguments in behalf of a denial of discretion are convincing arguments. They lend strong support to those who advocate a policy of full enforcement. If there was any indication that the breach between actual practice and the concept of full enforcement was narrowing, one might be encouraged to lean even more strongly in the direction of supporting a policy of full enforcement. The opposite, however, is true. The gulf between the ideal and reality in criminal law enforcement is growing wider. Every police official is keenly aware that the demands for his services are constantly increasing and that he is not given a proportionate increase in the resources with which to meet these demands. Crime is on the increase and gives no sign of leveling off. But, beyond this, there is evidence of a growing concern on the part of the public for a problem toward which there has more commonly been an attitude of complete apathy. The public no longer tolerates mental illness, unemployment, poor housing, or dropouts from high school. They do something about these social problems and there is an increasing indication that they intend to do more about crime. As this concern increases, the demands on law enforcement agencies will similarly increase.

How, then, does the dilemma posed here relate to improved law enforcement? How would its resolution better enable us to cope with present problems and those which develop in the future?

Law enforcement agencies cannot make progress so long as they remain on the defensive. They cannot win public support if they fail to level with the public. They cannot solve their problems if they fail to identify these problems.

There are a number of advantages to be gained by the police by being forthright in acknowledging the role which the police play in determining whether or not to invoke the criminal process. Let us examine the major ones.

Once and for all, acknowledging discretion would enable the police to climb out from underneath the impossible burden which has been placed upon them and which has placed them on the defensive in dealing with the public. And they would be doing so, not by abdicating their legal responsibilities, but by simply acknowledging the true magnitude of their responsibilities. It is the function of the police to demonstrate the impossibility of full enforcement to the community— making citizens aware that the enactment of laws does not cure a problem unless consideration is given to the means for enforcement. And appeal must be made to the public to accept the best judgment and efforts of the police in their approach to the total problem of criminal law enforcement. The community can be given the alternatives of providing additional funds for a level of enforcement closer to full enforcement, of relieving the police of non-police functions which deplete the effort devoted to criminal law enforcement, or of providing the police with more realistic legal guidance in how to fulfill their broad responsibilities. Citizens will choose a level of enforcement, if it is put to them in terms of cost. Somewhere between the extremes of having a police officer for each citizen and having none, a determination must be made as to the number of officers to be employed. Placed in these terms, the degree to which full enforcement can be achieved is a matter known not only to the police agency but to the community as a whole.

In the administration of governmental affairs, respect for the law takes a second place only to the need for honesty in dealing with the public. Because police officials have been placed in so awkward a position for so long and have felt compelled to deny the obvious, the public typically reacts with initial shock and subsequent pleasure when a police official is refreshingly forthright in his public pronouncements. Keeping the public well informed on police problems, including police shortcomings, clearly develops support for good law enforcement — and public support is the key to the solution of most police problems.

What are some of the specific implications of a policy which recognizes the discretion exercised by the police? At the present time, new legislation is enacted without regard to its enforceability. The assumption is that the police will, as always, assume responsibiliy for the new task much as a sponge absorbs water. Rarely is consideration given to possible problems of enforcement—or to the manpower which may be required. If the police are articulate on such occasions, legislative groups may be less likely to act without regard to considering enforcement.

It is not, in the long run, to the advantage of law enforcement agencies to have laws on the books which are widely ignored. The police have an obligation to help build respect among all citizens for law and order. A law which is known to exist and which is honored more in the breach than by compliance, tends to breed contempt for law enforcement — and usually among the very element in whom there is the greatest need for building respect. Knowledgeable in the techniques of enforcement, the police are probably in a better position to seek repeal of an obsolete or unenforceable law than any other element in the community. Their position need not be based on whether the conduct ought to be criminal, but rather on what are the practical aspects of enforcement.

The unworkability or inappropriateness of a legislative provision becomes apparent to a law enforcement agency more rapidly than it does to a legislative body. To persist in adhering to these legal requirements is nonsensical; such a policy tends only to harass citizens and lessen respect for the police. Applause will greet the police administrator who takes what the community terms an enlightened approach to such problems—publicly acknowledging the inappropriateness of the legislative provision.

Until this past year, members of the Chicago Police Department issued a summons to any motorist having a faulty headlight. This policy had been followed for years. It was, after all, the law. Had an effort been made, it is doubtful if one could have devised a more effective way of antagonizing the public. The violator rarely was aware of his violation.

A department memorandum was issued. It said, in clear language, that a police officer need not arrest a motorist with a defective light when the police officer was of the belief that the light would be repaired immediately. And further criteria were set forth:

> Where more than one lighting fixture is inoperative or where one is in such a state of disrepair as to indicate that it was not a recent, temporary malfunction, or where the lighting violation was the cause of an accident, or is only one of several violations, the operator will be cited.[3]

The reaction on the part of the press was that the public had causes to rejoice, that the department was "thinking big," that the policy was fair, and that the

---

[3] Chicago Police Department, Department Memorandum No. 63-35.

motorist who purposely breaks the law deserves to be punished. The police, they declared, were finally sensible about faulty car lights.

Taking the initiative in these matters has another advantage. A person who is unnecessarily aggrieved is not only critical of the procedure which was particularly offensive to him. He tends to broaden his interest and attack the whole range of police procedures which suddenly appear to him to be unusually oppressive; he may consider the police devoid of concern for civil rights; and perhaps, in moments of extreme delirium, he may even accuse them of fascistic or communist tendencies. Regrettably, such a person usually resorts to the therapy of letterwriting to vent his emotions, with carbon copies clearly labeled and sent in all directions. The pattern is a familiar one.

Police officials too often fail to recognize that there are many in the communities which they serve who have an inherent distaste for authority — and especially police authority. Joining with others of the same view and those whose beliefs are more firmly grounded in a support for our democratic processes, these people closely guard against the improper use of authority by the police. It behooves law enforcement officials to refrain from unnecessarily creating a situation which annoys such individuals. Such situations can often be avoided through the exercise of proper discretion.

One of the greatest needs in law enforcement is effective leadership. Presently, because of its defensive posture, law enforcement agencies have too often cultivated a form of defensive leadership. Many law enforcement officials today fulfill the need for defensive leadership in their respective organizations, but are not equal to the challenge of the times. Unfortunately, this type of need places a premium on the police administrator who can successfully dodge the issue of why he fails to provide full enforcement, who can create the impression that he is endeavoring to enforce all of the laws all of the time, who can take repeated attacks and onslaughts of public criticism, and who can be devious and less than forthright in his dealings with the public. While such leadership may have served some purpose in the past, it has not given law enforcement the type of guidance and impetus which is required to meet the problems of the 1960's.

Open recognition of basic police problems gives the police leader a clean atmosphere in which to operate. He becomes a leader rather than a defender. Police service today demands a bolder, more aggressive individual who is adept at articulating police problems in a forthright manner and developing community support for their solution.

The police have sought professional status. But, professional status does not normally accrue to individuals performing ministerial functions. One of the marks of a true profession is the inherent need for making value judgments and for exercising discretion based upon professional competence. To deny that discretion is exercised gives support to those citizens who maintain that the job of a police officer is a simple one, that it is not worthy of professional status. By acknowledging the discretionary role the police do fulfill, the drive toward a higher degree of respect and recognition for law enforcement personnel is given impetus.

The Choice and the Task

The real choice for a police administrator is not between "full enforcement" and "discretion" but rather more precisely between the ideal and reality. As the public becomes increasingly intolerant of crime, pressures will develop to improve and streamline not only our police organizations, but the laws and procedures under which they operate. An essential first step will then be to inform the public, to challenge some of our basic concepts, to take stock of the total responsibilities of the police, to recognize the limitations under which the police operate, and to acknowledge the need for the exercise of discretion. It is then likely that a new atmosphere will be created which will foster some new thinking and some new developments to aid in the improvement of the total system for the administration of criminal justice.

This is a big task. It is not a function for the police alone. Law — and the enforcement of law—is a vital element in our form of government. In law enforcement, one comes to grips with some of the basic legal, political and social concerns and issues of our time. Clearly, it warrants more than it has received in attention from not only the public, but from our universities and colleges as well. There is need for a much greater body of knowledge and understanding of our present operations. Such knowledge and understanding is essential if we are to develop intelligent solutions to our present and future problems.

Police Planning and Research, as Related to Police–Community Relations*

A. C. GERMANN

(Then) Head of the Department of Police Science and Administration, Long Beach State College, Long Beach, California

MAY 23, 1961

Police planning and research units are relatively new innovations within the American police service. When the Chief of Police collects, studies, and compares data relating to his operations and administrative responsibilities, whether he does such by himself, or delegates the task to a subordinate or special unit, he is engaging in research. When the Chief of Police makes decisions relating to future operations or administrative responsibilities, whether he does such by himself, or delegates the task to a subordinate or special unit, he is engaging in planning. Thus, planning and research can be an independent personal activity of the Chief, or delegated to others.

Planning and research activities are closely integrated as functions, for no adequate planning can be done without the exhaustive inquiry we term research, and no productive research can be accomplished without providing for the implementation of its necessary recommendations through prudent planning.

Many of our police agencies do a great deal of planning and research in the areas of organization, fiscal operations, personnel management, policy, procedures, strategy and tactics. *Very few* do an appreciable amount of planning and research in the police–community relations area.

---

* Reprinted with permission from POLICE Magazine, Vol. 6, No. 3, January–February, 1962, pp. 36-39; Charles C Thomas, Publisher, Springfield, Ill.

I have checked with the police planning and research units of Chicago, Los Angeles, Los Angeles County, Oakland, and Philadelphia, asking for opinions and information as to studies and surveys being done in "public relations, press relations, legal relations, school relations, race relations, processing of public complaints or recommendations, or other police–community based subject matters." My thought was to get a sampling of attitudes and practices.

Chicago's response indicated that its unit had begun operation in May, 1960, and since its inception had been able to concern itself only with reorganization and department operation. The Director of the Planning Division indicated that the unit "will, in the future, of course, undertake extensive study in all of these areas." He further stated:

> It is my opinion that police planning is vitally important to police–community relations. Since these relations consist essentially of the pride the police have in themselves and the respect the general public has for the integrity, ability and effectiveness of members of the police agency, the police department must be progressive and its operations must be businesslike and effective. The public, if it is to have faith in the police agency, must be informed on police problems, on what the police are doing about these problems, and the public must believe that what the police are doing is intelligent and effective.

> As you are aware, many police departments in the country, Chicago being an outstanding example, have failed to progress primarily because there has been no machinery within the organization for seeking out and developing progressive techniques and procedures. Just as in private business, the police administrator needs to keep abreast of all developments in his field. It is my observation that in most police departments where one or more selected individuals are not charged with this specific assignment, the tendency is to maintain the same procedures, techniques, equipment and practices which have served the department in years past. This is true because change is uncomfortable and makes the job more difficult.

> Where an organizational unit is specifically charged with responsibility for research and planning, this unit must have as its sole aim the searching out of better ways to do the job. If the unit is successful in this aim, department operations will be improved and police–community relations require this as an initial basis for development.

Oakland's response indicated that it was not doing planning and research in police–community relations "in the narrow sense," but that the general planning and research activities had an ultimate effect upon public relations. The Officer in Charge of the Planning and Research Section in Oakland indicated that the unit had contributed to several training bulletins dealing with press relations, public relations, and school relations.

Philadelphia's response indicated that the primary mission of their unit was the improvement of procedures and methods, and that they were "seldom involved in pure police–community relations planning or studies." Their Director of Research and Planning indicated that their work in developing a Juvenile Crime Index had community relations overtones.

The Commander of the Los Angeles Police Department's Division of Planning and Research indicated to me, by telephone, that their work was primarily in the techniques and procedures area, and that very little planning and research was done in the police–community relations area.

The Los Angeles County Sheriff's Department sent the status report of the Public and Foreign Relations Bureau. The Bureau of Research and Statistics indicated that Part II of the report, entitled "Community Relations," was particularly applicable. This section, a research into community relations, dealt with press groups, the public and the police, detailing "key failures of the past (research) in the light of what can be done to overcome them in the future (planning)."

The journal POLICE, published by Charles C Thomas, since last July has regularly listed planning and research activities of many different police agencies. An examination of the research study titles indicates that the great majority of researches are in the field of police operations and general administration — certainly an understandable phenomenon, for most agencies are vitally interested in improving the basic efficiency of their operations, and find it difficult to justify research projects that might be labeled as exotic.

Nonetheless, it is my opinion that police planning and research units can, and should devote substantial attention to the police–community relations area.

Assuming proper facilities, the necessary equipment, and trained planning and research personnel, the agency might follow research along these lines:

I. Identification of agency goals

II. Criteria of successful goal accomplishment

III. Identification of factors relating to success criteria

IV. Evaluation of agency policy and procedure affecting factors related to success criteria

V. Recommendations for changes in policy and procedure

Let us briefly analyze this frame of reference, with particular reference to police–community relations.

I. *Identification of agency goals*

Certainly one can list major police goals: the neutral, impartial, objective protection of life and property; preservation of the peace; the prevention and repression of crime; the regulation of noncriminal conduct; the extension of miscellaneous services; the minimization of community hazards; etc.

Yet a variety of opinion prevails that gives different emphasis to such goals. Various *levels of police service* — federal, state, county, and local — place differing accents upon such goals. Various *regions of the country* place differing priority on such goals. And, very often, *community opinion* differs from law enforcement opinion relative to the applicability of such goals. There are no universally *accepted* or *imposed* standards for police administration and operations; for one reason, there does not exist one nationalized police in our nation, and for another, the philosophy of local autonomy prevents the imposition of a single pattern of policing. Thus, practically, the police face a conflict between their *responsibilities* to *generally stated police goals,* and their *responsiveness* to *community opinion* which may or may not support such goals.

The first major objective of police planning and research in this area is, then, to identify the goals of the agency, not only with respect to generally stated objectives, but also with a genuine recognition of local community values.

II. *Criteria of successful goal accomplishment*

Certainly one can list major criteria: the absence of crime, accidents, congestion, and conflicts in the community; adequate rates of recovery of stolen property, case clearances, and successful convictions; low employee ratios and low per capita costs per population consistent with effective performance; the absence of community complaints regarding police personnel and services; etc.

Yet, here, too, a variety of opinion exists that places differing emphasis upon such criteria — depending upon level of service, regional location, and community norms.

The second major objective of police planning and research in this area is, then, to identify the criteria of successful goal accomplishment, not only with respect to generally stated norms, but also with a genuine recognition of local community values.

Thus, what we are saying is that agency goals or objectives, and the criteria or measuring rods for evaluating success in meeting those goals or objectives are closely identified with the local environment, with the philosophy of the local police agency, with the force of community opinion, and with the value system of that particular region or area.

This is *not* to say that we have not developed *any* nationwide goals for police — for we can always turn to the formulations of nationally recognized police experts and note their agreement in terms of general objectives.

This is *not* to say that we have not developed *any* nationwide criteria — for we can always make judgments relative to morality against the criteria of the Natural Law or Ten Commandments; we can always make judgments relative to legality against the criteria of the U. S. Constitution and its interpretation by the U. S. Supreme Court; and we can always make judgments relative to efficiency against the criteria of Uniform Crime Report statistics.

This *is* to say that *this* particular police agency must be considered with respect to *its* particular goals, and with respect to *its* particular criteria, in its particular environment *before* it is considered with respect to general goals and general criteria. To do otherwise is to get the cart before the horse.

III. *Identification of factors relating to success criteria*

Certainly the identification of factors relating to success criteria must be done by each individual agency — not imposed from outside — for these factors will vary with agency goals, criteria, and specific characteristics of the agency and community in question.

Major factors are usually obvious: adequacy of administrative talent to plan, organize, direct, coordinate, control and evaluate agency activities; adequacy of organization and management to ensure the propriety, legality, morality, and efficiency of agency policies and procedures; adequacy of fiscal processes to provide necessary facilities, equipment, and manpower; adequacy of personnel processes to provide for proper manpower selection, decent salaries, complete training programs, regulation of conduct by effective discipline, and motivation of personnel by exemplary leadership; adequate public relations to ensure public cooperation and goodwill, etc.

The third major objective of police planning and research in this area is, then, to identify those factors which relate to success criteria in that particular community.

It is in this area that a great number of police–community relations issues may be found. ANY FACTOR DEEMED TO BE RELATED, OR SUSPECTED OF BEING RELATED, TO THE SUCCESSFUL ACCOMPLISHMENT OF AGENCY GOALS IS PROPERLY AN AREA OF INQUIRY. For example, in one or another community, the following areas of inquiry could properly be undertaken by a police planning and research unit:

1. The extent of public knowledge of how a member of the general public should proceed with respect to a law enforcement problem confronting him.

2. Investigation of the propriety of specialized police activities that duplicate other community activities — juvenile recreation, management of correctional facilities, etc.

3. Evaluation of specific police activities which generate great public opposition and hostility.

4. Investigation of areas of possible joint research with local colleges and universities.

5. Evaluations of the utilization of police personnel who are themselves members of minority groups (Negro, Latin American, Oriental, etc.).

6. Value conflicts on the part of the law enforcement personnel: (enforcing the law vs. supporting the law; individual liberties vs. community security; maximum efficiency vs. constitutional guarantees; necessary operational secrecy vs. free and full public communication; letter of the law vs. spirit of the law; etc.).

7. Value conflicts on the part of the general public: (suporting the law vs. enforcing the law; community security vs. individual liberties; constitutional guarantees vs. maximum efficiency; free and full public communication vs. necessary operational secrecy; spirit of the law vs. letter of the law; etc.).

8. Development of ecological maps related to types of crimes.

9. Effects of police contacts with the juvenile offender.

10. Effects of police contacts with the first offender.

11. Knowledge of the law (and proper application and limitations) by law enforcement personnel.

12. Knowledge of the law (and proper application and limitations) by general public.

13. Communications problems and semantical difficulties involving police and public.

14. Police conceptions of: A. criminals; B. police; C. public; D. law enforcement processes.

15. General public conceptions of: A. criminals; B. police; C. public; D. law enforcement processes.

16. Particularized group conceptions of: A. criminals; B. police; C. public; D. law enforcement processes.

17. Role expectations of police relative to: A. police; B. public.

18. Role expectations of public relative to: A. police; B. public.

19. Evaluation of public complaints relative to police personnel and services.

20. Evaluation of agency complaints relative to public support and cooperation.

    IV. *Evaluation of agency policy and procedure affecting factors related to success criteria*

    V. *Recommendations for changes in policy and procedure*

The fourth and fifth major objectives of police planning and research in this area can be considered together. Certainly, one can understand that these processes will be highly specific, and will require objective and candid analysis of the agency operations by members of the agency.

This is much easier to state than to accomplish.

We occasionally find police executives who resist change, resent internal questioning of policy or procedure as disloyal, and are overly sensitive to any kind of criticism, positive or negative, whether made from within the organization or from without. Police executives are human beings and are subject to the human frailty of pride, which greedily feeds on praise and haughtily rejects censure. Nonetheless, many law enforcement administrators and supervisors are most highly motivated, have a genuine loyalty to the goal of a genuinely professional service, and are quite willing to review policies and procedures, and if they find them to be illegal, immoral, or inefficient, make immediate corrections.

The finest police planning and research unit will become frustrated and comatose if the top-level leadership does not proceed to implement obviously necessary recommendations, and install audit and follow-up processes to guarantee complete and continuing implementation. Thus, there is a heavy responsibility placed on the shoulders of the police executive who installs a planning and research unit — for their studies may recommend, and adequately justify, changes which are radical and which may upset decades of unquestioned practices, and thus place the executive squarely on the spot. If he makes an implementation of the recommendations he upsets the equanimity of all his personnel who are absolutely committed to the *status quo;* if he tables the recommendations, he may be tabbed as a bottleneck to progress. That is why it is most encouraging to note the rapid development of planning and research units in the police service, the implementation of their feasible and practicable recommendations, and their increased prestige — for that kind of development reflects great credit upon the Chief of Police and his commitment to the highest ideals of the American police service.

Conclusions

Police planning and research has a *genuine* and *proper* role in police–community relations. It accomplishes much now by promoting *efficiency* in general police administration, supervision, and operations. It can accomplish a great deal more in the future by interesting itself in promoting *morality* and *legality,* and by assisting in the elimination of any harmful attitudes and practices of police which contribute to the maintenance of a gap between police and public. And it can accomplish a great deal more in the future by interesting itself in promoting *public awareness* of *public responsibilities,* and by assisting in the elimination of any harmful attitudes and practices of the public which contribute to the maintenance of a gap between public and police.

In that fashion, the police planning and research unit will contribute to the achievement of ordered liberty in a democratic society, to responsible and responsive policing, and to community acceptance of the fact that the police are the public, and the public are the police—a unity dedicated to the Common Good.

Planning and Research in Law Enforcement
as Related to the Public View of the Police

ROBERT R. J. GALLATI

Director, New York State Identification and Intelligence System,
Assistant Chief Inspector
Director of Planning (on leave), New York City Police Department

MAY 20, 1964

This topic strikes very close to my heart. Today in the year 1964, law enforcement has come a long way from where it was way back in 1940, when I was a rookie in the New York City Police Department. At that time, police education and training was held in very low esteem. The Police Academy was in an old building underneath the Brooklyn Bridge. The staff were part-time people, brought in to share their experiences with us in their relatively ill-prepared courses. However, the greater part of our learning experience was on-the-job training. I recall vividly my first tour of foot patrol duty during such training, while still a recruit assigned to the Academy and with only a couple of weeks of classroom instruction.

I was assigned to the 34th precinct in Manhattan, which is uptown, near the George Washington Bridge. It is an area of five-story walk-up apartment houses. I was assigned to a tour of patrol with a senior police officer; a hard-bitten old-timer who was to teach me what I was supposed to know. I remember we were on foot patrol along Audubon Avenue on that beautiful June afternoon, when a building superintendent rushed up to us as we strolled along and excitedly told us there was gas escaping from one of his top floor apartments. We dashed up the five flights of stairs and traced the leak to the apartment kitchen; we broke open the door and found a fairly well-dressed man with his head in the oven and all the jets turned on. On a table nearby was a partly finished bottle of Scotch whiskey. Having attempted resuscitation to no avail and assuring ourselves that the gentleman was indeed "DOA," we looked for a phone in the apartment to make the necessary notifications. There being no phone to be found in the apartment, my old-time partner ordered me to go down to the corner candy store to phone the precinct, call the morgue wagon, etc. When I got back, I climbed up the five flights of stairs again and as I entered the kitchen, I found my erstwhile partner sitting on the table, imbibing freely from the bottle of Scotch.

"For God's sake, don't drink that," I shouted. "It might be poison."

He turned to me with a very deprecating look and said: "Now learn 'dis, rookie, if 'dis stuff was poison, 'dat guy neva' woulda' hadda' stick his head in da oven."

Police training has come a long way since that time, particularly in the broader concept of education for the law enforcement profession. There are now hundreds of colleges and universities in the country offering police administration courses. And New York City, not long ago, spent ten million dollars on a new police academy. It has a wonderful college level police training program. We are even seeing the beginning of police training programs on a mandatory basis, as in New York and New Jersey and elsewhere. We are now at the point where education and training for the police is accepted.

How about research? We've accepted education and training. Why not research? There is very little being done in research in law enforcement. A recent issue of a police journal indicated some of the types of research that *are* being done by various departments — such as the length of a nightstick; the use of rippled-soled shoes; the quality of decals for police car insignia. This is hardly the kind of research which makes a profession.

Actually, of course, it is encouraging to note that the police are no longer saying, "For a hundred years, we've had nightsticks this length; that's the way they'll stay." We've opened our minds, anyway. But why haven't we had more real in-depth research? Why haven't we used the social sciences to a larger extent? We have been entranced by the physical sciences. You can ask for and get in your budget a spectrograph costing $50,000 that will be used maybe once or twice a year. But try to get that much for a project in the social sciences. I know most of us couldn't get such in our police budgets. So we have sort of despaired of the social sciences. Yet we are basically engaged in the practice of the social sciences, and we urgently need research in this area.

We are concerned that we have developed so little in the way of a professional literature, yet we simply don't reduce what we do know to writing, so others can benefit from it. Recently in New York, we had two detectives retire who had almost a hundred years of experience between them. They have not, nor do they intend to write. And these men have solved three or four homicides a week! This is all too true of most of us. Some say that enforcement is largely a matter of common sense. What do we need research for? If that's true, anybody can be an expert. Anybody can be a second-guesser.

If policing is not an art or a science, how can we rail against the reporter who second-guesses us? He can claim he is as much an expert as we are. We ignore research at our peril. There are those who say that law enforcement is bankrupt; that we are losing the battle. They cite the fact that crime is rising at a rate many times that of the population. But we don't conduct research as to *why* this should be so. If we ran a business that way, I'm afraid we'd be out of business in a hurry. We have almost no developed strategic or tactical documented plans and policies or research designs for the solution of our problems.

There is almost no literature that tells us how to patrol, how to do the very important things that are basic elements of our profession. Have we got the "feedback" mechanism that would tell us definitely about the value of preventive patrol? As a result of this inability to justify our patrol purpose, we find ourselves handling ambulance cases, and mental cases, and cats in trees — things we were never truly trained or hired to do. Until very recently the police in Chicago were supposed to be dogcatchers, along with everything else they have to do. We permit ourselves, by virtue of the fact that we haven't had the research on which to base our expertise, to be made out to be the villain, not only in the area of civil rights, but also in the matter of statistics. It is not our doing that there is an increase in crime, and yet we take a defensive attitude immediately, as soon as crime statistics are flashed at us.

In the area of civil rights, as professional policemen, we have only one reason for being, and that is to protect the freedom of the individual. That is our whole purpose and the object of all our efforts — to preserve the delicate balance so that ordered liberty may thrive. And yet we permit ourselves to be cast as the villain, largely because we have no research, no developed rationale to support our position scientifically. In the meantime, industry is spending 15 billions of dollars every year on research. The Defense Department is spending vast sums to send people up into space, and we are getting — how much in the way of federal funds — for peace and security here on earth and in our own homes and communities? Just try to get some federal funding for law enforcement and social science research.

It is not enough for our profession to think only in terms of education and training. We must have research upon which to base the education and training. They complement each other. And on the basis of research, we will ultimately be able to raise our scientific posture and develop a science of police that will truly demonstrate that common sense is not enough. We have big problems coming up, and we must act as social scientists in meeting them. Not long ago, a member of one of the large philanthropic foundations asked a member of one of this nation's outstanding enforcement agencies how much his department spent over the last decade on research. He reached in his pocket and pulled out a handful of change, and said that was how much they'd spent! If that department had done so little, it is not likely that other departments have done much.

Yes, we'll be faced with many problems. But the silver lining in the situation is that, through research, I am confident we will find that the solutions of the problems are inherent in the problems themselves. We have with us a developing civil rights revolution. And this goes far beyond race problems. We are in an era of concern for the civil rights of all the people — right down the line. A new concern is abroad for true justice for all. In operation at the present time, in New York, is the Vera Foundation project on bail, and another on the use of summonses in lieu of arrest, both of which have very significant implications across the board in terms of protecting the liberty and freedom of all of us.

We have, concurrent with the revolution in civil rights, a revolution in education. Community colleges are cropping up all over the country. The average person, in a very short period of time, will have had at least two years of college. This means, in terms of recruiting policemen, that we must at least keep our selection of personnel up to the average of the community. It also means that many young people are unable to keep up with this new surge toward higher education and the pursuit of excellence. The result is that we have dropouts, and this creates new social problems for us. It is safe to say that this new wave of advanced education for the general population is going to result in greater respect for the social sciences, among which the police profession is perhaps the most vital to the maintenance of ordered liberty.

We must also take cognizance of the urban revolution, the growth of city and suburb, which will involve us with criminal mobility and regional coordination and cooperation. In New York City, we have formed the Metropolitan Regional Council Law Enforcement Committee, which is effectively bringing together the 600 police departments of the metropolitan area to discuss mutual problems and to develop communication with each other. New York State is developing a statewide computer-based information retrieval system serving all the 3,600 agencies of criminal justice in the State. These types of advances are the hallmarks of our new age, an age of rapid change.

Tied into all this ferment is the cybernetic revolution. This is the development which is going to hit law enforcement right where it helps, and possibly where it hurts. This will generate the problems of excess leisure, of the unskilled workers, the middle-management people who are to be replaced by computers, and of the many new services which the computers are going to supply that will replace mere people. We police are in a service business. Computers are now researching law cases, providing diagnoses for doctors, and aiding all kinds of research. Computers have within themselves not only the solution to the problems they themselves have created or enlarged, but also the solutions to our problems, if we but use them!

What are our problems? They include the rising crime rate, traffic safety, maintaining peace and order during community conflict, etc. We have done very little to research their solution. We have developed very few theories, and very few hypotheses to help us solve these problems. I'd like to suggest some of the areas where we might seek solutions to the problems we now have, and to the problems we may anticipate. These are largely research oriented problems.

First, *planning as a function of police* — the need for planning units to get away from the idea of getting along from day to day in our procedures and techniques — to think in terms of long-range planning. Recently, we had to plan for the New York World's Fair. This was a very important yet relatively low level of planning. However, a five-year research job to develop a new method of searching latent fingerprints would be high level planning. We need also to stimulate and reward innovation and protect zealously the right to make mistakes. Believe it or not, until very recently, we were still designing station houses in New York the same way we did before the Civil War. And we still have the same blotters we've had for 100 years!

Second, *we need to know more about preventive patrol*. There must be ways of measuring it. Preventive patrol is the biggest job of the police, and yet there is little significant literature on it. I'm sure that the social scientists can give us the answers about how to check the utility of our methods. We need new yardsticks and other criteria than just the number of arrests. The number of arrests made is no certain clue to the effectiveness of enforcement procedures. We must have better standards for the quantification of data and the interpretation of the statistics derived therefrom.

We need living laboratories, to look into real situations, to develop new controls on a pilot basis at least, so that we'll get feedback, and not just pronouncements from an ivory tower.

Third, *we need to know about police discretion*. The most amazing thing to me is that we are told from the first to the last day we're in the police profession that we have discretion in enforcing the law. Yet nowhere is there anything in the law of the land that gives us the right to exercise discretion. As a matter of fact, every time we exercise discretion we are doing it at our own legal peril. Can we avoid making an arrest when we see a crime being committed? Yet, can we possibly enforce the law as to all offenses? There is no legal resolution of this problem. Prosecutors don't have to prosecute every case that comes to them. The law is clear as to their discretion, but quite unclear as to what the parameters of our discretion could possibly be.

I would like to describe very briefly the design of the New York State Identification and Intelligence System as an example of the type of long-range research program that is so necessary for the future of the administration of criminal justice. Throughout the State, as in most states, there are six major agencies for the administration of criminal justice. The cornerstone of the whole criminal justice system is the police. In addition, we have the prosecutors, the court system, probation, parole and correction authorities. As police officers, we are dependent upon the subsequent processes of the criminal justice system, just as they are, in turn, dependent upon us. Let us not forget the 97 percent of the people who are convicted come back to society, and are our problems again. To the extent that the DA's, judges, probation, parole and correction authorities do the job well, these 97 percent are that much less a problem for us. These six major areas are the building blocks of the administration of justice and must stand together or surely fall apart.

Where is our communication with one another? Each of these agencies makes out its own pedigree sheet on each arrested offender. Much of the record keeping on the individual is needlessly duplicated and there is little information exchange or communication between and among the agencies concerning the persons they jointly process. A major purpose of the New York State Identification and Intelligence System is to convey data rapidly to all agencies concerned from a common data base serving all, to communicate essential information so that it is available at the point of decision.

Only with modern computer technology can the full impact of a massive information retrieval system be brought to bear upon the problem of crime and criminal behavior.

The System will have the ability to handle an unlimited number of requests. For example, in New York City, by taking a position at the entrance to the Battery-Brooklyn Tunnel and checking routinely all the license plates of cars entering the tunnel, we were able to identify, before the car could leave the tunnel, those cars which were stolen, had stolen license plates or were otherwise wanted. With a computer, we could enter the plate numbers into the computer, instantly communicate them to the arresting unit at the other end of the tunnel, and actually eliminate to a great extent, by such methods, the stolen car problem as it exists today. We've done it on a manual basis, and we know it can be done by computers. As of now, many kids get away with stealing cars and showing them off to their friends on the street corners. This method of apprehending car thieves while the perpetrator is still in the vehicle could cause a substantial reduction in car thefts.

Other types of computer science development could be used to help solve burglaries, identify latent fingerprints and scene-of-the-crime fingerprints, and the like. Today it takes 10 to 14 days to obtain a criminal history record from the Identification Bureau in Albany, New York. With the computer, response could be accomplished within two hours. Computers and computer aided scientific research can help us lower the crime rate and solve many of our problems.

I'd like to close with some recommendations. We should tie in university theses with actual police work. Let's not work in a vacuum. Let's get the social scientist together with the practical people. We need more literature and a greater number of publications by the professional police. We need a vehicle to receive and dispense funds and donations for police research. We need to develop new tactical concepts based upon rigorous analysis and evaluation of alternatives. But most important, we must remember that our chief reason for being, for the very existence of police forces, is to protect the freedom of the people, and with all our development of new techniques, we must be ever conscious of the ultimate importance of the individual, his rights, his liberties and his human dignity.

Ordered liberty which enhances the quality of life while protecting person and property from depredation is the goal we seek. When the public becomes aware that we are seeking these goals through the application of the most advanced methodologies and scientific techniques, the public view of police will spiral to new heights of support which will, in turn, create the means for even greater effectiveness — and police professionalism will have arrived.

Youth and Police

JAMES J. BRENNAN

*(Then) Professor, School of Police Administration and Public Safety,
Michigan State University, East Lansing, Michigan*

MAY 18, 1965

Introduction

There are many social problems affecting the welfare of the communities of this country. All of these call for concerted effort by a variety of people if we are to further the ideals of the democratic way of life.

However, there is no single problem of greater importance than the moral, physical, social, and mental well-being of our youth. They are the future of this country. When we work to preserve their worth, we work for a continuance of our form of society.

There is one way in which we can help our youth. We can join forces in every community to combat delinquency. Here is a challenge for all police. Police can do much to prevent delinquency and to redirect erring youth.

The Problem

The "cold facts" of juvenile delinquency and adolescent crime are even more serious than current periodical attention would indicate. There is always a certain superficiality about public attention to social problems. All too frequently, public interest is maintained only when the problems warrant bold headlines. A new problem arises, a new crisis fills the pages of newspapers, and public attention is diverted from the old and transferred to the new.

At one moment, youth and its delinquencies hold the spotlight. Another day, and youth will be forgotten. Then more teen-age crime, and again public attention will focus on youth.

All across this nation conferences are being held, and remedial proposals are being advanced. There are advocates of stern measures and advocates of coddling. Solemn pronouncements are made, yet tomorrow American society will be attentive to some other problem. But the problem of youth will remain with us, and the degeneration of children will continue.

There is a confusion, partly understandable, surrounding society's efforts to improve the lot of its youth. One can sympathize with some of the lay public's lack of appreciation, inertia, and emotionalism. They are besieged by conflicting theories of prevention and control.

Confusing Concepts

Statistically, we are told that delinquency and adolescent crime is increasing seriously. There are some who hold that this increase is simply a reflection of our having more youth, or being more aware of their delinquencies.

In terms of causation, we are presented with a multiplicity and variety of theories: world tensions, the aftermath of war, lack of educational facilities, lack of recreation. Some people accept these as causative factors. Others are confused. World tension exists for all youth, yet all are not delinquent. The same is true of war's aftermath. There is much head-shaking in regard to education. Some believe we are the most literate people in the world and yet have the most delinquency. Then, too, lack of recreation confuses some who see many delinquent youths in communities with extensive recreational facilities, and yet find many non-delinquents in areas lacking such recreational aids.

Slums, large families, and poor economic conditions are offered as causes, yet many, many non-delinquents are observed living in such social environment.

Areas of Agreement

There are certain concepts accepted by thinking, concerned people. These people may not be specialists, but using God-given sense to see and hear and intellects to think, have arrived at certain conclusions.

First, there is a feeling that 3 percent or 2 percent or 1 percent of our youth becoming delinquent and potentially criminal is entirely too much of a national waste — socially, economically, and morally.

Second, these "unscientific" but thinking people observe a change in the character of delinquent acts that frighten them. They sense, in youthful killings, rapes, robberies, and vandalisms, a moral depravity or a psychopathic quality that is difficult enough to accept in a few, but a tragedy of civilization to see spreading more and more among our young. These people sense a breakdown in morality, a breakdown in authority.

The people are no longer impressed by conflicting statistics, conferences upon conferences, the seemingly studious avoidance of coming to grips with the real problems, as specialists continue to study the obscure. These people, intensely concerned with our youth, their value and worth to God and society, are seeking a means of articulating a deep conviction. When expressed, it will sound like a clarion call to those who can and will help. At the same time, it will be a tolling bell for the passing of the fadists and fashionists, the dwellers in libido, the particularists, in short, for those who would be scientific but are not scientists, those who would sacrifice more youth while they try to discover more remedial programs that do not remedy.

The Pressing Need

There are many sane, sensible people who want to act, want to fight this evil, want to protect the integrity of our youth. These people have been confused. They lack weapons, they lack guidance and direction. These people need leaders — leaders who will forge the weapons, form the lines, and continue the fight — not for a day, a week, a month, a year, but for always. Police officials, along with their colleagues in every community in this country, can and must provide that leadership.

Policemen bind themselves by oath to protect the lives and property of the people they serve. Frequently, policemen offer their lives in performing that duty. No policeman is unmindful of the value of youth, our most priceless heritage. They deserve the best that police can give in time, talent, devotion, and sacrifice. Protect them, preserve them, and you protect and preserve our very way of life, our democratic society, our nation.

What Can Police Do?

There is a definite need to recognize the part police can and must play in meeting this challenge to law and order. While police cannot accept total responsibility, there is need for a realistic appraisal of the problem.

While many public and private agencies must join forces to help youth, close examination of agency responsibility indicates that no other single agency has the degree of responsibility that is incumbent on police. The charters of most police organizations, in spelling out the duties of that group, charge them with the prevention of crime. Intelligent crime prevention must begin with delinquency prevention.

Prevention of delinquency and crime is not to be confused with crime suppression. Prevention is of a different character. Here, concern is with contributing factors. Prevention is concerned with motivation for behavior. Having diagnosed a youth's behavior, we try to provide the treatment, the guidance, the interest, the help necessary to redirect his behavior along more morally and socially desirable lines.

Since the turn of the century, our police have been cognizant of the need to reevaluate the concept of police crime prevention. As a result of this new thinking, formal, organized police prevention programs have come into existence in many communities. While no one of these programs is as complete in function as one would desire to see, a study of police programs indicates several well-defined areas of operation which police can establish in order to realistically meet the problem of delinquency and adolescent crime.

Control Aspects

We must direct sustained attention and action toward the persons, places, and conditions which contribute to delinquency and adolescent crime. All too often these situations exist in violation of law, seemingly immune to police activity.

We appreciate the fact that police are not prosecutors nor prison administrators and therefore, cannot guarantee the conviction or imprisonment of persons who contribute to delinquency. However, we can offer no excuse for inaction on the part of police to secure evidence and arrest those who, by their activities, contribute in any way to delinquency or adolescent crime. The Fagin, the sex pervert, the promoter of prostitution, the drug pusher, the tavern owner who sells to minors — all who contaminate the youth of our communities — should be dealt with promptly, adequately, and if necessary, frequently.

No policeman, except a moral degenerate, would, for any type of favor or goodwill, tolerate for an hour the presence of such vermin in our communities.

All police work carries with it civil, social, and moral responsibility to do the job and do it well. None is more morally demanding than the protection of the minds, souls, and bodies of our young people.

Those who would tamper with our youth should come to realize, and quickly, that they could pick no more dangerous business as far as police reaction to their doings is concerned.

By intelligently presenting our problems to prosecutors, judges, and through our press, to the public we serve, we can expect, we can demand, that our police actions against these are not wasted through indifference, favoritism, or political conniving. In regard to these conditions, let us not be concerned with making bad friends — those who aid in any way to prevent the prosecution of the violators of youth are not fit to be friends with decent people.

The Individual Delinquent

Throughout the past and long before any police department ever established a "youth division," there were policemen who, avoiding the indiscriminate use of their power of arrest, gave advice and counsel to erring youth, and frequently were rewarded by seeing these youngsters become worthwhile citizens.

In contrast, policemen everywhere are witnesses to the fact that arrest, court action, and commitment to institutions does not always result in the individual becoming a law-abiding person.

It was this thinking that led police to more formally apply the principle of understanding youth and attempting to secure adequate help for those in need of such attention. The reasoning is sound, the procedure most desirable.

If a youngster, guilty of a minor offense, is subject to intelligent and sympathetic understanding, we may discover the factors that are contributing to his behavior.

In proposing this approach to the individual delinquent, there is no intention of suggesting that we fall prey to the theorists who would have us believe that delinquents must be deliquents, that criminals have no choice, that people's actions are predetermined, and that they must act as they act because of many psychological and sociological influences. Those who have stressed this theory to the exclusion of any area of choice of action have, willingly or not, attempted to reduce man to the status of an animal.

Yet while we refuse to deprive man of his free will, we can and must recognize that there are many influences that affect the use of that will. The intellect can be undeveloped or can contain false principles, false objectives. The will can be influenced and weakened. Conscience can be made false by wrong training.

Without trying to be confusing, the premise is asserted that we can recognize the intellect and free will in man and, at the same time, recognize the need to discover the wrongful influences, the erroneous training that motivates youth to undesirable behavior. Having discovered these liabilities in the development of character, we can hope to diminish them and at the same time increase the positive, good, and desirable influences.

Police engaged in youth work are gradually coming to understand the importance of such "diagnosis" for the purpose of putting the youngster into the hands of the agency that can best help him.

This type of work depends on training. There is need to know as much as is knowable about the development of personality and character in the individual. The normative and behavioral sciences have much to tell us. Police, through experience, have much to contribute.

The treatment of offenses will not help. We cannot cure burglary, auto theft, vandalism. Like doctors, we must go beneath the symptomatic act and put our hands on the things or conditions or thinking that prompt such action. Were a doctor to treat a symptom and not the cause of an illness, there is every likelihood that the patient would die.

Police programs designed to help youth can begin modestly. There can be limitations in terms of age, sex, and type of offense for which this proposed procedure will be used. In cooperation with judges, probation officers, and other agencies concerned, police can establish the area in which they will begin this type of work. As they progress, they can extend the area to include others in this new, treatment approach.

Community Resources for Treatment

Having made a "gross" diagnosis of a youngster's need, police should refer the case to an agency in their community capable of providing the treatment needed. Wherever possible, police should avoid the treatment process itself.

The social agencies, schools, churches, recreation facilities, mental and medical clinics can and should service the youth whom police refer for treatment. In some communities, a lack of professional facilities will pose a problem. But we must use what we have, and do what we can ourselves. A generation of children cannot be lost while we wait for promised facilities.

Community Organization

Delinquency control and prevention cannot become the sole responsibility of the police department nor, for that matter, of any other single agency. There are responsibilities encumbent upon parents, the church, the school, the local government, and other agencies of the community.

Police can and should be concerned with bringing together all of the moral and social influences of the community to stimulate them, coordinate their activities, and direct their attention to the problems that must be solved.

This area of police prevention work, community organization — community action — is one with the greatest potential for successful delinquency prevention. Unfortunately, too few police departments have moved into this field. Their deficiency has been due to a lack of understanding of how to organize, how to guide without imposing the rigid controls of police procedure.

Police are in a unique position to initiate such a program. Police are neutral in terms of service, but not in objective. Public sentiment would support and those who want to help youth will rally around such a police program. Community resentment will be aroused against individuals or agencies who attempt to block such an effort.

Through community organization, better use of existing facilities will ensue. The need for new facilities will be exposed. The attention of agencies will be retained.

There is another objective for such a community activity. Situations that are dangerous to the morals of youth, but which do not exist in violation of law, can be dealt with most effectively by the power of public opinion. An aroused public can be most effective in dealing with conditions that cannot be removed by statutory law. Community organization can help arouse the public.

What's Needed to Do the Job?

First and foremost, the will to do the job. A recognition by police that of all the services they can give to their community, none is more important than preserving youth.

We need a recognition and firm belief in the dignity and worth of the human being. Let us recognize in him a creature composed of body and soul, one who is made not for time, but for eternity.

We need to realize the value, the tremendous value, to ourselves, our communities and our country, in helping a boy or a girl grow up to become a socially, economically, and morally useful individual. If we believe in these values honestly and sincerely, the rest will be relatively easy.

Within our departments, large or small, there should be an organized program for the prevention and control of delinquency. Our personnel should be carefully chosen in terms of interest in the work, interest in youth, personality, adaptability, and education. They should be selected in that order. Education can be supplied, but not interest.

Training, guidance, and direction will be needed. The police can seek out such help from their local colleges and universities. There are many ways to gain the necessary knowledge.

Everyone in your community should know what you have done, are doing, and are planning to do. All local newspaper, radio, and television facilities should be enlisted to be your mouthpiece — to sustain the interest of everyone. Do not for a moment underestimate the power of the press. Allied with you, it can be a most potent weapon in this continuing struggle.

Conclusion

Some years ago, I spent an uncomfortable evening — a dreary, lonesome, fretful evening — watching a clock move ever so slowly to eleven. A twenty-two year old boy was to be electrocuted at Sing Sing. He came from a home that lacked everything a home should have. There was no love, no affection, no security. He had been arrested many times. There were several convictions and a few commitments. There never was an intelligent understanding of his needs and an attempt to help him.

This is no maudlin, sympathetic wail for a convicted murderer. It is a challenge to the effectiveness of punishing without first trying to understand — first trying to help.

Another incident comes to my mind. A young policeman graduated from the police academy of New York. He had made mistakes as a youth, but in his case, police understanding, police and community help proved effective. He became a policeman and had a serious concern. This young policeman was hopeful that in his twenty years of service, he could help straighten out one "kid." What a thought, what an ambition, what a hope for the youth of America! Policemen straightening out kids — even one kid!

There is little need for more conferences on what to do. There is need for a conference on what has been done. Police officers have done much to advance the professional character of police work. By this they evidence a sincere wish to serve, and serve well, the people of their community.

Here is a challenge. We have the welfare of youth at heart. Let each of us highly resolve that he will refuse to be frightened or confused by the problem of delinquency — that he will refuse to let this problem continue while more conferences are held. Here and now resolve to accept the challenge and move against this scourge of youth.

Let us confer again, to be sure. But let that conference be one concerned with things done, with programs started. The nation needs determined, steadfast, continued action. The youth of today who do not want to rot in prison or die in electric chairs need that help. The police of this nation can give it.

Administration of Criminal Justice: from Arrest to Sentence

EDMOND F. DeVINE

(Then) Prosecuting Attorney, Washtenaw County, Ann Arbor, Michigan

MAY 21, 1958

About a month ago, thousands of downtown shoppers in New York City witnessed what the newspapers called a real cops and robber drama, featuring a demonstration of uncommon courage by an underwear salesman, and a policeman who shot himself and the bandit with the same bullet. It was an example of the criminal law in action, of what may be involved in the practical administration of criminal justice, if you will, where members of the community play an active part. A masked and armed bandit first held up a citizen in the rest room of the Waldorf Cafeteria on 7th Avenue, then threatened the cashier, and scooped up sixteen hundred dollars in front of her. Going outside, the bandit got in a taxi; the cabbie became suspicious, and drove his cab up to a traffic officer. "This guy's not kosher" the driver told the surprised policeman. Equally surprising was the fact that the cab door opened, and an automatic was shoved under the officer's nose, accompanied by the order, "Get in or I'll kill you." The officer got in, but the cab driver got out, and ran off shouting "Help, stick up." By this time, running off seemed to have some merit, and the bandit also abandoned the cab, and took off down 34th Street, followed at a distance by the officer. Then the underwear salesman, weighing a mere 140 pounds, stepped in, dropped his sample case and tackled the armed bandit. Both fell. The bandit broke loose, started off, and the underwear salesman tackled him again. This brought up the panting patrolman, who grabbed the robber with his left hand and fired a bullet, which unfortunately went through the officer's hand before it lodged in the fleeing gunman's chest. In a few moments, to quote the underwear salesman, actually the hero of the day, "there was a sea of cops," and justice finally triumphed.

About the same time, in Detroit, an elderly man — in his late 60's — saw an obviously drunken driver strike down and kill a woman on a busy street. The driver didn't stop then, but had to come to a halt in the traffic at the next intersection. No one seemed to pay any attention to the hit-runner, and our elderly citizen — call him Mr. Smith — got mad. Running down the street, he managed to get up to the car involved, hang onto the window, dragging along side the car while it turned around the corner, and finally caused the driver to stop. The police were soon there, and the driver was held for manslaughter. He had become drunk after leaving the brewery where he worked, and claimed not to know he had killed the victim.

These two cases emphasize that the administration of criminal justice is not a fleshless thing — not a mere matter of theory — the concern solely of a specialized group, but a vital part of the operation of our communities, preventing the dominance of the law of the jungle. Our citizens developed our system of criminal justice — of criminal procedure. Properly applied, it protects them. They want the security of law enforcement — they will support it — and as our cases indicate, they often take a direct heroic part in it. Here then, ideally, is true team play. The police are not an agency apart — an antagonistic group. No citizen worthy of

the name would have the bully terrorize the neighborhood, would allow the burglar or rapist sanctuary on his street. Where therefore the criminal law operates
ideally, it has and it is bound to have, complete community support. There is no
place in such a system for oppression, for bias, for favoritism or prejudice. Where
these operate, one part of the body politic is injuring the other — it is like the
right hand striking the left.

How in fact does the administation of criminal justice operate? It is achieving this ideal of community protection for the common good? Let us examine it.

Arrest

The cases I described above had to do with arrest. It is here that the ordinary
citizen who is content to leave to someone else the actual protection of his rights,
and sometimes, the enforcement of his duties, is most likely to encounter the law
in action. Often here, he builds up a misconception as to the character of law
enforcement — his own strong right arm — treating it rather as an opposing
force, and transmitting this attitude sometimes to his children and associates. We
must be aware of this tendency — to fail to recognize *his* guardians of the peace,
and we must not contribute to it. We must remember, after all, that men enforce
the law and men, of varying circumstances, not all bad, violate it. At the same
time, our officers must not be allowed to forget that they are the special representatives of the law-abiding citizens of the community, and not a totally independent
force.

Arrest, of course, may be made in two ways: with a warrant, and without a
warrant. It is arrest without a warrant that poses most of the problems for police
and laymen alike. The foundations for such arrests are ancient, going back to the
very development of the common law. An officer may arrest without a warrant
when:

1. A misdemeanor (or greater crime) has been committed in his presence; or
2. He has reason to believe the man committed a felony. The officer in our New
   York case had sufficient grounds. A felony had been committed in his presence.
   Attempting to work out the nature of reasonable grounds for arrest is a matter
   of interest to the trained officer.

If an officer is informed that a certain man committed an assault and battery,
he may not, in Michigan, arrest this man until first, a warrant has been obtained
by the person giving the information. Here we deal with a misdemeanor offense,
and the needs of society for instant apprehension are not as great as the desire
that a man charged merely with a misdemeanor, not committed in the officer's
presence, shall be arrested only after a judge has issued a warrant.

The law of arrest without a warrant is fairly settled. How does it work in
practice?

The fact is, in metropolitan areas particularly, many thousands of arrests without a warrant are made yearly, which cannot be justified upon the legal grounds
given. The fact that in all but a few of such cases, no public outcry is raised may
be attributed to a number of factors:

1. The ignorance of the affected members of the public as to their rights, the
   law — and the corresponding duties of the police — in this area.
2. The inability, in any case, of those arrested to vindicate their rights.
3. The economic and social condition of those arrested.

4. The possible public need for a period of temporary detention for investigation on suspicion only.

You may wonder about these illegal arrests. Do they really happen? It is at least privately agreed, in the administration of some of the large police departments — not all — that harrassment arrests, temporary detention and release without the filling of charges, are required to combat metropolitan vice and crime generally. So periodically, members of the racket squad kick down doors and raid places generally known to be used for gambling. Those assembled may be taken to a precinct station and released without charges. Outstanding traffic charges, incidentally, may be cleared against some of those brought in. Suspected prostitutes are arrested and brought to jail for an overnight check. They seldom complain later. Suspected narcotic violators and other probable vice participants are picked up, usually on well founded "suspicion," or the sixth sense some detectives seem to possess that by no means adds up to reasonable belief. The same policy is often utilized to harass homosexuals and probable liquor law violators.

A police officer has stated:

"The Disorderly Person Investigation" arrest is a form of harassment which the department uses as an alternative to legal arrests and subsequent prosecutions: extra-legal arrests of street-walkers, panderers and mutuals men, made without the slightest intention of bringing such offenders to court, serve to antagonize, harass and interrupt. The police department has been forced into the harassment program by the attitude of the court.

Another statement of the harrassment program is as follows:

Now if our police patrol certain areas in the city, and they find two women standing on a corner, they go back an hour later, and those two are still there, and they are persons who have heretofore been arrested as prostitutes, what conclusion do the police come to? They are prostitutes. Yet there has been no offense committed by the prostitutes in the presence of the officer. He makes the arrest to accomplish several purposes. First, to get them off the street; second, as a means of harassment. These particular women I have reference to are not only prostitutes, but they are decoys for the so called "Murphy Game." There have been persons murdered who come in contact with them. As a general rule, in fact almost invariably, these women are out there at two o'clock when the saloons close, when the prospective customers have a lot of liquor in them, and they don't want to go home; they are looking for strange experiences. And we've had murders. We had one fellow that was found in a trash can. Now what should we do under those circumstances? We have no crime committed in the presence of the police officer, nothing that legally warrants the arrest. Shall we say, "Well now, because our hands are tied, we are going to let these women alone!!"

So, too, arrest of the suspected narcotics agent, or numbers operator, or "suspicious person" generally may result in the solution of crime, detection of fugitives and the like in our transient society. Accordingly, it is argued that the police should be granted the right to detain, on pure suspicion, for a limited period of questioning and investigation.

It may be that this power is needed to combat crime in the modern community, and to bring some police practices into the open, but such a power is also subject to abuses, and this request for extension of police power is not likely to be popular in the present climate of the law.

In any case, we must be sure that arrests are not made on the basis of a calculated risk that members of this racial or economic group are not so likely to have the means or inclination to complain, or the audience to hear the grievance. Law enforcement moves in our democracy, after all, not on the basis of force, but on that of acceptance and cooperation, and in evoking this spirit in place of hostility lies our progress toward a future law-abiding community.

Arrest with a Warrant

All of us realize that criminal laws, in impressive numbers, are churned out at every session of the legislature. These deal with misdemeanors, for the most part. Lawyers are hard pressed to keep up with them, and poor John Citizen has to rely often on a kind of intuition to keep out of the orbit of criminal law. Conscience will not afford the necessary guidance here, since the laws of which I speak are *malum prohibitum* only, i.e. — if the legislature did not prohibit or command the act, the doing or omission would in no sense be wrong. There are all kinds of possible violations in the area of weights and measures, selling, operation of businesses, etc., that have nothing to do with fraud or evil intent. It is a matter, sometimes unwittingly, of doing a prohibited act. Ignorance of the law, after all, is no excuse. Where it is a misdemeanor for a restaurant proprietor to fail to maintain a certain solution of dishwater, the idea is to see that he maintains the proper standard, at penalty of a fine, for the public safety, not so much to make him a criminal. But such is the effect. The same result obtains where it is a misdemeanor to violate zoning and building laws, to permit a dog to run at large, etc. A bill was brought before the last Michigan Legislature making it a high misdemeanor (so-called) for an employer to threaten to discharge an employee who is serving on a jury. It is a violation for a railway company to have a train block a road more than 5 minutes. In all these cases, it would seem that sending an officer out with a warrant for the arrest of a citizen, whose real part in the commission of the offense may only be ownership of a store or business, or dog, is a harsh procedure, and an unnecessary humiliation, breeding justified resentment and hostility for the future. There are alternatives. One is for an officer unofficially to call up the man named in the warrant, and invite him to come to court voluntarily. This is, of course, a hit-and-miss affair, unlikely to be utilized to any extent in a large community. The other alternative is for the state to permit the magistrate to issue a summons in place of a warrant, and mail it to the defendant requesting his voluntary appearance. This system, replacing the warrant with a summons in many misdemeanor cases, appears a real advance in the practical administration of our criminal law, and should be promoted. Some states now use the judicial summons successfully in this area.

No discussion of the Administration of Criminal Justice would be complete without some reference to search and seizure. We have generally recognized the right of officers, without a search warrant, to search a limited area, as an incident to a lawful arrest. The U. S. Supreme Court has now expressly repudiated its one-time view that a search without a search warrant is illegal if the officers had time to get the search warrant, although the time factor may be considered with other facts indicative of illegal search. Certainly the officers making a legal arrest may now again search the person of the arrestee. How else will they provide for their own safety, and the safety of others, including that of the arrested man? Since they may do this, they may take from the man the fruits or product of the crime he committed, as well as any weapons they may find. But what if he is arrested in his house or office? The officers may search only a limited area here — that under the immediate control of the defendant, and necessarily passed through by them to get to the defendant in making the valid arrest. In any case, brutal methods of search will not be permitted. So it has been held unlawful to use a stomach pump to recover narcotics the defendant swallowed on arrival of the officers.

Since we have progressed beyond the point of arrest, about here the defendant needs to consider hiring legal counsel. Ahead of him, in a felony case, lie a number of possibilities for disposition of his case. The Prosecuting Attorney has discretion in charging the offense, and may be impressed with factors requiring a less severe charge than the maximum available. A woman who steals bread to feed her children, for example, hardly needs to be charged with the felony of larceny in a building. There are obvious equities on her side. The Prosecutor considers such factors, but the defendant's counsel often brings them to his attention. The examination provides a kind of filter through which the criminal felony case must pass on its way to circuit court. Many cases wash out here, and rightly so, in this first test of available witnesses brought under judicial scrutiny. Competent counsel is necessary for the defendant here, however, if this protective device is to be made effective for him. The United States Supreme Court has forcefully recognized the indigent defendant's right to counsel and the duty of the trial court to advise him of his right to counsel appointed at the public's expense. The Michigan Statute provides for the appointment of counsel for indigent defendants at the time of examination, as well as at the time of trial. It is apparent that this legal representation, while the case is in its early stages, is much more effective for the defendant without money to engage his own counsel, especially since it is the fact, as shown by American Bar Foundation studies, that a large percentage of criminal cases are dismissed at the time of examination. And generally, whether the office of Public Defender exists, or whether the bar provides legal aid in this area, or the court appoints counsel, there is national recognition of the principle that free legal counsel must be available to the indigent person to guide him through what is to him the wilderness of criminal procedure.

Assuming our felony case survives the hazards of examination, with charge and witnesses intact, our defendant represented by counsel is ready for arraignment — plea of guilty, or not guilty (he may stand mute), and if the latter, for trial by jury. We might note, at this stage, the influence of mental deficiencies on the administration of criminal justice.

If we may assume that our defendant has been convicted of the felony charged, by the verdict of the jury, he is subject, within the limit provided by statute, to the court's order of sentence. He is in the same condition, of course, if he has dispensed with trial by jury, by an earlier plea of guilty.

Here the trial court quite properly looks for help. Here the law looks closely at the character of the defendant, taking into account for the first time many factors that could not be brought into the case, or before the court earlier. The judge whose sole responsibility it is, as a general rule, to assess the sentence, may consider:

1. The report of the probation officer — this will be a detailed history of the defendant, his antecedents, the nature of his crime, and his possible future.
2. Police reports or recommendations.
3. Recommendation of the Prosecutor or District Attorney.
4. Psychiatric or medical reports.
5. Representations of the defendant's family, friends, minister and counsel.
6. Representations by concerned members of the community generally.
7. The attitude of the victim or his associates or family.
8. Effect of a given sentence on the public generally — confidence in law enforcement, etc.
9. Settled law enforcement policies (jail for gamblers, etc.).
10. Gravity of crime.
11. Possible restitution.
12. Previous record.

With all the avenues of information available to the sentencing judge, we might assume he will generally avail himself of them. Unfortunately, such is not always the case. Recent hearings in Congress on bills affecting sentencing procedure indicated quite clearly that the judicial function of sentence was often arbitrarily exercised, sometimes in a mistaken belief in judicial independence, without the available assistance that would make for intelligent sentencing. Much has been said about the need for uniform sentencing procedure. This may be desirable where uniform sentences may not. After all, individuals vary greatly in their actual and potential danger to society. Generally, legislatures and appellate courts have been able to curb excessive zeal on the part of sentencing judges.

Conclusion

We have proceeded somewhat summarily between arrest and sentence. Our subject consumes many hours of the law school curriculum, and its coverage here must necessarily be somewhat sketchy. What we should note is that the administration of criminal justice is no theoretical affair. It concerns you and me. It obliges us to observe the rights of our fellow citizens at the peril of liberty itself. Its aims are lofty — directly the general welfare — the safety and security of all. It may be improved, but its practical experience should not lightly be tossed aside. It must be administered without bias, or corruption or prejudice, so as to be itself a working force to eradicate these devisive elements in our community.

The Administration of Justice: the Correctional Process

RICHARD A. McGEE

(Then) Director of Corrections, State of California

MAY 21, 1958

The title which has been assigned me reminds me of an incident which occurred several years ago in a hearing of an applicant for parole before the

California Adult Authority. The prisoner in question had a long, bad criminal record and had been in prison several times. After the Board had finished its questioning, the chairman asked the inmate the usual question: "Is there anything more you would like to say in your own behalf before closing the interview?" Very fervently and emphatically, he said, "Gentlemen, all I want is justice!" Whereupon he got up from his chair and walked halfway to the door, then turned around and, looking a little sheepish, said, "I am sorry, gentlemen, I would like to change that statement. I think I have had all the justice I can take — what I really want now is mercy."

I don't mean to suggest by this that I am going to embark upon a philosophical discussion of the meaning of justice, or the degree to which justice should be tempered with mercy. It is important to emphasize at the outset, however, that until relatively recent years — by which I mean chiefly within the last half century — the administration of criminal justice meant principally apprehension, detention, a plea of guilty or trial, and the imposition of a sentence which was intended primarily as punishment — retributive punishment, if you will — which was society's revenge for a wrongful act and a warning to all others that similar acts would be dealt with in the like manner.

Again, I need not review the history of crime and punishment for a sophisticated audience such as this, except to make the point that in a cruder and less complex society than we have today, those punishments more often than not entailed physical suffering and had no other purpose than retribution and deterrence. In passing, we might also remind ourselves of the period of geographical banishments — during which England populated far away Australia and our own Carolinas, France created Devils Island in French Guiana, and Russia sent people to Siberia. All such expressions of popular emotions in dealing with serious offenders soon became impractical, and also ran afoul of the rising tide of democratic feeling in the Western World, as well as the basic tenets of Christianity.

Man has never been pleased, in his saner and more thoughtful moments, with what he has had to do to carry out the sanctions of the penal law. And from the very beginning, this great new Republic of ours in the western hemisphere has generally frowned upon brutal, savage and unnecessarily severe punishment. This is expressed first in the Eighth Amendment of the Constitution of the United States, which says, "Excessive bail shall not be required, nor excessive fines imposed, nor cruel and unusual punishment inflicted."

Since America has prized liberty so highly, it is only natural that it has always seemed to our leadership that the rightful punishment of an offender who has the high privileges of citizenship in a democracy, should be the loss of his liberty. Therefore, confinement in prisons, reformatories, or correctional institutions of various grades and types became the preferred method of punishment. But we were not satisfied with this because the question then immediately arose, how much liberty should be taken from a man's life, and how much should be taken for one offense as compared with another? This problem has not been solved to this moment. There is wide disparity in the sentencing laws in the many criminal jurisdictions of this country, and there are even wider differences between this country and the other countries of the world. In addition, there is extreme variance between the sentencing practices of different courts within the same jurisdiction. This very often is as broad as the ratio of one to ten.

We have also been struck, during the past generation or two, with another anomaly in this question of the imposition of penal servitude, and that is the realization that keeping men in prison for long periods of time, with the full intention of releasing them eventually, but without doing anything to prepare them for that release, may be a greater crime against society than that committed by the offender himself.

A third problem has also arisen since the growth of industrialization in our country, and that is the waste of a great potential labor force and tremendously expanding costs for the operation of custodial institutions. Our prisons were becoming mere human warehouses, living mausoleums, from which little but hostility, perversion and degeneration could be expected.

During the period of 1951 to 1955, I believe that history will record that there was almost a complete breakdown of prison administration in most of the states of this country. This breakdown became apparent to the general public through riots, mutinies, sit-down strikes, arson, kidnapping and murder, in some of our major state facilities. In 1953, I was asked to serve as chairman of a committee of leaders in the American Prison Association, which was charged with the responsibility of attempting to make an analysis of the causes of this breakdown, and to make a public statement in the name of the Association, in an attempt to interpret this problem to the public and to our political leaders. This little pamphlet, entitled PRISON RIOTS AND DISTURBANCES was issued in May, 1953. Permit me to quote briefly from some of the opening paragraphs of that report:

> "Prison riots should be looked upon as costly and dramatic symptoms of faulty prison administration. The causes of these faults may exist within the prison or outside of it. Therefore, a discussion of such riots must begin with a consideration of the basic causes of poor prison administration.
>
> "The immediate causes given out for a prison riot are usually only symptoms of more basic causes. Bad food usually means inadequate budgets reflected in insufficient supplies, poor equipment, poor personnel and, often, inept management. Mistreatment of prisoners, or lax discipline, usually has behind it untrained employees and unwise or inexperienced management. And thus it goes.
>
> "The fundamental causes of prison maladministration may be categorized under a number of general heads:
>
> A. Inadequate financial support, and official and public indifference.
> B. Substandard personnel.
> C. Enforced idleness.
> D. Lack of professional leadership and professional programs.
> E. Excessive size and overcrowding of institutions.
> F. Political domination and motivation of management.
> G. Unwise sentencing and parole practices.
>
> "The above list is offered merely for emphasis and convenience of discussion. There is obvious overlapping between categories. Political motives of some nature are usually involved in budget making. Low budgets affect salaries and numbers of personnel, as well as overcrowding. Poor personnel affects professional programs, and enforced idleness is the result of political pressures."

Now I do not wish to emphasize unduly the place of the adult prison in correction, but it is one of the oldest of the family of correctional processes, and in the public mind it is the most dramatic, and it may very well be that it is far from being the most effective. What I would like to emphasize at this point is the rather obvious fact that we have come to a turning place in the road on the whole question of what to do with the offender after he has been convicted and society has marked him for special treatment because of his behavior.

We must make a clear-cut decision between two courses: *One: Shall we pin our faith on punishment and the threat of punishment?* Or, *Two: Shall we exert every known skill we possess to bring about psychological and social changes in and with the offender, aiming at rehabilitation and acceptable adjustment as free and responsible persons?*

The first has been tested for centuries, with little positive effect except temporary control. The second has been given lip service for 150 years, but has really never been given a full and fair test. This is so for many reasons which space permits me only to enumerate in part:

1. Such a program costs much more initially than merely locking the offenders behind bars.
2. We have not yet developed enough skilled professional workers to do the job even if the money were provided.
3. We have confused in our own minds and in the public mind constructive rehabilitative programs with the idea of softness or laxity in the treatment of criminals. Nothing is or should be further from the fact.
4. We do not as a general thing keep adequate statistics and records; hence we lack the quantitative tools to test our own effectiveness.
5. We have done no really significant research to find the answers to the basic questions which must be resolved before we can be sure of the best techniques for handling each of the numerous types of human maladjustment which come into our hands.
6. The political instability of management in both local and state governments has prevented the emergence of any significant number of really enlightened, objective and able leaders in our field. Without able leadership, no program and no idea will go far.

The overwhelming majority of professional leaders in the correctional field are committed to the concept that while convicted offenders must be controlled, they must also be trained, treated and readjusted to the fullest extent to which our knowledge and resources permit. Therefore, at any point in time, we must make the best choices available to us in determinating what can best be done with each individual offender.

The first question we must ask is, how many of these offenders must be institutionalized for any period of time, bearing in mind that institutionalization at its best — or as its worst — is the most expensive choice of the several choices available? Let us start with the first step, after arrest and preliminary hearing. I recently made an inspection of the Los Angeles County Jail, which serves a population of 5,661,000. This institution is located on the top floors of the Hall of Justice, and is designed to deal with people awaiting disposition by the courts. It has a capacity of about 900. On the day that I visited it, there were 3,001 men in this facility. Some of them would be set free, some would receive fines, many would receive sentences to other county facilities for misdemeanor offenses. A smaller number would be convicted of felonies for which the law prescribes the possibility of a prison sentence. Of these, 45 percent would be placed on probation, 20 percent would have their charges reduced to misdemeanors and sent to county facilities, 27 percent would be sent to state prison, and 8 percent would go to the Youth Authority.*

Now, the question arises, how many of these men and women could safely have been released on bail or on their own recognizance? I make no pretense of knowing what the percentage is, but I am sure that it is substantial. With the explosive growth that is taking place in California, especially in Southern California, the county authorities estimate that by 1970, assuming that present practices continue, Los Angeles County will need a detention jail, or jails, with a total capacity of 5,000. Such a facility will cost the taxpayers 50 million dollars, plus several million dollars per year of operating costs. I would be insensitive to my own experience if I failed to state that it would be unrealistic and naive to arbitrarily release any large percentage of these detention cases and expect them to appear for the judicial proceedings. I do believe, however, that a careful screening of these persons, by skilled interviewers and investigators during the first few days after arrest, would make it possible to release a substantial percentage of them without risk to the public welfare and at a great saving, certainly, to the economy. Some of the money to be saved on architecture, on food, and on institutional supervision would, of necessity, have to be spent for investigators, counselors, and classification personnel. All of this ignores, in addition, the tremendous social damage that is done by the moral and criminal contamination that occurs in these jails, which were referred to many years ago by Fischman as "crucibles of crime."

I am not the first to observe that the county jail — of which there are more than three thousand in this country and which process in the neighborhood of four million people per year — is the lowest form of social institution on the American scene. A few of them are intelligently managed, but almost none of them is adequately supported financially, and while I readily grant the necessity for places of temporary detention for most offenders, and for more prolonged detention for many offenders, I am constrained to begin this discussion on the rather sorry note that the initial step in the correctional process is often more destructive than corrective. We are in desperate need of innovations and new demonstrations to point the way to dealing with this problem on a higher level of decency and effectiveness, and with at least the minimum objective of making this function in the administration of criminal justice fulfill its purpose, that of immediate public protection and police control, without doing the untold social and psychological damage that has been so obvious to every student of this problem for the past 50 years.

Now let us move to the next step in the ladder process. What do we do with the man or woman who is convicted of a misdemeanor and sentenced to confinement in a local jail, usually for periods of a few days to a year? In the small jurisdictions, where these persons are kept confined in the same jail with the detention cases, this problem is handled no better than that of the cases awaiting adjudication. For many years the leadership in this field has recommended the establishment, either of state misdemeanant farms or regional misdemeanant institutions, operated on a cooperative basis by several counties. There are a

---

* Editor's Note: The *new* Los Angeles County Jail is much larger, and its facilities are among the finest in the world.

mere handful of such institutions operated at the state level in the United States, and as for regional cooperative institutions of this kind, I know of none. The State of California has had a permissive law on its books for many years, but never has it been possible for two or more counties to get together on an agreed program. All that can be said at this point about this recommendation is that it is theoretically sound, but so far, has been politically unworked.

Many of the larger jurisdictions are making some progress. The City of New York and several of the larger counties in New York State have provision for county penitentiaries. The Penitentiary of the City of New York at Rikers Island is an example of this type of operation. San Diego County, Los Angeles County and Alameda County in California are excellent examples of populous jurisdictions which have established misdemeanant institutions outside the metropolitan areas for the sentenced misdemeanant. Generally speaking, however, few of these institutions have adequate work programs, medical programs, educational programs, or programs of after-care supervision.

In 1938, I helped to organize and was the first president of the National Jail Association, which was established with the hope that something more constructive than the mere storage of these millions of human beings in short time institutions could be accomplished. Twenty years have passed since then. Here and there, there are glimmerings of hope, and we have at least some clearer notions today than we had then of some of the constructive things that might be done to rehabilitate and redirect the petty offender. But as a nationwide proposition, extremely little progress has been made. The petty offender is not so much a menace to society as he is an expensive nuisance. We seem to have hung our hope over these many decades on the idea that if we harass these people enough, and throw them into jail often enough, and float them from town to town, that sooner or later they will see the light and become honest, upright citizens. Those of us who are in this work, whether we be police, correctional workers, social workers, psychologists, psychiatists, or whatnot, know that we are merely chasing this problem through a huge revolving door. The very volume of it is frightening! Here again we need to take a new look at this problem. We need to determine whether or not, if we had adequate probation services at the local level, many of these people could be supervised more adequately and constructively in the community; whether many of them could be helped by outpatient clinics for alcoholics or public psychiatric clinics. I am not here to say that any of these is a panacea, but merely that what we are doing now serves little useful purpose, and that police and jailers alike grow cynical in their frustrations, while no one seems to have the authority, or the money, or the will, to examine the total problem and demonstrate programs that can be proven by experience.

Perhaps I should end this discussion of the correctional process as it applies to the short term offender with the understatement of the day — we are doing a poor job of it. And may I say also that in this country, where we place so much reliance upon the basic values of local government, here is a challenge to local government which it has never met. I hope that some community in the near future will be able to make a demonstration which will serve as a model to the rest of the country.

Since the turn of the century, a new concept and a new practice have entered into the treatment of offenders following the imposition of sentence. This concept is that convicted offenders may, under certain circumstances, be controlled and rehabilitated without being institutionalized. Generally speaking, this idea has taken two forms: one, that of probation, which means supervision in lieu of institutionalization, under prescribed conditions, and with the further provision that if these conditions are violated the offender may then be committed to an institution. The second application of the same concept is that of so-called after-care supervision, which generally is referred to in this country as parole. In other words, supervision in the community following a period of institutional experience and under prescribed conditions which if violated, may result in the subject's being returned to an institution as a parole violator.

The arguments advanced in favor of both probation and parole are varied and compelling. First there is the economic argument, for it can easily be established that the cost of reasonably adequate supervision of these persons in the community is about one-tenth that of holding them in an institution. In addition to this, there is the argument that men in institutions represent a great economic waste of manpower, and that these same persons in the community, under close supervision, are required to work, and not only support themselves and make a contribution to the economy, but also support their dependents who often would otherwise be on public relief. Then there is the social argument — that, by and large, these persons are inadequate human beings, emotionally unstable, morally irresponsible, and socially maladjusted. This being the case, supervision, assistance and guidance by trained caseworkers should be helpful in bringing a large proportion of them to such a position of social and psychological stabilization that they can carry their own weight in society and avoid continued illegal and antisocial behavior.

Even the severest critics of probation and parole have generally accepted the validity of the theory upon which they are based. The continued criticism of these two types of services relates primarily either to the alleged careless administration of the judgmental features of the programs, or to the inadequacy of the supervision presumed to be given these persons. In addition to these criticisms, which usually are leveled at probation and parole by the general public and by police agencies, there are criticisms not so often heard, coming from correctional specialists themselves. One of these is that we have not yet arrived at sound standards to guide the courts in the selection of persons for probation, or of parole boards in the granting of discretionary parole release from institutions.

A recent study made of probation in the State of California will illustrate the rather obvious lack of unanimity of policy with respect to this matter. This study revealed that while 43.5 percent of all felony convictions in the superior courts of the State are granted probation, this percentage varied from county to county and from court to court from as low as 10 percent in some jurisdictions to as high as 92 percent in others. (Excluding from consideration the smallest counties, which have very few cases, the variation is from 12.5 to 62 percent.) Further analysis indicated that some of the widest disparities existed between adjoining counties wherein the economy, the social structure and the ethnic composition of the population was almost identical. The difference in practice must rest, then, with the difference in attitudes on the part of judges, prosecutors, and probation officers. These judgments are obviously influenced far more by prejudice and emotional considerations than by professional standards established by scientific analysis. Not long ago, a lawyer in one of our counties wrote a letter to the Governor, recommending himself for appointment to a judgeship of the superior court. He gave as his major qualification for the job, in addition to that of being a member of the Bar, that he would pledge himself to place no criminal case appearing before him on probation. Needless to say, he was not appointed, but this illustrates an extreme point of view which, if followed universally in our State, would add about 60 million dollars a year to the tax bill and require the construction of from two or three times as many prisons as we now have, at an additional cost of more than two hundred million dollars.

Another criticism coming from the professional students in the correctional field relates to the inadequacy of financial support to maintain caseloads sufficiently small to make the theory of case supervision operative. A probation or parole officer can give minimum supervision under normal circumstances to no more than 60 cases. The National Probation and Parole Association recommends a caseload of not to exceed 50. I can point out to you, from my personal knowledge, situations in which as many as 350 probationers are assigned to the supervision of one officer. There are cases on record in this country of one parole officer being responsible for the supervision of all the parolees in the state. This is gross maladministration, and a complete violation of the theory of probation and parole.

Another criticism of these services is the lack of personnel standards in many jurisdictions. The larger, better organized jurisdictions will usually have a merit system with reasonably adequate salary scales and minimum qualifications for entry to the service. On the other hand, there are instances like the one where an appointing authority in a small jurisdiction appointed a 50-year-old housewife, who happened to be the widow of the late court bailiff, to the position of probation officer.

What I am saying is that probation and parole are new services; they hold great promise, but they must be implemented with sound standards and high levels of professional competence among the personnel and administrators charged with this work. We are moving in that direction, but as we view the problem on a national basis, we are far from having reached it as at this point.

I would not wish to leave the impression that the parole and probation supervisory services are generally inadequate or inept. But as we gain more experience with these functions, and as our personnel becomes more professionalized, and as these services are given supportive assistance from other community resources, they will continue to grow in strength and have the potentiality of vastly reducing the cost of dealing with the convicted offender, and at the same time reduce, to some degree, the extent of recidivism.

I referred to the need for supporting these agencies with other community resources. Even the best trained probation or parole officer, no matter how energetic or how dedicated he may be, cannot be expected to meet within himself all of the needs and problems of his diverse caseload and the associations with which they are involved. He has, for example, the need for assistance in finding employment for these persons. He needs some kind of specialized employment service to deal with this difficult group of clientele. He needs cooperation of employers and the cooperation of organized labor. Also he needs to have clinics to which he can refer badly disturbed cases of emotional maladjustment. He needs to have a close understanding with the police agencies of his community, such an understanding that will avoid either one compromising the work of the other, or resulting in unnecessary friction and mutual criticism. He needs to have available the resources of social agencies, of religious groups, and of public welfare organizations.

Since the correctional process deals with the offender after conviction, it is essentially concerned first with the control of the offender, and second with his adjustment to normal living, if this is possible.

There are difficult and challenging objectives at best, but it is unrealistic to expect even a modicum of success unless caseloads are realistically small, officers are thoroughly qualified for their jobs, and the other resources of the community lend a helping hand.

No discussion of the correctional process in America would be complete without some special reference to release procedures from institutional commitment. In the mind of the general public, this is usually thought of as parole. As a matter of fact, offenders may be released from prisons or correctional institutions by discharge at the expiration of sentence, by pardon, by parole, or by mandatory statutory release. The number released by executive pardon is so small that it can be ignored for purposes of this discussion. Those released without any supervision whatever, at the expiration of sentence, account for almost all of the misdemeanant releases, and for a substantial proportion of those released from state prisons. The Federal Prison System reports that 46 percent of those released during the year ending June 30, 1957, were discharged without supervision. There are still a few state jurisdictions which have no parole system, where almost one hundred percent are released without supervision. In the State of California, about 20 percent are released without supervision. According to the last report available to me, the State of Washington released no one without supervision. Thus, we have wide disparity throughout the country with respect to the question of post-institutional supervision of persons released from institutions for adults.

In the case of correctional institutions for juveniles, it is probably fair to say that the general practice is to release almost all of them under some kind of supervision.

It is, of course, true that some releasees do not require supervision either for their readjustment or for the protection of society. It is also true that it is impractical to attempt to supervise some types of releases under our present system. The most obvious example of this is the nomadic, misdemeanant alcoholic. The time may come when we will find a scheme organized on a national basis which will enable us to bring these persons under restraint and control and require them to submit to rehabilitative measures, but that time has not yet come, particularly when we consider that as a national proposition, we are not doing much more than half of the job of supervising released felons.

It should also be pointed out that there are wide differences in the sentencing and release laws of our many jurisdictions. In states like California, with an indeterminate sentence law, with wide discretion being given to the paroling agency, this type of law is regarded as a mandate by the Legislature to provide post-institutional supervision for as large a percentage of releases as practical. In a jurisdiction like the federal government, a definite sentence is pronounced by the courts, with a provision for eligibility for parole at one-third of the sentence, and mandatory release under supervision in a certain proportion of the cases after serving about two-thirds of the sentence. Other states, with a modified indeterminate sentencing practice, wherein the judge specifies both the minimum and the maximum term, provide another type of situation.

The 1957 Annual Report of the United States Board of Parole indicates that less than one-third of those released from prison were released on parole, as opposed to discharge or mandatory release. It is to be assumed that this was the most promising third. The report goes on to say that four out of five make good on parole, but no records are available as to what happened to the other two-thirds who were released without parole. I cite this, not by way of criticism, but only to call attention to the disparities of boards' actions and laws, and consequently, the impossibility of comparing on an equitable basis parole statistics from one state with another, or from one jurisdiction to another.

I believe in the principle of parole. I believe in the desirability and the efficacy of supervising most men and women and juveniles for at least two years after release, and in some cases much longer. We are faced here with an area of public misunderstanding due to the confused and inadequate manner in which parole is administered. As an important phase of the correctional process, we have a nationwide problem, not because a few parole boards have made occasional mistakes in judgment in individual cases, but because we have no consistent policy throughout the country; we have no clear-cut standards of release criteria, or of caseloads size, or of supervision techniques.

We should remember that probation supervision and post-institutional supervision, as substitutes for institutional commitment and as complementary services to institutions, is a relatively new idea in the correctional process. They are barely half a century old, and their widespread use has developed within the lifetime of most adults now living. This phase of the correctional process is growing and maturing. It holds great promise for the future, but new development, new research, new demonstration, and the constant reexamination of old practices must be the order of the day if probation and parole are to eventually realize their full potentialities.

Now let us look at the administration and programs of prisons and correctional institutions. As I have previously remarked, up until quite recently in the history of this country, commitment to an institution has been the preferred treatment for the convicted offender.

In order to discuss this phase of the correctional process without more confusion than necessary, we should first identify the three generally accepted types of such institutions. The first of these, of course, is the prison or penitentiary for adults who have been committed after conviction for a felonious act. With rare exceptions these institutions are operated by the state governments or by the federal government. There are still a few jurisdictions in which felons may be committed to county institutions. There are also some jurisdictions in which misdemeanants may be committed to state institutions. The general pattern, however, throughout the country is that adult felons are committed to state-operated prisons.

Correctional schools and institutions for wards of the juvenile courts represent a somewhat different group of problems, and in many of the states are administered by an agency separate from that which administers the adult prisons. The question of who may be sent to a correctional school, as compared with a prison, is deeply involved with the many diverse attitudes found amongst the general public on the question of what to do about the juvenile delinquent, and the further question of when a juvenile delinquent becomes an adult criminal.

The upper age jurisdiction of a juvenile court varies from state to state from age 16 to age 21. In the eastern part of the country, the most common age limit for juvenile court jurisdiction is 16, in the western states it is 18, and in a few, 17 and 21. This in itself is an expression of our society's confusion as to the age in which a person, for purposes of criminal prosecution, should be treated as a child, and since a child does not become an adult overnight, we have a kind of chronological and psychological intermediate group between ages 16 and 25 which contribute most heavily to the criminal problem, and contribute even more to our confusion as to what we should do about it.

Therefore, in spite of the fact that we have had reformatories in this country since 1880 for this intermediate age group, there is even yet no clear-cut, well-understood program as to the treatment of this group, as separated from juveniles or as separated from adults. Therefore, the institution for handling this inter-mediate problem calls for some special consideration.

State and federal prisons for adults, have a current population of about 190,000 men and women, and an annual turnover of about 96,000. Of those committed to prison, only about 2 percent die there. The remainder are released after periods of time ranging from about 6 months to as much as 40 or 50 years. The average time served by offenders released from prison in most jurisdictions is between two and three years. Administrative and operating problems of main-taining this huge establishment for persons held in custody against their will, are difficult and complex, but in addition to this, the nature of the American prison is constantly changing.

In the beginning there was a long period, when the nation was young and there was an acute shortage of manpower, when there was little concern on the part of public administrators with ideas of readjustment to society, when prison was primarily an instrument of punishment, and when the labor of the prisoner was exploited for the benefit of private interests under the old contract system. This type of prison management came to an end, to a large extent, during the 70's and 80's. From that time and until the advent of the first World War, an effort was made to industrialize the prisons in order to make use of the prisoner's labor for the benefit of the taxpayer. The warden who could claim that his prison was one hundred percent self-supporting, or almost self-supporting, was considered the most successful. During both of these periods little concern was expressed for the welfare of the prisoner as a human being, or for the notion that it might be in the public interest to exert some effort and spend some money in an attempt to control the future behavior of these persons. The outstanding exception to all of this was to be found in the interest of religious groups. From the very beginning of our national history, the Quakers made this problem one of their major social concerns. The basic standard formula for prison treatment was then "religion and hard work," and not a bad formula either, had we been able to apply it with full public and political support. However, the bottom began falling out of this program more than forty years ago.

For a long time, the country has been becoming more materialistic in its outlook, and religious programs were often more tolerated than supported by the political managements in the institutions. Both organized business and organ-ized labor began a campaign to curtail the use of prison labor. Both the Federal government and the state governments have gradually been placing more limits upon the disposition of prison-made products. So that now, since 1930, with the exception of the period of the second World War, when most of these laws were suspended, from 20 to 40 percent of the prisoners in most state prisons are, for all practical purposes, without constructive work.

It has also been during the last 40 or 50 years that the so-called behavioral sciences have been developing and reaching maturity. I mean, of course, psychology, anthropology, sociology and psychiatry. Each of these sciences has its special application to the disordered behavior of criminal offenders, as well as to the behavior of the rest of the population. So now, in 1958, after having gone through one of the worst holocausts of prison administration in our country's history during the first five years of this decade, we are faced with the necessity of taking a new look at our prisons, of revamping our programs and of establishing new sets of values.

We are now going through a period when most of the state governments are struggling with the problem of how to maintain professional leadership and direction for correctional programs at the state level of government. I made a survey of the laws of the 48 states several years ago, to determine the various forms of administrative structure for fitting the correctional services of the states into state government as a whole. I found, at that time, nine different methods for state administration of the correctional functions, and it is even now difficult to find two states with identical systems. The structure includes those in which the individual institution heads are appointed directly by the Governor, without any intervening authority, especially in the small states. In other states, there is multiplicity of different kinds of boards, or of organizations in which the correctional system is integrated into other state agencies responsible for public welfare or public safety. Then there are those states which have a separate department of corrections, headed by a professional administrator responsible either directly to the Governor, or to an intervening lay board. The separate department of corrections, with a single administrative head appointed either by the Governor or by an intervening lay board, is the organizational form which appears to get the best leadership and the best administration. This is the form, also, which the American Correctional Association has endorsed as the preferred organizational pattern. This is particularly true in states of large population and with a number of institutions. The needs of various states must, of necessity, be different because of size. It is hardly to be expected that a department of corrections like those found in California, Michigan or New York would be justifiable in states like Nevada, Utah and Delaware. On the other hand, the principle is the same; the correctional function is important enough and difficult enough to warrant high level leadership, undiluted by needs of other state functions at the top level of state administration.

Now what does the public have a right to expect of a prison administration? The most obvious expectation is that of security. When offenders are deprived of their liberty for the protection of society and committed to a state prison, penitentiary or reformatory, certainly the public expects, and properly so, that adequate restraint be imposed to prevent excessive escapes and unnecessary risks to the lives of employees.

As a close corollary to security comes the matter of orderly administration within the institution, which will prevent excessive violence, criminal acts and lax and sometimes dishonest administration. The ideal internal atmosphere of an institution is one of a professional, non-emotional approach to dealing with inmates, which will keep the controls in the hands of management and the exercise of just that much restraint and threat of force as is absolutely necessary to carry out the basic purpose of the institution. Unnecessarily harsh disciplinary measures and rigid regimentation are often as destructive as extreme laxity.

Prisons are not only filled with people, they are also run by people. Therefore, too much emphasis cannot be placed on the necessity of raising the standards of prison personnel and inculcating in them the professional attitude toward their work which cannot be accomplished without a well organized and aggressive program of personnel development and training. If I were asked to name a single factor of more importance than all others in the improvement and advancement of prison administration, I would say without hesitancy, personnel development. Good personnel will beget good programs, and good programs will attract good personnel. Beyond the obvious and essential housekeeping functions which are required to run any institution, the first concern of the institutional manager should be to provide constructive programs which will fill the otherwise empty days of the inmates with activities which, it may be hoped, will prepare them for the day of their release.

The first step in such a program is that of diagnosis. Each case, upon receipt, should be thoroughly studied and investigated as a human being and as a member of the social system of which he is a part. Knowing his offense, age, race and previous criminal record is obviously not enough. Before embarking him upon a treatment program aimed at his rehabilitation, every bit of knowledge about him which professional skill can uncover should be analyzed and recorded.

The next step is classification and induction into a program. It should always be borne in mind that prisons can sometimes do an individual more harm than good, and so the initial tests of an individual prisoner's program are: (1) Is it safe to place him in this program? (2) Does this program reduce to a minimum the possibilities of the experience doing him damage? (3) Is the program suited to his peculiar needs? (4) Are the probabilities in favor of the program having constructive future effect on his outlook and behavior? (5) Is it expedient to place him in a given program if so doing will deprive some hopeful case of the opportunities which limited facilities provide? Obviously, we cannot enumerate or discuss in detail all of the desirable programs which should be in force in a prison or correctional institution, but certainly they should include, in all events, constructive work, education, vocational training, directed recreation, religious worship and instructive casework management, psychiatric treatment and counseling.

The institution manager of today who feels that he is doing an adequate job if he maintains control, has few escapes and no riots, falls far short of meeting the standard which should be set. The correctional institution may no longer be regarded as a place of retribution only, but rather one in which there is an intensive effort to retain, reeducate, and recast disordered lives.

Some of the things which I have said about prisons apply with equal force, or with even greater force, to the so-called intermediate institution of youths and young men convicted of felonies and sentenced to reformatories or correctional schools for the age group consisting primarily of those between 17 and 22. Part of our confusion in dealing with this age group grows out of the fact that some boys at 23 are less mature in their outlook and behavior than others of 18, and consequently, while I am convinced of the necessity for a separate institution for this intermediate group, I am also convinced of the desirability of flexibility in the assignment of young men to this particular type of institution. Very often an especially immature boy of 18 or 19 will fit into a program with boys of 15 or 16 much better than he will with the older age group. This, I believe, is generally recognized. A problem that isn't so often recognized is that a certain percentage of 18- and 19-year-olds are extremely troublesome and difficult to deal with in the reformatory type institution, but will adjust and accept programs in a prison for adults. This is a function which should not be left to the courts; it should be delegated to the administration of the state correctional agency. The flexibility which we have in California which permits us to move older correctional schools boys from the Preston School of Industry to the Deuel Vocational Institution, which is our reformatory, or vice versa, and to move young men from Deuel to the medium security prison at Soledad, has been a blessing which is appreciated by inmates and management alike.

It is usually easier to obtain facilities for education and other types of treatment for the intermediate age group than it is for the older offenders, but there are some special problems worthy of mention. First of these is that this particular age group is screened far more thoroughly in the counties which have good probation services than are the older age groups. Consequently, the group sent to this particular type of institution is a far more difficult group to handle, and there is a tendency not to keep these persons in prison or in custody for as long a period of time as with the older group beyond age 21. There has been a tendency growing out of past history to pin our faith pretty largely, in such institutions, upon trade training, and this is still a sound portion of the program. But it has weaknesses: first, because of the short sentences served, it is usually only possible to get an individual boy started well along the road to learning a craft before he is released; consequently, there must be a close tie-in with the subsequent apprentice program while the boy is on parole, otherwise the investment in his training is to a large extent vitiated. The second problem grows out of the fact that the negative selectivity of this group presents a disproportionate number of emotionally maladjusted young men who are in desperate need of psychiatric treatment and counseling. The two things this group needs, most, beyond the restraints of the correctional process, are instruction in how to earn a living honestly, and treatment for their emotional maladjustments. Both of these cost money. Accordingly, it can be expected that if the intermediate, reformatory-type institution is to fulfill its purposes, it can be expected that its per capita cost will exceed that of adult institutions by as much as 50 per cent. If the institution is small, the unit cost may be more than double.

There are many experienced men in our field who have seen the so-called reformatory movement grow and develop for half a century, and who have felt that it has been, by and large, a failure and that these institutions are often not as good as many of the adult prisons. It is not difficult to look for the reasons: part of the fault has lain in the law which permits the courts to sentence directly to such an institution. This often has the effect of injecting into the population of such establishments persons who have no business to be there, and who damage the rest of the program. The other fault has lain in the failure of the political administration to provide adequate funds to support a really functioning program. A reformatory can become as much of a storehouse as a maximum security prison.

Correctional schools for wards of the juvenile court are fitted into the structure of state government in as many diverse ways as are the prisons. In some states, they are in the department of institutions, some in the department of social welfare, some in the department of corrections, and in some, under a youth authority. Since the advent of the growth of probation, which had its first and most vigorous growth in the treatment of youth offenders, correctional schools, as such, have been getting an even more negative clientele than have the intermediate institutions and the prisons. And it is also wrong to assume that these places are primarily for young children. In a well organized state, while most of the state laws permit commitment as young as age 8, those under age 12 are rare, and the average age is more likely to be in the neighborhood of 15. This type of institution was originally conceived primarily as a kind of disciplinary school for school age children who were neglected as much as delinquent. Since most of the children committed to these institutions were of school age, the schools have always maintained academic programs often very closely patterned after the public schools, and have offered some vocational training. However, these programs have often been very lean, because vocational instruction is expensive. The attitude has usually been held by the managers of these institutions that badly adjusted, emotionally unstable and near-psychotic cases were not suitable for their schools, but unfortunately, there was no place else to send them. The obviously psychotic could go to mental hospitals; the obviously feeble-minded could go to schools for the feeble-minded, but a substantial number of hard-core, difficult behavior problems, which were neither insane nor feeble-minded, have been pushed into these schools because they were not amenable to community supervision, and the institutions were not prepared to deal with them. Many of these youngsters are far more in need of psychiatric treatment and the understanding guidance of a responsible adult than they are of anything else. This small number of hard-core, difficult behavior problems emerging early in the teen-age period, and not dealt with adequately in most of our correctional schools through no particular fault of their own, have been the recruiting grounds for the habitual criminals of ten and fifteen years later.

Two years ago, some of the judiciary of our state became so distressed at the inadequate means for dealing with this group that through their influence, an interim committee of the State Legislature made a full investigation of the whole problem. It was their conclusion that no matter what the treatment of this group cost, it should be provided when they were first identified, and not after they have cost the taxpayers many thousands of dollars by criminal activity, and perhaps many human lives. Accordingly, there is now being established, under the jurisdiction of the California Youth Authority, four psychiatric treatment teams to be set up in four of the correctional institutions to deal with this special problem of the so-called "acting out" non-feeble minded, non-psychotic delinquent teenager. The annual per capita basic cost of operating these programs seems shockingly large, in comparison with the figures to which we are accustomed. Consequently, we must look upon these programs as experimental, but if they can prevent as much as another 10 percent of those who pass through them from graduating into the ranks of habitual adult criminals, the price is still very low.

In closing, to recapitulate very briefly, it seems to me that we are passing through a generation of tremendous change in all phases of human experience.

These changes are, and will be reflected in the administration of criminal justice. There are a number of particulars in which new emphasis is indicated and indicated now.

1. Better standards of selection and diagnosis of offenders at the court level before the imposition of sentence.

2. More emphasis on community programs aimed at getting at the causes for the development of criminal behavior at its inception. Criminals and delinquents are not born — they are made. They are made in the families and in the communities. This must be the starting point. Consequently, do not expect miracles from either the police or the correctional agencies. Most of the damage has been done before we get hold of the problem.

3. There is need for better implementation of probation and parole. More officers, better officers, better standards, more resources, more cooperation with other community agencies.

4. There is need for fuller implementation of training and treatment programs in institutions, at all age levels and of all types.

5. More emphasis needs to be placed on breaking through the barriers of misunderstanding between the various agencies who deal with specialized features of the total process of the administration of criminal justice. I am always distressed at the mutual criticism and lack of understanding that often takes place between probation and parole workers and institutional staff, between correctional workers and police, between the police and correctional workers and the courts, and so on around the circuit. We are all doing the same thing, we are unified — or we should be a unified, thoroughly coordinated, mutually supportive fabric of officialdom, for dealing with one of the most perplexing problems of our times. Perhaps much of this could be overcome if we would get better acquainted.

6. Now that we have virtually abandoned the concept that retributive punishment alone will accomplish our purpose, particularly with the bizarre types of maladjusted people with whom we are required to deal, we are then faced with acquiring a whole new set of skills, some of which have not yet even come into existence. I call your attention to the fact that a bare year ago, no one knew how to put an artificial moon into orbit; now it has been done five times. Only a handful of years ago, we knew nothing about how to immunize people against polio — and so we can go through the whole gamut of new developments and new skills that have arisen, one after another, in the physical sciences during our lifetime. How has it been possible to do this? The answer is to be found in a single word: *RESEARCH*. The application of the tools of science in finding the answers to a question. In the field of the administration of criminal justice, and especially in the phase of it that has to do with the treatment of maladjusted offenders, we have more questions than we have answers. We can't expect to get the answers except by the approach that has been used in other scientific endeavors. We must have more research, and it must start at once because this type of research is expensive, it is difficult and time-consuming. I am willing to predict that at this time 25 years from now, we will know so much more about how to deal with the types of cases that perplex us now that we will wonder how we could have been so stupid in 1958! But I can only make this prediction on the assumption that vast sums of money and able, dedicated researchers devote their lives to finding these answers. I certainly couldn't make the assumption on the basis of historical development, because I have been in this work myself

more than 25 years, and we do not have very many more answers today than we had then.

No country in the world is as dedicated to developing its human resources through education, recreation and character-building community efforts as we are. We not only give it lip service, but we spend billions on these efforts. And when these mass medicines fail, as they do in a small percentage of cases, we grow angry and can think of no better remedy than to get tough, even though we know it doesn't help. Because of this some people assume that if extreme toughness doesn't work, then extreme permissiveness and softness will — and this may be even worse. Both toughness and softness are emotional reactions. What we need is scientific objectivity and an unremitting search for new knowledge, new skills, and new methods.

Problems in Communication and Cooperation in the Administration of Criminal Justice

ROBERT H. SCOTT

Deputy Director, Michigan Department of Corrections

MAY 26, 1967

The administration of criminal justice, viewed as a totality, may seem to be a continuous and coordinated process. However, when examined at close hand, serious gaps and barriers become apparent. Inconsistencies inhibit cooperation; chasms cut communications. The process of criminal justice becomes a series of segments, separated from each other by differences in philosophy, purpose and practice. Moreover, the segments themselves are often characterized by internal conflicts and confusion. The blanket of the administration of justice, when seen at close range, becomes a patchwork quilt.

One of these patches is a matter of the age of the offender. When the latter is below a certain age, prescribed by statute, he is subject to juvenile court rather than criminal court. These age limits vary from jurisdiction to jurisdiction, but most states specify one of the three following birthdays: 16th, 17th, or 18th — as the upper limit. The special procedures of juvenile justice are characterized by privacy, informality, and a concern for the offender rather than the offense. Strict rules of evidence and adversary proceedings (representation by counsel) are de-emphasized. Recently, however, more attention is being paid to due process of law. Future trends in juvenile justice will probably go toward more formal procedures and emphasis upon the traditional protections of the criminal law for the juvenile before the court. (See in re Gault, Supreme Court, U.S., May 15, 1967).

The special proceedings of juvenile courts have spread to the other two parts of the justice triangle — police and corrections. Police agencies have emphasized specialization in work with juveniles. Larger departments have established juvenile divisions. Police officers have been trained in special juvenile procedures. Emphasis has been placed upon prevention and treatment. Police have, in some instances, acted as the informal equivalents of probation staff. By placing juveniles "on visits," some cases have been handled by police without referral to either social agencies or to the court. Both social agencies and the courts have criticized this exercise of discretion as social work by unqualified persons to the detriment of primary duties, on the one hand, and the denial of due process of law to the accused, on the other. This area of discretion will undoubtedly be more carefully circumscribed and delineated in the future. The upper limits of police power are prescribed by police departments as co-terminous with juvenile court jurisdiction so persons under 17 years (to select one jurisdiction) are handled by police as juveniles and those over 17 as adult offenders.

A special and separate corrections process has been developed for juveniles in many jurisdictions. The detention home replaces the county jail for the custodial care of juveniles awaiting court disposition (the requirement for safekeeping of juveniles separate from adults results in problems where no separate facilities are provided). The juvenile's stay in the detention home is often utilized for testing, treatment, and educational purposes. The detention home is not intended to be used for long-term care before adjudication, not for disposition by the court after adjudication.

The juvenile court often combines jurisdiction over dependent and neglected children with delinquents. The trend has been away from the use of juvenile correctional dispositions for the dependent and neglected. Basically, the training school is intended for the adjudicated delinquent only. Specialists in juvenile corrections have tended to favor separation of administration from adult systems. This separation of juvenile and adult corrections has contributed to competition and confusion among the agencies concerned with the administration of justice.

Another area of confusion — the youthful offender — lies athwart the fields of juvenile delinquency and adult crime. No longer a child, not yet an adult, the youth beyond the mid-teens traditionally has come under the adult criminal code. The reformatory designed for his special care nearly a century ago has increasingly come to resemble an adult institution. The calendar, rather than the character of the offender, became the arbiter of the youth's future. In most cases, he bore the mark of an adult offender for the rest of his life. Courts could draw no legal distinction between a sophisticated, difficult youth of 18 and an immature, situational offender of 19. The only individual distinctions possible were the use of probation and the length of sentence involved. The introduction of the Model Youth Authority Act in California in the early 1940's, followed closely by a similar act in Minnesota, brought a new corrections program for youthful offenders into being. Statutes in New York and the United States courts, and more recently in Michigan, have established a separate legal category of youthful offender (youthful trainee in Michigan).

Another line of separation in the judicial process is determined by the nature of the offense involved — whether it is a felony or a misdemeanor. The felon's place of imprisonment is the state institution, but the sentenced misdemeanant goes normally to the county jail. The jail serves a dual purpose. It confines both those awaiting trial and those serving sentence. County jail treatment programs are few and far between. For the most part, jails are places for the secure storage of prisoners with little chance of treatment. In too many cases, that storage takes place in substandard buildings — indeed, some jails are condemned as unsafe. Here another inconsistency presents itself. Prisoners who thus far are charged only with a crime — and who therefore must be presumed innocent — may be held in jail, often for long periods of time, awaiting trial.

The correctional process concentrates upon the serious offender and has neither the authority nor the wherewithal to mount treatment programs for the misdemeanant, be he serving time or on probation. Parole or after-care services for the misdemeanant are virtually nonexistent. Yet a large percentage of those who wind up in prison have first "done time" in the county jail. Thus, there is no coherent system of justice for the adult offender. Rather, there is one system for the misdemeanant and another for the felon.

The next division among the major components of the administration of criminal justice is that of function. The function of law enforcement may generally be described as the prevention of crime, the preservation of the peace, and the protection of life and property. These functions involve such matters as the detection and apprehension of offenders, searches, and the investigation of offenses, including the taking of statements. In the face of increasing police problems — mobility, civil rights demonstrations, new technologies, and a host of other problems — it is not surprising that police view with concern any limitation upon their powers. Recent decisions dealing with due process and civil liberties and restricting the power of the police to take confessions and requiring legal aid at many more stages of the proceedings have caused consternation to many police officers.

Since these restrictions are court-imposed, many police officers view recent court trends with caution and skepticism. Law enforcement tends to regard persons convicted of crimes as a high risk group. Consequently, the use of probation by courts and of parole by corrections are often seen by the police as "mollycoddling the offender," or "getting soft."

On their part, courts are concerned with due process and the protection of individual rights. Criminal law is not only a way by which the guilty may be punished. It is the means by which innocent persons are protected even though appearances and public opinion may be against them. These protections can and do result in guilty persons going free since their conviction must be "according to law." Courts are the means by which due process in the administration of criminal justice is ensured.

The third leg of the justice triangle is corrections. Its mandate is to carry out the sentence of the court. Its ultimate purpose is the rehabilitation of the offender, but it must do so within the limits of the court's disposition. When the offender is sentenced to imprisonment, it is the task of corrections to retrain as well as restrain the offender and to effectuate his release at the optimum time within the limits of the sentence. This responsibility may bring the corrections segment into disagreement with both the courts and the police. This difficulty can arise in various ways. First, probation may be viewed differently by the police than corrections. In principle, probation means the restoration of the selected offender under guidance and supervision. The cost of probation is about 1/10th that of imprisonment; the destructive impact upon the offender is far less, and the hardship on the offender's family is not so great.

Yet, the police officer may see as mere softness permitting an offender to remain at large when the officer has gone to a great deal of trouble to detect and apprehend that same offender. To him the judgment of the court may appear as only a "slap on the wrist." Furthermore, the police may regard the criminal as part of a high risk group, the temporary removal of which from the community lessens the likelihood of crime. Much the same reasoning can apply to police reaction to parole. On the other hand, corrections workers may believe that police have used excessive zeal in the arrest of parolees. Admittedly, the known offender group constitutes a higher risk and the "modus operandi theory" may have encouraged a "throw out the dragnet" attitude. However, overreadiness to arrest may cause bitterness and resentment in the parolee and foster "what's the use" attitude on the part of the offender. A very practical hardship to the parolee and his family may result in the form of loss of employment.

One can speculate that the broader power to arrest parolees ("where there is reasonable ground to believe that he has violated a condition of pardon, probation, or parole") may result in more arrests. It is easier to arrest a probationer or parolee than other citizens.

None of these instances, however, is typical of all or even most police officers or corrections workers. The stereotypes represent overgeneralizing about the attitudes of all from the actions of some. It can only be said that each profession in the justice network represents certain opportunities for attitude formation. One cannot generalize from these possibilities that all police officers or corrections workers will feel or react in a particular way.

Within the major functions of law enforcement, courts and corrections specialization provides further ground for conflict. In large city police departments, one can find such functions as patrol, criminal investigation, traffic, records, and youth work. The detective who investigates a crime committed by a juvenile may feel frustrated by his inability to enter school premises to question suspects. His responsibility for obtaining information leading to arrest and conviction represents an investment in his own professional and personal interests which may be in conflict with principles of police work with juveniles. This conflict may cause him to be critical, either overtly or covertly. The police officer who is concerned with traffic or scientific criminal investigation may, on the other hand, be similarly critical of the work of a community relations unit in the police department.

Courts also specialize; juvenile courts, municipal courts, superior courts, and appellate courts all have different emphases. The order of promotion is usually from municipal or juvenile court to superior court and thence to an appellate court. The volume of criminal work is to be found in the magistrate courts in larger cities, but judges of these courts tend to seek promotion to courts of higher jurisdiction which often de-emphasize criminal work.

Similarly one finds within corrections a specialization that provides grounds for difficulties arising from different perspectives. Perhaps the most prominent among these is the split between custody and treatment. The difficulty arises from the dual directions of corrections — namely, the confinement of the offender for the term of his sentence and the rehabilitative efforts required during that sentence. The difficulty, however, is often more apparent than real. The goals of custody and treatment are not inconsistent, but represent two principles, each of which must modify the other. Any conflict arises not so much from inherent inconsistency between a custodial worker and a treatment worker as from the ways in which the respective roles are structured and defined. If the job responsibility and expectation of the custodial worker describes custody as exclusively his, then the possibility of conflict between him and the treatment worker is increased and vice versa. If, however, the role of each is so described and structured as to include both custody and treatment in appropriate ways, the possibilities of conflict are reduced. The task of corrections administration is to coordinate these roles into realistic teamwork. In so doing, the contribution of the corrections officer and the work supervisor to changes in the attitude and behavior of the inmate can be incorporated by the treatment worker into the record of progress and used for further growth. Change does not take place in a vacuum and the officer and supervisor are important parts of the inmate's daily environment. Thus, treatment becomes the management of the environment toward production of desired growth. Certain differences between probation and parole officer functions were potential sources of different role definition and resulting conflict. These differences were largely a matter of training and selection of personnel and administrative emphasis. Probation officers often saw themselves as more casework oriented while parole officers tended to emphasize supervision and control. However, recent developments in corrections have tended to merge these two functions with a resultant communication of concepts toward common principles and techniques. Differences between the two are beginning to disappear.

Differing philosophies vie for supremacy in the administration of justice. The theory of punishment holds that fear deters the potential violator and modifies the behavior of the actual offender. We must make sure that crime does not pay. The moralistic or exhortatory approach seeks to influence or motivate the individual to change his behavior through appeals to his conscience, reason, and sense of duty. Proponents of education as the universal answer hope that by increasing the individual's knowledge and skills, he will be motivated and enabled to avoid further antisocial behavior. Psychologists urge an understanding of human behavior and motivation, although there are marked differences of thought between the followers of Freud and the new school of "Reality Therapy." Sociology has brought some new and penetrating insights to bear upon the influence of the culture on the behavior of the individual. Conflicts arise between permissive and authoritarian approaches. The "permissive approach" is viewed as influencing human behavior by understanding of motivation, awareness, and problem-solving behavior. The "authoritarian approach" is seen as influencing behavior by external controls. All of these views exist contemporaneously in the administration of justice and are not merely benchmarks in the historical progress toward the solution of crime problems.

Professional education is another area of controversy. The proponents of social work education, counselling and guidance, and psychology — to mention only a few — view their professional education as the most effective for correctional work. Currently the matter of manpower training is under careful consideration and the findings of a joint commission on that subject should point the way toward more effective professional and sub-professional development.

Nor do these professional preoccupations take place separate from the community. Public sentiment and support play an important part. Levels of community tolerance for different kinds of behavior vary from area to area. Cries of "get tough," "stop handcuffing the police," and similar slogans are heard increasingly. Complex social problems add to our difficulties as we seek simplified solutions.

In order to develop a united front in the battle to solve the problems of crime and delinquency, we need to avoid our professional prejudices and our insular

interests. Crime and delinquency prevention and treatment are a unitary phenomenon. The importance of special skills should not blind us to the necessity
of a coordinated approach. The area of crime and delinquency is not a neat
compartment with many subdivisions — rather, its sub-areas blend with each
other and have many ties to general community agencies — education and welfare, to mention only two. The current thrust of federal programs of poverty
and education draw our attention to the totality of the field. The old rigid lines
between professions are disappearing. We now are problem oriented rather than
agency bound. Task forces replace standing committees. As professionals we
will exercise our own responsibilities more effectively if we are aware of the
contribution of our colleagues with related responsibilities but with different
training and orientation. Greater objectivity toward ourselves and others can
reduce defensiveness and confusion. Research can help rid our minds of in-
accuracy and our practices of inefficiencies. With patience, sensitivity, and good
will, we will learn to communicate and to cooperate in the solution of these
grave problems.

Police–Press Relations

PATRICK V. MURPHY

(Then) Deputy Chief Inspector, Commanding Officer,
Police Academy, New York City Police Department

MAY 20, 1965

Good police–press relationships are desirable for both the police and the
press, but they are even more important for the best interest of the people.

The public has a right to be informed. The press has a duty and an obligation to keep the public informed. The police, for their part, have the same duty
and obligation to keep the public advised of their successes and failures in the
constant war against crime and violence. They do so mainly through the press.

In addition, the public has the absolute right to the fullest protection which
can be provided by law, in accordance with the safeguards established by the
Constitution. This includes protection against illegal arrest, illegal invasion of
privacy, and the harm which can be caused by premature disclosure.

The press relations of a police department are unique. They are in sharp
contrast to press relations in industries or in other government agencies. The
principal reason lies in the nature of police work, which must keep pace with
the constant, dynamic and rapid pulsebeat of big city life.

In New York, for example, 26,000 policemen guard 8,000,000 residents and
more than a million visitors daily. There are contacts between police and public
every minute of the day and night, and each contact can be either good or bad
publicity for the Police Department. Because police work consists mainly of
"people meeting people," each such meeting can contain an element of drama
not often present in other agencies or situations. Because of this human drama
generated by almost every police response to calls for aid, there is news value
in police activity in the minds of most editors and newspapermen — far beyond
almost any other type of event. For this reason, the press covers a police depart-

ment twenty-four hours a day, seven days a week so that, in effect, there is a perpetual spotlight focused on all police activities, large and small.

The most important advice that can be given to any police department is to make certain, as far as is humanly possible, that the conduct of all members of the department is above reproach. In this way, no avoidable ammunition is furnished which could blast the reputation of the department and cause a loss of public respect and confidence.

Simply phrased in traditional Madison Avenue terms, this means that nobody can sell an inferior product for more than a very brief period. No matter how high-sounding the publicity is phrased, no matter how flamboyant the claims, no matter how well-worded the press releases or the speeches of the police chief or commissioner, the press and the public will soon become aware of the inferiority and will resent the attempts to sugar-coat bitter pills.

To win the confidence and support of the public, police service must be superior. It must be dedicated to the safety and protection of the public. Police service must be devoted exclusively to the service of all the people. In my opinion, it is the task of not only the police administrator, but of the policemen themselves, to convince the public of their sincerity through deeds, not merely words.

Edmond Burke said, "The one thing necessary to the triumph of evil is that good men do nothing." This adage applies to the police, the press and the public. To win the battle against crime, the police need the support of the public. They cannot effectively fight the criminal and defend the citizens whom they are sworn to protect without the support of those citizens.

Public support for a police department cannot be created by publicity stunts, self-serving oratory or other shortcuts. Public support can be won only by faithful, honest and effective police service.

There must be a conscious and conscientious effort on the part of each and every member of the force to conduct both his official and private life such that he will inspire the confidence and trust of the people. Some people seem to delight in ridiculing police. The police should do more than "grin and bear it." They should make certain that the unfortunate stereotype of the stupid cop is eliminated, by eliminating stereotyped behavior.

Police service, if it is to be of value, must be dependable. Dependability arises through appreciation and acceptability of the total responsibility of the police job. The policeman must be punctual, attentive, accurate and courteous if he is to be depended upon. Dependability is the end product of respect, and it is predicated upon how well a person has recognized his responsibilities in the performance of his duties — in short, how well he has achieved the sincerity of purpose that can be counted upon.

I would like now to try to pinpoint the problems involved in developing good press relations, in the hope that there may be some ideas here which will be of value to all of us. We must first examine the reason for the many conflicts and frictions which develop between the police and the press. There is little good reason for such conflicts. They come mainly because of personality clashes and poor understanding. I think that the prime reason is a misunderstanding of the other's goals and purposes. Too often the press, while dimly realizing the reasons for certain police action, consciously or unconsciously forgets them in their eagerness to obtain the story. Too often the police, while dimly realizing the reasons for press attention in any particular incident, consciously or unconsciously ignore these reasons because of their own prime interest in solving the case. The goals of the police cannot be overlooked. The rights of both must be respected, but the press must realize that the police duty of protection and apprehension must take priority.

Another roadblock to smooth police–press relations is the time element. The press is always under pressure and seems always impatient. The newspapers work under the deadline of editions; radio and television reporters work under the even harsher deadline of on-plunging minutes. The area of possible friction with police doubles because of the constant demand for speed in getting the story.

The police, for their part, are concerned — and rightly so — about matters other than deadlines. They are concerned with obtaining the facts and obtaining the evidence necessary for arrest and future court presentation. Here is the area of greatest and most frequent clashes between the two. Here is where each side must be understanding and tolerant of the other. The reporters must understand that they cannot get the story until the police do — that the fast and inaccurate story, while serving an immediate need, can be more harmful to the persons involved and to the police than the full and complete facts which may be — and often are — harder to develop. The police must realize the time element under which the press operates and do their best within all legal means to provide information as soon as it may be used. This may sound like wishful thinking, but it can be done. There should be no conflict, for both the press and the police have a similar goal, whether they realize it or not, and that goal is to serve the public, in the search for truth.

Because the nature of police work is so wide and varied, because its pace is so rapid, no panacea cures can be developed to solve all situations. Police–press relations have to be "ad-libbed" in most of the encounters concerning fast breaking or "hot" stories. In contrast, information on administrative matters, programs, procedures and operations, can and are handled by press releases. But the events which occur on the street and which are unpredictable must be handled on the spur of the moment, under the conditions found at the scene. It is here that intelligence, good judgment and recognition of press needs count the most.

There are certain guidelines, however, which can be followed. For example, I would advise policemen and police officials never to lie or evade answering a reporter's question that is based either on information or on a rumor he is trying to check out. If there is no truth to the rumor or the "tip" he has, say so — and say so emphatically. If there is a germ of truth to it, but the version he has received is distorted, then explain it as fully as possible. If there is truth to it — yet for one reason or another the police feel that they cannot confirm it without hurting their case, then they should *not* deny it. They may, if they know the reporter well enough, speak to him off the record and ask him to respect the confidence, or if they feel that they cannot "go off the record," there is nothing wrong with that two-word lifesaver: "No Comment." The reporter will respect the police more for their refusal to comment, which to him is an indication that there may be some truth to the query which the police are not yet free to disclose, than for their denial if the reporter later learns that the story was true. Once a policeman becomes known as evasive or as a "double-talker," any statements he makes in the future are grudgingly accepted, if accepted at all.

There may be many occasions when a big story from a newspaper viewpoint, and an important case from a police viewpoint, is developing and bits of it leak out to the press — to the dismay of the investigators of the case. When this occurs, and if the newspaperman is conscientious enough to seek confirmation before printing the meager information he has, then it is advisable to seek his cooperation in withholding the story until it is fully developed. Some cynics might say that this is like trying to hold back the tide but, believe it or not, it works. It has worked in New York City, and I am sure it has worked in other areas. Most members of the press are conscientious and reasonable men and women. Unless they feel that they are being deceived, they will cooperate in most cases. For example, several years ago, our Narcotics Bureau planned a city-wide roundup of drug pushers who had been under surveillance for months. The roundup operations, it was estimated, would take at least twelve hours. It was scheduled to begin at 8 P.M. and end at 8 A.M. The then Commanding Officer of the Narcotics Bureau was concerned that there would be leaks. Most of the arrests would of necessity take place on the street, and there would be telephone calls to the press and inquiries from the press. He felt that any premature disclosures might send the drug pushers into hiding. Several hours before the roundup was due to begin, we called the press representatives to Police Headquarters and explained the problem to them. We urged their cooperation and promised that a full and detailed story on all persons arrested and the listing of quantities of narcotics seized would be available when the roundup was completed. To the credit of all the newspapers the roundup was a complete success.

Press cooperation can be obtained whenever necessary if the full facts and problems are explained. The press appreciates being taken into police confidence. It puts them in "the know," and it helps to wipe away the long-standing misconception that the police jealously guard all secrets until they are pried from them. I have heard that the prevailing sentiment among newspapermen — a sentiment which I am afraid is prevalent in many quarters — is that police headquarters and every police stationhouse are dungeons, concealing thousands of deep, dark secrets, and that if a reporter could dig into these dungeons, he would find a treasure trove of stories well worth his efforts. Our policy has been to disabuse the press as much as possible of this notion by opening our stationhouses and headquarters to them. Certainly we do not allow the press to sit in on interrogations or investigations. But we do keep them apprised of developments, and in this way we have convinced them that we are not trying to hide anything.

Another method used to kill the myth is to "beat" the reporter to the story. Announce it as fast as possible before there are leaks and distortions. This is not always possible, but it should be done whenever possible. Let me give you an example of what can occur when a distorted story is withheld by the police. Several months ago, a Deputy Police Commissioner was awakened at 3 A.M. at home by a telephone call from a newspaper reporter who said in effect, "I learned that three policemen have been arrested for burglary in a Bronx precinct, and the old iron curtain has dropped." He added in a bitter tone, "It's the same old runaround. Everyone clamps down on information as soon as a policeman is involved." The Commissioner asked him not to jump to conclusions but to let him check the story. He called the precinct and learned, happily, that the information the reporter had received was wrong. What actually had occurred was that two of three men were being arrested for burglary; neither of them was a policeman.

The third man, however, was a police officer, and this is what brought about the distortion. He was not being arrested. He, as a matter of fact, was responsible for the arrest. He was an off-duty policeman who had been asked by two neighborhood youths who knew him to take part in a burglary. He asked for time to think it over. He consulted with his commanding officer who advised him to play along with the two burglars, both with records. He met the men again and told them he would join them. The three visited an apartment house, and the two thugs cornered the building superintendent who had several hundred dollars in rent collections in his possession. Before they could seize the money or harm the man, the patrolman drew his gun.

Armed with these facts, the Commissioner called the reporter back and the complexion of the story was changed. However, even had the story turned out to be true, the reporter would still have been given all the facts, because it *did* happen and we could not and would not conceal it.

The practice in New York is to print orders indicating the assignments, transfers and dismissals of members of the force. Orders have always been a source of news for the reporters, and rightly so. However, we now do more than merely issue the order. When there are transfers which have news interest, we announce them before the order is printed, rather than wait for the inevitable queries. The same applies to dismissals. In the past, the order merely cited the name of the man dismissed, which immediately brought a press search for the reasons. Because the full facts could not always be obtained by a reporter, the story was harmful not only to the man involved but to the department. Now we offer the story of dismissal to the newspapers, giving charges, disposition and the reasons for the penalty *before* the printed order is issued. The practice has now become so routine that in most cases the reporters are not interested in dismissals unless they have an outstanding news angle.

The matter of news angles constantly perplexes police. They are often surprised to find a story which they considered to have little news value blown into a page one spread. They are often puzzled that a story that they consider important, that *is* important to *them*, gets buried deep in the wonderfully complex minds of editors and reporters. But there is one guide to this type of newspaper play and it is "the unusual angle." Anything which has an unusual aspect makes news, particularly police news. For example, narcotics arrests have become routine in the press's mind, but when narcotics detectives posed as beatniks to round up gangs of narcotics pushers in Greenwich Village, that made news.

"Bad" stories about police often get more space than "good" stories. It simply comes down to this: the public and the press expect a policeman to do a good job, and when he does it, they say, "That's what he's getting paid for." But when he does a bad job and violates his oath of office and his trust, it is unusual and therefore makes news — unfortunate, but a harsh fact of life which the police must realize and live with.

There is a tendency on the part of some police to view the press as a sort of opponent. The same idea is present in the mind of some members of the press. Admittedly there are times when legitimate interests of the press and of the police conflict. But friction between press and police often results from personality conflicts which can be erased by the exercise of patience and the control of tempers. The police should always remember that when they talk to an individual reporter, they may be talking beyond him to hundreds of thousands and sometimes millions of readers, listeners or viewers in their communities. Reporters on their part should always remember that although they may be dealing with an individual officer, he represents the police department and all the authority of the law and of government.

The minds of both groups must be disabused of the idea that they are on opposite sides. It is important for the police to remember that the press can be, and often is, of aid. Press cooperation can be and has been helpful in search for criminals. To cite brief examples, the arrest of the "Mad Bomber" came about through press cooperation, and one of the slayers of two Brooklyn detectives was turned over to police after he surrendered to a newspaper.

Facilities of the press, television and radio are always open to police news, whether it be news of traffic bottlenecks, appeals for manpower or public compliance or for such special tasks as printing and distributing sketches of wanted criminals. This type of cooperation should be encouraged and developed for the mutual benefit of the police, the press and the public.

It should be realized that both the police and the press, in their respective areas, have great powers and great responsibilities. Under law a policeman has the power to deprive a person of his liberty by legal arrest; to injure a person by the use of justifiable force and in the most extreme circumstances, to take a life under the doctrine of justifiable homicide. These are truly awesome powers and they must never be abused. The police must also remember their responsibilities to the public and act in the highest traditions of democratic government.

The press too has frightening power to help or to harm. Its members have a great responsibility to use the truth as a vehicle of improvement, to use the spotlight of publicity to prevent abuse of power, by anyone. Yet in their zeal to protect the innocent and to prevent abuse of power, they must make certain that they too do not in turn abuse.

Each should work together for the common good. They have done so in the past. They should continue to do so — and improve their relationships — in the future, to strengthen democracy and to demonstrate to all the world that the free state will prevail over all police states.

Communication Within the Community

WILLIAM R. CARMACK

(Then) Director, Center for Human Relations Study,
University of Oklahoma

MAY 23, 1963

Man learns primarily through experience. Some things, relatively few, we experience directly, but a great many more things we know from vicarious experience — the experience of others communicated to us. This latter method of learning is the thing that gives man his advantage over lesser forms of life. We can bind our knowledge in time and pass it from one generation to another through communication. Further, we can benefit from the trials and errors of others by attending to their communication of their experiences. Communication makes it possible to organize men into a society and establish norms or rules of conduct.

Without the ability to communicate, we would each behave independently and without reference to the needs of others — we would live in a complete state of anarchy. So, in talking about communication, we are talking about the cohesive force which makes social action and cooperation possible.

But to be more specific, communication is the technique through which the laws that govern society are made, disseminated, and enforced. The mere fact that a law has been enacted does not mean that it will be known of or respected by the public. Further, knowledge of the law may not mean respect for and acceptance of the law. Police represent the branch of society charged with the enforcement of the laws that the majority, through their elected representatives, make and claim to want enforced. Yet, as the police go about their work, they do so knowing that, while *society* may value their enforcement function in the abstract, the particular *individual* whose behavior must be checked is not likely to value their activity. And in many instances, the mass of people tend to identify with the lawbreaker.

Thus, it becomes necessary for the policeman to understand the role that he is called upon to play in the community, and for the community to understand fully the nature and function of the policeman. The image of the policeman is too often a negative one — that of a person interfering with or abridging the freedom of movement of another. His positive role and function is not quite so clear, because in the performance of that function he is seldom involved in "news." Thus, collectively and individually, one of the important tasks of the police is to interact or communicate with the community more fully.

I appreciate the fact that there is no "s" on the term communication in my topic. I do not want to talk specifically about any form of communication — the print media, the electronic media, public speaking, group discussion, or what have you. Rather, I would like to identify a few factors important to communicative success in any and all situations. We might briefly note some of the components of the process of communication.

Obviously, communication must begin with a *source*. This may be a person about to say something — someone who has a "psychic itch." It could be a machine, but let's think primarily of human communication.

The concept or idea to be shared is a *message*. But messages cannot be transferred from the mind of one person to another directly. We must employ some code system which is capable of containing the concept to be communicated. Of course, in our society, the most common code is the English language, but we use a great many other kinds, such as standard insignia and signs. The code, whatever it is, must be common to both the source and the receiver, and it must be one that both have facility in using. We learn to attach meaning to the code only through experience in using it, just as an infant learns to attach meaning to words only as he experiences their association with objects that he knows about.

The chief point here is that meanings are in people, not in messages. Their previous experiences structure the meanings they attach to our codes. Thus, the police person who speaks of statutes and technical concepts may or may not be understood by the average citizen. In this matter, as in all other aspects of communication, the criterion must be: What does the receiver know of this, and how does he feel about it?

Little need be said here about a third aspect of the process of communication — the *channel*. All messages must be transmitted through some medium or channel. This may be in the form of a mass medium, like books, newspapers, radio and television, or it may be the non-mechanical medium of person-to-person communication. We have all had occasion to consider the relative merits of the various media, and much is written on this. We also know that, where possible, it is desirable to employ more than one channel in the transmission of the message. Thus, a visual aid may be valuable to accompany a verbal explanation of a process. Or, a brief telephone conversation might supplement a memorandum.

But we have noted only three components of the process of communication, the source, the message and the channel. We have said more about the message and channel than the source, because it is difficult to speak of the source apart from the fourth component we need to identify — the *receiver*. The message is important, the treatment of it is important, and the channel is also important. But the most important determinant of the success of any communication is the quality of the interaction between the source and the receiver.

Aristotle said that the chief determiner of communicative success was *ethos,* by which he meant the receiver's estimate of the character and trustworthiness of the source. Today, some researchers call this "source credibility," but the basic idea is the same. A story of an experiment done recently at the University of Oklahoma will indicate the role of source credibility in communication. A researcher had a speech professor tape record a speech advocating Medicare. The speech was evaluated by several faculty members who considered the logical and emotional appeals of the speech and termed it a good one. Four sections of the beginning speech course were tested as to their attitude toward medicare, each section heard the tape recording, and they were tested again. There were wide differences in the responses of the groups, even though they had heard the same speech. There was a major difference. One group had been told by the instructor that the tape was a recording of a speech made by a sophomore student fulfilling an assignment, another group was told that it was a speech by a Russian doctor visiting this country, a third group believed that the speech was by the Surgeon General of the United States, and the final group was told that the speech was by General Douglas MacArthur. Except for these impressions of the source, the other factors in the situation were the same for all of the classes of audiences. Perhaps you know what happened. Of course, the group that thought they were hearing the sophomore student were not moved to alter their opinions to the topic either way. Those who thought they heard a Russian doctor tended to lower their opinions toward the topic. But the next statement may be a surprise. The group that moved most in the direction of favoring the topic was the group that thought they were hearing General MacArthur. Although, logically, the Surgeon General could be expected to know more about this topic, it turns out that the factor most responsible for attitude change is really the audience's prior assessment of the source as to his trustworthiness. The students had a generalized respect for MacArthur, which caused them to place high credence on what he said, or they thought he said.

We will be able to illustrate this still further when we speak of opinion leadership in group situations. But you have only to look at newspaper, magazine and television ads to see this every day. Athletes and movie stars endorse foods, automobiles, or anything else. Logically, we know that an athlete may know nothing about automobiles, not being trained as an engineer, but the advertisers have learned that some of us are profoundly influenced to accept communication as a result of our prior attitude toward the source *in a general way.*

It is easy to see the relevance of this for police–community communication. The acceptance of any given message from the police is, in a sense, filtered through all previous experiences and attitudes relating to the police. Here we are fighting the same problem that faces communication from any minority group — stereotyping. As long as the press insists upon playing up negative instances regarding police, as long as the public considers primarily the *enforcement* function of the police, then subsequent messages will be less than completely effective because of low source credibility. The stories of the graft in police departments in Denver, and the telecast of the shooting of a Negro man in Fort Worth make it more difficult for the police of Lansing or anywhere else to communicate with the public effectively.

Up to now, we have considered the receiver as an individual, and we have spoken of his reactions on an individual basis. But for our topic, it may be more important to consider the individual as part of a community and as a member of numerous groups.

If we could view the receiver of a communication in isolation, as we can draw one card from a deck of cards, our task of predicting the possible effect of a message upon him would be much simpler. But not many games are played with single cards. Most games require that cards be viewed as parts of hands or tricks, and it is in relation to the other cards in the hand or the trick that they take their value. So receivers do not exist in an isolated state, but are parts of groups, and it is as parts of social groups that they must be studied.

Our society is made up of many overlapping groups, bound together by lines of communication. These groups have been classified as primary and secondary, formal and informal, small and large. The family is a primary group. Southerners comprise an informal group. The Democratic Party is a large group. And one person can easily belong to these three and perhaps dozens of other groups. Most of us have group affiliations with a family, a church, a school (past or present), a community, a state, a nation, various professional societies, one or more social clubs, perhaps several civic and service organizations.

All of these groups influence us, but they do not all influence us in the same way. Some of them influence us so indirectly that we scarcely notice it. Since we contributed to that national charity, we have not even thought about it. But we did contribute, and although membership in this group has not changed our pattern of behavior appreciably, it did cause at least one response, the initial act of making a contribution. On the other extreme, the family group to which we belong influences us profoundly and directly. We would hesitate to make major decisions or purchases, for example, without considering their possible impact upon our family group. This is all very important to communication because group loyalties influence an individual's reception of a message.

One of the first ways that groups tend to influence their members in receiving communication is through the norms that groups develop.

We know that opinions held by individuals are stronger if they are reinforced by the group. Attempts to change individual opinions are more likely to prove successful if the incoming communication (the stimulus to change) is consistent with the established norms of the group. On the other hand, any message communicated to a group member is likely to be rejected. Of course, this is usually not a conscious process, since the influence of our group norms is not often obvious to us. Norms are so much a part of the group that they are seldom isolated for consideration.

To complicate the role of norms in the communication process, it may happen that sets of norms held by several groups, to which a single individual belongs, conflict. For example, a boy may refuse to tell his school teacher about some mischief of which a friend is guilty. Although one of the values associated with his school group is to obey the teacher, a stronger value associated with his play group is not to tattle. In a case of this sort, the stronger loyalty influences behavior more. Thus it is clear that any account of the changes in opinion that an individual group member undergoes must recognize, not only the communication directed to him, but the norms his groups share, and the communication that takes place within the groups about the new idea. Police see evidence of this constantly in dealing with juvenile gangs, or other sub-groups in society. It becomes necessary for them to understand more fully the norms by which these groups behave. It would be helpful, further, to study carefully the unspoken norms of our own group to consider how many of them are understood by the general public.

A final factor in communicating to the total community is important. If people are organized into groups, and if these groups influence the thinking of their members, it might be profitable to trace briefly the process by which ideas and opinions reach members within groups.

Most of us will, at first, think of the mass media. But I am convinced that we place too much reliance on the mass media to change opinion. The media inform us and entertain us, but they do not play nearly as major a role in inducing opinion changes as we once thought. There is a major function the media have of reinforcing us in our opinions, but I am speaking here of the matter of opinion change. Recent research indicates that an important step must take place between the mass communication and the final opinion adopted by a given individual. Research by Elihu Katz and Paul Lazarsfeld has identified an "opinion leader" in each group, who tends to mediate the media message for the members, or interpret it for them and structure their reactions to it.

For several years, it has been assumed that to understand the effect of a given message on an individual, we must consider not only the message, but the sender and the receiver as well. This concept was useful for a time, and true as far as it went. But as a result of studies in the area of voting behavior, Katz, Lazarsfeld and others concluded that the picture is complicated by other factors. They were not able to observe direct and immediate effects as a result of messages sent by radio, for example. They developed the hypothesis that we have noted briefly, i.e., that a man's social environment will help to determine the influence of a given message upon him. Men do not exist alone, but are members of groups with values (norms). They tend to receive only those communications which strengthen their social relationships. Therefore, it would be reasonable to say that in some way, the group is mediating messages to its members from outside sources.

Actually, the mass medium sends a message to the opinion leader, who evaluates the message and responds favorably or unfavorably. Then he makes use of the channels of communication which exist within the group to relay the message and his evaluation to the other members.

There are several problems with this concept. While it is generally accurate, it is dangerously oversimplified. In the real world, there is not one group only, but many overlapping groups. Further, messages are not sent just to opinion leaders, but to everyone. The members of a group hear a political speech on television as soon as their opinion leader hears it. They do not depend upon him for an account of the message contents; rather, they tend to depend upon him for an *evaluation* of the worth of the message.

The picture is still much too simple. We seem to give the impression that there are opinion leaders within groups who are easily identified and static, like fathers in family groups. This appears not to be the case. Opinion leadership in a group is a dynamic thing, constantly shifting from one person to another.

What makes a person an opinion leader? Katz and Lazarsfeld discovered that among other things, an opinion leader is more likely to receive messages from outside the group than new messages. The others in the group come to realize this, consciously or not, and to rely on this person more and more for evaluating new ideas.

Let us illustrate the process by considering a teenage daughter (Girl A) and her family. If her parents were to decide to see a movie, they might be unable to make an intelligent choice by consulting the advertisements in the newspaper. Perhaps they attend the movies so infrequently that they do not know the names of any of the current stars. They might well turn to their daughter for advice on which movie they would most enjoy. She would probably be in a position to help them predict the quality of the various pictures because of her acquaintance with the names and reputations of the stars. In other words, she would be an opinion leader in the family group on the subject of motion pictures, by virtue of having more relevant information about the question at hand from outside the group than the others.

Let us suppose that this daughter is also a member of a small, informal group of girls in the neighborhood, and that this group decides to attend a motion picture. They consult the advertisements in the paper and all agree that only three possibilities are worth considering. However, they may be unable to agree which of the three is best, and finally act on the recommendation of Girl B, who attends movies daily and has read accounts of all of the pictures in the fan magazines. Girl A, who was an opinion leader among the members of her family on the subject of movies, respects the opinion of Girl B, who has read much more relevant material than she. Thus, a person can belong to two or more groups and be an opinion leader on a given topic for one of the groups, but not for the others.

Implied in the example of the two girls and the question about movies is another generalization which we can make about opinion leadership. Opinion leadership changes as issues change. If the family were considering an area other than entertainment, the daughter might not be consulted for leadership. In the area of politics, for example, we would expect the father to exert opinion leadership in the family group. Whether or not his political views are taken seriously among the men at work, his political views are regarded as significant at home. If the family has a problem concerning interpersonal relations, it may be that the mother will lead their thinking. Opinion leadership changes with the nature of the problem, as well as from group to group.

Perhaps we can summarize thus far. Communication takes place in a social setting which has a profound influence upon it. Individuals belong to many groups in our society. Communication networks exist in these groups which make it possible for the members to share ideas and opinions with each other. Groups establish norms by which they behave and judge others' behavior. A message which violates the norms of a group is likely to be rejected by that group. Opinion leaders exist within groups and tend to evaluate outside messages for the group in the light of shared norms. These opinion leaders seem to be selected by the others because of their wider and more frequent channels of communication outside the group. Opinion leaders change from group to group and within the same group, as the problems and issues change. Their function is to mediate outside messages. Although everyone may receive the message, the others tend to wait until they understand the view of the opinion leader before establishing their own view or changing a previous view.

A few suggestions specifically related to police–community communication might be warranted. First, the focus that must be kept in mind is the receiver or intended receiver of the messages, not just the messages themselves. We must consider the things that interest and motivate the receiver. We must also recall that the meanings of our messages are not so much in the language or codes that we use as in the mind of the receiver as a result of his previous background and experiences. We will be relatively unsuccessful until we consciously adapt the message to the intended receiver.

But we should recall the role that the receiver's various group identifications play in structuring his reaction to communication. While the mass media can support a community-wide educational or persuasive campaign, we cannot overlook the role of opinion leaders in all sorts of community groups who will be influential with the people. They should be identified and an effort should be made to acquire their understanding and support. This, of course, is work. It often requires "walking a change through" them, one by one. But this is the lesson that political campaigners have learned and employ. Programs where police personnel become involved in desirable roles supporting other community groups like the schools, civic clubs, fund drives, and the like are helpful in two ways. They give the public a view of the police officer in a favorable role, and they permit a firsthand acquaintance between the officer and the opinion leaders of the community. Community organizations like the "Citizens for Police Improvement" group in Oklahoma City serve this purpose also in that they draw from many other groups, and allow the leaders to understand police problems firsthand.

Police and Community — as Viewed by a Religious Leader

PAUL O. CARDWELL

(Then) Executive Secretary, Board of Education,
North Texas Conference of the Methodist Church, Dallas, Texas

MAY 18, 1966

I am not speaking for any organization or association of people. I am speaking for myself only. However, I shall be mindful of many facets of organized and institutional religion as interpreted by churches and synagogues.

Institutional religion, which I shall hereafter call *the church*, although I shall be including the synagogue, is vulnerable from its critics at two points. First, I suppose there is a bit of truth in the accusation, "If the church performed its role with fidelity, we would not be harassed by crime." Second, no segment of the community basically is more interested in crime prevention than is organized religion.

Let us look at the first of these. In those communities historically dominated by a single denomination or sect, overt crime is kept at a minimum because the church not only sets the standards of conduct, but also is the enforcement agency through social pressure or threat of excommunication. This was especially true of the colonial days of our country when the establishment of a state church accompanied the advent of any colony. It is still true in those rare self-contained communities where the power structure is the expression of a single approach to religious faith. These are the self-segregated sect communities like those of the Amish; or the community that was settled for the propagation of the Catholic faith, and the cathedral dominates the landscape and the priest is the person of greatest influence; or the southern rural town where the leaders in all areas are of the dominant Protestant denomination; or where Jewry has been forced into an economic ghetto.

Because of the very nature of ethical religion, the church should be the most concerned of all segments of community life in the prevention of crime. However, the city that pays the greatest lip service to religion may be a city with unimaginable crime problems. This, alas, is sometimes true because organized religion is too much wrapped up in the perpetuation and aggrandizement of its own institutionalism. This also may be true because we are more interested in maintaining a stance of respectability than in shouldering our cross in the midst of the sweat, blood and tears of human suffering and need. As a designated leader in the field of religion, I cannot make a plea of "not guilty" for the church.

However, in my judgment, the two factors that have contributed most to the seeming impotence of the church in the prevention of crime are the rise of religious pluralism, and the secularization of our American culture.

The community that is dominated by a single religious point of view is rare — and daily is getting rarer. My own city of Dallas was once considered a *Protestant* city — under the influence, for the most part, of the Baptist and Methodist. This is no longer true. The voices of Rabbi Olan and Bishop Gorman increasingly are heard with respect. The once all-Protestant and all-white Dallas Pastors Association had as its president, two years ago, the Rev. Zan W. Holmes, Jr., a Negro, and now its chief officer is Father Joseph W. Drew, a Roman Catholic of the Paulist order. Rabbi Gerald Klein is a member of the executive committee. For the past two years, the Roman Catholics have had officer "observers" (except for voting, they participated as any member would) in attendance at the annnal assembly of the Texas Council of Churches, and are now in serious conversation with the possibility of becoming members of the Council, as Catholics have done in some of the other states. Ecumenical lay conversations are coming into being all over our section of the country, and "ecumenism" is becoming a more significant word than "parochialism."

If the church can no longer speak with "authority," as it did when a single denomination virtually controlled a community, what, if any, are the signs of hope that religion can still be influential in the behavior of persons, especially in the prevention of crime? I give you four signs of hope, although there are others.

1. *The serious emphasis on renewal.* This is a turning from the selfish devotion to self-perpetuation to the sacrificial giving of one's self to making this world a better place in which a larger number of persons can live with dignity and freedom. This recurring note was heard in Vatican Council II. There is no denominational assembly where "renewal" is not urged.

2. *From sanctuary to marketplace.* The church is no longer being considered as a refuge from the defilement of a dirty world; but a place where we go for worship, teaching and fellowship to enable us to go back into the world to change it. In the recent demonstrations for human rights, leaders in the field of religion joined in the struggle for human dignity, and most of the martyrs in that conflict have been persons in whom religion was a driving force. Not a facet of human need and depravity has been overlooked — from the black ghetto of Harlem to the ministry to the homosexuals of North Beach, San Francisco. Recently, a friend of mine, a clergyman, served on the grand jury. After weeks of being exposed to the sordidness of human depravity, one of his fellow jurors said, "I suppose you never imagined anything like this existed." To which my friend replied, "I have not seen nor heard one thing that I haven't already met in my responsibilities as pastor and counselor."

3. *Lay participation.* We find today a renewed emphasis on the lay ministry of the church. This means that it is not sufficient to have professional religious servants. Every man and woman, youth and child, must find his or her place of service in the name of religion. Frequently I hear the query, "Why doesn't the church do so-and-so?" or, in terms of our interest here, "What is the church doing in the prevention of crime?" I am guessing that most of the men and women interested in police–community relations are members of a church or synagogue. If so, YOU are the church. If you are a religious law enforcement officer, then religion IS at work in the prevention of crime.

4. *The ecumenical movement.* As I previously stated, we are joining hands in our common tasks across denominational boundaries. We are in transition from the self-interest of many religious groups to the recognition of our religious pluralism. When we have come into full faith in the ecumenical movement, then the influence of religion will be felt within and above the cultural secularism of our American civilization.

Police–Community Relations — A Personal View

JACKIE ROBINSON

Chairman of the Board, Freedom National Bank of New York City, Baseball Hall of Famer

MAY 19, 1966

I want to say that I feel that if we are to be successful, we must learn how to work together. Some of the fears that the fellows on the Brooklyn baseball club had, as I understood it, were what would happen to them when and if Jackie

Robinson joined the ball club. In athletics, as you know, the restrooms and locker rooms have to be shared equally. Some of the fellows were so concerned, they weren't able to join together as a team, until all of a sudden, they realized that nothing really was happening from their association with me; then we started to work together and become a better ball club, and we understood one another better. I think that because of the groundless fear that had no justification, we were able to do the kind of job that made a good club. I must admit that nothing happened to me in that time either, so I felt pretty good about it, too.

I feel that in community relations, as far as the police are concerned, that if they, too, take the kind of attitude that the Brooklyn baseball club had (and get over the fears that some people on the police force have), they'd have the basis of a better understanding about the community, especially the Negroes. I think that when the police departments in certain sections of our country truly understand what the desires and wants of Negro Americans are, they will truly have a good working relationship. So many police are fearful of the people in many minority areas, fearful that they are trying to cause problems, and fearful that they are going to retaliate for some of the conditions that they have faced over the years. I can honestly say, from my associations in the early years, that I was somewhat fearful about the police in my community, because we had heard stories. I am sure that some of the police were fearful of us, because they too had heard stories. There were certainly many problems between the minority groups and the police. But one of the things that helped us overcome these fears that we both had was that we got a chance to get to know one another just a little bit.

I was grateful, out in Pasadena, because we were members of the gang of youngsters, about 13 or 14 years of age, who were from underprivileged homes, whose mothers and fathers were out working from early morning till late at night, thus giving us opportunities to be in the streets and getting into difficulties. I remember that the big thrill we had was that just before we went home at night, we would raise some kind of disturbance so that the police would be called out, and when they got out of their cars, we'd fling dirt on them, and the chase was on. I recall that one night, after one of our gang was caught, he told on the rest of us. The officer chased us through a maze of barbed-wire, which we knew very well and he didn't. He came up to my door, and I had been in bed "for a long period of time." He was dripping blood from the barbed wire, so I let him know our feelings. And later, the police talked to us about where we were headed, and we began to think a little differently. Along with the help of a new gang, we started working in our community to better ourselves and get people to work with us. Our little gang turned out to be a pretty good bunch of kids.

Because of our financial problems, we had difficulties, naturally. But the most important thing that we learned was that we must try to work together. There was a police captain out in California who talked to us constantly. We had to laugh when we'd be called down about our little adventures, of which he didn't approve. The gang consisted of white fellows, and Japanese, and Negroes and Mexicans. We were all called in separately, and would go back and compare notes. The Negroes were told that they'd get in trouble by associating with the Japs, and the Japs were told they'd get in trouble by going with those "niggers," and so on. We had to laugh, of course, but I am sure that it was an attempt to make us better citizens. Obviously, the police were trying to do a job and were trying to help. And, of course, I now know that the great body of our policemen are tremendously dedicated to the job that they have to do. Occasionally, there are just a few who take advantage of their uniforms, and feel that they have a superiority over the community, and then incidents of police brutality result. I am positive that the great number of our police want to end all our difficulties, and that we are seldom going to have the kind of incident that I ran into in Pasadena.

I remember coming home from a baseball game, and we had an argument with a white man; one of the fellows in the car jumped out, and we had a tremendous discussion, and we asked him if he wanted to get into battle. The man said, "No. I'm in the neighborhood and if I get into a fight, I'll be ganged upon." We tried to insist that if he wanted to fight one member of the gang, that was his business and we wouldn't interfere. About that time a young policeman came up, and in his inexperience, he immediately pulled out his gun. He was shaking like a leaf in a windstorm, and in my view he was about ready to create a problem that didn't have to come about. There were several Negroes present and a few whites. I think he became disturbed, and he started pushing us around to show his authority because he had the gun in his hand. We couldn't have cared less about the gun he had, and we let him know so. He started putting everybody under arrest, and I was included. Finally, when a sergeant appeared, we were picked up for suspicion of robbery and other charges which had nothing to do with what had gone on.

Fortunately, when the case came up, nothing happened, and it was dropped. But I think that these kinds of incidents are the causes of misunderstanding between people in the community and the police. For instance, when we went to Birmingham, Alabama — Floyd Patterson, myself and some others — to involve ourselves in the situation in Birmingham, the bombings were going on and we were fearful of going out to get something to eat. The local people told us to be careful, not to cross the street against the light, and so on, because "you're going to be watched, and followed and arrested, if they can do it." Finally, since the restaurant in the hotel had been bombed out, and we couldn't get anything to eat, a young girl said we had nothing to fear, that she would go with us. From the moment we started leaving the hotel till we got to the restaurant, we were trailed. I don't know if anything would have happened if we had crossed the street, but I know we had been forewarned. We went to the church and upon leaving there, a police car pulled up in front of us, deliberately trying to provoke some kind of incident. We merely turned our car around and went the other way. When we got to the next church, we were met by a bunch of Negro people who had been protecting people coming in from out of the city. Upon leaving the church the second time, we were met by these fellows and we said, "Now what?" They said nothing was going to happen — they were well prepared. If we had started anything, I don't know what could have happened.

What I am saying is that there is so much misunderstanding in so many communities today that the Negro has become pretty well fed up with the kind of incidents that are provoked without any warnings or justification. Unless we are ready to take a real look at what the Negro is really asking for, we can expect a tremendously hot summer.

What bothers us, again, is in New York City. There is the head of the Police Benevolent Association, who disturbs the Negroes in the community. He is so much opposed to Mayor Lindsay's Police Review Board that his statements make no sense at all. The Mayor has appointed some of the top citizens of New York to investigate other top people, so he can appoint a Civilian Review Board. The only thing they want to do is investigate when and if there are incidents in New York that need investigation. And yet, the head of the Police Benevolent Association is yelling so loud that the people of Harlem are asking, "What are the police trying to hide? Why are they afraid of men and women who have made a reputation in New York, who will investigate and make a fair decision on their findings?"

I know that there are questions that the police have; they feel they are being unduly judged; but, for the life of me, I can't understand it.

The Negro police organization in New York, the Guardians Association, has fully supported the Police Review Board. I've had the opportunity to talk to white policemen who agree with the Negroes, and they feel that they too can be protected better if there is an outside board, rather than their immediate superiors, although there will be three of the police officers on the Board. If we are to gain respect, if we are to have a better relationship, the police should not throw into the minds of people a notion that the police have something to hide. I feel very strongly about this. I know that there may be real reasons for the objections, but I think we should get together and spell them out.

I want to say, also, that there are many questions being raised as to why so many of us are involving ourselves in the struggle for equal opportunity. I remember receiving a newspaper clipping from down in Florida, where a newspaper man was extremely critical of Jackie Robinson for involving himself. He pointed out that, if it had not been for Branch Rickey, a white man, Jackie Robinson wouldn't be where he is today. Mr. Rickey took me out of Pasadena, put me on the Brooklyn baseball club, gave me an opportunity to make the kind of living that I am making today, and then — after my baseball career was over — it was a white man, William Black, the President and Chairman of the Board of the Chock-Full-of-Nuts organization, who hired me as Vice-President for Personnel, and made me a member of the Board, and as this newspaper reporter pointed out, gave me a job that many people in this country envied. Why, then, should someone, who has been given such opportunities by white men, involve himself in the struggle for equal opportunity? Why am I "rocking the boat?" The reporter pointed out that Jackie Robinson, of all people in this country, has it made.

I sat down and wrote this reporter a letter, and explained to him exactly why I am involved. I pointed to Nat King Cole who went to Birmingham a few years ago, trying to do things that he knew how to do best. I said that Nat King Cole had a fantastic ability with his trio and his ability to sing, and the opportunity he had of making money; but he tried to sing in Birmingham, and out of the crowd came individuals who beat Nat King Cole for no reason other than that he was a Negro, trying to do what he knew how to do best.

And then I pointed out that Lena Horne, wanting to go to a night club in Los Angeles to enjoy herself one evening, was so heckled and so abused that it took most of the newspapers of the country to explain what had happened. I think you know the great talents that Lena Horne has: her beauty, her voice, the opportunity that she has of making money. Lena Horne has it made, as well; but being a Negro in these United States, she was subjected to the same kind of abuse.

In my profession of baseball, when the San Francisco Giants moved out there, Willie Mays tried to buy a home in what was then an all-white district. He was subjected to so much abuse that the Mayor said that Willie was such a fine man that he could come and live in his home, if he liked. So Willie Mays, though he is considered the greatest name in baseball, is subjected to the same kind of abuse as any other Negro.

So I humbly submit that, if we are to solve our problems, we can't go around talking about those of us who have had opportunities. We must look at the people who are still struggling to make a go of it here in this country, the great percentage of the people who are not making enough money to get out of the poverty classification. We keep pointing out that with all of this kind of thing happening to people who are not so fortunate, there is not one single Negro in this country who "has it made," until each of these people, struggling to get out of poverty, has it made! And as I concluded my letter to this reporter, being white in this country doesn't mean that anybody "has it made" either.

We must take a good look at this whole world of ours, and realize that it is made up of some 80 percent colored people. In Communist China, the political leaders are saying to colored people the world over: "Let's unite against our white oppressors; if we unite we can get back at the whites for some of the things they have done to us over the years." Fortunately, the Negro in this country is not interested in what happened yesterday. He feels very strongly that he has as much right to the opportunity that exists here as anybody else; we have a tremendous love for our country, and we're going to fight for its future. We're not interested in fighting something that has been done to us over the years. Most of the Negro leaders are trying to avoid friction. We are grateful for the poverty program. We're very much concerned about the fact that, in some cities, the poverty programs are being eliminated. More than anything else, I think, the great majority of our Negro leaders are interested in a united effort, a better communication between the whites of this country and the Negro; also the Puerto Ricans of this country and the whites, and so on down the line. Unless we are able to establish some kind of rapport, some communication with one another, I think we're going to go on having incidents.

Try to understand that the great majority of Negroes are really not interested in "getting back." When we move into a neighborhood, it doesn't mean that we're interested in getting into your kitchen, eventually into your living room, and finally into your bedroom. A Negro in this country is more interested in being your brother than he is in being your brother-in-law!

I know that some of you don't particularly care about some of the things I have to say. The day has come when the Negro is no longer interested in saying the things he thinks will please Mr. Charlie; he is saying the things he thinks Mr. Charlie ought to know. We think this country is a tremendous country. We believe, as I said earlier, that it should afford us the same opportunity that it affords any other person, and we're not going to allow the Negro to be held down any longer without shouting to the housetops. We're going to get our rights here in this country because we believe that the Constitution was written for us as well as for anyone else, and we know full well that as long as any group of people attempt to hold the Negro down, he, too, has to remain down. As long as any group has to remain down, our country is weakened by that much.

I have a son who is on his way back from Vietnam, who has spent one year over there fighting for some of you. There are thousands of Negro youngsters fighting because they believe in our country, and they're not protesting against their involvement in this tragic war. I would hate to have them come back to this country and face the same kind of problems that we've talked to them about for so many years. Our Negro youngsters who've been involved over there are not going to come back just to face the same old problems. They are no longer afraid of death. I think, as has been demonstrated in the deep South, that this is the feeling of the masses of the young Negroes. They are going to get their rights, come Hell or high water. We think it's going to be a lot easier if all of us join together and work together in an effort to eliminate the kind of problems we've been discussing.

It's true, I've been a fortunate individual. I am grateful for the opportunities that I've had, and grateful for the things that are before me; but I'm not so grateful that I'm willing to sit idly by on the sidelines and not participate in the struggle so that all of our children in this country will have a fair and equal chance. I am sure that you recognize that building up false security in the young whites today is bad, because then they too are hurt as much as the young Negro students are hurt when they cannot compete.

We have come a long way in the struggle. We've come this distance, not because of the great desire of the Negro alone, but because of the fact that there have been thousands upon thousands of white Americans who feel strongly about the democracy of this country of ours. It was demonstrated so well in the March on Washington a few years ago, when 250,000 people walked down Constitution Avenue, and Negroes found whites walking with them because they all believed in the Constitution.

I think that the reason for the police department to be concerned about where they're going is because you are the group most affected. You have a terrific opportunity; and those of us who know the problems that you have want to work with you to do whatever we can possibly do to make it easier for you. It was pointed out by the NAACP, in a letter to a state police conference in New York, that "in view of the dangers of the coming months, I feel it advisable that we take immediate progressive, constructive steps to promote a better relationship between police and minority groups. The great harm done to all police by reckless and irresponsible and unreasonable public statements being made in the name of the police department in New York, in my opinion, is causing tremendous harm and misunderstanding in minority communities."

Police–Citizen Interaction as a Problem in Communication

HIDEYA KUMATA

Professor of Communications, Michigan State University

MAY 23, 1967

We have a tendency to relegate problems, particularly sticky problems of human relations, to faulty communications, and then to feel that since we have named the problem, we have solved it.

I believe that increased communication can bring about desirable consequences under certain conditions. However, where lines are drawn, where images are set, where prejudices are ingrained, these conditions are seldom met. Let me point out that increasing communication under hostile conditions increases hostility. It is not a blessing just to increase the flow of communication. This says that perhaps we should not look at communication in terms of messages, so much as we should look at the conditions under which messages are transmitted.

Let me relate a story, to illustrate what I mean. In 1943, I was promoted to Sergeant in the United States Army. To give you some background, I happen to be of Japanese ancestry. I got a three-day pass as a consequence of being promoted to Sergeant. I decided to use these 72 hours by visiting Chicago. Coming from a relatively small city on the West Coast, I had never visited a large city before. My Army friends, said, "Kumata, you are a very young man and we know what you are going to do. You will go to the Museum of Science and Industry, you will go to the Museum of Natural History, you will go to the Shedd Aquarium, the Chicago Art Gallery, then sit around the USO, come home, and say you had a good time. But be sure and visit, before you are through, on West Madison Street." In 1943, West Madison Street in Chicago was nothing but a series of establishments meant to catch GI trade, all of which had floor shows. I walked into one of these places. The Master of Ceremonies came out, and he said, "Ladies and Gentlemen, before we start our evening's festivities, let's all give a hand to our gallant Chinese allies." At which point everybody applauded, and so did I, until of course I realized that he referred to me, so I got up, took a bow, and sat down. That is all there is to the story, a rather innocent one, but I think it illustrates some of the problems in communications. I could have made a big noise there, and explained in meticulous detail what I was, and why he shouldn't have referred to me in that fashion. It just wasn't worth the effort.

On the other hand, that particular Master of Ceremonies did some things which all of us do, which makes the problem of communication especially difficult. We take what is obvious, and add details which will make the obvious more obvious. Therefore, the cue is not the message which was sent out in terms of words; the cue was a message which was sent out in terms of my physiognomy. And what this did was to give him a sort of a check list of things — who looks like that around here in 1943? You can't come up with anybody but Chinese, especially with a uniform on, and he switched the American uniform to a Chinese one. I think this is the crucial part of this operation.

When we talk about communication, merely increasing communication will do no good whatsoever, until we can do something about the basis of expectations or perceptions upon which the communication is based.

Therefore, let me start out with some very pessimistic views about communication:

1. I think the research shows that the main effect of most communication is reinforcement. This is both good and bad. What I means by reinforcement is that it strengthens the belief systems which people already have. I think we ought to ponder this quite seriously. A major brunt of most communication is reinforcement of existing attitudes, not change. This is especially true when the mass media are used. The mass media at times has a hopelessness about it in that once the message is out, there is no more control over it. On the part of the audience, furthermore, there is a selectivity in which things which might be disquieting and uncomfortable and clarifying are avoided by the reader or listener.

2. Changes occur through communication, but they are very small. I can demonstrate to you that we can change attitudes through communication; however, when we look at the research, most of it deals with inconsequential attitudes which nobody cares about one way or the other. So they change. Attitude change research oftentimes is upon subjects such as "What do you think of prohibition in Missouri?" And you are living in Michigan! Or "What do you think of late hours for coeds?" Research tends to deal with subjects in which there is no deep, vested interest by any other parties. Then you can get great changes. When you get people who have a vested interest in the subject matter, communication does not change people very much, if at all. So my second point is that in effective communication, changes are very small.

3. Conversion, which means a switch from negative to a positive attitude, or a switch from a positive to a negative, is very unlikely. That is not a very encouraging state of affairs, but I am afraid that as we look at the research, cause for optimism is not greater than this.

4. The communication of statements of fact seldom convinces anybody. That is, parading what the state of affairs is, in terms of an "objective" display of statements of fact, without some explanation or interpretation of what these facts are, means that people will interpret these facts to suit their particular purposes. Some may dispute this, but let me give you an example. A great many of us, perhaps some of you, through television, watched the Michigan State–Notre Dame football game last fall. The same statements of fact were televised and were seen by all. But today, if you compare a Notre Dame fan and a Michigan State fan, there is some question as to who Number One was! My point is that the business of changing people by communication is an arduous and long process, and does not come about simply because people feel good about it and attempt to increase communication.

I cite for you, for example, the famous Starr study in Cincinnati, about the United Nations. If you'll recall, in the early fifties, there was a six-month campaign, using radio, billboards, ministers from the pulpit and what have you, trying to get the people of Cincinnati to become more aware of what the United Nations was and become more favorable to it. The before–after study showed that after six months of this sort of campaigning, the people who were affected the most were those who already believed in the United Nations — that the campaign had not succeeded very well in changing viewpoints.

There was a television program, about three years ago, when the late Edward R. Murrow narrated a program on "The Great Holiday Massacre." There was a before–after study in Chicago, with selected families. During that particular program of 60 minutes, less commercial time, the major emphasis was to make people more careful in their driving, and to bring home to people that their own particular driving habits have a great deal to do with the accident rate. This was released immediately prior, if I recall, to the Thanksgiving holiday. They were trying to cut down the number of accidents. The before–after study showed what? There was a less-than-a-minute segment in that particular program, which showed a highway patrolman flagging down a motorist on the turnpike. The motorist was obviously inebriated. This was just a short excerpt, to show that drunkenness was also a contributor to the accident rate. When the program was over, in the after study, the results showed that most people had shifted whatever opinions they had before the program to a position which said that most accidents are caused by drunken driving, an interesting kind of outcome. Given an opportunity to escape from blame, given an opportunity to validate their own belief systems about how good they are as drivers, given an excuse to put blame on somebody else, the audience chose this alternative, even though the proportion of time spent in that message on drunken driving in this particular dramatization was $\frac{1}{60}$ or less.

What can we do about this sort of thing, especially in some very sticky community relations problems? I think, rather than have do's and don'ts, I would like to emphasize a *point of view* in approaching communication. The intent is not to change any style of communication; I don't think anyone should be uncomfortable in communicating at all — but I think a point of view is necessary. And these things might well be kept in mind in approaching community relations problems:

1. The notion of perfect communication in any particular message transaction is nonsense. I would take that as a point of view. I view communication as a successive approximation procedure, at the end of which both parties may not feel exactly the same about what transpired, but they are close enough. I think that at our present stage of research and development, this is about the best we can ask.

Therefore, saying that we will have an immense publicity program or public relations program, which will be pushed for a period of one month or two months will not do the trick. If communication is a process of successive approximation by small changes, it means that a very, very long term should be devoted to including communication and improving community relations.

2. I would take the general semantics notion that meanings are in *people*, not in words. This prevents us from making some errors. It prevents us from looking at a piece of writing, or a speech, or a movie and expecting that particular message to have all the meaning that you want in it. I think it is much better to say the message is but a stimulator or evoker of meanings which already exist, and that the words or pictures in and of themselves are devoid of meaning until somebody puts meaning in them. Therefore, to argue that this place of writing said this, and you say this and you're wrong, is a waste of time. We should start to work at trying to understand what are the reservoir of meanings available to the people with whom we wish to communicate, before we start sending messages.

3. Another point of view I would take is that which says any kind of communication effort by responsible authorities is mostly sponsor-centered. By sponsor-centered I mean, it is the police department, it is the human relations commission, it is the social workers who have the need and are expressing the kind of world they would like to have.

Very seldom in the communication process can we get to a position where we become what I would consider, receiver-oriented. Effective communication, from my point of view, is to ask what is it that is out there, and then to probe a little bit and hope that the kinds of messages we send will stimulate enough until we get to a point where we will be satisfied, assuming that we will never get perfection. This is a rather dismal outlook, but I think it is a realistic one.

4. Another point of view I would like to suggest is that perhaps when we think of channels of communication, we have been educated to feel that the channel which is most efficient is that which uses print. Let me give you some citation on this. In terms of mass media consumption today, for example, the

"average American" views television about 22-24 hours a week. He listens to radio another 10 hours a week. He reads — 95 percent of American adults are exposed to one or more newspapers, but his time spent is about 20 minutes a day which means about 2⅓ hours a week for most people. Magazine reading takes about 2 hours. The exact figures are not important, but the relationship is. That is, given our "druthers," people have a way of receiving messages that select seeing or hearing over reading. Yet, when I say we rely on channels that are most inefficient, I am saying that a lot of our campaigns are based upon materials which are written.

I might point out another kind of datum. About seven years ago, Bernard Berelson noted that 70 percent of American adults read less than one book a year. I think what I am trying to point out is that the American public is not a reading public at all. And yet, in some sorts of communication situations, we feel quite secure in putting out written communications. When we do put out written communications, we tend to make them so long that people do not stick to the main point of the message. Even for people who are highly literate, whose business it is to read, when you give them materials which are lengthy, but which are of only moderate interest to them, they tend to give it a quick shake. That is, they ask what is it about, what does it say? — flip through the pages and out. Perhaps from a communication standpoint, we should look at what it is that's out there in terms of preference patterns, and work with that, rather than to satisfy the needs of the sponsor in that he can display a lot of brochures the next time a conference is held.

Let me suggest another kind of position. Let me introduce the notion of feedback. It is a popular term nowadays. But may I suggest that in order to estimate effect, the best way we know is the old-fashioned way of having people respond back to us. This says that communication is a cyclical process. Unless you close the loop by having somebody respond to your messages, you will never know how well you do. Now this is a harsh criticism for people who do not do this, but I think we often feel that educated guesses as to effects will suffice. We should go out and find out what happened. If we do not invite feedback, we will be floating around in a Never-Never Land of guessing what the probable effect of our message was. This assumes serious proportions in a community where sources which put out messages assume certain kinds of effect, and never check out what effect these messages actually had. Oftentimes, increasing communication just increases what I would consider noise in the environment.

At some point, then, some check on our communication system is desirable, to see that it has a "closed loop."

That's a point of view I have about communication. I cannot wholly justify it, in terms of research. I cannot say that there is no such thing as perfect communication, but I feel that such a position in approaching communication is much better assuming one can produce perfect messages.

I also think that although you may dislike certain ways of communicating, if they are the easiest way that people receive the message, we ought to use them. Although you will hear some very, very nasty things sometimes in feedback, you had better get them or you will not know how you are doing.

The problem of feedback is not only difficult technically, in terms of communicating with a lot of people, but it is also difficult psychologically. Often we assume we have feedback, but our feedback comes from the wrong sources. For example, a great many community programs of uplift, in which a lot of people volunteer their time and energy, get a great deal of enthusiasm back from people who say the program is good, and it turns out they're talking to other people like themselves. In fact, most of us do not want to talk to people who are unlike ourselves, because you may get hurt in the process. Therefore, we may have some circles of communication going which are self-sealing systems, devoid of any touch with reality.

In terms of communication we should increase face-to-face communication whenever possible, this being the best way to get immediate feedback, whether you like it or not. If you write a letter, you can ward off anything coming back. If you appear on television, you don't have to consider the audience. If you put up a poster, you can blithely say that it was a good poster because other artists speak of it favorably. But in the face-to-face, eyeball-to-eyeball situation, you cannot avoid the kind of messages you are going to get back. The problem then, for all of us, is not only to get into this nexus of face-to-face, but to be able to read feedback in terms in which we are not fending defensively. What I'm suggesting is that of all the things we can use for communication, our marvelous technology says we can hit a lot of people at one time. However, the most effective means of changing people (remember, changes are small), is when you can alter the message immediately, on the spot, which occurs best when people are face-to-face. That these occasions do not arise often enough is a fault of ourselves. I think partially we are somewhat afraid of having these confrontations.

On the other hand, I will admit that when conditions seem especially tough, it is hard to engage in some sort of interaction situation. I will also admit that when hostility arises, we tend to cut communication rather than to increase it. I would suggest, from what little we know from communication research, that when hostility is present, some skillful means of establishing face-to-face interation should be sought at all costs. This is not indiscriminate face-to-face contact; this is *planned* face-to-face contact, in which there will be a clear understanding on both sides that defensiveness will be thrown by the board. Now this is an ideal state of affairs, and I think maybe we will depart from it, but I think the attempt should be made.

I have not given you any kind of advice as to how to do communication or what to do, or what to do in particularly sticky situations. What I have been trying to do is to set a framework, in which we look at the whole problem of communication, such that when people say communication is at the root of the problem, we start to think of more angles than just increasing the sheer amount of messages in the environment. One might point out, in just increasing communication with some people, you wouldn't want to know them after you knew more about them.

Let me suggest another thing in terms of attitude change and communication. I said changes were small. I said that conversion is very, very unlikely. However, this obtains in the situation where you try communication in trying to persuade people reasonably to change their minds, and under these circumstances, given strong positions, you get very little change. There is another option; this option has to be exercised with care, I believe, but you reverse the procedure. Reversing the procedure says you make a person commit or do something, and then make him change himself and the communication now supports what he did. From a research standpoint doing, and then changing attitudes, is oftentimes much easier than telling another to change attitudes, and measuring the results afterward. The fact that one does something (and I think it is crucial that he does it in front of other people he thinks are important) commits him to that action, and given the choice of rejecting the action or changing his view of the situation, it's easier to change his view. In this fashion, he doesn't feel that he has been coerced to change to a position that perhaps he wouldn't have thought of originally.

If we can get somebody to do something in front of what he feels are important others, and then put in communication to support his behavior, we may get better results. This says the kind of things which are "do-able" for people might be a good way to get the first wedge into a reconsideration of their stances. In this respect, there is a great deal of merit in saying, let us put in laws which make people's behavior conform. This says you may justify what you are doing later, by reasoning it out yourself, rather than having some sort of outside source forever yammering at you to do this and do that.

I said I was going to be pessimistic; I think I have been pessimistic but realistic. I hope, however, that this pessimism that I express will not be a cause for you to cease seeking ways to ease community relations.

It says that we must find situations where the positions are not so strongly drawn that communication may engender more hostility. In the case of the police, if I may make a small suggestion, they should get into interaction situations which are outside the expectations of ordinary police interaction with citizens. If police–citizen contacts are always within the accepted role pattern, there are some very strong attitudes afoot which will cut off the effect of any communication. Although it means more work for the same pay, I would very strongly suggest that situations for communicating face-to-face with citizens be sought which are somewhat outside of the normal, expected pattern of contact. This also says that people who are working for better community relations, who are not police, have a very heavy responsibility in being the mediators of reasonable positions when they find the opportunity. Again, the way these people are seen will determine whether increased communication will result.

The Police and Their Problems*

MARVIN E. WOLFGANG

Professor of Sociology, Center for Studies in Criminology and Criminal Law, University of Pennsylvania

MAY 17, 1965

There have been some studies of the police, and there are many observations made in a somewhat clinical and anthropological way. I have been fairly close to the police department in Philadelphia for about 14 years, having spent three intensive years working closely with the homicide squad. Our own research activi-

* Reprinted with permission from POLICE Magazine, Vol. 10, No. 4, pp. 50-56, Charles C Thomas, Publisher, Springfield, Ill.

ties at the University of Pennsylvania's Center of Criminological Research are intimately linked with the Philadelphia police department, without whose cooperation we would not have been able to conduct some of our meaningful work. Thus, at least in our own area, we enjoy that kind of peculiar position which permits us entree and rapport while granting us freedom to make suggestions — hopefully constructive and criticism of the police organization and of the community's attitudes and relationships with the police.

To ask "Who are they?" poses more than one question because we can hardly speak of a collective consciousness, a community consensus in this regard. The police represent not only persons of subgroup in a society, but also a symbol of social values, of authority, of formal and codified rules of conduct. The police are the guardians of a system of values that have historical continuity and contemporary coherency; they are the executors of middle class values reflected in the criminal law and community norms of right and wrong conduct. They are the front line reconnaisance troops of these values; their functional role is to discover, detect and deter deviance from those values, while protecting vulnerable victims from the offensiveness of others. In this sense, the community of individuals is primarily composed of persons who accept, internalize, and themselves teach and represent in their roles the very values the police are expected to uphold.

But most communities are also made up of interest groups, at least two sexes, different ethnic groups, social classes, important age differences, occupational categories, wealth and poverty, a power elite and impotent minority. These are only broad and gross classifications that we use to simplify analysis; there are obviously many more. But these suffice to show the range of variation in differential perspectives relative to the police and their functions. Moreover, there is a dichotomy that we must never forget — e.g., that the community is composed of criminals and non-criminals, delinquents and non-delinquents. The attitudes of these groups toward the police serve both to divide the community response to police power, and cause a response in the policeman's psychology. Sometimes, as we shall see, the police tend to exaggerate this response and view the community of citizens and of criminals as either saints or sinners, as respectably good or irrefutably bad. Instead, the community comprises a continuum, a distribution-like IQ ranging along an axis from good to bad, with most of us in the model sweep of the bell-shaped curve.

We must also keep in mind that the police themselves do not represent an entirely homogeneous group. Having a police badge does not make men alike. The uniform does not cause uniformity of ideas, hopes, aspirations and achievement. While there may be more similarities among persons in a police organization than in the community at large, each officer comes to his profession with his own peculiar personality, abilities and talents to handle ideas and people. If there are sadists in the police force, they must be extremely rare, and the idea is more of a myth than a reality. But there are some men more aggressive, more prone to violence, more hostile, more prejudicial than others. To say that these same variations exist in all occupations is not a sanguine response, however, for the police are in a special kind of relationship to the community that most other occupational groups do not enjoy (or suffer).

Therefore, to speak of the police in general, as one is required to do in a short space like this, is somewhat in violation of our recognition of heterogeneity among the police. But we shall nonetheless keep this fact in mind.

I have said that we don't know enough about the social organization of the police and of the community's attitudes. We have more than rumors, however, and are better off than in many other things where our notions are only rumors. My grandfather reminded me during the Second World War of a jingle popular during the First World War:

> "My aunt's charwoman's sister's son
> Heard a policeman in his beat
> Say to a nursemaid down the street
> That he knew a man who had a friend
> And he could tell when the war would end."

We are better off than this, and before saying more about the specific relationship between the police and the community, let me pay my debts generally to some writers and researchers whose work has influenced my thinking on these matters. I am referring, for example, to the unpublished material of Dr. Jerome Skolnick[1] at the Center for the Study of Law and Society at Berkeley, California; to the newly published work by Michael Banton in England, THE POLICE-MAN IN THE COMMUNITY,[2] to David Matza's DELINQUENCY AND DRIFT,[3] to William Westley's *Violence and the Police,* [4] and others. I do not always agree with all of these writings but I do occasionally draw upon them.

1. The Role of the Police in Relation to the Community, as This Role Affects Attitudes in Both Directions

It is axiomatic that the police officer's role represents a conflict of values in many specific situations. Policemen participate in the same community as the people whose conduct they are supervising. William Foote Whyte noted in STREET CORNER SOCIETY, in his account of the social structure in a Massachusetts Italian neighborhood, the contradiction between the policeman's formal obligations and the relationships he needs to build up in such a community, if he is to keep the peace. Taking a strictly legalistic view of duties cuts him off from the personal relations necessary to enable him to serve as mediator of disputes in his area. Yet the policeman who develops close ties with the local people is unable to act against them with the vigor prescribed by the law.[5] Accepting free coffee or meals, shirts or hams at Christmastime, may be innocuous behavior in one sense and at one time, but it creates ties of trouble between the generous citizen and the policeman. It is not merely that the police officer may be more lenient in permitting minor violations by his benefactors. Even if the gift-giving citizen performs any law violation, the actual conflict is potentially present, and there-fore promotes a moral conflict harbored by the organization of the police, if not by the officer himself.

As an organization, the police are expected to perform successfully. The police, like any other group, wish to be successful, to conceive of themselves as performing their roles with efficiency, for efficiency is one of the main virtues in the American *ethos.* Similarly, the community wants the police to function efficiently. But the measures of success of this organization are probably harder to obtain than for most organizations. The automobile industry and most businesses measure success by economic rewards, by net profits. A university is performing its role if it teaches, does research, grows in quantity or quality; a professor by his publications, research, and teaching and administrative skills. There are, of course, problems of weighing these ingredients, but they are consistent and form a logic of function. For the police organization, there are conflicting values expressed by the community itself. The police must meet many criteria, and it is difficult to compare the value of success in one direction at the expense of shortcomings in another. A police force which solves more crimes, but which treats suspects with undue severity, is in one sense more efficient, but its practices would excite public protest. The police have a variety of objectives, but they are simultaneously subjected to many restrictions about the ways in which they attain them, and the interplay between ends and means is much more complex than in most organizations. The efficiency of the police may be less important than their responsiveness to the community they are required to serve.[6]

Moreover, the structure of the police organization, the way information upon which to act is fed into the system, and the way supervision in the bureaucracy is performed, help to promote ambiguities and sometimes conflicts. As the density of population increases and police work becomes more complex, with greater division of labor and specialized skills, a bureaucratic system emerges. We are not using bureaucracy in a pejorative sense, but in a sociologically descriptive way. Bureaucracies create hierarchies of command and impersonalized regulations. But unlike most formal social organizations — industry, hospital staffs, business — where directives come from above, from upper echelon, as the basis for dealing with people from the outside, most police activities are originated by members of the public — motorists, drunks, lost children, crowds, burglars. Information about these events, as Banton points out, reaches the organization through the men at the bottom. The patrolman first on the scene must make a judgment, and this decision may affect the entire organization. His supervisors are, in a real sense, dependent on him. Yet while these cases are fed into the system from the bottom, and the supervisors cannot be looking over the shoulders of the officers at all times, the men at the top must control their subordinates. Discretion at the bottom is permitted, and this creates a break in the link of supervision.

This issue of discretion is an important one, both from a constitutional or legal perspective and from the viewpoint of community values. Police power is a mighty force for many objectives. How that power is used is a function of how the community perceives the police and how the police perceive the community. If there is inadequate communication between these two groups — as I fear there is — then a condition that David Matza calls "pluralistic ignorance" is maintained; that is, both groups are ignorant of or inadequately informed of, one another's wishes and expectations. As Michael Banton suggests, "the only long-term solution to the problem of police discretion is for the police and the public to share the same norms of propriety."[7]

Now the community often sees the police as employees of the state, not as public servants, and rarely, if ever, as the formal guardians of the community's sentiments. As I shall emphasize shortly the heterogeneity of our American communities, with many different social groups and classes, has much to do with the fact that there is not *one* community, but many which the police serve on one hand and contain on the other. And while I referred earlier to the police functioning as guardians and executors of middle class values — at least from a sociologist's functional view of society — the community as a whole probably does not share this perspective. The police are invested, the community generally feels, with *legal power* only. Although it is true that the police officer does not enjoy many more rights, privileges or power than the ordinary citizen, the police officer does perform a role that clusters certain rights and responsibilities and power that the citizen has only in a diffuse and uncommitted sense. That is, the police officer — when he takes a salary and signs up for the job — is committed to performing certain limited activities that express this power, while the citizen is working in a factory, an office, or a classroom and does not use this same power. The investment of time, labor and ego make the difference.

But if the police officer has power, concentrated in his role, he also wants authority — that is, rightful or moral authority. And it is this kind of authority the community often appears unwilling to grant. Power itself is not necessarily rightful. As has been said elsewhere, legal power itself "gives one man the ability to force another to do his will. But if this power is seen as rightful, as authority, the second man will probably comply with the former's wishes because he feels morally obliged to do so." [8] In these terms, policemen could possess both authority and power. Many criminals and many law-breakers (if I may assume the difference is being communicated) do not consciously recognize policemen as having moral authority over them. In most situations, the police expect that the persons with whom they deal will regard the police as being morally justified in dealing with them as they do. The police try to get offenders to recognize what the norm of proper conduct is, and to agree to observe it in the future. If the "client" must be made a "captive," the police really prefer that the offender believe that he deserved it. This is one of the reasons that homicide squad officers generally have less trouble with the parties they arrest. Most homicide offenders who killed their spouses or loved ones or friends in a quarrel express remorse, shame or guilt, and in expressing it, accept the moral authority of the officer who is obliged to make the arrest. This is the same reason that accounts for the American police officer's general reluctance to make arrests, as well as his explaining or arguing with the persons he arrests — to confirm his moral authority.

The police officer, we have said, is himself a member of the community whose norms he must enforce. But the community does not make the police and the norms moral equivalents. This difference means that the policeman often does not receive the moral support of his community. I shall point out later that one of the reasons for the lack of moral support is the police emphasis on their own solidarity, and the community's apathy and forced isolation. The police officer really wants the goodwill, even of the offender, and will sometimes treat him leniently in order to be thought a "human" and good-hearted person. When he must make an arrest, he is often in a conflict situation and is almost in one sense "betraying" the arrestee. Banton [9] draws a parallel to the agents in society who are responsible for having persons committed to a mental hospital. This unattractive status requires restricting a man's freedom while simultaneously trying to suggest that it is for his own good and for the good of others.

The police are known to complain that the lower or higher courts often release offenders they (the police) felt firmly about as real criminals. Lack of evidence, legal technicalities, and political corruption may separately or concomitantly be responsible for the releases, or for light sentences. The conflict between protection of society and protection of private individual rights plays a part in these disparities between what the police believe and what the courts may do. The police are more interested in security; the courts, it seems, are more concerned with freedom. Whatever the reason for the disparate views — arrests too readily made without sufficient evidence, or release by the courts because of overconcern for technical freedom — there is no denying that the police view the arrested offender who's back on the street the next day as a negative judgment of the policeman's role and moral authority. Either the specific circumstances causing this judgment must be changed, or the police should re-evaluate their role so as not to perceive this kind of event as an indictment of their authority. Under present conditions, the police are forced to retreat into themselves, and become less identified with the community that seems not to support them. As Durkheim, a French sociologist, said, one of the purposes of punishment is to reinforce the social norms of right and wrong conduct. [10] When the police are rebuffed, they can no longer be seen or see themselves as executors of that reinforcement process. When this happens, their moral authority is chipped away until only legal power, which is in itself ineffective, remains. The motorist who is stopped comes, then, to be intimidated by the legal power of the police to make an arrest, but does not comply with requests out of a belief in the officer's rightful authority to require conformity. The more society is in this condition, the weaker are the police, the more alienated they become, and the less secure is the community.

Finally, within this context of the policeman's role and community attitudes, let me suggest that there is much similarity in values regarding the degree of offensiveness of certain crimes. Being members of the community, we have said, policemen share the same values as many other members. In a study designed to measure people's attitudes regarding the seriousness of delinquency, Thorsten Sellin and I studied police officers, juvenile court judges and many university students. [11] These are admittedly and generally representatives of middle class values. We found no significant differences among the three groups with respect to their ratings of seriousness. This finding reveals that the police do, in fact, share the same relative perspective on crimes as do these other groups. But it further indicates the rightful authority the police should have to perform their roles of enforcement.

   II. The Social Isolation, Alienation and Solidarity of the Police — Their Effect on the Police and the Community.

The police are often attacked by the community for not being sufficiently aggressive in apprehending an offender. But if the police are too aggressive and use too severe yet efficient means of solving a crime and making an arrest, the American Civil Liberties Union, the NAACP, the courts and other agencies will attack them for undue process of law. When the police perform their duties with alacrity and comprehensiveness, often the paradoxical situation occurs that crimes seem to go up. The more they work, the more they discover. The more thorough the policeman is, the more he may offend some groups — like catching speeding motorists. If he is lenient, he does not discourage; if too harsh, he's criticized for discourtesy (although this is a reaction of particular segments of the class structure). In short, he is vulnerable to abuse by his very role, not by his personality; and this kind of community reaction generates alienation from the public. The cleavage is crowned by the need to stick together. In sociological terms and generalization, the more the outgroup attacks the ingroup, the more prominent become the differences between the outgroup and the ingroup, and the greater is the solidarity of the ingroup. The similarities rather than the differences between members of the ingroup are stressed. In our specific context, the police fraternity become a solidified front, both as a protection against the outside and as a status-retaining force within. In England, we are told by one author: "British policemen have much less cause than American ones to feel that they must keep together in face of the public. Their organization can therefore tolerate more internal strains than could be the case across the Atlantic.

There is no longer hierarchy of ranks in Britain; pay differentials are greater; the sense of opposition between the men and the bosses (and vice versa) seems stronger; discipline is stricter; constables show less solidarity with one another, and more competitiveness." (12)

There is another point to keep in mind: the police officer in certain neighborhoods is viewed as alien by definition. He is apart, and his separateness makes him lonely except for his own neighborhood of officers. James Baldwin describes some of this feeling of the soldier walking through enemy territory in NOBODY KNOWS MY NAME:

> .... The only way to police a ghetto is to be oppressive. None of the Police Commissioner's men, even with the best will in the world, have any way of understanding the lives led by the people and they swagger about in twos and threes controlling. Their very presence is an insult, and it would be, even if they spent their entire day feeding gumdrops to children. They represent the force of the white world, and that world's criminal profit and ease, to keep the black man corraled up here, in his place. The badge, the gun in the holster, and the swinging club make vivid what will happen should his rebellion become overt ...
>
> It is hard, on the other hand, to blame the policemen, blank, good-natured, thoughtless, and insuperably innocent, for being such a perfect representative of the people he serves. He, too, believes in good intentions and is astounded and offended when they are not taken for the deed. He has never, himself, done anything for which to be hated — which of us has? — and yet he is facing, daily and nightly, people who would gladly see him dead, and he knows it. There is no way for him not to know it: there are few things under heaven more unnerving than the silent, accumulating contempt and hatred of a people. He moves through Harlem, therefore, like an occupying soldier in a bitterly hostile country; which is precisely what, and where he is, and is the reason he walks in twos and threes. (13)

A policeman expressed his isolation to a researcher recently in terms of the following incident:

> I try not to bring my work home with me, and that includes my social life. I like the men I work with, but I think it's better that my family doesn't become a police family. I try to put my police work into the background, and try not to let people know I'm a policeman. Once you do, you can't have normal relations with them (14)

III. Danger and Violence

The exposure to danger and potential violence is one of the most important ingredients separating the policeman from the "civilian." Policemen may be assaulted or insulted just because of their occupation; they are more likely to be assaulted or murdered in executing their duty than are others. Hence, policemen have sympathy for any of their own members who makes an error in judgment, as when an officer shoots an innocent person in a dark alley, believing him to be a dangerous suspect or escapee from prison, etc. The public is quick to condemn; the police have sympathy where there is public indignity. And in the light of our previous remarks, it is understandable that the police rally around their own member to protect him, and symbolically expect a similar display of sympathy should any of them perform the same kind of error.

In 1962, 78 law-enforcement employees were killed in the line of duty; 48 officers were victims of direct attack by criminals, most of them dying by gunfire.

Over a 3-year period, 26 percent of police officers killed by felons were responding to "disturbance" calls (family quarrels, man with a gun, etc.); 12 percent were investigating burglaries in progress; 22 percent pursuing robbers; 25 percent were attempting arrests or transporting prisoners; 11 percent were investigating suspicious persons; 4 percent were killed without warning by deranged persons. Of every 100 police officers, 10 were assaulted at some time during the year. [15] Part of the reason for much of this is the ease with which guns are acquired, and the association between the gun and virility in regions of American culture. When people possess guns, there is a standing temptation to use them when circumstances do not justify their use, and this fact increases the policeman's burden.

It should be noted that because the policeman lives under a more constant threat — if not actual use — of violence, he tends to collect, like a clinician, certain clues of danger: the black leather jacket, a particular strut, the demeanor and language, particularly juveniles, and the gesture toward a pocket that is quick and threatening. Living on the threshold of violence, whether or not he ever experiences it, creates suspicion. And this cognitive awareness again sets him apart from civilians.

Dealing with criminals, as most nonpolice persons do not, tends to develop a defensive reaction, often in the form of violence by the police themselves. In one classic study in the Midwest, William Westley asked policemen under what circumstances they thought officers were justified in "roughing a man up." More frequently mentioned than any other reason was the reply that violence might be justified when a man showed disrespect for the police — 27 out of 73 men (or 37 percent) felt this way. According to Westley, if a policeman uses violence to make a difficult offender show respect for the police, he is requiring that the man show respect for him as an individual; his action is not meant to exact respect for law and order and the policeman as its representative, but simply for him as an individual. [16]

The police tend to view flagrant disrespect as a personally ego-deflating experience, partly because of the lack of court and public support. In England, I doubt that this is the case. As one officer in Westley's study put it:

> There was the incident of a fellow I picked up. I was on the beat and I was taking him down to the station. There were people following us. He kept saying that I wasn't in the army. Well, he kept going on like that, and I finally had to bust him one. I had to do it. The people would have thought I was afraid otherwise. [17]

As one who handles violence, the policeman becomes associated, in the eyes of the community, with something dirty and nasty. Moreover, the citizen, realizing the necessity for such work, wants to be disengaged from it and those who do it. Keep in mind that one idea of power, status and respectability of a group is their ability to tolerate having jokes made about them. Psychiatrists can afford to have jokes made about their profession. The police have not been able to enjoy such a level of tolerance.

IV. Social Variables in the Community: Attitudes Towards the Police

In my conversations with middle class women, asking them how they felt about the police, the answer was almost invariably that they had been treated with respect and dignity. They felt either warmly protected by the police ("I like to see patrolmen on my street"), or had a sense of social distance, as if the police were impersonalized agents of the body politic. This protective feeling is probably much more commonly a female than a male response. A father or big brother image is fairly common.

But there is a difference by social class. When a police officer rings the bell of a home in a middle class residential area, the respondent's expectations are centered around such items as the following: "Is he going to tell me that my little daughter is lost? That someone was seen prowling around the house? Or that he has tickets to sell to the policeman's ball?" In a lower class neighborhood, the respondent has more focal concerns around "trouble." "What did my kid do now? Did Bill (the husband) get drunk again last night?"

The lower class gets into trouble more often, and comes to view the policeman as an unfriendly intruder in the neighborhood. And in a sense, he is, as the excerpt from Baldwin graphically states. The reaction of the police officer is affected by the social class of the offender, or by the suspect he must question and arrest.

Relative to the slum dweller, the police is socially superior. When the lower class suspect tells the officer to go to hell, the officer can respond with swearing (thus giving the other party a kind of privileged familiarity), or he can remain aloof with an air of dignified middle class morality, representing that morality in appropriate conduct. But the interaction between officer and suspect should be reduced to physical force *only* by the suspect, else the inference of moral authority is lost by the officer, and it is only the legal and physical power that remain as weapons of control. That the latter are necessary many times is not to be denied; but the ready resort to violence by the police is more degenerating to the police than to the offender.

Deference to middle or upper class status in suspects is probably less common in the United States than in England, but it is there, nonetheless. Particularly in dealing with traffic violators does this kind of interaction occur. When the officer receives comments, such as — "Who do you think you are, anyway? You should be spending your time chasing criminals" — from the Cadillac owner, the policeman may either feel a sense of deference to superior social and economic status as he projects beyond the immediate situation; or he may enjoy the experience of exercising a moral authority over the offender by reminding him of his duty to obey the law. In either case, the upper class offender's attitude is a personal rebuke that is best responded to by an impersonal stance represented in the law's requirement of obedience, and the officer's being the representative guardian of social harmony and order.

In the lower class area, the police are perceived more as the "long arm of the law," reaching into a subculture easily vulnerable to detection of deviance. In the middle and upper class area, the police represent rules established by the group itself. But too often, the policeman is viewed as a hired hand, a servant, rather than a mirrored and visible reflection of the mores.

Juveniles comprise another group attitude toward the police. They generally reflect their parents' attitudes, which vary by social class. But do the police represent authority figures to adolescents? In an interesting study in up-state Pennylvania, Edwards Rothstein questioned junior and senior high school students who were nondelinquents, and he did the same with delinquent boys. He found that the leading authority figures of all boys were in rank order, mother, father, judges. The police, clergymen and teachers were lowest for both delinquents and nondelinquents, but whereas nearly 70 percent of the nondelinquents rated the police as being important authority figures, only 31 percent of the delinquents did so.[18]

Once again, the right of the policeman to feel that he signifies society's moral authority is shown to be in conflict with that segment of the juvenile population which fails to see him in this role, and which also is the group most likely to violate the law.

We do not have time to analyze special interest groups, juvenile gangs, minority populations, and so forth in further detail. But obviously, they each contain their own attitudes towards the police. The professional criminal who sees all life as a racket too often finds reinforcement for his view in the handout to the police. The informant for the police requires some moral compromises for the sake of expediency. The rioting strikers, the militant minorities, the drug pushers, and the friendly prostitutes form different subsocieties of response to the police. "If they're not with us, they're against us" may be a common and illogical perspective. They all contribute to the isolation and insularity which the police feel in relation to these clusters of clients.

V. Conclusion

In a society that permits as many alternatives and as much personal freedom as does a democracy, deviance that takes the form of crime may be viewed as the price we pay for permitting these liberties. We should remember that there are many offenses committed by generally law-abiding citizens, and that total efficiency in law enforcement would mean totalitarianism and would be unthinkable. The community of citizens cannot expect perfect security from wrongdoers. The role of the police should be viewed as an integral part of that effort to strengthen and sustain the chief values of our culture — freedom from attack on our persons and our property. They are part of our collectivity, and need the confidence of the community in order to perform their roles. They should be freed from conflicts that occur in their tasks. They should be less required than they are to take solace in their own solidarity, and be made to feel more a part and reflection of the larger community, of which they are in fact and in attitude. The police will always be a special agency of society, facing changes and having experiences most of us will never really know. But they should be seen not *apart from*, but as *part of*, the community in which they work and live.

References

1. Jerome Skolnick, JUSTICE WITHOUT TRIAL (New York: Science Editions, John Wiley & Sons, 1966).
2. Michael Banton, THE POLICEMAN IN THE COMMUNITY (London: Tavistock, 1964).
3. David Matza, DELINQUENCY AND DRIFT (New York: John Wiley & Sons, 1964).
4. William Westley, *Violence and the Police,* AMERICAN JOURNAL OF SOCIOLOGY, Vol. 59 (July 1953) 34–41.
5. William Foote Whyte, STREET CORNER SOCIETY (Chicago: University of Chicago Press, 1943), p. 136.
6. Banton, *op. Cit.,* pp. 105, 106.
7. *Ibid.,* p. 146.
8. *Ibid.,* p. 147.
9. *Ibid.,* p. 150, n. 1.
10. Emil Durkheim, RULES OF SOCIOLOGICAL METHOD (Glencoe, Ill.: The Free Press, 1950), pp. 65–73.

11. Thorsten Sellin and Marvin E. Wolfgang, THE MEASURE-MENT OF DELINQUENCY (New York: John Wiley & Sons, 1964).

12. Banton, *op. cit.*, pp. 118–119.

13. James Baldwin, NOBODY KNOWS MY NAME (New York: Dial Press, 1962), pp. 65–67, cited by Skolnick, *op. cit.*

14. Skolnick, *op. cit.*

15. Data cited by Banton, *op. cit. p.* 111, from J. Edgar Hoover, CRIME IN THE UNITED STATES (Boston: The Beacon Press, 1961) pp. 21–23, 110.

16. Westley, *op. cit.*, p. 38.

17. *Ibid.*, p. 39.

18. Edward Rothstein, *An Analysis of Status Images as Perception Variables Between Delinquent and Non-Delinquent Boys* (New York University doctoral dissertation, 1961). See also this author's *Attributes Related to High Social Status: A Comparison of the Perceptions of Delinquent and Non-Delinquent Boys*, JOURNAL OF SOCIAL PROBLEMS, Vol. 10 (Summer 1962) pp. 75–83.

It is September, 1967 as this book is concluded. The longest and hottest of the "long, hot summers" is too recent for calm and detached assessment. Social researchers have flocked to Newark and Detroit as they did to Watts, each seeking a distinctive "angle" and a ready source of funding. They encounter people still stunned, still "shell-shocked," still incredulous — "it could not happen here" — but somehow, it did, and catastrophically.

This is not the place to undertake some sort of analysis of what happened, and why. But there is an obvious connection between the tragedies of civic disorder in the summer of 1967 and the theme of this book. The point need not be dramatized nor belabored.

Our concern is that the essential message of the summer's violence will not get through. There is widespread evidence, currently, of this possibility, and should it eventualize, it will be the greater tragedy. It occurs to us that this "essential message" of the summer — and of the many who have contributed to this book — are one and the same. What is this "essential message," as we see it?

Look at our cities today. Generally speaking, the panorama is one characterized by Maurice Stein as "the eclipse of community." New terms, such as "megalopolis," have been coined for it. There is anger, hatred, bigotry, bitterness, discrimination, injustice — all these things, and more. There is segregation, separation, exploitation, second-class citizenship, despair and alienation. These are the abrasives of the festering problems of metropolis, spelling out social and moral bankruptcy, loud and clear. Superintendent Neil Sullivan of the Berkeley, California, Schools has described the situation as follows:

> Can you imagine the year 1976 when there could be more than 20,000,000 Negroes living tightly packed in ghettos, attending segregated schools? To allow this process to continue would seem a collision

course which could lead to a Revolution 1976 and make the Revolution of 1776 look like a tea party. There is among separated and segregated white youth in city and suburb a growing preoccupation with despair, a retreat from the world of the establishment into the bizarre hair-do, dress, behavior and temporary, if debilitating, surcease of narcotics. Teachers, parents, the adult community, stand by in shocked, helpless sorrow, as alienation grows, in self-righteous rage. And students contend against the adult world and among each other in perfect carica-ture of adult behavior in community and in school. The end, unless all bestir ourselves, can only be self-destruction as varieties of alienation and hostility break into violent combat in the cites and the suburbs.*

Superintendent Sullivan is chiefly concerned about teacher training and the implications of the conditions he describes for schools of educa-tion. He calls for a "massive revolution," to meet the personal, individual and group needs of this generation of children and youth. "Teacher edu-cation," he says, "must prepare a new quality professional for the way ahead." He pleads for development of a teaching atmosphere and style capable of creating a nation of "critically conscious problem-solvers."

He might as well have been speaking to police officers! For this, as we see it, is "the essential message." It is not singularly a message for the police, nor for teachers. Others are "involved in mankind," certainly. But it is a message of particular significance for those whose responsi-bilities are at the base of our social institutions in the free society. The changes that are called for may mean a new way of life—in police organi-zations, for example. So be it!

For the solutions to the major problems of our society today are not simply in terms of money, in and of itself. More and better housing, more and better jobs, more and better education, more and better health, recreation and welfare services — these things are important, surely. But "the essential message" of the summer of 1967 in our cities is more subtle, more fundamental. It has to do with the gnawing need of "nobodies" for *identity*, for something to engender self-respect, for ways of feeling that one is *involved*, that one has something to say that others will hear. Riot is the communication of utter despair and hopelessness.

No one has put it more poignantly than Ralph Ellison:

I can hear you say, "What a horrible, irresponsible bastard!" And you're right. I leap to agree with you. I am one of the most irresponsible beings that ever lived. Irresponsibility is part of my invisibility; any way you face it, it is a denial. But to whom can I be responsible, and why should I be, when you refuse to see me?†

Can police help to build a sense of community, where none exists? The consensus among those who have contributed to this book is emphati-

---

* Neil V. Sullivan, *Let's Take a Good Hard Look at Teacher Training;* THE COM-MUNITY SCHOOL AND ITS ADMINISTRATION, Michigan State University, Vol. V, No. 10, June, 1967.

† Ralph Ellison, INVISIBLE MAN. New York: Random House, Inc., 1947; *Prologue.*

cally in the affirmative. If so, how? Again, the views expressed by the numerous contributors to this book provide some partial answers to this question. Even the basic question of what is meant by "community" has been discussed: a community is where a person can have a realistic belief in a decent life. It is argued that the police *alone*, under the best conditions of police–community relations, cannot supply this goal. Granted; but on the other hand, is humane, impartial, truly professional police service (and attitude!) to be available only to the affluent, to those with power and influence, to white people, "somebodies"? If so, then we had better face realistically the conclusion that our entire system of government by law is in peril.

How does a person learn to respect himself, whether police officer or ghetto dweller? He learns this, in large part, by how others treat him. One discovers who he is through the actions of others toward him. It is of vital importance who these "others" are. A police officer is an important symbolic figure; therefore, his treatment of people is particularly noteworthy. Alone, he cannot change "the system." But from the viewpoint of economically marginal people, the "power-less," the "alienated," the "nobodies," it is of cardinal importance that the police be seen as "our police."

For still too many police officers and police executives today, this concept of police work is regarded as "social work" — the "sociological cop." Apparently, their three-ply prescription for today's problems must prevail, viz., (1) Find a scapegoat (e.g., Communism, "outside agitators," etc.); (2) Beef up law and order (violent repression vs. violent rebellion); and (3) Apply some token "mustard plaster" to the problem area, conduct an investigation, set up a committee to make a study, etc. — in short, do everything possible to *avoid* dealing with the real problem.

On the other hand, there is another — and we think, a better — way. By and large, it is the way charted by the President's Commission on Law Enforcement and Administration of Justice, in its report published earlier this year. While we do not agree with every finding, conclusion and recommendation of the Commission, we are in sufficient agreement so as to make a rechronicling of that report unnecessary here.

We conclude with the central idea with which we began: the solution to all of the challenging problems of law enforcement in the free society is to be found in the direction of closer partnership between police and community.

The Editors

A Selected Bibliography on Police and Community Relations

Compiled by

MARTIN G. MILLER

Instructor and Assistant Director, National Center on Police and Community Relations, Michigan State University

Our society's transition from rural to urban and the resulting conflicts between the perceptions of the functions and roles of law enforcement by police and citizens, has caused the task of social control to become increasingly difficult. These police and community problems have attracted the interest of both academicians and practitioners. The materials relating to this subject matter are vast and continue to grow daily. This selected bibliography represents our judgment of the prime references from the voluminous literature on police and community relations.

The reference items selected were drawn from the bibliographic files of the National Center on Police and Community Relations. These files are kept up-to-date to facilitate the publication of the National Center's annual bibliography. References are accumulated from the fields of administration, community relations, civil rights, law, minority group relations, mass media, youth problems, psychology, sociology and political science. This diversity depicts our philosophy of the interdisciplinary nature of the field of police and community relations.

I. Books

Aaron, Thomas J. THE CONTROL OF POLICE DISCRETION: THE DANISH EXPERIENCE. Springfield, Ill.: Charles C Thomas, Publisher, 1966.

A NATIONAL SURVEY OF POLICE AND COMMUNITY RELATIONS. National Center on Police and Community Relations, School of Police Administration and Public Safety, Michigan State University, Field Survey V. Washington, D.C.: Superintendent of Documents, U.S. Government Printing Office, 1967.

Ashenhurst, Paul H. POLICE AND THE PEOPLE. Springfield, Ill.: Charles C Thomas, Publisher, 1957.

Banton, Michael. THE POLICEMAN IN THE COMMUNITY. New York: Basic Books Inc., 1964.

Berson, Lenora E. CASE STUDY OF A RIOT: THE PHILADELPHIA STORY. New York: Institute of Human Relations Press, American Jewish Committee, 1966.

Biderman, Albert D., Louise A. Johnson, Jennie McIntyre, and Adrianne W. Weir. REPORT ON A PILOT IN THE DISTRICT OF COLUMBIA ON VICTIMIZATION AND ATTITUDES TOWARD LAW ENFORCEMENT—FIELD SURVEYS I. Washington, D.C.: Superintendent of Documents, U.S. Government Printing Office, 1967.

Bordua, David J. (ed.). THE POLICE: SIX SOCIOLOGICAL ESSAYS. New York: John Wiley & Sons, 1967.

Brennan, James, and Donald W. Olmsted. POLICE WORK WITH DELINQUENTS: ANALYSIS OF A TRAINING PROGRAM. East Lansing: Social Sciences Research Bureau, Michigan State University, 1965.

Chapman, Samuel G. (ed.). POLICE PATROL READINGS. Springfield, Ill.: Charles C Thomas, Publisher, 1964.

Chapman, Samuel G., and T. Eric St. Johnston. THE POLICE HERITAGE IN ENGLAND AND AMERICA; A DEVELOPMENTAL SURVEY. East Lansing: Institute for Community Development and Services, Continuing Education Service, Michigan State University, 1962.

Cramer, James. THE WORLD'S POLICE. London: Cassell, 1964.

Cray, Ed. THE BIG BLUE LINE: POLICE POWER VERSUS HUMAN RIGHTS. New York: Coward-McCann, Inc., 1967.

Curry, Jesse E., and Glen D. King. RACE TENSIONS AND THE POLICE. Springfield, Ill.: Charles C Thomas, Publisher, 1962.

Fichter, Joseph H. POLICE HANDLING OF ARRESTEES: A RESEARCH STUDY OF POLICE ARRESTS IN NEW ORLEANS. New Orleans: Department of Sociology, Loyola University of the South, 1964.

Fosdick, Raymond B. AMERICAN POLICE SYSTEMS. New York: The Century Co., 1920.

Gellhorn, Walter. OMBUDSMEN AND OTHERS: CITIZENS' PROTECTORS IN NINE COUNTRIES. Cambridge, Mass.: Harvard University Press, 1966.

Gellhorn, Walter. WHEN AMERICANS COMPLAIN: GOVERNMENTAL GRIEVANCE PROCEDURES. Cambridge, Mass.: Harvard University Press, 1966.

Germann, A.C., Frank D. Day, and Robert G. Gallati. INTRODUCTION TO LAW ENFORCEMENT. Springfield, Ill.: Charles C Thomas, Publisher, 1962.

Gourley, G. Douglas. PUBLIC RELATIONS AND THE POLICE. Springfield, Ill.: Charles C Thomas, Publisher, 1953.

GUIDE TO RACE RELATIONS FOR PEACE OFFICERS. Sacramento: Division of Criminal Law and Enforcement, California State Department of Justice, 1952.

Holcomb, Richard L. THE POLICE AND THE PUBLIC. Springfield, Ill.: Charles C Thomas, Publisher, 1957.

JUSTICE (VOLUME V). United States Commission on Civil Rights. Washington, D.C.: Superintendent of Documents, U.S. Government Printing Office, 1961.

Kamisar, Yale, Fred E. Inbau, and Arnold Thurman. CRIMINAL JUSTICE IN OUR TIME. Charlottesville: The University Press of Virginia, 1965.

Kephart, William M. RACIAL FACTORS IN URBAN LAW ENFORCEMENT. Philadelphia: University of Pennsylvania Press, 1957.

LaFave, Wayne R. ARREST: THE DECISION TO TAKE A SUSPECT INTO CUSTODY. New York: Little, Brown & Co., 1965.

LAW ENFORCEMENT, A REPORT ON EQUAL PROTECTION IN THE SOUTH. Washington, D.C.: Superintendent of Documents, U.S. Government Printing Office, 1965.

Lawler, Irvin D. TRAINING PROGRAM IN HUMAN RELATIONS FOR CADET AND IN-SERVICE OFFICERS. Detroit: Detroit Police Department, 1952.

Lohman, Joseph D. THE POLICE AND MINORITY GROUPS. Chicago: Chicago Park Police, 1947.

Lohman, Joseph D., and Gordon E. Misner. THE POLICE AND THE COMMUNITY: THE DYNAMICS OF THEIR RELATIONSHIP IN

A CHANGING SOCIETY—VOLUMES 1 AND 2, FIELD SURVEYS IV. Washington, D.C.: Superintendent of Documents, U.S. Government Printing Office, 1967.

McEntire, Davis, and Robert B. Powers. POLICE TRAINING BULLETIN: A GUIDE TO RACE RELATIONS FOR POLICE OFFICERS. Sacramento: California State Department of Justice, 1946.

McMillan, George. RACIAL VIOLENCE AND LAW ENFORCEMENT. Atlanta, Georgia: Southern Regional Council, May, 1964.

Misner, Gordon E. THE DEVELOPMENT OF "NEW CAREERIST" POSITIONS IN THE RICHMOND POLICE DEPARTMENT. Walnut Creek, Calif.: Contra Costa Council of Community Services, 1967.

Momboisse, Raymond M. COMMUNITY RELATIONS AND RIOT PREVENTION. Springfield, Ill.: Charles C Thomas, Publisher, 1967.

Myren, Richard A., and Lynn D. Swanson. POLICE WORK WITH CHILDREN: PERSPECTIVES AND PRINCIPLES. Washington, D.C.: Children's Bureau, U.S. Department of Health, Education and Welfare, 1962.

Newman, Donald J. CONVICTION: THE DETERMINATION OF GUILT OR INNOCENCE WITHOUT TRIAL. Boston: Little, Brown & Co., 1966.

Niederhoffer, Arthur. BEHIND THE SHIELD: THE POLICE IN URBAN SOCIETY. New York: Doubleday & Co., Inc., 1967.

O'Connor, George W., and Nelson A. Watson. JUVENILE DELINQUENCY AND YOUTH CRIME, THE POLICE ROLE. AN ANALYSIS OF: PHILOSOPHY, POLICY, OPINION. Washington, D.C.: International Association of Chiefs of Police, 1965.

PAPERS ON POLICE ADMINISTRATION AND CIVIL DISOBEDIENCE. New York: New York University Graduate School of Public Administration, 1963.

Pfiffner, John M. THE FUNCTION OF THE POLICE IN A DEMOCRATIC SOCIETY. Los Angeles: School of Public Administration, Civic Center Campus Center for Training and Career Development, University of Southern California, 1967.

POLICE–MINORITY GROUP RELATIONS IN LOS ANGELES AND THE SAN FRANCISCO BAY AREA. California Advisory Committee to the United States Commission on Civil Rights, G.P.O. Pamphlet 1839. Washington, D.C.: Superintendent of Documents, U.S. Government Printing Office, 1963.

Preiss, Jack J., and Howard J. Ehrlich. AN EXAMINATION OF ROLE THEORY: THE CASE OF THE STATE POLICE. Lincoln: University of Nebraska Press, 1966.

PUBLIC RELATIONS AND THE POLICE. Houston Police Department. Houston, Texas: Department of Public Safety, 1961.

REPORT (AND APPENDIX) OF THE PRESIDENT'S COMMISSION ON CRIME IN THE DISTRICT OF COLUMBIA. Washington, D.C.: Superintendent of Documents, U.S. Government Printing Office, 1966.

Reiss, Albert, Jr. STUDIES IN CRIME AND LAW ENFORCEMENT IN MAJOR METROPOLITAN AREAS. VOLUMES 1 AND 2, FIELD SURVEYS III. Washington, D.C.: Superintendent of Documents, U.S. Government Printing Office, 1967.

Rolph, C. H. THE POLICE AND THE PUBLIC: AN INQUIRY. London: Heinemann, 1962.

Rowat, Donald C. (ed.). THE OMBUDSMAN: CITIZEN'S DEFENDER. Toronto: University of Toronto Press, 1965.

Rudwick, Elliot M. THE UNEQUAL BADGE: NEGRO POLICEMEN IN THE SOUTH. Atlanta, Georgia: Southern Regional Council, 1962.

Senn, Milton A. STUDY OF POLICE TRAINING PROGRAMS IN MINORITY RELATIONS. Los Angeles: Los Angeles County Conference on Community Relations, 1952.

Siegel, Arthur I., Philip J. Federman, and Douglas G. Schultz. PROFESSIONAL POLICE–HUMAN RELATIONS TRAINING. Springfield, Ill.: Charles C Thomas, Publisher, 1963.

Skolnick, Jerome H. JUSTICE WITHOUT TRIAL: LAW ENFORCEMENT IN DEMOCRATIC SOCIETY. New York: John Wiley & Sons, Inc., 1966.

Smith, Bruce. POLICE SYSTEMS IN THE UNITED STATES, 2d Ed. New York: Harper, 1960.

Sowle, Claude R. (ed.). POLICE POWER AND INDIVIDUAL FREEDOM: THE QUEST FOR BALANCE. Chicago: Aldine Publishing Co., 1962.

Stahl, David, Frederick B. Sussman, and Neil J. Bloomfield. THE COMMUNITY AND RACIAL CRISES. New York: Practicing Law Institute, 1966.

TASK FORCE REPORT: THE POLICE. President's Commission on Law Enforcement and Administration of Justice. Washington, D.C.: Superintendent of Documents, U.S. Government Printing Office, 1967.

THE ADMINISTRATION OF JUSTICE—HEARINGS: VOLUME II. United States Commission on Civil Rights. Washington, D.C.: Superintendent of Documents, U.S. Government Printing Office, 1965.

THE CHALLENGE OF CRIME IN A FREE SOCIETY. President's Commission on Law Enforcement and Administration of Justice. Washington, D.C.: Superintendent of Documents, U.S. Government Printing Office, 1967.

THE HANDLING OF JUVENILES FROM OFFENSE TO DISPOSITION. 7 vols. School of Criminology, University of California. Berkeley: University of California, 1965.

THE POLICE AND THE CIVIL RIGHTS ACT. Washington, D.C.: International Association of Chiefs of Police, 1965.

Towler, Juby E. THE POLICE ROLE IN RACIAL CONFLICTS. Springfield, Ill.: Charles C Thomas, Publisher, 1964.

Trebach, Arnold S. THE RATIONING OF JUSTICE: CONSTITUTIONAL RIGHTS AND THE CRIMINAL PROCESS. New Brunswick, N.J.: Rutgers University Press, 1964.

Vollmer, August. THE POLICE AND MODERN SOCIETY. Berkeley: University of California Press, 1936.

Waskow, Arthur I. FROM RACE RIOT TO SIT-IN. Garden City, N.Y.: Doubleday & Co., 1966.

Watson, Nelson A. (ed.). POLICE AND THE CHANGING COMMUNITY: SELECTED READINGS. Washington, D.C.: International Association of Chiefs of Police, 1965.

Watson, Nelson A. POLICE–COMMUNITY RELATIONS. Washington, D.C.: International Association of Chiefs of Police, Research and Development Division, 1966.

Watson, Nelson A., and Robert N. Walker (eds.). JUVENILE DELINQUENCY IN POLICE EDUCATION: PROCEEDINGS OF WORKSHOP FOR POLICE PROFESSORS, MICHIGAN STATE UNIVERSITY, 1966. Washington, D.C.: International Association of Chiefs of Police, 1966.

Wilson, O. W. POLICE ADMINISTRATION, 2d Ed. New York: McGraw-Hill Book Co., 1963.

WITH JUSTICE FOR ALL: A GUIDE FOR LAW ENFORCEMENT OFFICERS. New York: Anti-Defamation League of B'nai B'rith and the International Association of Chiefs of Police, Publication No. G-363, 1959.

Wolfgang, Marvin E. CRIME AND RACE: CONCEPTIONS AND MISCONCEPTIONS. New York: Institute of Human Relations Press, American Jewish Committee, 1964.

II. Articles

Abernathy, M. Glenn. *Police Discretion and Equal Protection,* SOUTH CAROLINA LAW QUARTERLY, 14 (1962), 472–486.

Allman, James J. *Establishing a Police Community Relations Office Within a Police Department,* THE POLICE CHIEF, 32 (3), (1965), 11–14.

Banton, Michael. *Social Integration and Police,* THE POLICE CHIEF, 30 (4), (1963), 8–20.

Barrett, Edward J. *Police Practices and the Law — From Arrest to Release or Charge,* CALIFORNIA LAW REVIEW, 50 (1), (1962), 11–55.

Beral, Harold, and Marcus Sisk. *The Administration of Complaints by Civilians Against the Police,* THE POLICE CHIEF, 31 (2), (1964), 12–14+.

Blum, Sam. *The Police,* REDBOOK, 128 (4), (February 1967), 76–77.

Bordua, David J. *Recent Trends: Deviant Behavior and Social Control,* THE ANNALS OF THE AMERICAN ACADEMY OF POLITICAL AND SOCIAL SCIENCE, 369 (1967), 149–161.

Bray, Robert J., Jr. *Philadelphia's Police Advisory Board — A New Concept in Community Relations,* VILLANOVA LAW REVIEW, 7 (1962), 656–673.

Brown, Lee P. *Black Muslims and the Police,* THE JOURNAL OF CRIMINAL LAW, CRIMINOLOGY AND POLICE SCIENCE, 56 (1), (1965), 119–126.

Brown, Lee P. *Police Review Boards: An Historical and Critical Analysis,* POLICE, 10 (6), (1966), 19–29.

Brown, William P. *The Police and Community Conflict,* THE POLICE CHIEF, May–June 1964, 51–59.

Carmack, William R. *Practical Communication Tools for Group Involvement in Police–Community Problems,* THE POLICE CHIEF, March 1965, 34–36.

Chwast, Jacob. *Value Conflicts in Law Enforcement,* CRIME AND DELINQUENCY, 11 (2), (1965), 151–161.

Clark, John P. *Isolation of the Police: A Comparison of the British and American Situations,* THE JOURNAL OF CRIMINAL LAW, CRIMINOLOGY AND POLICE SCIENCE, 56 (3), (1965), 307–319.

Clark, John P., and Eugene P. Wenninger. *The Attitude of Juveniles Toward the Legal Institution,* THE JOURNAL OF CRIMINAL LAW, CRIMINOLOGY AND POLICE SCIENCE, 55 (4), (1964), 482–489.

Cross, Granville J. *Negro, Prejudice, and the Police,* THE JOURNAL OF CRIMINAL LAW, CRIMINOLOGY AND POLICE SCIENCE, 55 (3), (1964), 405–411.

Cumming, E., I. Cumming, and L. Edell. *Policeman as Philosopher, Guide and Friend,* SOCIAL PROBLEMS, 12 (3), (1965), 276–286.

Derbyshire, Robert L. *The Social Control Role of the Police in Changing Urban Communities,* EXCERPTA CRIMINOLOGICA, 6 (3), (1966), 315–321.

Edwards, George. *Order and Civil Liberties: A Complex Role for the Police,* MICHIGAN LAW REVIEW, 64 (1), (1966), 47–62.

Edwards, George. *The Constitution, the Citizen and the Police,* MICHIGAN STATE BAR JOURNAL, 40, (1961), 26–32.

Falk, Gerhard J. *The Police Dilemma in England and America,* PAPERS OF THE AMERICAN SOCIETY OF CRIMINOLOGY, (1964), 109–121.

Foote, Caleb. *Tort Remedies for Police Violations of Individual Rights,* MINNESOTA LAW REVIEW, 39, (1955), 493–516.

George, B. J., Jr. *Juveniles and the Police,* MICHIGAN STATE BAR JOURNAL, 43, (1964), 24.

Germann, A. C. *Police Planning and Research as it Affects Police–Community Relations,* POLICE, 6 (3), (1962), 36–39.

Goldstein, Herman. *Administrative Problems in Controlling the Exercise of Police Authority*, THE JOURNAL OF CRIMINAL LAW, CRIMINOLOGY AND POLICE SCIENCE, 58 (2), (1967), 160–172.

Goldstein, Joseph. *Police Discretion Not To Invoke the Criminal Process: Low-Visibility Decisions in the Administration of Justice*, YALE LAW JOURNAL, 69, (1960), 543–594.

Grimshaw, Allen D. *Actions of Police and the Military in American Race Riots*, PHYLON, 24, (1963), 271–289.

Grimshaw, Allen D. *Police Agencies and the Prevention of Racial Violence*, THE JOURNAL OF CRIMINAL LAW, CRIMINOLOGY AND POLICE SCIENCE, 54 (1), (1963), 110–113.

Hale, E.C. *Police, Minorities, and Mobs*, NEW SOUTH, (September 1961), 8–12.

Handlin, Oscar. *Community Organization as a Solution to Police – Community Problems*, THE POLICE CHIEF, 32 (3), (1965), 16–22.

Jacobs, Paul. *The Los Angeles Police*, THE ATLANTIC MONTHLY, (December 1966), 95–101.

Jones, Marshall E. *Police Leadership and Human Relations*, POLICE, 10 (5), (1966), 42–53.

Kadish, Sanford H. *Legal Norm and Discretion in the Police and Sentencing Processes*, HARVARD LAW REVIEW, 75, (1963), 904–931.

Kennedy, Robert F. *Crime in the Cities: Improving the Administration of Criminal Justice*, THE JOURNAL OF CRIMINAL LAW, CRIMINOLOGY AND POLICE SCIENCE, 58 (2), (1967), 142–154.

Lacouture, R. *The Police, the Press and Public Relations*, POLICE, 5 (6), (1961), 38–41.

LaFave, Wayne R. *Improving Police Performance Through the Exclusionary Law*, MISSOURI LAW REVIEW, 30 (3), (1965), 391–458.

LaFave, Wayne R. *The Police and Non-Enforcement of the Law*, WISCONSIN LAW REVIEW, (January–March 1962), 104–137, 179–239.

LaFave, Wayne R., and Frank J. Remington. *Controlling the Police— The Judge's Role in Making and Reviewing Law Enforcement Decisions*, MICHIGAN LAW REVIEW, 63 (6), (1965), 987–1012.

Leary, Howard R. *Role of Police in Riotous Demonstrations. (Symposium.)* NOTRE DAME LAW JOURNAL, 40, (1965), 499.

Lieberson, Stanley, and Arnold R. Silverman. *The Precipitants and Underlying Conditions of Race Riots*, AMERICAN SOCIOLOGICAL REVIEW, (December 1965), 887–898.

Littman, Sol. *The Policeman Looks at Himself*, (New York), Anti-Defamation League of B'nai B'rith, (1967).

Lundstedt, Sven. *Social Psychological Contributions to the Management of Law Enforcement Agencies*, THE JOURNAL OF CRIMINAL LAW, CRIMINOLOGY AND POLICE SCIENCE, 56 (3), (1965), 375–381.

McManus, George. *Human Relations Training for Police*, INTERRACIAL REVIEW (Catholic Interracial Council), (November 1955), 188–191.

Mihanovich, Clement S. *Programming for Citizen Participation in Police Action Programs*, THE POLICE CHIEF, 32 (3), (1965), 27–31.

Mills, Robert B. *Police–Community Relations: A Psychologist's Viewpoint*, (Cincinnati), National Conference of Christians and Jews, 1964.

Nelson, E. K., Jr. *Organizational Disparity in Defintions of Deviance and Uses of Authority: Police, Probation, and the Schools*, in SCHOOLS IN A CHANGING SOCIETY, Albert J. Reiss, Jr., (ed.). (New York: The Free Press, 1966). 21–47.

Norris, Harold. *Constitutional Law Enforcement is Effective Law Enforcement: Toward a Concept of Police in a Democracy and a Citizens' Advisory Board*, UNIVERSITY OF DETROIT LAW JOURNAL, 43 (2), (1965), 203–234.

Packer, Herbert L. *Policing the Police: Nine Men Are Not Enough,* NEW REPUBLIC, 153 (8), (1965), 17–21.

Parker, William H. *The Police Role in Community Relations,* (New York), National Conference of Christians and Jews, 1955. 31 pp.

Pierce, Chester M. *Psychiatric Aspects of Police–Community Relations,* MENTAL HYGIENE, 46 (1), (1962), 107–115.

Piliavin, Irving, and Scott Briar. *Police Encounters With Juveniles,* THE AMERICAN JOURNAL OF SOCIOLOGY, 70 (2), (1964), 206–214.

POLICE–COMMUNITY RELATIONS IN ST. LOUIS—EXPERIENCE REPORT 103. Washington, D.C.: Community Relations Service, U.S. Conference of Mayors. 7 pp.

POLICE–COMMUNITY RELATIONS POLICIES AND PRACTICES: A NATIONAL SURVEY. Washington, D.C.: International Association of Chiefs of Police and the U.S. Conference of Mayors. 11 pp.

Pomrenke, Norman E., C.E. Cherry, and H. Barton. *A New Approach to Crime Prevention—Community Services,* THE POLICE CHIEF, 34 (3), (1967), 33–41.

Price, Carroll S. *Ethics and Professionalization in American Law Enforcement,* POLICE, 7, (1963) 6–12.

Radelet, Louis A. *Implications of Professionalism in Law Enforcement for Police–Community Relations,* POLICE, 10 (6), (1966), 82–86.

Radelet, Louis A. *Police and Community Relations: On the National Scene,* THE POLICE CHIEF, 31 (9), (1964), 40–44.

Radelet, Louis A. *Police Community Programs: Nature and Purpose,* THE POLICE CHIEF, 32 (3), (1965), 38–40.

Reiss, Albert, Jr., and David Bordua. *Command, Control and Charisma: Reflections on Police Bureaucracy,* THE AMERICAN JOURNAL OF SOCIOLOGY, 72, (1966), 68–76.

Remington, Frank J. *The Role of Police in a Democratic Society,* THE JOURNAL OF CRIMINAL LAW, CRIMINOLOGY AND POLICE SCIENCE, 56, (1965), 361–365.

Rudwick, Elliot M. *The Southern Negro Policeman and the White Offender,* JOURNAL OF NEGRO EDUCATION, 30, (1961), 426–431.

Salomon, Frederic, Walker L. Walker, Garrett J. O'Connor, and Jacob R. Fishman. *Civil Rights Activity and Reduction in Crime Among Negroes,* ARCHIVES OF GENERAL PSYCHIATRY, 12, (1965), 227–236.

Shallow, Robert S. *Reinforcing Police Neutrality in Civil Rights Confrontations,* THE JOURNAL OF APPLIED BEHAVIORAL SCIENCE, 1 (3), (1965), 243–254.

Sheehan, Thomas M. *Urbanism and Jane Jacobs: A Note for the Police,* POLICE, (November–December 1965), 27–29.

Stinchcombe, Arthur L. *Institutions of Privacy in the Determination of Police Administration Practice,* THE AMERICAN JOURNAL OF SOCIOLOGY, 69 (2), (1963), 150–160.

Terry, Robert M. *The Screening of Juvenile Offenders,* THE JOURNAL OF CRIMINAL LAW, CRIMINOLOGY AND POLICE SCIENCE, 58 (2), (1967), 173–181.

Toch, Hans H. *A Note on Police "Experience,"* POLICE, 11 (4), (1967), 87–89.

Toch, Hans H. *Psychological Consequences of the Police Role,* POLICE, 10 (1), (1965), 22–25.

Toch, Hans H., and R. Schulte. *Readiness to Perceive Violence as a Result of Police Training,* BRITISH JOURNAL OF PSYCHOLOGY, 52 (4), (1961), 389–393.

Watson, Nelson A. *Police and Group Behavior,* THE POLICE CHIEF, 30 (11), (1963), 8–10+.

Watson, Nelson A. *The Police and Human Relations,* MUNICIPAL YEAR BOOK, 1965, 415–422.

Wattenberg, William W., and Noel Bufe. *Effectiveness of Police Youth Bureau Officers,* THE JOURNAL OF CRIMINAL LAW, CRIMINOLOGY AND POLICE SCIENCE, 54 (4), (1963), 470–475.

Westley, William A. *Secrecy and the Police,* SOCIAL FORCES, 34 (3), (1956), 254–257.

Westley, William A. *Violence and the Police,* THE AMERICAN JOURNAL OF SOCIOLOGY, 59 (1), (1953), 34–41.

Williams, Gerald O. *Crime News and its Relation to Police/Press Policies,* POLICE, 8 (4), (1964), 10–16.

Wilson, James Q. *The Police and the Delinquent in Two Cities,* in CONTROLLING DELINQUENTS, Stanton Wheeler (ed). New York: John Wiley & Sons, 1966.

Wilson, James Q. *The Police and Their Problems: A Theory on Why Misconduct Occurs Chiefly in Big-City Departments,* PUBLIC POLICY, (Yearbook of the Graduate School of Public Administration, Harvard University). Cambridge, Mass.: 1963. 189–216.

Wilson, O. W. *Police Authority in a Free Society,* THE JOURNAL OF CRIMINAL LAW, CRIMINOLOGY AND POLICE SCIENCE, 52 (2), (1963), 175–177.

Wirths, Claudine Gibson. *The Development of Attitudes Toward Law Enforcement,* POLICE, 3, (1958), 50–52.

Wolfgang, Marvin E., (ed.). *Patterns of Violence,* THE ANNALS OF THE AMERICAN ACADEMY OF POLITICAL AND SOCIAL SCIENCE, 364, (1966), 1–248.

Vedder, Clyde B., and Keller J. Oliver, Jr. *The Police and Middle Class Conflicts,* POLICE, 9, (1965), 6–8.

III. Unpublished Materials

Brown, William P. *The Review Board Proposals Do Not Go Far Enough.* Paper presented at the 71st National Conference on Government, New York, November 17, 1965.

Reichert, Irving. *The Background of the Interrelationship and Possible Problems of Balance—A Historical Perspective on the Roles of Law, Courts and Law Enforcement.* Paper presented at the 7th annual San Francisco Police–Community Relations Institute, San Francisco, California, January 21, 1966.

Stinchcombe, Arthur L. *Municipal Police and Civil Liberty.* Unpublished manuscript.

Stinchcombe, Arthur L. *The Control of Citizen Resentment in Police Work.* Unpublished manuscript.

Yinger, J. Milton. *Who Are We?* Paper presented at the Northern Ohio Institute on Police and Community Relations, Cleveland, Ohio, November 21, 1964.